*and Harlem*

Upper
West
Side

*Central
Park*

Upper
East
Side

Upper
Midtown

Lower
Midtown

EAST RIVER

**PAGES 220–31**
*Street Finder maps
19–20*

**PAGES 166–81**
*Street Finder maps
12, 13–14*

0 kilometres    1

0 miles    0.5

**PAGES 150–65**
*Street Finder maps
9, 12, 13*

**PAGES 210–19**
*Street Finder maps
11–12, 15–16*

**PAGES 122–9**
*Street Finder maps
8, 9*

**PAGES 182–203**
*Street Finder maps
12–13, 16–17*

**PAGES 204–9**
*Street Finder maps
12, 16*

**PAGES 116–21**
*Street Finder maps
4, 5*

EYEWITNESS TRAVEL

# NEW YORK CITY

# EYEWITNESS TRAVEL

# NEW YORK CITY

MAIN CONTRIBUTOR: ELEANOR BERMAN

DK

LONDON, NEW YORK,
MELBOURNE, MUNICH AND DELHI
www.dk.com

PROJECT EDITOR Fay Franklin

ART EDITOR Tony Foo

EDITORS Donna Dailey, Ellen Dupont, Esther Labi

DESIGNERS Steve Bere, Louise Parsons, Mark Stevens

EDITORIAL ASSISTANT Fiona Morgan

CONTRIBUTORS
Lester Brooks, Patricia Brooks, Susan Farewell

PHOTOGRAPHERS
Max Alexander, Dave King, Michael Moran

ILLUSTRATORS
Richard Draper, Robbie Polley, Hamish Simpson

This book was produced with the assistance of
Websters International Publishers.

Reproduced by Colourscan (Singapore)
Printed and bound by South China Printing Co. Ltd, China.

First published in Great Britain in 1993
by Dorling Kindersley Limited
80 Strand, London WC2R 0RL

**Reprinted with revisions 1994, 1995 (twice),
1997, 1999, 2000, 2001, 2002, 2003, 2004, 2005, 2006, 2007, 2008**

Copyright 1993, 2008 © Dorling Kindersley Limited, London
A Penguin Company

ALL RIGHTS RESERVED. NO PART OF THIS PUBLICATION MAY BE REPRODUCED,
STORED IN A RETRIEVAL SYSTEM, OR TRANSMITTED IN ANY FORM OR BY ANY MEANS,
ELECTRONIC, MECHANICAL, PHOTOCOPYING, RECORDING OR OTHERWISE, WITHOUT
THE PRIOR WRITTEN PERMISSION OF THE COPYRIGHT OWNER.

A CIP CATALOGUE RECORD IS AVAILABLE FROM THE BRITISH LIBRARY.

ISBN: 978-1-40532-104-4

THROUGHOUT THIS BOOK, FLOORS ARE REFERRED TO IN ACCORDANCE WITH
AMERICAN USAGE, IE THE "FIRST FLOOR" IS AT GROUND LEVEL.

*Front cover main image: Brooklyn Bridge and downtown skyline*

**The information in this
DK Eyewitness Travel Guide is checked annually.**
Every effort has been made to ensure that this book is as up-to-date
as possible at the time of going to press. Some details, however,
such as telephone numbers, opening hours, prices, gallery hanging
arrangements, and travel information are liable to change. The
publishers cannot accept responsibility for any consequences arising
from the use of this book, nor for any material on third party
websites, and cannot guarantee that any website address in this
book will be a suitable source of travel information. We value the
views and suggestions of our readers very highly. Please write to:
Publisher, DK Eyewitness Travel Guides, Dorling Kindersley,
80 Strand, London WC2R 0RL, Great Britain.

◁ **Towering skyscrapers in central New York**

# CONTENTS

HOW TO USE THIS
GUIDE **6**

Baseball star
**Babe Ruth
(1895–1948)**

## INTRODUCING
## NEW YORK

FOUR GREAT DAYS IN
NEW YORK **10**

PUTTING NEW YORK
ON THE MAP **12**

THE HISTORY OF
NEW YORK **16**

NEW YORK
AT A GLANCE **34**

NEW YORK THROUGH
THE YEAR **50**

THE MANHATTAN
SKYLINE **54**

**South Manhattan skyline**

Vesuvio Bakery, SoHo

Trump Tower, Upper Midtown

The New York City Ballet

Riverfront promenade in Brooklyn

Bagel from a New York deli

Solomon R. Guggenheim Museum, Upper East Side

# HOW TO USE THIS GUIDE

This Eyewitness Travel Guide helps you get the most from your stay in New York with the minimum of practical difficulty. The opening section, *Introducing New York*, locates the city geographically, sets modern New York in its historical context and describes the highlights of the year. *New York at a Glance* is an overview of the city's attractions. Section two, *New York Area by Area*, guides you through the city's sightseeing areas. It describes all the main

sights with maps, photographs and detailed illustrations. In addition, seven planned walks take you step-by-step through special areas.

Well-researched tips on where to stay, eat, shop, and on sports and entertainment are in section three, *Travelers' Needs. Children's New York* lists highlights for young visitors, and section four, *Survival Guide*, shows you how to do everything from mailing a letter to using the subway.

## NEW YORK AREA BY AREA

Manhattan has been divided into 15 sightseeing areas, each described separately. Each area opens with a portrait, summing up the area's character and history and listing all the sights to be covered. Sights are numbered and clearly located on an *Area Map*. After this comes a large-scale *Street-by-Street Map* focusing on the most interesting part of the area. Finding your way around each area is made simple by the numbering system. This refers to the order in which sights are described on the pages that follow.

### 1 The Area Map

*For easy reference, the sights in each area are numbered and located on an* Area Map. *To help the visitor, the map also shows subway stations, heliports and ferry embarkation points.*

### 2 The Street-by-Street Map

*This gives a bird's-eye view of the heart of each sightseeing area. The most important buildings are illustrated, to help you spot them easily as you walk around.*

**Photographs** of facades and distinctive details of buildings help you locate the sights.

**Color-coding** on each page makes the area easy to find in the book.

**A locator map** shows you where you are in relation to surrounding areas. The area of the *Street-by-Street Map* is shown in red.

**Trump Tower ❷** is also shown on this map.

**Sights at a Glance** lists the sights in the area by category, including: Historic Streets and Buildings, Modern Architecture, Museums and Galleries, Churches, Monuments, and Parks and Squares.

**The area** covered in greater detail on the *Street-by-Street Map* is shaded red.

**Numbered circles** pinpoint all the listed sights on the area map. Trump Tower, for example, is ❷

**Travel tips** help you reach the area quickly by public transportation.

**Stars** indicate the sights that no visitor should miss.

**A suggested route** for a walk takes you past some of the area's most interesting sights.

## NEW YORK AT A GLANCE

Each map in this section concentrates on a specific theme: *Museums, Architecture, Multicultural New York,* and *Celebrated New Yorkers.* The top sights are shown on the map; other sights are described on the two pages following and cross-referenced to their full entries in the *Area by Area* section.

**Each sightseeing area** is color-coded.

**The theme** is explored in greater detail on the pages following the map.

### 3 Detailed information on each sight
*All important sights in each area are described in depth here. They are listed in order, following the numbering on the opening Area Map. Practical information is also provided.*

### PRACTICAL INFORMATION
Each entry provides all the information needed to plan a visit to the sight. The key to the symbols is inside the back cover.

**Address**

**Map reference to Street Finder at back of book**

**Sight Number**

## Trump Tower ②

725 5th Ave. **Map** 12 F3. **Tel** 832-2000. **M** 5th Ave-53rd St. **Garden level, shops open** 10am–6pm Mon–Sat. **Building open** 8am–10pm daily. **Adm free.** See **Shopping** p311.
📷 🅿 **Concerts.** 🍴 🛗 🎦

**Opening hours**

**Telephone number**

**Services and facilities available**

**Nearest subway station**

### 4 New York's major sights
*These are given two or more full pages in the sightseeing area in which they are found. Important buildings are dissected to reveal their interiors; museums have color-coded floor plans to help you find particular exhibits.*

**The Visitors' Checklist** provides the practical information you will need to plan your visit.

**The facade** of each major sight is shown to help you spot it quickly.

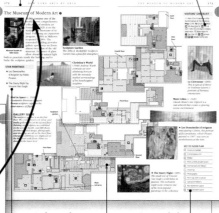

**Stars** indicate the most important exhibits or works of art on display inside, or the most interesting architectural details of the building.

**A color key** helps you find your way easily around the collection.

**Floors** are referred to in accordance with American usage, i.e., the "first floor" is at ground level.

# INTRODUCING
# NEW YORK

# FOUR GREAT DAYS IN NEW YORK

At first glance New York may seem a bit overwhelming, but these four great days are planned to give you a taste of the Big Apple, with much of the city's best in architecture, shopping, museums, and fun. Each day offers a mix of things to see and do, and the schedules are not meant to

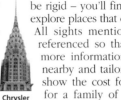

Chrysler pinnacle

be rigid – you'll find ample time to explore places that catch your fancy. All sights mentioned are cross-referenced so that you can find more information, check what's nearby and tailor the day. Prices show the cost for two adults or for a family of two adults and two children including lunch.

## CITY LANDMARKS

- A tour of the UN
- Modern, Art Deco and Beaux-Arts edifices
- Lights of Times Square
- Empire State Building

**TWO ADULTS** allow at least $115

### Morning
Start at the East River with a guided tour of **United Nations headquarters** (see pp160–63), with its striking modern architecture. Then head to 42nd Street, detouring into the unique residential enclave of **Tudor City** (see p158), and dropping in to admire the Art Deco interior of the **Chrysler Building** (see p155). Next is **Grand Central Terminal**, a great Beaux-Art landmark (see pp156–7; free tours Wed, Fri 12:30pm). Admire the Main Concourse and explore the shopping gallery, colorful food market and a food court with everything from sushi to Southern barbecue to New York cheesecake. Another lunchtime option is

chowder or a platter of Long Island oysters at the **Grand Central Oyster Bar** (see pp306).

### Afternoon
Back on 42nd Street is another Beaux-Arts creation, the **New York Public Library** (see p146; free one-hour tours at 11am and 2pm Tue–Sat). The marble halls, stairways, Main Reading Room and Periodicals Room are highlights. Check your e-mail for free in the Bill Blass Public Catalog Room. Look out also for current exhibits. Behind the library is **Bryant Park** (see p145), a welcome oasis of green in midtown. Ahead is New York's most famous crossroads, **Times Square** (see p147), gateway to the glittering neon of Broadway. The new 42nd Street is just beyond, now a bright avenue of restored theaters, giant movie palaces and Madame Tussaud's Wax Museum, with 200 true-to-life celebrities. Hail a cab to the **Empire State Building** (see pp136–7) and end the day with a fine twilight view of the city from the 86th-floor observatory.

**Glistening Prometheus Statue and Lower Plaza at Rockefeller Center**

## ART AND SHOPPING

- A morning of modern art
- Lunch at Rockefeller Center
- Fifth Avenue shopping
- Tea at the The Pierre

**TWO ADULTS** allow at least $135

### Morning
The spectacular **Museum of Modern Art** (MOMA) (see pp172–5) will easily fill your morning with its wonderful art. Allow a couple of hours to enjoy its great works, including Van Gogh's *The Starry Night* and Claude Monet's *Water Lilies*, as well as Picasso's *Les Demoiselles d'Avignon*, to name just a few. Don't miss the design exhibits on floor three; one of MOMA's best-known facets. Leave the museum and stroll over to the **Rockefeller Center** (see p144) for lunch at the Rock Center Café, where you can watch the ice skaters in action in winter.

**The neon lights of Times Square, the city's famous crossroad**

◁ New York harbor and 42nd Street in 1946

In summer the rink is transformed into a leafy garden, where you can dine at the Rink Bar.

## Afternoon

After lunch head for **St. Patrick's Cathedral** (see pp178–9), the largest Catholic cathedral in the US and one of the city's finest places of worship. Then continue along **Fifth Avenue** for an afternoon of upscale shopping. Saks Fifth Avenue is just across the street from St. Patrick's at 50th Street. Heading uptown, the temptations include Cartier (52nd St), Henri Bendel (55–56th sts), Prada, Fendi and Trump Tower (56–57th sts), Tiffany (57th St), and Bergdorf Goodman (57–58 sts). End the day on 61st Street with a final splurge – have a lavish English-style tea amid the murals at the **The Pierre** (see p290).

Statue of Liberty

## HISTORIC NEW YORK

• A boat trip to Ellis Island and the Statue of Liberty
• Lunch at Fraunces Tavern
• A tour of Old New York

**TWO ADULTS** allow at least $120

## Morning

At Battery Park, board the ferry to the **Statue of Liberty** (see pp74–5) and on to **Ellis Island** (see pp78–9), the point of arrival for many immigrants (round trip includes both stops). On your return, exit the park at **Bowling Green**, the city's oldest park (see p73). Walk to the **Fraunces Tavern Block Historic District** (see p76), New York's last block of 18th-century commercial buildings. The recreated Tavern includes a museum of the revolutionary period and a restaurant that

Central Park, a vast area of fun rides, animals, and places to play

is the perfect choice for an atmospheric lunch.

### Afternoon

A block away is Stone Street Historic District, rebuilt after a fire in 1835. Look for India House (see p56), once the New York Cotton Exchange, now **Harry's Café**. Take William Street to Wall Street and **Federal Hall** (see p68) with exhibits on the US Constitution. Nearby is the **New York Stock Exchange** (see pp70–1) and **Trinity Church** (see p68), built in 1839. Go up Broadway to **St. Paul's Chapel** (see p91), miraculously unscathed after the World Trade Center fell behind it. Ahead is **City Hall** (see p90). Finally, head for the **South Street Seaport Historic District**, heart of the 19th-century port (see pp82–3) with a view of the awesome **Brooklyn Bridge** (see pp86–9).

## A FAMILY FUN DAY

• A morning in Central Park
• Lunch at the Boathouse
• Dinosaurs at the American Museum of Natural History

**FAMILY OF 4** allow at least $175

## Morning

**Central Park** (see pp205–9) was made for family fun. Ride the vintage Carousel, watch model boats in action at Conservatory Pond, visit the Zoo, then watch the animal parade on the Delacorte clock on the half hour. There are themed playgrounds to please all ages: Safari at West 91st Street (2–5 years); Adventure at West 67th Street (6–12 years). The Swedish Cottage Marionette Theater, at West 79th, presents classic fairy tales (Tue–Fri: 10:30am and noon, Sat: 1:00pm, book in advance). Rent bikes or take a boat out on the lake, then lunch at the Boat House snack bar, which has a view of the lake. In winter, you can ice skate at the Wollman rink.

## Afternoon

Depending on ages and interests, choose between the interactive **Children's Museum** (see p219), or the famous dinosaurs and dioramas at the **American Museum of Natural History** (see pp216–17). Finish up on West 73rd Street for a "wee tea" at Alice's Tea Cup.

Ellis Island, the view greeting early immigrants to New York

# Putting New York on the Map

New York is a city of eight million people, covering 301 sq miles (780 sq km). The city gives its name to the state of New York, the capital of which is Albany, 156 miles (251 km) to the north. New York is also a good base from which to visit the historic towns of Boston and Philadelphia, as well as the nation's capital, Washington, DC.

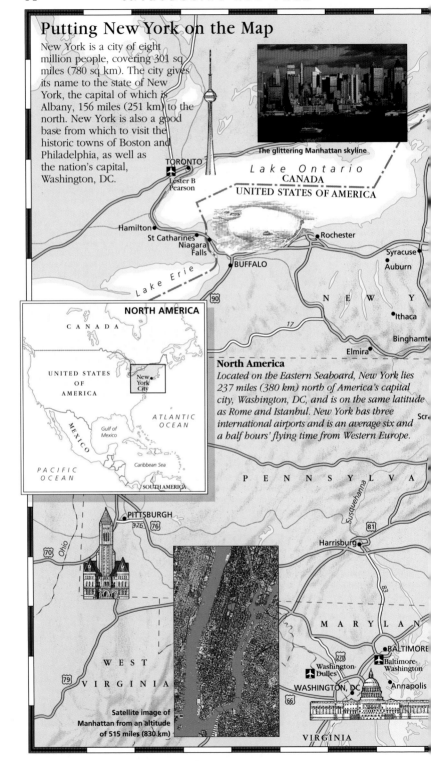

The glittering Manhattan skyline

TORONTO
Lester B Pearson

*Lake Ontario*

CANADA
UNITED STATES OF AMERICA

Hamilton
St Catharines
Niagara Falls
BUFFALO

Rochester

Syracuse
Auburn

*Lake Erie*

90

N   E   W      Y

Ithaca

17

Binghamt

Elmira

## North America

*Located on the Eastern Seaboard, New York lies 237 miles (380 km) north of America's capital city, Washington, DC, and is on the same latitude as Rome and Istanbul. New York has three international airports and is an average six and a half hours' flying time from Western Europe.*

NORTH AMERICA

C A N A D A

UNITED STATES
OF
AMERICA

New York City

ATLANTIC OCEAN

M
E
X
I
C
O

Gulf of Mexico

Caribbean Sea

PACIFIC OCEAN

SOUTH AMERICA

P   E   N   N   S   Y   L   V   A

Susquehanna

Scr

PITTSBURGH
376   76

81

Harrisburg

70

Ohio

Baltimore

M   A   R   Y   L   A   N

270

Washington-
Dulles

Baltimore-
Washington

WASHINGTON, DC

Annapolis

W E S T

79

V I R G I N I A

66

VIRGINIA

Satellite image of
Manhattan from an altitude
of 515 miles (830 km)

**GREATER NEW YORK**

**Greater New York**
*New York City is made
of five distinct boroughs:
Manhattan (where the
vast majority of sights are
located), the Bronx, Queens,
Brooklyn, and Staten Island.
Details of important sights
inside central New York but
within the city's boundaries
can be found on pages
133–55. Day trips in New
York State and beyond are
suggested on page 393.*

**KEY**

Greater New York

Airport

Interstate highway

State highway

Major railroad line

International border

Shipping route

State line

# Manhattan

This guide divides Manhattan into 15 areas, each with
its own chapter. Many of New York's oldest and newest
buildings rub shoulders in Lower Manhattan. It is
from here, too, that you can take the Staten Island
ferry, for breathtaking views of the city's famous
skyline and the Statue of Liberty. Midtown includes
the Theater District and Fifth Avenue's glittering
shops. Museum Mile, alongside Central Park on
Upper East Side, is a cultural paradise. To the north
lies Harlem, America's most famous black community.

**Grand Central Terminal**
*This Beaux Arts station has
been a gateway to the city
since 1913. Its concourse is
a vast pedestrian area with
a high-vaulted roof
(see pp156–7).*

**Morgan Library & Museum**
*One of the world's finest collections of rare
manuscripts, prints, and books is on display in
this palazzo-style building (see pp164–5).*

**Statue of Liberty**
*Presented as a gift from the
French to the American people
in 1886, this towering statue
has become a symbol of
freedom throughout the
world (see pp74–5).*

**Cathedral of
St. John the Divine**
*When it is finished, at
some time after the mid-
21st century, this great
cathedral will be the
largest in the world. It is
also a theater and music
venue (see pp226–7).*

kilometers               2

miles               1

**United Nations**
*New York is the headquarters of the global organization set up to preserve world peace and security (see pp160–63).*

**Empire State Building**
*This is the tallest skyscraper in New York and a symbol of the city. Built in the 1930s, it has since attracted more than 110 million visitors (see pp136–7).*

**KEY**

 Major Sight

**Metropolitan Museum of Art**
*With a stunning collection of artifacts dating from prehistoric times to the present, this is one of the world's greatest museums (see pp190–97).*

**Brooklyn Bridge**
*This bridge spans the East River between Manhattan and Brooklyn. Built in 1883, it was the largest suspension bridge and the first to be constructed of steel (see pp86–9).*

**Solomon R. Guggenheim Museum**
*A masterpiece of architecture by Frank Lloyd Wright, this unique building contains a fine collection of 19th- and 20th-century painting (see pp188–9).*

# THE HISTORY OF NEW YORK

From its first sighting almost 500 years ago by Giovanni da Verrazano, New York's harbor was the prize that all of Europe wanted to capture. The Dutch first sent fur traders to the area in 1621, but they lost the colony they called New Amsterdam to the English in 1664. The settlement was re-christened New York and the name stayed, even after the English lost the colony in 1783, at the end of the Revolutionary War.

A shell-work cloak worn by an Indian chief

### THE GROWING CITY

In the 19th century, New York grew rapidly and became a major port. Ease of shipping spawned manufacturing, commerce was king and great fortunes were made. In 1898, Manhattan was joined with the four outer boroughs to form the world's second-largest city. From 1800 to 1900, the population grew from 79,000 to 3 million people. New York City became the country's cultural and entertainment mecca as well as its business center.

### THE MELTING POT

The city continued to grow as thousands of immigrants came seeking a better life. Overpopulation meant that many at first lived in slums. Today, the mix of cultures has enriched the city and become its defining quality. Its eight million inhabitants speak some 100 languages.

Manhattan's skyline took shape as the city grew skyward to make space for its ever-increasing population. Throughout its history, the city has experienced alternating periods of economic decline and growth, but in both good times and bad, it remains one of the world's most vital cities.

The following pages illustrate significant periods in New York's history.

A deed signed by New Amsterdam's last Dutch governor, Peter Stuyvesant, in 1664

◁ The southern half of Manhattan and part of Brooklyn in 1767

# Early New York

**Indian husk mask**

Manhattan was a forested land populated by Algonquian-speaking Natives when the Dutch West India Company established a fur trading post called New Amsterdam in 1625. The first settlers built houses helter-skelter, so even today the streets of Lower Manhattan still twist. Broadway, then called by the Dutch name *Breede Wegh*, began as an Indian trail known as the Weekquaesgeek Trail. Harlem has also kept its Dutch name. The town was unruly until Peter Stuyvesant arrived to bring order. But the colony did not produce the expected revenues, and in 1664 the Dutch let it fall to the English, who renamed it New York.

**GROWTH OF THE METROPOLIS**

■ 1664    □ Today

**Seal of New Netherland**
*The beaver pelt and wampum (Indian shell beads) on the seal were the currency of the colony of New Netherland.*

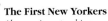

## FIRST VIEW OF MANHATTAN (1626)
*The southern tip of Manhattan resembled a Dutch town, down to the windmill. Although shown here, the fort had not yet been built.*

**The First New Yorkers**
*Algonquian-speaking Natives were the first inhabitants of Manhattan.*

Dutch ships

**Iroquois Pot**
*Iroquois Indians were frequent visitors to early Manhattan.*

**Indian Village**
*Some Algonquians lived in longhouses on Manhattan before the Dutch arrived.*

Native canoe

## TIMELINE

**1524** Giovanni da Verrazano sails into New York harbor

**1626** Peter Minuit buys Manhattan from the Natives

**1653** Wall is built for protection from attack; adjacent street is called Wall Street

**1625** Dutch establish first permanent trading post

**1600**

**1620**

**1640**

**1609** Henry Hudson sails up the Hudson River in search of the Northwest Passage

**1625** First black slaves brought from Africa

**1643–45** Indian skirmishes end with temporary peace treaty

**1647** Peter Stuyvesant becomes colonial governor

**1654** First Jewish settlers arrive

**Dutch Delftware**
*Colonists brought this popular tin-glazed earthen-ware pottery from Holland.*

**Manhattan Skyline**
*The Strand, now Whitehall Street, was the site of the city's first brick house.*

*Tiger* timbers

## WHERE TO SEE DUTCH NEW YORK

Dug up by workmen in 1916, these remnants of a Dutch ship, the *Tiger*, which burned in 1613, are the earliest artifacts of the period and are now in the Museum of the City of New York *(see p199)*. Rooms in this museum, as well as in the Morris-Jumel Mansion *(see p235)* and the Van Cortlandt House Museum *(see p240)*, display Dutch pottery, tiles and furniture.

**Purchase of Manhattan**
*Peter Minuit bought the island from the Natives in 1626 for $24 worth of trinkets.*

Dutch windmill

Fort Amsterdam

**Peter Stuyvesant**
*The last Dutch governor was a tyrant who imposed strict laws – such as an edict closing all the city's taverns at 9 o'clock.*

---

**1660** First city hospital established

**1664** British forces oust Dutch without a fight and change name to New York

**1676** Great Dock built on East River

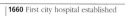

**1698** Trinity Church dedicated

**1660** | **1680** | **1700**

*The surrender of New Amsterdam to the British*

**1680s** Bolting Laws give New York exclusive right to process and ship grain

**1683** First New York city charter established

**1689** Merchant Jacob Leisler leads revolt against taxes and takes over the city for two years

**1693** Ninety-two cannons installed for protection; area becomes known as the Battery

**1691** Leisler sentenced to death for treason

# Colonial New York

Colonial gentleman

Under British rule, New York prospered and the population grew rapidly. The bolting of flour (grinding grain) was the main commercial enterprise. Shipbuilding also flourished. As the city prospered, an elite emerged that could afford a more refined way of life, and fine furniture and household silver were made for use in their homes during the Colonial period. During more than a century of governing New York, Britain proved more interested in profit than in the welfare of the colony. The Crown imposed hated taxes, and the spirit of rebellion grew, although especially in New York, loyalties were divided. On the the eve of Revolution, New York was the second-largest city in the 13 colonies, with 20,000 citizens.

Colonial currency

**GROWTH OF THE METROPOLIS**

▨ *1760*    ☐ *Today*

Bedroom

**Colonial Street**
*Pigs and dogs roamed free on the streets of Colonial New York.*

Dining room

**Kas**
*This Dutch-style pine wardrobe was made in New York's Hudson River valley around 1720.*

**Shipping**
*Trade with the West Indies and Britain helped New York prosper. In some years, 200 or more vessels visited the port.*

## TIMELINE

**1702** Lord Cornbury appointed Colonial governor; he often wore women's clothes

**1711** Slave market set up at the foot of Wall Street

**1720** First shipyard opens

| 1700 | 1710 | 1720 | 1730 |
|---|---|---|---|

**1710** Iroquois chief Hendrick visits England

**1732** First city theater opens

**1725** *New York Gazette*, city's first newspaper, is established

## Captain Kidd

*The Scottish pirate William Kidd was a respected citizen, lending a block and tackle to help build Trinity Church (see p68).*

## VAN CORTLANDT HOUSE

*Frederick Van Cortlandt built this Georgian-style house in 1748 on a wheat plantation in what is now the Bronx. Today a museum (see p240), it shows how a well-to-do Dutch-English family once lived.*

West parlor

### WHERE TO SEE COLONIAL NEW YORK

Colonial buildings are open to the public at Historic Richmond Town on Staten Island *(see p254)*. Fine examples of Colonial silver and furniture are on display at the Museum of the City of New York *(see p199)*.

Richmond Town General Store

## Colonial Kitchen

*Plain white cheese, called "white meat," was often served in place of meat. Waffles, introduced by the Dutch, were popular. Fresh fruit was rare, but preserved fruits were eaten.*

Pewter baby bottle

Cheese mold

Waffle iron

### Decorative Carvings

*A face carved in stone peers over each of the front windows.*

Sucket fork, for eating preserved fruits

---

**1734** John Peter Zenger's libel trial upholds freedom of the press

**1741** Slave uprising creates hysteria; 31 slaves are executed, 150 imprisoned

**1754** French and Indian War begins; King's College (now Columbia University) founded

*British soldier*

**1759** First jail built

**1740**  **1750**  **1760**

**1733** Bowling Green becomes first city park; first ferries to Brooklyn

*King's College*

**1762** First paid police force

**1763** War ends; British gain control of North America

# Revolutionary New York

**George Washington, Revolutionary general**

Dug up into trenches for defense, heavily shelled by British troops and scarred by recurring fires, New York suffered during the American Revolution. But despite the hardships, many continued to enjoy cricket games, horse races, balls and boxing matches. After the British took the city in 1776, it became their headquarters. The Continental army did not return to Manhattan until November 25, 1783, two years after the fighting ended.

**GROWTH OF THE METROPOLIS**

▮ *1776* ☐ *Today*

**Battle Dress**
*The Continental (Patriot) army wore blue uniforms, while the British wore red.* **British soldier**

## TOPPLING THE KING

*New Yorkers tore down the statue of King George III in Bowling Green and melted it down to make ammunition.*

**Soldier's Haversack**
*American soldiers in the War of Independence carried their supplies in haversacks.*

**American soldier**

**Battle of Harlem Heights**
*Washington won this battle on September 16, 1776. But he did not have enough troops to hold New York so retreated, leaving it to the British.*

**Patriot**

**Death of a Patriot**
*While working behind British lines in 1776, Nathan Hale was captured and hanged by the British without trial for spying.*

## TIMELINE

**1765** British pass Stamp Act; New Yorkers protest; Sons of Liberty formed

**1767** New duties imposed with Townshend Act; after protests, the act is repealed

**1770** Sons of Liberty fight British in the "Battle of Golden Hill"

**1774** Rebels dump tea in New York harbor to protest taxes

1

**1766** St. Paul's Chapel completed; Stamp Act repealed; Statue of George III erected on Bowling Green

*St. Paul's Chapel*

*General William Howe, commander in chief of the British troops*

**1776** War begins; 500 ships under General Howe assemble in New York harbor

**Leather fire bucket**

## Fire Fighters
*Fires had long threatened the city, but during the war a series of fires nearly destroyed it. In the wake of the patriot retreat, on September 21, 1776, a devastating fire razed Trinity Church and 1,000 houses.*

## Flags of the Revolution
*Washington's army flew the Continental colors, with a stripe for each of the 13 colonies and a Union Jack in the corner. The Stars and Stripes became the official flag in 1777.*

**First Stars and Stripes**

**Continental colors**

**Statue of George III**

## General Washington Returns
*Washington received a hero's welcome when he reentered New York on November 25, 1783, after the British withdrawal.*

**Cheering patriots**

## WHERE TO SEE THE REVOLUTIONARY CITY

In 1776, George Washington used the Morris-Jumel Mansion in upper Manhattan as a headquarters *(see p235)*. He also slept at the Van Cortlandt House *(see p21 and p240)*. After the war he bade farewell to his officers at Fraunces Tavern *(see p76)*.

**Morris-Jumel mansion**

**1783** Treaty of Paris signed, US wins independence; British evacuate New York

**1785** New York named US capital

**1784** Bank of New York chartered

**1789** George Washington inaugurated as first president at Federal Hall

**1790** US capital is moved to Philadelphia

**1794** Bellevue Hospital opens on the East River

**1790**

**1792** Tontine Coffee House built – first home of the Stock Exchange

**1791** New York Hospital, city's oldest, opens

*Washington's inauguration*

**1801** *New York Post* founded by Alexander Hamilton

**1800**

**1804** Vice President Aaron Burr kills political rival Alexander Hamilton in a duel

# New York in the 19th Century

**Governor De Witt Clinton**

Firmly established as the nation's largest city and preeminent seaport, New York grew increasingly wealthy. Manufacturing increased due to the ease of shipping; tycoons like John Jacob Astor made millions. The rich moved uptown; public transportation followed. With rapid growth came fires, epidemics and financial panics. Immigrants from Ireland, Germany, and other nations arrived. Some found prosperity; others crowded into slums in Lower Manhattan.

**GROWTH OF THE METROPOLIS**

☐ *1840*        ☐ *Today*

**Sheet Music**
*The Stephen Foster ballad* Jeanie With the Light Brown Hair *was popular at this time.*

**Croton Distributing Reservoir** was built in 1842. Until then, New Yorkers had no fresh drinking water – they relied on deliveries of bottled water.

**Keeping Fit**
*Gymnasiums such as Dr. Rich's Institute for Physical Education were established in New York in the 1830s and 1840s.*

**Omnibus**
*The horse-drawn omnibus was introduced for public transportation in 1832 and remained on New York streets until World War I.*

## TIMELINE

**1805** First free state schools established in New York

**1811** Randel Plan divides Manhattan into grid pattern above 14th Street

**1812–14** War of 1812; British blockade New York harbor

*The* Constitution, *most famous ship in War of 1812*

**1835** Much of old New York razed in city's worst fire

| 1810 | 1820 | 1830 |
|---|---|---|

**1807** Robert Fulton launches first steamboat, on the Hudson River

**1822** Yellow fever epidemic; people evacuate to Greenwich Village

**1823** New York surpasses Boston and Philadelphia to become nation's largest city

**1827** New York abolishes slavery

**1837** New Yorker Samuel Morse sends first telegraph message

**The Brownstone**
*Many brownstone row houses were built in the first half of the century. The raised stoop allowed separate entry to the parlor and ground-floor servants' quarters.*

**Crystal Palace** was an iron and glass exhibition hall erected for the 1853 World's Fair.

## NEW YORK IN 1855
*Looking south from 42nd Street, Crystal Palace and the Croton Distributing Reservoir stood where the main public library and Bryant Park are today.*

## THE PORT OF NEW YORK
New York's importance as a port city grew by leaps and bounds in the early 19th century. Robert Fulton launched his first steamboat, the *Clermont*, in 1807. Steamboats made travel much quicker – it now took 72 hours to reach Albany, which was both the state capital and the gateway to the West. Trade with the West by steamboat and canal boat, and with the rest of the world by clipper ship, made the fortunes of many New Yorkers.

The steamboat *Clermont*

**Crystal Palace in Flames**
*On October 5, 1858, New York's Crystal Palace exhibition hall burned to the ground, just as its predecessor in London did.*

**Grand Canal Celebration**
*Ships in New York harbor lined up to celebrate the 1825 Erie Canal opening. In connecting the Great Lakes with Albany, the state capital, on the Hudson River, the canal opened a water link between the Midwest and the Port of New York. New York realized huge profits.*

---

*Early baseball player*

*Crowds in Central Park*

**1849** Astor Place riots; ships set sail for California Gold Rush

**1851** *New York Times* first published

**1861** Civil War begins

**1863** Draft riots last four days, many die

**1853** New York hosts World's Fair

**1857** Financial panic and depression

**1865** Abraham Lincoln lies in state in City Hall

**1840**     **1850**     **1860**

**1845** New York Knickerbockers, first organized baseball team chartered

*Clipper ship card*

**1858** Vaux and Olmsted design Central Park; Macy's founded

**1842** Croton Reservoir built

FREE TRADE

# The Age of Extravagance

**Industrialist
Andrew Carnegie**

As New York's merchant princes grew ever wealthier, the city entered into a gilded era during which many of its most opulent buildings went up. Millions were lavished on the arts with the founding of the Metropolitan Museum, Public Library and Carnegie Hall. Luxury hotels like the Plaza and the original Waldorf-Astoria were built, and elegant department stores arose to serve the wealthy. Such flamboyant figures as William "Boss" Tweed, political strongman and king of corruption, and circus man Phineas T. Barnum were also larger than life.

**GROWTH OF THE METROPOLIS**
🔲 1890  ☐ Today

**Overlooking the Park**
*The Dakota (1880) was the first grand luxury apartment house on the Upper West Side (see p218).*

**Palatial Living**
*Mansions lined Fifth Avenue. When it was built in 1882, W.K. Vanderbilt's Italianate palace at 660 Fifth Avenue, was one of the farthest north.*

**Fashion City**
*Lord & Taylor built a new store on Broadway's Ladies' Mile; 6th Avenue between 14th and 23rd streets was known as Fashion Row.*

**BATHING SUITS.**

A GREAT SPECIALTY AT
**LORD & TAYLOR'S, Broadway and 20th Street, N.Y.**

**THE ELEVATED RAILROAD**
*By the mid 1870s, elevated railroads or "Els" ran along 2nd, 3rd, 6th and 9th avenues. They made travel faster, but left noise, grime and pollution in their wake.*

## TIMELINE

**1867** Brooklyn's Prospect Park completed

**1868** First elevated railroad built on Greenwich Street

**1869** First apartment house built on 18th Street; Black Friday financial crisis hits Wall Street

*The interior of the Stock Exchange*

**1870** J.D. Rockefeller founds Standard Oil

**1871** The first Grand Central Depot opens on 42nd St.; "Boss" Tweed is arrested and imprisoned

**1872** Bloomingdale's opens

**1873** Banks fail: Stock Exchange panics

**1877** A.G. Bell demonstrates the telephone in New York

**1879** St. Patrick's Cathedral completed; first city telephone exchange opened on Nassau Street

1865 1870 1875

**Mark Twain's Birthday**
*Mark Twain, whose 1873 novel* The Gilded Age *portrayed the decadent lifestyle of New Yorkers, celebrated his birthday at Delmonico's.*

## WHERE TO SEE THE AGE OF EXTRAVAGANCE

The Gold Room in the Henry Villard Houses *(see p176)* is a good place to experience the city's past. Formerly the Music Room, it is now a venue for afternoon tea. The Museum of the City of New York also has period rooms (p199)

Elevated train

Bowery

Streetcar

**Rural Fifth Avenue**
*This painting by Ralph Blakelock shows a shanty-town at 86th Street. Today it is one of New York's most expensive addresses.*

### The Tweed Ring
*William "Boss" Tweed led Tammany Hall, which dominated city government. He stole millions in city funds.*

Nast's cartoon of "Boss" Tweed

### Tammany Tiger
*The Museum of the City of New York has "Boss" Tweed's cane, which sports a gold Tammany Tiger mascot on its handle.*

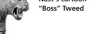

**1880** Canned fruits and meats first appear in stores; Metropolitan Museum of Art opens; streets lit by electricity

**1883** Metropolitan Opera opens on Broadway; Brooklyn Bridge completed

**1886** Statue of Liberty unveiled

**1891** Carnegie Hall opens

**1880**          **1885**          **1890**

**1888** Great Blizzard dumps 22 in (56 cm) of snow

**1890** First moving picture shows appear in New York

*Grand display of fireworks over Brooklyn Bridge, 1883*

**1892** Cathedral of St. John the Divine begun; Ellis Island opens

# New York at the Turn of the Century

**Horse-drawn carriage**

By 1900, New York was a hub of American industry: 70% of the country's corporations were based there, and the port handled two-thirds of all imported goods. The rich got richer, but in the crowded slums, disease spread. Even so, immigrants kept their rich traditions alive, and political and social reform emerged. In 1900, the International Ladies' Garment Workers' Union was founded to battle for the rights of the women and children who toiled in dangerous factories for low wages. The Triangle Shirtwaist Factory fire in 1911 also sped reform.

**GROWTH OF THE METROPOLIS**

▨ *1914*   ☐ *Today*

**Gateway to America**
*Almost five times as crowded as the rest of New York, the Lower East Side was the most densely populated place in the world.*

**Crowded Conditions**
*Tenements were unhealthy and overcrowded. They often lacked windows, air shafts or proper sanitary facilities.*

## WHERE TO SEE TURN-OF-THE-CENTURY NEW YORK

The Lower East Side Tenement Museum *(see p97)* has exhibits on tenement life.

**Tailor's scissors**

**Hip bath**

**Inside a Sweatshop**
*Workers toiled long hours for low wages in the overcrowded sweatshops of the garment district. This view of Moe Levy's shop was taken in 1912.*

**Streetcars on Broadway**

## TIMELINE

**1895** Olympia Theater is first to open in the Broadway area

**1898** Five boroughs merge to form world's second-largest city

**1901** Macy's opens Broadway department store

**1895**

**1900**

**1896** First bagel served in a Clinton Street bakery

**1897** Waldorf-Astoria Hotel opens: the largest hotel in the world

**1900** Mayor Robert Van Wyck breaks ground for city's first subway with silver shovel

**1903** Lyceum Theater opens – oldest Broadway house still in use

## FLATIRON BUILDING

*Overlooking Madison Square where Broad-way, Fifth Avenue and 23rd Street meet, the 21-story tower was one of the city's first sky-scrapers (1902). Triangle-shaped, it was dubbed the Flatiron Building (see p127).*

Underlying steel structure

Elaborate limestone facade

Only 6 ft (185 cm) wide at apex of triangle

### Supper in the Saddle
*Decadent parties were all the rage. C.K.G. Billings's horseback dinner at Sherry's restaurant in 1903 was the talk of all New York.*

### Plaza Promenade
*The section of Fifth Avenue in front of the Plaza Hotel was considered the most elegant in the city.*

Ventilated hairpiece

### High Fashion
*In 1900 styles were stiff, with wire hoops and bustles worn beneath ornate dresses. Later, clothes became softer and more practical.*

Long bustle

Wire hoops

**1906** Architect Stanford White shot at Madison Square Garden, which he had built in 1890

**1909** Wilbur Wright flies first plane over New York

**1910** Pennsylvania Station opens

**1913** Woolworth Building is world's tallest; new Grand Central Terminal opens; Harlem's Apollo Theater opens

**1905**

**1910**

**1905** First crossing of the Staten Island Ferry

**1907** First metered taxicabs; first Ziegfield Follies

**1911** Triangle Shirtwaist Factory fire kills 146 sweatshop workers; New York Public Library completed

*Woolworth Building*

# New York Between the Wars

**Entrance card to the Cotton Club**

The 1920s were a time of high living for many New Yorkers. Mayor Jimmy Walker set the pace, whether squiring chorus girls, drinking in speakeasies or watching the Yankees. But the good times ended with the 1929 stock market crash. By 1932, Walker had resigned, charged with corruption, and one-quarter of New Yorkers were unemployed. With Mayor Fiorello La Guardia's 1933 election, New York began to recover and thrive.

**GROWTH OF THE METROPOLIS**
  1933     Today

**Exotic Costumes**
*Chorus girls were a major Cotton Club attraction.*

**THE COTTON CLUB**
*This Harlem nightclub was host to the best jazz in town, as first Duke Ellington and then Cab Calloway led the band. People flocked from all over the city to hear them.*

**Defying Prohibition**
*Although alcohol was outlawed, speakeasies – semi-secret illegal drinking dens – still sold it.*

**Home-Run Hitter**
*In 1927, baseball star Babe Ruth hit a record 60 home runs for the Yankees. Yankee Stadium (see p241) became known as "the house that Ruth built."*

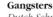

Sawed-off shotgun concealed in violin case

**Gangsters**
*Dutch Schultz was the kingpin of an illegal booze racket.*

## TIMELINE

**1918** End of World War I

**1919** 18th Amendment bans alcohol, launches Prohibition Era

**1920** US women get the vote

*Opening of the Holland Tunnel*

**1926** Jimmy Walker becomes mayor

**1931** Empire State Building becomes world's tallest

1920

1925

1930

**1924** Novelist James Baldwin is born in Harlem

**1925** *The New Yorker* magazine is launched

**1927** Lindbergh flies across the Atlantic; first talking movie, *The Jazz Singer*, opens; Holland Tunnel opens

**1929** Stock market crash; Great Depression begins

**1930** Chrysler Building completed

### Big Band Leaders
*Banned from many downtown clubs, black artists like Cab Calloway starred at the Cotton Club.*

### Broadway Melodies
*The 1920s were the heyday of the Broadway musical, with a record number of plays opening.*

### THE GREAT DEPRESSION
The Roaring Twenties ended with the stock market crash of October 29, 1929, which set off the Depression. New York was hard hit: squatters' shacks sprang up in Central Park and thousands were out of work. But art flourished as artists went to work for the Works Projects Administration (WPA), creating outstanding murals and artworks throughout the city.

**Waiting to receive benefits in 1931**

**Lindbergh's plane, *Spirit of St. Louis***

**Breakfast menu**

### Lindbergh's Flight
*New Yorkers celebrated Lindbergh's nonstop solo flight across the Atlantic in 1927 in a variety of ways, including a breakfast in his honor.*

### Rockefeller Center
*Millionaire John D. Rockefeller drives the final rivet to celebrate the opening of Rockefeller Center on May 1, 1939.*

### Mass Event
*Forty-five million people visited the 1939 World's Fair in New York.*

**1933** Prohibition ends; Fiorello LaGuardia begins three terms as mayor

**1940** Queens-Midtown Tunnel opens

**1942** Times Square blacked out during World War II; Idlewild International Airport (now JFK) opens

**1935**

**1940**

**1945**

**1936** Parks Department headed by Robert Moses; new parks created

**1939** Rockefeller Center is completed

**1941** US enters World War II

**1944** Black leader Adam Clayton Powell elected to Congress

# Postwar New York

Since World War II, New York has seen both the best of times and the worst. Although established as the financial capital of the world, the city itself almost went bankrupt in the 1970s. Wall Street hit its peak in the 1980s, then experienced its worst crash since 1929. Since the early 1990s, New York has seen a dramatic drop in the crime rate and an increase in the restoration and renewal of such landmarks as Grand Central Terminal and the "new" Times Square. This constant rebuilding is emblematic of the city's position at the cultural and financial hub of the United States.

**1967** Hippie musical *Hair* opens on Off-Broadway, then transfers to the Biltmore Theater

**1971** Pop artist Andy Warhol has a retrospective show of his work at the Whitney Museum

**1966** Newspaper and transit strikes

**1953** Merce Cunningham founds dance company

**1963** Pennsylvania Station razed

**1959** Guggenheim Museum opens

**1945** End of World War II

**1975** Federal loan saves New York from bankruptcy

**1946** UN headquarters established in New York

**1954** Ellis Island closes

| 1945 | 1950 | 1955 | 1960 | 1965 | 1970 | 1975 |
|------|------|------|------|------|------|------|
| MAYORS: | IMPELLITERI WAGNER | | | LINDSAY | | BEAME |
| 1945 | 1950 | 1955 | 1960 | 1965 | 1970 | 1975 |

**1947** Jackie Robinson, first black baseball player in the major leagues, signs with Brooklyn Dodgers

**1964** New York World's Fair; race riots in Harlem and Bedford-Stuyvesant; Verrazano Narrows Bridge links Brooklyn and Staten Island; Beatles play at Shea Stadium

**1973** World Trade Center completed

*Souvenir scarf*

**1968** 20,000 anti-establishment hippies gather in Central Park; student sit-ins at Columbia University

*Andy Warhol with actresses Candy Darling and Ultra Violet*

**1983** Economic boom: property prices skyrocket; Trump Tower completed by real estate tycoon Donald Trump, who symbolizes the "yuppie" wealth of the 1980s

**1981** New York regains solvency

**1988** Twenty-five percent of New Yorkers live below the poverty line

**1990** David Dinkins, New York's first black mayor, takes office; Ellis Island reopens as an immigration museum

**2001** Terrorist attack on the World Trade Center; Mayor Giuliani is a great support to the people of New York. President George W Bush declares war on terrorism

**1987** Stock market crash

**1994** Rudolph Giuliani takes office as mayor

| 1980 | 1985 | 1990 | 1995 | 2000 | 2005 |
|------|------|------|------|------|------|

KOCH            DINKINS    GIULIANI          BLOOMBERG

| 1980 | 1985 | 1990 | 1995 | 2000 | 2005 |
|------|------|------|------|------|------|

**1986** Shock of corruption scandals rock Mayor Koch's administration; Centennial of Statue of Liberty

**2000** Population reaches just over 8 million

**2003** A major power outage on August 14 leaves 50 million people in the North East (including New York City), mid-West, and ports of Canada, blacked out for up to 24 hours

**1995** The neglected Chelsea Piers are renovated and open as a mammoth sports and entertainment complex (*see p138*)

**2002** The lights go on in a regenerated 42nd Street, which crosses Broadway at Times Square. Along with neighboring Chelsea and its cutting-edge galleries, the area out-shines SoHo as the city's chic spot

# NEW YORK AT A GLANCE

There are almost 300 places of interest described in the Area by Area section of this book. They range from the bustling New York Stock Exchange *(see pp70–71)* to Central Park's peaceful Strawberry Fields *(see p208)*, and from historic synagogues to dazzling skyscrapers. The following 14 pages provide a time-saving guide to New York's most interesting sights. Museums and architecture each have a section, and there are guides to the people and cultures that have given the city its unique character. Each sight is cross-referenced to its own full entry. Below are the top ten tourist attractions to start you off.

## NEW YORK'S TOP TEN TOURIST ATTRACTIONS

**Empire State Building**
*See pp136–7.*

**Ellis Island**
*See pp78–9.*

**South Street Seaport**
*See p84.*

**Museum of Modern Art**
*See pp172–5.*

**Rockefeller Center**
*See p144.*

**Central Park**
*See pp204–9.*

**Statue of Liberty**
*See pp74–5.*

**Metropolitan Museum of Art**
*See pp190–97.*

**Brooklyn Bridge**
*See pp86–9.*

**Chinatown**
*See pp96–7.*

◁ Park Avenue's relentless flow of traffic

# New York's Best: Museums

New York's museums range from the vast scope of the Metropolitan Museum to the personal treasures of financier J. Pierpont Morgan's own collection. Several museums celebrate New York's heritage, giving visitors an insight into the people and events that made the city what it is today. This map features some highlights, with a detailed overview on pages 38 and 39.

**Museum of Modern Art**
*Picasso's Goat (1950) is among the impressive collection in the renovated and expanded Museum of Modern Art.*

***Intrepid* Sea-Air-Space Museum**
*This naval museum also traces the progress of flight exploration. The large aircraft carrier housing it is currently docked in New Jersey for restoration.*

**Morgan Library & Museum**
*One of the world's finest collections of manuscripts, prints and books includes this rare French Bible from 1230.*

**Merchant's House Museum**
*This perfectly preserved 1832 house belonged to a wealthy trader.*

**Ellis Island**
*This museum vividly re-creates the experiences of many millions of immigrant families.*

Upper West Side

Theater District

Chelsea and the Garment District

Lower Midtown

Gramercy and the Flatiron District

Greenwich Village

East Village

SoHo and TriBeCa

Lower East Side

Lower Manhattan

Seaport and the Civic Center

Ellis Island

0 kilometers    2

0 miles    1

**American Museum of Natural History**
*Dinosaurs, meteorites and much more have fascinated generations of visitors here.*

*Morningside Heights and Harlem*

*Central Park*

*Upper East Side*

*Upper Midtown*

**Museum of the City of New York**
*Costumes, works of art and household objects (such as this 1725 silver dish) create an intricate and detailed picture of New York's past.*

**Cooper-Hewitt Museum**
*A wealth of decorative arts is displayed in industrialist Andrew Carnegie's former Upper East Side mansion.*

**Solomon R. Guggenheim Museum**
*Painting and sculpture by almost all major avant-garde artists of the late 19th century to the end of the 20th fill this unique building by Frank Lloyd Wright.*

**Metropolitan Museum of Art**
*Of the millions of works in its collection, this 12th-dynasty Egyptian faïence hippo is the museum's own mascot.*

**Frick Collection**
*The collection of 19th-century rail-road magnate Henry Clay Frick is displayed in his former home. Master-pieces include* St. Francis in the Desert *(about 1480) by Giovanni Bellini.*

**Whitney Museum of American Art**
*This exceptional collection includes many views of New York. One of the best is* Brooklyn Bridge: Variation on an Old Theme *(1939), by Joseph Stella.*

# Exploring New York's Museums

**Richmond Town tobacco tin**

You could devote an entire month to visiting New York's museums and still not do them justice. There are more than 60 museums in Manhattan alone, and half that number again in the other boroughs. The wealth of art and the huge variety of offerings – from Old Masters to old fire engines, dinosaurs to dolls, Tibetan tapestries to African masks – is equal to that of any city in the world. Note that some museums close on Monday as well as on another day. Many stay open late one or two evenings a week, and some have one evening when admission is free. Not every museum charges for admission, but donations are always welcome.

## PAINTING AND SCULPTURE

New York is best known for its art museums. The **Metropolitan Museum of Art** houses an extensive collection of American art, as well as world-famous masterpieces. **The Cloisters**, a branch of the "Met" in Upper Manhattan, is a treasury of medieval art and architecture. The **Frick Collection** has a superb display of Old Masters. In contrast, the **Museum of Modern Art (MoMA)** houses Impressionist and modern paintings. **The Whitney Museum of American Art** and the **Solomon R. Guggenheim Museum** also specialize in modern art, the Whitney's biennial show being the foremost display of work by living artists. Today's cutting-edge art is at the **New Museum of Contemporary Art**, and the work of untrained artists can be seen at the

**American Folk Art Museum**. The **National Academy Museum** displays a collection of 19th- and 20th-century art, donated by academy members. In Harlem, the **Studio Museum** shows the work of black artists.

## CRAFTS AND DESIGN

If you are interested in textiles, porcelain and glass, embroideries and laces, wallpaper, and prints, visit the **Cooper-Hewitt Museum**, the decorative arts out-post of Washington's Smithsonian Institu-tion. The design collections at **MoMA** trace the history of design from clocks to couches. The **Museum of Arts and Design** offers the finest work of today's skilled artisans in mediums from furniture to art glass, and the **American Folk Art Museum** presents folk forms, from quilts to canes. Silver collections are notable at the **Museum of the City of New York**. The fine displays of native art at the **National Museum of the American Indian** include jewelry, rugs and pottery.

## PRINTS AND PHOTOGRAPHY

The **International Center of Photography** is the only museum in New York that is totally devoted to this medium. Collections can also be seen at the **Metropolitan Museum of Art** and there are many examples of early photography at the **Museum of the City of New York** and **Ellis Island**.

Prints and drawings by such great book illustrators as Kate Greenaway and Sir John Tenniel are featured at the **Morgan Library & Museum**. The **Cooper-Hewitt Museum** has examples of the use of prints in the decorative arts.

## FURNITURE AND COSTUMES

The annual exhibition of the Costume Institute at the **Metropolitan Museum of Art** is always worth a visit. Also impressive is the American Wing, with its 24 rooms of original furnishings tracing life from 1640 to the 20th century. Period rooms depicting New York in various settings, beginning with the 17th-century Dutch, are on display at the **Museum of the City of New York**.

**Corn husk doll, American Museum of Natural History**

There are also some house museums that give a realistic picture of life and furnishings in old New York. The **Merchant's House Museum**, a preserved residence from 1832, was occupied by the same family for 98 years. **Gracie Mansion** was the residence of mayor Archibald Gracie, who bought it in 1798 from a shipping merchant, and it is open periodically for public tours. The **Theodore Roosevelt Birthplace** is the brownstone where the 26th president of the United States grew up, and the **Mount Vernon Hotel Museum** was an early 19th-century resort.

*The Peaceable Kingdom* (c.1840–45) by Edward Hicks, at the Brooklyn Museum

## HISTORY

Palm pistol at the New
York City Police Museum

American history unfolds
at **Federal Hall**, the United
States' first capitol, where
George Washington took
his oath as America's first
president on the balcony
in April 1789.

Visit the **Fraunces Tavern
Museum** for a glimpse of
colonial New York. **Ellis
Island** and **Lower East Side
Tenement Museum** re-create
the hardships faced by immi-
grants. The new **Museum of
Jewish Heritage** in Battery
City is a living memorial
to the Holocaust. The **New
York City Fire Museum** and
the **New York City Police
Museum** chronicle heroism
and tragedy, while the **South
Street Seaport Museum** re-
creates early maritime history.

## TECHNOLOGY AND
NATURAL HISTORY

Forest-dwelling bonga, American
Museum of Natural History

Science museums hold exhibitions from nature to space-age
technology. The **American
Museum of Natural History**
has vast collections covering
flora, fauna and cultures from
around the world. Its Rose
Center/Hayden Planetarium
offers a unique view of space.
The *Intrepid* Sea-Air-Space
Museum is a repository of
technology that chronicles
military progress. It is based on
the decks of an aircraft carrier.

If you missed a classic Lucille
Ball sitcom or footage of the
first man on the moon, the
place to visit is the **Museum
of Television and Radio**, which
holds these and many other
classics of TV and radio.

## ART FROM OTHER
CULTURES

Egyptian
mummy,
Brooklyn
Museum

Artwork of other
nations is the focus
of several special
collections.
Oriental art is the
specialty of the
**Asia Society**
and the **Japan
Society**. The
**Jewish Museum**
features major
collections of
Judaica and has
changing exhibi-
tions of various
aspects of Jewish
life. **El Museo
del Barrio** is
dedicated to the
arts of Puerto Rico,
including many
Pre-Columbian
artifacts. For an
impressive review
of African-American
art and history, visit
the **Schomburg
Center for Research
in Black Culture**. Finally, the
**Metropolitan Museum of Art**
excels in its multicultural
displays, ranging from the
art of ancient Egypt to that
of contemporary Africa.

## LIBRARIES

New York's notable libraries,
such as the **Morgan Library
& Museum**, offer superb art
collections as well as a
chance to view pages from
ancient manuscripts and rare
books. The **New York Public
Library**'s collection includes
historic documents and manuscripts of many famous works.

## BEYOND MANHATTAN

Other museums worth a visit
include the **Brooklyn Museum
of Art**, with a huge collection
of artifacts from across the

world and over one million
paintings. The **Museum of the
Moving Image** in Queens has
a unique collection of motion-
picture history. The **Jacques
Marchais Museum of Tibetan
Art** is a rare find on Staten
Island as is **Historic Richmond
Town**, a well-restored village
dating from the 1600s.

## FINDING THE MUSEUMS

# New York's Best: Architecture

Even when following world trends, New York has
given its own twist to the turns of architectural
fashion, the style of its buildings influenced by both
geography and economy. An island city, with space
at a premium, must look upward to grow. This
trend was reflected early on with tall, narrow town

**Apartment Buildings**
*The Majestic is one of five
Art Deco twin-towered
apartment buildings
on Central
Park
West.*

houses and later with
the city's apartment
buildings and sky-
scrapers. Building
materials such as cast-
iron and brownstone
were chosen for their
local availability and
practical appeal. The
result is a city that has
developed by finding
flamboyant answers to
practical needs. A more
detailed overview of
New York's architecture
is on pages 42 to 43.

**Cast-Iron Architecture**
*Mass-produced cast-iron was often
used for building facades. SoHo has
many of the best examples, such as this
building at 28–30 Greene Street.*

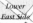

Theater District

Chelsea and the Garment District

Greenwich Village

Gramercy and the Flatiron District

SoHo and TriBeCa

East Village

Lower East Side

Lower Manhattan

**Post-Modernism**
*The quirky, yet elegant, shapes
of buildings like the World
Financial Center, built in 1985
(see p69) mark a bold departure
from the sleek steel-and-glass
boxes of the 1950s and 1960s.*

**Brownstones**
*Built from local sand-
stone, brownstones
were favored by the
19th-century middle
classes. India House,
built in a Florentine
palazzo style on Wall
Street, is typical of
many brownstone
commercial buildings.*

19th-Century Mansions
The Jewish Museum (see p186), *formerly the home of Felix M. Warburg, is a fine example of the French Renaissance style that typified these mansions.*

Beaux Arts
Opulent style, created for the richest of owners, is exemplified by the Beaux Arts grandeur of the Frick mansion.

Modernism
The Seagram Building's sleek bronze-and-glass walls, scant decoration and monumental scale typify postwar architecture (see p177.)

The Skyscraper
The glory of New York architecture, these buildings expressed a perfect blend of practical engineering skill together with fabulous decoration, such as this gargoyle on the Chrysler Building.

Federal Architecture
Federal style was popular in civic architecture of the 19th century; City Hall combines it with French Renaissance influences.

Tenements
Constructed as an economic form of housing, for many these buildings were a stark introduction to new lives. Mainly built on the Lower East Side, the apartments were hopelessly overcrowded. In addition, the buildings' design, with inadequate air shafts, resulted in apartments with little or no ventilation.

# Exploring New York's Architecture

**A Federal-style front door**

During its first 200 years, New York, like all of America, looked to Europe for architectural inspiration. None of the buildings from the Dutch colonial period survive in Manhattan today; most were lost in the great fire of 1776 or torn down to make way for new developments in the early 1800s. Throughout the 18th and 19th centuries, the city's major architectural trends followed those of Europe. With the advent of cast-iron architecture in the 1850s, the Art Deco period and the ever-higher rise of the skyscraper, New York's architecture came into its own.

## FEDERAL ARCHITECTURE

This American adaptation of the Neoclassical Adam style flowered in the early decades of the new nation, featuring square buildings two or three stories tall, with low hipped roofs, balustrades and decorative elements – all carefully balanced. **City Hall** (1811, John McComb, Jr. and Joseph François Mangin) is a blend of Federal and French Renaissance influences. The restored warehouses of **Schermerhorn Row** (c. 1812) in the Seaport district are also in Federal style.

## BROWNSTONES

Plentiful and cheap, the brown sandstone found in the nearby Connecticut River Valley and along the banks of the Hackensack River in New

**A typical brownstone with stoop leading up to the main entrance**

Jersey was the most common building material in the 1800s. It is found all over the city's residential neighborhoods, used for small homes or small apartments – some of the best examples of brownstone can be found in **Chelsea**. Because street space was limited, these buildings were very narrow in width, but also very deep. A typical brownstone has a flight of steps, called a stoop, leading up to the living floors. Separate stairs lead down to the basement, which was originally the servants' quarters.

## TENEMENTS

Tenements were built to house the huge influx of immigrants who arrived from the 1840s up to World War I. The six-story blocks, 100 ft (30 m) long and 25 ft (8 m) wide, offered very little light and air except from tiny sidewall air shafts and windows at each end, leaving the middle rooms in darkness. The tiny apartments were called railroad flats after their similarity to railroad cars. Later designs had air shafts between buildings, but these helped the spread of fire. The **Lower East Side Tenement Museum** has scale models of the old tenements.

## CAST-IRON ARCHITECTURE

An American architectural innovation of the 19th century, cast iron was cheaper than stone or brick and allowed ornate features to be prefabricated in foundries from molds and used as building facades. Today, New York has the world's largest concentration of full and partial cast-iron facades. The best, built in the 1870s, are in the **SoHo Cast-Iron Historic District**.

**The original cast-iron facade of 72–76 Greene Street, SoHo**

## BEAUX ARTS

This French school of architecture dominated the design of public buildings and wealthy residential properties during New York's gilded age. This era (from 1880 to about 1920) produced many of the city's most prominent architects, including Richard Morris Hunt (**Carnegie Hall**, 1891; **Metropolitan Museum of Art**, 1895), who in 1845 was the first American architect to study in Paris; Cass Gilbert (**Custom House**, 1907; **New York Life Insurance**

## ARCHITECTURAL DISGUISES

Some of the most fanciful forms on the New York skyline were devised by clever architects to disguise the city's essential but utilitarian – and rather unattractive – rooftop water tanks. Look skyward to discover the ornate cupolas, spires and domes that transform the most mundane of features into veritable castles in the air. Examples that are easy to spot are atop two neighboring Fifth Avenue hotels: the Sherry Netherland at 60th Street and the Pierre at 61st Street.

**Standard water tower**

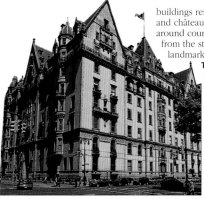

The Dakota Apartments, built in 1884, on the Upper West Side across from Central Park

buildings resembled castles and châteaux, and were built around courtyards not visible from the street. Favorite landmarks are the five **Twin Towers** on Central Park West, the San Remo, Eldorado, Century, the Beresford, and the Majestic. Built during the peak of Art Deco (1929 to 1931), they create the distinctive skyline seen from the park.

**Building**, 1928; the **US Courthouse**, 1936); the teams of Warren & Wetmore (**Grand Central Terminal**, 1913; **Helmsley Building**, 1929); Carrère & Hastings (**New York Public Library**, 1911; **Frick Mansion**, 1914); and McKim, Mead & White, the city's most famous firm of architects (**Villard Houses**, 1884; **United States General Post Office**, 1913; **Municipal Building**, 1914).

## APARTMENT BUILDINGS

As the city's population grew and space became ever more precious, family homes in Manhattan became much too expensive for most New Yorkers, and even the wealthy joined the trend toward communal living. In 1884 Henry Hardenbergh's Dakota (*see p218*), one of the first luxury apartment buildings, started a spate of turn-of-the-century construction on the Upper West Side. Many of the

## SKYSCRAPERS

Although Chicago gave birth to the skyscraper, New York has seen some of the greatest innovations. In 1902 Daniel Burnham, a Chicago architect, built the **Flatiron Building**, so tall at 300 ft (91 m) that skeptics said it would collapse. By 1913, the **Woolworth Building** had risen to 792 ft (241 m). Soon, zoning laws were passed requiring "setbacks" – upper stories were stepped back to allow light to reach street level. This suited the Art Deco style. The **Chrysler Building** (1930) was the world's tallest until the

Art Deco arched pattern on the spire of the Chrysler Building

**Empire State Building** (1931) was completed. Both are Art Deco classics, but it was Raymond Hood's **Group Health Insurance Building**, formerly the McGraw-Hill Building, that represented New York in 1932 in the *International Style* architectural survey.

The World Trade Center (*see p72*) was New York's tallest building until September 2001 (*see p54*). It represented the "glass box" Modernist style, now superseded by the Post-Modern style, such as the **Citigroup Center** (1977).

## WHERE TO FIND THE BUILDINGS

**245 Fifth Avenue (Apartment Building)**

**60 Gramercy Park North (Brownstone)**

**The Pierre (Beaux Arts)**

**Sherry Netherland Hotel (Beaux Arts)**

# Multicultural New York

Wherever you go in New York, even in pockets
of the hectic high-rise city center, you will find
evidence of the richly ethnic flavor of the city.
A bus ride can take you from Madras to Moscow,
Hong Kong to Haiti. Immigrants are still coming to
New York, though numbers are fewer than in the
peak years from 1880 to 1910, when 17 million
people arrived. In the 1980s, a million newcomers,
largely from Caribbean countries and Asia, arrived
and found their own special corner of the city.
Throughout the year you will encounter crowds
celebrating one of many festivals. To
find out more about national
celebrations and parades,
see pages 50 to 53.

**Hell's Kitchen**
*For a while called "Clinton"
to reflect a new neighborhood
mix, this was the first home
of early Irish immigrants.*

**Little Ukraine**
*Services are held at T.
Shevchenko Place as
part of the May 17
festivities to mark the
Ukrainians' conversion
to Christianity.*

**Little Korea**
*Not far from Herald
Square, a small
enclave of Koreans has
made a niche.*

Theater
District

Chelsea
and the
Garment
District

Gramercy
and the
Flatiron
District

Greenwich
Village

**Little Italy**
*For ten days in September, the Italian
community gathers around the
Mulberry Street area, and the streets
are taken over by the celebrations of the
Festa di San Gennaro.*

SoHo and
TriBeCa

East Village

**Chinatown**
*Every year, in
January or
February,
Mott Street is
packed as
residents
celebrate the
Chinese
New Year.*

Seaport
and the
Civic
Center

Lower
Manhattan

Lower East
Side

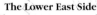

**The Lower East Side**
*The synagogues around
Rivington Street reflect
the religious traditions
of this old Jewish area.*

| 0 kilometers | 2 |
| 0 miles | 1 |

Morningside
Heights and
Harlem

Upper West
Side

Central
Park

Upper East
Side

Upper
Midtown

Lower
Midtown

**Harlem**
*The Sunday morning
gospel service at the
Abyssinian Baptist
Church is one of
Harlem's finest.*

**El Barrio**
*The vibrant
Hispanic
community
of Harlem's
El Barrio
district is
centered
around the
street
market, La
Marquetta.*

**Yorkville**
*Only a few cafés
and bierkellers
remain to keep the
flavor of this
former uptown
German district.
The Steuben Day
Parade is still held
here each September.*

**Upper East Side**
*The magnificent St. Nicholas
Russian Orthodox Cathedral
on East 97th Street is a
reminder of the dispersed White
Russian community. Mass is
held in Russian each Sunday.*

**Little India**
*The restaurants of East 6th Street offer
Eastern atmosphere at affordable prices.*

# Exploring New York's Many Cultures

**Stained glass at the Cotton Club**

Even "native" New Yorkers have ancestral roots in other countries. Throughout the 17th century, the Dutch and English settled here, establishing trade colonies in the New World. Soon America became a symbol of hope for the downtrodden elsewhere in Europe. Many flocked across the ocean, some penniless and with little knowledge of the language. The potato famine of the 1840s led to the first wave of Irish immigrants, followed by German and other European workers displaced by political unrest and the Industrial Revolution. Immigrants continue to enrich New York in countless ways, and today an estimated 100 languages are spoken.

the 1940s, they were the city's fastest-growing and most upwardly mobile ethnic group, extending the old boundaries of Chinatown and establishing new neighborhoods in parts of Brooklyn and Queens. Once a closed community, Chinatown now bustles with tourists exploring the streets and markets, and sampling the restaurant food.

## THE HISPANIC AMERICANS

**Hispanic religious carving at El Museo del Barrio (see p231)**

Puerto Ricans were in New York as early as 1838, but it was not until after World War II that they arrived in large numbers in search of work. Most live in El Barrio, formerly known as Spanish Harlem. Professionals who fled Fidel Castro's Cuba have moved out of the city itself but are still influential in Hispanic commerce and culture. Parts of Washington Heights have large Dominican and Colombian communities.

**Turkish immigrants arriving at former Idlewild Airport in 1963**

## THE JEWS

There has been a Jewish community in New York since 1654. The city's first synagogue, Shearith Israel, was established by refugees from a Dutch colony in Brazil and is still active today. These first settlers, Sephardic Jews of Spanish descent, included such prominent families as the Baruchs. They were followed by the German Jews, who set up successful retailing enterprises, like the Straus brothers at Macy's. Russian persecution led to the mass immigration that began in the late 1800s. By the start of World War I, 600,000 Jews were living on the Lower East Side. Today, this area is more Hispanic and Asian than Jewish, but it holds reminders of its role as a place of refuge and new beginnings.

## THE GERMANS

The Germans began to settle in New York in the 18th century. From John Peter Zenger onward *(see p21)*, the city's German community has championed the freedom to express ideas and opinions. It has also produced giants of industry, such as John Jacob Astor, the city's first millionaire.

## THE ITALIANS

Italians first came to New York in the 1830s and 1840s. Many came from northern Italy to escape the failing revolution at home. In the 1870s, poverty in southern Italy drove many more Italians across the ocean. In time, Italians became a potent political force in the city, exemplified by Fiorello La Guardia, one of New York's finest mayors.

## THE CHINESE

The Chinese were late arrivals to New York. In 1880, the population of the Mott Street district was a mere 700. By

**Eastern States Buddhist Temple, in central Chinatown (see pp96–7)**

## THE IRISH

The Irish, who first arrived in New York in the 1840s, had to overcome harsh odds. Starving and with barely a penny to their names, they labored hard to escape the slums of Five Points and Hell's Kitchen, helping to build the modern city in the process. Many joined the police and fire-fighting forces, rising to high rank through dedication to duty. Others set up successful businesses, such as the Irish bars that act as a focus for the now-scattered New York Irish community.

## THE AFRICAN AMERICANS

Perhaps the best-known black inner-city community in the Western world, Harlem is noted for the Harlem Renaissance of writing *(see pp30–31)* as much as it is for great entertainment, gospel music and soul food. The move of black African Americans from the South to the North began with emancipation in the 1860s and increased markedly in the 1920s, when Harlem's black population rose from 83,000 to 204,000. Today Harlem is undergoing revitalization in many areas. The African American population has also dispersed throughout the city.

## THE MELTING POT

Other New York cultures are not distinctly defined but are still easily found. Ukrainians gather in the East Village, around St. George's Ukrainian Catholic Church on East 7th Street. Little India can be spotted by the restaurants along East 6th Street. Koreans own many of the small grocery stores in Manhattan, but most tend to live in the Flushing area of Queens. The religious diversity of New York can be seen in the Islamic Center on Riverside Drive, the

**A woman celebrating at the Greek Independence Day parade**

Russian Orthodox Cathedral on East 97th Street *(see p199)*; and the new Islamic Cultural Center on 96th Street – Manhattan's first major mosque.

## THE OUTER BOROUGHS

Brooklyn is by far the most international borough of New York. Caribbean newcomers from Jamaica and Haiti are

**The New York police, a haven for Irish Americans**

one of the fastest-growing immigrant groups. West Indians tend to cluster along Eastern Parkway between Grand Army Plaza and Utica Avenue, the route of the lavish, exotically costumed West Indian Day Parade in September. Recently arrived Russian Jewish immigrants have turned Brighton Beach into "Little Odessa by the Sea," and the Scandinavians and Lebanese have settled in Bay Ridge and the Finns in Sunset Park. Borough Park and Williamsburg are home to Orthodox Jews, and Midwood has an Israeli-Middle East accent. Italians live in the Bensonhurst area. Greenpoint is little Poland, and Atlantic Avenue is home to the largest Arab community in America.

The Irish were among the earliest groups to cross the Harlem River into the Bronx. Japanese executives favor the more exclusive Riverdale area. One of the most distinctive ethnic areas is Astoria, Queens, which has the largest Greek population outside the motherland. Jackson Heights is home to a large Latin American quarter, including 300,000 Colombians. Indians also favor this area and neighboring Flushing. But it is the Asians who have transformed Flushing, so much so that the local train is popularly known as "The Orient Express."

## NEWCOMERS WHO MADE THEIR MARK see also pp48–9.

*The dates mark the year these immigrants entered the US via New York.*

**1893** Irving Berlin (Russia), musician

**1894** Al Jolson (Lithuania), singer

**1906** "Lucky" Luciano (Italy), gangster (deported 1946)

**1908** Bob Hope (England), comedian

**1909** Lee Strasberg (Austria), theater director

**1921** Bela Lugosi (Hungary), star of *Dracula*

**1932** George Balanchine (Russia), ballet choreographer

**1933** Albert Einstein (Germany), scientist

| 1890 | 1895 | 1900 | 1905 | 1910 | 1915 | 1920 | 1925 | 1930 | 1935 | 1940 |
|---|---|---|---|---|---|---|---|---|---|---|

**1896** Samuel Goldwyn (Poland), movie mogul

**1902** Joe Hill (Sweden), labor activist

**1903** Frank Capra (Italy), film director

**1904** Hyman Rickover (Russia), developer of nuclear submarine

**1912** Claudette Colbert (France), film star

**1913** Rudolph Valentino (Italy), film star

**1923** Isaac Asimov (Russia), scientist and writer

**1938** von Trapp family (Austria), singers

# Remarkable New Yorkers

New York has nourished some of the best creative talents since the beginning of the 20th century. Pop Art began here, and Manhattan is still the world center for modern art. The alternative writers of the 1950s and '60s – known as the Beat Generation – took inspiration from the city's jazz clubs. And as it is the financial capital, many leading world financiers have made New York their home.

**Pop artist Andy Warhol**

## WRITERS

**Novelist James Baldwin**

Much great American literature was created in New York. *Charlotte Temple, A Tale of Truth*, first published in 1791 by Susanna Rowson (c. 1762–1824), was a tale of seduction in the city and a best-seller for 50 years.

America's first professional author was Charles Brockden Brown (1771–1810), who came to New York in 1791. The novels of Edgar Allan Poe (1809–49), the pioneer of the modern detective story, expanded the thriller genre. Henry James (1843–1916) published *The Bostonians* (1886) and became the master of the psychological novel, and his friend Edith Wharton (1861–1937) became known for her satirical novels about American society.

American literature finally won international recognition with Washington Irving's (1783–1859) satire, *A History of New York* (1809). It earned him $2,000. Irving coined the names "Gotham" for New York and "Knickerbockers" for New Yorkers. He and James Fenimore Cooper (1789–1851), whose books gave birth to the "Western" novel, formed the Knicker

bocker group of US writers. Greenwich Village has always attracted writers, including Herman Melville (1819–91) whose masterpiece, *Moby Dick* (1851), was very poorly received at first.

Jack Kerouac (1922–69), Allen Ginsberg, and William Burroughs all went to Columbia University and drank at the San Remo Café in Greenwich Village. Dylan Thomas (1914–53) lived at the Chelsea Hotel (*see p139*). Novelist Nathanael West (1902–40) worked in the Gramercy Park Hotel, and Dashiell Hammett (1894–1961) wrote *The Maltese Falcon* while living there. James Baldwin (1924–87), born in Harlem, wrote *Another Country* (1963) on his return to New York from Europe.

## ARTISTS

The New York School of Abstract Expressionists founded the first influential American art movement. It was launched by Hans Hofmann (1880–1966) with Franz Kline and Willem de Kooning, whose first job in America was as a house-painter. Adolph Gottlieb, Mark Rothko (1903–70), and Jackson Pollock (1912–56) went on to popularize this style. Pollock, Kline and de Kooning all had their studios on the Lower East Side.

Pop Art began in New York in the 1960s with Roy Lichtenstein and

Andy Warhol (1926–87), who made some of his cult films at 33 Union Square. Keith Haring (1958–90) was a very prolific graffiti artist whose work as a pop artist is now receiving recognition.

Robert Mapplethorpe (1946–89) acquired notoriety for his homoerotic photos of men. Jeff Koons has now superseded him as the *bête noire* of the art establishment.

The illusionistic murals by Richard Haas enliven many walls throughout the city.

## ACTORS

In 1849 the British actor Charles Macready started a riot by saying Americans were vulgar. A mob stormed the Astor Place Opera House, where Macready was playing Macbeth, police opened fire, and 22 rioters were killed. In 1927 Mae West (1893–1980) spent 10 days in a workhouse on Roosevelt Island and was fined $500 for giving a lewd performance in her Broadway show *Sex* . Marc Blitzstein's radical pro-labor opera *The Cradle Will Rock* produced by Orson Welles (1915–85) and John Houseman (1902–88), was immediately banned and the show had

**Vaudeville actress Mae West**    to move to

another theater. The actors managed to get around the ban by buying tickets and singing their roles from the audience.

The musical has been New York's special contribution to the theater. Florenz Ziegfeld's (1869–1932) *Follies* ran from 1907 to 1931. The opening of *Oklahoma!* on Broadway in 1943 began the age of musicals by the famous duo Richard Rodgers (1902–79) and Oscar Hammerstein, Jr. (1895–1960).

Off Broadway, the Province-town Players at 33 MacDougal Street were the first to produce Eugene O'Neill's (1888–1953) *Beyond the Horizon* (1920). His successor as the major innovative force in US theater was Edward Albee, author of *Who's Afraid of Virginia Woolf?* (1962).

## MUSICIANS AND DANCERS

Leonard Bernstein (1918–90) followed a long line of great conductors at the New York Philharmonic, including Bruno Walter (1876–1962), Arturo Toscanini (1867–1957) and Leopold Stokowski (1882–1977). Maria Callas (1923–77) was born in New York but moved to Europe.

Carnegie Hall *(see p148)* has featured Enrico Caruso (1873–1921), Bob Dylan and the Beatles. A record concert attendance was set in 1991 when Paul Simon drew a million people for his free concert in Central Park.

The legendary swinging jazz clubs of the 1930s and 1940s are now gone from 52nd Street. Plaques on "Jazz Walk" outside the CBS building honor such

**Musical producer Florenz Ziegfeld**

**Josephine Baker**

famous performers as Charlie Parker (1920–55) and Josephine Baker (1906–75).

Between 1940 and 1965, New York became a world dance capital, with the establishment of George Balanchine's (1904–83) New York City Ballet and the American Ballet Theater. In 1958, choreographer Alvin Ailey (1931–89) set up the American Dance Theater, and Bob Fosse (1927–87) changed the course of musicals.

## INDUSTRIALISTS AND ENTREPRENEURS

**Tycoon Cornelius Vanderbilt**

The rags-to-riches story is an American dream. Andrew Carnegie (1835–1919), "the steel baron with a heart of gold," started with nothing and died having given away $350 million. His beneficiaries included public libraries and universities throughout America. Many other foundations are the legacies of wealthy philanthropists. Some, like Cornelius Vanderbilt (1794–1877), tried to shake off their rough begin-nings by patronizing the arts.

In business, New York's "robber barons" did what they liked with apparent impunity. Financiers Jay Gould (1836–92) and James Fisk (1834–72) beat Vanderbilt in the war for the Erie Railroad by manipu-lating stock. In September 1869 they caused Wall Street's first "Black Friday" when they tried to corner the gold market, but fled when their fraud was discovered. Gould died a happy billionaire, and Fisk was killed in a fight over a woman.

Modern entrepreneurs include Donald Trump *(see p33)*, owner of Trump Tower, and Leona and the late Harry Helmsley. Despite Leona's imprisonment for tax evasion, their property empire remains intact and includes such New York sites as the Helmsley Building *(see p158)*.

## ARCHITECTS

Cass Gilbert (1858–1934), who built such Neo-Gothic sky-scrapers as the Woolworth Building of 1913 *(see p91)* was one of the men who literally shaped the city. His caricature can be seen in the lobby, clutching a model of his masterpiece. Stanford White (1853–1906) was as well known for his scandalous private life as for his fine Beaux Arts buildings, such as the Players Club *(p128)*. For most of his life, Frank Lloyd Wright (1867–1959) spurned city architecture. When he was persuaded to leave his mark on the city, it was in the form of the Guggenheim Museum *(pp188–9)*. German-born Ludwig Mies van der Rohe (1886–1969), who built the Seagram Building *(p177)*, did not believe in "inventing a new architecture every Monday morning," although some might argue that this is just what New York has always done best.

# NEW YORK THROUGH THE YEAR

Springtime in New York sees Park Avenue filled with blooms, while Fifth Avenue goes green for St. Patrick's Day, the first of the year's many big parades. Summer in the city is hot and humid, but it is worth forsaking an air-conditioned interior to step outside, where parks and squares are the setting for free open-air music and theater. The first Monday in September marks Labor Day and the advent of comfortable temperatures and the orange-red colors of autumn. Then, as Christmas nears, the shops and streets begin to sparkle with dazzling window displays.

Dates of the events on the following pages may vary. For details consult the listings magazines *(see p369)*. The New York Convention and Visitors Bureau *(see p368)* also issues a useful quarterly free calendar of events.

## SPRING

Every season in New York brings its own tempo and temptations. In spring, the city shakes off the winter with tulips and cherry blossoms in the parks and spring fashions in the stores. Everyone window shops and gallery hops. The hugely popular St. Patrick's Day Parade draws the crowds, and thousands don their finery for the Easter Parade down Fifth Avenue.

Inventive Easter bonnets in New York's Easter Parade

## MARCH

**St. Patrick's Day Parade** *(Mar 17)*, Fifth Ave, from 44th to 86th St. Green clothes, beer and flowers, plus bagpipes.
**Greek Independence Day Parade** *(Mar 25)*, Fifth Ave, from 49th to 59th St. Greek dancing and food.
**New York City Opera Spring Season** *(Mar–Apr)*, Lincoln Center *(p350)*.
**Ringling Bros and Barnum & Bailey Circus** *(Mar–Apr)*, Madison Square Garden *(p135)*.

## EASTER

**Easter Flower Show** *(week before Easter)*, Macy's department store *(pp134–5)*.
**Easter Parade** *(Easter Sun)*, Fifth Ave, from 44th to 59th St. Paraders in costumes and outrageous millinery gather around St. Patrick's Cathedral.

## APRIL

**Cherry Blossom Festival** *(late Mar–Apr)*, Brooklyn Botanic Garden. Famous for Japanese cherry trees and beautifully laid out ornamental gardens.
**Annual Earth Day Festival Activities** *(varies)*.
**Baseball** *(Apr–May)*, Major league season starts for Yankees and Mets *(p360)*.
**New York City Ballet Spring Season** *(Apr–Jun)*, New York State Theater and Metropolitan Opera House in Lincoln Center *(p214)*.

## MAY

**Five Boro Bike Tour** *(early May)*, a 42-mile (68-km) ride ending with a festival with live music, food and exhibitions. **Cuban Day Parade** *(early May)*, a lively carnival on Sixth Ave, between 44th St and Central Park South.

Parading in national costume on Greek Independence Day

**Ninth Avenue Street Festival** *(mid-May)*, from W 37th to W 57th St. A feast of ethnic foods, music and dance.
**Washington Square Outdoor Art Exhibit** *(last weekend May, first weekend Jun)*.
**Memorial Day** Activities *(last weekend)* A parade down Fifth Ave, festivities at South Street Seaport.

Yellow tulips and cabs shine on Park Avenue

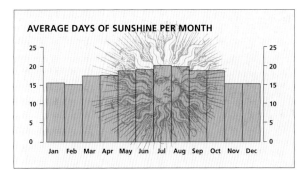

**AVERAGE DAYS OF SUNSHINE PER MONTH**

**Days of Sunshine**
*New York enjoys long hours of summer sun from June to August, with July the month of greatest sunshine. The winter days are much shorter, but many are clear and bright. Autumn has more sunshine than spring, although both are sunny.*

## SUMMER

New Yorkers escape the hot city streets when possible, for picnics, boat rides and the beaches. Macy's fireworks light up the Fourth of July skies, and more sparks fly when the New York Yankees and Mets baseball teams are in town. Summer also brings street fairs, outdoor concerts, and free Shakespeare and opera in Central Park.

**Policeman dancing in the Puerto Rican Day Parade**

### JUNE

**Puerto Rican Day Parade** *(early Jun)*, Fifth Ave, from 44th to 86th St. Floats and marching bands.
**Museum Mile Festival** *(second Tue)*, Fifth Ave, from 82nd to 105th St. Free entry to museums.
**Central Park Summerstage** *(Jun–Aug)*, Central Park. Music and dance of every variety, almost daily, rain or shine.
**Metropolitan Opera Parks Concerts**. Free evening concerts in parks throughout the city *(pp350–51)*.
**Goldman Memorial Band Concerts** *(Jun–Aug)*, Lincoln Center *(p214)*. Traditional band concerts.

**Shakespeare in the Park** *(Jun–Sep)*. Star actors take on the bard at Delacorte Theater, Central Park *(p347)*.
**Lesbian and Gay Pride Day Parade** *(Jun)*, from Columbus Circle along Fifth Ave to Washington Sq *(p115)*.
**JVC Jazz Festival** *(late Jun–early Jul)*. Top jazz musicians perform in various halls in the city *(p353)*.

### JULY

**Macy's Firework Display** *(Jul 4)*, East River. High point of the city's Independence Day celebrations, featuring the best fireworks in town.
**American Crafts Festival** *(mid Jun–early Jul)*, Lincoln Center *(p214)*. High-quality crafts.
**Mostly Mozart Festival** *(end Jul–end Aug)*, Avery Fisher Hall, Lincoln Center *(pp350-51)*.
**NY Philharmonic Parks Concerts** *(late Jul–early Aug)*. Free concerts in parks

**Festivities at a summer street fair in Greenwich Village**

throughout the city *(p351)*.
**Lincoln Center Festival** *(Jul)*, Dance. opera, other performing arts from around the world.

### AUGUST

**Harlem Week** *(mid-Aug)*. Films, art, music, dance, fashion, sports and tours.
**Out-of-Doors Festival** *(Aug)*, Lincoln Center. Free dance and theater performances *(p346)*.
**US Open Tennis Championships** *(late Aug–early Sep)*, Flushing Meadows *(p360)*.

**Crowds of spectators flock to the US Open Tennis Championships**

**AVERAGE MONTHLY TEMPERATURE**

**Temperature**
*The chart shows the average minimum and maximum temperatures for each month in New York. With top temperatures averaging 84° F (29° C), the city can become hot and humid. In contrast, the months of winter, although rarely below freezing, can seem bitterly cold.*

## AUTUMN

Labor Day marks the end of the summer. The Giants and the Jets kick off the football season, the Broadway season begins and the Festa di San Gennaro in Little Italy is the high point in a succession of colorful neighborhood fairs. Macy's Thanksgiving Day Parade is the nation's symbol that the holiday season has arrived.

## SEPTEMBER

**Richmond County Fair**
*(Labor Day weekend)*, in the grounds of Historic Richmond Town *(p254)*. New York's only authentic county fair.
**West Indian Carnival**
*(Labor Day weekend)*, Brooklyn. Parade, floats, music, dancing and food.
**Brazilian Festival**
*(early Sep)*, E 46th St, between Times Sq and Madison Ave.

Exotic Caribbean carnival costume in the streets of Brooklyn

Brazilian music, food, and crafts.
**New York is Book Country** *(mid-Sep)*, Fifth Ave, from 48th to 59th Sts. Book fair.
**Festa di San Gennaro** *(third week)*, Little Italy *(p96)*. Ten days of festivities and processions.
**New York Film Festival** *(mid-Sep–early Oct)*, Lincoln Center *(p214)*. American films and international art films.
**Von Steuben Day Parade** *(third week)*, Upper Fifth Ave. German-American celebrations.
**American Football** *(season begins)*, Giants Stadium, home to the Giants and the Jets *(pp360–61)*.

## OCTOBER

**Columbus Day Parade** *(2nd Mon)*, Fifth Ave, from 44th to 86th Sts. Parades and music to celebrate Columbus's first sighting of America.
**Pulaski Day Parade** *(Sun closest to Oct 5)*, Fifth Ave, from 26th to 52nd Sts. Celebrations for Polish-American hero Casimir Pulaski.
**Halloween Parade** *(Oct 31)*, Greenwich Village. Brilliant event with fantastic costumes.
**Big Apple Circus** *(Oct–Jan)*, Damrosch Park, Lincoln Center. Special themes are presented each year *(p365)*.
**Basketball** *(season begins)*, Madison Square Garden. Local team is the Knicks *(pp360–61)*.
**New York City Marathon** *(early Nov)*. From Staten Island through all the city boroughs.

Huge Superman balloon floating above Macy's Thanksgiving Day Parade

## NOVEMBER

**Macy's Thanksgiving Day Parade** *(fourth Thu)*, from Central Park West and W 79th St to Broadway and W 34th St. A joy for children, with floats, huge balloons and Santa.
**Rockefeller Center Ice Skating Rink** *(Oct–Mar)*, Open to the public. You can skate beneath the famous Christmas Tree.
**Christmas Spectacular** *(Nov–Dec)*, Radio City Music Hall. Variety show, with the Rockettes.

Revelers in Greenwich Village's Halloween Parade

## AVERAGE MONTHLY RAINFALL

MM    Inches
100    4
80    3
60    2
40    1
20
0    0
Jan Feb Mar Apr May Jun Jul Aug Sep Oct Nov Dec

### Rainfall

*March and August are the months of heaviest rainfall in New York. Rainfall in spring is usually unpredictable, so be prepared. Sudden heavy snowfalls in winter can cause chaos in the city.*

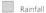 Rainfall

Snowfall

## WINTER

New York is a magical place at Christmas – even the stone lions at the Public Library don wreaths for the occasion, and shops become works of art. From Times Square to Chinatown, New Year celebrations punctuate the season, and Central Park becomes a winter sports arena.

**Statue of Alice in Wonderland in Central Park**

## DECEMBER

**Tree-Lighting Ceremony** *(early Dec)*, Rockefeller Center *(p144)*. Lighting of the giant Christmas tree in front of the RCA Building.
**Messiah Sing-In** *(mid-Dec)*, Lincoln Center *(p214)*. The audience rehearses and performs under the guidance of various conductors.
**Hanukkah Menorah** *(mid-late Dec)*, Grand Army Plaza, Brooklyn. Lighting of the huge menorah (candelabra) every night during the eight-day Festival of Lights.
**New Year's Eve**. Fireworks display in Central Park *(pp206-7)*; festivities in Times Square *(p147)*; 5-mile (8-km) run in Central Park; poetry reading in St. Mark's Church.

## JANUARY

**National Boat Show** *(Jan)*, Jacob K. Javits Convention Center *(p138)*.
**Chinese New Year** *(late Jan/Feb)*, Chinatown *(pp96-7)*. Dragons, fireworks and food.
**Winter Antiques Show** *(Jan)*, Seventh Regiment Armory *(p187)*. NYC's most prestigious antiques fair.

## FEBRUARY

**Black History Month**. African-American events take place throughout the city.
**Empire State Building Run-Up** *(early Feb)*. Runners race to the 102nd floor *(pp136-7)*.
**Lincoln and Washington Birthday Sales** *(Feb 12-22)* Big department stores sales throughout the city.
**Westminster Kennel Club Dog Show** *(mid-Feb)*, Madison Square Garden *(p135)*. Major dog show.

**Chinese New Year celebrations in Chinatown**

## PUBLIC HOLIDAYS

**New Year's Day** (Jan 1)
**Martin Luther King Day** (3rd Mon, Jan)
**President's Day** (mid-Feb)
**Memorial Day** (end May)
**Independence Day** (Jul 4)
**Labor Day** (1st Mon, Sep)
**Columbus Day** (2nd Mon, Oct)
**Election Day** (1st Tue, Nov)
**Veterans Day** (Nov 11)
**Thanksgiving Day** (4th Thu, Nov)
**Christmas Day** (Dec 25)

**The giant Christmas tree and decorations at Rockefeller Center**

**LOCATOR MAP**

■ *The Southern Tip*

# The Southern Tip of Manhattan

This view of Lower Manhattan, seen from the Hudson River, encompasses some of the most striking modern additions to the New York skyline, including the distinctively topped quartet of the World Financial Center. You will also catch glimpses of an earlier Manhattan: Castle Clinton set against the green space of Battery Park and, behind it, the noble Custom House building. From 1973 until September 2001 the area also boasted the World Trade Center, in its day the city's tallest building. Its landmark towers were destroyed in a terrorist attack on the city.

## DESTRUCTION OF THE WORLD TRADE CENTER

On September 11, 2001, two planes bound for Los Angeles were hijacked and targeted at the World Trade Center. Hundreds of people died in the impact, but thousands more were killed when the twin towers collapsed. Two other planes were also hijacked that morning; the first struck the Pentagon, while the second came to ground near Pittsburgh. The death toll exceeded the number of troops killed in the Revolutionary War *(see pp22–3),* and comparisons were made with the bombing of Pearl Harbor. Images of the destruction were seen across the world, drawing wide support for a "war against terrorism."

**World Financial Center**
*At the heart of this complex is the Winter Garden – a place to shop, dine, be entertained, or just enjoy the Hudson River views (see p69).*

**World Trade Center**
*Twin 110-story towers dominated the sky- line (see p72).*

**Detail from The *Upper Room***

**The Upper Room**
*This walk-around sculpture by Ned Smyth is one of many works of art in Battery Park City (see p72).*

**An Earlier View**
*This 1898 photograph shows a skyline now changed beyond recognition.*

**Skyscraper Museum**
Located at the southern tip of Battery Park City, the Skyscraper Museum celebrates and explores New York's rich architectural heritage.

**US Custom House**
*This magnificent 1907 Beaux Arts building now houses the Museum of the American Indian (see p73).*

**East Coast War Memorial**
*In Battery Park, a huge bronze eagle by Albino Manca honors the dead of World War II.*

**26 Broadway**
*The tower of the former Standard Oil Building resembles an oil lamp. The interior is still decorated with company symbols.*

Bank of New York

17 State Street

26 Broadway

1 Liberty Plaza

Liberty View

Castle Clinton     US Custom House

**American Merchant Mariners' Memorial** (1991)
*This sculpture by Marisol is on Pier A, the last of Manhattan's old piers. The pier also has a clock tower that chimes the hours on ships' bells.*

**Shrine of Mother Seton**
*The first US-born saint lived here (see p76).*

# Lower Manhattan from the East River

At first sight, this stretch of East River shoreline, running up from the tip of Manhattan Island, is a seamless array of 20th-century office buildings. But from sea level, streets and slips are still visible, offering glimpses of old New York and the Financial District to the west. On the skyline itself, a few of the district's early skyscrapers still proudly display their ornate crowns above their more anonymous modern counterparts.

**LOCATOR MAP**

■ *East River View*

**India House**
*The handsome brownstone at One Hanover Square is one of the finest of its kind.*

**Vietnam Veterans Plaza**
*An engraved green-glass memorial dominates the former Coenties Slip, a wharf filled in to make a park in the late 19th century (see p76).*

**Hanover Square**
*A statue of one of the Dutch mayors, Abraham De Peyster, sits near the house where he was born in 1657.*

**One New York Plaza**

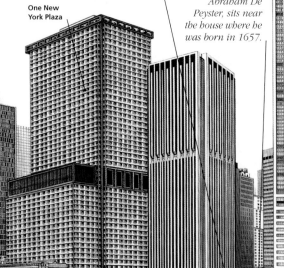

**55 Water Street**

**Barclay's Bank Building**

**Downtown Heliport**
*Air-Sea Rescue and sightseeing flights operate from here.*

**Battery Maritime Building**
*This historic ferry terminal serves only Governors Island (see p77).*

**Delmonico's**
*High society dined here a century ago.*

**New York Stock Exchange**
*Although hidden from view
by more modern edifices,
this is still the hub of the
hectic Financial
District (see
pp70–71).*

**40 Wall Street**
*In the 1940s, the
pyramid-topped tower
of the former Bank of
Manhattan was hit
by a light aircraft.*

**70 Pine Street**
*Replicas of this
elegant Gothic-
style tower can
be seen near
the Pine and
Cedar Street
entrances.*

**Bank of New York**
*This serene 1928 interior
is part of the bank set up
in 1784 by Alexander
Hamilton (see p23).*

**Morgan Bank**
*Columns from lobby to
rooftop are the theme
of this striking modern
building.*

1 Financial Square

New York
Stock
Exchange

Chase Manhattan
Bank Tower

120 Wall
Street

Citibank Building

**100 Old Slip**
*Now in the
shadow of One
Financial Square,
the small palazzo-
style First Precinct
Police Department
was the city's most
modern police
station when it was
built in 1911.*

Carved
medallion, 100
Old Slip

***Queen Elizabeth* Monument**
*The ocean liner that sank in
1972 is remembered here.*

# South Street Seaport

As the Financial District ends, the skyline, as seen from the East River or Brooklyn, changes dramatically. The corporate headquarters are replaced by the piers, low-rise streets and warehouses of the old seaport area, now restored as the South Street Seaport *(see pp82–3)*. The Civic Center lies not far inland, and a few of its monumental buildings can be seen. The Brooklyn Bridge marks the end of this stretch of skyline. Between here and midtown, apartment blocks make up the majority of riverside features.

**LOCATOR MAP**

■ *South Street Area*

**Pier 17**
*A focal point of the Seaport, this traditional-style leisure pier is packed with exciting shops, vendors and restaurants.*

Stonework on the Woolworth Building

**Woolworth Building**
*The handsomely decorated spire marks the headquarters of F.W. Woolworth's empire. It is still the finest "cathedral of commerce" ever built (see p91).*

Fleet Bank Building

Seaport Plaza

Transportation Building

Bogardus Building

**Maritime Crafts Center**
*At Pier 15, craftspeople demonstrate traditional seafaring skills such as woodcarving and modelmaking.*

**Titanic Memorial**
*The lighthouse on Fulton Street commemorates the sinking of the Titanic, the largest steam ship ever built.*

**Police Plaza**
Five in One *(1971–4),* in Police Plaza, is a sculpture by Bernard Rosenthal. It represents the five boroughs of New York.

**United States Courthouse**
*The Civic Center is marked on the skyline by the golden pyramid of architect Cass Gilbert's courthouse (see p85).*

**Municipal Building**
*Among the offices of this vast building is the Marriage Chapel, where weddings "at City Hall" actually take place. The copper statue on the skyline is* Civic Fame *by Adolph Weinman (see p85).*

**Surrogate's Court and Hall of Records**
*Archives dating back to 1664 are stored and displayed here (see p85).*

Verizon Telephone Company

Police Plaza

Pace University

Southbridge Towers

**Con Edison Mural**
*In 1975, artist Richard Haas re-created the Brooklyn Bridge on the side wall of a former electrical substation.*

**Brooklyn Bridge**
*Views of, and from, the bridge have made it one of New York's best-loved landmarks (see pp86–9).*

# Midtown Manhattan

The skyline of Midtown Manhattan is graced with some of the city's most spectacular towers and spires – from the familiar beauty of the Empire State Building's Art Deco pinnacle to the dramatic wedge shape of Citicorp's modern headquarters. As the shoreline progresses uptown, so the architecture becomes more varied; the United Nations complex dominates a long stretch, and then Beekman Place begins a strand of exclusive residential enclaves that offer the rich and famous some seclusion in this busy part of the city.

**LOCATOR MAP**

■ Midtown

**Chrysler Building**
*Glinting in the sun by day or lit up by night, this stainless-steel spire is, for many, the ultimate New York skyscraper (see p155).*

**Grand Central Terminal**
*Now dwarfed by its neighbors, this landmark building is full of period details, such as this fine clock (see pp156–7).*

**Empire State Building**
*At 1250 ft (381 m), this was the tallest building in the world for many years (see pp136–7).*

The Highpoint

MetLife Building

**Tudor City**
*Built in the 1920s, this complex is mock Tudor on a grand scale, with over 3,000 apartments (see p158).*

**United Nations**
*Works of art from member countries include this Barbara Hepworth sculpture, a gift from Britain (see pp160–63).*

**1 and 2 UN Plaza**
*Angular glass towers house offices and the UN Millennium Plaza Hotel (see p158).*

**General Electric Building**
*Built of brick in 1931, this
Art Deco building has a
tall spiked crown that
resembles radio waves.*
(see p176).

**Waldorf–Astoria**
*The splendid interior of
one of the city's finest
hotels lies beneath twin
copper-capped towers*
(see p177).

**Citigroup Center**
*St. Peter's Church nestles in one
corner of the Citigroup Center,
with its raked tower (see p177).*

**Rockefeller Center**
*The outdoor skating
rink and walkways of
this complex of office
buildings are a great
place to people watch*
(see p144).

General
Electric
Building

*The Nail*, by
Arnoldo
Pomodoro,
St. Peter's
Church,
Citicorp
Center

100 UN
Plaza

866 UN
Plaza

Trump World
Tower

**Japan Society**
*Japanese culture, from avant-
garde plays to ancient art, can
be seen here (see p158–9).*

**Beekman
Tower**
*Now an all-
suite hotel, this
Art Deco tower
was built in
1928 as a hotel
for women who
were members
of US college
sororities.*

**St. Mary's Garden**
*The garden at Holy
Family Church is a
peaceful haven.*

**Dusk view of Manhattan skyline** ▷

# NEW YORK
# AREA BY AREA

# LOWER MANHATTAN

The old and the new converge at Lower Manhattan, where Colonial churches and early American monuments stand in the shadow of skyscrapers. New York was born here, and this was the site of the nation's first capitol. Commerce has also flourished here since 1626, when Dutchman Peter Minuit purchased the

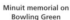

Minuit memorial on Bowling Green

island of Man-a-hatt-ta from the Algonquian Indians for goods valued at $24 *(see p19)*. At the time of revising this guide a number of landmark buildings in the area were still being repaired following the destruction of the World Trade Center *(see p54)*. Visitors are advised to call all sights to check opening times and transport information.

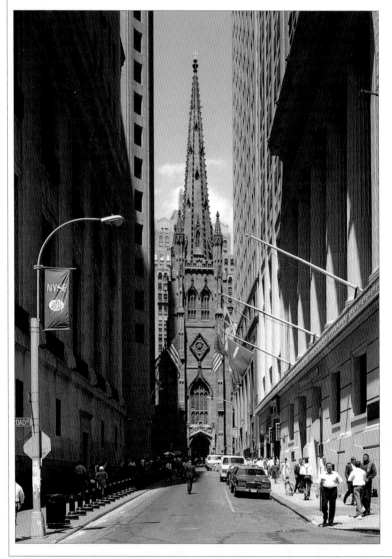

Trinity Church at the foot of Wall Street

## SIGHTS AT A GLANCE

**Historic Buildings and Important Sites**
Battery Maritime Building ⑯
Federal Hall ②
Federal Reserve Bank ①
Fraunces Tavern Museum ⑬
*New York Stock Exchange pp70–71* ③
World Trade Center Site ⑥

**Museums and Galleries**
Castle Clinton National Monument ⑳
*Ellis Island pp78–9* ⑱
Museum of Jewish Heritage ㉑

Skyscraper Museum ⑧
US Custom House ⑪

**Monuments and Statues**
Charging Bull ⑨
*Statue of Liberty pp74–5* ⑰

**Parks and Squares**
Battery Park ⑲
Bowling Green ⑩
Vietnam Veterans' Plaza ⑭

**Boat Trips**
Staten Island Ferry ⑮

**Churches**
Shrine of Saint
Elizabeth Ann Seton ⑫
Trinity Church ④

**Modern Architecture**
Battery Park City ⑦
World Financial Center ⑤

**GETTING THERE**
The best subway routes to
the tip of Manhattan are the
Lexington Ave 4 or 5 trains to
Bowling Green; R or W to
Whitehall St; or the 7th Ave
1 train to South Ferry. For
Wall St, take subways 2, 3, 4,
or 5 to Wall St, or 1, R, or W
to Rector St. The M1, M6,
and M15 buses and the
M22 crosstown route
all serve the area.

0 meters       500

0 yards       500

**KEY**

▨ Street-by-Street map

Ⓜ Subway station

⏬ Ferry boarding point

🚁 Heliport

# Street by Street: Wall Street

No intersection has been of greater importance to the city, past or present, than the corners of Wall and Broad streets. Three important sites are located here. Federal Hall National Monument marks the place where, in 1789, George Washington was sworn in as president. Trinity Church is one of the nation's oldest Anglican parishes. The New York Stock Exchange, founded in 1817, is to this day a financial nerve center whose ups and downs cause tremors around the globe. The surrounding buildings are the very heart of New York's famous financial district.

**Trinity Building**, an early 20th-century Gothic skyscraper, was designed to complement nearby Trinity Church.

**The Marine Midland Bank** rises straight up 55 stories. This dark, glass tower occupies only 40% of its site. The other 60% is a plaza in which a large red sculpture by Isamu Noguchi, *Cube*, balances on one of its points.

**The Equitable Building** (1915) deprived its neighbors of light, prompting a change in the law: skyscrapers had to be set back from the street.

★ **Trinity Church**
*Built in 1846 in a Gothic style, this is the third church on this site. Once the tallest structure in the city, the bell tower is now dwarfed by the skyscrapers that surround it. Many famous early New Yorkers are buried in the churchyard* ❹

**Wall Street subway** (lines 4, 5)

**The Irving Trust Company**, built in 1932, has an outer wall patterned to look like fabric. In the lobby is an Art Deco mosaic in shades of flame and gold.

**26 Broadway** was built as the home of the Standard Oil Trust. An oil lamp rests on top of it.

**New York Stock Exchange ★**
*The hub of the world's financial markets is housed in a 17-story building constructed in 1903* ❸

**The Liberty Tower** is clad in white terracotta and is in the Gothic style. It was later turned into apartments.

**The Chamber of Commerce** is a fine Beaux-Arts building of 1901.

## STAR SIGHTS

★ Federal Hall National Monument

★ Federal Reserve Bank

★ New York Stock Exchange

★ Trinity Church

**LOCATOR MAP**
See Manhattan Map pp14–15

### KEY

– – – Suggested route

| 0 meters | 100 |
| 0 yards | 100 |

**Chase Manhattan Bank and Plaza** has the famous Jean Dubuffet sculpture, *Four Trees*, located in the plaza.

### ★ Federal Reserve Bank
*In the style of a Renaissance palace, this is a bank for banks. US currency is issued here* ❶

**Louise Nevelson Plaza** is a park containing Nevelson's sculpture *Shadows and Flags*.

**Wall Street** is named for the wall that kept enemies and warring Indians out of Manhattan – the street is now the heart of the city's business center.

**Wall Street in the 1920s**

### ★ Federal Hall National Monument
*Originally the US Custom House, this classical building, refurbished in 2006, usually houses an exhibit about the Constitution* ❷

# Federal Reserve Bank ❶

33 Liberty St. **Map** 1 C2. **Tel** (212) 720-6130. Ⓜ Fulton St–Broadway Nassau. ◑ 8:30am–5pm Mon–Fri. ● public hols. 🍴 ♿ 🎦 free (reservations required). **www**.newyorkfed.org

**Entrance to Federal Reserve Bank**

This is a government bank for banks – it is one of the 12 Federal Reserve banks, and therefore issues US currency. You can identify bank notes originating from this branch by the letter B in the Federal Reserve seal on each note.

Five stories below ground is one of the largest storehouses for international gold. Each nation's hoard is stored in its own compartment within the subterranean vault, guarded by 90-ton doors. Payments between nations used to be made by physical transfers of gold. An exhibition of "The History of Money," with 800

items, runs from 10am to 4pm. Designed by York & Sawyer in the Italian Renaissance style, the 1924 building occupies a full block and is adorned with fine wrought-iron grillwork.

# Federal Hall ❷

26 Wall St. **Map** 1 C3. **Tel** (212) 825-6888. Ⓜ Wall St. ◑ 9am–5pm Mon–Fri. ● public hols. 📷 ♿ 🎦 🛗 **www**.nps.gov/feha

A bronze statue of George Washington on the steps of Federal Hall marks the site where the nation's first president took his oath of office in 1789. Thousands of New Yorkers jammed Wall and Broad Streets for the occasion. They roared their approval when the Chancellor of the State of New York shouted, "Long live George Washington, President of the United States." The present structure, under renovation until 2007, was built between 1834 and 1842 as the US Customs House. It is one of the finest Classical designs in the city. Display rooms off the Rotunda include the Bill of Rights Room and an interactive computer exhibit about the Constitution.

# New York Stock Exchange ❸

See pp70–71.

**Trinity Churchyard**

# Trinity Church ❹

Broadway at Wall St. **Map** 1 C3. **Tel** (212) 602-0800. Ⓜ Wall St, Rector St. ◑ 7am–6pm Mon–Fri, 8am–4pm Sat, 7am–4pm Sun (church); 7am–4pm (5pm DST) Mon–Fri, 8am–3pm Sat & public hols, 7am–3pm Sun (churchyard). 🛗 12.05pm Mon–Fri, 9am & 11:15am Sun. 📷 except during services. 🎦 2pm daily; also Sun after 11:15am service. **Concerts** 1pm Thu. 🛗 💻 **www**.trinitywallstreet.org

This square-towered Episcopal church at the head of Wall Street is the third one on this site. Designed in 1846 by Richard Upjohn, it was among the grandest churches of its day, marking the beginning of the best period of Gothic Revival architecture in America. Richard Morris Hunt's design for the sculpted brass doors was inspired by Lorenzo Ghiberti's Doors of Paradise at the Baptistery in Florence.

Restoration has uncovered the original rosy sandstone, long buried beneath layers of city grime. The 280-ft (86-m) steeple, the tallest structure in New York until the 1860s, still commands respect despite its towering neighbors.

Many prominent early New Yorkers are buried in the graveyard: statesman Alexander Hamilton; steamboat inventor Robert Fulton; and William Bradford, founder of New York's first newspaper in 1725.

**Marble-columned rotunda within Federal Hall**

LOWER MANHATTAN

69

## World Financial Center ❺

West St. **Map** 1 A2. **Tel** (212) 945-
2600. Ⓜ A, C and J, M, Z, and
2, 3, 4, 5 to Fulton St, E to WTC
Station, R, W to Cortlandt St and
1 to Rector St. 🅾 ♿ 🚻 🖦 🏧
**www**.worldfinancialcenter.com

A model of urban design by
Cesar Pelli & Associates, this
development is a vital part
of the revival of Lower
Manhattan, and its damage
in the World Trade Center
attack was attended to as a
matter of urgency. Four office
towers soar skyward, housing
the headquarters of some of
the world's most important
financial companies. At the
heart of the complex lies the
dazzling Winter Garden, a
vast glass-and-steel public
space (all 2,000 panes of
glass had to be replaced),
flanked by 45 restaurants
and shops, opening onto
a lively piazza and marina
on the Hudson River. The
sweeping marble staircase
leading down to the Winter
Garden (re-opened September
2002) often doubles as seating
for free arts and events,

**Main floor of the Winter Garden**

**The atrium** is a sparkling vault of
glass and steel, 120 ft (36 m) high.

**The "hourglass"
staircase** is used as
extra seating during
concerts in the
Winter Garden.

**An esplanade** borders the Hudson.

**Cafés and shops** line the atrium.

varying from classic to
contemporary in music,
dance and theater. Sixteen
*Washingtonia robusta* palm
trees, 40 ft (15 m) high,
have been replaced in this
contemporary version of the
"palm court" of yesteryear.
   Inaugurated in 1988, the
building has been hailed
as the Rockefeller Center
of the 21st century.

**World Financial Center viewed from the Hudson River**

# New York Stock Exchange ❸

In 1790, trading in stocks and shares took place haphazardly on or around Wall Street, but in 1792, 24 brokers who traded at 68 Wall Street signed an agreement to deal only with one another: the basis of the New York Stock Exchange (NYSE) was formed. The NYSE has weathered a succession of alternating slumps ("bear markets") and booms ("bull markets"), growing from a local market-place into a financial center of global importance. Membership is strictly limited. In 1817, a "seat" cost $25; in recent "bullish" years, the prices ran as high as $4 million. In 2006, the NYSE became a for-profit public company, and all the seats were exchanged for cash and stock settlements. Traders now buy one-year licenses.

**Ticker-tape Machine**
*Introduced in the 1870s, these machines printed out up-to-the-minute details of purchase prices on ribbons of paper tape.*

**Computerized stock tickers** flash a steady stream of prices as fast as the human eye is able to read them.

## WHAT A TRADING POST DOES

The 17 trading posts each consist of 22 groups, or "sections," of traders and technology, each trading the stock of up to 10 listed companies. Commission brokers work for brokerage firms, and rush between booth and trading post, buying and selling securities (stocks and bonds) for the public. A specialist trades in just one stock at a time, quoting bids to other brokers, and independent floor brokers handle orders for busy brokerage firms. Clerks process the orders that come into the trading post via SuperDOT computer into the Exchange's Market Data System. The pages help on the busy exchange floor, bringing orders from the booths to the brokers and specialists. Post display units

**Trading post**

show stock prices, and flat screens show prices and trades for the specialist. As of January 24, 2007, all NYSE stocks can also be traded via an electronic hybrid market.

**The 48 -Hour Day**
*During the 1929 Crash, stock exchange clerks worked nonstop for 48 hours. Their mood stayed cheerful despite the panic outside.*

**VISITORS' CHECKLIST**

20 Broad St. **Map** 1 C3.
**Tel** (212) 656-3000. Ⓜ 2, 3, 4, 5 to Wall St, R, W to Rector St. 🚌 M1, M6, M15. ⬤ visitors' gallery closed for security reasons. 📷 for educational purposes only. Highly restricted.
♿ **www**.nyse.com

Public viewing gallery

Trading post

**Trading Floor**
*On a typical day, some 3.5 billion shares are traded for more than 2,000 listed companies. The advanced electronics that support the Designated Order Turnaround (SuperDOT) computer are carried above the chaos of the trading floor in a web of gold piping.*

**Great Crash of 1929**
*On Tuesday, October 29, over 16 million shares changed hands as the stock market crashed. Investors thronged Wall Street in bewilderment but, contrary to popular myth, traders did not leap from windows in panic.*

Members' entrance, Wall Street

**TIMELINE**

**1792** Buttonwood Agreement signed on May 17

**1844** Invention of the telegraph allows trading nationwide

**1867** Ticker-tape machines introduced

**1903** Present Stock Exchange building opens

**1976** DOT system replaces ticker tape

**1981** Trading posts upgraded with electronic units

**1987** "Black Monday" crash, October 19. Dow Jones Index drops 508 points

| 1750 | 1800 | 1850 | 1900 | 1950 | 2000 | 2010 |

**1817** New York Stock & Exchange Board created

*Crowds gather outside during the 1929 Crash*

**1863** Name changed to New York Stock Exchange

**1865** New Exchange Building opens at Wall and Broad Streets

**1869** "Black Friday" gold crash, September 24

**1929** Wall St. Crash, October 29

**2001** After 8 years of bull markets, economy falters after September 11

**2006** The NYSE merges with Archipelago Holdings to become a for-profit public company

# World Trade Center Site ❻

**Map** 1 B2 Ⓜ Chambers St, Rector St. ⃝ Viewing wall on Church St. **www**.projectrebirth.org **www**.renewnyc.org

Immortalized by film-makers and photographers, the twin towers of the World Trade Center dominated the skyline of Manhattan for 27 years, until September 2001's terrorist attack (see p54). The enormous weight of each building was supported by an inner wire cage, which melted from the heat of the fire caused by the two passenger aircraft that were flown into the towers.

These towers were part of a buildings complex consisting of six office blocks and a hotel, connected by a vast underground concourse lined with shops and restaurants. A bridge linked the complex to the World Financial Center (see p69), which survived the attack. The World Trade Center was home to some 450 companies with 50,000 employees.

Large numbers of visitors used to come to see the unparalleled views from the observation deck or the rooftop promenade at Two World Trade Center. The elevator took 58 seconds to reach the 107th floor. At One World Trade Center, this speedy ascent could be taken to the Windows on the World restaurant on the 107th floor. One of the Center's most memorable days was on August 7, 1974, when Philippe Petit stepped onto a tightrope between the two towers and entertained crowds of office workers for almost an hour with a high-rise balancing act.

New buildings are already beginning to reoccupy "Ground Zero". Plans to erect a new skyscraper, designed by architect Daniel Libeskind, have been controversial and construction may not be finalized until 2011. Several memorials will also be included in the new complex.

The tightrope act in progress

Philippe Petit about to step out between the two towers in 1974

# Battery Park City ❼

**Map** 1 A3. Ⓜ 1 to Rector St. 📷 ♿ 🍴 ⃝ **www**.batteryparkcity.org

Governor Mario Cuomo set the tone for this project in

Battery Park City esplanade

1983 when he urged the developers, "Give it a social purpose – give it a soul." The ambitious new neighborhood is on 92 reclaimed acres (37 ha) along the Hudson River.

The restaurants, apartments, sculptures, and gardens are built on a human scale.

Battery Park City is designed to house more than 25,000 people. The most visible part of it is the World Financial Center (see p69) and total costs are estimated at $4 billion.

The 1.2-mile (2-km) walk along the river offers unobstructed views of the Statue of Liberty.

# Skyscraper Museum ❽

39 Battery Pl. **Map** 1 A3. **Tel** (212) 968-1961. Ⓜ 4, 5 to Bowling Green; 1, R, W to Rector St. ⃝ noon–6pm Wed–Sun. 📷 ⃝ **www**.skyscraper.org

Adjacent to the Ritz Carlton hotel, this museum celebrates New York's architectural heritage and examines the historical forces and individuals that shaped the city's skyline. There is a permanent exhibition on the World Trade Center and a digital reconstruction of how Manhattan has changed over time, as well as temporary exhibitions that analyze tall buildings as objects of design, products of technology, sites of construction, real-estate investments, and places of work and residence.

The airy Skyscraper Museum

Arturo Di Modica's iconic bull statue, at the southern end of Broadway

# US Custom House ⓫

1 Bowling Green. **Map** 1 C4.
Ⓜ Bowling Green. **National Museum of the American Indian. Tel** (212) 514-3700.
◷ 10am–5pm daily (to 8pm Thu).
● Dec 25. ♿ ▯
www.nmai.si.edu

One of New York's finest Beaux Arts designs, this 1907 granite palace by Cass Gilbert is a fitting monument to the city's role as a great seaport, decorated by the best sculptors and artists of the time. Forty-four Ionic columns stand guard, with an ornate frieze. Heroic sculptures by Daniel Chester French depict four continents as seated women: Asia (contemplative), America (facing optimistically forward), Europe (surrounded by symbols of past glories) and Africa (still sleeping).

# Charging Bull ⓽

Broadway at Bowling Green.
**Map** 1 C4. Ⓜ Bowling Green.

At 1am on December 15, 1989, sculptor Arturo Di Modica and 30 friends unloaded his 7,000-lb (3,200-kg) *Charging Bull* bronze statue in front of the New York Stock Exchange. The group had eight minutes between police patrols to place the sculpture, but they managed to carry out the deed in just five. The bull was later taken away for obstructing traffic and lacking a permit. Due to the large outcry, however, the Parks Department gave it a "temporary" stomping ground on Broadway, just north of Bowling Green, where it remains to this day, the unofficial mascot of Wall Street.

Di Modica created the sculpture after the 1987 stock-market crash, to symbolize the "strength, power, and hope of the American people for the future." It took him two years to complete at a personal cost of $350,000.

# Bowling Green ⓾

**Map** 1 C4. Ⓜ Bowling Green.

This triangular plot north of Battery Park was the city's earliest park, used first as a cattle market and later as a bowling ground. A statue of King George III stood here until the signing of the Declaration of Independence, when, as a symbol of British rule, the statue was hacked to pieces and smelted for ammunition *(see pp22–23)*. The wife of the governor of Connecticut is said to have melted down enough pieces to mold 42,000 bullets.

The fence, erected in 1771, is still standing, but minus the royal crowns that once adorned it. They met the same fate as the statue. The Green was once surrounded by elegant homes. Beyond it is the start of Broadway, which runs the length of Manhattan and, under its formal name of Route 9, all the way north to the State capital in Albany.

**Top of a column at the US Custom House**

Inside, murals by Reginald Marsh decorate the fine marble rotunda, showing the progress of ships into the harbor. Opposite the entrance is a portrait of movie star Greta Garbo giving a press conference on board ship. In 1973 the US Customs Service moved out, leaving the building empty but for a small bankruptcy court.

The Custom House took on a new function in 1994, when the George Gustav Heye Center of the **Smithsonian National Museum of the American Indian** was unveiled on three floors of the building. The museum's outstanding collection of about a million artifacts along with an archive of many thousands of photographs, spans the breadth of the native cultures of North, Central and South America.

Exhibitions include works by contemporary Native American artists as well as changing displays drawn from the permanent collection.

**Fountain at Bowling Green**

# Statue of Liberty ⑰

A gift from the French to the American people, the statue was the brainchild of sculptor Frédéric-Auguste Bartholdi and has become a symbol of freedom throughout the world. In Emma Lazarus's poem, which is engraved on the base, Lady Liberty says: "Give me your tired, your poor,/ Your huddled masses yearning to breathe free." Unveiled by President Grover Cleveland on October 28, 1886, the statue was restored in time for its 100th anniversary in 1986. Visitors were able to go right up to the crown, but this was closed after the terrorist attack of September 11, 2001. However, the base is still open.

★ **Golden Torch**
*In 1986, a new torch replaced the corroded original. The replica's flame is coated in 24-carat gold leaf.*

**The crown** cannot currently be visited.

**The frame** was designed by Gustave Eiffel, who later built the Eiffel Tower. The copper shell hangs on iron bars from a central iron pylon.

**A central pylon** anchors the 225-ton statue to its base.

**354 steps** lead from the entrance to the crown.

**Observation deck and museum**

## THE STATUE
*With a height of 305 ft (93 m) from ground to torch, the Statue of Liberty dominates New York harbor*

**The pedestal** is set within the walls of an army fort. It was the largest concrete mass ever poured.

**From Her Toes to Her Torch**
*Three hundred molded copper sheets riveted together make up Lady Liberty.*

★ **Statue of Liberty Museum**
*Posters featuring the statue are among the items on display.*

**The original torch** now stands in the main lobby.

★ **Ferries to Liberty Island**
*Ferries cross New York Harbor to Liberty Island, where the Statue offers some of the city's finest views.*

**Portrait of Liberty**
*Bartholdi's mother was the model for Liberty. The seven rays of her crown represent the seven seas and seven continents.*

**Making the Hand**
*To mold the copper shell, the hand was made first in plaster, then wood.*

**A Model Figure**
*A series of graduated scale models enabled Bartholdi to build the largest metal statue ever constructed.*

**FREDERIC-AUGUSTE BARTHOLDI**

The French sculptor who designed the Statue of Liberty intended it as a monument to the freedom he found lacking in his own country. He said "I will try to glorify the Republic and Liberty over there, in the hope that someday I will find it again here." Bartholdi devoted 21 years of his life to making the statue a reality, even traveling to America in 1871 to talk President Ulysses S. Grant and others into funding it and installing it in New York's harbor.

**STAR FEATURES**

★ Ferries to
  Liberty Island

★ Golden Torch

★ Statue of Liberty
  Museum

**Restoration Celebration**
*On July 3, 1986, after a $100-million restoration, the statue was unveiled. The $2-million fireworks display was the largest ever seen in America.*

# St. Elizabeth Ann Seton Shrine

7 State St. **Map** 1 C4. **Tel** (212) 269-6865. Ⓜ Whitehall, South Ferry. ◯ 6:30am–5pm Mon–Fri. 🕭 8:05am, 12:15pm, 1:05pm Mon–Fri; 11am Sun. �📷

**Elizabeth Ann Seton**

Elizabeth Ann Seton (1774–1821), the first native-born American to be canonized by the Catholic Church, lived here from 1801 to 1803. Mother Seton founded the American Sisters of Charity, the first order of nuns in the United States.

After the Civil War, the Mission of Our Lady of the Rosary turned the building into a shelter for homeless Irish immigrant women – 170,000 passed through on their way to a new life in America. The adjoining church was built in 1883. The Mission established and maintains the shrine to Mother Seton.

# Fraunces Tavern Museum ⓭

54 Pearl St. **Map** 1 C4. **Tel** (212) 425-1778. Ⓜ Wall St, Broad St, Bowling Green. ◯ noon–5pm Tue–Fri, 10am–5pm Sat. ⬤ public hols, day after Thanksgiving. 🎟

🖥 groups only. **Lectures, films.** 🕚 🌐 www.frauncestavernmuseum.org **NYC Police Museum** 100 Old Slip, South St. **Map** 1 D3. **Tel** (212) 480-3100. ◯ 10am–5pm Mon–Sat. Donation suggested. 🖥 groups only. www.nycpolicemuseum.org

New York's only remaining block of 18th-century commercial buildings contains an exact replica of the 1719 Fraunces Tavern where George Washington said farewell to his officers in 1783. The tavern had been an early casualty of the Revolution: the British ship *Asia* shot a cannonball through its roof in August 1775. The building was bought in 1904 by the Sons of the Revolution. Its restoration in 1907 was one of the first efforts to preserve the nation's heritage. The ground floor restaurant has wood-burning fires and great charm. An upstairs museum has changing exhibits interpreting the history and culture of early America. The **New York City Police Museum** (see p84) is at South Street. Exhibits include NYPD artifacts, interactive displays, seminars, and special events. Visit the Hall of Heroes and try your hand at the firearms training simulator.

**The 18th-century Fraunces Tavern Museum and restaurant**

# Vietnam Veterans' Plaza ⓮

Between Water St and South St. **Map** 2 D4. Ⓜ Whitehall, South Ferry.

This multilevel brick plaza has an upscale shopping mall below. However, in its center is a huge wall of translucent green glass, engraved with excerpts from speeches, news stories and moving letters to families from servicemen and women who died in the war.

**Staten Island Ferry – one of the city's best bargains**

# Staten Island Ferry ⓯

Whitehall St. **Map** 2 D5. **Tel** 311. Ⓜ South Ferry. ◯ 24 hrs. Free. 📷 ♿ www.siferry.com

The first business venture of a promising Staten Island boy named Cornelius Vanderbilt, who later became the railroad magnate, the ferry has operated since 1810, carrying island commuters to and from the city and offering visitors an unforgettable close-up of the harbor, the Statue of Liberty, Ellis Island and lower Manhattan's incredible skyline. The fare is still the city's best bargain: it's free.

## Battery Maritime Building

11 South St. **Map** 2 D4.
M *South Ferry.* ⬤ *to the public.*

From 1909 to 1938, the municipal terminal for ferries to Brooklyn operated here on the site of a small wharf known as Schreijers Hoek, from which Dutch Colonial ships once set sail for the mother country. At the height of the ferry era, 17 lines made regular runs from these bustling piers, which are used now only by the Coast Guard service for Governors Island.

The building was designed in 1907. Arriving boats face 300-ft (91-m) arched openings guarded by tall, ornately scrolled columns and adorned with latticework, molding and rosettes typical of the Beaux Arts period. This is actually a false front of sheet metal and steel, painted green to resemble copper.

**Ironwork railing on the Battery Maritime Building**

## Statue of Liberty ⬤

*See pp74–5.*

## Ellis Island ⬤

*See pp78–9.*

**Castle Clinton National Monument in Battery Park**

## Battery Park ⬤

**Map** 1 B4.
M *South Ferry, Bowling Green.*

Named for the cannons that once protected the harbor, the park is one of the best places in the city for gazing out to sea. Over the years, landfill has extended the greenery far beyond its original State Street boundary.

The park is rimmed with statues and monuments, such as the Netherlands Memorial

**Beaux Arts subway entrance at the corner of Battery Park**

Monument and memorials to New York's first Jewish immigrants and the Coast Guard. Fritz Koenig's *The Sphere*, a sculpture that once stood in the World Trade Center Plaza, is now here, serving as a memorial to those who died in the 9/11 terrorist attack.

## Castle Clinton National Monument ⬤

Battery Park. **Map** 1 B4. *Tel (212) 344-7220.* M *Bowling Green, South Ferry.* ⬤ *8:30am–5pm daily.* ⬤ *Dec 25.* ⬤ ⬤ ⬤ *Concerts.* ⬤ *www.nps.gov/cacl*

Castle Clinton was built in 1811 as an artillery defense post 300 ft (91 m) offshore,

connected to Battery Park by a causeway; but landfill gradually linked it to the mainland. None of its 28 guns was ever used in battle.

The fort was enclosed in 1824 to become a fashionable theater, where Phineas T. Barnum introduced "Swedish nightingale" Jenny Lind in 1850. In 1855 it preceded Ellis Island as the city's immigration point, processing over 8 million newcomers. In 1896, it became the New York Aquarium, which moved to Coney Island in 1941 *(see p249).*

Now it is a monument and visitors' center for Manhattan's National Park Service sites, with historical panoramas of the city. The complex is the departure point for the Statue of Liberty–Ellis Island ferry *(see p369).*

## Museum of Jewish Heritage ⬤

36 Battery Place. **Map** 1 B4. *Tel (646) 437-4200.* M *Bowling Green, South Ferry.* 🚌 *M1, 6, 9, 15, 20.* ⬤ *10am–5:45pm Sun–Tue, Thu, 10am–8pm Wed, 10am–3pm Fri and eve of Jewish holidays.* ⬤ *Sat, Jewish holidays, Thanksgiving.* ⬤ ⬤ ⬤ ⬤ ⬤ *Lectures.* www.mjhnyc.org

The museum has a core exhibition of more than 2,000 photographs, 800 artifacts and 24 documentary films about Jewish life, before, during and after the Holocaust. The newly expanded museum now contains a state-of-the-art theater for films, lectures and performances; a memorial garden; classrooms; a resource center and library; a family history center; expanded gallery space for temporary exhibitions; offices; a cafe and event hall.

# Ellis Island ⑱

Half of America's population can trace its roots to Ellis Island, which served as the country's immigration depot from 1892 until 1954. Nearly 12 million people passed through its gates and dispersed across the country in the greatest wave of migration the world has ever known. Centered on the Great Hall or Registry Room, the site today houses the three-story *Ellis Island Immigration Museum.* Much of this story is told with photos and the voices of actual immigrants, and an electronic database traces ancestors. Outside, the *American Immigrant Wall of Honor* is the largest wall of names in the world. No other place explains so well the "melting pot" that formed the character of the nation. Visit early to avoid the crowds.

**Main building**

**The railroad office** sold tickets onward to the final destination.

**Rail Ticket**
*A special fare for emigrants led many on to California.*

★ **Dormitory**
*There were separate sleeping quarters for male and female detainees.*

## THE RESTORATION

In 1990 a $156-million project by the Statue of Liberty-Ellis Island Foundation, Inc., renewed several ruined buildings, replacing the copper domes and restoring the interior with original fixtures.

The ferry office sold tickets to New Jersey.

★ **Baggage Room** *The immigrants' meager possessions were checked here on arrival.*

Great Hall ★
*Immigrant families were made to wait for "processing" in the Registry Room. The old metal railings were replaced with wooden benches in 1911.*

The metal and glass awning is a re-creation of the original.

Main entrance

**Arrival** *Steerage passengers crowd the deck as the ship approaches Ellis Island.*

**Immigrant Family**
*An Italian mother and her children arrive in 1905.*

**Medical Examining Rooms**
*Immigrants with contagious diseases could be refused entry and sent back home.*

**STAR FEATURES**

★ Baggage Room

★ Dormitory

★ Great Hall

# SEAPORT AND
# THE CIVIC CENTER

Manhattan's busy Civic Center is the hub of the city and the state, of the federal governments' court systems and the city's police department. In the 1880s it was the heart of the newspaper publishing business as well. The area is still a handsome enclave of imposing architecture with fine landmarks from every period in the city's history, from the 20th-century Woolworth Building to 19th-century City Hall and 18th-century St. Paul's

Chapel, New York's oldest building in continuous use. Nearby is South Street Seaport. Called the "street of sails" in the 19th century because of the many ships that were moored there, the seaport underwent a decline when sailing ships became unprofitable. The area has now been restored and is home to a museum and many shops and restaurants. The Brooklyn Bridge, once the largest suspension bridge in the world, lies to the north.

Ship's figurehead, South Street Seaport

## SIGHTS AT A GLANCE

### Historic Streets and Buildings
AT&T Building **14**
*Brooklyn Bridge pp86–9* **3**
City Hall **10**
Criminal Courts Building **4**
Municipal Building **7**
New York County Courthouse **5**
Old New York County Courthouse **9**
Schermerhorn Row **2**
South Street Seaport **1**
Surrogate's Court, Hall of Records **8**
United States Courthouse **6**
Woolworth Building **12**

### Churches
St. Paul's Chapel **13**

### Parks and Squares
City Hall Park and Park Row **11**

### GETTING THERE
Many subway lines serve the area: the 7th Ave/Broadway 2 and 3 trains to Park Pl or Fulton St; the Lexington Ave 4, 5 and 6 to Brooklyn Bridge; the 8th Ave A, C and E to Chambers St and the R or W to City Hall. By bus take the M1, M6, M9, M10, M15, M101/102 or the M22 crosstown.

### SEE ALSO

**KEY**
▦ Street-by-Street map
Ⓜ Subway station
⛴ Riverboat boarding point

0 meters 500
0 yards 500

◁ South Street Seaport

# Street by Street: South Street Seaport

Part commercial, part historical, the development of South Street Seaport has turned the former heart of the 19th-century port of New York, which had long been neglected, into a lively part of the city. Shops and cafés abound; tall ships are once again moored here. The South Street Seaport museum tells the story of New York's maritime past through craft demonstrations, ship tours, and river cruises. Workers from Wall Street come here to eat and drink.

★ **South Street Seaport**
*Once full of sailors and sailing ships, the seaport is now a lively complex of shops, restaurants, and museums* ❶

**Cannon's Walk** is a 19th- and 20th-century block of buildings, with an outdoor café, shops, and a very lively marketplace.

**The Titanic Memorial** is a lighthouse built in 1913 in memory of those who died on the *Titanic*. It now stands on Fulton Street.

To Fulton St. subway (4 blocks)

**Schermerhorn Row**
*Built as warehouses in 1813 and due to house The World Port New York exhibit, the Row contains the South Street Seaport Museum and Brookstone* ❷

**The Boat-Building Shop** lets you watch as skilled craftspeople build and restore small wooden vessels.

**At the Maritime Crafts Center** woodcarvers and painters can be seen at work on models, ship carvings, and figureheads.

**Ship in a bottle**

**The Pilothouse** was originally from a steam tugboat built in 1923 by New York Central. The Seaport's admission and information center is to be found here.

## STAR SIGHTS

★ Brooklyn Bridge

★ South Street Seaport

**The Consolidated Edison**
electrical substation, built in
1975, has an illusionistic
mural of the Brooklyn
Bridge by Richard Haas on
one side to help it blend
in with its historic
neighbors.

**LOCATOR MAP**
See Manhattan Map pp14–15

**KEY**

− − − Suggested route

| 0 meters | 100 |
| 0 yards | 100 |

**Meyer's
Hotel**,
built in
1873, became
a hotel in 1881.
Now a bar, it retains a feel of days
gone by when markswoman
Annie Oakley stayed here.

**★ Brooklyn Bridge**
*An engineering wonder when it was
built in 1883, the bridge is still
remarkable. From the pedestrian
walkway there are fine views of the
city and the bridge itself* ❸

**Pier 17** offers three
floors of shops,
restaurants, and
food stands in an
impressive glass and
steel pavilion. From
the top floor there
are great views
of the Brooklyn
Bridge and historic
ships moored in
the harbor.

**The schooner**
*Pioneer* is used for
river cruises from the
Seaport. The 1908
*Ambrose* lightship,
which guided ships
into port, is also
moored here.

The Ambrose lightship at a South Street Seaport pier on the East River

# South Street Seaport ❶

Fulton St. **Map** 2 E2. **Tel** (212) SEA-
PORT. 🅼 Fulton St. ◗ Nov–Mar:
10am–7pm Mon–Fri, 11am–6pm Sun;
Apr–Oct: 10am–9pm Mon–Sat, 11am–
8pm Sun. 🔲 ♿ 🅕 **Concerts.** 🎭
🏛 **South Street Seaport Museum**
12 Fulton St. 📳 (212) 748-8600.
◗ Apr–Oct: 10am–6pm Tue–Sun;
Nov–Mar: 10am–5pm Fri–Mon.
◗ Jan 1, Thanksgiving, Dec 25. 🆔
🔲 ♿ 🅕 **Lectures, exhibits, films.**
🎭 🏛 www.southstseaport.org

The heart of New York's
19th-century seaport has been
given an imaginative new lease
on life. Glitzy stores and
restaurants sit harmoniously
beside seafaring craft, historic
buildings, and museums, with
spectacular views of Brooklyn
Bridge and the East River from
the cobblestone streets. Historic
ships berthed here range from
the little tugboat *W.O. Decker*
to the great four-masted sailing
ship *Peking*. Mini-trips on the
schooner *Pioneer* are a great
way to see the river.
   The **Museum** covers the
12 blocks of what was once
America's leading port. Not

only is it home to the largest
fleet of privately maintained
historic vessels in the US, but
there are also over 20,000
artifacts, artworks, and documents from the 19th- and early
20th-century maritime world.
   The New York City Police
Museum *(see p76)* chronicles
the history of law enforcement.
Exhibits include weapons, the
art of fingerprinting and
forensics, and the arrest
records of famous criminals.
   Fulton Fish Market, which
was a popular attraction at
Seaport for more than 150
years, moved to a new home
in the Bronx in 2006.

# Schermerhorn Row ❷

Fulton and South Sts. **Map** 2 D3.
🅼 Fulton St.

This is Seaport's architectural
showpiece. Constructed in
1811 by shipowner and
chandler Peter Schermerhorn
on land reclaimed from the
river, the buildings were
originally warehouses and
counting-houses. With the
opening of the Brooklyn
Ferry terminus in
1814 and of Fulton
Market in 1822, the
block became
desirable property.
   The Row has been
restored as part of
the South Street
developmen, and
it now houses 24
museum galleries,
as well as shops,
and restaurants.

# Brooklyn Bridge ❸

See pp86–9.

# Criminal Courts Building ❹

100 Centre St. **Map** 4 F5.
🅼 Canal St. ◗ 9am–5pm Mon–Fri.
◗ public hols. ♿

This 1939 building is Art
Moderne in style, with towers
reminiscent of a Babylonian
temple. The three-story-high
entrance is set back in a
court, behind two huge,
square, free-standing granite
columns – an intimidating
sight for the accused. The
building also houses the
Manhattan Detention Center
for Men, which was formerly
across the street in a building
known as "The Tombs"
because of its Egyptian-style
architecture. The nickname
has stuck, although the
original is long gone. An
aerial walkway, or "bridge
of sighs," links the courts
with the correctional facility
across Centre Street.
   The building also houses
the night courts, where cases
are heard from 5pm to 1am
on weekdays.

**Entrance to the Criminal
Courts Building**

# New York County Courthouse ❺

60 Centre St. **Map** 2 D1.
🅼 Brooklyn Br-City Hall. ◗ 9am–
5pm Mon–Fri. ◗ public hols. ♿

Built to replace the Tweed
Courthouse *(see p90)*, this
new county supreme court-
house was completed in 1926.

Restored buildings on Schermerhorn Row

The fluted Corinthian portico at the top of a wide staircase is the main feature of the hexagonal building. The austere exterior is offset by a circular-columned interior rotunda featuring Tiffany lighting fixtures and a series of rich marble and ceiling murals by Attilio Pusterla on themes of law and justice. Six wings radiate from the rotunda, each housing a single court and its facilities.

The courtroom drama *Twelve Angry Men,* starring Henry Fonda, was filmed here.

**New York County Courthouse**

# United States Courthouse ❻

40 Centre St. **Map** 2 D1. Ⓜ
*Brooklyn Br-City Hall.* ◯ *9am–5pm Mon–Fri.* ◯ *public hols.* ♿

This courthouse was the last project undertaken by noted architect Cass Gilbert, designer of the Woolworth Building *(see p91).* Begun in 1933, the year before his death, it was finished by his son. The

**United States Courthouse**

31-story structure is a pyramid-topped tower set on a classical temple base. The bronzework on the doors is handsome, but the interior lacks the colorful decoration Gilbert had outlined in his sketchbooks. Aerial walkways link the building with its Police Plaza Annex.

# Municipal Building ❼

1 Centre St. **Map** 1 C1. Ⓜ
*Brooklyn Br-City Hall.* ◯ ♿

The Municipal Building, constructed in 1914, dominates the Civic Center and straddles Chambers Street. It was McKim, Mead & White's first skyscraper and houses government offices and a marriage chapel. The exterior, in harmony with City Hall, has no excess detail to detract from the earlier building. The most notable feature is the top, a fantasy of towers capped by Adolph Wienman's statue *Civic Fame.*

A railway passage (no longer in use) through the base, and the plaza joining the Municipal Building to the entrance of the IRT subway station were built as concessions to modern transportation needs. The building has had a far-reaching influence on architectural style; the main building at Moscow University is said to have been modeled on its design.

# Surrogate's Court, Hall of Records ❽

31 Chambers St. **Map** 1 C1.
Ⓜ *City Hall.* ◯ *9am–5pm Mon–Fri.*
◯ *public hols.* ◯ ♿ ☑

A Beaux Arts triumph, the original Hall of Records was begun in 1899 and completed in 1911. The elaborate columned facade is of white Maine granite, with a high mansard roof. The figures by Henry K. Bush-Brown in the roof area represent life's stages from childhood to old age; the statues by Philip Martiny over the colonnade are of notable New Yorkers such as Peter

**Municipal Building**

Stuyvesant. Martiny also made the representations of New York in its infancy and New York in revolutionary times at the Chambers Street entrance.

The Paris Opéra Garnier was the inspiration for the twin marble stairways and painted ceiling of the dazzling central hall. The ceiling mosaic by William de Leftwich Dodge features the signs of the zodiac and symbols of record keeping.

Recently restored, the Hall of Records holds public records dating back to 1664. A permanent exhibition, *Windows on the Archives,* features historical papers, drawings, letters and photographs illustrating what life was like in New York from 1626 to the present.

**Surrogate's Court**

# Brooklyn Bridge ❸

Completed in 1883, the Brooklyn Bridge was the largest suspension bridge and the first to be constructed of steel. Engineer John A. Roebling conceived of a bridge spanning the East River while ice-bound on a ferry to Brooklyn. The bridge took 16 years to build, required 600 workers and claimed over 20 lives, including Roebling's. Most died of caisson disease (known as "the bends") after coming up from the underwater excavation chambers. When finished, the bridge linked Manhattan and Brooklyn, then two separate cities.

Souvenir medal cast for the opening of the bridge

**BROOKLYN BRIDGE**
*From making the wire to sinking the supports, the bridge was built using new techniques.*

**Anchorage**
*The ends of the bridge's four steel cables are fastened to a series of anchor bars held in place by anchor plates. These are held down by giant granite vaults up to three stories high. Their vast interiors, once used for storage, are now used for summer art displays.*

Granite vault

Cable to tower

Anchor bar

**Caisson**
*The towers rose up above caissons, each the size of four tennis courts, which provided a dry area for underwater excavation. As work went on, they sank deeper beneath the river.*

Shaft

**Anchor Plates**
*Each of the four cast-iron anchor plates holds one cable. The masonry was built up around them after they were placed in position.*

Anchor plates

Anchor plate

Vault

Central span is 1,595 ft (486 m) long

Vault

Roadway from anchorage to anchorage is 3,579 ft (1,091 m)

### First Crossing
*Master mechanic E.F. Farrington in 1876 was the first to cross the river on the bridge-in-progress, using a steam-driven traveler rope. His journey took 22 minutes.*

### Steel Cable Wire
*Each cable contains 3,515 miles (5,657 km) of wire, galvanized with zinc for protection from the wind, rain, and snow.*

FOUNDATION LINE

### Brooklyn Tower (1875)
*Two Gothic double arches, each 271 ft (83 m) high, one in Brooklyn, the other in Manhattan, were meant to be the portals of the cities.*

### Inside the Caisson
*Immigrant workers broke up rocks in the riverbed.*

### JOHN A. ROEBLING
The German-born Roebling designed the bridge. In 1869, just before construction started, his foot was crushed between an incoming ferry and the ferry slip. He died three weeks later. His son, Washington Roebling, finished the bridge, but in 1872 he was taken from a caisson suffering from the bends and became partly paralyzed. His wife, under his tutelage, then took over.

## MAKING THE CABLES

Thickness of steel wire
(actual size)

End of
wire

### How the Cables Were Made
*Each of the four main cables has
19 strands, each made of 278
steel wires. The wires were not
twisted, but laid parallel.*

The 19 strands of a
main cable

**The strands** were laid in order: after
the bottom 12 strands were laid, the
center strands were bound together.

Iron clamp

Bolt

### Cable Wrapping
*Wire was wound
off the drum and
around the cable
to form a
tight final
wrapping.*

**A massive iron clamp**
compressed all the
strands into an even
cylinder once they had
been positioned.

**1983 Centennial Fireworks over the Brooklyn Bridge**
*Celebrating the bridge's 100th year, this display was awesome.*

### Bustling Bridge
*This 1883 view from
the Manhattan side
shows the original two
outer lanes for horse-
drawn carriages, two
middle lanes for cable
cars, and the elevated
center walkway.*

**Panic of May 30, 1883**
*After a woman tripped on the
bridge, panic broke out. Of the
estimated 20,000 people on the
bridge, 12 were crushed to death.*

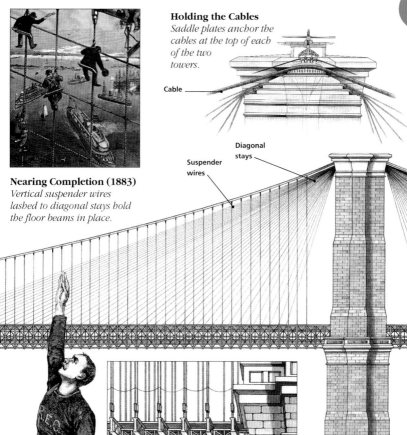

**Nearing Completion (1883)**
*Vertical suspender wires lashed to diagonal stays hold the floor beams in place.*

**Holding the Cables**
*Saddle plates anchor the cables at the top of each of the two towers.*

Cable

Diagonal stays

Suspender wires

**Floor Beams**
*The steel floor beams weigh 4 tons each.*

**Odlum's Jump**
*Robert Odlum was the first to jump off the bridge, on a bet, in May 1885. He later died from internal bleeding.*

**Elevated Walkway**
*Poet Walt Whitman said that the view from the walkway – 18 ft (5.5 m) above the road – was "the best, most effective medicine my soul has yet partaken."*

# Old New York County Courthouse ❾

52 Chambers St. **Map** 1 C1.
Ⓜ *Chambers St-City Hall.*
🖼 *included in City Hall tour.*

This building is best known for the scandal it caused. It is nicknamed the "Tweed Courthouse" for the political boss who spent 20 times the budget for the building and pocketed $9 million of the total $14 million cost. "Boss" Tweed even bought a marble quarry and sold materials to the city at huge profit. Public outrage eventually led to his downfall in 1871 – ironically, he was tried in his own courthouse and died in a New York jail *(see p27).*

After an $85 million restoration, including the 85-ft (26-m) rotunda and the grand staircase, this vibrant 19th-century landmark became the home of the Department of Education.

City Hall's imposing early 19th-century facade

# City Hall ❿

City Hall Park. **Map** 1 C1. **Tel** 311.
Ⓜ *Brooklyn Br-City Hall Park Pl.*
☐ *for prearranged tours only.* 📷
♿ 🖼 *(212) 788-2170.*

City Hall has been the seat of the New York city government since 1812, and is one of the finest examples of early 19th-century American architecture. A stately Federal-style building (with some influences from the French Renaissance), it was

P.T. Barnum's museum blazes as crowds watch from City Hall Park

designed by John McComb, Jr., the first prominent American-born architect, and the French emigré Joseph Mangin.

Marble cladding was not used for the building's rear, since it was not expected that the city would ever develop farther to the north. In 1954, a program of restoration remedied this and the interior was refurbished.

Mangin is usually given credit for designing the exterior, and McComb for the beautiful interior with its fine domed rotunda encircled by 10 columns. The space beneath it opens onto an elegant marble stairway, leading to the splendid second-floor City Council chambers and the Governor's Room, which houses a portrait gallery of early New York leaders. This magnificent entrance has welcomed rulers and heroes for nearly 200 years. In 1865 Abraham Lincoln's body lay in state in this hall.

Stand on the steps and look to your right to see a statue of Nathan Hale, a US soldier hanged by the British as a spy in September 1776 during the Revolutionary War. His last words – "My only regret is that I have not more lives than one to offer in the service of my country" – won him a permanent place in the history books and hearts of America.

# City Hall Park and Park Row ⓫

**Map** 1 C2. Ⓜ *Brooklyn Br-City Hall Park Plc.*

This was New York's village green 250 years ago, complete with stocks and whipping post. It was the scene of pre-Revolution protests against English rule, and there is a memorial to the "Liberty Poles" (symbols of revolt) on City Hall's west lawn. The Declaration of Independence was read to George Washington and his troops here on July 9, 1776.

Later, Phineas T. Barnum's American Museum at the park's southern tip drew crowds from 1842 until it burned down in 1865. The Park Row building was the site of the Park Theater. From 1798 to 1848, the best actors of the day, such as Edmund Kean and Fanny Kemble, performed there. Park Row runs along the east side of City Hall Park. Once called "Newspaper Row," it was lined with the lofty offices of the *Sun, World, Tribune,* and other papers.

Statue of Benjamin Franklin in Printing House Square

Printing House Square has a statue of Benjamin Franklin with his *Pennsylvania Gazette*. In 1999 City Hall Park underwent major renovations; its clean, open space is a fine place to sit and relax.

# Woolworth Building ⓬

233 Broadway. **Map** 1 C2. M *City Hall Park Pl.*

**Bas-relief caricature of architect Gilbert in the Woolworth lobby**

In 1879, salesclerk Frank W. Woolworth opened a new kind of store, where shoppers could see and touch the goods, and everything cost five cents. The chain of stores that followed made him a fortune and changed retailing forever.

The 1913 Gothic headquarters of his empire was New York's tallest building until 1930. It set the standard for the great skyscrapers.

Architect Cass Gilbert's soaring two-tiered design, adorned with gargoyles of bats and other wildlife, is topped with a pyramid roof, flying buttresses, pinnacles, and four small towers. The marble interior is rich with filigree, sculptured reliefs, and painted decoration, and has a high glass-tile mosaic ceiling that almost seems to glow. The lobby is one of the city's treasures. Gilbert showed his sense of humor here, in bas-relief caricatures of the founder counting out his fortune in nickels and dimes; of the real estate broker closing a deal; and of Cass Gilbert himself cradling a large model of the building. Paid for with $13.5 million in cash, the building has never had a mortgage. Woolworth's went out of business in 1997. The building is now owned by the Witkoff Group.

# St. Paul's Chapel ⓭

209–211 Broadway. **Map** 1 C2. **Tel** (212) 233-4164. M *Fulton St.* ☐ *10am–6pm Mon–Sat, 9am–4pm Sun.* ● *most public hols.* ✝ *12:30pm Wed; 8am, 10am Sun.* ☐ ☑ *by appt.* **Concerts** *1pm Mon.* **www**.saintpaulschapel.org

Miraculously untouched when the World Trade Center towers collapsed in 2001, St. Paul's is

**The Georgian interior of St. Paul's Chapel**

Manhattan's only remaining church built before the Revolutionary War. It is a Georgian gem. The colorful interior, lit by Waterford chandeliers, is the setting for free concerts. The pew where newly inaugurated George Washington prayed has been preserved. In the churchyard, the Actor's Monument commemorates George F. Cooke, who played many great roles at the Park Theater; he drank himself to death at the Shakespeare Tavern on Fulton Street.

# AT&T Building ⓮

195 Broadway. **Map** 1 C2. M *Broadway-Nassau Fulton St.* ☐ *office hours.*

Columns, columns everywhere mark this former headquarters designed by Welles Bosworth from 1915 to 1922. The facade is said to have more columns than any other building in the world, and the interior is a forest of marble pillars. The whole edifice looks like a gigantic square-topped layer cake.

**A sea sprite above the door of the AT&T (American Telephone and Telegraph) Building**

# LOWER EAST SIDE

owhere does the strong
ethnic flavor of New
York come through
more tangibly than in Lower
Manhattan, where immigrants
began to settle in the late 19th
century. Here Italians, Chinese
and Jews established distinct
neighborhoods, preserving
their languages, customs,
foods and religions in the midst of a
strange land. This neighborhood of

19th-century tin,
Lower East Side
Tenement Museum

low-rise buildings is steadily
becoming gentrified, but
the old flavor remains. The
area brims with restaurants,
bars, and trendy stores, but
still offers some of the city's
greatest bargains and has a
spirit found nowhere else.
The composer Irving Berlin,
who grew up here, famously
said: "Everybody ought to have a
Lower East Side in their life."

## SIGHTS AT A GLANCE

**Historic Streets and
Buildings**
Chinatown ❹
Delancey Street ❿
East Houston Street ⓫
Engine Company No. 31 ⓮
Home Savings of America ❶
Little Italy ❸
Orchard Street ❽
Police Headquarters
   Building ❷
Puck Building ⓬

**Parks and Squares**
Columbus Park ❺

**Museums and Galleries**
FusionArts Museum ⓳
Lower East Side Tenement
   Museum ❼
New Museum of
   Contemporary Art ⓰

**Shops and Markets**
Economy Candy ⓱
Essex Street Market ⓴
The Pickle Guys ⓯

**Churches and Synagogues**
Angel Orensanz Center ⓲
Bialystoker Synagogue ❾
Eldridge Street Synagogue ❻
Old St. Patrick's Cathedral ⓭

### GETTING THERE
Chinatown and Little Italy can
be reached by subway on the
N, R, Q, W, J, M, or 6 trains to
Canal St, or on the M1 or
M103 bus. The Lower East Side
is served by the B and D trains
to Grand St, the F to Delancey
St, the J, M, or Z to Essex St, or
by the M9, M14A, or M15 bus.

**SEE ALSO**

• *Street Finder*, maps 4, 5

• *Where to Stay* p280

• *Restaurants* pp296–7

• *Lower East Side Walk*
   pp258–9

0 meters          500

0 yards           500

**KEY**

▢ Street-by-Street map

Ⓜ Subway station

◁ **Dragon puppet in Chinatown at Chinese New Year**

# Street by Street: Little Italy and Chinatown

New York's largest and most colorful ethnic neighborhood is Chinatown, which is growing so rapidly that it is overrunning nearby Little Italy as well as the Lower East Side. Streets here teem with grocery stores, gift shops and hundreds of Chinese restaurants; even the plainest offer good food. What is left of Little Italy can be found at Mulberry and Grand streets, where old-world flavor abounds.

★ **Little Italy**
*The scents of Italy still waft from the restaurants and bakeries of this area, once home to thousands of immigrants* ❸

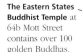

**The Market on Canal Street** has a wide range of bargains in new and used clothes and fresh produce.

Ⓜ **Canal Street subway (lines R, W, N, Q, 6)**

★ **Chinatown**
*Home to a thriving – and still expanding – community of Chinese immigrants, this area is famous for its restaurants and hectic street life. The area truly comes alive around the Chinese New Year in January or February* ❹

**The Eastern States Buddhist Temple** at 64b Mott Street contains over 100 golden Buddhas.

**The Wall of Democracy** on Bayard Street is covered with newspapers and posters describing the situation in China.

**Columbus Park**
*In the 19th century this park was the site of New York's worst slum* ❺

**Confucius Plaza** is marked by sculptor Liu Shih's monument to the Oriental philosopher.

**Chatham Square** has a memorial to Chinese-American war dead.

**Police Headquarters Building**
*The dome of this Baroque civic building towers over the City Hall area. In 1973, the police moved out; ten years later the building was turned into apartments* ❷

**LOCATOR MAP**
See Manhattan Map pp14–15

**KEY**
− − − Suggested route

0 meters 100
0 yards 100

**Home Savings of America**
*Stanford White designed this in 1894 for the old Bowery Savings Bank* ❶

**Umbertos Clam House,** known as the place where Mafia boss Joey Gallo was shot in 1972, once occupied this location on Mulberry Street.

★ **Eldridge Street Synagogue**
*Built in 1887, this was the first large temple built in the US by European Jews* ❻

**Bloody Angle,** where Doyers Street turns sharply, was the gruesome site of many gangland ambushes during the 1920s.

**STAR SIGHTS**

★ Chinatown

★ Eldridge Street Synagogue

★ Little Italy

## Home Savings of America **❶**

130 Bowery. **Map** 4 F4.
Ⓜ *Grand St, Bowery.*

Imposing inside and out, this Classical Revival building was built for the Bowery Savings Bank in 1894. Architect Stanford White designed the ornamented lime-stone facade to wrap around the rival Butchers' and Drovers' Bank, which refused to sell the corner plot. The interior is decorated with marble pillars and a ceiling scattered with gilded rosettes.

By the middle of the 20th century, the bank was a contrast to the Bowery with its vagrants and flophouses. It is now the site of Capitale, and open only for special events.

**Detail from Home Savings of America**

## Police Headquarters Building **❷**

240 Centre St. **Map** 4 F4.
Ⓜ *Canal St.* ⓞ *to the public.*

Completed in 1909 this was a fitting home for the city's new professional police force. The main portico and end pavilions have Corinthian columns and the dome dominates the sky-line. However, lack of space meant the headquarters had to fit into a wedge-shaped site in the midst of Little Italy.

For nearly three-quarters of a century, this was where "New York's finest" came to

work. During Prohibition, Grand Street from here to the Bowery was known as "Bootleggers' Row," and alcohol was easily obtained except when a police raid was due. The liquor merchants paid handsomely for a tip-off from inside police headquarters. The police moved to new headquarters in 1973, and in 1985 the building was converted into a luxury cooperative apartment project.

## Little Italy **❸**

Streets around Mulberry St.
**Map** 4 F4. Ⓜ *Canal St.*
**www**.littleitalynyc.com

The southern Italians who came to New York in the late 19th century found themselves living in the squalor of "dumbbell" apartments. These were built so close together that sunlight never reached the lower windows or backyards. With over 40,000 people living in 17 small, unsanitary blocks, diseases such as tuberculosis were rife.

Despite the privations of life on the Lower East Side, the community that grew up around Mulberry Street was lively with the colors, flavors, and atmosphere of Italy. These have lingered on, though the Italian population has dwindled to 5,000 and

Chinatown has encroached on the traditional "Little Italy."

The most exciting time to visit is during the Feast of San Gennaro around September 19 *(see p52)*. For nine days Mulberry Street is renamed Via San Gennaro. On the saint's day, his shrine and relics are paraded through the streets. Throughout the feast there is music, dancing, and sideshows, and stalls selling Italian food and drink, as well as other ethnic cuisines.

Little Italy's restaurants offer simple, rustic food served in friendly surroundings at reasonable prices.

NoLIta, North of Little Italy, is filled with boutiques. Actresses, models, and the fashionable flock here for the coolest small labels.

**A street scene in Little Italy**

## Chinatown **❹**

Streets around Mott St.
**Map** 4 F5. Ⓜ *Canal St.*
**Eastern States Buddhist Temple**
64b Mott St. ⓞ *9am–6pm daily.*
**www**.explore chinatown.com

The Chinatown of the early 20th century was primarily a male community, made up of immigrants who had first gone to California. Wages were sent home to their families in China, who were prevented from joining them by US immigration laws. The men relaxed by gambling at mahjong. The community remained isolated from the rest of the city, financed and controlled by its own secret organizations, the Tongs. Some of the Tongs were simply family associations who provided loans. Others, such as the On Leong and the Hip Sing, who were at war with one another, were criminal fraternities. Tiny, crooked Doyers Street was

**Stonework figures adorning the Police Headquarters Building**

A Chinese grocer tending his shop on Canal Street

called "Bloody Angle"; enemies were lured there and set upon by gang members waiting around the bend.

A truce between the Tongs in 1933 brought peace to Chinatown. By 1940 it was home to many middle-class families. Immigrants and businesses from Hong Kong also brought postwar prosperity to the community. Today over 80,000 Chinese-Americans live here.

Many visit the neighborhood to sample the cuisine, but there is more to do here than eat. There are galleries, antiques and curio shops, and Oriental festivals *(see p53)*. To glimpse another side of Chinatown, step into the incense-scented Eastern States Buddhist Temple at 64b Mott Street, where offerings are piled up and over 100 golden Buddhas gleam in the candlelight.

## Columbus Park ❺

**Map** 4 F5. Ⓜ *Canal St.*

The tranquillity of Columbus Park today could not be further removed from the scene near this site in the early 1800s. The area, known as Mulberry Bend, was a red-light district, part of the infamous Five Points slum. Gangs with names like the Dead Rabbits and the Plug Uglies roamed the streets. A murder a day was common-place; even the police were afraid to pass through. Partly as a result of the writings of reformer Jacob Riis *(see p49)*, the slum was taken down in 1892. The park is now the only open space in Chinatown.

## Eldridge Street Synagogue ❻

12 Eldridge St. **Map** 5 A5. **Tel** *(212) 219-0888.* Ⓜ *East Broadway.* ◯ *11am–4pm Tue–Thu, Sun.* ◯ *Fri sundown, Sat 10am onward.* 🖼 🚫 📷 *11am, noon, 1pm, 2pm, 3pm.* 📷 **www.***eldridgestreet.org*

When this house of worship was built by the Orthodox Ashkenazi from Eastern Europe in 1887, it was the most flamboyant temple in the neighborhood. But many immigrant Jews saw the Lower East Side as just

the beginning of a new life, and later moved out of this massive synagogue.

In the 1930s, the huge sanctuary, rich with stained glass, brass chandeliers, marbleized wood paneling, and fine carving, was closed. Three decades later a group of citizens raised funds for preservation, and restoration is underway. The synagogue has become a vibrant cultural center, with concerts and other special programs.

Even after years of neglect, the facade, with touches of Romanesque, Gothic and Moorish designs, is impressive. Inside, the Italian hand-carved ark and sculpted wooden balcony show why this build-ing was the pride of the area.

## Lower East Side Tenement Museum ❼

108 Orchard St. **Map** 5 A4. **Tel** *(212) 431-0233.* Ⓜ *Delancey, Grand St.* ◯ *for* 🔲 *only (book ahead), 1:20–4:45pm Tue–Fri; 11am–5pm Sat, Sun.* ● *Jan 1, Thanksgiving, Dec 25.* 🖼 🚫 📽 ***Lectures, films, videos.*** 📷 *(daily).* **www.***tenement.org*

**Street vendor's pushcart (1890s), Lower East Side Tenement Museum**

The interior of this building was restored to re-create apartments as they appeared in the late 1870s, in 1916, 1918, and 1935. There were no regulations on tenement living conditions until 1879. Many rooms had no windows, and indoor plumbing was rare. The rooms give a sense of the cramped and deplorable conditions in which so many lived. The museum program includes the newest exhibit, "The Sweatshop Apartment", and offers excellent walking tours of the area.

Window, Eldridge Street Synagogue

## Orchard Street ❽

**Map** *5 A3.* Ⓜ *Delancey, Grand St.*
See ***Shopping** p320.*
www.lowereastsideny.com

Jewish immigrants founded the
New York garment industry
on this street, named for the
orchards that once stood here
on James De Lancey's Colonial
estate. For years the street was
filled with pushcarts loaded
with goods for sale. The
pushcarts are long gone, and
not all the shopkeepers are
Jewish, but the flavor remains.
On Sunday there is an outdoor
market, and shoppers fill the
street from Houston to Canal,
looking for clothing bargains.
  Orchard Street is also at the
heart of the Lower East Side's
gentrification. Trendy boutiques
and vintage stores nestle
alongside bars, restaurants,
and the boutique Blue Moon
hotel, formerly a tenement.

**Mural featuring a sign of the
zodiac in Bialystoker Synagogue.**

## Bialystoker
Synagogue ❾

*7–11 Willett St.* **Map** *5 C4.*
***Tel** (212) 475-0165.* Ⓜ *Essex St.*
🔲 *frequent services.*
🔳 *prearranged only.* 📷
www.bialystoker.org

This 1826 Federal-style
building was originally the
Willett Street Methodist
Church. It was bought in
1905 by Jewish immigrants
from the Bialystok province
of Poland, who converted it
into a synagogue. For this

**Vegetable stall at an outdoor market in Canal Street**

reason, it faces west in
the tradition of Christian
churches instead of east.
  The synagogue has a
beautiful interior, with lovely
stained-glass windows, a
three-story carved wooden
ark, and murals representing
the signs of the zodiac and
views of the Holy Land.

## Delancey Street ❿

**Map** *5 C4.* Ⓜ *Essex St.*
See ***Shopping** p320.*
***Bowery Ballroom** 6 Delancey St.*
***Tel** (212) 533-2111. See website
for shows schedule.* 📷 *no flash.*
♿ www.boweryballroom.com

Once a majestic boulevard,
Delancey Street these days
is little more than an
obligatory entrance to the
Williamsburg Bridge. The
street was named for James
De Lancey, whose farm was
situated here in Colonial

days. During the American
Revolution *(see pp22–3),*
De Lancey remained loyal
to King George III. After
the war, he fled to England,
and his land was seized.
  At 6 Delancey sits the
**Bowery Ballroom**, a three-
story theater completed
only weeks before the
stock market crash of
1929 *(see p31).* Throughout
the Great Depression and
World War II, the building
was deserted. Later, it
served as a retail space,
housing a haberdashery,
a jeweler's boutique, and
Treemark Shoes, until
its resurrection as a live-
music venue in the late
1990s. Much of the theater's
original structure is still in
place, including such
decorative details as the
brass rails, the copper-
vaulted plaster ceiling
of the mezzanine bar,
and the brass and iron
exterior metalwork.

**Live music at the Bowery Ballroom, in a stylish 1920s theater**

# East Houston Street ⓫

East Houston St. **Map** *4 F3, 5A3.*
Ⓜ *Second Avenue.*

The dividing line between the Lower East Side and the East Village, East Houston between Forsyth and Ludlow streets clearly demonstrates the

**Trays of bagels at a traditional Jewish bakery in East Houston Street**

changing mix of old and new in the area. Between Forsyth and Eldridge is a new small hotel next door to the Yonah Schimmel Knish Bakery, a fixture for more than 90 years, still with its original showcases. Further down the block is the Sunshine Theater, constructed as a Dutch Church in the 1840s and later used as a boxing arena and a Yiddish vaudeville theater. Today it shows art films.

While much of the Jewish flavor of the Lower East Side has disappeared, there are two survivors further along East Houston. Russ and Daughters is a culinary landmark, a third-generation family business that began on a pushcart, circa 1900. At this location since 1914, the store has seen its fortunes change with the neighborhood. It is famed for traditional smoked fish and herring, and has an impressive stock of caviar. At the corner of Ludlow Street is perhaps the best-known survivor, the bustling Katz's Delicatessen, well past its

100th birthday and still packing them in for pastrami and corned beef sandwiches and spicy hot dogs.

# Puck Building ⓬

295–309 Lafayette St. **Map** *4 F3.*
Ⓜ *Lafayette.* ◯ *to the public during business hours.* **Tel** *(212) 274-8900.*

This block-square architectural curiosity was built in 1885 by Albert and Herman Wagner. It is an adaptation of the German *Rundbogenstil,* a mid-19th-century style characterized by horizontal bands of arched windows and the skillful use of molded red brick.

From 1887 to 1916 the building housed the satirical magazine *Puck,* and at the turn of the century it was the largest building in the world devoted to lithography and publishing.

Today it is the site of some of New York's most stylish parties and artiest fashion-photography shoots. The only connection remaining to the mythical Puck is the gold-leaf statue on the corner of Mulberry and Houston, and the smaller version over the entrance on Lafayette Street.

**Statue of Puck on the northeast corner of the Puck Building**

**Facade of Old St. Patrick's Cathedral, now a parish church**

# Old St. Patrick's Cathedral ⓭

263 Mulberry St. **Map** *4 F3.* **Tel** *(212) 226-8075.* Ⓜ *Prince St.* ◯ *8am–12:30pm & 3:30–6pm Thu–Tue.* ✝ *9am, noon Mon–Fri; 5:30pm Sat; 9:15am, 12:45pm Sun; Spanish: 11:30am Sun.* **www**.oldsaintpatricks.com

The first St. Patrick's was begun in 1809, and it is one of the oldest churches in the city. When fire destroyed the original in the 1860s, it was rebuilt much as it is today. When the archdiocese transferred the see to the new St. Patrick's Cathedral uptown *(see pp178–9),* Old St. Patrick's became the local parish church, and it has flourished despite a constantly changing ethnic congregation.

Below the church are vaults containing the remains of, among others, one of New York's most famous families of restaurateurs, the Delmonicos. Pierre Toussaint was also buried here, but in 1990 his remains were moved from the old graveyard beside the church to a more prestigious burial place in a crypt in the new St. Patrick's Cathedral. Born as a slave in Haiti in 1766, Toussaint was brought to New York, where he lived as a free man and became a prosperous wig-maker. He later devoted himself to caring for the city's poor, also tending cholera victims and using his money to build an orphanage. The Vatican is now considering the philanthropic Toussaint for sainthood.

# Engine Company No. 31 ⓮

87 Lafayette St. **Map** *4 F5.*
**Tel** *(212) 966-4510.* M *Canal St.*
● *to the public.*

In the 19th century, fire stations were considered important enough to merit a building of architectural importance and the Le Brun firm was the acknowledged master of the art. This 1895 station is one of their best. The building resembles a Loire château, with its steep roof, dormers and towers, seeming almost fairy tale-like in this location.

The present-day tenant is the Downtown Community Television Center, which offers courses and workshops to members. However, the building is no longer open to the public.

Facade of Engine Company No. 31, in the style of a French château

# The Pickle Guys ⓯

49 Essex St. **Map** *5 B4.* **Tel** *(212) 656-9739.* M *Grand St.*
○ *9am–4pm Fri, 9am–6pm Sun–Thu.* **www**.nycpickleguys.com

The scent of pickles permeates this little section of Essex Street, just as it did in the early 1900s when Jewish pickle shops filled the area. True to the old Eastern European recipe, The Pickle Guys store their pickles in barrels filled with brine, garlic and spices; this mixture preserves the pickles for months on end. Pickle varieties include full sour, three-quarters sour, half sour, new, and hot. No

chemicals or preservatives are added and the shop operates to strict Kosher rules.

The store also carries pickled tomatoes, pickled celery, olives, mushrooms, hot peppers, sun-dried tomatoes, sweet kraut, sauerkraut, and herring. It is run like a family business, with a friendly, chatty atmosphere, which perpetuates the neighborhood's traditions.

# New Museum of Contemporary Art ⓰

235 Bowery St. **Map** *4 E3.* **Tel** *(212) 219-1222.* M *Spring St, Bowery.* ○ *noon–6pm Tue–Sat, noon–8pm Thu.* 🏛 🚫 ♿ 🛍 **Lectures, readings.** 🏛 **www**.newmuseum.org

Marcia Tucker left her post as the Whitney Museum's Curator of Painting and Sculpture in 1977 to found this museum. Her aim was to exhibit the kind of work she felt was missing from more traditional museums. She created one of New York's most cutting-edge exhibition spaces, which includes an innovative Media Lounge for digital art, video installations, and sound works.

There is no permanent collection here but instead three to four major shows are produced each year. Jeff Koons and the late John Cage were among

those whose work featured in early shows.

The museum has recently relocated to its present address. The striking new building, designed by Tokyo-based architects Sejima & Nishizawa, is the first art museum building to be constructed in downtown Manhattan in over a century. It has 60,000 sq ft (5,574 sq m) of exhibition space, a theater, a café, and a rooftop terrace offering stunning views of the city.

Sweets on the densely packed shelves at Economy Candy

# Economy Candy ⓱

108 Rivington S. **Map** *5 B3.* **Tel** *1-800 352-4544.* M *Second Ave–Houston St.* ○ *10am–5pm Sat, 9–6pm Sun–Fri.* **www**.economycandy.com

A Lower East Side landmark since 1937, this family-owned candy store stocks hundreds of varieties of candy, nuts, and dried fruit. Lined with floor-to-ceiling shelves packed with old-fashioned dispensers, the store is one of

Entrance to The Pickle Guys' store, with traditional pickling barrels

the few businesses on Lower East Side that has remained almost unchanged in name and specialty throughout the neighborhood's fluctuating fortunes over 50 years.

This is due in no small part to Jerry Cohen's enterprise in transforming his father's "Nosher's Paradise" from a penny candy store to a national company. The shop carries sweets and treats from all over the world, as well as numerous food items dipped in chocolate and 21 colors of candy-covered chocolate buttons.

**Interior of the Angel Orensanz Center, once a large synagogue**

## Angel Orensanz Center ⓲

172 Norfolk St. **Map** 5 B3. **Tel** (212) 529-7194. Ⓜ Essex St, Delancey St. ⓘ by appt. ♿ www.orensanz.org

Built in 1849, this cherry-red Neo-Gothic structure was once the oldest synagogue in New York. With ceilings 54 ft (15 m) high and seating for 1500, it was also the largest in the Unites States at the time. It was designed by the Berlin architect Alexander Saelzer in the tradition of the German Reform movement, and closely resembles Cologne Cathedral and the Friederichwerdeschekirche in the Mitte in Berlin.

After World War II and the decline of Lower East Side's Yiddish population, the synagogue was one of many to close. In 1986, the

building was acquired by the Spanish sculptor Angel Orensanz, who turned it into an art studio. It now serves as a spiritual and cultural center with a program of artistic, musical, and literary events.

## FusionArts Museum ⓳

57 Stanton St. **Map** 5 A3. **Tel** (212) 995-5290. Ⓜ Second Ave-Houston St. ⓘ noon–6pm Sun–Wed, noon–8pm Thu, noon–3pm Fri. ⓘ ♿ ⓘ www.artnet.com

With psychedelic metal sculptures that give a foretaste of the pieces displayed inside, the entrance to this museum is hard to miss. It is dedicated to showing "fusion art", defined as art in which various artistic disciplines, such as painting, sculpture, photography, and video, meld to form a distinct new genre in themselves. The museum's out-of-the-way location gives it access to an underground art scene that uptown contemporary art museums often neglect, and it also offers lesser-known artists the opportunity to exhibit their work in a reputable gallery.

Many New York City artists who have been creating fusion art on the Lower East Side for more than two decades have already shown their work in group exhibitions here.

**Metal sculptures at the entrance of the FusionArts Museum**

## Essex Street Market ⓴

120 Essex St. **Map** 5 B3. **Tel** (212) 312-3603/388-0449. Ⓜ Essex St, Delancey St. ⓘ 8am–6pm Mon–Sat. ⓘ ⓘ ⓘ www.essexstreetmarket.com

The market was created in 1938 by Mayor Fiorello H. La Guardia to bring pushcart vendors together and out of the way of traffic, especially police cars and fire trucks that used the narrow streets.

Two dozen meat, cheese, produce, and spice stalls now fill the recently renovated market. One of the oldest vendors is Jeffrey's butcher store, which has been at the market since 1939. Also here are the Essex Restaurant, which servies Latin/Jewish fare, and Cuchifritos, an art gallery showing the work of the neighborhood's artists.

**Cut of meat on a butcher's display at the indoor Essex Street Market**

# SOHO AND TRIBECA

Art and architecture are the twin lures that have transformed these formerly industrial districts. SoHo (south of Houston) was threatened with demolition in the 1960s until preservationists drew attention to the rare historic cast-iron architecture. The district was saved, and artists began to move into the loft

**Storefront of a SoHo bakery**

spaces. Galleries, cafés, shops and then boutiques followed. Brunch and gallery hopping in SoHo is now a favorite weekend outing. As rents rose, many artists were priced out of SoHo and moved to TriBeCa (triangle below Canal). Now, trendy TriBeCa has galleries, many new restaurants, and the Tribeca Film Festival in May.

## SIGHTS AT A GLANCE

**Historic Streets and Buildings**
Greene Street ❸
Harrison Street ❽
Haughwout Building ❶
St. Nicholas Hotel ❷
Singer Building ❹
White Street ❾

**Museums and Galleries**
Children's Museum of the Arts ❺
New York City Fire Museum ❼
New York Earth Room ❻

**GETTING THERE**
Take the F, V, B, or D subway to Broadway-Lafayette; the 6 to Bleecker St or Spring St; or the N or R to Prince St. For TriBeCa, take the 1 to Franklin St, or the 1, 2, 3, A, or C to Chambers St. Bus routes are the M1 or M6, the M21 Houston St crosstown for SoHo, and the M6 or M20 for TriBeCa.

## SEE ALSO

- **Street Finder,** map 4
- **SoHo Walk** pp260–61
- **Restaurants** pp297–9
- **Where to Stay** p281

## KEY

▨ Street-by-Street map

Ⓜ Subway station

◁ **Cast-iron facades on Greene Street**

# Street by Street: SoHo Cast-Iron Historic District

The largest concentration of cast-iron architecture in the world *(see p42)* survives in the area between West Houston and Canal streets. The heart of the district is Greene Street, where 50 buildings erected between 1869 and 1895 are found on five cobblestoned blocks. Most of their intricately designed cast-iron facades are in the Neo-Classical Revival style, with Corinthian columns and pediments. Mass-produced in a foundry, they were relatively inexpensive to produce and easy to erect and maintain. Now they rare works of industrial art, well suited to the present character of this district.

**West Broadway**, as it passes through SoHo, combines striking architecture with a string of art galleries, art shops, designer boutiques, and small restaurants.

**72–76 Greene Street**, the "King of Greene Street," is a splendid Corinthian-columned building. It was the creation of Isaac F. Duckworth, one of the masters of cast-iron design.

**The Broken Kilometer**, at 393 West Broadway, is an installation by Walter De Maria *(see p107)*. Its 500 brass rods are arranged to play tricks with perspective. Laid end to end, the rods would measure 1 km.

**Performing Garage** is a tiny experimental theater that pioneers the work of avant-garde artists.

**★ Greene Street**
*Of all Greene Street's fine cast-iron architecture, one of the best is 28–30, the "Queen," which was built by Duckworth in 1872, and has a tall mansard roof* ❸

**Canal Street-Broadway subway** (2 blocks)

**10–14 Greene Street** dates from 1869. Note the glass circles in the risers of the iron stoop, which allowed daylight to reach the basement.

**15–17 Greene Street** is a late addition from 1895, in a simple Corinthian style.

**★ Singer Building**
*This terra-cotta beauty was built in 1904 for the famous sewing machine company* ❹

**Richard Haas**, the prolific muralist, has transformed a blank wall into a convincing cast-iron frontage.

**LOCATOR MAP**
*See Manhattan Map pp14–15*

**KEY**

– – – Suggested route

**Prince Street subway station (lines N, R)**

**Dean & DeLuca** is one of the best gourmet food stores in New York. Its range includes a global choice of coffee beans *(see p336).*

**101 Spring Street**, with its simple, geometric facade and large windows, is a fine example of the style that led to the skyscraper.

**Spring Street subway station**

**St. Nicholas Hotel**
*During the Civil War, this former luxury hotel was used as a headquarters for the Union Army* ❷

0 meters 100

0 yards 100

**STAR SIGHTS**

★ Greene Street

★ Singer Building

**Haughwout Building**
*In 1857 this was an elegant store, featuring the first Otis safety elevator* ❶

# Haughwout Building ❶

488–492 Broadway. **Map** 4 E4.
Ⓜ *Canal St, Spring St.*

**Haughwout Building facade**

This cast-iron building was erected in 1857 for the E.V. Haughwout china and glassware company, which once supplied the White House. Beneath the grime, the design is superb: rows of windows are framed by arches set on columns flanked by taller columns. Mass-produced sections repeat the pattern over and over. The building was the first to use a steam-driven Otis safety elevator, an innovation that made the skyscraper a possibility.

# St. Nicholas Hotel ❷

521–523 Broadway. **Map** 4 E4.
Ⓜ *Prince St, Spring St.*

English parliamentarian W. E. Baxter, visiting New York in 1854, reported of the recently opened St. Nicholas Hotel: "Every carpet is of velvet pile; chair covers and curtains are made of silk or satin damask … and the embroidery on the mosquito nettings itself

**St. Nicholas Hotel in its heyday in the mid-19th century**

might be exhibited to royalty." It is small wonder, then, that it cost over $1 million to build – and with profits of over $50,000 for that year it must have seemed money well spent. Its glory was short-lived, however. In the Civil War it served as a Union Army headquarters. Afterward, the better hotels followed the entertainment district uptown, and by the mid-1870s the St. Nicholas had closed. There is little left on the ground floor to attest to its former opulence, but look up to the remains of its once-stunning marble facade.

# Greene Street ❸

**Map** 4 E4. Ⓜ *Canal St.*

**Haas mural on Greene Street**

This is the heart of SoHo's Cast-Iron District. Along five cobblestoned blocks are 50 cast-iron buildings dating from 1869 to 1895. The block between Broome and Spring streets has 13 full cast-iron facades and from 8–34 is the longest row of cast-iron buildings anywhere. Those at 72–76 are known as the "King of Greene Street," but 28–30, the "Queen," is considered to be the finest. The architecture is best appreciated as a streetscape, with row upon row of columned facades. Walk into any of the galleries housed within to see the spacious interior lofts.

At the corner of Greene and Prince streets, the illusionistic muralist Richard Haas has created an eye-catching work, disguising a plain brick side wall as a cast-iron frontage. Look for the detail of the little gray cat, which sits primly in an "open window."

# Singer Building ❹

561–563 Broadway. **Map** 4 E3.
Ⓜ *Prince St.*

The "little" Singer Building built by Ernest Flagg in 1904 is the second and smaller Flagg structure by this name, and many critics think it superior to the 41-story tower on lower Broadway that was torn down in 1967. The charmingly ornate building is adorned with wrought-iron balconies and graceful arches painted in striking dark green. The 12-story facade of terracotta, glass and steel was advanced for its day, a forerunner of the metal and glass walls to come in the 1940s and 1950s. The building was an office and warehouse for the Singer sewing machine company, and the original Singer name can be seen cast in iron above the entrance to the store on Prince Street.

**Early electric-powered Singer sewing machine**

# Children's Museum of the Arts ❺

182 Lafayette St. **Map** 4 F3. *Tel (212) 941-9198.* Ⓜ *Prince St.* M1, M6. ◯ *noon–5pm Wed, Fri, Sat, Sun, noon–6pm Thu.* **Movie Night** *1st Wed of the month 4:30–6pm.* 📷 ♿ **www.cmany.org**

Founded in 1988, this innovative museum aims to make the most of children's artistic potential by providing plenty of hands-on activities, sing-alongs, workshops, and performances. Children aged 1-12 can busy themselves with paint, glue, paper and other messy materials to create their own drawings and sculptures. For inspiration, displays of work

**Brightly-colored exhibition space at the Children's Museum of the Arts**

by local artists are exhibited alongside examples of children's art from around the world. Kids can also play around in the dressing-up room and the ball pond, and every month there is a movie night complete with popcorn and juice.

# New York Earth Room ❻

141 Wooster St. **Map** 4 E3. *Tel (212) 989-5566.* Ⓜ *Prince St.* ◯ *noon–3pm & 3:30–6pm Wed–Sun.* ♿ **www.earthroom.org**

Of the three Earth Rooms created by conceptual artist Walter De Maria, this is the only one still in existence. Commissioned by the Dia Art Foundation in 1977, the interior earth sculpture consists of 280,000 lbs (127,000 kg) of dirt piled 22 in (56 cm) deep in a 3,600 sq ft (335 sq m) room. *The Broken Kilometer,* another sculpture by De Maria, can be seen at 393 West Broadway *(see p104).* It is composed of 500 solid brass rods arranged in five parallel rows.

**1901 La France horse-drawn steam pumper in the City Fire Museum**

# New York City Fire Museum ❼

278 Spring St. **Map** 4 D4. *Tel (212) 691-1303.* Ⓜ *Spring St.* ◯ *10am–5pm Tue–Sat, 10am–4pm Sun.* ◯ *public hols.* 📷 📷 ♿ 🏪 **www.nycfiremuseum.org**

This splendid museum is housed in a Beaux Arts–style 1904 firehouse. New York City's unsurpassed collection of fire-fighting equipment and memorabilia from the 18th century to 1917 includes scale models, bells, and hydrants. Upstairs, fire engines are neatly lined up for an 1890 parade. An interactive fire simulation, available for groups, gives an insight into fire-fighting.

# Harrison Street ❽

**Map** 4 D5. Ⓜ *Chambers St.*

Surrounded by modern high-rise blocks, this rare row of eight beautifully restored Federal town houses, with their pitched roofs and distinctive dormer windows, almost seems like a stage set. The houses were constructed in the late 1700s and early 1800s. Two of the buildings were designed by John McComb, Jr., New York's first major native-born architect, and were moved from Washington Street, their original site, for preservation purposes. The houses had previously been used as warehouses and were about to be razed to the ground, when, in 1969, the Landmarks Preservation Commission intervened and helped secure the necessary funding to enable them to be completely restored. They are now privately owned.

On the other side of the high-rise complex is Washington Market Park. This area was formerly the site of New York City's wholesale produce center. The market moved from this historic district and relocated to the Bronx at the beginning of the 1970s.

# White Street ❾

**Map** 4 E5. Ⓜ *Franklin St.*

While not as fine and intricate as some of the SoHo blocks, this sampling of TriBeCa cast-iron architecture shows a considerably wide range of styles. The house at No. 2 has carefully balanced Federal features and a rare gambrel roof, in contrast with the mansard roof of No. 17. Numbers 8 to 10 White, designed by Silesian-born Henry Fernbach, in 1869, have impressive Tuscan columns and arches, with Neo-Renaissance shorter upper stories to give an illusion of height. In contrast, 38 White is the home of neon artist Rudi Stern's gallery, Let There Be Neon.

**Rudi Stern's Let There Be Neon gallery in White Street**

# GREENWICH VILLAGE

New Yorkers call it "the Village," and it began as a country village, an escape for city dwellers during the yellow fever epidemic of 1822. The crazy-quilt pattern of streets, reflecting early farm boundaries or streams, makes it a natural enclave that has been a bohemian haven and home to many celebrated artists and writers.

Jazz club flag on West 3rd Street

A popular gay district is here, but the area has become mainstream and expensive. Near Washington Square, it is dominated by New York University students. Once cheaper, the East Village attracts a trendy crowd from all over the city. The Meatpacking District, which still functions as such, has become overwhelmed with smart boutiques and restaurants.

## SIGHTS AT A GLANCE

**Historic Streets and Buildings**
75½ Bedford Street **2**
Grove Court **4**
Isaacs-Hendricks House **3**
Jefferson Market Courthouse **7**
Meatpacking District **5**
New York University **14**

Patchin Place **8**
St. Luke's Place **1**
Salmagundi Club **10**
Washington Mews **13**

**Museums and Galleries**
Forbes Magazine Building **9**

**Churches**
Church of the Ascension **12**
First Presbyterian Church **11**
Judson Memorial Church **15**

**Parks and Squares**
Sheridan Square **6**
Washington Square **16**

### GETTING THERE
By subway, take lines A, C, E, F, or V to West 4th St-Washington Sq, the 1 to Christopher St-Sheridan Sq or Houston St, or the N or R to 8th St. By bus take the M1, M5, M6, or the M8 crosstown.

### SEE ALSO

• *Street Finder*, maps 3–4
• *Village Walk* pp260–61
• *Where to Stay* p281
• *Restaurants* pp299–301

### KEY

Street-by-Street map

**M** Subway station

◁ **People enjoying relaxed café culture in leafy Greenwich Village**

# Street by Street: Greenwich Village

A stroll through historic Greenwich Village is a feast of unexpected small pleasures – charming row houses, hidden alleys, and leafy courtyards. The often quirky architecture suits the bohemian air of the Village. Many famous people, particularly artists and writers, such as playwright Eugene O'Neill and actor Dustin Hoffman, have made their homes in the houses and apartments that line these old-fashioned narrow streets. By night, the Village really comes alive. Late-night coffeehouses and cafés, experimental theaters and music clubs, including some of the best jazz venues, beckon you at every turn.

**The Lucille Lortel Theater** is at No. 121 Christopher Street; it opened in 1955 with *The Threepenny Opera*.

**Christopher Street**, a part of New York's gay community, is lined with all kinds of shops, bookstores, and bars.

**Twin Peaks** at No. 102 Bedford Street began life in 1830 as an ordinary house. It was rebuilt in 1926 by architect Clifford Daily to house artists, writers, and actors. Daily believed that the quirky house would help their creativity flourish.

**Grove Court**
*Six houses dating from 1853–1854 are set at the back of a quiet leafy courtyard* ❹

**Chumley's** at No. 86 Bedford Street *(see p317)*, once a speakeasy, now a restaurant, still seems secret. There is no sign outside, just a small menu.

★ **St. Luke's Place**
*This beautiful row of Italianate houses was built in the 1850s* ❶

To Houston Street subway (2 blocks)

**No. 75½ Bedford Street**
*Built in 1873 in an alley, this is the city's narrowest house* ❷

**The Cherry Lane Theatre** was founded in 1924. Originally a brewery, it was one of the first of the Off-Broadway theaters.

### Patchin Place

*Built in 1848 to house waiters from the Brevoort Hotel, it was later home to poet e e cummings and other famous writers of the 1920s and 1930s* ⑦

To W 14th St subway (3 blocks)

Christopher St subway

GREENWICH AVENUE

PERRY ST

W 10TH STREET

WAVERLEY

STREET PLACE

WASHINGTON PLACE

SIXTH AVENUE

TENTH AVENUE

**LOCATOR MAP**
*See Manhattan Map pp14–15*

CHELSEA & THE GARMENT DISTRICT

Hudson River

GRAMERCY & THE FLATIRON DISTRICT

GREENWICH VILLAGE

SOHO & TRIBECA

EAST VILLAGE

### STAR SIGHTS

★ Jefferson Market Courthouse

★ St. Luke's Place

### ★ Jefferson Market Courthouse

*The courthouse was built in 1877, and has been voted the fifth most beautiful building in the US. It was converted into a public library in 1967* ⑥

**KEY**

— — — Suggested route

0 meters 100
0 yards 100

To West 4th Street subway (2 blocks)

**The Northern Dispensary** began offering free medical care to the poor in 1827. Edgar Allan Poe was treated here for a cold in 1837. It is now a hostel for the disabled.

GAY St
ONE WAY
ANYTIME
*Gemini* CLEANERS

**Gay Street** attracted many aspiring artists, writers, and musicians during the 1920s. It was the setting for Ruth McKenney's novel, *My Sister Eileen*, and the film *Carlito's Way*.

Row houses on St. Luke's Place, a street with literary associations

## St. Luke's Place **❶**

**Map** 3 C3. **M** *Houston St.*

Fifteen attractive row houses, dating from the 1850s, line the north side of this street. The park opposite is named for a previous resident of St. Luke's Place, Mayor Jimmy Walker, the popular dandy who ran the city from 1926 until he was forced to resign after a financial scandal in 1932.

In front of the house at No. 6 are the tall lamps that always identify a mayor's home in New York. More recently, the most recognizable house on the block has been No. 10, the home of the Huxtable family in *The Cosby Show* (although the series sets it in Brooklyn). This is also the block where *Wait Until Dark* was filmed, starring Audrey Hepburn as a blind woman living at No. 4. Theodore Dreiser was one of several writers, including the poet Marianne Moore, who lived here. Dreiser wrote *An American Tragedy* while living at No. 16. One block north, the corner of Hudson and Morton Streets marked the edge of the Hudson River three centuries ago.

Mayor's lamp at No. 6

## 75½ Bedford Street **❷**

**Map** 3 C2. **M** Houston St. ◉ *to the public.* **www**.cherrylanetheatre.com

New York's narrowest home, just 9½ ft (2.9 m) wide, was built in 1893 in a former passageway. The poet Edna St. Vincent Millay lived here briefly, followed by the actor John Barrymore, and later Cary Grant. The three-story building, now renovated, is marked by a plaque.

Just around the corner, at 38 Commerce Street, Miss Millay founded the Cherry Lane Theater in 1924 as a site for avant-garde drama. It still premieres new works. Its biggest hit was the 1960s musical *Godspell*.

## Grove Court **❸**

**Map** 3 C2. **M** *Christopher St/ Sheridan Sq.*

An enterprising grocer named Samuel Cocks built the six town houses here, in an area formed by a bend in the street. (The bends in this part of the Village originally marked divisions between colonial properties.) Cocks reckoned that having residents in the empty passage between 10 and 12 Grove Street would help his business at No. 18.

But residential courts, now highly prized, were not considered respectable in 1854, and the lowbrow residents attracted to the area earned it the nickname "Mixed Ale Alley." O. Henry later chose this block as the setting for his 1902 work *The Last Leaf*.

Isaacs-Hendricks House

## Isaacs-Hendricks House **❹**

77 Bedford St. **Map** 3 C2. **M** *Houston St.* ◉ *to the public.*

This is the oldest surviving home in the Village, built in 1799. The old clapboard walls are visible on the sides and rear; the brickwork and third floor came later. The first owner, John Isaacs, bought the land for $295 in 1794. Next came Harmon Hendricks, a copper dealer and associate of revolutionary Paul Revere. Robert Fulton, who used copper for the boilers in his steamboat, was one of Hendricks's customers.

## Meatpacking District **❺**

**Map** 3 B1 **M** *14th St (on lines A, C, E); 8th Av L; Christopher St/ Sheridan Sq.*

Once the domain of butchers in blood-stained aprons hacking at sides of beef, these days (and particularly nights) the Meatpacking District is very different. Squeezed into an area south of 14th Street and west of 9th Avenue, the neighborhood is now dotted with trendy clubs, lounges and boutique hotels that swell

The mid-19th-century town houses at Grove Court

with New Yorkers out for a good time. The neighborhood's hipness quotient rose when Soho House, the New York branch of the London private members' club, moved in, followed by the smart Hotel Gansevoort, with rooftop swimming pool. Hip clothiers, including Stella McCartney and Alexander McQueen, now have outlets here, and upscale restaurants have opened.

The great allure of the Meatpacking District is, of course, that chic urbanites like some edginess to their nighttime recreation, and this is where the district delivers. The face of the neighborhood may be forever changed, but club-hoppers might still catch the occasional whiff of the meat-processing business that gave the area its name.

## Sheridan Square ❻

**Map** 3 C2. M *Christopher St-Sheridan Sq.*

This square, where seven streets converge, is the heart of the Village. It was named for the Civil War General Philip Sheridan who became commander in chief of the US Army in 1883. His statue stands in nearby Christopher Park.

The Draft Riots of 1863 took place in the square. Over a century later, another famous disturbance rocked the square. The Stonewall Inn on Christopher Street was a gay bar that had stayed in business (it was then illegal for gays to gather in bars) by paying off the police. However, on June 28, 1969, the patrons rebelled, and in the pitched battle that ensued police officers were barricaded inside the bar for hours while crowds taunted them from outside. It was a landmark moral victory for the budding Gay Rights movement. The inn that stands today is not the original. The Village remains a focus for the city's gay community.

"Old Jeff", the pointed tower of Jefferson Market Courthouse

## Jefferson Market Courthouse ❼

425 Ave of the Americas. **Map** 4 D1. *Tel (212) 243-4334.* M *W 4th St-Washington Sq.* ◯ *noon–8pm Mon & Wed, 10am–6pm Tue, noon–6pm Thu, 1–6pm Fri, 10am–5pm Sat.* ● *public hols.* ♿ **www**.nypl.org

This treasured Village landmark was saved from the wrecking ball and converted into a branch of the New York Public Library through a spirited preservation campaign that began at a Christmas party in the late 1950s.

The site became a market in 1833, named after former president Thomas Jefferson. Its fire lookout tower had a giant bell that was rung to alert the neighborhood's volunteer fire fighters. In 1865, the founding of the municipal fire department made the bell obsolete, and the Third Judicial District, or Jefferson Market, Courthouse was built. With its Venetian Gothic-style spires and turrets, it was named one of the 10 most beautiful buildings in the country when it opened in 1877. The old fire bell was installed in the tower. Here, in 1906, Harry Thaw was tried for Stanford White's murder *(see p126).*

**Statue of General Sheridan in Christopher Park**

By 1945, the market had moved, court sessions had been discontinued, the four-sided clock had stopped and the building was threatened with demolition. In the 1950s, preservationists campaigned first to restore the clock and then the whole building. Its renovation was undertaken by architect Giorgio Cavaglieri, who preserved many of the original details, including the stained glass and a spiral staircase that now leads to the library's dungeonlike reference room.

Facade and an ailanthus tree at Patchin Place

## Patchin Place ❽

W 10th St. **Map** 4 D1. M *W 4th St-Washington Sq.*

One of many delightful and unexpected pockets in the Village is this tiny block of small residences. It is lined with ailanthus trees that were planted in order to "absorb the bad air." The houses were built in the mid-19th century for Basque waiters working at the Brevoort Hotel on Fifth Avenue.

Later the houses became fashionable addresses, with many writers living here. The poet e e cummings lived at No. 4 from 1923 until his death in 1962. The English poet laureate John Masefield also lived on the block, as did the playwright Eugene O'Neill and John Reed, whose eyewitness account of the Russian Revolution, *Ten Days That Shook The World* was made into a film, *Reds,* directed by Warren Beatty.

Toy battleship from the
Forbes Magazine Collection

## Forbes Magazine Building ❽

60 5th Ave. **Map** 4 E1. **Tel** (212) 206-
5548. Ⓜ 14th St-Union Sq. **Galleries**
Ⓞ 10am–4pm Tue–Wed, Fri–Sat (times
may vary). No strollers. ⛔ Thu groups
only. ♿ Ⓞ public hols.

Some architectural critics have
called this 1925 limestone
cube by Carrère & Hastings
pompous. It was originally
the headquarters of the
Macmillan Publishing
Company. When Macmillan
moved uptown, the late
Malcolm Forbes moved in
with his financial magazine,
*Forbes*. The Forbes Magazine
Galleries here show Forbes's
diverse tastes, with over 500
antique toy boats; Monopoly
games; trophies; 12,000 toy
soldiers; and a signed copy of
Abraham Lincoln's Gettysburg
Address, among other historical
memorabilia. Paintings, from
French to American Military
works, are also on display.

## Salmagundi Club ❾

47 5th Ave **Map** 4 E1. **Tel** (212)
255-7740. Ⓜ 14th St-Union Sq.
Ⓞ 1–5pm daily. ⊘
**www**.salmagundi.org

America's oldest artists club
resides in the last remaining
mansion on lower Fifth
Avenue. Built in 1853 for Irad
Hawley, it now houses the
American Artists' Professional
League, the American Water-
color Society and the

Greenwich Village
Society for Historic
Preservation.
Washington Irving's
satiric periodical, *The
Salmagundi Papers*, gave the
club its name.
  Founded in 1871, the club
moved here in 1917. Periodic
art exhibits open the late 19th-
century interior to the public.

Exterior of the Salmagundi Club

## First Presbyterian Church ❿

5th Ave at 12th St. **Map** 4 D1. **Tel**
(212) 675-6150 Ⓜ 14th St-Union Sq.
Ⓞ 11:45am–12.30pm Mon, Wed,
Fri, 11am–12:30pm Sun. ⛪ 6pm
Wed in chapel. **www**.fpcnyc.org

Designed by Joseph C. Wells
in 1846, this Gothic church was
modeled on the Church of
St Saviour in Bath, England.
The church is noteworthy for
its brownstone tower. The
carved wooden plaques on
the altar list every pastor since
1716. The south transept by
McKim, Mead & White was
added in 1893. The fence of
iron and wood was built in
1844 and restored in 1981.

## Church of the Ascension ⓫

5th Ave at 10th St. **Map** 4 E1.
**Tel** (212) 254-8620 Ⓜ 14th St-
Union Sq. Ⓞ noon–2pm,
5–7pm daily. ⛪ 6pm Mon–Fri,
9am, 11am Sun. Ⓞ (except
during services). **www**.
ascensionnyc.org

Church of the Ascension

This English Gothic Revival
church was designed in
1840–41 by Richard Upjohn,
architect of Trinity Church. The
interior was redone in 1888 by
Stanford White, with an altar
relief by Augustus Saint-
Gaudens. Above the altar
hangs *The Ascension*, a mural
by John La Farge, who also
designed some of the stained
glass. The belfry tower is lit at
night to show off the colors.
In 1844 President John Tyler
married Julia Gardiner here;
she lived in nearby
Colonnade Row (see p120).

## Washington Mews ⓬

Between Washington Sq N and
E 8th St. **Map** 4 E2. Ⓜ W 4th St.

Built originally as stables, this
hidden enclave was turned
into carriage houses around
1900. The south side was
added in 1939. Gertrude
Vanderbilt Whitney, founder
of the Whitney Museum (see
pp200–01), once lived here.
  At No. 16 is NYU's French
House, remodeled in a French
style. Movies, lectures, and
classes in French are held
here, most of them free.

# New York University ⑬

Washington Sq. **Map** 4 E2.
**Tel** (212) 998-1212, (212) 998-4636. Ⓜ W 4th St. ◔ 8:30am–8pm Mon-Fri. **www**.nyu.edu

Originally called the University of the City of New York, NYU was founded in 1831 as an alternative to Episcopalian Columbia University. It is now the largest private university in the US and extends for blocks around Washington Square.

Construction of the school's first building on Waverly Place sparked the Stone-cutters' Guild Riot of 1833: contractors protested the use of inmates from a state prison to cut stone. The National Guard restored order. The original building no longer exists, but a memorial with a piece of the original tower is on a pedestal set into the pavement on Washington Square South. Samuel Morse's telegraph, John W. Draper's first-ever photographic

*Bust of Sylvette* **by Picasso, between Bleecker and West Houston streets**

portrait and Samuel Colt's six-shooter were invented here.

The Brown Building, on Washington Place near Greene Street, was the site of the Triangle Shirtwaist Company. In 1911, 146 factory workers died in a fire here, leading to new fire safety and labor laws.

A 36-ft (11-m) enlargement of Picasso's *Bust of Sylvette* is in University Village.

# Judson Memorial Church ⑭

55 Washington Sq S. **Map** 4 D2.
**Tel** (212) 477-0351. Ⓜ W 4th St. ◔ 10am–1pm, 2pm–6pm Mon–Fri. ☗ Sun 11am. **www**.judson.org

Built in 1892, this McKim, Mead & White church is an impressive Romanesque building with stained glass by John La Farge. Designed by Stanford White, it is named after the first American missionary sent to foreign soil, Adoniram Judson, who served in Burma in 1811. A copy of his Burmese translation of the Bible was put in the cornerstone when the building was dedicated.

It is the unique spirit of this church, not the architecture, that makes it stand out. Judson Memorial has played an active role in local and world concerns and has been the site of activism on issues ranging from AIDS to the arms race. It is also home to avant-garde art exhibitions and off-Off Broadway plays.

**Arch on the north side of Washington Square**

# Washington Square ⑮

**Map** 4 D2. Ⓜ W 4th St.

Now one of the city's most vibrant open spaces, Washington Square was once marshland through which the quiet Minetta Brook flowed. By the late 1700s, the area had been turned into a public cemetery – when excavation began for the park, some 10,000 skeletal remains were exhumed. The square was used as a dueling ground for

a time, then as a site for public hangings until 1819. The "hanging elm" in the northwest corner remains. In 1826 the marsh was filled in and the brook diverted underground, where it still flows; a small sign on a fountain at the entrance to Two Fifth Avenue marks its course.

The magnificent marble arch by Stanford White, completed in 1895 and newly refurbished, replaced an earlier wooden arch that spanned lower Fifth Avenue to mark the centenary of George Washington's inauguration. A stairway is hidden in the right side of the arch. In 1916, a group of artists led by Marcel Duchamp and John Sloan broke in, climbed atop the arch, and declared the "free and independent republic of Washington Square, the state of New Bohemia."

Across the street is "the Row." Now part of NYU, this block was once home to New York's most prominent families. The Delano family, writers Edith Wharton, Henry James, and John dos Passos, and artist Edward Hopper all lived here. Number 8 was once the mayor's official home.

Today students, families and free spirits mingle and enjoy the park side by side. A few drug dealers frequent the park, but it is safe by day.

**Window on the corner of West 4th Street and Washington Square**

# EAST VILLAGE

eter Stuyvesant had
a country estate in
the East Village, and
in the 19th century, the
Astors and Vanderbilts
lived here. But around
1900, high society moved
uptown and immigrants
moved in. The Irish,
Germans, Jews, Poles,
Ukrainians and Puerto Ricans all left
their mark in the area's churches and
landmarks, and the city's most varied

**Mosaic, facade of St. George's Ukrainian Catholic Church**

and least expensive ethnic
restaurants. In the 1950s
low rents attracted the
"beat generation." Later,
hippies were followed by
punks, and experimental
music clubs and theaters
still abound. Astor Place
buzzes with students. To
the east are Avenues A, B,
C, and D, an area known as "Alphabet
City," which has been transformed
into one of New York's trendiest areas.

## SIGHTS AT A GLANCE

**Historic Streets and Buildings**
Bayard-Condict Building ❽
Colonnade Row ❸
Cooper Union ❶

**Museums and Galleries**
Merchant's House Museum ❹

**Churches**
Grace Church ❻
St. Mark's-in-the-Bowery Church ❺

**Parks and Squares**
Tompkins Square ❼

**Famous Theaters**
Public Theater ❷

**SEE ALSO**

• *Street Finder,* map 4, 5

• *Where to Stay* pp281–2

• *Restaurants* pp301–2

**GETTING THERE**
By subway, the 6 train stop at
Astor Pl. is the most
convenient or the F or V to
2nd Ave for Alphabet City;
the area is also served by the M9,
M14A, M15, and M103 buses
and the M8 crosstown bus.

**KEY**

| | Street-by-Street map |
| **M** | Subway station |

0 meters       500
0 yards        500

**Gothic bas-relief on the facade of Grace Church**

◁ **The interior of McSorley's Old Ale House**

# Street by Street: East Village

At the spot where Tenth and Stuyvesant streets now intersect, Peter Stuyvesant's country house once stood. His grandson, also named Peter, inherited most of the property and had it divided into streets in 1787. Among the prize sites of the St. Mark's Historic District are the St. Mark's-in-the-Bowery Church, the Stuyvesant-Fish house and the 1795 home of Nicholas Stuyvesant, both on Stuyvesant Street. Many other homes in the district were built between 1871 and 1890 and still have their original stoops, lintels and other architectural details.

**Astor Place** subway (line 6)

**Astor Place** saw rioting in 1849. English actor William Macready, playing Hamlet at the Astor Place Opera House, criticized American actor Edwin Forrest. Forrest's fans revolted and there were 34 deaths.

**Alamo** is the title of the 15-ft (4.5-m) steel cube in Astor Place designed by Bernard Rosenthal. It revolves when pushed.

**Colonnade Row**
*Now in shabby disrepair, these buildings were once expensive town houses. The houses, of which only four are left, are unified by one facade in the European style. The marble was quarried by Sing Sing prisoners* ❸

**Public Theater**
*In 1965 the late Joseph Papp convinced the city to buy the Astor Library (1849) as a home for the theater. Now restored, it sees the opening of many famous plays* ❷

## STAR SIGHTS

★ Cooper Union

★ Merchant's House Museum

★ **Merchant's House**
*This museum contains the house's original Federal, American Empire and Victorian furniture* ❹

★ **Cooper Union**
*Founded by self-made man Peter Cooper in 1859, it still provides a free education to its students* ❶

**The Stuyvesant-Fish House**
(1803–04) was constructed out of brick. It is a classic example of a Federal-style house.

**Renwick Triangle**
is a group of 16 houses built in the Italianate style in 1861.

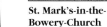

**St. Mark's-in-the-Bowery-Church**
*The church was built in 1799 and the steeple added in 1828* ❺

**LOCATOR MAP**
*See Manhattan Map pp14–15*

**Stuyvesant Polyclinic**
was founded in 1857 as the German Dispensary, and it is still a health clinic. The facade is decorated with the busts of many famous physicians and scientists.

**St. Mark's Place** was once the main street of hippie life. It is still the hub of the East Village youth scene. Funky shops now occupy many of the basements.

0 meters 100
0 yards 100

**Little India**, the row of Indian eateries on the south side of East Sixth Street, offers a taste of India at budget prices.

**KEY**

--- Suggested route

**Little Ukraine** is home to 30,000 Ukrainians. The hub is St. George's Ukrainian Catholic Church.

**McSorley's Old Ale House** still brews its own ale and serves it in surroundings seemingly unchanged since it opened in 1854 *(see p317.)*

Great Hall at Cooper Union, where Abraham Lincoln spoke

# Cooper Union **❶**

7 East 7th St. **Map** 4 F2.
**Tel** (212) 353-4000. **M** Astor Pl.
🕐 11am–7pm Mon–Fri, 11am–5pm
Sat, and for lectures and concerts in
Great Hall. ● Jun–Aug, public hols.
🚫 ♿ www.cooper.edu

Peter Cooper, the wealthy
industrialist who built the first
US steam locomotive, made
the first steel rails and was a
partner in the first trans-
atlantic cable venture, had no
formal schooling. In 1859 He
founded New York's first free,
non-sectarian coeducational
college specializing in design,
engineering, and architecture.
Still free, the school inspires
intense competition for
places. The six-story building,
renovated in 1973–4, was the
first with a steel frame, made
of Cooper's own rails. The
Great Hall was inaugurated
in 1859 by Mark Twain, and
Lincoln delivered his "Right
Makes Might" speech there
in 1860. Cooper Union still
sponsors a Public Forum.

# Public Theater **❷**

425 Lafayette St. **Map** 4 F2. **Tel** (212)
239-6200 (tickets). Admin (212) 539-
8500. **M** Astor Pl. See also **Entertainment** p344. www.publictheater.org

This large redbrick and brownstone building began its life in
1849 as the Astor Library, the
city's first
free library,

The Public Theater on Lafayette Street

now part of the New York
Public Library. It is a prime
American example of German
Romanesque Revival style.
  When the building was
threatened with demolition in
1965, Joseph Papp, founder of
the New York Shakespeare
Festival, which became The
Public Theater,
persuaded New York
City to buy it as a
home for the
company. Renovation
began in 1967,
and much of the
handsome interior
was preserved
during conversion
into six theaters.
Although much of
the work shown is
experimental, The
Public Theater was
the original home
of hit musicals *Hair*
and *A Chorus Line*.
The latter moved
uptown to become a long-
running Broadway production.

# Colonnade Row **❸**

428–434 Lafayette St. **Map** 4 F2.
**M** Astor Pl. ● to the public.

The Corinthian columns
across these four buildings
are all that remain of a once-
magnificent row of nine Greek
Revival town houses. They
were completed in 1833 by
developer Seth Geer and
were known as "Geer's Folly"
by skeptics who
thought no one
would live so far
east. They were
proved wrong
when the houses
were taken by
such eminent
citizens as John

Jacob Astor and Cornelius
Vanderbilt. Washington Irving,
author of *Rip Van Winkle* and
other classic American tales,
lived here for a time, as did
two English novelists, William
Makepeace Thackeray and
Charles Dickens. Five of the
houses were lost when the
John Wanamaker Department
Store razed them in the early
20th century to make room
for a garage. The remaining
buildings are falling to ruin.

# Merchant's House Museum **❹**

29 E 4th St. **Map** 4 F2. **Tel** (212)
777-1089. **M** Astor Pl., Bleecker St.
🕐 noon–5pm Mon, Thu–Sun and by
appt. 🎫 🚫 (no flashes permitted).
🎦 📷 www.merchantshouse.com

The original 19th-century iron stove in the
kitchen of the Merchant's House Museum

This remarkable Greek
Revival brick town house,
improbably tucked away on
an East Village block, is a
time capsule of a vanished
way of life. It still has both
its original fixtures and its
kitchen, and is filled with the
actual furniture, ornaments,
and utensils of the family that
lived here for almost 100
years. Built in 1832, it was
bought in 1835 by Seabury
Tredwell, a wealthy merchant,
and stayed in the family until
Gertrude Tredwell, the last
member, died in 1933. She
had maintained her father's
home just as he would have
liked it, and a relative
opened the house as a
museum in 1936. The first-
floor parlors are very grand,
a sign of how well New
York's merchant class lived
in the 1800s.

## St. Mark's-in-the-Bowery Church ❺

131 E 10th St. **Map** 4 F1. **Tel** (212) 674-6377. Ⓜ Astor Pl. ◗ 8:30am–4pm Mon–Fri unless Poetry Project rehearsals taking place. 🕁 6pm Wed, 11am Sun; in Spanish 5:30pm Sat. **www**.stmarkschurch-in-the-bowery.com

One of New York's oldest churches, this 1799 building replaced a 1660 church on the *bouwerie* (farm) of Governor Peter Stuyvesant. He is buried here with seven generations of descendants and many other prominent early New Yorkers. Poet W.H. Auden was a parishioner and is also commemorated here.

In 1878, a grisly kidnapping took place when the remains of department store magnate A.T. Stewart were removed and held for $20,000 ransom.

The church rectory at 232 East 11th Street dates from 1900 and is by Ernest Flagg, who achieved renown for his Singer Building *(see p106)*.

## Grace Church ❻

802 Broadway. **Map** 4 F1. **Tel** (212) 254-2000. Ⓜ Astor Pl, Union Sq. 🚌 M1. 🕁 Jul–Aug: 10am, 6pm Sun; Sep–Jun: 9am, 11am, 6pm Sun. 🚻 ♿ **Concerts.** **www**.gracechurchnyc.org

James Renwick, Jr., the architect of St. Patrick's Cathedral, was only 23 when he designed this church, yet many consider it his finest achievement. Its delicate early Gothic lines have a grace befitting the church's name. The interior is just as beautiful, with Pre-Raphaelite stained glass and a handsome mosaic floor.

The church's peace and serenity were briefly shattered in 1863, when Phineas T. Barnum

**Tom Thumb and his bride at Grace Church**

staged the wedding of midget General Tom Thumb here; the crowds turned the event into complete chaos.

The marble spire replaced a wooden steeple in 1888 amid fears that it might prove too heavy for the church – and it has since developed a distinct lean. The church is visible from afar, because it is on a bend on Broadway. Henry Brevoort forced the city to bend Broadway to divert it around his apple orchard.

**Grace Church altar and window**

## Tompkins Square ❼

**Map** 5 B1. Ⓜ 2nd Ave, 1st Ave. 🚌 M9, M14A.

This English-style park has the makings of a peaceful spot, but its past has more often been dominated by strife. It was the site of America's first organized labor demonstration in 1874, the main gathering place during the neighborhood's hippie era of the 1960s and, in 1991, an arena for violent riots when the police tried to evict homeless people who had taken over the grounds. The square also contains a poignant monument to the neighborhood's greatest tragedy. A small statue of a boy

and a girl looking at a steamboat commemorates the deaths of over 1,000 local residents in the *General Slocum* steamer disaster. On June 15, 1904, the boat caught fire during a pleasure cruise on the East River. The boat was crowded with women and children from this then-German neighborhood. Many local men lost their entire families and moved away, leaving the area and its memories behind.

## Bayard-Condict Building ❽

65 Bleecker St. **Map** 4 F3. Ⓜ Bleecker St.

The graceful columns, elegant filigreed terra-cotta facade and magnificent cornice on this 1898 building mark the only New York work by Louis Sullivan, the great Chicago architect who taught Frank Lloyd Wright. He died in poverty and obscurity in Chicago in 1924.

Sullivan is said to have objected vigorously to the sentimental angels supporting the Bayard-Condict Building's cornice, but he eventually gave in to the wishes of Silas Alden Condict, the owner.

Because this building is squeezed into a commercial block, it is better appreciated from a distance. Cross the street and walk a little way down Crosby Street for the best view.

**The Bayard-Condict Building**

# GRAMERCY AND THE FLATIRON DISTRICT

our squares were laid out in this area by real estate developers in the 19th century to emulate the quiet, private residential areas in many European cities. Gramercy Park, still mainly residential, was one of them. The townhouses around this square were designed by some of the

Lizard on a statue in
**Union Square**

country's best architects, such as Calvert Vaux and Stanford White, and occupied by some of New York's most prominent citizens. Today, not far away, boutiques, trendy cafés, and high-rise apartments have taken over the stretch of lower Fifth Avenue just south of the famous Flatiron Building.

## SIGHTS AT A GLANCE

### Historic Streets and Buildings
Appellate Division of the Supreme Court of the State of New York ❸
Block Beautiful ⓫
Con Edison Headquarters ⓮
Flatiron Building ❺
Gramercy Park Hotel ⓬
Ladies' Mile ❻
Metropolitan Life Insurance Company ❹

National Arts Club ❽
New York Life Insurance Company ❷
The Library at the Players ❾

### Museums and Galleries
Theodore Roosevelt Birthplace ❼

### Churches
The Little Church Around the Corner ⓰

### Parks and Squares
Gramercy Park ❿
Madison Square ❶
Stuyvesant Square ⓭
Union Square ⓯

### SEE ALSO

- *Street Finder*, maps 8, 9
- *Where to Stay* p282
- *Restaurants* pp302–3

## GETTING THERE
The closest subway stations are at 23rd St, where the N, R, F, V, and 6 trains stop, and Union Sq, where the N, Q, R, W, L, 4, 5, and 6 trains stop. Buses to the area include the M101–3 on 3rd Ave, the M1–3 or M5 on 5th and Madison Aves, and the M6 and M7 on Broadway.

### KEY

Street-by-Street map

Ⓜ Subway station

0 meters 500
0 yards 500

◁ **Con Edison Headquarters by night**

# Street by Street: Gramercy Park

Gramercy Park and nearby Madison Square tell a tale of two cities. Madison Square is ringed by offices and traffic and is used mainly by those who work nearby, but the fine surrounding commercial architecture and statues make it well worth visiting. It was once the home of Stanford White's famous pleasure palace, the old Madison Square Garden, a place where revelers always thronged. Gramercy Park, however, retains the air of dignified tranquility it has become known for. Here, the residences and clubs remain, set around New York's last private park, for which only those who live on the square have a key.

Statue of Diana atop the old Madison Square Garden

**★ Madison Square**
*The Knickerbocker Club played baseball here in the 1840s and was the first to codify the game's rules. Today office workers enjoy the park's many statues of 19th-century figures, among them Admiral David Farragut* ❶

**23rd Street subway (lines N, R)**

**★ Flatiron Building**
*The triangle made by Fifth Avenue, Broadway, and 23rd Street is the site of one of New York's most famous early skyscrapers. When it was built in 1903, it was the world's tallest building* ❺

**A sidewalk clock** found in front of 200 Fifth Avenue marks the very end of the once-fashionable shopping area, known as Ladies' Mile.

**Ladies' Mile**
*Broadway from Union Square to Madison Square was once New York's finest shopping area.* ❻

**Theodore Roosevelt Birthplace**
*The house is a replica of the one in which the 26th American president was born* ❼

**KEY**

– – – Suggested route

0 meters      100

0 yards      100

**National Arts Club**
*This is a private club for the arts, on the south side of the park* ❽

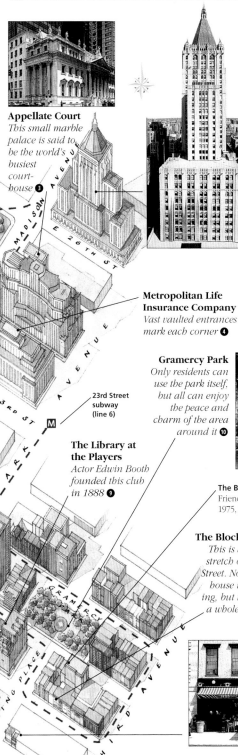

**Appellate Court**
*This small marble palace is said to be the world's busiest courthouse* ❸

**New York Life Insurance Company**
*This spectacular building by Cass Gilbert bears his trademark pyramid-shaped top* ❷

**STAR SIGHTS**

★ Flatiron Building

★ Madison Square

**Metropolitan Life Insurance Company**
*Vast vaulted entrances mark each corner* ❹

**Gramercy Park**
*Only residents can use the park itself, but all can enjoy the peace and charm of the area around it* ❿

23rd Street subway (line 6)

Ⓜ

**The Library at the Players**
*Actor Edwin Booth founded this club in 1888* ❾

**The Brotherhood Synagogue** was a Friends' Meeting House from 1859 to 1975, when it became a synagogue.

**The Block Beautiful**
*This is a tree-lined stretch of East 19th Street. No particular house is outstanding, but the street as a whole is lovely* ⓫

**Pete's Tavern** has been here since 1864. Short story writer O. Henry, a well-known chronicler of the city, wrote "The Gift of the Magi" in the second booth.

## Madison Square ❶

**Map** 8 F4. Ⓜ *23rd St.*

**Farragut's statue, Madison Square**

Planned as the center of a fashionable residential district, this square became a popular entertainment center after the Civil War. It was bordered by the elegant Fifth Avenue Hotel, the Madison Square Theater, and Stanford White's Madison Square Garden. The torch-bearing arm of the Statue of Liberty was exhibited here in 1884.

Quiet once again, it is a lunchtime spot for neighborhood office workers, and a place to stroll and admire the sculptures. The 1880 statue of Admiral David Farragut is by Augustus Saint-Gaudens, with a pedestal by Stanford White. Farragut was the hero of a Civil War sea battle; figures representing Courage and Loyalty arising from the waves are carved on the base. The statue of Roscoe Conkling commemorates a US senator who died of exposure during the great blizzard of 1888. The Eternal Light flagpole, by Carrère & Hastings, honors the soldiers who fell in France during World War I.

## New York Life Insurance Company ❷

51 Madison Ave. **Map** 9 A3. Ⓜ *28th St.* 🕐 *office hours.*

This imposing building was designed in 1928 by Cass Gilbert of Woolworth Building fame. The interior is a masterpiece, adorned with enormous hanging lamps, bronze doors and paneling, and a grand staircase leading, of all places, to the subway station.

Other famous buildings have stood on this site. Barnum's Hippodrome was here in 1874, then the first Madison Square Garden opened in 1879. A wide range of entertainments were put on, including the prizefights of heavyweight boxing hero John L. Sullivan in the 1880s. The next Madison Square Garden – Stanford White's legendary pleasure palace – opened on the same site in 1890. Lavish musical shows and social events were attended by New York's elite, who paid over $500 for a box at the prestigious annual horse show.

The building had street-level arcades and a tower modeled on the Giralda in Seville. A gold statue of the goddess Diana stood atop the tower. Her nudity was shocking, but far more scandalous was the decadent life and death of White himself. In 1906, while watching a revue in the roof garden, he was shot dead by millionaire Harry K. Thaw, the husband of White's former mistress, showgirl Evelyn Nesbit. The headline in the journal *Vanity Fair* summed up popular feeling: "Stanford White, Voluptuary and Pervert, Dies the Death of a Dog." The ensuing trial's revelations about decadent Broadway high society leave modern soap operas far behind.

**New York Life Insurance Company's golden pyramid roof**

## Appellate Division of the Supreme Court of the State of New York ❸

E. 25th St. at Madison Ave. **Map** 9 A4. Ⓜ *23rd St.* 🕐 *9am–5pm Mon–Fri (court in session from 2pm Tue–Thu, from 10am Fri).* ● *public hols.* 🚫

Appeals relating to civil and criminal cases for New York and the Bronx are heard here, in what is widely considered to be the busiest court of its kind in the world. James Brown Lord designed the small yet noble Palladian Revival building in 1900. It is decorated with more than a

**Statues of *Justice* and *Study* above the Appellate Court**

dozen handsome sculptures, including Daniel Chester French's Justice flanked by Power and Study. During the week, the public is invited to step inside to admire the fine interior, designed by the Herter brothers, including the courtroom when it is not in session. Among the elegant details worth looking for are the fine stained-glass windows and dome, the murals, and the striking cabinetwork.

Displays in the lobby often feature some of the more famous –and infamous – cases that have been heard in this court. Among the celebrity names that have been involved in appeals settled here are Babe Ruth, Charlie Chaplin, Fred Astaire, Harry Houdini, Theodore Dreiser, and Edgar Allan Poe.

Clock tower of the Metropolitan Life Insurance Company building

## Metropolitan Life Insurance Company ❹

1 Madison Ave. **Map** 9 A4.
Ⓜ 23rd St. ◯ banking hours. ⍉

In 1909, the addition of a 700-ft (210-m) tower to this 1893 building ousted the Flatiron as the tallest in the world. The huge four-sided clock has minute hands said to weigh 1000 lb (454 kg) each.The building is lit up at night, and is a familiar part of the evening skyline. It served as the company symbol "the light that never fails."
A series of historical murals by N.C. Wyeth, the famed illustrator of such classics as *Robin Hood*, *Treasure Island* and *Robinson Crusoe* (and the father of painter Andrew Wyeth), once graced the walls of the cafeteria. The building now houses First-Boston Crédit-Suisse.

## Flatiron Building ❺

175 5th Ave. **Map** 8 F4. Ⓜ 23rd St.
◯ office hours.

Originally named the Fuller Building after the construction company that owned it, this building by Chicago architect David Burnham was the tallest in the world when it was completed in 1902. One of the first buildings to use a steel frame, it heralded the era of the skyscrapers.
It soon became known as the Flatiron for its unusual triangular shape, but some called it "Burnham's folly," predicting that the winds created by the building's shape would knock it down. It has withstood the test of time, but the winds along 23rd Street did have one notable effect. In the building's early days, they drew crowds of males hoping to get a peek at women's ankles as their long skirts got blown about. Police officers had to keep people moving along, and their call, "23-skidoo" became slang for "scram."
The stretch of Fifth Avenue to the south of the building was, until recently, rather run down but is fast coming to life with chic shops such as Emporio Armani and Paul Smith, giving the area new cachet and a new name, "the Flatiron District."

Flatiron Building during its construction

## Ladies' Mile ❻

Broadway (Union Sq. to Madison Sq.).
**Map** 8 F4–5, 9 A5. Ⓜ 14th St, 23rd St.

Arnold Constable store

In the 19th century, the "carriage trade" came here in shiny traps from their town houses nearby, to shop at stores such as Arnold Constable (Nos. 881–887) and Lord & Taylor (No. 901). The ground-floor exteriors have changed beyond recognition; look up to see the remains of once-grand facades.

President Teddy Roosevelt

## Theodore Roosevelt Birthplace ❼

28 E. 20th St. **Map** 9 A5. **Tel** (212) 260-1616 Ⓜ 14th St.-Union Sq-23rd St. ◯ 9am–5pm Tue–Sat (last adm: 4pm). ⬤ public hols. 📷 ◯ ⬛ hourly. **Lectures, concerts, films, videos.** ⬛ www.nps.gov/thrb

The reconstructed boyhood home of the colorful 26th president displays everything from the toys with which the young Teddy played to campaign buttons and emblems of the trademark "Rough Rider" hat that Roosevelt wore in the Spanish-American War. One exhibit features his explorations and interests; the other covers his political career.

**Bas-relief faces of great writers at the National Arts Club**

# National Arts Club ❽

15 Gramercy Pk S. **Map** 9 A5. **Tel** (212) 475-3424. **M** 23rd St. ◯ noon–5pm Mon–Fri during exhibitions. **www**.nationalartsclub.org

This brownstone was the residence of New York governor Samuel Tilden, who condemned "Boss" Tweed (see p27) and established a free public library. He had the facade redesigned by Calvert Vaux in 1881–4. In 1906 the National Arts Club bought the home and kept the original high ceilings and stained glass by John La Farge. Members have included most leading American artists of the late 19th and early 20th century, who were asked to donate a painting or sculpture in return for life membership; these gifts form the permanent collection. The club is open to the public for exhibitions only.

# The Library at the Players ❾

18 Gramercy Pk S. **Map** 9 A5. **Tel** (212) 228-7610. **M** 23rd St. ◯ except for pre-booked group tours. 📷

This two-story brownstone was the home of actor Edwin Booth, brother of John Wilkes Booth, President Lincoln's assassin. Architect Stanford White remodeled the building as a club in 1888. Although intended primarily for actors, members have included White himself, author Mark Twain, publisher Thomas Nast and Winston Churchill, whose mother, Jennie Jerome, was born nearby. A statue of Booth playing Hamlet is across the street in Gramercy Park.

**Decorative grille at The Players club**

# Gramercy Park ❿

**Map** 9 A4. **M** 23rd St, 14th St-Union Sq.

Gramercy Park is one of four squares (with Union, Stuyvesant and Madison) laid out in the 1830s and 1840s to attract society residences. It is the city's only private park, and residents in the surrounding buildings have keys to the park gate as the original owners once did. Look through the railings at the southeast corner to see Greg Wyatt's fountain, with giraffes leaping around a smiling sun.

The buildings around the square were designed by some of the city's most famous architects, including Stanford White, whose house was located on the site of today's Gramercy Park Hotel. Particularly fine are 3 and 4, with graceful cast-iron gates and porches. The lanterns in front of 4 serve as symbols marking the house of a former mayor of the city, James Harper. Number 34 (1883) has been the home of the sculptor Daniel Chester French, the actor James Cagney and circus impresario John Ringling (who had a massive pipe organ installed in his apartment).

# Block Beautiful ⓫

E 19th St. **Map** 9 A5. **M** 14th St-Union Sq, 23rd St.

**House facade on the Block Beautiful on East 19th Street**

This is a serene, tree-lined block of 1920s residences, beautifully restored. None of them is exceptional on its own, but together they create a wonderfully harmonious whole. Number 132 had two famous theatrical tenants: Theda Bara, silent movie star and Hollywood's first sex symbol, and the fine Shakespearean actress Mrs. Patrick Campbell, who originated the role of Eliza Doolittle in George Bernard Shaw's Pygmalion in 1914. The hitching posts outside 141 and the ceramic relief of giraffes outside 147–149 are two of the many details to look for as you walk along the block.

**Fountain with sun and giraffes by Greg Wyatt in Gramercy Park**

# Gramercy Park Hotel ⓬

2 Lexington Ave at 21st St. **Map** 9 B4. *Tel* *(212) 475-4320.* M *14th St-Union Sq, 23rd St.* **www**.gramercyparkhotel.com

Located on the site of Stanford White's house, this hotel has, for more than 60 years, been a home away from home for many international visitors and New Yorkers alike. It is also right next to the only private park in Manhattan.

The shabby-chic hotel drew all types, from old matrons, to wealthy young rock stars. Then Ian Schrager, of Studio 54 fame, began a $200-million renovation, in which the 185-room hotel was given an "eclectic-Bohemian" look by artist Julian Schnabel. The conversion included 23 condominiums that range in price from $5 million to $10 million each. Two bars and a Chinese restaurant are open to the public.

# Stuyvesant Square ⓭

**Map** 9 B5. M *3rd Ave, 1st Ave.*

This oasis, in the form of a pair of parks divided by Second Avenue, was part of Peter Stuyvesant's original farm in the 1600s. It was still in the Stuyvesant family when the park was designed in 1836; Peter G. Stuyvesant sold the land to the city for the nominal sum of $5 (much to the delight of those living nearby, who saw real estate values jump). A statue of Stuyvesant by Gertrude Vanderbilt Whitney stands in the park. The park separated the Stuyvesant area from the poorer Gas House district.

# Con Edison Headquarters ⓮

145 E 14th St. **Map** 9 A5. M *3rd Ave, 14th St-Union Sq.* ● *to the public.*

The clock tower of this building, which dates from 1911, is a local landmark. Originally conceived by Henry Hardenbergh, the

The towers of Con Edison (right), Metropolitan Life and the Empire State

architect best known for such buildings as the Dakota *(see p218)* and the Plaza *(see p181)*. The 26-story tower was built by the same firm who designed Grand Central Terminal. Near the top of the tower, a 38-ft (11.6-m) bronze lantern was built as a memorial to Con Ed's employees who died in World War I. The tower itself is not as tall as nearby Empire State Building, but when it is lit up at night, it makes an attractive showpiece, in addition to a potent symbol of the company that keeps Manhattan and the other four boroughs shining.

# Union Square ⓯

**Map** 9 A5. M *14th St-Union Sq.* **Farmers' Market** ○ *8am–6pm Mon, Wed, Fri, Sat.*

**Greenmarket day at Union Square**

Opened in 1839, this park joined Bloomingdale Road (now Broadway) with the Bowery Road (Fourth Avenue or Park), and hence its name. Later, the center of the square

was lifted up for a subway to run beneath it. The park became popular with soapbox orators. During the Depression in 1930, more than 35,000 unemployed people rallied here, before marching on to City Hall to demand jobs. The square hosts a popular greenmarket where farmers from all over New York State sell fresh and organic produce.

# The Little Church Around the Corner ⓰

1 E 29th St. **Map** 8 F3. *Tel* *(212) 684-6770.* M *28th St.* ○ *8am–6pm daily.* ✟ *12:10pm Mon–Fri; 8:30am, 11am Sun.* ○ & ✦ *Sun, after 11am service.* **Lectures, concerts, recitals.** **www**.littlechurch.org

Built from 1849 to 1856, the Episcopal Church of the Transfiguration is a tranquil retreat. It has been known by its nickname since 1870 when Joseph Jefferson tried to arrange the funeral of fellow actor George Holland. The pastor at a nearby church refused to bury a person of so lowly a profession. Instead, he suggested "the little church around the corner." The name stuck and the church has had special ties with the theater ever since. Sarah Bernhardt attended services here.

The south transept window, by John La Farge, shows Edwin Booth playing Hamlet. Jefferson's cry of "God bless the little church around the corner" is commemorated in a window in the south aisle.

# CHELSEA AND THE GARMENT DISTRICT

This was open farmland in 1750. By the 1830s it was a suburb, and in the 1870s, with the coming of the elevated railroads *(see pp26–7)*, it had become commercial. Music halls and theaters lined 23rd Street. Fashion Row grew in the shadow of the El, with department stores serving middle-class New York. As fashion moved uptown, Chelsea drifted downhill. It became a warehouse district, until the Els were removed and New Yorkers rediscovered its town houses. When Macy's arrived at Herald Square to the north, the retailing and garment districts grew around it, along with the flower district. Today Chelsea is filled with art galleries and antique shops and has a large gay community.

**Statue of garment worker, at 555 7th Avenue**

Inside Chelsea's Empire Diner

## SIGHTS AT A GLANCE

**Historic Streets and Buildings**
Chelsea Historic District ⑫
*Empire State Building*
  *pp136–7* ②
General Post Office ⑦
General Theological
  Seminary ⑪

Hugh O'Neill Dry Goods
  Store ⑭

**Churches**
Marble Collegiate Reformed
  Church ①
St. John the Baptist Church ⑤

**Modern Architecture**
Chelsea Piers Sports and
  Entertainment Complex ⑨
    Jacob K. Javits Convention
      Center ⑧

Madison Square
  Garden ⑥

**Monuments**
Worth Monument ⑮

**Parks and Squares**
Herald Square ③

**Landmark Hotels and Restaurants**
Chelsea Hotel ⑬
Empire Diner ⑩

**Landmark Stores**
Macy's ④

**0 meters          500**

**0 yards          500**

**GETTING THERE**
To Chelsea, take the 1 subway
train to 18th or 23rd St. The
C and E trains go to 23rd St.
Buses include the M11 and
M20. For the area around
Macy's, take the 1, 2, or 3
express trains to 34th St/Penn
Station. The A, C, and E trains
also stop at 34th St, and the
B, D, F, V, N, R, Q, and W
trains stop at Herald Sq.

**KEY**

▨ Street-by-Street map

Ⓜ Subway station

🚁 Heliport

***SEE ALSO***

• *Street Finder*, maps 7–8

• *Where to Stay* pp283–4

• *Restaurants* p304

# Street by Street: Herald Square

Herald Square is named for the New York *Herald*, which had its office here from 1894 to 1921. Today full of shoppers, the area was once one of the raunchiest parts of New York. During the 1880s and '90s, it was known as the Tenderloin District and was filled with dance halls and bordellos. When Macy's opened in 1901, the focus moved from flesh to fashion. New York's Garment District now fills the streets near Macy's around Seventh Avenue, also known as Fashion Avenue. To the east on Fifth Avenue is the Empire State Building, with the city's best eagle's-eye views from the observation deck.

**Manhattan Mall**, the site of Gimbel's, Macy's former archrival, holds 90 stores, a huge food court, and a floor for children's wares.

**Fashion Avenue** is another name for the stretch of Seventh Avenue around 34th Street. This area is the heart of New York's garment industry. The streets are full of men pushing racks of clothes.

**34th Street subway (1, 2, 3)**

**The Ramada Hotel Pennsylvania** was a center for the 1930s big bands – Glenn Miller's song "Pennsylvania 6-5000" made its telephone number famous.

**St. John the Baptist Church**
*A beautiful set of carved Stations of the Cross is hung on the walls of the white marble interior of this church* ❺

**The SJM Building** is at 130 West 30th Street. Mesopotamian-style friezes adorn the outside of the building.

**The Fur District** is at the southern end of the Garment District. Furriers ply their trade between West 27th and 30th streets.

**The Flower District**, around Sixth Avenue and West 28th Street, hums with activity in the early part of the day as florists pack their vans with their highly scented, brightly colored wares.

**28th Street subway (lines N, R)**

## ★ Macy's

*The biggest department store in the world has something for everyone* ❹

**The Greenwich Savings Bank** (now the HSBC) is a Greek temple to banking with huge columns on three sides.

**34th Street subway** (lines B, D, F, N, Q, R, V, W)

### Herald Square

*The New York Herald Building's clock now is situated where Broadway meets Sixth Avenue* ❸

**LOCATOR MAP**
See Manhattan Map pp14–15

### KEY

– – – Suggested route

0 meters 100
0 yards 100

**Greeley Square** is more of a traffic island than a square, but it does have a fine statue of Horace Greeley, founder of the New York *Tribune*.

## ★ Empire State Building

*The observation deck of this quintessential skyscraper is a great place to view the city* ❷

**Little Korea** is an area of Korean businesses. In addition to shops, there are restaurants nearby on West 31st and 32nd streets.

**The Life Building** at 19 West 31st Street housed *Life* magazine when it was a satirical weekly. Carrère &Hastings designed the building in 1894. It is now a hotel.

### Marble Collegiate Church

*This 1854 church was built in the Gothic Revival style. It became famous when Norman Vincent Peale was pastor here* ❶

### STAR SIGHTS

★ Empire State Building

★ Macy's

Marble Collegiate's Tiffany stained-glass windows

# Marble Collegiate Reformed Church ❶

1 W. 29th St. **Map** 8 F3. **Tel** (212) 686-2770. **M** 28th St. 🕐 8:30am–8:30pm Mon–Fri, 9am–4pm Sat, 8am–3pm Sun. 🔵 public hols. ✝ 11:15am Sun. 📷 during services. ♿ **Sanctuary** 3 W 29th St. 🕐 10am–noon, 2–4pm Mon–Fri. **www**.marblechurch.org

This church is best known for its former pastor Norman Vincent Peale, who wrote *The Power of Positive Thinking*.

Another positive thinker, future US president Richard M. Nixon, attended services here when he was a lawyer in his pre-White House days.

The church was built in 1854 using the marble blocks that give it its name. Fifth Avenue was then no more than a dusty country road, and the cast-iron fence was there to keep livestock out.

The original white and gold interior walls were replaced with a stenciled gold *fleur-de-lis* design on a soft rust background. Two stained-glass Tiffany windows, depicting Old Testament scenes, were placed in the south wall in 1893.

# Empire State Building ❷

*See pp136–7.*

# Herald Square ❸

6th Ave. **Map** 8 E2. **M** 34th St-Penn Station. *See* **Shopping** p321.

Named after the New York *Herald*, which occupied a fine arcaded, Italianate Stanford White building here from

1893 to 1921, the square was the hub of the rowdy Tenderloin district in the 1870s and 1880s. Theaters, such as the Manhattan Opera House, dance halls, hotels, and restaurants kept the area humming with life until reformers clamped down on sleaze in the 1890s. The ornamental Bennett clock, named for James Gordon Bennett Jr., publisher of the *Herald*, is now all that is left of the Herald Building.

The Opera House was razed in 1901 to make way for Macy's and, soon after, other department stores followed, making Herald Square a mecca for shoppers. One such store was the now-defunct Gimbel Brothers Department Store, once arch rival to Macy's. (The rivalry was affectionately portrayed in the New York Christmas movie *A Miracle on 34th Street*). In 1988 the store was converted into a vertical mall with a glittery neon front. Although most of the old names have gone, Herald Square is still a key shopping district.

# Macy's ❹

151 W. 34th St. **Map** 8 E2. **Tel** (212) 695-4400 **M** 34th St-Penn Station. 🕐 10am–9:30pm Mon–Sat; 11am–8:30pm Sun. 🔵 public hols. *See* **Shopping** p319. **www**.macys.com

The "world's largest store" covers a square block, and the merchandise inside covers just about any item you could imagine in every price range.

Macy's was founded by a former whaler named Rowland Hussey Macy, who opened a small store on West 14th Street in 1857. The store's red star logo came from Macy's tattoo, a souvenir of his sailing days.

By the time Macy died in 1877, his little store had grown to a row of 11 buildings. It was to expand further under two brothers, Isidor and Nathan Straus, who had operated Macy's china and glassware department. By 1902 Macy's had outgrown its 14th Street premises, and the firm acquired its present site. The eastern facade has a new

Macy's 34th Street facade

The nave of St. John the Baptist Church

entrance but still bears the bay windows and Corinthian pillars of the 1902 design. The 34th Street facade still has its original caryatids guarding the entrance, along with the clock, canopy, and lettering. Inside, many of the original wooden escalators are still in good working order.

The sea featured again in Macy's history in 1912 – a plaque by the main entrance commemorates the death of Isidor and his wife in the sinking of the *Titanic*.

Macy's sponsors New York's renowned Thanksgiving Day parade and the Fourth of July fireworks. The store's popular Spring Flower Show draws thousands of visitors.

## St. John the Baptist Church ❺

210 W 31st St. **Map** 8 E3. **Tel** (212) 564-9070. Ⓜ *34th St-Penn Station.* ◷ *6:15am–6pm daily.* ✝ *8:45am, 10:30am, 5:15pm daily.* ◎ ♿ 🛉

Founded in 1840 to serve a congregation of newly arrived immigrants, today this small Roman Catholic church is almost lost in the heart of the Fur District. The exterior has a single spire. Although the brownstone facade on 30th Street is dark with city soot, many treasures lie within this dull exterior. The entrance is through the modern Friary on 31st Street.

The sanctuary by Napoleon Le Brun is a marvel of Gothic arches in glowing white marble surmounted by gilded capitals. Painted reliefs of religious scenes line the walls; sunlight streams through the stained-glass windows. Also off the Friary is the Prayer Garden, a small, green and peaceful oasis with religious statuary, a fountain and stone benches.

## Madison Square Garden ❻

4 Pennsylvania Plaza. **Map** 8 D2. **Tel** (212) 465-6741. Ⓜ *34th St-Penn Station.* ◷ *Mon–Sun, times vary according to shows.* 📧 See **Entertainment** p360. **www**.thegarden.com

There's only one good thing to be said for the razing of the extraordinarily lovely McKim, Mead & White Pennsylvania Station building in favor of this undistinguished 1968 complex: it so enraged city preservationists that they formed an alliance to ensure that such a thing would never be allowed to happen again.

Madison Square Garden itself, which sits atop underground Pennsylvania Station, is a cylinder of precast concrete, functional enough as a 20,000-seat, centrally located home for the famous New York Knickerbockers (the Knicks) basketball, Liberty (women's basketball), and New York Rangers hockey teams. It has a packed calendar of other events: rock concerts, championship tennis and boxing, outrageously staged wrestling, the Ringling Bros. and Barnum & Bailey Circus, an antiques show, a dog show and more. There is also a 5,600-seat theater.

Despite renovation work, Madison Square Garden lacks the panache of its earlier location, which combined a stunning Stanford White building with extravagant entertainment *(see p126)*.

The massive interior of Madison Square Garden

## General Post Office ❼

421 8th Ave. **Map** 8 D2. **Tel** (800) ASK-USPS. Ⓜ *34th St-Penn Station.* ◷ *24 hrs a day, every day (incl public hols).* See **Practical Information** p377.

Designed by McKim, Mead & White in 1913, in a style to complement their 1910 Pennsylvania Station across the street, the General Post Office is a perfect example of a public building of the Beaux Arts period. The imposing, two-block-long structure has a broad staircase leading to a facade with 20 Corinthian columns and a pavilion at each end. The 280-ft (85-m) inscription across it is based on a description of the Persian Empire's postal service, from around 520 BC: "Neither snow nor rain nor heat nor gloom of night stays these couriers from the swift completion of their appointed rounds."

The Corinthian colonnade of the General Post Office

# Empire State Building ❷

**102nd-floor observatory**

The Empire State Building is the tallest skyscraper in New York. Construction began in March 1930, not long after the Wall Street Crash, and by the time it opened in 1931, space was so difficult to rent that it was nicknamed "the Empty State Building." Only the immediate popularity of the observatories saved the building from bankruptcy – to date, they have attracted more than 120 million visitors – and the building soon became a symbol of the city the world over.

**Empire State Building**

**The Empire State** was planned to be 86 stories high, but a then 150 ft (46 m) mooring mast for zeppelins was added. The mast, now 204 ft (62 m), transmits TV and radio to the city and four states.

**Colored floodlighting** of the top 30 floors marks special and seasonal events.

**High-speed** elevators travel at up to 1,000 ft (305 m) a minute.

**Symbols of the modern age** are depicted on these bronze Art Deco medallions placed throughout the lobby.

## CONSTRUCTION

*The building was designed for ease and speed of construction. Everything possible was prefabricated and slotted into place at a rate of about four stories per week*

**The framework** is made from 60,000 tons of steel and was built in 23 weeks.

**Aluminum panels** were used instead of stone around the 6,500 windows. The steel trim masks rough edges on the facing.

**Ten million bricks** were used to line the whole building.

**Nine minutes** 33 seconds is the record for racing up the 1,575 steps from the lobby to the 86th floor, in the annual Empire State Run-Up.

**Sandwich space** between the floors houses the wiring, pipes and cables.

**Over 200 steel** and concrete piles support the 365,000-ton building.

## STAR FEATURES

★ Fifth Avenue Entrance Lobby

★ Views from the Observatories

## VISITORS' CHECKLIST

350 5th Ave. **Map** 8 F2.
*Tel* (877) NYC-VIEW. Ⓜ *A, B,
C, D, E, F, N, Q, R, 1, 2, 3 to
34th St.* 🚌 *M1–5, M16, M34,
Q32.* **Observatories** ◯ *8am–
2am (last adm: 1:15am); 9am–
5pm Dec 24; 11am–7pm Jan 1
and Dec 25.* 🎦 📷 🛗 🍴
www.esbnyc.com

### ★ Views from the Observatories

*The 86th-floor outdoor observation decks offer superb views
of Manhattan. The 102nd-floor observatory, 1,250 ft (381 m)
high, can be visited for an additional fee payable only at
the Visitors' Center on the second floor, not online.*

### A Head for Heights

*As the building took
shape, construction
workers often showed
great bravery. Here,
a worker clings to a
crane hook. The
Chrysler Building and
other skyscrapers in the
background appear
surprisingly small.*

**Empire State
1454 ft (443 m)
with mast**

**Eiffel Tower
1045 ft
(319 m)**

**Great Pyramid
350 ft (107 m)**

**Big Ben 220 ft
(67 m)**

### Pecking Order

*New Yorkers are justly proud of their city's symbol,
which towers above the icons of other countries.*

### Lightning Strikes

*The Empire State is a
natural lightning
conductor, struck up
to 100 times a year.
The observation deck
is closed during
unfavorable weather.*

### ★ Fifth Avenue
### Entrance Lobby

*A relief image of the
skyscraper is superimposed
on a map of New York State
in the marble-lined lobby.*

### ENCOUNTERS IN THE SKY

The Empire State Building has been
seen in many films. However, the finale
from the 1933 classic *King Kong* is easily its
most famous guest appearance, as the giant
ape straddles the spire to do battle with army
aircraft. In 1945 a real bomber flew too low
over Manhattan in fog and struck the
building just above the 78th floor. The
luckiest escape was that of a young elevator
operator whose cabin plunged 79 floors.
The emergency brakes saved her life.

# Jacob K. Javits Convention Center ❽

655 W. 34th St. **Map** 7 B2. **Tel** (212) 216-2000. Ⓜ 34th St-Penn Station, 42nd St. 🚌 M34, M42. 🔘 only on show days – times vary. 🎨 📷 ♿ 🍽 www.javitscenter.com

**The Convention Center – modern New York architecture at its best**

Strikingly modernistic in appearance, this glass building facing the Hudson, which opened in 1986, was designed by I.M. Pei to give New York the space for large-scale expositions. The 18-story building is constructed of 16,000 panes of glass, the two main halls can accommodate thousands of delegates, and the lobby is high enough to hold the Statue of Liberty. In 1989 the construction of the Galleria River Pavilion added another 40,000 sq ft (3,750 sq m) of open space to the building, and two outdoor terraces overlooking the river.

# Chelsea Piers Complex ❾

11th Ave (17th to 23rd Sts) **Map** 7 B5. **Tel** (212) 336-6666. Ⓜ 14th St, 18th St, 23rd St. 🚌 M14, M23. 🔘 daily. 🎨 www.chelseapiers.com

This mammoth complex, which opened in 1995, has converted four neglected piers into a center for a vast range of sports and leisure activities (see p33). The facilities include skating rinks, running tracks, a golf driving range, a marina, and 11 TV and film production sound stages.

# Empire Diner ❿

210 10th Ave. **Map** 7 C4. **Tel** (212) 243-2736. Ⓜ 23rd St. 🔘 24hrs daily. ⚫ 4–8am Mon. 🚌 M11, M23.

This Art Deco beauty is a faithful refurbishing of a classic 1929 American diner, complete with stainless steel bar and black and chrome trim. Bette Davis reputedly declared this to be her favorite diner. Both the cuisine and the clientele here are up-to-date New York style.

**A 15th-century music manuscript in the General Theological Seminary**

# General Theological Seminary ⓫

175 9th Ave. **Map** 7 C4. **Tel** (212) 243-5150. Ⓜ 23rd St. 🔘 noon–3pm Mon–Fri, 11am–3pm Sat. 🕇 11:45am Mon, Wed–Fri, 6pm Tue, Sun. 📷 ♿ www.gts.edu

Founded in 1817, this block-square campus accepts 150 students at a time to train for the priesthood. Clement Clarke Moore, a professor of Biblical Learning, donated the site, officially known as Chelsea Square. The earliest remaining building dates from 1836; the most modern, St. Mark's Library, was built in 1960 and holds the largest collection of Latin Bibles in the world.

The campus can be entered from Ninth Avenue only. Inside, the garden is laid out in two quadrangles like an English cathedral close: it is especially lovely in spring.

**The Empire Diner before hungry club-goers arrive for breakfast**

# Chelsea Historic District ⑫

W. 20th St from 9th to 10th Aves.
**Map** 8 D5. Ⓜ *18th St.* 🚌 *M11.*

Although he is better-known as the author of the poem "A Visit from St. Nicholas" than as an urban planner, Clement Clarke Moore owned an estate here and divided it into lots in the 1830s, creating handsome rows of town houses. Restoration has since rescued many of the original buildings here.

Of these, the finest are seven houses known as Cushman Row, running from 406 – 418 West 20th Street, which were built from 1839 –1840 for Don Alonzo Cushman. He was a merchant who also founded the Greenwich Savings Bank. He joined Moore and James N. Wells in the development of Chelsea. Rich in detail and intricate ironwork, Cushman Row is ranked with Washington Square North as supreme examples of Greek Revival architecture. Look for cast-iron wreaths around attic windows and the pineapples on the newel posts of two of the houses – old symbols of hospitality.

Farther along West 20th Street, from 446 – 450, there are fine examples of the Italianate style for which Chelsea is also renowned.

A house on Cushman Row

The detailed brickwork arches of windows and fanlights subtly implied the wealth of the owner, being able to afford this expensive effect.

**Hugh O'Neill Dry Goods Store**

# Chelsea Hotel ⑬

222 W. 23rd St. **Map** 8 D4.
**Tel** *(212) 243-3700.* Ⓜ *23rd St.*
*www.hotelchelsea.com*
See **Where to Stay** *p283.*

Few hotels can match the Chelsea for artistic and literary heritage – and notoriety. Many former guests have been commemorated in the brass plaques on the hotel's facade. They include Tennessee Williams, Mark Twain, Jack Kerouac, and Brendan Behan. Dylan Thomas spent his last years here. In 1966 Andy Warhol's movie *Chelsea Girls* was set here, reviving its cult status, and in 1978 punk band member Sid Vicious killed his girlfriend in the hotel. The Chelsea still draws musicians, artists, and writers who hope their names will one day be remembered. Stop by the bar to soak in the decadent decay of this creative atmsphere.

# Hugh O'Neill Dry Goods Store ⑭

655–671 6th Avenue. **Map** 8 E4.
Ⓜ *23rd St.*

Though the store is long gone, the 1876 cast-iron columned and pilastered facade clearly shows the scale and grandeur of the emporiums that once lined Sixth Avenue from 18th to 23rd streets, the area known as Fashion Row. O'Neill, whose sign can still be seen on the facade, was a showman and super-salesman whose trademark was a fleet of shiny delivery wagons. His customers came in droves via the conveniently close Sixth Avenue El. They were not the "carriage trade" enjoyed by Ladies' Mile *(see p127),* but their numbers allowed the Row to flourish until the turn of the century, when the retailing district continued its move uptown. Now mostly restored, the buildings have turned into superstores and the headquarters of bargain places like Filene's Basement.

# Worth Monument ⑮

5th Ave and Broadway. **Map** 8 F4.
Ⓜ *23rd St-Broadway.*

Hidden away behind a water meter on a triangle amid city traffic is an obelisk erected in 1857 to mark the grave of the one public figure to be buried under the streets of Manhattan. That honor belongs to General William J. Worth, a hero of the Mexican wars of the mid-1800s. A cast-iron fence of swords embedded in the ground surrounds the monument.

**The Worth Monument**

---

A guest's-eye view of the Chelsea Hotel's cast-iron stairwell

# THEATER DISTRICT

It was the move of the Metropolitan Opera House to Broadway at 40th Street in 1883 that first drew lavish theaters and restaurants to this area. In the 1920s, movie palaces added the glamour of neon to Broadway, the signs getting bigger and brighter until eventually the street became known as the "Great White Way." After World War II, the pull of

Lee Lawrie design in Rockefeller Center

the movies waned and the glitter was replaced by grime. In recent years, however, a redevelopment program has brought the public and the bright lights back. Pockets of calm also exist away from the bustle. Explore the Public Library or relax in Bryant Park. For the best of both worlds, though, visit the landmark Rockefeller Center.

**The heart of the Theater District, around Times Square**

## SIGHTS AT A GLANCE

### Historic Streets and Buildings

Alwyn Court Apartments **18**
Group Health Insurance Building **12**
New York Public Library **8**
New York Yacht Club **5**
Paramount Building **13**
Shubert Alley **14**
Times Square **10**

### Museums and Galleries

International Center of Photography **9**
*Intrepid* Sea-Air-Space Museum **19**
Museum of Arts and Design **20**

### Modern Architecture

MONY Tower **15**
Rockefeller Center **1**

### Parks and Squares

Bryant Park **6**

### Famous Theaters

Carnegie Hall **17**
City Center of Music and Dance **16**
Lyceum Theater **3**
New Amsterdam Theater **11**

### Landmark Hotels and Restaurants

Algonquin Hotel **4**
Bryant Park Hotel **7**

### Landmark Stores

Diamond Row **2**

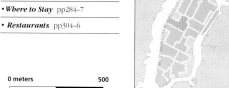

### GETTING THERE

Subway lines A, C, and E go to the Port Authority and connect to the 1, 2, 3, N, Q, R, W, S, and 7 at Times Sq. The B, D, F, V, and 7 lines stop at Bryant Park. The 1, N, R, W, C, and E lines also stop at the north end of Times Sq. Bus routes through the area are the M1–7, M10, M20, M27 and M104, and the M42, M50, M57 crosstown.

### KEY

| | |
|---|---|
| ▨ | Street-by-Street map |
| **M** | Subway station |
| 🛥 | Riverboat boarding point |

### SEE ALSO

• *Street Finder,* maps 8, 11–12
• *Where to Stay* pp284–7
• *Restaurants* pp304–6

0 meters 500
0 yards 500

# Street by Street: Times Square

Named for the 25-story New York Times Tower, which
opened in 1906, Times Square has been at the heart
of the city's theater district since 1899, when Oscar
Hammerstein built the Victoria and Republic theaters.
Since the 1920s, the glowing neon of theater billboards
has combined with the *Times'* illuminated newswire
and other advertising to create a spectacular lightshow.
After a period of decline starting in the 1930s, which
saw sex shows taking over many of the grand theatres,
rejuvenation of the district began in the 1990s. Old-
style Broadway glamour again rubs shoulders with
modern entertainment in this enticing part of the city.

**Paramount Hotel**
This hotel, designed by
Philippe Starck, is the
hip haunt of the theater
crowd who drink in
the late-night Whiskey
Bar *(see p285).*

**MTV Studios**
Crowds gather outside at 3pm
Monday through Friday to
watch interviews being filmed
in the second-floor studios.
Roving cameras often seek
reactions on the street.

**Westin Hotel**
One of the newest buildings in
Manhattan, this striking 45-story
hotel consists of a prism split by
a curving beam of light.

**Sardi's**
In Times Square since 1921,
Sardi's walls are lined with
caricatures of Broadway
stars of yesterday
and today.

★ **E Walk**
This entertainment and retail complex
has a multiplex cinema, restaurants, a
hotel, and the BB King Blues Club.

★ **Times Square**
*Every New Year's Eve at midnight,
the famed crystal ball drops from
the top of One Times Square. There
are great views from the front of this
New York landmark* ⓾

0 meters     100
0 yards      100

★ **New Victory
Theater**
Renovated in 1995,
this classic Broadway
theater reopened as
a young people's
performance space.

**Electronic Ticker Tape**
The figures on the Morgan Stanley LED tickertape are 10 feet (3 m) high. It is only one of the eye-catching lighting displays that illuminate Times Square day and night. City ordinances require office buildings to carry neon advertising.

**LOCATOR MAP**
*See Manhattan Map pp14–15*

**KEY**

– – – Suggested route

## STAR SIGHTS

★ E Walk

★ New Victory Theater

★ Times Square

**McGraw-Hill Building**

**J.P. Stevens Tower**

**Celanese Building**

**Times Square Information Center**

**Duffy Square**
A statue of actor, composer, and writer George M Cohan, responsible for many of Broadway's hits, stands proud in this small square. Duffy Square is named for World War I hero, "Fighting" Father Duffy, immortalized in a statue. It is also home to the **TKTS** booth, where cut-price theater tickets are sold daily.

GEORGE · M · COHAN
1878–1942

**Lyceum Theater**
*The oldest Broadway theater, the Lyceum has a beautifully ornate Baroque facade* ❸

**Belasco Theater**
Built in 1907 by producer David Belasco, it was the most technically advanced theater of its time. Original Tiffany glass and Everett Shinn murals decorate the interior. It is rumored that Belasco's ghost still treads the boards some nights.

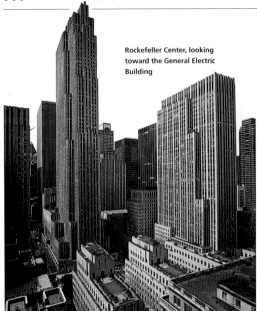

Rockefeller Center, looking toward the General Electric Building

In December 1932, Radio City Music Hall opened within the complex. It still hosts its famous Christmas and Easter shows here. Later, NBC opened their TV studios here.

The latest attraction is Top of the Rock, an observatory on the 67th–70th floors that offers a dizzying 360° panoramic view of the city.

## Diamond Row ❷

47th St, between 5th and 6th Aves. **Map** 12 F5. Ⓜ 47th-50th Sts. See **Shopping** p328.

Nearly every shop window on 47th Street glitters with gold and diamonds. The buildings are filled with booths and workshops where jewelers vie for customers while, upstairs, millions of dollars change hands. The diamond district was born in the 1930s, when the Jewish diamond cutters of Antwerp and Amsterdam fled to America to escape Nazism.

Hasidic Jews with black hats, beards, and long earlocks are still an integral part of the scene. Although mainly a wholesale district, individual customers are welcome. Bring cash, compare prices, haggle, and stay away if you know nothing about the value of diamonds.

Diamond Row's main commodity

## Rockefeller Center ❶

**Map** 12 F5. Ⓜ 47th–50th Sts. **Tel** (212) 332-6868 (information). 📷 ♿ 🍴 🖥 🗂 NBC, Rockefeller Center, daily. **Tel** (212) 664-7174 (reservations advised). Radio City Music Hall, daily. **Tel** (212) 247-4777. Top of the Rock, daily. **Tel** (212) 698-2000. **www**.rockefellercenter.com **www**.nbc.com **www**.radiocity.com **www**.topoftherocknyc.com

When the New York City Landmarks Preservation Commission unanimously voted to declare Rockefeller Center a landmark in 1985, they rightly called it "the heart of New York . . . a great unifying presence in the chaotic core of midtown Manhattan."

It is the largest privately owned complex of its kind and the inspiration for many cities to emulate its perfect urban mix. The Art Deco design was by a team of top architects headed by Raymond Hood. Works by 30 artists can be found in foyers, on facades, and in the gardens.

The site, once a botanic garden owned by Columbia University, was leased in 1928 by John D. Rockefeller, Jr., as an ideal central home for a new opera house. When the 1929 Depression scuttled these plans, Rockefeller, stuck with a long lease, went ahead with his own development. The 14 buildings erected between 1931 and 1940 provided jobs for as many as 225,000 people during the Depression and by 1973 there were a total of 19 buildings.

**Wisdom** by Lee Lawrie, on the GE Building

## Lyceum Theater ❸

149 W 45th St. **Map** 12 E5. **Tel** Telecharge (212) 239-6200. Ⓜ 42nd, 47th St, 49th St. See **Entertainment** p345.

The oldest New York theater still active is a Baroque-style bandbox as frilly as a wedding cake. This 1903 triumph was the first theater by Herts and Tallant, later renowned for their extravagant style. The Lyceum made history with a record run of 1,600 performances of the comedy Born Yesterday. It was the first theater to be designated a historic landmark and though the Theater District has shifted westward, there are still many shows here.

The Rose Room in the
Algonquin Hotel

# Algonquin Hotel ❹

59 W 44th St. **Map** 12 F5.
*Tel* (212) 840-6800. M *42nd St.*
*See* **Where to Stay** *p285.*
www.algonquinhotel.com

The exterior is a bit fussy –
iron bay windows in vertical
rows, red brick, too much
detail – but it is the ambience,
not the 1902 architecture, that
makes the Algonquin Hotel
special. In the 1920s, the Rose
Room was home to America's
best-known luncheon club,
the Round Table, with literary
lights such as Alexander
Woollcott, Franklin P. Adams,
Dorothy Parker, Robert
Benchley, and Harold Ross.
All were associated with the
*New Yorker* (Ross was the
founding editor), whose 25
West 43rd Street headquarters
had a back door opening into
the hotel.
    Renovations have preserved
the old-fashioned, civilized
feel of the Rose Room,
as well as the cozy,
paneled lobby
where publishing
types and
theater-goers
still like
to gather
for drinks,
settling into
comfortable
armchairs
and ringing
a small
brass bell
in order to
summon
the waiters.

# New York Yacht Club ❺

37 W 44th St. **Map** 12 F5. *Tel* (212)
382 1000. M *42nd St.* ⬤ *to the*
*public (members only).* **www**.nyyc.org

A whimsical 1899 creation,
this private club has the
carved sterns of 16th-century
Dutch galleons in the three
bay windows. The
prows of the ships
are borne up by
sculpted dolphins and
waves that spill over
the windowsills and
splash down to the
pavement. (The
building, just over
100 years old, has
been spruced up for
its next century.) This
is the birthplace of
the Americas Cup
yacht race, which
was based in the
US from 1857 to
1983. That was
the year the
much coveted
prize was
taken from
the table
where it had
stood for more than a
century, when the *Australia II*
sailed to a historic victory.

**The Americas Cup, the
coveted yachting prize**

# Bryant Park ❻

**Map** 8 F1. M *42nd St.*
**www**.bryantpark.org

In 1853, with the New York
Public Library site still occupied
by Croton Reservoir, Bryant
Park (then Reservoir Park)
housed a dazzling Crystal
Palace, built for the World's
Fair of that year *(see p25)*.
    In the 1960s the park was a
hangout for drug dealers and
other undesirables. In 1989
the city renovated the
park, reclaiming it for
workers and visitors
to relax in. In spring
and fall, world-famous
fashion shows take
place here; in the
summer, classic
movies are screened.
Over seven
million books lie
in storage stacks
beneath the park.

**Statue of poet William Cullen
Bryant in Bryant Park**

# Bryant Park Hotel ❼

40 W 40th St. **Map** 8 F1.
*Tel* (212) 869-0100. M *42nd St.*
www.bryantparkhotel.com

The American Radiator
building (now the Bryant Park
Hotel) was the first major
New York work by Raymond
Hood and John Howells,
who went on to design the
Daily News Building *(see
p155)*, the McGraw-Hill
building, and Rockefeller
Center. The 1924 structure is
reminiscent of one of Hood's
best-known Gothic
buildings, Chicago's
Tribune Tower. Here, the
design is sleeker, giving the
building the illusion of being
taller than its actual 23 stories.
The black brick facade is set
off by gold terracotta trim,
evoking images of flaming
coals: a comparison that
would have suited its
original owners well,
since they made
heating equipment.
The building is now
a luxury hotel *(see p288)*
across the street from
Bryant Park and boasts
the New York outpost of
trendy LA eatery Koi.

**The Bryant Park Hotel, formerly the
American Radiator Building**

# The New York Public Library 🔞

5th Ave and 42nd St. **Map** 8 F1.
*Tel (212) 930-0830.* M *42nd St-Grand
Central, 42nd St-5th Ave.* ⏱ *Tue–Sun,
hours vary.* 🌐 *public hols.* 📷 ♿ ✔
*Lectures, workshops, readings.* 🏛

**Doorway leading to New York
Public Library's Main Reading Room**

In 1897 the coveted job of
designing New York's main
public library was awarded to
architects Carrère & Hastings.
The library's first director
envisaged a light, quiet, airy
place for study, where millions
of books could be stored and
yet be available to readers as
promptly as possible. In the
hands of Carrère & Hastings,
his vision came true, in what
is considered the epitome of
New York's Beaux Arts period.

Built on the site of the
former Croton Reservoir
*(see p24)*, it opened in 1911
to immediate
acclaim,
despite
having
cost the
city $9
million.

**One of the library's two stone lions, named
Patience and Fortitude by Mayor LaGuardia**

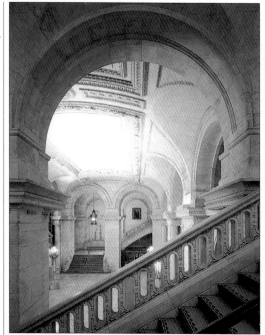

**Barrel vaults of carved
white marble over the
stairs in the Astor Hall**

The vast, paneled Main
Reading Room stretches
two full blocks and is
suffused with daylight
from the two interior
courtyards. Below it
are 88 miles (140 km) of
shelves, holding over
seven million volumes.
A staff of over 100 and
a computerized dumb-
waiter can supply any
book within 10 minutes.

The Periodicals Room
holds 10,000 current
periodicals from 128
countries. On its walls
are murals by Richard
Haas, honoring New York's
great publishing houses. The
original library combined the
collections of John Jacob
Astor and James Lenox.
Its collections today
range from Thomas
Jefferson's hand-
written copy of the
Declaration of
Independence to
T.S. Eliot's typed
copy of "The
Waste Land." More
than 1,000 queries

**The Main Reading Room, with its
original bronze reading lamps**

are answered daily, using the
vast database of the CATNYP
and LEO computer catalogs.

This library is the hub of a
network of 82 branches, with
nearly seven million users.
Some branches are very well
known, such as the New York
Public Library for the Performing Arts at the Lincoln Center
*(see p212)* and the Schomburg
Center in Harlem *(see p229)*.

# International Center of Photography **9**

*1133 Avenue of the Americas (43rd St).* **Map** *8 F1.* **Tel** *(212) 857-0000.* Ⓜ *42nd St.* ◯ *10am–6pm Tue–Thu, Sat & Sun; 10am–8pm Fri.* ◐ *4 Jul.* ◪ Ⓐ Ⓞ *10am–5pm Tue–Sun.* ◱ **www**.icp.org

This museum was founded by Cornell Capa in 1974 to conserve the work of such photojournalists as his brother Robert, who was killed on assignment in 1954. The collection of 12,500 original prints contains work by many top photographers, including Ansel Adams and Henri Cartier-Bresson. Special exhibitions are organized from the ICP'S archive as well as from outside sources. There are also films, lectures, and classes.

# Times Square **10**

**Map** *8 E1.* Ⓜ *42nd St-Times Sq.* ℹ *Times Square Information Center, 1560 Broadway (46th St) 8am–8pm daily.* ◪ *noon Fri, (212) 869-1890.* **www**.timessquarenyc.org

The 1990s saw a transformation in Times Square, reversing a decline that began during the Depression. The square is now a safe and vibrant place where Broadway traditions comfortably coexist with modern innovations.

Although the *New York Times* has moved on from its original headquarters at the south end of the square, the glistening ball (now of Waterford crystal) still drops at midnight on New Year's Eve, as it has since the building opened with fanfare and fireworks in 1906. New buildings, such as the Bertlesmann and the fashionably minimalist Condé Nast offices, sit comfortably alongside the classic Broadway theaters.

Broadway's fortunes have also revived. Many theaters have been renovated and are again housing new productions; theatergoers

throng the area's bars and restaurants each evening.

The newest landmark is the 57-story skyscraper designed by Miami architects Arquitectonica, that tops the E Walk entertainment and retail complex at 42nd Street and Eighth Avenue *(see p142)*. Other attractions include an outpost of Madame Tussaud's Wax Museum at 42nd Street, between Seventh and Eighth Avenues; ESPN Zone, a huge sports bar and video game complex at 1472 Broadway and 42nd Street; and Toys 'R' Us at 1514 Broadway.

W.C. Fields (far left) and Eddie Cantor (holding top hat, right) in the 1918 *Ziegfeld Follies* at the New Amsterdam Theater

# New Amsterdam Theater **11**

*214 W 42nd St.* **Map** *8 E1.* **Tel** *(212) 282-2900.* Ⓜ *42nd St-Times Sq.* ◪ *10am–3pm Mon–Tue, 10am–11am Thu–Sat, 10am Sun; (212) 282-2907.*

This was the most opulent theater in the United States when it opened in 1903, and the first to have an Art Nouveau interior. It was owned for a time by Florenz Ziegfeld, who produced his famous *Follies* revue here between 1914 and 1918 – with Broadway's first $5 ticket price. He remodeled the roof garden into another theater, the Aerial Gardens. This is one of the fine early theaters on 42nd Street that fell on hard times. With the rehabilitation of Times Square its fortunes rose again and it is once more in Show Business.

# Group Health Insurance Building **12**

*330 W 42nd St.* **Map** *8 D1.* Ⓜ *42nd St-8th Ave.* ◯ *office hours.*

This 1931 design by Raymond Hood was the only New York building selected for the influential International Style survey of 1932 *(see p43)*. Its unusual design gives it a stepped profile seen from east and west, but a slab effect viewed from the north or south. The exterior's horizontal bands of blue-green terracotta have earned it the nickname "jolly green giant." Step inside to see the classic Art Deco lobby of opaque glass and stainless steel.

One block west is Theater Row, a pleasant group of Off-Broadway theaters and cafés.

# Paramount Building **13**

*1501 Broadway.* **Map** *8 E1.* Ⓜ *34th St.*

The fabulous ground-floor movie theater where bobby-soxers stood in line in the 1940s to hear Frank Sinatra perform is gone, but there's still a theatrical feel to the massive building designed by Rapp & Rapp in 1927. On each side 14 symmetrical setbacks rise to an Art Deco crown – a tower, clock, and globe. In the heyday of the "Great White Way," the tower was lit, with an observation deck at the top. The Hard Rock Cafe is now here, along with a retail store and a concert area.

Art Deco top of the Paramount Building

# Shubert Alley ⓮

Between W 44th and W 45th St.
**Map** 12 E5. Ⓜ 42nd St-Times Sq.
See **Entertainment** p342.

The playhouses on the streets west of Broadway are rich in theater lore – and in notable architecture. Two classic theaters built in 1913 are the Booth (222 West 45th Street), named after actor Edwin Booth, and the Shubert (225 West 44th), after theater baron Sam S. Shubert. They form the west wall of Shubert Alley, where aspiring actors lined up, hoping for a casting in a Shubert play.

A *Chorus Line* ran at the Shubert until 1990, for a record 6,137 performances; Katharine Hepburn starred earlier in *The Philadelphia Story*. Across from the 44th Street end of the alley is the St. James, where Rodgers and Hammerstein made their debut with *Oklahoma!* in 1941, followed by *The King and I*. Nearby is Sardi's, the restaurant where actors waited for opening-night reviews. Irving Berlin staged *The Music Box Revue* opposite the other end of the alley in 1921. His Music Box Theater has since housed many famous shows.

The tiled Moorish facade of the City Center of Music and Dance

## MONY Tower ⓯

1740 Broadway. **Map** 12 E4.
Ⓜ 57th St. ⚫ to the public.

Built in 1950, the head office of the Mutual of New York insurance company (now MONY Financial Services) has a weather vane that tells you everything except the wind direction. The mast turns green for fair, orange for cloudy, flashing orange for rain and white for snow. Lights moving up the mast mean warmer weather; lights going down mean get out your overcoat!

## City Center of Music and Dance ⓰

131 W 55th St. **Map** 12 E4.
**Tel** (212) 581-1212. Ⓜ 57th St.
🚫 ♿ See **Entertainment** p346.
**www**.citycenter.org

This highly ornate Moorish structure with its dome of Spanish tiles was designed in 1924 as a Masonic Shriners' Temple. It was saved from the developers by Mayor LaGuardia, becoming home to the New York City Opera and Ballet in 1943. When the troupes moved to Lincoln Center, City Center lived on as a major venue for dance. Renovation work has preserved the delightful excesses of the architecture.

## Carnegie Hall ⓱

154 W 57th Street. **Map** 12 E3.
**Tel** (212) 247-7800. Ⓜ 57th St,
59th St. **Museum** 🕐 11am–4:30pm
daily & after concerts. ⚫ Wed.
🚫 ♿ 🎥 Mon–Fri, during season.
🎫 See **Entertainment** p350.
**www**.carnegiehall.org

Financed by millionaire philanthropist Andrew Carnegie, New York's first great concert hall opened in 1891 in what was then a suburb of the city. The terra-cotta and brick Renaissance–style building has among the best acoustics in the world. On opening night, Tchaikovsky was a guest conductor and New York's finest families

Auditorium of the Shubert Theater, built by Henry Herts in 1913

Carnegie Hall offering some of the best acoustics in the world

attended. For many years
Carnegie Hall was home to
the New York Philharmonic,
under such conductors as
Arturo Toscanini, Leopold
Stokowski, Bruno Walter, and
Leonard Bernstein. Playing
Carnegie Hall quickly became
an international symbol of
success for both classical
and popular musicians.

A campaign led by violinist
Isaac Stern in the 1950s saved
the site from re-
development, and
in 1964 it was
made a national
landmark.
Renovation in
1986 brought
the bronze
balconies and
the ornamental
plaster back to
their original
splendor. In
1991, a museum
opened next to
the first-tier
level, telling the
story of the first
100 years of "The
House that Music
Built." In 2003,
the Judy and Arthur Zankel
Hall re-established the lower
level as a performance venue.

**Millionaire
Andrew
Carnegie**

Top orchestras and
performers from around the
world still fill Carnegie Hall,
and the corridors are lined
with memorabilia of artists
who have performed here.

# Alwyn Court
# Apartments ⓲

180 W 58th St. **Map** 12 E3.
Ⓜ *57th St.* ⬤ *to the public.*

You can't miss it – not
with the fanciful crowns,
dragons, and other French
Renaissance-style terracotta
carvings covering the exterior
of this 1909 Harde and Short
apartment building. The
ground floor has lost its
cornice, but the rest of the
building is intact, and it's
one of a kind in the city.

The facade follows the
style of François I, whose
symbol, a crowned salamander, can be seen above the
entrance to the building.

The interior courtyard
features a dazzling display
of the illusionistic skills of
artist Richard Haas, in which
plain walls are transformed
into "carved" stonework.

The crowned salamander, symbol
of François I, on Alwyn Court

# Intrepid Sea-Air-
# Space Museum ⓳

Pier 86, W 46th St. **Map** 11 A5. 🚻
(877) 957-SHIP. 🚌 M16, M42, M50.
⬤ Apr–Sep: 10am–5pm Mon–Fri;
10am–6pm Sat, Sun and hols; Oct–
Mar: 10am–5pm Tue–Sun and hols.
🎫 🏪 www.intrepidmuseum.org

Exhibits on board this World
War II aircraft carrier include
fighter planes from the 1940s,
the A-12, the world's fastest
spy plane, and the *Growler*,
a guided-missile submarine.

The workings of today's
super-carriers are traced in
Stern Hall, while Technologies
Hall looks at the rockets of
the future and includes two
flight simulators. Mission
Control offers live coverage
of NASA shuttle missions.

The *Intrepid* was docked in
New Jersey in 2007 for an over-
haul. It will reopen in 2008.

The flight deck of the Intrepid with
fighter and spy planes on display

# Museum of Arts
# and Design ⓴

2 Columbus Circle. **Map** 12 D3. **Tel**
(212) 956-3535. Ⓜ *5th Ave-53rd St.*
⬤ 10am–6pm daily (to 8pm Thu). ⬤
public hols. 🎫 📷 ♿ 🏪 **Lectures,
films.** 🏪 www.madmuseum.org

The leading American cultural
institution of its kind, this
museum is dedicated to
contemporary objects in an
array of media ranging from
clay and glass to wood, metal,
and fiber. The permanent
collection includes over 2,000
artifacts by international
craftsmen and designers. The
store also offers visitors the
chance to purchase items by
top-class American designers.

# LOWER MIDTOWN

From Beaux Arts to Art Deco, this section of midtown boasts some fine architecture. Quiet, residential Murray Hill was named for a country estate that once occupied the site. By the turn of the century, it was home to many of New York's first families, including the financier J.P. Morgan, whose library,

**Brass door, Fred F. French Building**

now a museum, reveals the grandeur of the age. The commercial pace quickens at 42nd Street, near Grand Central Terminal, where tall office buildings line the streets. However, few of the newer buildings have equaled the Beaux Arts Terminal itself or such Art Deco beauties as the Chrysler Building.

## SIGHTS AT A GLANCE

**Historic Streets and Buildings**
Chanin Building ❹
Chrysler Building ❺
Daily News Building ❻
Fred F. French Building ⓬
*Grand Central Terminal pp156– 7* ❷
Helmsley Building ❽
Home Savings of America ❸
Sniffen Court ⓯
Tudor City ❼

**Museums and Galleries**
Japan Society ⓫
*Morgan Library & Museum pp164– 5* ⓮

**Modern Architecture**
MetLife Building ❶
Nos. 1 and 2 United Nations Plaza ❾
*United Nations pp160–63* ❿

**Churches**
Church of the Incarnation ⓭

**GETTING THERE**
By subway, take the Lexington Avenue 4, 5 or 6 trains to 42nd Street–Grand Central. Buses M15, M101/102, M1, M2, M3 and M4 run along the area's avenues, while the M34 and M42 are the crosstown buses.

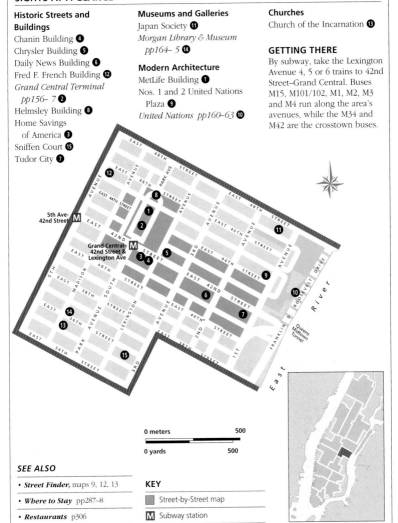

0 meters    500
0 yards    500

**KEY**

▨ Street-by-Street map

Ⓜ Subway station

◁ **The stainless-steel–coated spire of the Chrysler Building**

# Street by Street: Lower Midtown

A walk in the neighborhood allows you to see an eclectic mix of New York's architectural styles. Step back to appreciate the contours of the tallest skyscrapers, and step inside to experience the many fine interiors, from modern atriums such as those in the Philip Morris Building and Ford Foundation buildings to the ornate details of the Home Savings Bank and the soaring spaces of Grand Central Terminal.

**MetLife Building**
*This skyscraper, built by Pan Am in 1963, towers above Park Avenue* ❶

★ **Grand Central Terminal**
*The vast, vaulted interior is a splendid reminder of the heyday of train travel* ❷

Grand Central-42nd St. subway (lines S, 4, 5, 6, 7)

**The Philip Morris Building** is the headquarters of a tobacco company. It houses a branch of the Whitney Museum, which specializes in modern American art.

## STAR SIGHTS

- ★ Chrysler Building
- ★ Daily News Building
- ★ Grand Central Terminal
- ★ Home Savings of America

**Chanin Building**
*Built for self-made real estate mogul Irwin Chanin in the 1920s, this building has a fine Art Deco lobby* ❹

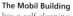

**The Mobil Building** has a self-cleaning stainless steel facade that is embossed in geometric patterns to prevent it from warping. It was built in 1955.

**Brass door, Home Savings Bank**

★ **Home Savings of America**
*Formerly the headquarters of the Bowery Savings Bank, this is one of the finest bank buildings in New York. Architects York & Sawyer designed it to resemble a Romanesque palace* ❸

## Helmsley Building
*Straddling Park Avenue between 45th and 46th, its ornate entrance symbolized the wealth of its first occupants, New York Central Railroad* **8**

**Mailbox in the Chrysler Building**

**LOCATOR MAP**
*See Manhattan Map pp14–15*

**KEY**

– – – Suggested route

| 0 meters | 100 |
| 0 yards | 100 |

## ★ Chrysler Building
*O rnamented with automotive motifs, this Art Deco delight was built in 1930 for the Chrysler car company* **5**

**Worker resting during construction of the Chrysler Building**

**The Ford Foundation Building**
is the headquarters of Ford's philanthropic arm. It has a lovely interior garden surrounded by a cube-shaped building made of pinkish gray granite, glass, and steel.

**Ralph J. Bunche Park**

## ★ Daily News Building
*The Art Deco former home of the newspaper has a revolving globe in the lobby* **6**

## Tudor City
*This 1928 private residential complex has 3,000 apartments. Built in the Tudor style, it features fine stonework details* **7**

# MetLife Building ❶

200 Park Ave. **Map** 13 A5.
Ⓜ *42nd St-Grand Central.*
◯ *office hours.* 🍸 🍴

**Lobby of the MetLife Building**

Once, the sculptures atop the Grand Central Terminal stood out against the sky. Then this colossus, formerly called the Pan Am Building and designed by Walter Gropius, Emery Roth and Sons, and Pietro Belluschi, rose up in 1963 to block the Park Avenue view. It dwarfed the terminal and aroused universal dislike. At the time it was the largest commercial building in the world, and the dismay over its scale helped thwart a later plan to build a tower over the terminal itself.

It is ironic that the New York skies were blocked by Pan Am, a company that had opened up the skies as a means of travel for millions of people. When the company began in 1927, Charles Lindbergh, fresh from his solo trans-atlantic flight, was one of their pilots and an adviser on new routes. By 1936, Pan Am managed to introduce the first trans-Pacific passenger route, and in 1947 they introduced the first round-the-world route.

The building's famous roof-top heliport was abandoned in 1977 after a freak accident showered debris on to the surrounding streets. Now Pan Am itself has gone, too, and in 1981 the entire building was sold to the Metropolitan Life organization.

# Grand Central Terminal ❷

*See pp156–7.*

# Home Savings of America ❸

110 E 42nd St. **Map** 9 A1. Ⓜ *42nd St- Grand Central.* ◯ *by appointment only.* **Tel** *Cipriani (212) 499 0599*

Many consider this 1923 building the best work of the best bank architects of the 1920s. York & Sawyer chose the style of a Romanesque basilica for the uptown offices of the venerable Bowery Savings Bank (now Home Savings of America). An arched entry leads into the vast banking room, with a high beamed ceiling, marble mosaic floors, and marble columns that support the stone arches that soar overhead.

**Facade of Home Savings of America building**

Between the columns are unpolished mosaic panels of marble from France and Italy. The rich detailing includes symbolic animal motifs, such as a squirrel representing thrift and a lion for power.

# Chanin Building ❹

122 E 42nd St. **Map** 9 A1.
Ⓜ *42nd St-Grand Central.*
◯ *office hours.*

**Stonework detail on the Chanin Building**

Once the headquarters of Irwin S. Chanin, one of New York's leading real estate developers, the 56-story tower was the first skyscraper in the Grand Central area, a harbinger of things to come. It was designed by Sloan & Robertson in 1929 and is one of the best examples of the Art Deco period. A wide bronze band, patterned with birds and fish, runs the full length of the facade; the terracotta base is decorated with a luxuriant tangle of stylized leaves and flowers. Inside, Radio City's sculptor René Chambellan worked on the reliefs and the bronze grills, elevator doors, mailboxes, clocks, and pattern of waves in the floor. The vestibule reliefs chart the career of Chanin, who was a self-made man.

**Carved detail in the banking hall of Home Savings of America**

# Chrysler Building ●

405 Lexington Ave. **Map** 9 A1.
*Tel* (212) 682-3070. Ⓜ *42nd St-Grand Central.* ◯ *office hours (7am–6pm), lobby only.* 📷 ♿

Stainless-steel gargoyle on the Chrysler Building

Walter P. Chrysler began his career in a Union Pacific Railroad machine shop, but his passion for the motor car helped him rise swiftly to the top of the new industry, to found, in 1925, the corporation bearing his name. His wish for a headquarters in New York that symbolized his company led to a building that will always be linked with the golden age of motoring. Following Chrysler's wishes, the stainless-steel Art Deco spire resembles a car radiator grill; the building's series of stepped setbacks are emblazoned with winged radiator caps, wheels and stylized automobiles; and there are gargoyles modeled on hood ornaments from the 1929 Chrysler Plymouth.

It stands at 1,046ft (320 m) but it lost the title of tallest building in the world to the Empire State Building a few months after its completion in 1930. William Van Alen's 77-story Chrysler Building and its shining crown are still among the city's best-known and most-loved landmarks.

The crowning spire was kept a secret until the last moment, when, having been built in the fire shaft, it was raised into position through the roof, ensuring that the building would be higher than the Bank of Manhattan, then just completed downtown by Van Alen's great rival, H. Craig Severance.

Van Alen was poorly rewarded for his labors. Chrysler accused him of accepting bribes from contractors and refused to pay him. Van Alen's career never recovered from the slur.

The stunning lobby, once used as a showroom for Chrysler cars, was perfectly restored in 1978. It is lavishly decorated with patterned marbles and granite from around the world and has chromed steel trim. A vast painted ceiling by Edward

Elevator door at the Chrysler Building

Trumball shows transportation scenes of the late 1920s.

Although the Chrysler Corporation never occupied the building as their headquarters, their name remains, as firm a fixture as the gargoyles.

Entrance to the Daily News Building

# Daily News Building ●

220 E 42nd St. **Map** 9 B1.
Ⓜ *42nd St-Grand Central.*
◯ *8am–6pm Mon–Fri.*

The Daily News was founded in 1919, and by 1925 it was a million-seller. It was known, rather scathingly, as "the servant girl's bible," for its concentration on scandals, celebrities, and murders, its readable style and heavy use of illustration. Over the years it has stuck to what it does best, and the formula paid off handsomely. It revealed stories such as the romance of Edward VIII and Mrs. Simpson, and has become renowned for its punchy headlines that sum up the mood of the moment. Its circulation figures are still among the highest in the United States.

Its headquarters, designed by Raymond Hood in 1930, has rows of brown and black brick alternating with windows to create a vertical striped effect. Hood's lobby is familiar to many as that of the *Daily Planet* in the 1980s *Superman* movies. It includes the world's largest interior globe, and bronze lines on the floor indicate the direction of world cities and the position of the planets. At night, the intricate detail over the front entrance of the building is lit from within by neon. The newspaper's offices are now on West 33rd Street, and the future of the building is in some doubt.

# Grand Central Terminal ❷

In 1871 Cornelius Vanderbilt opened a
railway station on 42nd Street. Although
often revamped, it was never large enough
and was finally demolished. The present
station opened in 1913. This Beaux Arts
gem has been a gateway to and symbol of
the city ever since. Its glory is the soaring
main concourse and the way it separates
pedestrian and train traffic. The building
has a steel frame covered with plaster and
marble. Reed & Stern were in charge of
the logistical planning; Warren & Wetmore
for the overall design. The restoration by
architects Beyer
Blinder Belle
is awesome.

**42nd Street colonnaded facade**

**Statuary on the 42nd Street Facade**
*Jules-Alexis Coutans sculptures of Mercury,*
*Hercules, and Minerva crown the main entrance.*

**Main Concourse Level**

**Circumferential Road**

**Subway**

**Cornelius Vanderbilt**
*The railroad magnate was*
*known as the "Commodore."*

**Commuters** use the terminal.
Half a million people pass
through it each day. An escalator
leads up into the MetLife
Building, where there are
specialty shops and restaurants.

**Vanderbilt Hall**, adjacent to
the Main Concourse, is a
good example of Beaux Arts
architecture. It is decorated
with gold chandeliers and
pink marble.

**Grand Central Oyster Bar**
*This popular spot (see p306),*
*with its yellow Guastavino*
*tiles, is one of the many*
*eateries in the station. The*
*dining concourse is*
*enormous, with food,*
*snacks, and drinks to suit*
*all tastes.*

## STAR SIGHTS

★ Central Information

★ Grand Staircases

★ Main Concourse

## VISITORS' CHECKLIST

E 42nd St at Park Ave. **Map** 13 A5.
**Tel** (212) 532-4900. Ⓜ 4, 5, 6,
7, S to Grand Central. 🚌 M1–5,
M42, M98, M101–104, Q32.
🕐 5:30am–1:30am daily. 📷 ♿
📅 12:30pm Wed & Fri (free);
(212) 340-2347. 🍴 🖥 🛄
**Baggage check; lost & found**
(212) 340 2555
**www**.grandcentralterminal.com

### ★ Main Concourse
*This vast pedestrian area with its high vaulted ceiling is dominated by three great arched windows, 75 ft (23 m) high on each side.*

### Vaulted Ceiling
*A medieval manuscript provided the basis for French artist Paul Helleu's zodiac design containing over 2,500 stars. Lights pinpoint the major constellations.*

**The Lower Level**
is linked to the other levels by stairways, ramps, and brand new escalators.

### Grand Staircase
*There are now two of these double flights of marble steps, styled after the staircase in Paris' Opera House, and a vivid reminder of the glamorous days of early rail travel.*

### ★ Central Information
*This four-faced clock tops the travel information booth on the main concourse.*

# Tudor City ❼

E 41st–43rd St between 1st and 2nd Aves. **Map** 9 B1. Ⓜ *42nd St-Grand Central.* 🚌 *M15, M27, M42, M50, M104.* **www**.tudorcity.com

Dating from 1925–8, this early urban renewal effort by the Fred F. French Company was designed as a middle-class city within the city. Rents were modest, thanks to the "large-scale production." There are 12 buildings containing 3,000 apartments, a hotel, shops, restaurants, a post office, and two small private parks, all built in the Tudor Gothic style.

In the mid-19th century the area was the haunt of gangs and criminals and was known as Corcoran's Roost, after Paddy Corcoran, the leader of the notorious "Rag Gang." The East River shore was lined with glue factories, slaughter-houses, breweries, and a gasworks. Some were still there when Tudor City was planned, so its buildings have only a few outward-facing windows from which residents might enjoy what is now a great view of the river.

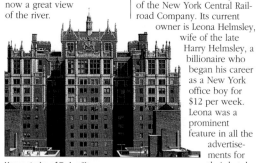

**Upper stories of Tudor City**

# Helmsley Building ❽

230 Park Ave. **Map** 13 A5. Ⓜ *42nd St-Grand Central.* ⭘ *office hours.*

One of the great New York views looks south down Park Avenue to the Helmsley Building straddling the busy traffic flow beneath. There is just one flaw – the monolithic MetLife Building (which was built by Pan Am as its corporate headquarters in

**Performance at the Japan Society**

1963) that towers behind it, replacing the building's former backdrop, the sky.

Built by Warren & Whetmore in 1929, the Helmsley Building was originally the headquarters of the New York Central Railroad Company. Its current owner is Leona Helmsley, wife of the late Harry Helmsley, a billionaire who began his career as a New York office boy for $12 per week. Leona was a prominent feature in all the advertisements for their hotel chain – until her imprisonment in 1989 for tax evasion on a grand scale. Many observers believe that the extravagant glitter of the building's face-lift is due to Leona's over-blown taste in decor.

# 1 & 2 United Nations Plaza ❾

**Map** 13 B5. Ⓜ *42nd St-Grand Central.* 🚌 *M15, M27, M42, M50, M104.*

These two great columns of blue-green mirrored glass are set at an angle to each other; the play of light and reflections on their gleaming sides and sloping setbacks make them seem a giant, ever-changing, work of modern art. The marble and mirrored interiors are also stunning. They house streamlined modern offices and, in No. 1, the Millennium United Nations Plaza Hotel. Here, the guest list frequently includes many UN delegates from all over the world as well as a number of visiting heads of state. Even the stresses of international diplomacy must ease when one is floating lazily in the glassed-in swimming pool, enjoying the bird's-eye views of the city and the United Nations itself.

# United Nations ❿

*See pp160 –63.*

# Japan Society ⓫

333 E 47th St. **Map** 13 B5. *Tel* (212) 832-1155. Ⓜ *42nd St-Grand Central.* 🚌 *M15, M27, M50.* *Gallery* ⭘ *11am–6pm Tue–Thu, 11am–9pm Fri, 11am–5pm Sat–Sun.* 🚫 ♿ 🎫 **www**.japansociety.org

The headquarters of the Japan Society, founded in 1907 to foster understanding and cultural exchange between Japan and the US, was built with the help of

**Roman gods reclining against the Helmsley Building clock**

John D. Rockefeller III, who underwrote costs of some $4.3 million. The striking black building with its delicate sun grilles was designed by Tokyo architects Junzo Yoshimura and George Shimamoto in 1971. It includes an auditorium, a language center, a research library, a museum gallery, and traditional Oriental gardens.

Changing exhibits include a variety of Japanese arts, from swords to kimonos to scrolls. The society offers programs of Japanese performing arts, lectures, language classes, and many business workshops for American and Japanese executives and managers.

## Fred F. French Building **12**

521 5th Ave. **Map** 12 F5.
**M** 42nd St-Grand Central.
**O** office hours.

Built in 1927 to house the best-known real estate firm of the day, this is a fabulously opulent creation.
It was designed by French's chief architect, H. Douglas Ives, in collaboration with Sloan & Robertson, whose

**Tiffany stained-glass window in the Church of the Incarnation**

other work included the Chanin Building (see p154). They handsomely blended Near Eastern, ancient Egyptian and Greek styles with early Art Deco forms.

Multicolored faïence ornaments decorate the upper facade, and the water tower is hidden in a false top level of the building. Its disguise is an elaborate one, with reliefs showing a rising sun flanked by griffins and bees and symbols of virtues such as integrity and industry. Winged Assyrian beasts ride on a bronze frieze over the entrance. These exotic themes continue into the vaulted lobby, with its elaborate polychrome ceiling decoration and 25 gilt-bronze doors.

This was the first building project to employ members of the Native Canadian Caughnawaga tribe as construction workers. They did not fear heights and soon became highly sought-after as scaffolders for many of the city's most famous skyscrapers.

**Lobby of the Fred F. French Building**

## Church of the Incarnation **13**

209 Madison Ave. **Map** 9 A2. **Tel** (212) 689-6350. **M** 42nd St-Grand Central, 33rd St. **O** 11:30am–2pm Mon–Fri (also 4–7pm Tue, 5–7pm Wed), 1–4pm Sat, 8:15am–12:30pm Sun. **†** 12:15pm & 6:30pm Wed, 12:45pm Fri, 8:30am & 11am Sun. **◎ ♿ ✉** By appointment.
**www**.churchoftheincarnation.org

This Episcopal church dates from 1864, when Madison Avenue was home to the elite. Its patterned sandstone and brownstone exterior is typical of the period. The interior has an oak communion rail by Daniel Chester French; a chancel mural by John La Farge; and stained-glass windows by La Farge, Tiffany, William Morris and Edward Burne-Jones.

## Morgan Library & Museum **14**

See pp164–5.

## Sniffen Court **15**

150–158 E 36th St. **Map** 9 A2.
**M** 33rd St.

Here is a delightful, intimate courtyard of ten brick Romanesque revival carriage houses, built by John Sniffen in the 1850s. They are perfectly and improbably preserved off a busy block in modern New York. The house at the south end was used as a studio by the American sculptor Malvina Hoffman, whose plaques of Greek horsemen decorate the exterior wall.

**Malvina Hoffman's studio**

# United Nations 🔟

Founded in 1945 with 51 members, the United Nations now numbers 189 nations. Its aims are to preserve world peace, to promote self-determination, and to aid economic and social well-being around the globe. New York was chosen as the UN headquarters, and John D. Rockefeller, Jr. donated $8.5 million for the purchase of the site. The chief architect was American Wallace Harrison, who worked with an international Board of Design Consultants. The 18-acre (7-ha) site is an international zone, with its own stamps and post office. In 2006, the UN's General Assembly approved a $1.6-billion renovation of the complex that will take several years to complete; visitors should phone ahead to check access.

**Flag of the United Nations**

**United Nations headquarters**

**Secretariat building**

**The Conference Building** houses meeting rooms for the Security Council, the Trusteeship Council and the Economic and Social Council.

**★ Security Council**
*Delegates and their assistants confer around the horseshoe-shaped table while verbatim reporters and other UN staff members sit at the long table in the center.*

**Trusteeship Council**

**Economic and Social Council**

**STAR FEATURES**

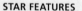

★ General Assembly

★ Peace Bell

★ Reclining Figure

★ Security Council

**★ Peace Bell**
*Cast from the coins of 60 nations, this gift from Japan hangs on a cypress pagoda shaped like a Shinto shrine.*

**Rose Garden**
*Twenty-five varieties of roses adorn the manicured gardens on the East River.*

★ **Reclining Figure** (1982)
*This bronze statue was a gift from the Henry Moore Foundation.*

## VISITORS' CHECKLIST

1st Ave at 46th St. **Map** 13 C5.
**Tel** (212) 963-8687. Ⓜ 4, 5, 6, 7 and S to 42nd St-Grand Central Terminal. 🚌 M15, M27, M42, M104. ⬜ Mar–Dec: 9:30am–4:45pm Mon–Fri, 10am–4:30pm Sat–Sun; Jan–Feb: Mon–Fri. ⬤ Jan 1, President's Day, Eid, Thanksgiving, Dec 25 (limited hours during year-end hols). 📷 ♿ 🎦 in 17 languages. **Lectures, films.** 🍴 🛍 www.un.org

**General** ★ **Assembly**
*This is the only UN organ in which all member states are represented. One regular, three-month session is held each year.*

**Colors of the World**
*Flags of member nations fly in front of the UN complex.*

**Non-Violence** (1988)
*Luxembourg donated this peace sculpture by Karl Fredrik Reutersward.*

**The statue of peace** was a gift from Yugoslavia.

**Visitors' entrance**

**Let Us Beat Swords Into Plowshares**
*This bronze statue (1958) by Soviet sculptor Evgeny Vuchetich symbolizes the main goal of the United Nations.*

# The Work of the United Nations

The goals of the United Nations are pursued by three UN councils and a General Assembly comprising all of its member nations. The Secretariat carries out the administrative work of the organization. Guided tours allow visitors to see the Security Council Chamber. Often there is a chance to briefly observe a meeting.

**Secretary General**

**Translators** interpret debates in Arabic, Chinese, French, Russian, Spanish, or English.

**Reporters**

**Nation delegates** sit in alphabetical order by country, but who sits at the front is decided before every session by drawing lots.

**Public gallery**

**Public entrance**

**GENERAL ASSEMBLY HALL**

## GENERAL ASSEMBLY

The General Assembly is the governing body of the UN and has regular sessions each year from mid-September to mid-December. Special sessions are also held when the Security Council or a majority of members request one. All member states are represented with an equal vote, regardless of size. The General Assembly may discuss any international problem raised by the members or by other UN bodies. Although it cannot enact laws, recommendations strongly influence world opinion; these require a two-thirds majority vote.

Lots are drawn before each session to determine the seating in the chamber for the delegations. All 1,898 seats in the chamber are equipped with earphones that offer simultaneous translations in

several languages. The General Assembly also appoints the Secretary General (on the recommendation of the Security Council), approves the UN budgets and elects the non-permanent members of

*Foucault's Pendulum* (Holland); its slowly rotating swing is proof of the earth's rotation on its axis

the Councils. Together with the Security Council, it also appoints the judges of the International Court of Justice, based in the Netherlands.

## SECURITY COUNCIL

The most powerful part of the UN is the Security Council. It strives to achieve international

**Mural symbolizing peace and freedom by Per Krohg (Norway)**

peace and security and intervenes in crises such as the fighting in Iraq and Afghanistan. It is the only body whose decisions member states are obliged to obey as well as the only one in continuous session.

Five of its members – China, France, the Russian Federation, the United Kingdom, and the United States – are permanent. The other nations are elected by the General Assembly to serve two-year terms.

When international conflicts arise, the Council first tries to seek agreement by mediation. If fighting breaks out, it may issue cease-fire orders and impose military or economic sanctions. It could also decide to send UN peace-keeping missions into troubled areas to separate opposing factions until issues can be resolved through diplomatic channels.

Military intervention is the Council's last resort. UN forces may be deployed, and peace-keeping forces are resident in such places as Cyprus and the Middle East.

## TRUSTEESHIP COUNCIL

The smallest of the councils, this is the only UN body whose workload is decreasing. The council was established in 1945 with the goal of fostering peaceful independence for non-self-governing territories or colonies. Since then, more than 80 colonies have gained self-rule, and the number of people living in dependent territories has been reduced from 750 million to about 3 million. The Trusteeship Council currently consists of the five permanent members of the Security Council.

Zanetti mural (Dominican Republic) in the Conference Building depicting the struggle for peace

Trusteeship Council Chamber

## ECONOMIC AND SOCIAL COUNCIL

The 54 members of this Council work to improve the standard of living and social welfare around the world, goals that consume 80% of the UN's resources. It makes recommendations to the General Assembly, to each member nation and to the UN's specialized agencies. The Council is assisted by commissions dealing with regional economic problems, human rights abuses, population, narcotics, and women's rights. It also works with the International Labor Organization, the World Health Organization, UNICEF, and other global welfare organizations.

## SECRETARIAT

An international staff of 16,000 works for the Secretariat to carry out the day-to-day work of the United Nations. The Secretariat is headed by the Secretary General, who plays a key role as a spokesperson in the organization's peace-keeping efforts. The Secretary

General is appointed by the General Assembly for a five-year term. On January 1, 2007, Ban Ki-moon of South Korea became the latest Secretary General.

## IMPORTANT EVENTS IN UN HISTORY

Soviet premier Krushchev speaking to the General Assembly in 1960

The UN depends on voluntary compliance and military support from its members to keep the peace in the event

of disputes. In 1948, the UN declared South Korea the legitimate government of Korea; two years later, it played a leading role in defending South Korea against North Korea. In 1949, the UN helped negotiate a cease-fire between Indonesia and the Netherlands and set up a conference that led to the Dutch granting independence to Indonesia, returning in 2002 to supervise elections in East Timor.

In 1964 a UN military force was sent to Cyprus to keep peace between the Greeks and Turks, and still remains. Persistent problems in the Middle East have kept UN forces in the area since 1974, the year that the People's Republic of China – long refused membership in favor of Taiwan – gained UN membership. In the 1990s, the UN was heavily involved in the break-up of Yugoslavia, and more recently in the conflicts in Afghanistan and Iraq. A 2004 UN mission to Congo was plagued by accusations of sexual abuse by UN peace-keepers.

At any given time at least half a dozen missions are active somewhere in the world. The UN was awarded the Nobel Peace Prize in 1988 and 2001.

## WORKS OF ART AT THE UN

The UN Building has acquired numerous works of art and reproductions by major artists; many have been gifts from member nations. Most of them have either a peace or international friendship theme. The legend on Norman Rockwell's *The Golden Rule* reads "Do unto others as you would have them do unto you." Marc Chagall designed a large stained-glass window as a memorial to former Secretary General Dag Hammarskjöld, who was accidentally killed while on a peace mission in 1961. There is a Henry Moore sculpture in the grounds (limited access) and many other sculptures and paintings by the artists of many nations.

*The Golden Rule* (1985), a large mosaic by Norman Rockwell

# Morgan Library & Museum ⑭

The Morgan Library reopened in 2006 after an expansion program. The collection, accumulated by banker Pierpont Morgan, is housed in a magnificent palazzo-style 1902 building by architects McKim, Mead & White. Morgan's son, J.P.Morgan, Jr., made it a public institution in 1924. One of the world's finest collections of rare manuscripts, prints, books, and bindings is on display in a complex that includes the original library and the home of J.P. Morgan, Jr.

**Exterior of the original library building**

**The Song of Los** *(1795)*
*Mystic poet William Blake designed and engraved this plate for one of his most innovative works.*

Morgan House

Main entrance

Gallery

## KEY TO FLOOR PLAN

☐ Exhibition space

▨ Non-exhibition space

**Gutenberg Bible** *(1455)*
*Printed on vellum, this volume is one of only eleven surviving copies.*

## STAR EXHIBITS

★ The West Room

★ The Rotunda

★ East Room

**The Nursery Alice**
*Lewis Carroll's characters are immortalized in John Tenniel's classic illustrations (c. 1865).*

## LIBRARY GUIDE

*Mr. Morgan's Study and the original library contain some of his favorite paintings, objets d'art and rare acquisitions. Changing exhibitions provide visitors access to some of the world's most significant cultural artifacts.*

**West Room (Mr. Morgan's study)**

### Mozart's Horn Concerto in E-flat Major

*The six surviving leaves of this score are written in different colored inks.*

**★ East Room**
*The walls are lined from floor to ceiling with triple tiers of bookcases. Murals show historical figures and their muses, and signs of the zodiac.*

**★ The Rotunda** *(1504)*
*The entrance foyer of the Library has marble columns and pilasters; the marble floor is modeled on the floor in Villa Pia in the Vatican gardens.*

**★ The West Room**
*Renaissance art and an antique, Florentine wooden ceiling adorn this room.*

### PIERPONT MORGAN

Pierpont Morgan (1837–1913) was not only a leading financier but also one of the great collectors of his time. Rare books and original manuscripts were his passion, and inclusion in his collection was an honor. In 1909, when Morgan requested the donation of the manuscript of *Pudd'nhead Wilson*, Mark Twain responded, "One of my high ambitions is gratified."

# UPPER MIDTOWN

pscale New York in all its diversity is here, in this district of churches and synagogues, clubs and museums, grand hotels and famous stores, as well as trend-setting skyscrapers and pockets of luxury living. For almost 30 years from 1833, Upper Midtown was home

1946 Cisitalia in the MoMA

to society names such as Astor and Vanderbilt. In the 1950s, architectural history was made when the Lever and Seagram buildings were erected. These first great modern towers marked midtown Park Avenue's change from a residential street to a prestigious office address.

## SIGHTS AT A GLANCE

### Historic Streets and Buildings
Beekman Place ⓲
Fuller Building ㉑
General Electric Building ⑪
Roosevelt Island ⑲
Sutton Place ⑰
Villard Houses ⑨

### Modern Architecture
Citigroup Center ⑮
IBM Building ③
Lever House ⑬
Seagram Building ⑭
Trump Tower ②

### Museums and Galleries
American Folk Art Museum ⑥
*Museum of Modern Art (MoMA) pp172–5* ⑤

Museum of Television and Radio ⑦

### Churches and Synagogues
Central Synagogue ⑯
St. Bartholomew's Church ⑩
*St. Patrick's Cathedral pp178–9* ⑧
St. Thomas Church ④

### Landmark Hotels
Plaza Hotel ㉒
Waldorf–Astoria ⑫

### Landmark Stores
Bloomingdale's ⑳
Fifth Avenue ①

## KEY

| | |
|---|---|
| ▨ | Street-by-Street map |
| Ⓜ | Subway station |

0 meters  500
0 yards  500

## SEE ALSO
- *Street Finder,* maps 12, 13–14
- *Where to Stay* pp288–9
- *Restaurants* pp306–8

### GETTING THERE
Take the 6 subway to 51st St or the 4, 5, or 6 to 59th St, the N, R, or W to 60th St, or the E or V to 53rd St-5th Ave or 53rd St-Lexington. Bus routes are the M1–4, M15, or M101–3. Crosstown buses are the M27 and M50, and the M31 and M57.

◁ **View down Fifth Avenue**

# Street by Street: Upper Midtown

The luxury stores that are synonymous with Fifth Avenue first blossomed as society moved on uptown. In 1917, Cartier's acquired the mansion of banker Morton F. Plant in exchange for a string of pearls, setting the style for other retailers to follow. But this stretch of midtown is not simply for shoppers. There are three distinctive museums and an equally diverse assembly of architectural styles to enjoy, too.

**Fifth Avenue**
*The popular carriage rides offer tourists a taste of past elegance and a leisurely way to view some of the main sights around this thoroughfare* ❶

**The University Club** was built in 1899 as an elite club for gentlemen.

W 55TH ST

**St. Thomas Church**
*Much of the interior carving was designed by sculptor Lee Lawrie* ❹

**★ Museum of Modern Art**
*One of the world's finest collections of modern art* ❺

**Museum of Television and Radio**
*Exhibitions, seasons of special screenings, live events and a vast library of historic broadcasts are offered at this media museum* ❼

**Fifth Avenue subway (lines E, V)**

**Saks Fifth Avenue** has offered goods in impeccable taste to generations of New Yorkers. *(See p319.)*

**★ St. Patrick's Cathedral**
*This, the largest Catholic cathedral in the United States, is a magnificent Gothic Revival building* ❽

**Olympic Tower**
combines offices, apartments and a skylit atrium within its sleek walls.

**Villard Houses**
*Five handsome brownstone houses now form part of the New York Palace Hotel* ❾

## STAR SIGHTS

★ Museum of Modern Art

★ St. Patrick's Cathedral

**Trump Tower**
*Donald Trump's tower houses many expensive shops* ❷

**Paley Park** is a tiny green oasis, known as a "vest-pocket" park.

**IBM Building**
*A restful atrium is to be found at the base of this polished black granite building* ❸

**Sony Building** has a very distinctive "Chippendale" top.

**Lever House**
*This building is one of the most prominent "glass-box" buildings in New York* ⓭

**LOCATOR MAP**
*See Manhattan Map pp14–15*

**KEY**

– – –   Suggested route

| 0 meters | 100 |
| 0 yards | 100 |

**Tiffany & Company** is renowned for its discreet luxury. The store contains many precious jewels. *(See p329.)*

**Park Avenue Plaza** is a bulky glass prism containing an airy atrium.

**General Electric Building**
*The spiky pinnacle of this building, built in 1931, is meant to symbolize electrical waves* ⓫

**Racquet Club**, a Renaissance palazzo–style building, provides squash and tennis courts for its members.

**St. Bartholomew's Church**
*A Byzantine dome sets this place apart from other Midtown churches* ❿

**51st Street subway (line 6)**

**Waldorf-Astoria**
*Old-world elegance has attracted many famous guests to this hotel, including the late Duke and Duchess of Windsor* ⓬

**Window display at Bergdorf Goodman (see p319)**

# Fifth Avenue ❶

**Map** 12 F3–F4. **M** *5th Ave-53rd St, 5th Ave-59th St.*

In 1883, when William Henry Vanderbilt built his mansion at Fifth Avenue and 51st Street, he started a trend that resulted in palatial residences stretching as far as Central Park, built for top families such as the Astors, Belmonts, and Goulds. Only a few remain to attest to the grandeur of the era.

One of these is the Cartier store at 651 Fifth Avenue, once the home of Morton F. Plant, millionaire and commodore of the New York Yacht Club. As retailers swept north up the avenue – a trend that began in 1906 – society gradually moved to better locations uptown. In 1917, Plant moved to a new mansion at 86th Street, and legend has it that he traded his old home to Pierre Cartier for a perfectly matched string of pearls.

Fifth Avenue has been synonymous with luxury goods ever since. From Cartier at 52nd Street to Tiffany and Bergdorf Goodman at 57th, you will find a range of great brands symbolizing wealth and social standing today, just as Vanderbilt and Astor did over a century ago.

# Trump Tower ❷

725 5th Ave. **Map** 12 F3. *Tel (212) 832-2000.* **M** *5th Ave-53rd St, 5th Ave-59th St.* **Garden level, shops** ◯ *10am–6pm Mon–Sat, noon–5pm Sun.* **Building** ◯ *8am–10pm daily.* ◙ ♿ *Concerts.* 🍴 ▣ 🛈

A glittering, exorbitantly expensive apartment and office tower rises above a lavish six-story atrium with layers of exclusive shops and cafés. Designed in 1983 by Der Scutt of Swanke, Hayden, Connell & Partners, the public space has pink marble, a waterfall, mirrors and glitz. It is the most opulent example of the trend toward vertical shopping centers. The tower is a flamboyant monument to affluence by the developer Donald Trump, a symbol of the excesses of the 1980s (see p33).

Next door, 727 Fifth Avenue is a complete contrast: the location of Tiffany & Co., the prestigious jewelers founded in 1837. Famed for exquisite window displays, the store uses understated but elegant blue packaging as a status symbol in itself. Tiffany's was immortalized by Truman Capote in his 1958 novel *Breakfast at Tiffany's.*

**Entrance to Tiffany and Co., the exclusive jewelry emporium**

# IBM Building ❸

590 Madison Ave. **Map** 12 F3. **M** *5th Ave.* **Garden Plaza** ◯ *8am–10pm daily.* ◙ ♿ **Dahesh Museum of Art**; *(212) 759-0606.* ◯ *11am–6pm Tue–Sun (until 9pm 1st Thu in the month).* ⬤ *public hols.* 🎟 *(free 1st Thu of the month.)* ▣ www.daheshmuseum.org

Completed in 1983, this 43-story tower was designed by Edward Larrabee Barnes. It is a sleek, five-sided prism of gray-green polished granite, with a cantilevered corner at 57th Street. The **Garden Plaza** is open to the public. Near the atrium is a work by American sculptor Michael Heizer, entitled *Levitated Mass.* Inside a low, stainless-steel tank is a huge slab of granite that seems to float on air.

The **Dahesh Museum**, at 580 Madison Avenue, contains paintings, drawings, prints, photographs, and sculptures by popular 19th- and early 20th-century European artists.

**Interior of the Trump Tower atrium**

# St. Thomas Church ❹

1 W 53rd St. **Map** 12 F4. *Tel (212) 757-7013.* Ⓜ *5th Ave-53rd St.* ⏱ *7am–6pm daily.* ✝ *frequent.* 🚫 ♿ 📷 *after 11am service & concerts.* **www**.saintthomaschurch.org

This is the fourth home for this parish and the second on this site. Today's church was built between 1909 and 1914 to replace an earlier structure destroyed in a fire in 1905. The previous building had provided the setting for many of the glittering high-society weddings of the late 19th century. The most lavish of these was in 1895 when heiress Consuelo Vanderbilt married the English Duke of Marlborough.

The limestone building, in French–Gothic style, has a single asymmetrical tower and an off-center nave, novel solutions to the architectural problems posed by its corner position. The richly carved, shimmering white screens behind the altar were designed by architect Bertram Goodhue and sculptor Lee Lawrie. Carvings in the choir stalls, dating from the 1920s, include modern inventions such as the telephone, Presidents Roosevelt and Wilson, and Lee Lawrie himself.

# Museum of Modern Art ❺

*See pp172–5.*

# American Folk Art Museum ❻

45 W 53rd St. **Map** 12 F4. *Tel (212) 265-1040.* Ⓜ *5th Ave-53rd St.* ⏱ *10:30am–5:30pm Tue–Sun (7:30pm Fri).* 📷 ♿ 📷 💻 📷 **www**.folkartmuseum.org

The permanent home for the appreciation and study of American folk art is here, in the first free-standing art museum built in New York since 1966. Designed by the innovative architectural firm of Tod Williams Billie Tsien & Associates and built in 2001,

Beatles Paul, Ringo and John on the "Ed Sullivan Show" in 1964

the structure is clad in panels of white tombasil, a white bronze alloy. The museum has 30,000 sq ft (2,787 sq m) of exhibition space on eight levels. The museum still retains the Eva and Morris Feld Gallery at the Lincoln Square location *(see p214).*

The American Folk Art Museum

# Museum of Television and Radio ❼

25 W 52nd St. **Map** 12 F4. *Tel (212) 621-6800.* Ⓜ *5th Ave-53rd St.* ⏱ *noon–6pm Tue–Sun (8pm Thu). Theaters and screening rooms close 9pm Fri.* ⏱ *public hols.* 📷 🚫 ♿ 📷 💻 **www**.mtr.org

In this one-of-a-kind repository museum, visitors can watch and listen to news and a collection of entertainment and sports documentaries from radio and television's earliest

days to the present. Pop fans can see the early Beatles or a young Elvis Presley making his television debut. Sports enthusiasts can relive classic Olympic competitions. World War II footage might be chosen by students of history or by those who lived through the war. Six choices at any one time can be selected from a computer catalogue that covers a library of over 50,000 programs. The selections are then played on small private areas. There are larger screening areas and a theater for 200, where retrospectives of artists, directors, and topics are shown. There are also photo exhibits, posters and memorabilia.

The museum was the brainchild of William S. Paley, a former head of the CBS TV network. It opened in 1975 as the Museum of Broadcasting on East 53rd Street. It proved so popular that in 1991 it moved into this hi-tech $50 million home in a building reminiscent of an antique radio set.

1960s television star Lucille Ball

# The Museum of Modern Art ❺

**Museum facade on 54th Street**

MoMA contains one of the world's most comprehensive collections of modern art. Founded in 1929, it set the standard for museums of its kind. Following an expansion program, MoMA in Midtown reopened in 2004. The renovated building provides gallery space over six floors, almost twice that of the old museum. Expanses of glass allow abundant natural light both to penetrate inside the building and to bathe the sculpture garden.

**Sculpture Garden**
*The Abby A. Rockefeller Sculpture Garden has a peaceful atmosphere.*

### STAR PAINTINGS

★ Les Demoiselles d'Avignon by Pablo Picasso

---

★ The Starry Night by Vincent Van Gogh

**Christina's World**
*(1948) Andrew Wyeth contrasts an overwhelming horizon with the minutely-studied surroundings of his handicapped neighbor.*

**Bird in Space** *(c. 1928)*
*Constantin Brancusi's elegant bronze sculpture captures the sheer essence of flight.*

### GALLERY GUIDE
*The sculpture garden is on the first floor. The contemporary art, print, and media galleries are on the second floor. Painting and sculpture are exhibited on the second, fourth, and fifth floors. Architecture and design, photography, and drawings are all on the third floor. Changing exhibitions are displayed on the third and sixth floors. Films are shown on the lower level.*

Sculpture garden

First floor

Main entrance

**VISITORS' CHECKLIST**

11 West 53rd St between Fifth
Ave & Avenue of the Americas.
**Map** 12 F4. *Tel* (212) 708-9400.
M 5th Ave-53rd St. M1–4,
M27, M50. 10:30am–5:30pm,
Wed–Mon, 10:30am–8pm Fri.
Tue, Dec 25. groups
www.moma.org

**La Clownesse** *(1896)*
*This is typical of Henri
de Toulouse-Lautrec's
portraits of Parisian
entertainers.*

**Water Lilies** *(c. 1920)*
*Claude Monet's late triptych is a
vast artwork that creates a glowing,
serene environment.*

★ **Les Demoiselles d'Avignon**
*Anticipating Cubism, this portrait
of five prostitutes, which Picasso
painted in 1907, was seen as
revolutionary at the time.*

**KEY TO FLOOR PLAN**

- Sculpture Garden
- Contemporary Art
- Media
- Prints and Illustrated books
- Architecture and Design
- Drawings
- Photography
- Paintings and Sculpture
- Special exhibitions
- Non-exhibition space
- Non-accessible space

★ **The Starry Night** *(1889)*
*The small size of Vincent
Van Gogh's work belies its
passion. This turbulent
night scene remains one
of the most popular
paintings in the collection.*

# Exploring the Collection

The Museum of Modern Art has approximately 150,000 works of art ranging from Post-Impressionist classics to an unrivaled collection of modern and contemporary art, from fine examples of design to early masterpieces of photography and film.

## 1880S TO 1940S PAINTING AND SCULPTURE

*The Persistence of Memory* **by the Surrealist Salvador Dalí (1931)**

Paul Cézanne's monumental *The Bather* and Vincent van Gogh's passionate and transcendent *The Starry Night* are two of the seminal works in the museum's collection of late 19th-century painting. Both Fauvism and Expressionism are well represented with works by Matisse, Derain, Kirchner, and others, while Pablo Picasso's *Les Demoiselles d'Avignon* marks a transition to a new style of painting.

The collection also has an unparalleled number of Cubist paintings, providing an overview of a movement that radically challenged our perception of the world. Among the vast range are Picasso's *Girl with a Mandolin*, Georges Braque's *Man with a Guitar* and *Soda*, and *Guitar and Flowers* by Juan Gris. Works by the Futurists, who brought color and movement to Cubism to depict the dynamic modern world, include Gino Severini's *Dynamic Hieroglyphic of the Bal Tabarin* and *Dynamism of a Soccer Player* by Umberto Boccioni, plus works by Balla, Carrà, and Villon.

The geometric abstract art of the Constructivists is included in a strong representation of Lissitzky, Malevich, and Rodchenko: De Stijl's influence is seen in paintings by Piet Mondrian, such as *Broadway Boogie Woogie*. There is a large body of work by Matisse, such as *Dance I* and *The Red Studio*. Dalí, Miró, and Ernst feature among the bizarre, strangely beautiful Surrealist works.

## POSTWAR PAINTING AND SCULPTURE

The extensive collection of postwar art includes works by Bacon and Dubuffet, and has a particularly strong representation of American artists. The collection of Abstract Expressionist art, for example, includes Jackson Pollock's *One [Number 31, 1950]*, Willem de Kooning's *Women, I*, Arshile Gorky's *Agony*, and *Red, Brown, and*

*The Bather,* **an oil painting by French Impressionist artist Paul Cézanne**

*Black* by Mark Rothko. Other notable works include Jasper Johns' *Flag*, Robert Rauschenberg's *First Landing Jump*, composed of urban refuse, and *Bed,* which consists of bed linen. The Pop Art collection includes Roy Lichtenstein's *Girl with Ball* and *Drowning Girl*, Andy Warhol's famous *Gold Marilyn Monroe*, and Claes Oldenburg's *Giant Soft Fan*.

Works after about 1965 include pieces by Judd, Flavin, Serra, and Beuys, among many others.

## DRAWINGS AND OTHER WORKS ON PAPER

*Man with a Hat* **by Pablo Picasso (1912), a collage with charcoal**

More than 7,000 artworks ranging in size from tiny preparatory pieces to large mural-sized works are among MoMA's holdings. Many drawings use conventional materials, such as pencil, charcoal, pen and ink, pastel, and watercolor. However, there are also collages and mixed-media works composed of paper ephemera, natural products, and man-made goods.

The collection provides an overview of Modernism, from the late 19th century to the present day, including movements such as Cubism, Dadaism, and Surrealism. Drawings by famous and well-established artists, such as Picasso, Miró, and Johns, are exhibited alongside a growing number of works by talented emerging artists.

## PRINTS AND ILLUSTRATED BOOKS

*American Indian Theme II* by
Roy Lichtenstein (1980)

All significant art movements from the 1880s onward are represented in this extensive collection, which provides an overview of printed art. With more than 50,000 items in the department's holdings, there are wide-ranging examples of historical and contemporary printmaking. Works created in such traditional media as etchings, lithographic prints, screenprints, and woodcuts are displayed alongside pieces created using more experimental techniques.

There are some particularly fine examples of works by Pablo Picasso, who is widely considered to be the most important printmaker of the 20th century. There are also many illustrations and prints by other artists including Redon, Munch, Matisse, Dubuffet, Johns, Lichtenstein, and Warhol. The works are displayed in the galleries on a rotating basis.

## PHOTOGRAPHY

The photography collection begins with the invention of the medium around 1840. It includes pictures by fine artists, journalists, scientists, and entrepreneurs, as well as amateur photographers.

Among the highlights of the collection are some of the best-known works by American and European photographers including Atget, Stieglitz, Lange, Arbus, Steichen, Cartier-Bresson, and Kertesz. There is also a range of contemporary practitioners,

## FILM DEPARTMENT

With a collection of some 10,000 films and four million stills, the collection can offer a wide range of programs, including retrospectives of individual directors and actors, films in specific genres and experimental work, as well as a broad range of other exhibitions. Film conservation is a key part of the department's work. Today's top directors are donating copies of their films to help fund this expensive but vital work.

Film still of Charlie Chaplin and
Jackie Coogan in *The Kid* (1921)

most notably Friedlander, Sherman, and Nixon.

The photographers have covered an extensive variety of subject matter in both colour and black and white– delicate landscapes, scenes of urban desolation, abstract imagery, and stylish portraiture, including some

*Sunday on the Banks of the Marne,* photographed by
Henri Cartier-Bresson in 1939

beautiful silver-gelatin print nudes by the French Surrealist Man Ray. Together, they form a complete history of photographic art and represent one of the finest collections in existence.

## ARCHITECTURE AND DESIGN

The Museum of Modern Art was the first art museum to include utilitarian objects in its collection. These range from household appliances such as stereo equipment, furniture, lighting, textiles, and glassware to industrial ball bearings and silicon chips. Architecture is represented in the collection of photographs, scale models, and drawings of buildings that have been or might have been built.

Graphic design is shown in typography and posters. Larger exhibits that look as if they belong in a museum of transportation include Pinin Farina's Cisitalia car and the Bell helicopter.

Reclining
rocking chair
of steam-bent beech
and cane by Gebrüder
Thonet (c. 1900)

## St. Patrick's Cathedral ❽

*See pp178–9.*

## Villard Houses ❾

457 Madison Ave (New York Palace Hotel). **Map** 13 A4. **Tel** *(800) NY PALACE.* Ⓜ *51st St.* **www**.newyork palace.com **Urban Center** ◯ *10am–7pm Mon–Thu, 10am–6pm Fri, 10am–5:30pm Sat.* **Tel** *(212) 935 3595.* ◙ ♿ ▣ **www**.mas.org

Henry Villard was a Bavarian immigrant who became publisher of the *New York Evening Post* and founder of the Northern Pacific Railroad. In 1881, he bought the land opposite St. Patrick's Cathedral and hired McKim, Mead & White to design town houses, one for himself, the rest for sale. The inspired result has six four-story houses set round a central court opening to the street and the church. The south wing was Villard's, but financial difficulties forced him to sell before it was finished.

Ownership passed to the Roman Catholic archdiocese, but when the church outgrew its space in the 1970s the houses were threatened. The problem was solved when the Helmsley chain purchased air rights for the 51-story Helmsley (now New York) Palace Hotel.

The center wing now comprises the hotel's formal entrance and the Villard Bar & Lounge, from which the grand public rooms of the Villard suite can be admired. The **Urban Center** occupies the north wing, and its bookshop is the best place in New York for architectural books on the city.

St. Bartholomew's Church

## St. Bartholomew's Church ❿

109 E 50th St. **Map** 13 A4. **Tel** *(212) 378-0222.* Ⓜ *51st St.* ◯ *8am–6pm daily (to 7:30pm Thu & 8:30pm Sun).* ✝ *frequent.* ◙ ♿ **Lectures, concerts.** ◙ ◙ *after 11am Sunday services.* ▯ *(212) 888-2664.* **www**.stbarts.org

Known fondly to New Yorkers as "St. Bart's," this Byzantine structure with its ornate detail, pinkish brick, open terrace and a polychromed gold dome brought color and variety to Park Avenue in 1919.

Architect Bertram Goodhue incorporated into the design the Romanesque entrance portico created by Stanford White for the original 1903 St. Bartholomew's on Madison Avenue, and marble columns from the earlier church were used in the chapel.

St. Bartholomew's program of concerts is well known, as is its theater group, which mounts three productions here each year.

## General Electric Building ⓫

570 Lexington Ave. **Map** 13 A4. Ⓜ *Lexington Ave.* ⚫ *to the public.*

In 1931 architects Cross & Cross were commissioned to design a skyscraper that would be in keeping with its neighbor, St. Bartholomew's Church. Not an easy task, but the result won unanimous acclaim. The colors were chosen to blend and contrast, and the design of the tower complemented the church's polychrome dome.

The General Electric Building on Lexington Avenue

View the pair from the corner of Park and 50th to see how well it works. However, the General Electric is no mere backdrop but a work of art in its own right and a favorite part of the city skyline. It is an Art Deco gem from its chrome and marble lobby to its spiky "radio waves" crown.

Walk one block north on Lexington Avenue to find a place much cherished by movie fans. It is right at this spot that Marilyn Monroe, in a billowing white frock, stood so memorably in the breeze from the Lexington Avenue subway grating in the movie *The Seven-Year Itch.*

Villard Houses, now the entrance to the New York Palace Hotel

# Waldorf–Astoria ⓬

301 Park Ave. **Map** 13 A5.
***Tel*** *(212) 355-3000.* Ⓜ *Lexington Ave, 53rd St. See* **Where to Stay** *p289.* **www**.waldorf.com

This Art Deco classic, which covers an entire city block, was designed by Schultze & Weaver in 1931. The original Hotel at 34th Street was demolished to make way for the Empire State Building.

**Winston Churchill and New York philanthropist Grover Whalen at the Waldorf–Astoria in 1946**

Still deservedly one of New York's most prestigious hotels, the Waldorf–Astoria serves, too, as a reminder of a more glamorous era in the city's history. The 625-ft (190-m) twin towers, where the Duke and Duchess of Windsor lived, have hosted numerous celebrities, including every US president since 1931. The giant lobby clock, executed for the Chicago World's Fair of 1893, is from the original hotel, and the piano in the Peacock Alley cocktail lounge belonged to Cole Porter when he was a resident of the hotel's exclusive Towers.

# Lever House ⓭

390 Park Ave. **Map** 13 A4.
Ⓜ *5th Ave-53rd St.* **Lobby and building** 🔵 *to the public.* 🍴
*See* **Where to Eat** *p308.*

Imagine a Park Avenue lined with sturdy, residential buildings – and then imagine the sensation when they were suddenly reflected here in the first of the city's glass-walled skyscrapers, one of the most influential buildings of the modern era. The design, by Skidmore, Owings & Merrill,

**The pool at the Four Seasons in the Seagram Building**

is simply two rectangular slabs of stainless steel and glass, one laid horizontally, the other stacked to stand tall above it, to allow light in from every side. The crisp and bright design was intended to symbolize many of the Lever Brothers' products – they make soaps and other cleaning products.
Revolutionary though it was in 1952, Lever House is now dwarfed by its many imitators, but its importance as an architectural pacesetter remains undiminished. The Lever House restaurant is a VIP scene.

**Lever House on Park Avenue**

# Seagram Building ⓮

375 Park Ave. **Map** 13 A4. Ⓜ *5th Ave-53rd St.* 🕐 *9am–5pm Mon–Fri.* 🍴 *See* **Where to Eat** *p309.*

Samuel Bronfman, the late head of Seagram distillers, was prepared to put up an ordinary commercial building until his architect daughter, Phyllis Lambert, intervened and persuaded him to go to the best – Mies van der Rohe.

The result, which is widely considered the finest of the many Modernist buildings of the 1950s, consists of two rectangles of bronze and glass that let the light pour in.
Within is the exclusive Four Seasons Restaurant *(see p289)*, a landmark in its own right. Designer Philip Johnson has created a remarkable space, with the centerpiece of one room a pool, and another a bar topped by a quivering Richard Lippold sculpture.

**Office workers at lunch in the spacious Citigroup Center atrium**

# Citigroup Center ⓯

153 E 53rd St. **Map** 13 A4. Ⓜ *53rd St-Lexington Ave.* 🕐 *7am–11pm daily.* 🍴 🏛 **St. Peter's Lutheran Church** 619 Lexington Ave. ***Tel*** *(212) 935-2200.* 🕐 *9am–9pm daily.* 🏛 *12:15pm Mon–Fri, 6pm Wed, 8:45am & 11am Sun.* **Jazz vespers** *5pm Sun.* **Concerts** *noon Wed.* **York Theater at St. Peter's;** ***Tel*** *(212) 935-5820.* **www**.saintpeters.org

An aluminum-clad spire built on ten-story stilts with a sliced-off roof, Citigroup Center is unique; it caused a sensation when it was completed in 1978. The unusual base design had to incorporate St. Peter's Lutheran Church. The church is separate both in space and design, a granite sculpture below a corner of the tower. Step inside to see the striking interior and the Erol Beker Chapel by sculptor Louise Nevelson. The church is well known for its organ concerts, jazz vespers, and theater presentations. Citigroup's slanting top never functioned as a solar panel as intended, but it is an unmistakable landmark on the skyline.

# St. Patrick's Cathedral

**The cathedral's Fifth Avenue facade**

The Roman Catholic Church originally intended this site for use as a cemetery, but in 1850 Archbishop John Hughes decided to build a cathedral instead. Many thought that it was foolish to build so far beyond the (then) city limits, but Hughes went ahead anyway. Architect James Renwick built New York's finest Gothic Revival building, the largest Catholic cathedral in the United States. The cathedral, which seats 2,500 people, was completed in 1878, though the spires were added from 1885 to 1888.

**★ Lady Chapel**
*This chapel honors the Blessed Virgin. The stained-glass windows portray the mysteries of the rosary.*

**Pietà**
*American sculptor William O. Partridge created this Pietà in 1906. The statue stands at the side of the Lady Chapel.*

**★ Baldachin**
*The great baldachin rising over the high altar is made entirely of bronze. Statues of the saints and prophets adorn the four piers supporting the canopy.*

## STAR FEATURES

★ Baldachin

★ Great Bronze Doors

★ Great Organ and Rose Window

★ Lady Chapel

**Cathedral Facade**
*The exterior wall is built of white marble. The spires rise 330 ft (101 m) above the pavement.*

**Stations of the Cross**
*Carved of Caen stone in Holland, these reliefs won first prize in the field of religious art at the Chicago World's Fair in 1893.*

**Shrine of St. Elizabeth Ann Seton**
*The bronze statue and screen depict the life of the first American to be canonized a saint. She founded the Sisters of Charity (see p76).*

**★ Great Organ and Rose Window**
*Measuring 26 ft (8 m) in diameter, the rose window shines above the great organ, which has more than 7,000 pipes.*

Main entrance

**★ Great Bronze Doors**
*The massive doors weigh 20,000 lb (9,000 kg) and are adorned with important religious figures in New York.*

# Central Synagogue 16

652 Lexington Ave. **Map** 13 A4.
**Tel** (212) 838–5122. Ⓜ 51st St,
Lexington Ave. 🕙 noon–2pm Tue–
Wed. 📷 12:45 Wed. ♿ ✡ 6pm
Fri, also 10am Sat (Jul–Aug),
10.30am Sat (Sep–Jun).
**www**.centralsynagogue.org

This is New York's
oldest building in
continuous use as a
synagogue. It was
designed in 1870 by
Silesian-born Henry
Fernbach, America's
first prominent Jewish
architect. He also
designed some of
SoHo's finest cast-iron
buildings. Restored
after a 1999 fire, the
Synagogue is considered
the city's best example
of Moorish-Islamic
Revival architecture.
The congregation was
founded in 1846 as
Ahawath Chesed (Love
of Mercy) by 18 new
immigrants, most of
them from Bohemia,
on Ludlow Street on
the Lower East Side.

**The stenciled interior** is a colorful mix of red, blue, ocher and gilt and was inspired by Victorian prints of a Moorish Palace in Spain called the Alhambra.

**Banded "horseshoe" arches** are an Hispano-Mooresque design.

**The ark** holds the sacred scrolls of the Jewish Holy Book, The Torah.

**The twin towers** represent the two columns that stood outside Solomon's Temple. The domed minarets, which rise 122 ft (37 m), are onion-shaped and made of green copper.

**The facade** is an understated Moorish design in local brownstone.

# Sutton Place 17

**Map** 13 C3. Ⓜ 59th St, 51st St.
🚌 M15, M31, M57

Sutton Place is a posh and
pleasant neighborhood,
delightfully devoid of busy
traffic, made up of elegant
low-rise apartment houses
and town houses designed by
noted architects. The arrival of
New York society in the 1920s
transformed an area that had
once been the province of
factories and tenements.
Three Sutton Square is the
residence of the secretary-
general of the United Nations.
Look beyond Sutton Square
and 59th Street for a glimpse
of Riverview Terrace, a
private street of five ivy-
covered brownstones fronting
on the river. The tiny parks
at the end of 55th Street and
jutting out at 57th Street offer
views of the river and the
Queensboro Bridge.
   After much neighborhood
opposition, Bridgemarket
opened in 2000. Located
between the huge vaults
under the Queensboro
Bridge, there is an upscale
Terence Conran's for
housewares and a Food
Emporium supermarket.

**Park at Sutton Place, looking toward Queensboro Bridge and
Roosevelt Island**

# Beekman Place 18

**Map** 13 C5. Ⓜ 59th St, 51st St.
🚌 M15, M31, M57.

Smaller than Sutton Place,
and even more tranquil, is
Beekman Place, a virtually
private two-block enclave
of 1920s town houses and

small-scale apartments. Famous residents here have included Gloria Vanderbilt, Rex Harrison, Irving Berlin and members of the large Rockefeller family.

At Turtle Bay Gardens, restored brownstone houses dating from the 1860s hide a charming Italianate garden. Among the residents enticed by this privacy have been the film stars Tyrone Power and Katharine Hepburn, composer Stephen Sondheim, and writer E.B. White.

## Roosevelt Island ⓳

**Map** 14 D2. Ⓜ *59th St. Tram, Roosevelt Island station (F).* **www**.rioc.com

Since 1976 a Swiss cable car has offered a quick ride across the East River to Roosevelt Island, with eagle's-eye views of the city and the Queensboro Bridge.

Near the tram station are the remains of the Blackwell farmhouse, which stood from 1796 to 1804 and gave the island its name until real estate development began in the 1920s. From then until the 1970s, the island housed a succession of hospitals, an almshouse, a jail, a workhouse and an insane asylum, and became known as Welfare Island. In 1927, Mae West was held in the penitentiary here after a "lewd performance." The ruins of 19th-century hospitals still remain, as does an 1872 lighthouse built by an asylum inmate.

The tram departs from 2nd Avenue at 60th Street and affords a thrilling ride and some fine city views.

Bloomingdale's store sign

## Bloomingdale's ⓴

1000 3rd Ave. **Map** 13 A3. *Tel* (212) 705-2000. Ⓜ *59th St.* ◯ *10am–8:30pm Mon–Fri, 10am–7pm Sat, 11am–7pm Sun. See* ***Shopping*** *p319.* **www**.bloomingdales.com

For a while in the booming 1980s, "Bloomies" was synonymous with the good life. Founded by Joseph and Lyman Bloomingdale in 1872, this famous department store had a bargain-basement image until the 3rd Avenue El was taken down in the 1960s. Then came the store's transformation to the epitome of trendy, sophisticated shopping. But the late 1980s brought new ownership and eventual bankruptcy. While not as flashy as in the past, Bloomingdale's is open every day and remains one of the city's best-stocked stores. A second store has opened in SoHo at 504 Broadway.

## Fuller Building ㉑

41 E 57th St. **Map** 13 A3. *Peter Findlay Gallery.* **Tel** (212) 644-4433; *James Goodman Gallery.* **Tel** (212) 593-3737. ◯ *10am–6pm Tue–Sat.* Ⓜ *59th St.*

This slim-towered black, gray and white 1929 beauty by Walker & Gillette is a prime example of geometric Art Deco design. The striking statues on either side of the clock above the entrance are by Elie Nadelman. Step inside to admire the intricate mosaic tile floors; one panel shows the Fuller Company's former home in

the famous Flatiron Building on Fifth Avenue (*see 127*). The Fuller Building is a hive of exclusive art galleries, most of which are open to the public daily.

French Renaissance–style facade of the Plaza Hotel

## Plaza Hotel ㉒

5th Ave & Central Park South. **Map** 12 F3. Ⓜ *59th St.*

The city's grande dame of hotels was designed by Henry J. Hardenbergh, known for the Dakota (*see p218*) and the original Waldorf–Astoria. Completed in 1907 at the exorbitant cost of $12.5 million, the Plaza was proclaimed "the best hotel in the world," with 800 rooms, 500 baths, a two-story ballroom, five marble staircases, and 14- to 17-room apartments for such families as the Vanderbilts and the Goulds (*see p49*).

The 18-story cast-iron structure resembles a French Renaissance château on a larger scale. Much of the interior decoration came from Europe. The Palm Court still has mirrored walls and Italian carvings of the four seasons as supporting columns.

Already lavishly restored by its former owner Donald Trump, the building underwent a $350-million conversion into a mix of apartments, hotel condominiums, and a 130-room hotel in time for its 100th birthday in 2007. There are also six floors of luxury retail and upscale dining.

The clock statues above the Fuller Building entrance

# UPPER EAST SIDE

A t the turn of the century, New York society moved to the Upper East Side – and stayed. Many of the Beaux-Arts mansions in this district are now museums and embassies, but the well-to-do still occupy the grand apartment buildings on Fifth and Park avenues. Chic shops and galleries line

**African urn, Metropolitan Museum of Art**

Madison Avenue. Farther east, the area includes what is left of German Yorkville in the East 80s, Hungarian Yorkville to the south, and little Bohemia, with its Czech population, below 78th Street. Although many of these ethnic groups no longer inhabit the area, their churches, restaurants, and shops still remain.

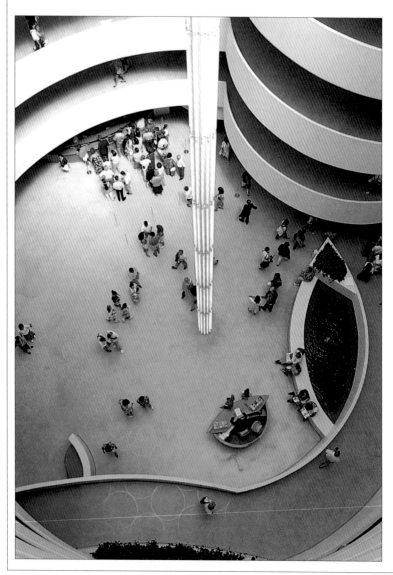

**Bird's-eye view of the lobby at the Solomon R. Guggenheim Museum**

# SIGHTS AT A GLANCE

## Historic Streets and Buildings
Gracie Mansion **16**
Henderson Place **14**
Seventh Regiment Armory **10**

## Museums and Galleries
Asia Society **9**
Cooper-Hewitt National Design Museum **3**
*Frick Collection pp202–3* **8**
Jewish Museum **2**
*Metropolitan Museum of Art pp190–97* **6**
Mount Vernon Hotel Museum and Garden **13**
Museum of the City of New York **19**
National Academy Museum **4**
Neue Galerie New York **1**
Society of Illustrators **12**
*Solomon R. Guggenheim Museum pp188–9* **5**
*Whitney Museum of American Art pp200–1* **7**

## Churches and Synagogues
Church of the Holy Trinity **17**
St. Nicholas Russian Orthodox Cathedral **18**
Temple Emanu-El **11**

## Parks and Squares
Carl Schurz Park **15**

**Statue of Diana, National Academy of Design**

**0 meters**    500
**0 yards**    500

## KEY

Street-by-Street map

**M** Subway station

## SEE ALSO

- *Street Finder,* maps 12–13, 16–18, 21
- *East Side Walk pp264–5*
- *Where to Stay pp289–90*
- *Restaurants pp308–9*

## GETTING THERE
The Lexington Ave 4 and 5 express trains stop at 59th and 86th sts. The local (No. 6) stops at 68th, 77th, and 96th sts. The F stops at 63rd St, the N, R, and W at 5th Ave and 59th St. Buses include: M1, M2, M3, and M4 on Fifth/Madison aves, M101–3 on Lexington/Third and M15 on First/Second. The crosstown buses are the M66, M72, M79, M86, and M96.

# Street by Street: Museum Mile

Many of New York's museums are clustered on the Upper East Side, in homes ranging from the former Frick and Carnegie mansions to the modernistic Guggenheim, designed by Frank Lloyd Wright. The displays are as varied as the architecture, running the gamut from Old Masters to photographs to decorative arts. Presiding over the scene is the vast Metropolitan Museum of Art, America's answer to the Louvre. Many of the museums stay open late on Tuesday evenings, and some offer free admission.

**Jewish Museum**
*The most extensive collection of Judaica in the world is housed here. It includes coins, archaeological objects, and ceremonial and religious artifacts* ❷

★ **Cooper-Hewitt National Design Museum**
*Ceramics, glass, furniture and textiles are well represented here* ❸

**The Church of the Heavenly Rest** was built in 1929 in the Gothic style. The madonna in the pulpit is by sculptor Malvina Hoffman.

**National Academy Museum**
*The Academy, founded in 1825, moved here in 1940. Its fine collection includes paintings and sculptures by its members* ❹

**Graham House** is an apartment building with a splendid Beaux Arts entrance. It was built in 1892.

★ **Solomon R. Guggenheim Museum**
*Floodlit at dusk, architect Frank Lloyd Wright's building looks purple. It is in the form of a spiral. Take the elevator to the top and walk down to see one of the world's best collections of modern art* ❺

## STAR SIGHTS

★ Cooper-Hewitt Museum

★ Solomon R. Guggenheim Museum

**The facade of the Squadron A Armory** is all that remains of the original building. It is now the west wall of the playground of Hunter High School. The school was built to complement the style of the armory.

**LOCATOR MAP**
*See Manhattan Map pp14–15*

UPPER WEST SIDE

East Side

CENTRAL PARK

UPPER EAST SIDE

Roosevelt I.

UPPER MIDTOWN

Queens

**KEY**

– – – Suggested route

0 meters 100
0 yards 100

**Public basketball court**

**To 96th Street subway (2 blocks)**

**The William G. Loew Mansion** (1931), now part of the Spence School, is in the "American Adams" style.

**The Synod of Bishops of the Russian Orthodox Church Outside of Russia** is housed in a lovely 1918 mansion.

**Night Presence IV** (1972), a modern work in rusting steel, was created by Louise Nevelson. Some New Yorkers feel it is out of place among its staid, old-fashioned neighbors on Park Avenue.

At **120 and 122 East 92nd Street** are two of the few wooden houses left in Manhattan. Built in 1859 and 1871, respectively, they have a charming Italianate air.

**The Marx Brothers** spent their boyhoods in a three-bedroom apartment in a modest row house at 179 East 93rd Street.

## Neue Galerie New York ❶

1048 5th Ave at E 86th St. **Map** 16 F3. **Tel** (212) 628-6200. Ⓜ 86th St. 🚌 M1–4. 🕐 11am–9pm Fri, 11am–6pm Sat–Mon, Thu. ⬤ public hols. 🖼 📷 🚫 🍴 Café 9am–6pm Mon–Wed, 9am–9pm Thu–Sun. 🔲 ♿ **www**.neuegalerie.org

This museum was founded by art dealer Serge Sabarsky and philanthropist Ronald Lauder. Its objective is to collect, research, and exhibit the fine and decorative arts of Germany and Austria from the early 20th century.

The Louis XIII-style Beaux-Arts structure was completed in 1914 by Carrère & Hastings, who also designed and built the New York Public Library (*see p146*). The building has been designated a landmark and is considered to be one of the most distinguished buildings on Fifth Avenue. Once occupied by Mrs. Cornelius Vanderbilt III, the mansion was purchased by Lauder and Sabarsky in 1994. The ground floor houses the entrance, a bookshop, and the Café Sabarsky, which draws its inspiration from the Viennese cafés of old. The second floor is devoted to the works of Klimt, Schiele, and Wiener Werkstätte objects. The upper floors feature works from Der Blaue Reiter (artists such as Klee, Kandinsky), the Bauhaus (Feininger, Schlemmer) and Die Brücke (Mies van der Rohe, Breuer).

## Jewish Museum ❷

1109 5th Ave. **Map** 16 F2. **Tel** (212) 423-3200 Ⓜ 86th St, 96th St. 🚌 M1–4. 🕐 11am–5:45pm Sun–Wed, 11am–8pm Thu, 11am–3pm Fri. ⬤ Sat, public & Jewish hols. 🖼 🚫 ♿ 🔲 🔲 **www**.thejewishmuseum.org

The exquisite château-like residence of Felix M. Warburg, financier and leader of the Jewish community, was designed by C. P. H. Gilbert in 1908. It now houses one of the world's largest collections of Jewish fine and ceremonial art, and historical Judaica. The stonework in a new extension is by the stonemasons of St. John the Divine (*see pp226– 7*).

Objects have been brought here from all over the world, some at great risk of persecution to the donors. Covering 4,000 years, artifacts include Torah crowns, candelabras, kiddush cups, plates, scrolls, and silver ceremonial objects.

There is a Torah ark from the Benguiat Collection, the exquisite faience entrance wall of a 16th-century Persian synagogue, and the powerful *Holocaust* by sculptor George Segal. Changing exhibitions reflect Jewish life and experience around the world.

**19th-century ewer and basin from Istanbul at the Jewish Museum**

## Cooper-Hewitt National Design Museum ❸

2 E 91st St. **Map** 16 F2. **Tel** (212) 849-8400 Ⓜ 86th St, 96th St. 🚌 M1–4. 🕐 10am–5pm Mon–Sat (to 9pm Fri & 6pm Sat), noon–6pm Sun. ⬤ Jan 1, Thanksgiving, Dec 25. 🖼 🚫 ♿ 🔲 🔲 🔲 **www**.ndm.si.edu

One of the largest design collections in the world, this museum occupies the former home of industrialist Andrew Carnegie. The collection was amassed by the Hewitt sisters, Amy, Eleanor, and Sarah. The museum opened in 1897 at Cooper Union (*see p120*); the Smithsonian Institution acquired the collections in 1967, and the Carnegie Corporation offered the mansion.

Carnegie asked for "the most modest, plainest, and most roomy house in New York," but the house set new trends

**Cooper-Hewitt Museum entrance**

with central heating, private elevator, and air-conditioning. Note the wooden staircase, rich paneling and carving, and the sunny solarium.

## National Academy Museum ❹

1083 5th Ave. **Map** 16 F3. **Tel** (212) 369-4880 Ⓜ 86th St. 🚌 M1–4. 🕐 noon–5pm Wed–Thu, 11am–6pm Fri–Sun. ⬤ public hols. 🖼 🚫 ♿ 🔲 **www**.nationalacademy.org

More than 6,000 paintings, drawings, and sculptures, including works by Thomas Eakins, Winslow Homer, Raphael Soyer, and Frank Lloyd Wright, comprise the collection of the National Academy Museum, founded in 1825 by a group of artists. The group's mission was (and is) to train artists and exhibit their work.

In 1940, Archer Huntington, an art patron and philanthropist, donated his house, an attractive building with patterned marble floors and decorative plaster ceilings. The grand entrance foyer has a statue of Diana by sculptor Anna Hyatt Huntington.

**Statue of Diana in the National Academy Museum entrance foyer**

# Solomon R. Guggenheim Museum ❺

*See pp188–9.*

# Metropolitan Museum of Art ❻

*See pp190–97.*

# Whitney Museum of American Art ❼

*See pp200–01.*

# Frick Collection ❽

*See pp202–03.*

# Asia Society ❾

725 Park Ave. **Map** 13 A1. *Tel* (212) 288-6400. Events: 517-ASIA. Ⓜ 68th St. ◯ 11am–6pm Tue–Sun (to 9pm Fri). ◯ public hols. 🎦 12:30pm Tue–Sat, 6:30pm Fri, 2:30pm Sun. 🚫 ♿ 📷 📚 www.asiasociety.org

Founded by John D. Rockefeller III in 1956 to increase understanding of Asian culture, the society is a forum for 30 countries from Japan to Iran, Central Asia to Australia.

The 1981 eight-story building was designed by Edward Larrabee Barnes and is made of red granite. After a complete renovation in 2001, the museum has greatly increased gallery space. One gallery is permanently devoted to Rockefeller's own collection of Asian sculptures, amassed by him and his wife on frequent trips to the East.

Changing exhibits show a wide variety of Asian arts, and the society has a full program of films, dance, concerts, and lectures and a well-stocked bookshop.

**South Asian sculpture at the Asia Society**

**Entrance Hall of the Seventh Regiment Armory**

# Seventh Regiment Armory ❿

643 Park Ave. **Map** 13 A2. Ⓜ 68th St. ◯ to the public, except for special events. 🚫 ♿

From the War of 1812 through two world wars, the Seventh Regiment has played a vital role. They were an elite corps of "gentlemen soldiers" from prominent families, and their armory is unlike any other in the US. Within the stern fortresslike exterior are extraordinary rooms filled with lavish furnishings of the Victorian era, objets d'art, and regimental memorabilia.

The design by Charles W. Clinton, a veteran of the regiment, had offices facing Park Avenue, with a vast drill hall stretching behind to Lexington Avenue. The reception rooms include the Veterans' Room and the Library by Louis Comfort Tiffany. The drill hall is now the site of the Winter Antiques Show (*see p53*) and a favorite place to hold the city's many charity balls.

# Temple Emanu-El ⓫

1 E 65th St. **Map** 12 F2. *Tel* (212) 744-1400 Ⓜ 68th St, 63rd St. ◯ 10am–5pm Sun–Fri, 12:30pm–4:45pm Sat (last adm on Fri 3:30pm) ◯ Jewish hols. ✡ 5:30pm Sun–Thu, 5:15pm Fri, 10:30am Sat. 📷 ♿ 📚 🏛 www.emanuelnyc.org

This impressive limestone edifice of 1929 is the largest synagogue in the world, with seating for 2,500 in the main sanctuary alone. It is home to the oldest Reform congregation in New York, and the wealthiest members of Jewish society worship here.

Among the synagogue's many fine details are the bronze doors of the Ark, which represent an open Torah scroll. The Ark also has stained glass depicting biblical scenes and showing the tribal signs of the houses of Israel. These signs also appear on a great recessed arch that frames a magnificent wheel window, the dominant feature of the Fifth Avenue facade.

The synagogue stands on the site of the palatial home of Mrs. William Astor, the legendary society hostess. Lady Astor moved to the Upper East Side after a feud with her nephew, who lived next door. Her wine cellar and three marble fireplaces still remain at the synagogue.

**The Ark at Temple Emanu-El**

# Solomon R. Guggenheim Museum ❺

Home to one of the world's finest collections of modern and contemporary art, the building itself is perhaps the museum's greatest masterpiece. Designed by Frank Lloyd Wright, the shell-like facade is a veritable New York landmark. The spiral ramp curves down and inward from the dome, passing works by major 19th-, 20th-, and 21st-century artists. The museum has just undergone a major program of restoration to its exterior, which has been plagued by cracks almost since it first opened in 1959.

**Fifth Avenue facade**

**Paris Through the Window**
*The vibrant colors of Marc Chagall's 1913 masterpiece illumine the canvas, conjuring up images of a magical and mysterious city where nothing is quite what it appears to be.*

Small Rotunda

Sculpture terrace

Main entrance

THE SOLOMO

**Woman Ironing** (*1904*)
*A work from Pablo Picasso's Blue Period, this painting is his quintessential image of hard work and fatigue.*

**Yellow Cow** (*1911*)
*Franz Marc's work was influenced by a German back-to-nature movement.*

**Nude** (*1917*)
*This sleeping figure is typical of Amedeo Modigliani's stylized work.*

## MUSEUM GUIDE

*The Great Rotunda features special exhibitions. The Small Rotunda shows some of the museum's celebrated Impressionist and Post-Impressionist holdings. The new Tower galleries feature exhibitions of work from the permanent collection as well as contemporary pieces. A fifth-floor sculpture terrace overlooks Central Park. Not all of the collection is on display at any one time.*

**Before the Mirror** *(1876)*
*In trying to capture the flavor of 19th-century society, Edouard Manet often used the image of the courtesan.*

Tower

Great
Rotunda

**Woman Holding a Vase**
*Fernand Léger incorporated elements of Cubism into this work from 1927.*

**Black Lines** *(1913)* This is
one of Vasily Kandinsky's
earliest examples of his work
in "non-objective" art.

G G E N H E I M    M U S E U M

**Woman with Yellow Hair**
*(1931) The gentle, voluptuous figure of Picasso's mistress often appears in his work.*

### FRANK LLOYD WRIGHT

During his lifetime, Wright was considered the great innovator of American architecture. Characteristic of his work are Prairie-style homes and office buildings of concrete slabs, glass bricks, and tubing. Wright received the Guggenheim commission in 1942 and it was completed after his death in 1959, his only New York building.

**Interior of the Guggenheim's Great Rotunda**

# Metropolitan Museum of Art ⑥

Founded in 1870 by a group of artists and philanthropists who dreamed of an American art institution to rival those of Europe, this collection is thought to be the most comprehensive in the Western world. Works date from prehistoric times to the present. The museum opened here in 1880 and houses collections from all continents. Part of the first floor is under renovation, but will reopen in 2007 with a new Roman Court and Etruscan gallery.

The entrance of the Metropolitan Museum of Art

★ **Gertrude Stein** *(1905–6) This portrait of the American writer Gertrude Stein is by Pablo Picasso. The masklike face is evidence of his debt to African and Roman art.*

**Pendant Mask**
*The kingdom of Benin (now part of Nigeria) was renowned for its art. This mask was made in the 16th century.*

**Seated Man with Harp**
*This statuette was made in the Cyclades c. 3,000 BC.*

## GALLERY GUIDE

*Most of the collections are housed on the two main floors. Works from 19 curatorial areas are in the permanent galleries, with designated sections for temporary exhibitions. Central on the first and second floors are European painting, sculpture, and decorative art. The Costume Institute is situated on the ground level, directly below the Egyptian galleries on the first floor.* Robert Lehman Collection

**The Marriage Feast at Ca**
*This rare 16th-century par painting by Juan de Fland is part of the Linsky Collec*

**Bust of Diderot** (1773)
*Jean Antoine Houdon's bust was made for a Russian count.*

**★ Portrait of the Princesse de Broglie**
*This portrait, painted in 1853, was J.A.D. Ingres' last.*

First floor

Stairs to Costume Institute

Main entrance

**Byzantine Galleries**
*This marble panel with a griffin is from Greece or the Balkans (c.1250). It is just one of the pieces on display in the Byzantine Galleries.*

## STAR EXHIBITS

★ Byzantine Galleries

★ Gertrude Stein by Pablo Picasso

★ Portrait of the Princesse de Broglie by Ingres

★ Temple of Dendur

## KEY TO FLOOR PLAN

☐ Robert Lehman Collection
☐ European painting, sculpture and decorative arts
☐ Art of Africa, Oceania, and the Americas
☐ Modern art
☐ American art
☐ Egyptian art
☐ Greek and Roman art
☐ Medieval and Byzantine art
☐ Arms and armor
☐ Non-exhibition space

**English Armor**
*This was made for Sir George Clifford around 1580.*

**★ Temple of Dendur** *(15 BC)*
*The Roman emperor Augustus built this three-room temple. He is shown in its reliefs making offerings.*

# Metropolitan Museum of Art: Upper Levels

**Marrakech**
*This 1964 work is one of Frank Stella's "Moroccan" paintings. Within a square format, fluorescent strips form the painting's main focus.*

**Sculpture Garden**
*These modern sculptures, on top of the Modern Art wing, are changed annually.*

**Card Players** *(1890)*
*Paul Cézanne departed here from his traditional landscapes, still lifes and portraits to paint this scene of peasants intently playing cards.*

Under renovation

First floor

Second floor

**★ Cypresses** *(1889)*
*Vincent Van Gogh painted this the year before he died. The heavy brushstrokes and the swirling style mark his later work.*

## STAR EXHIBITS

- ★ Cypresses by Vincent Van Gogh

- ★ Diptych by Jan van Eyck

- ★ George Washington Crossing the Delaware by Leutze

- ★ Self-portrait of 1660 by Rembrandt

**Eagle-headed Winged Being Pollinating the Sacred Tree** *(about 900 BC)*
*This relief comes from an Assyrian palace.*

★ **Diptych**
*(1425–30)*
*Flemish painter
Jan van Eyck was
one of the earliest
masters of oil
painting. These
scenes of the
Crucifixion and
Last Judgment
show him to be
a forerunner of
realism, too.*

★ **Washington Crossing the Delaware**
*In 1851 Emanuel Gottlieb Leutze painted
this romanticized – and inaccurate –
view of the famous crossing.*

**KEY TO FLOOR PLAN**

| | |
|---|---|
| ☐ | European painting, sculpture and decorative arts |
| ☐ | Art of Africa, Oceania, and the Americas |
| ☐ | Ancient Near Eastern, and Islamic art |
| ☐ | Modern art |
| ☐ | American art |
| ☐ | Asian art |
| ☐ | Cypriot art |
| ☐ | Musical instruments |
| ☐ | Drawings, prints and photographs |
| ☐ | Non-exhibition space |
| ☐ | Special exhibitions |

Astor Court

**The Death of Socrates** *(1787)
Jacques-Louis David shows
Socrates about to take poison
rather than renounce his beliefs.*

★ **Self-portrait** *(1660)
Rembrandt painted almost
100 self-portraits. This one
shows him at the age of 54.*

**THE ASTOR COURT**

In 1979, 27 crafts-
people from China,
responsible for the care
of Souzhou's historic
gardens, came to New
York to replicate a
Ming-style scholar's garden in the Metropolitan Museum.
They used centuries-old techniques and hand-made tools
that had been passed down for generations. It was the
first cultural exchange between the United States and the
People's Republic of China. The result is a quiet garden
for meditation, a Western parallel to Souzhou's Garden
of the Master of the Fishing Nets.

# Exploring the Metropolitan

The treasures of "the Met" include a vast collection of American art and more than 2,500 European paintings, including masterpieces by Rembrandt and Vermeer. There are also many Islamic exhibits, plus the greatest collection of Egyptian art outside Cairo.

## AFRICA, OCEANIA, AND THE AMERICAS

A painted gold funerary mask (10th–14th century) from the necropolis of Batán Grande, Peru

Nelson Rockefeller built the Michael C. Rockefeller Wing in 1982 in memory of his son, who lost his life on an art-finding expedition in New Guinea. The wing showcases a superb collection of over 1,600 objects from Africa, the islands of the Pacific and the Americas.

Among the African works, the ivory and bronze sculptures from the royal kingdom of Benin (Nigeria) are outstanding, as is the wooden sculpture by the Dogon, Bamana and Senufo peoples of Mali. From the Pacific come carvings by the Asmat people of New Guinea and decorations and masks from the Melanesian and Polynesian islands. From Mexico and Central and South America come pre-Columbian gold, ceramics and stonework. The wing also contains fine Native American artifacts by the Inuit and other groups.

## AMERICAN ART

Gilbert Stuart's portrait of George Washington, George Caleb Bingham's *Fur Traders Descending the Missouri,* John SingerSargent's notorious portrait of *Madame X,* and the monumental *Washington Crossing the Delaware* by Emanuel Leutze are among the icons in the American Wing. It holds not only one of the world's finest collections of American painting and sculpture but also of decorative arts from Colonial times to the beginning of the 20th century. Highlights range from elegant Neo-Classical silver vessels made by Paul Revere to innovative glassware by Tiffany & Co. In furniture section are settees, dining chairs, tables, bookcases, and desks from major centers of American cabinetmaking such as Boston, Newport, and Philadelphia.

Period rooms, with their original decorative woodwork and furnishings, range from the saloon hall in which George Washington celebrated his last birthday to the elegant prairie-style living room from the house that Frank Lloyd Wright designed for Francis W. Little in Wayzata, Minnesota, in 1912.

The Charles Engelhard Court is an indoor sculpture garden with large-scale architectural elements, including the lovely stained-glass and mosaic loggia from Louis Comfort Tiffany's Long Island estate and the facade of an 1824 United States Branch Bank that once stood on Wall Street.

## ANCIENT NEAR EASTERN AND ISLAMIC ART

Massive stone sculptures of winged, human-headed animals, once the guardians of the 9th-century BC Assyrian

Mysterious in identity and origin, a rare 5,000-year-old copper head from the Near East

palace of Ashurnasirpal II, stand at the entrance to the Ancient Near Eastern galleries. Inside is a collection spanning 8,000 years, rich in Iranian bronzes, Anatolian ivories and Sumerian sculptures, and Achaemenian and Sassanian silver and gold. An adjacent area, currently undergoing renovation, will contain Islamic art of the 7th to the 19th centuries; glass and metalwork from Egypt, Syria and Meso-potamia; royal miniatures from Persia and Mughal India; 16th- and 17th-century rugs; and an 18th-century room from Syria.

## ARMS AND ARMOR

Mounted knights in full armor charge at each other across the equestrian court here. These galleries are a favorite with children and anyone moved by medieval romance or thrilled by power.

There are suits of armor, rapiers and sabers with hilts of precious stones and gold, firearms inlaid with ivory and mother-of-pearl, plus colorful heraldic banners and shields.

The pistol of Holy Roman Emperor Charles V (16th century)

Highlights include the armor of gentleman-pirate Sir George Clifford, a favorite of Queen Elizabeth I. The rainbow-colored armor of a 14th-century Japanese shogun and a collection of Wild West revolvers that once belonged to gunmaker Samuel Colt are also exhibited here.

## ASIAN ART

*The Old Plum*, a Japanese paper screen from the early Edo period (about 1650)

Many outstanding galleries contain masterpieces of Chinese, Japanese, Korean, Indian, and Southeast Asian art, dating from the second millennium BC to the 20th century. A full-scale Ming-style Chinese scholar's garden was built by craftspeople from Souzhou as part of the first cultural exchange between the United States and the People's Republic of China. The museum also has one of the finest collections of Sung and Yuan paintings in the world, Chinese Buddhist monumental sculptures, fine Chinese ceramics and jade, and an important display of the arts of ancient China.

The full range of Japanese arts is represented in a breathtaking suite of 11 galleries featuring chronological and thematic displays of Japanese lacquer, ceramics, painting, sculpture, textiles, and screens. Indian, Southeast Asian, and Korean galleries display superb sculptures and other arts from these regions.

## COSTUME INSTITUTE

There is always a portion of the 75,000-piece collection of costumes, dating from the 17th century to the present, on display in these new state-of-the-art galleries. Here, the Institute maintains a definitive compendium of fashionable dress, from the elaborately embroidered dresses of the late 1600s to the shocking-pink evening dresses of Elsa Schiaparelli, complete with hats, scarves, gloves, handbags, and other accessories. There are also the designs of Worth, Quant, and Balenciaga, as well as gowns from the Napoleonic and Victorian eras, the costumes of the Ballets Russes and even David Bowie's sequined jockstrap.

The regional portion of the collection is rich with folk costumes from Europe, Asia, Africa, and the Americas.

The Institute is so sophisticated in its understanding of conservation techniques that it has been called upon to advise NASA on the cleaning of astronauts' spacesuits.

A 17th-century European silk-and-satin doublet

## DRAWINGS, PRINTS, AND PHOTOGRAPHS

A new gallery regularly displays selections from the museum's incredible holdings of drawings, prints, etchings, and photographs. The

Michelangelo's studies of a Libyan Sibyl for the ceiling of the Sistine Chapel (1508)

drawings collection is especially rich in Italian and French art from the 15th to the 19th century. Specific exhibits of the drawings in this collection are shown on a rotating basis because of the light-sensitive nature of works on paper.

Highlights among the 11,000 drawings include works by Michelangelo, Leonardo da Vinci, Raphael, Ingres, Goya, Rubens, Rembrandt, Tiepolo, and Seurat.

The encyclopedic print collection of nearly 1.5 million images and the 14,000 illustrated books includes major works by virtually every master printmaker, from an early German woodcut called *Virgin and Child* to some of Dürer's most accomplished works and Goya's *The Giant*. Influential gallery-owner Alfred Stieglitz's donation of his own extensive collection of photographs brought here such gems as Edward Steichen's *The Flatiron*. It formed the core of a photography collection that is now also particularly strong in Modernist works dating from between the world wars.

Ephemera such as posters and advertisements form another part of this collection.

## EGYPTIAN ART

One of the museum's best-loved areas is the ancient Egyptian wing, which displays every one of its thousands of holdings – from the prehistoric period to the 8th century AD. Objects range from the fragmented jasper lips of a 15th-century BC queen to the massive Temple of Dendur. Other amazing archaeological finds, most of them originating from museum-sponsored expeditions undertaken early in the 20th century, include sculptures of the notorious Queen Hatshepsut, who seized the Theban throne in the 16th century BC; 100 carved reliefs of Amenhotep IV's reign; and tomb figures like the blue faïence hippo that has become the museum's mascot.

**Fragment of the head of a pharoah's queen**

## EUROPEAN PAINTING, SCULPTURE, AND DECORATIVE ARTS

The heart of the museum is its awe-inspiring collection of 3,000 European paintings. The Italian works include

*Young Woman with a Water Jug* (1660) by Jan Vermeer

Botticelli's *Last Communion of Saint Jerome* and Bronzino's *Portrait of a Young Man*. The Dutch and Flemish canvases are among the finest in the world, with Brueghel's *The Harvesters*, several works by Rubens and Van Dyck, over a dozen Rembrandts, and more Vermeers than any other museum. The collection also has masterpieces by Spanish artists El Greco, Velázquez, and Goya, and by French artists Poussin and Watteau. Some of the finest Impressionist and Post-Impressionist canvases reside here: 34 Monets, including *Terrace at Sainte-Adresse;* 18 Cézannes; and Van Gogh's *Cypresses.*

In the Kravis wing and adjacent galleries are works from the 60,000-object collection of European sculpture and decorative arts, such as Tullio Lombardo's marble statue of Adam; a bronze statuette of a rearing horse, after a model by Leonardo; and dozens of pieces by Degas and Rodin. Period settings include the patio from a 16th-century Spanish castle and a series of ornate 18th-century French domestic interiors known as the Wrightsman Rooms. The Petrie European Sculpture Court features French and Italian sculpture in a beautiful garden setting reminiscent of Versailles in France.

## GREEK AND ROMAN ART

A Roman sarcophagus from Tarsus, donated in 1870, was the first work of art in the Met's collections. It can still be seen in the museum's superbly restored Greek and Roman galleries, along with breathtaking wall panels from a villa that was buried under the lava of Vesuvius in AD 79, Etruscan mirrors, Roman portrait busts, exquisite objects in glass and silver, and hundreds of Greek vases. A monumental 7th-century BC statue of a youth shows the movement toward naturalism in sculpture, and the Hellenistic *Old Market Woman* demonstrates how the Greeks had mastered realism by the 2nd century BC.

**An amphora by Exekias, showing a wedding (6th century BC)**

## EGYPTIAN TOMB MODELS

In 1920, a Met researcher's light illuminated a room, which had been closed for 2,000 years, in the tomb of the nobleman Meketre. Within were 24 tiny, perfect replicas of his daily life: his house and garden, fleet of ships and herd of cattle. Meketre is there, too, on his boat, inhaling a lotus's scent and enjoying the music of his singer and harpist. The museum has 13 of these delightful replicas.

## LEHMAN COLLECTION

What had been one of the the finest private art collections in the world, that of investment banker Robert Lehman, came to the museum in 1969. The Lehman Wing is a dramatic glass pyramid housing an extraordinarily varied collection rich in Old Masters and 19th-century French paintings, drawings, bronzes,

A panel from the stained-glass *Death of the Virgin* window, from the 12th-century cathedral of Saint Pierre in Troyes, France

Renaissance majolica, Venetian glass, furniture, and enamels. Among the canvases are works by north–European masters; Dutch and Spanish paintings, French masterworks, Post-Impressionists and Fauves.

## MEDIEVAL ART

The Metropolitan's medieval collection includes works dating from the 4th to the 16th century, roughly from the fall of Rome to the beginning of the Renaissance. The collection is split between the main museum and its uptown branch, the Cloisters *(see pp236–9)*. In the main building are a chalice once thought to be the Holy Grail, six silver Byzantine plates showing scenes from the life of David, a 1301 pulpit by Giovanni Pisano in the shape of an eagle, and several monumental sculptures of the Virgin and Child. Other exhibits include Migration jewelry, liturgical vessels, stained glass, ivories, and 14th- and 15th-century tapestries.

## MUSICAL INSTRUMENTS

The world's oldest piano, Andrés Segovia's guitars and a sitar shaped like a peacock are some of the features of a broad and sometimes quirky collection of musical instruments that spans six continents and dates from prehistory to the present. The instruments illustrate the history of music and performance, and most of them are conserved to remain in playable condition.

Worth particular mention are instruments from the European courts of the Middle Ages and the Renaissance; rare violins; spinets, and harpsichords; instruments inlaid with precious materials; a fully equipped traditional violin-maker's work-shop; there are also African drums, Asian *pi-pas*, or lutes; and Native American flutes. Visitors can use audio equipment to hear many of the instruments playing the music of their day.

**Stradivari violin from Cremona, Italy (1691)**

## MODERN ART

Since its foundation in 1870, the museum has been acquiring contemporary art, but it was not until 1987 that a permanent home for 20th-century art was built – the Lila Acheson Wallace Wing. Other museums in New York have larger collections of modern art, but this display space is considered among the finest. European and American works from 1900 onward are featured on three levels, startingwith Europeans such as Picasso, Kandinsky, and Bonnard. The collection's greatest strength lies in its collection of modern American art, with works by New York school "The Eight," including John Sloan; such Modernists as Charles Demuth and Georgia O'Keeffe; American Regionalist Grant Wood; Abstract Expressionists Willem de Kooning; and such Color Field painters as Clyfford Still.

**Grant Wood's view of *The Midnight Ride of Paul Revere* (1931)**

Special areas of the wing house Art Nouveau and Art Deco furniture and metalwork; a large collection of works on paper by Paul Klee; and the Sculpture Gallery, with its large-scale sculptures and canvases.

Gems of the collection include Picasso's portrait of Gertrude Stein, Matisse's *Nasturtiums* and *"Dance,1"* Demuth's *I Saw the Figure 5 in Gold*, Jackson Pollock's *Autumn Rhythm*, and Andy Warhol's last self-portrait.

Each year the Cantor Roof Garden at the top of the wing features a new installation of contemporary sculpture, especially dramatic against the backdrop of the New York skyline and Central Park.

**Book cover (1916) by illustrator N. C. Wyeth**

# Society of Illustrators ⑫

128 E 63rd St. **Map** 13 A2. **Tel** (212) 838-2560. Ⓜ Lexington Ave. ◐ 10am–8pm Tue, 10am–5pm Wed–Fri, noon–4pm Sat. ● public hols. ▣ & restricted. ▣ ▮ www.societyillustrators.org

Established in 1901, this society was formed to promote the illustrator's art. Its notable roster included Charles Dana Gibson, N. C. Wyeth, and Howard Pyle. It was at first concerned with education and public service, and held occasional exhibits. In 1981, the Museum of American Illustration opened in two galleries. Changing thematic exhibitions show the history of book and magazine illustration, with an annual exhibition of the year's finest American illustrations.

# Mount Vernon Hotel Museum ⑬

421 E 61st St. **Map** 13 C3. **Tel** (212) 838-6878. Ⓜ Lexington Ave, 59th St. ◐ 11am–4pm Tue–Sun (Tue in Jun & Jul: 6pm–9pm). ● Aug, public hols. ▣ ▣ ▣ ▮ www.mvhm.org

Built in 1799, the Mount Vernon Hotel Museum and Garden was once a country day hotel for New Yorkers who needed to escape from the crowded city, then only at the south end of the island. The stone building sits on land once owned by Abigail Adams Smith, daughter of President John Adams.

It was acquired by the Colonial Dames of America in 1924 and turned into a charming re-creation of a Federal home. Costumed guides show visitors through the rooms, pointing out the treasures, including Chinese porcelain, Aubusson carpets, Sheraton chests, and a Duncan Phyfe sofa. In one bedroom there is even a baby's cradle and children's toys. An 18th-century-style garden has been planted around the house.

# Henderson Place ⑭

**Map** 18 D3. Ⓜ 86th St. ▥ M31, M86.

**Queen Anne row houses at Henderson Place**

Now surrounded by modern apartment blocks, this enclave of 24 red-brick Queen Anne row houses was built in 1882. The row houses were commissioned by John C. Henderson, a hat-maker, as a self-contained community. The elegant Lamb & Rich design has gray slate roof gables, pediments, parapets, chimneys and dormer windows forming patterns, and a turret marking the corner of each block.

**Carl Schurz Park promenade**

# Carl Schurz Park ⑮

**Map** 18 D3. Ⓜ 86th St. ▥ M31, M86.

Laid out in 1891, this park along the East River has a wide promenade over the East River Drive. It offers fine vistas of the river and the turbulent waters of Hell Gate, where the river meets Long Island Sound. It is named after Carl Schurz, a native who became Secretary of the Interior (1869–75). The first part of the promenade is the John Finlay Walk, named for an editor of the *New York Times* known for his hiking prowess. One of the city's most pleasant green escapes, the park's grassy areas are filled with basking New Yorkers on sunny days.

# Gracie Mansion ⑯

East End Ave at 88th St. **Map** 18 D3. **Tel** (212) 570-4751. Ⓜ 86th St. ◐ Apr–mid-Nov:10am, 11am, 1pm, 2pm Wed for prebooked guided tours only. ▣ ▣ & ▮

This gracious, balconied wooden 1799 country home is the official mayor's residence. Built by wealthy merchant Archibald Gracie, it is one of the best Federal houses left in New York.

Acquired by the city in 1887, it was the first home of the Museum of the City of New York. In 1942 it became the official Mayoral Residence. When Fiorello LaGuardia

**Front view of Gracie Mansion**

moved in after nine years in office, preferring it to a 75-room palace on Riverside Drive, he said that even the modest Gracie Mansion was too fancy for him. "The Little Flower" (from Fiorello) had fought corruption in the city.

## Church of the Holy Trinity ⑰

316 E 88th St. **Map** 17 B3. **Tel** (212) 289-4100. Ⓜ 86th St. 🕙 9am–5pm Mon–Fri, 7:30am–2pm Sun. ✝ 8:45am Tue, Thu; 8am, 9:30am, 10:30am, 6pm Sun. 📷 **www**.holytrinity-nyc.org

**Arched doorway of the Church of the Holy Trinity**

Delightfully placed in a serene garden setting, this church was constructed in 1889 of glowing golden brick and terracotta in French Renaissance style. It boasts one of New York's best bell towers, which holds a handsome wrought-iron clock with brass hands. The arched doorway is richly decorated with carved images of the saints and prophets.

The complex was donated by Serena Rhinelander in memory of her father and grandfather. The land was part of the Rhinelander farm, which the family had owned for 100 years.

Farther down at 350 E. 88th Street is the Rhinelander Children's Center, also a gift, and the headquarters of the Children's Aid Society.

## St. Nicholas Russian Orthodox Cathedral ⑱

15 E 97th St. **Map** 16 F1. **Tel** (212) 876-2190. Ⓜ 96 St. 🕙 by appt. ✝ 10am, 6pm Sat; 10am, 5pm Sun (Russian). 📷 **www**.russianchurchusa.org

This really is "Moscow on the Hudson." Built in Muscovite Baroque style in 1902, it has five onion domes crowned with crosses, and blue and yellow tiles on a red brick and white stone facade. Among the early worshipers were White Russians who had fled the first uprisings at home, mostly intellectuals and aristocrats who soon became a part of New York society. Later, there were more waves of refugees, dissidents, and defectors.

The cathedral now serves a scattered community, and the congregation is small. Mass is celebrated in Russian with great pomp and dignity.

The cathedral is filled with the scent of incense. The high central sanctuary has marble columns with blue and white trim above. Ornate wooden screens trimmed with gold enclose the altar. It is unique, an unexpected find on a side street in this staid part of Manhattan.

**Facade and domes of St. Nicholas Russian Cathedral**

**Facade of the Museum of the City of New York**

## Museum of the City of New York ⑲

1220 5th Ave at 103rd St. **Map** 21 C5. **Tel** (212) 534-1672. Ⓜ 103rd St. 🕙 10am–5pm Tue–Sun. 🔴 Jan 1, Thanksgiving, Dec 25. 🖊 📷 ♿ ✂ 🖥 🎁 **www**.mcny.org

Founded in 1923 and at first housed in Gracie Mansion, this museum is dedicated to New York's development from its earliest beginnings up to the present and on to the future.

Housed in a handsome Georgian Colonial building since 1932, the museum contains period rooms from actual homes, including John D. Rockefeller's bedroom. Special exhibitions rotate throughout the year, covering such subjects as fashion and theater history. In addition there is a collection of toys, including an 18th-century dollhouse, and a state-of-the-art theatre. Newly renovated galleries focus on trade, with objects shown in the context of New York's growth as an economic center. The Alexander Hamilton Gallery contains furniture and paintings that once belonged to the first Secretary of the Treasury. A further collection in the basement includes antique fire equipment, paintings, maps, and prints, all relating to city history.

# Whitney Museum of American Art ❼

The Whitney Museum is the foremost showcase for American art of the 20th and 21st centuries. It was founded in 1930 by sculptor Gertrude Vanderbilt Whitney after the Metropolitan Museum of Art turned down her collection of works by living artists such as Bellows and Hopper. In 1966 the museum moved to the present inverted-pyramid building designed by Marcel Breuer. The Whitney Biennial, held in even years, is the most significant survey of new trends in American art.

**The cantilevered facade of the Whitney Museum**

**Green Coca-Cola Bottles**
*Andy Warhol's 1962 work is a commentary on mass production and monopoly.*

**The White Calico Flower**
*Georgia O'Keeffe's enlarged flower paintings have an abstract quality, as in this 1931 example.*

**Little Big Painting**
*The 1965 work by Roy Lichtenstein is a comic critique of Abstract Expressionist painting.*

## MUSEUM GUIDE
*The Leonard and Evelyn Lauder galleries on the fifth floor have permanent collections, showing works by Calder, O'Keeffe, and Hopper. Changing exhibitions occupy the lobby and the second, third, and fourth floors.*

**Early Sunday Morning** *(1930)*
*Edward Hopper's paintings often convey the emptiness of American city life.*

**Dempsey and Firpo**
*In 1924, George Bellows depicted one of the most famous prizefights of the century.*

### VISITORS' CHECKLIST

945 Madison Ave. **Map** 17 A5.
**Tel** (800) WHITNEY. M 6 to
77th St. M1–4, 30, M72,
M79. 11am–6pm Wed–Thu,
Sat, Sun, 1–9pm Fri. public
hols. **Lectures,
film/video presentations**.
www.whitney.org

**Three Flags** *(1958)*
*Jasper Johns's use of familiar objects in an abstract form was influential in the development of Pop Art.*

**Owh! In San Paõ** *(1951)*
*In this painting by Stuart Davis, abstract forms are combined with lettering to create a unique and distinctive American style.*

**Circus** *(1926–31)*
*Alexander Calder's fanciful creation is usually on display.*

**Tango** *(1919)*
*This is considered Polish-born Elie Nadelman's greatest wood sculpture.*

**Hudson River Landscape** *(1951)*
*This steel sculpture is one of David Smith's most influential works.*

# Frick Collection ❽

The priceless art collection of steel magnate Henry Clay Frick (1849–1919) is exhibited in a residential setting amid the furnishings of his opulent mansion, which provides a rare glimpse of how the extremely wealthy lived in New York's gilded age. Henry Frick intended the collection to be a memorial to himself and on his death he bequeathed the entire house to the nation. The collection includes important Old Master paintings, French furniture, rare Limoges enamels and beautiful Oriental rugs.

Fifth Avenue facade of the Frick Collection

**The Harbor of Dieppe** *(1826)*
*J.M.W.Turner was criticized by some skeptical contemporaries for depicting this northern European port suffused with light.*

Colonnade
Garden
Court

Library

West
Gallery

**The Polish Rider**
*The identity of the rider in this equestrian portrait, painted by Rembrandt in 1655, is unknown. The somber, rocky landscape creates an eerie atmosphere of unknown danger.*

## STAR PAINTINGS

★ Lady Meux by James McNeill Whistler

★ Mall in St. James's Park by Thomas Gainsborough

★ Officer and Laughing Girl by Johannes Vermeer

★ Sir Thomas More by Hans Holbein

★ **Sir Thomas More** *(1527)*
*Holbein's portrait of Henry VIII's Lord Chancellor was painted eight years before More's execution for treason.*

Living
Hall

## GALLERY GUIDE
*Of special interest are the West Gallery, with oils by Vermeer, Hals, and Rembrandt; the East Gallery, featuring Van Dyck and Whistler; the Oval Room, featuring Gainsborough; the Library and Dining Room, with English works; and the Living Hall, with works by Titian, Bellini, and Holbein.*

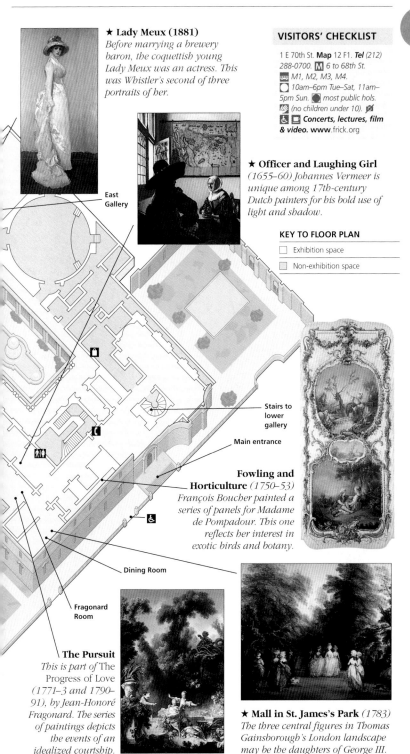

★ **Lady Meux** (1881)
*Before marrying a brewery baron, the coquettish young Lady Meux was an actress. This was Whistler's second of three portraits of her.*

East Gallery

**VISITORS' CHECKLIST**

1 E 70th St. **Map** 12 F1. *Tel* (212) 288-0700. M 6 to 68th St. M1, M2, M3, M4. 10am–6pm Tue–Sat, 11am–5pm Sun. most public hols. (no children under 10). Concerts, lectures, film & video. www.frick.org

★ **Officer and Laughing Girl**
*(1655–60) Johannes Vermeer is unique among 17th-century Dutch painters for his bold use of light and shadow.*

**KEY TO FLOOR PLAN**

☐ Exhibition space

☐ Non-exhibition space

Stairs to lower gallery

Main entrance

**Fowling and Horticulture** *(1750–53)*
*François Boucher painted a series of panels for Madame de Pompadour. This one reflects her interest in exotic birds and botany.*

Dining Room

Fragonard Room

**The Pursuit**
*This is part of* The Progress of Love *(1771–3 and 1790–91), by Jean-Honoré Fragonard. The series of paintings depicts the events of an idealized courtship.*

★ **Mall in St. James's Park** *(1783)*
*The three central figures in Thomas Gainsborough's London landscape may be the daughters of George III.*

# CENTRAL PARK

The city's "backyard" was created in 1858 by Frederick Law Olmsted and Calvert Vaux on an unpromising site of quarries, pig farms, swampland and shacks. Ten million cartloads of stone and earth turned it into the lush 843-acre (340-ha) park of today. There are scenic hills, lakes and lush meadows, dotted throughout with out-crops of Manhattan bedrock and planted with more than 500,000 trees and shrubs. Over the years the park has blossomed, with playgrounds and skating rinks, plus ball fields and spaces for every activity from chess and croquet to concerts and events. Cars are banned on weekends, giving bicyclists, in-line skaters and joggers the right-of-way.

Statues, Delacorte Theater (see p206)

## SIGHTS AT A GLANCE

**Historic Buildings**
Belvedere Castle ❸
The Dairy ❶

**Monuments and Statues**
Bethesda Fountain and Terrace ❺
Bow Bridge ❹
Strawberry Fields ❷

**Lakes and Gardens**
Central Park Wildlife Center ❼
Conservatory Garden ❽
Conservatory Water ❻

### SEE ALSO

• *Street Finder,* maps 12, 16, 21

**www**.centralparknyc.org

### GETTING THERE

Subway lines A, B, C, and D run the length of the park on the Upper West Side, with stops at 59th, 72nd, 81st, 86th, 96th, and 103rd Sts. The 59th St/Columbus Circle stop is served by the 1; the 2 and 3 stop at 110th Street; the N, R and W stop at 57th St and 5th Ave at the southern end of the park. Bus routes M1, M2, M3, and M4 run along the eastern edge of the park; M10 to the west, and M5 to the south.

**KEY**

| | |
|---|---|
| (shaded) | Tour map |
| **M** | Subway station |

0 meters 500
0 yards 500

◁ **Bird's-eye view of the park**

# A Tour of Central Park

On a short visit, a walking tour from 59th to 79th streets takes in some of Central Park's loveliest features, from the de nse wooded Ramble to the open formal spaces of Bethesda Terrace. Along the way, you will see artificial lakes and some of the 30 graceful bridges and arches, no two alike, that link some 58 miles (93 km) of footpaths, bridle paths, and roads in the park. In summer the park is often several degrees cooler than the city streets around it, and thus is a favorite retreat.

★ **Strawberry Fields**
*One of the park's most visited spots, this peaceful area was created in memory of John Lennon, who lived nearby* ❷

★ **Bethesda Fountain and Terrace**
*The richly ornamented formal terrace overlooks the Lake and the wooded shores of the Ramble* ❺

**Wollman Rink** was restored in the 1980s for future generations of skaters by tycoon Donald Trump.

**Central Park Wildlife Center**
*Three climate zones are home to over 100 species of animals* ❼

**The Pond**

**Plaza Hotel**
*(see p181)*

**Frick Collection**
*(see pp202–3)*

★ **The Dairy**
*This Victorian Gothic building houses the Visitor Center. Make it your first stop and pick up a calendar of park events* ❶

**Hans Christian Andersen's** statue is a favorite Central Park landmark for children. It is on the west side of Conservatory Water and is a popular site for storytelling in the summer.

**Bow Bridge**
*This cast-iron bridge links the Ramble with Cherry Hill by a graceful arch, 60 ft (18 m) above the Lake* ❹

**LOCATOR MAP**
See Manhattan Map pp14–15

**Alice in Wonderland** is immortalized in bronze at the northern end of Conservatory Water, along with her friends the Cheshire Cat, the Mad Hatter and the Dormouse. Children love to slide down her toadstool seat.

**STAR SIGHTS**

★ The Dairy

★ Strawberry Fields

★ Belvedere Castle

★ Bethesda Fountain

★ Conservatory Water

kota
ilding
e p218)

**San Remo Apartments**
*(see p214)*

**American Museum of Natural History**
*(see pp216–17)*

GREAT LAWN

**Metropolitan Museum** *(see pp190–97)*

**Obelisk**

**The Ramble** is a wooded area of 37 acres (15 ha), crisscrossed by paths and streams. It is a paradise for birdwatchers. Over 250 species of birds have been spotted in the park, which is on the Atlantic migration flyway.

**Reservoir**

**Guggenheim Museum**
*(see pp188–89)*

**★ Belvedere Castle**
*From the terraces there are unequaled views of the city and surrounding park. Within the stone walls is the Central Park Learning Center* ❸

**★ Conservatory Water**
*From March to November, this is the scene of model boat races each Saturday. Many of the tiny craft are stored in the boathouse that adjoins the Lake* ❻

The Carousel, part of the park's Children's District

# The Dairy ❶

**Map** 12 F2. **Tel** (212) 794-6564.
Ⓜ Fifth Ave. ◯ 10am–5pm
Tue–Sun. **Slide show.** 🖼
www.centralparknyc.org

Now used as Central Park's Visitor Center, this charming building of natural stone was planned as part of the "Children's District" of the park, which included a playground, the Carousel, a Children's Cottage, and stable. In 1873, there were cows grazing on the meadows in front of the Dairy, a ewe and her lambs feeding nearby, and chickens, guinea fowl, and peacocks roaming the lawn. City children could get fresh milk and other refreshments here. Over the years, the Dairy deteriorated, being used as a shed until restoration in 1979, done according to original photographs and drawings. The Dairy is the place to begin exploring the lush and leafy park; maps and details of events can be obtained here. The less energetic can rent chess and checkers sets for use on the pretty inlaid boards of the *kinderberg*, the charming little "children's hill" nearby.

# Strawberry Fields ❷

**Map** 12 E1. Ⓜ 72nd St.

The restoration of this teardrop-shaped section of the park was Yoko Ono's tribute in memory of her slain husband, John Lennon. They lived in the Dakota apartments overlooking this spot (*see p218*). Gifts for the garden came from all over the world. A mosaic set in the pathway, inscribed with the word *Imagine* (named for Lennon's famous song), was a gift from the city of Naples in Italy.

This broad expanse of the park's landscape was designed by Vaux and Olmsted. Now it is an international peace garden, with 161 species of plants (one from every country of the world), including jetbead, roses, witch hazel, birches – and strawberries.

# Belvedere Castle ❸

**Map** 16 E4. **Tel** (212) 772-0210.
Ⓜ 81st St. ◯ 10am–5pm Tue–Sun.
📷 ♿ to main floor only.

This stone castle atop Vista Rock, complete with tower and turrets, offers one of the best views of the park and the city from its lookout on the rooftop. Inside is the Henry Luce Nature Observatory, with a delightful exhibit telling inquisitive young visitors about the surprising variety of wildlife to be found in the park.

The view to the north from the castle allows you to look down into

Belvedere Castle with its lookout over the park

the Delacorte Theater, home to the free productions of Shakespeare in the Park every summer, featuring big-name stars (*see p347*). The theater was the gift of George T. Delacorte. Publisher and founder of Dell paperbacks, Delacorte was a delightful philanthropist who was responsible for many of the park's pleasures.

# Bow Bridge ❹

**Map** 16 E5. Ⓜ 72nd St.

This is one of the park's seven original cast-iron bridges and is considered one of the finest. It was designed by Vaux as a bow tying together the two large sections of the Lake. In the 19th century, when the Lake was used for ice skating, a red ball was hoisted from a bell tower on Vista Rock to signal that the ice was safe. The bridge offers expansive views of the park and the buildings bordering it on both the east and west sides.

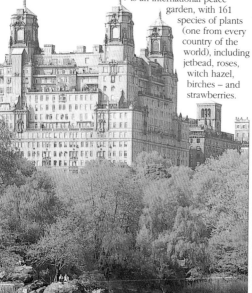
A tranquil scene in Central Park, overlooked by exclusive apartments

An 1864 print of Bethesda Fountain and Terrace

# Bethesda Fountain and Terrace ❺

**Map** 12 E1. Ⓜ *72nd St.*

Situated between the Lake and the Mall, this is the architectural heart of the park, a formal element in the naturalistic landscape. The fountain was dedicated in 1873. The statue, *Angel of the Waters*, marked the opening of the Croton Aqueduct system in 1842, bringing the city its first supply of pure water; its name refers to a biblical account of a healing angel at the pool of Bethesda in Jerusalem. The Spanish-style detailing, such as the sculptured double staircase, tiles, and friezes, is by Jacob Wrey Mould.

The terrace is one of the best spots to relax and take in some people-watching.

# Conservatory Water ❻

**Map** 16 F5. Ⓜ *77th St.*

Better known as the Model Boat Pond, this stretch of water is home to model yacht races every weekend.

At the north end of the lake, a sculpture of Alice in Wonderland is a delight for children. It was commissioned by George T. Delacorte in honor of his wife. He himself is immortalized in caricature as the Mad Hatter. On the west bank, free story hours are held at a statue of Hans Christian Andersen, portrayed reading from his own story, "The Ugly Duckling," while its hero

waddles at his feet. Like that of Alice, this statue is climbed on by small children, who especially like to snuggle in the author's lap.

Conservatory Water's literary links continue into adolescence: it is here that J. D. Salinger's Holden Caulfield comes to tell the ducks his troubles in *The Catcher in the Rye*.

# Central Park Wildlife Center ❼

**Map** 12 F2. *Tel* (212) 439-6500. Ⓜ *Fifth Ave between 63rd and 66th sts.* ⃝ *10am–5pm Mon–Fri, 10am–5:30pm Sat–Sun; Nov–Mar: 10am–4:30 daily. Last admission 30 mins before closing.* ⃠ ◻ ⛾ ◻ ◻ www.centralparkzoo.com

Reopened in 1988 after four years of reconstruction, this imaginative zoo won plaudits for its creative and humane use of small space. More than 130 species of animals are represented in three climate zones, the Tropics, the Polar Circle, and the California coast. An equatorial rain forest is home to monkeys and free-flying birds, while penguins and polar bears populate an Arctic landscape that allows views both above

and under water. At the Tisch Children's Zoo children can get close to goats, sheep, cows, and pot-bellied pigs. By its entrance is the much-loved Delacorte Clock, which plays nursery rhymes every half hour, as bronze musical animals (such as a goat playing pan pipes) circle around it. Toward Willowdell Arch is another favorite – the memorial to Balto, leader of a team of huskies that made a heroic journey across Alaska with serum for a diphtheria epidemic.

Statue of Balto, the heroic husky dog, Central Park Wildlife Center

# Conservatory Garden ❽

**Map** 21 B5. Ⓜ *Central Pk N, 103rd St.* *Tel* (212) 860-1382. ⃝ *8am–dusk.* ⛾

The Vanderbilt Gate on Fifth Avenue is the entry to a 6-acre (2.4-ha) park containing three formal gardens. Each one represents a different national landscape style. The Central Garden, with a large lawn, yew hedges, crabapple trees, and a wisteria pergola recreates an Italian style. The South Garden, spilling over with perennials, represents an English style, with a bronze statue in the reflecting pool of Mary and Dickon, from Frances Hodgson Burnett's *The Secret Garden*. Beyond is a slope with thousands of native wildflowers, spreading into the park beyond. The North Garden, in the French style, centers around the bronze *Fountain of the Three Dancing Maidens*. It puts on a brief but brilliant display of annuals each summer.

Polar bear in the Central Park Wildlife Center

# UPPER WEST SIDE

This district of New York became residential in the 1870s, when the Ninth Avenue elevated railroad (see pp26-7) made commuting to midtown possible. The Dakota, the city's first luxury apartment house, was built here in 1884, and the streets were graded and leveled. Buildings sprang

Indian mask, Museum of Natural History

up on Broadway and Central Park West, and cross streets, dating from the 1890s, still retain fine brownstone row houses. The area is bustling and diverse, with many cultural institutions, including the American Museum of Natural History, Lincoln Center, and Columbus Circle complex for Time Warner and CNN.

## SIGHTS AT A GLANCE

### Historic Streets and Buildings
Columbus Circle **7**
Pomander Walk **13**
Riverside Drive and Park **14**
The Dakota **9**
The Dorilton **17**
Twin Towers of Central Park West **1**

### Museums and Galleries
*American Museum of Natural History pp216–17* **11**
Children's Museum of Manhattan **15**
Hayden Planetarium **12**
New-York Historical Society **10**

### Famous Theaters
Avery Fisher Hall **6**
Lincoln Center for the Performing Arts **2**
Lincoln Center Theater **5**
Metropolitan Opera House **4**
New York State Theater **3**

### Landmark Hotels and Restaurants
Hotel des Artistes **8**
The Ansonia **16**

### GETTING THERE
By subway, take the A, B, C, D, or 1 to Columbus Circle, the 1, 2, or 3 along Broadway, or the B and C along Central Park West. Buses include the M10 (Central Park West), M7, M11, M104, and M5 or M66 or M72 crosstown buses.

### SEE ALSO
- **Street Finder**, maps 11, 15
- **Where to Stay** pp290–91
- **Restaurants** pp309–10

### KEY
Street-by-Street map
**M** Subway station

◁ **The facade of 14 Riverside Drive**

# Street by Street: Lincoln Center

Lincoln Center was conceived when both the Metropolitan Opera House and the New York Philharmonic required homes, and a large tract on Manhattan's west side was in dire need of revitalization. The notion of a single complex where different performing arts could exist side by side seems natural today, but in the 1950s it was considered both daring and risky. Today Lincoln Center has proved itself by drawing audiences of five million each year. Proximity to its halls prompts both performers and arts lovers to live nearby.

★ **Lincoln Center for the Performing Arts**
*Dance, music, and theater come together in this fine contemporary complex. It is also a great place to sit around the reflecting fountain and people-watch* ❷

**Lincoln Center Theater**
*The Vivian Beaumont and the Mitzi E. Newhouse theaters are both housed in this building* ❺

**Composer Leonard Bernstein's** famous musical *West Side Story,* which was based on the Romeo and Juliet theme, was set in the impoverished streets around what is now Lincoln Center. Bernstein was later instrumental in setting up the large music complex.

**The Guggenheim Bandshell** in Damrosch Park is the site of free concerts.

**The New York State Theater**
*This is the home of the New York City Ballet, as well as an opera company. The theater seats 2,737 people* ❸

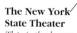

**The College Board Building** is an Art Deco delight that now houses condominiums and the administrative offices of the College Board, developers of the college entrance exam.

**Metropolitan Opera House**
*Lincoln Center's focus is the Opera House. The café at the top of the lobby offers wonderful plaza views* ❹

**Early American quilt**

**American Folk Art Museum**
Quilting and naïve painting are some of the arts displayed here.

**James Dean** once lived in a one-room apartment on the top floor at 19 West 68th Street.

### ★ Hotel des Artistes
*Artists Isadora Duncan, Noël Coward and Norman Rockwell once lived here. It also houses a much-praised restaurant (see p310)*
**8**

**LOCATOR MAP**
*see Manhattan Map pp14–15*

**KEY**

– – – Suggested route

| 0 meters | 100 |
| 0 yards | 100 |

**To 72nd Street subway (4 blocks)**

**An ABC-TV** sound stage for soap operas is housed in this castle-like building, formerly an armory.

W 67TH STREET

65TH STREET

WEST

**55 Central Park West** is the Art Deco apartment building that featured in the film *Ghostbusters*.

PARK

CENTRAL

**The Society for Ethical Culture** was one of the city's first Art Nouveau buildings. It also houses a school.

**To 59th Street subway (2 blocks)**

**Central Park West** is home to many celebrities, who like the privacy of its exclusive apartments.

**Century Apartments**
*The Century's twin towers are visible from the park, making it a New York landmark* **1**

### STAR SIGHTS

★ Lincoln Center

★ Hotel des Artistes

The San Remo, a twin-towered apartment house designed by Emery Roth

## Twin Towers of Central Park West ●

**Map** 12 D1, 12 D2, 16 D3, 16 D5.
Ⓜ *59th St-Columbus Circle, 72nd St, 81St, 86th St.* ⬜ *to the public.*

Among the most familiar landmarks on the New York skyline are the four twin-towered apartment houses on Central Park West. Built between 1929 and 1931, before the Great Depression halted all luxury construction, they are among the most highly sought-after residences in New York.

Admired today for their grace and architectural detail, they were designed in response to a city planning law allowing taller apartments if setbacks and towers were used.

Emery Roth designed the San Remo (145 CPW), whose tenants have included Dustin Hoffman, Paul Simon, and Diane Keaton. Turned down by the residents' committee, Madonna went to live close by at 1 West 64th Street. The towers of the Eldorado (300 CPW), also designed by Roth, were home to

Groucho Marx, Marilyn Monroe, and Richard Dreyfuss. The Majestic (115 CPW) and the Century (25 CPW) are both sleek classics by Art Deco designer Irwin S. Chanin.

## Lincoln Center for the Performing Arts ●

**Map** 11 C2. *Tel (212) 546-2656.*
Ⓜ *66th St.* ♿ 🖼 *(212) 875-5350.*
🍴 🅿 *See Entertainment pp350–51.* **www**.lincolncenter.org

In May 1959, President Eisenhower traveled to New York to turn a shovelful of earth, Leonard Bernstein lifted his baton, the New York Philharmonic and the Juilliard Choir broke into the Hallelujah Chorus –

and the city's most important cultural center was born. It soon covered 15 acres (6 ha) on the site of the slums that had been the setting for Bernstein's classic musical *West Side Story*. The plaza fountain is by Philip Johnson, and the sculpture, *Reclining Figure*, is by Henry Moore.

Jazz at the Lincoln Center has developed a state-of-the-art facility dedicated to jazz performances. It forms part of a major new complex at Columbus Circle *(see p215).*

## New York State Theater ●

Lincoln Center. **Map** 11 D2.
*Tel (212) 870-5560.* Ⓜ *66th St.*
♿ 🖼 🍴 🅿 *See Entertainment pp346–7.* **www**.nycballet.com

The home base for the highly acclaimed New York City Ballet and the New York City Opera, a troupe devoted to presenting opera at popular prices, is a Philip Johnson design. It was inaugurated in 1964.

Gargantuan white marble sculptures by Elie Nadelman dominate the vast four-story foyer. The theater seats 2,800 people. Because of its rhinestone lights and chandeliers both inside and out, some have described the theater as "a little jewel box."

## Metropolitan Opera House ●

Lincoln Center. **Map** 11 D2. *Tel (212) 362-6000.* Ⓜ *66th St.* ♿ 🖼 🍴 🅿 *See Entertainment pp350–51.* **www**.metopera.org; **www**.abt.org

Home to the Metropolitan Opera Company and the American Ballet Theater, "the Met" is the most spectacular of Lincoln Center's buildings. Five great arched windows offer views of the opulent foyer and two radiant murals by Marc Chagall. (You can't see them in the mornings when they are protected from the sun.)

Central plaza at Lincoln Center

Inside there are curved white marble stairs, miles of plush red carpeting, and exquisite starburst crystal chandeliers

**Concert at Guggenheim Bandshell, Damrosh Park, near the Met**

that are raised to the ceiling just before each performance. All the greats have sung here, including Maria Callas, Jessye Norman, and Luciano Pavarotti. First nights are glittering, star-studded occasions.

The Guggenheim Bandshell, in Damrosch Park next to the Met, is a popular concert site with music from opera to jazz. The high point of the season is the Lincoln Center Out-of-Doors Festival, which takes place in August.

# Lincoln Center Theater ❺

Lincoln Center. **Map** 11 C2. **Tel** (212) 362-7600 (Beaumont and Newhouse), (212) 870-1630 (Library). 800-432 7250 (tickets). M 66th St. 🅰 ✍ 🍴 🏠 See **Entertainment** pp350–51. www.lct.org

Two theaters make up this innovative complex, where eclectic and often experimental drama is presented.

The theaters are the 1000-seat Vivian Beaumont and the more intimate 280-seat Mitzi E. Newhouse. Works by some of New York's best modern playwrights have featured at the Beaumont. Among these was Arthur Miller's *After the Fall*, the theater's inaugural performance in 1962.

The size of the Newhouse suits workshop-style plays, but it can still make the news with theatrical gems such as Robin Williams and Steve Martin in a production

of Samuel Beckett's *Waiting for Godot*. The complex also houses the New York Public Library for the Performing Arts, which has exhibits including audio cylinders of early Met performances and original scores and playbills.

# Avery Fisher Hall ❻

Lincoln Center. **Map** 11 C2. **Tel** (212) 875-5030. M 66th St. 🅰 ✍ 🍴 🏠 See **Entertainment** pp350–51. www.newyorkphilharmonic.org

Located at the northern end of the Lincoln Center Plaza, Avery Fisher Hall is home to America's oldest orchestra, the New York Philharmonic. It also provides a stage for some of the Lincoln Center's own performers, and the Mostly Mozart Festival.

When the venue opened in 1962 as the Philharmonic Hall, critics initially complained about the acoustics. Several structural modifications, however, have rendered the hall an acoustic gem, comparing favorably with other great classical concert halls around the world. For a small fee, the public can attend rehearsals on Thursday mornings in the 2,738-seat auditorium.

# Columbus Circle ❼

Columbus Circle, New York. **Map** 12 D3. M 59th St. **Concerts** (212) 258 9800. www.jazzatlincolncenter.org

Presiding over this urban plaza at the corner of Central Park is a marble statue of explorer Christopher Columbus, perched on top of a tall granite column. The statue is one of the few remaining original features in this circle – which has become one of the largest building projects in New York's history.

New multi-use skyscrapers have been erected, attracting national and international businesses. Global

media company Time Warner has its headquarters in a new 80-storey skyscraper. The 2.8 million sq ft (260,000 sq m) building provides a retail, entertainment, and restaurant facility. Facilities include shops such as Hugo Boss, Williams-Sonoma, and Borders Books; dining at Per Se and Jean-George Vongerichten's Steakhouse; and the sixth hotel in the Mandarin Oriental chain.

The Time Warner Center is also home to Jazz at the Lincoln Center. The two venues here – The Frederic P. Rose Concert Hall and The Allen Room – together with a jazz club and education center, comprise the world's first performing arts facility dedicated to jazz.

Other notable buildings in Columbus Circle include Hearst House designed by British architect Norman Foster, Trump International Hotel, the Maine Monument, and the Museum of Arts and Design, due to open in spring 2008.

# Hotel des Artistes ❽

1 W 67th St. **Map** 12 D2. **Tel** (212) 877-3500 (café). M 72nd St.

Built in 1918 by George Mort Pollard, these two-story apartments were intended to be working artists' studios but they have attracted a variety of interesting tenants, including Alexander Woollcott, Norman Rockwell, Isadora Duncan, Rudolph Valentino, and Noël Coward. The Café des Artistes is well known for its misty, romantic Howard Chandler Christy murals and its fine cuisine.

**Decorative figure on the Hotel des Artistes**

# American Museum of Natural History ⑪

This is one of the world's largest natural history museums. Since the original building opened in 1877, the complex has grown to cover four city blocks, and today holds more than 30 million specimens and artifacts. The most popular areas are the dinosaurs, and the Milstein Hall of Ocean Life. The Rose Center for Earth and Space includes the Hayden Planetarium *(see p218)*.

The facade on 77th Street

## STAR EXHIBITS

★ Barosaurus

★ Blue Whale

★ Great Canoe

★ Star of India

### ★ Star of India
*This 563-carat gem is the world's largest blue star sapphire. Found in Sri Lanka, it was given to the museum by J. P. Morgan in 1900.*

## GALLERY GUIDE
*Enter at Central Park West onto the second floor to view the Barosaurus exhibit, African, Asian, Central and South American peoples and animals. First floor exhibits include ocean life, meteors, minerals and gems, and the Hall of Biodiversity. North American Indians, birds, and reptiles occupy the third floor. Dinosaurs, fossil fishes, and early mammals are on the fourth floor.*

### ★ Blue Whale
*The blue whale is the largest animal, living or extinct. Its weight can exceed 100 tons. This replica is based on a female captured off South America in 1925.*

### ★ Great Canoe
*This 63-ft (19.2-m) seafaring war canoe of the Haida Indians was carved from the trunk of a single cedar. It stands in the Grand Gallery.*

Entrance on W. 77th St

Dinosaurs

Fourth floor

Third floor

Second floor

First floor

Rose Center for Earth and Space
(see p218)

Central Park West entrance

## VISITORS' CHECKLIST

Central Park West at 79th St. **Map**
16 D5. **Tel** (212) 769-5100. **M** B,
C to 81st St. **M7, M10, M11,
M79, M104.** ◯ 10am–5:45pm
daily. (Rose Center open until
8:45pm 1st Fri of month). www.amnh.org

### Komodo Dragons

*The largest living
lizards, which can
grow to 10 ft (3 m), live
on Komodo and other
Indonesian islands.*

### African Elephants

*Four of the elephants in this group were collected
and mounted in the 1920s by Carl Akeley, who
created the museum's Hall of African Mammals.*

### ★ Barosaurus

*This exhibit, which shows
the skeletons of a mother
Barosaurus rearing up to
protect her baby from an
attacking predator, was
cast from original fossils.
The plant-eating dinosaur
lived 140 million years ago.*

### KEY TO FLOOR PLAN

| | |
|---|---|
| ▦ | Dinosaurs and other fossil vertebrates |
| ▦ | Birds |
| ▢ | Fishes |
| ▢ | Mammals |
| ▦ | Meteorites, minerals, and gems |
| ▢ | Human cultures |
| ▢ | Human origins |
| ▢ | Amphibians and reptiles |
| ▢ | Environment and ecology |
| ▢ | Rose Center for Earth and Space |
| ▢ | Special exhibitions |
| ▢ | Non-exhibition space |

### Giant Sequoia

*Sequoias are among the
world's longest-lived
plants. This section has
1,342 annual rings and
measures more than
16 ft (4.8 m) across.*

# The Dakota ❾

1 W 72nd St. **Map** 12 D1.
Ⓜ *72nd St.* ⬤ *to the public.*

The name and style reflect
the fact that this apartment
building was truly "way out
West" when Henry J. Hardenbergh, the architect responsible
for the Plaza Hotel, designed
it in 1880–84. It was New
York's first luxury apartment
house and was originally
surrounded by squatters'
shacks and wandering farm
animals. Commissioned by
Edward S. Clark, heir to the
Singer sewing machine
fortune, it is one of the city's
most prestigious addresses.
    The Dakota's 65 luxurious
apartments have had many
famous owners, including
Judy Garland, Lauren Bacall,
Leonard Bernstein, and Boris
Karloff, whose ghost is said
to haunt the place. It was the
setting for the film *Rosemary's
Baby,* and the site of the
tragic murder of former Beatle
John Lennon. His widow,
Yoko Ono, still lives here.

**Carved Indian head over the
entrance to the Dakota**

# New-York
# Historical Society ❿

170 Central Park West. **Map** 16 D5.
**Tel** *(212) 873-3400.* Ⓜ *81st St.*
**Galleries** ◯ *10am–6pm Tue–Sat.*
🖼 **Library** ◯ *10am–5pm Tue–Sun
(Tue–Fri in summer).* ⬤ *public hols.*
🚫 ♿ 📷 🖥 🏬
**www.nyhistory.org**

Founded in 1804, this society
houses a distinguished research
library and the city's oldest

**The Rose Center for Earth and Space**

museum. Its collections include
historical material relating to
slavery and the Civil War, an
outstanding collection of 18th-
century newspapers, all 435
watercolors of Audubon's
*Birds of America*, and the
world's largest collection of
Tiffany lamps and glasswork.
There are also fine displays of
American furniture and silver.

# American Museum
# of Natural
# History ⓫

*See pp216–17.*

# Hayden
# Planetarium ⓬

Central Park West at 81st St.
**Map** 16 D4. **Tel** *(212) 769-5100, for
Space Show tickets: (212) 769-5200.*
Ⓜ *81st St.* **www.**amnh.org/rose

On the northern side of the
American Museum of Natural
History *(see pp216–17)* is the
Hayden Planetarium, centerpiece of the spectacular new
Rose Center for Earth and
Space, designed by Polshek
and Partners. Housed within
an 87-ft (26-m) sphere, the
Planetarium contains a techno-
logically advanced Space
Theater, the Cosmic Pathway,
a 350-ft (107-m) spiral ramp
with a timeline chronicling
13 billion years of evolution,
and a Big Bang Theater, where
the origins of the universe
are explained.
    The Hall of Planet Earth,
centered around rock samples
and using state-of-the-art
computer and video displays
explaining how the Earth
works, explores our geologic
history. Exhibits in the Hall
of the Universe present the

discoveries of modern
astrophysics. Four
zones have hands-on
interactive exhibits.
Seen from the street at
night, the Rose Center
is simply breath-
taking; the exhibits
inside prove that,
as Carl Sagan said,
"We are starstuff."

# Pomander Walk ⓭

261–7 W 94th St. **Map** 15 C2.
Ⓜ *96th St.*

Look through the gate for
a delightful surprise – a
double row of tiny town
houses built in 1921 to look
like the London mews setting
of a popular play of the same
name. It was much favored as
a home by movie actors,
including Rosalind Russell,
Humphrey Bogart, and the
Gish sisters.

**Facade of a house on Pomander Walk**

# Riverside Drive
# and Park ⓮

**Map** 15 B1–B5, 20 D1–D5.
Ⓜ *79th St, 86th St, 96th St.*

Riverside Drive is one of the
city's most attractive streets –
broad, with shaded and
lovely views of the Hudson
River. It is lined with the
opulent original town houses
as well as newer apartment
buildings. At 40–46, 74–77,
81–89, and 105–107 Riverside
Drive are houses designed in
the late 19th century by local
architect Clarence F. True.
The curved gables, bays and

arched windows seem to suit the curves of the road and the flow of the river.

The bizarrely named Cliff Dwellers' Apartments at 243 (between 96th and 97th streets) is a 1914 building with a frieze showing early Arizona cliff dwellers, complete with masks, buffalo skulls, mountain lions, and rattlesnakes.

Riverside Park was designed by Frederick Law Olmsted in 1880. He also laid out Central Park *(see pp204–07)*.

**Soldiers' and Sailors' monument in Riverside Park**

# Children's Museum of Manhattan ⓳

212 W 83rd St. **Map** 15 C4. **Tel** *(212) 721-1234.* Ⓜ *79th St, 81st St, 86th St.* ◯ *10am–5pm Tue–Sun.* ◗ *Jan 1, Thanksgiving, Dec 25.* 🎫 📷 ♿ 🛈 **www**.cmom.org

This particularly imaginative participatory museum was founded in 1973 on the premise that children learn best through play. The Body Odyssey shows kids what they're made of in a fun-filled scientific ride through the body. The HP Inventor Center transports kids to this digital domain where they can rethink, revise, and reshape design solutions.

The Time Warner Media Center transforms children into budding camera operators, newscasters, animators, and

**Children's Museum entrance**

technicians in a state-of-the-art TV studio. On weekends and holidays there are guest performers, from puppeteers to storytellers, in the 150-seat theater. On Saturdays children have the opportunity to make their own books. There is also a gallery for free play and a Word Play area for early language acquisition.

# The Ansonia ⓰

2109 Broadway. **Map** 15 C5. Ⓜ *72nd St.* ◗ *to the public.*

This Beaux Arts gem was built in 1899 by William Earl Dodge Stokes, heir to the Phelps Dodge Company fortune, who brought French architect Paul E.M. Duboy to design a building to rival the Dakota. The hotel was converted to a condominium in 1992. The most prominent features are the round corner tower and the two-story mansard roof adorned with single and double dormers. The building had a roof garden (complete with Dodge's menagerie: ducks,

**Distinctive rounded turret of the Ansonia Hotel**

chickens, and a tame bear) and two swimming pools.

The hotel's thick, sound-muffling walls soon made it a favorite with the musical stars of yesteryear. Florenz Ziegfeld, Arturo Toscanini, Enrico Caruso, Igor Stravinsky, and Lily Pons were once regular guests there.

# The Dorilton ⓱

171 W 71st St. **Map** 11 C1. Ⓜ *72nd St.* ◗ *to the public.*

Opulent detail and an impressive high mansard roof adorn this apartment house. On the West 71st Street side of the building is a nine-story-high gateway. To the modern eye, the Dorilton is gloriously elaborate, but when it was first built in 1902 it provoked this reaction, reported by the *Architectural Record*: "The sight of it makes strong men

**Balcony on the Dorilton, supported by groaning figures**

swear and weak women shrink affrighted."

What would the critics have made of the Alexandria Condominium, at 135 West 70th Street, just a block away? Built in 1927 as the Pythian Temple, its current name stems from the lavish Egyptian-style motifs that adorned this former Masonic lodge. Many were stripped away when the building was converted to a condominium, but you can still see what the polychrome designs were like. There are lotus leaves, hieroglyphics, ornately carved columns, mythical beasts, and, in majestic splendor on the roof, two seated pharaohs.

# MORNINGSIDE HEIGHTS AND HARLEM

**St. Francis of Assisi, Museo del Barrio**

Morningside Heights, near the Hudson River, is home to Columbia University and two of the city's finest churches. Farther east is Hamilton Heights, situated on the border of Harlem, America's most famous black community. One way to see the district's highlights, which are spread over a large area, is by taking one of the tours offered, including a Sunday morning tour *(see p369)*. Many tours start in Hamilton Heights, move east to the St. Nicholas Historic District, stop to enjoy the gospel choir at the Abyssinian Baptist Church, and end with a southern-style brunch at Sylvia's, Harlem's best-known restaurant.

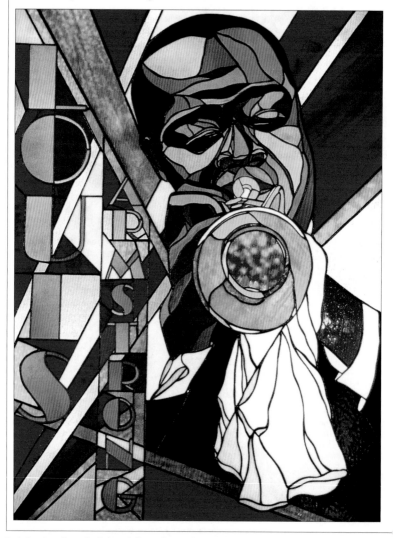

**Louis Armstrong in a stained-glass window at the new Cotton Club**

## SIGHTS AT A GLANCE

### Historic Streets and Buildings
City College of the City University of New York **7**
Columbia University **1**
Grant's Tomb **6**
Hamilton Grange National Memorial **8**
Hamilton Heights Historic District **9**
Low Library **3**
Mount Morris Historic District **17**
St. Paul's Chapel **2**
St. Nicholas Historic District **10**

### Museums and Galleries
Museo del Barrio **19**
Schomburg Center for Research into Black Culture **12**
Studio Museum in Harlem **16**

### Famous Theaters
Apollo Theater **15**
Harlem YMCA **13**

### Churches
Abyssinian Baptist Church **11**
*Cathedral of St. John the Divine pp226–7* **4**
Riverside Church **5**

### Parks and Squares
Marcus Garvey Park **18**

### Landmark Restaurants
Sylvia's **14**

Carved stone column,
**Cathedral of St. John
the Divine**

### SEE ALSO
- *Street Finder,* maps 19–21
- *Harlem Walk* pp272–3
- *Where to Stay* p291
- *Restaurants* p310

0 meters        500

0 yards        500

### KEY

▨ Street-by-Street map

**M** Subway station

### GETTING THERE
By subway, take the 7th Ave/Broadway local 1 train to 116th St/Columbia University. The M4, M5, M11, and M104 buses serve the area. For Harlem, take the A, B, C, D, 2, or 3 lines to 125th St, or the M1, M2, M7, or M100/101 buses.

# Street by Street: Columbia University

A great university is as much spirit as buildings. After admiring the architecture, linger awhile on Columbia's central quadrangle in front of the Low Library, where you will see the jeans-clad future leaders of America meeting and mingling between classes. Across from the campus on both Broadway and Amsterdam Avenue are the coffee-houses and cafés where students engage in lengthy philosophical arguments, debate the topics of the day or simply unwind.

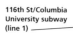

**Alma Mater** was sculpted by Daniel Chester French in 1903 and survived a bomb blast in the 1968 student demonstrations.

**116th St/Columbia University subway (line 1)**

**The School of Journalism** is one of Columbia's many McKim, Mead & White buildings. Founded in 1912 by publisher Joseph Pulitzer, it is the home of the Pulitzer Prize awarded for the best in letters and music.

**Butler Library** is Columbia's main library.

**Low Library**
*With its imposing façade and high dome, the library dominates the main quadrangle. McKim, Mead & White designed it in 1895–97* ❸

★ **Central Quadrangle**
*Columbia's first buildings were designed by McKim, Mead & White and built around a central quadrangle. This view looks across the quad toward Butler Library* ❶

### St. Paul's Chapel
*esigned by the architects Howells &
okes in 1907, this church is known
or its fine woodwork and magnificent vaulted interior. It is full of
light and has fine acoustics* ❷

**The Sherman
Fairchild
Center** was
built in 1977
to house the
university's
life sciences
departments.

**LOCATOR MAP**
*See Manhattan Map pp14–15*

**KEY**

− − − Suggested route

0 meters 100
0 yards 100

*116TH ST*

*MORNINGSIDE DRIVE*

**Student demonstrations** put Columbia
University in the news in 1968.
The demonstrations were sparked
by the university's plan to build a
gymnasium in nearby Morningside
Park. The protests forced the
university to build elsewhere.

**The Eglise de Notre Dame** was built for a
French-speaking congregation. Behind
the altar is a replica of the grotto at
Lourdes, France, the gift of a woman
who believed her son was healed there.

**★ Cathedral of St.
John the Divine**
*If this Neo-Gothic
cathedral is ever
finished, it will be
the largest in the
world. Although one third of the
structure has not yet been built, it
can hold 10,000 parishioners* ❹

**Carved
stonework**
decorates the
facade of the
Cathedral.

**STAR SIGHTS**

★ Cathedral of
St. John the Divine

★ Central
Quadrangle

*Alma Mater* statue at the Low Library, Columbia University

# Columbia University ❶

Main entrance at W 116th St and Broadway. **Map** 20 E3. **Tel** *(212) 854-1754.* Ⓜ *116th St-Columbia University.* 🔲 *11am, 2pm Mon–Fri.* **www**.columbia.edu

This is the third location of one of America's oldest universities. Founded in 1754 as King's College, it was first situated close to where the World Trade Center stood.

In 1814, when a move uptown was proposed, the university approached the authorities for funding but was instead given a plot of land valued at $75,000, on which to build a new home. The university never built on the land itself, but leased it out and spent the years from 1857 to 1897 in buildings nearby. It finally sold the plot in 1985 to the leaseholders, Rockefeller Center Inc., for $400 million.

The present campus was begun in 1897 on the site of the Bloomingdale Insane Asylum. Charles McKim, the architect, placed the university on a terrace, serenely above street level. Its spacious lawns and plazas still create a sense of contrast in the busy city.

Columbia, an Ivy League School, is noted for its law, medicine, and journalism schools. Its distinguished faculty and alumni, past and present, include over 50 Nobel laureates. Famous alumni include Isaac Asimov, J.D. Salinger, James Cagney, and Joan Rivers. Across the street is the affiliated Barnard College, a highly selective liberal arts college for women.

# St. Paul's Chapel ❷

Columbia University. **Map** 20 E3. **Tel** *(212) 854-1487, for concert info.* Ⓜ *116th St-Columbia Univ.* 🔲 *10am–11pm Mon–Sat (term time), 10am–4pm (breaks).* 🕆 *Sun.* 📷 ♿

Interior brick vaulting of St. Paul's Chapel dome

Columbia's most outstanding building, built in 1904, is a mix of Italian Renaissance, Byzantine, and Gothic. The interior Guastavino vaulting is of intricate patterns of aged red brick; the whole chapel is bathed in light from above.

The free organ concerts are an exceptionally fine way to appreciate the beauty and acoustics of this church. The Aeolian-Skinner pipe organ is renowned for its fine tone.

Facade of St. Paul's Chapel

# Low Library ❸

Columbia University. **Map** 20 E3. Ⓜ *116th St-Columbia University.*

A Classical, columned building atop three flights of stone stairs, the library was donated by Seth Low, a former mayor and college president. The statue in front of it, *Alma Mater* by Daniel Chester French, became familiar as the backdrop to the many 1968 anti-Vietnam War student demonstrations. The building is now used as offices, and its rotunda for a variety of academic and ceremonial purposes. The books were moved in 1932 to the Butler Library, across the quadrangle. The university's library collections total some six million volumes.

# Cathedral of St. John the Divine ❹

*See pp226 –7.*

# Riverside Church ❺

490 Riverside Dr at 122nd St. **Map** 20 D2. **Tel** *(212) 870-6700.* Ⓜ *116th St-Columbia Univ.* 🔲 *10:30am–5pm Tue–Sun.* 🕆 *10:45am Sun.* 📷 *with prior permission.* ♿ 🎵 **Carillon bell concerts**; *(212) 870-6784; noon, 3pm Sun.* **Theater**; *(212) 864-2929.* 🖥 **www**.theriversidechurchny.org

A 21-story steel frame with a Gothic exterior, the church design was inspired by the cathedral at Chartres. It was lavishly funded by John D. Rockefeller, Jr., in 1930. The Laura Spelman Rockefeller Memorial Carillon (in honor of Rockefeller's mother) is the largest in the world, with 74

Columbia University's main courtyard and the Low Library

bells. The 20-ton Bourdon, or hour bell, is the largest and heaviest tuned carillon bell ever cast. The organ, with its 22,000 pipes, is among the largest in the world.

At the rear of the second gallery is a figure by Jacob Epstein, *Christ in Majesty*, cast in plaster and covered in gold leaf. Another Epstein statue, *Madonna and Child*, stands in the court next to the cloister. The panels of the chancel screen honor eight men and women whose lives have exemplified the teachings of Christ. They range from Socrates and Michelangelo to Florence Nightingale and Booker T. Washington.

For quiet reflection, enter the small, secluded Christ Chapel, patterned after an 11th-century Romanesque church in France. For views, take the elevator to the 20th floor and then walk the 140 steps to the top of the 392-ft (120-m) bell tower for a fine panorama of Upper Manhattan from the windy observation deck. (This is definitely not recommended when the bells are tolling.)

Mosaic mural in Grant's Tomb showing Grant (right) and Robert E. Lee

## Grant's Tomb ❻

W 122nd St and Riverside Dr. **Map** 20 D2. **Tel** *(212) 666-1640.* Ⓜ *116th St–Columbia Univ.* 🚌 *M5.* ◯ *9am–5pm daily.* ● *Jan 1, Thanksgiving, Dec 25.* 📷 ♿ ♿
**www**.nps.gov/gegr

This grandiose monument honors America's 18th president, Ulysses S. Grant, the commanding general of the Union forces in the Civil War.

The mausoleum contains the coffins of General Grant and his wife, in accordance with the president's last wish that they be buried together. After Grant's death in 1885, more than 90,000 Americans contributed $600,000 to build the sepulcher, which was inspired by Mausoleus's tomb at Halicarnassus, one of the Seven Wonders of the Ancient World.

**General Grant on a Civil War campaign**

The tomb was dedicated on what would have been Grant's 75th birthday, April 27, 1897. The parade of 50,000 people, along with a flotilla of 10 American and 5 European warships, took more than seven hours to pass in review.

The interior was inspired by Napoleon's tomb at Les Invalides in Paris. Each sarcophagus weighs 8.5 tons. Two exhibit rooms feature displays on Grant's personal life and his presidential and military career. Surrounding the north and east sides of the building are 17 sinuously curved mosaic benches that seem totally out of keeping with the formal architecture of the tomb. They were designed in the early 1970s by the Chilean-born Brooklyn artist Pedro Silva and were built by 1,200 local volunteers, who worked under his supervision. The benches were inspired by the work of Spanish architect Antonio Gaudi in Barcelona. The mosaics depict subjects ranging from the Inuit to New York taxis to Donald Duck.

A short walk north of Grant's Tomb is another monument. An unadorned urn on a pedestal marks the resting place of a young child who fell from the riverbank and drowned. His grieving father placed a marker that simply reads: "Erected to the memory of an amiable child, St. Clair Pollock, died 15 July 1797 in his fifth year of his age."

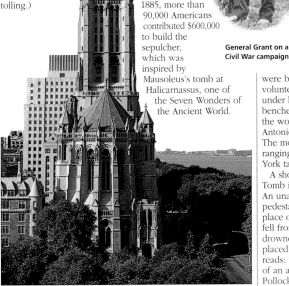

**The 21-story Riverside Church, from the north**

# Cathedral of St. John the Divine ❹

**Cram's Gothic West Front**

Started in 1892 and still only two-thirds finished, this will be the largest cathedral in the world. The interior is over 600 ft (180 m) long and 146 ft (45 m) wide. It was originally designed in Romanesque style by Heins and LaFarge; Ralph Adams Cram took over the project in 1911, devising a Gothic nave and west front. Medieval construction methods, such as stone on stone supporting buttresses, continue to be used to complete the cathedral, which is also a venue for theater, music, and avant-garde art.

**Choir**
*Each of the choir's columns is 55 ft (17 m) tall and made of polished gray granite.*

**Nave**
*Rising to a height of over 100 ft (30 m), the piers of the nave are topped by graceful stone arches.*

**Rose Window ★**
*Completed in 1933, the stylized motif of the Great Rose is symbolic of the many facets of the Christian Church.*

**★ West Front Entrance**
*The portals of the cathedral's west front are adorned with many fine stone carvings. Some are recreations of medieval religious sculpture, but others have modern themes. This apocalyptic vision of New York's skyline, by local stonemason Joe Kincannon, seems almost to predict the events of September 11, 2001 (see p54).*

## STAR FEATURES

★ Bay Altars

★ Peace Fountain

★ Rose Window

★ West Front Entrance

★ **Peace Fountain**
*The sculpture is the creation of Greg Wyatt and represents nature in its many forms. It stands within a granite basin on the Great Lawn, south of the cathedral.*

**Baptistry**
*The Gothic Baptistry has Italian, French and Spanish influences.*

**THE FINISHED DESIGN**

Crossing tower

South transept

West towers

The north and south transepts, the crossing tower, and the west towers have yet to be finished. When the money to fund their construction is raised, the proposed design will still take at least another 50 years to complete.

Pulpit

★ **Bay Altars**
*The bay altar windows are devoted to human endeavor. The sports window shows feats of skill and strength.*

**Bishop's Chair**
*This is a copy from the Henry VII chapel in Westminster Abbey.*

**St. Ambrose Chapel**
*Named after a 4th-century Italian bishop, the chapel is decorated with Renaissance-style ironwork.*

**TIMELINE**

| | |
|---|---|
| **1823** Cathedral planned for Washington Square | |

**1891** Site chosen and designated Cathedral Parkway

**1909** Pulpit designed by Henry Vaughan

**1911** Cram design replaces earlier ones

**2001** Major fire destroys interior and roof of north transept

| 1800 | 1850 | 1900 | 1950 | 2000 |
|---|---|---|---|---|

**1873** Charter granted

**1888** Competition to design cathedral won by Heins & LaFarge

**1892** December 27 (St. John's Day), cornerstone laid

**1916** Ground broken for nave

**1941** Work halted by World War II and does not resume until 1978

**1978–89** Third phase of building. Stonemasons' Yard opened and south tower heightened

# City College of the City University of New York **7**

Main entrance at W. 138th St. and Convent Ave. **Map** 19 A2. **Tel** (212) 650-7000. **M** 137th St-City College. **www**.ccny.cuny.edu

Set high on a hill adjoining Hamilton Heights, the original Gothic quadrangle of this college, built between 1903 and 1907, is very impressive. The material used for the buildings is Manhattan schist, a stone that had been excavated in building the IRT subway. Later, contemporary buildings were added to the school, which enrolls nearly 15,000 students.

Once free to all residents of New York, City College still offers an education at low tuition rates. Three-quarters of the students are from minority groups, and a large number of them are the first in their families to attend college.

**Shepard Archway at City College of the City University of New York**

# Hamilton Grange National Memorial **8**

287 Convent Ave. **Map** 19 A1. **Tel** (212) 283-5154. **M** 137th St-City College. ⏰ 9am–5pm Fri–Sun. ● public hols. 📷 📹 hourly. **www**.nps.gov/hagr

Squeezed between a church and apartments is one of the city's most historic buildings, the 1802 columned wooden country home of Alexander Hamilton. He was one of the architects of the federal government system, First Secretary of the treasury and founder of the National Bank.

**Statue of Alexander Hamilton at Hamilton Grange**

It is his face that appears on the $10 bill. Hamilton lived in The Grange for the last two years of his life. He was killed in a duel with political rival Aaron Burr in 1804.

The house was acquired by St. Luke's Episcopal Church in 1889 and moved two blocks to this "temporary" site, where it is undergoing renovation until early 2009.

# Hamilton Heights Historic District **9**

W 141st–W 145th St. and Convent Ave. **Map** 19 A1. **M** 137th St-City College.

Originally this was a setting for the impressive country estates of the wealthy. Also known as Harlem Heights, it was developed during the 1880s following the extension of the El line (see p26) into the neighborhood. The privacy of the enclave, on a high hill above Harlem, made it a very desirable location.

The section of Hamilton Heights known as Sugar Hill was highly favored by Harlem's elite – US Supreme Court Justice Thurgood Marshall, notable jazz musicians Count Basie, Duke

Ellington, and Cab Calloway, and world champion boxer Sugar Ray Robinson have all lived there.

The handsome three- and four-story stone row houses were built between 1886 and 1906 mixing Flemish, Romanesque and Tudor influences. In fine condition, many are used as residences by the faculty of City College.

**Row houses in Hamilton Heights**

# St. Nicholas Historic District **10**

202–250 W 138th & W 139th St. **Map** 19 B2. **M** 135th St (B, C).

A startling contrast to the rundown surroundings, the two blocks here, known as the King Model Houses, were built in 1891 when Harlem was considered a neighborhood for New York's gentry. They still comprise one of the city's most distinctive examples of row townhouses.

The developer, David King, chose three leading architects, who succeeded in blending their different styles to create a harmonious whole. The most famous of these was the firm of McKim, Mead & White,

**Houses in St. Nicholas district**

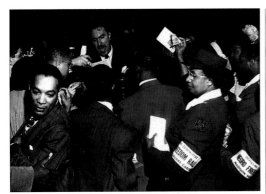

Adam Clayton Powell, Jr. (in dark suit) during a civil rights campaign

designers of the Pierpont Morgan Library *(see pp164–5)* and Villard Houses *(see p176),* who were responsible for the northernmost row of solid brick Renaissance palaces. Their homes featured ground floor entrances rather than the typical New York brownstone stoops. Also, the elaborate parlor floors have ornate wrought-iron balconies below, as well as carved decorative medallions above their windows.

The Georgian buildings designed by Price and Luce are built of buff brick with white stone trim. James Brown Lord's section of buildings, also Georgian in architectural style, feels much closer to Victorian, with outstanding red-brick facades and bases constructed of brownstone.

Successful blacks were attracted here in the 1920s and 1930s, giving it the nickname Strivers' Row. Among them were celebrated musicians W. C. Handy and Eubie Blake.

## Abyssinian Baptist Church ⓫

132 W 138th St. **Map** 19 C2. *Tel* (212) 862-7474. Ⓜ 135th St (B, C, 2, 3). 🕐 9am, 11am Sun. *Groups of 10 or more need reservations.* **www**.abyssinian.org

Founded in 1808, New York's oldest black church became famous through its charismatic pastor Adam Clayton Powell, Jr. (1908–72), a congressman and civil rights leader. Under his leadership it became the most powerful black church in America. A room in the church houses memorabilia from his life.

The church, a fine 1923 Gothic building, welcomes properly dressed visitors to Sunday services and to hear its superb gospel choir.

## Schomburg Center for Research into Black Culture ⓬

515 Malcolm X Blvd. **Map** 19 C2. Ⓜ 135th St (2, 3). *Tel* (212) 491-2200. 🕐 hours vary. ⬤ Mon, Sun, public hols. 📷 (212) 491-2207. ♿ 📷 **www**.schomburgcenter.org

Housed in a sleek contemporary complex opened in 1991, this is the largest research center of black and African culture in the United States. The immense collection was assembled by the late Arthur Schomburg, a black man of Puerto Rican descent, who was told by a teacher that there was no such thing as "black history." The Carnegie

Kurt Weill, Elmer Rice, and Langston Hughes at the Schomburg Center

Corporation bought the collection in 1926 and gave it to the New York Public Library; Schomburg was made curator in 1932.

The library was the unofficial meeting place for writers involved in what later became known as the black literary renaissance of the 1920s, including Langston Hughes, W.E.B. Du Bois, Zora Neale Hurston, and many other great writers of the day. It also hosted many literary gatherings and poetry readings.

The Schomburg Library has excellent facilities for conserving and making available the archive's treasures, which include rare books, photos, movies, art, and recordings. The library was planned and designed to double as a cultural center and includes a theater and two art galleries, which feature changing shows of art and photography.

## Harlem YMCA ⓭

180 W 135th St. **Map** 19 C3. *Tel* (212) 281-4100. Ⓜ 135th St (2, 3).

Sociologist W. E. B. Du Bois

Paul Robeson and many others made their first stage appearances here in the early 1920s. The Krigqa Players, organized by W. E. B. Du Bois in the basement in 1928, was founded to counter the derogatory images of blacks often presented in Broadway reviews of the time. The "Y" also provided temporary lodgings for some notable new arrivals in Harlem, including writer Ralph Ellison.

**Gospel singers performing at Sylvia's during Sunday brunch**

## Sylvia's ⑭

328 Lenox Ave. **Map** 21 B1.
**Tel** (212) 996-0660. Ⓜ 125th St
(2, 3). **www**.sylviassoulfood.com

Harlem's best-known soul food restaurant serves up southern-fried or smothered chicken, spicy ribs, black-eyed peas, collard greens, candied yams, sweet potato pie, and other Southern delicacies (see p310).

*Sylvia's*

Sunday brunch here is served to the accompaniment of Gospel singers.
 Take some time to explore the market at the corner of 125th Street and Lenox Avenue (opposite Sylvia's), extending for a block or more in either direction. It sells African clothing, jewelry, and art of varying quality.

## Apollo Theater ⑮

253 W 125th St. **Map** 21 A1.
**Tel** (212) 531-5304/5 (events); (212) 531-5337 (tours). Ⓜ 125th St.
◯ at showtimes. ⚑ Groups only.
♿ ⬛ See **Entertainment** p353.
**www**.apollotheater.com

The Apollo opened in 1913 as a whites-only opera house. Its great fame came when Frank Schiffman, a white entrepreneur, took over in 1934. He then opened the

theater to all races and turned it into Harlem's best-known showcase, with great artists such as Bessie Smith, Billie Holiday, Duke Ellington, and Dinah Washington.
 Wednesday Amateur Nights, (begun in 1935) with winners

**Apollo Theater**

determined by audience applause, were famous, and there was a long waiting list for performers. These amateur

nights launched the careers of Sarah Vaughan, Pearl Bailey, James Brown, and Gladys Knight, among others, and they still attract hopefuls.
 The Apollo was *the* place during the swing band era; following World War II, a new generation of musicians, such as Charlie "Bird" Parker, Dizzy Gillespie, Thelonius Monk, and Aretha Franklin, continued the tradition.
 Rescued from decline and refurbished in the 1980s, the Apollo once again features top black entertainers and hosts Amateur Nights.

## Studio Museum in Harlem ⑯

144 W 125th St. **Map** 21 B2. **Tel**
(212) 864-4500. Ⓜ 125th St (2, 3).
◯ 12–6pm Wed–Fri & Sun,
10am–6pm Sat. ● public hols. 🎫
Donations. 🚫 ♿ **Lectures,
children's programs, films.** 🎁 💻
**www**.StudioMuseum.org

The museum was founded in 1967 in a loft on upper Fifth Avenue with the mission of becoming the premier center for the collection and exhibition of the art and artifacts of African-Americans.
 The present premises, a five-story building on Harlem's main commercial street, was donated to the museum by the New York Bank for Savings in 1979. There are galleries on two levels for changing exhibitions featuring artists and cultural themes, and three galleries are devoted to the permanent collection of works by major black artists.
 The photographic archives comprise one of the most

**Exhibition space at the Studio Museum in Harlem**

complete records in existence of Harlem in its heyday. A side door opens onto a small sculpture garden.

In addition to its excellent exhibitions, the Studio Museum also maintains a national artist-in-residence program, and offers regular lectures, seminars, children's programs, and film festivals. An excellent small shop sells a range of books and various African crafts.

# Mount Morris Historical District ⑰

W 119th–W 124th Sts. **Map** 21 B2.
Ⓜ *125th St (2, 3).*

You can plainly see that the late 19th-century Victorian-style town houses near Marcus Garvey Park were once grand. This was a favorite neighborhood of German Jews moving up in the world from the Lower East Side. Time has not been kind, and this district shows how the area has deteriorated.

A few impressive churches, such as St. Martin's Episcopal Church, remain. There are also some interesting juxtapositions of faiths to be seen: the columned Mount Olivet Baptist Church, at 201 Lenox Avenue, was once Temple Israel, one of the most imposing synagogues in

**St. Martin's Episcopal Church on Lenox Avenue**

the city; and at the Ethiopian Hebrew Congregation, 1 West 123rd Street, housed in a former mansion, the choir sings in Hebrew on Saturdays.

# Marcus Garvey Park ⑱

120th–124th Sts. **Map** 21 B2.
Ⓜ *125th St (2, 3).*

**The flamboyant black nationalist leader Marcus Garvey**

This hilly, rocky, two-block square of green is the site of New York's last fire watch-tower, an open cast-iron structure built in 1856, with spiral stairs leading to the observation deck. The bell below the deck sounded the alarm. It may be best to view it from a distance, however, if you have any doubts about your safety.

Previously known as Mount Morris Park, it was renamed in 1973 in honor of Marcus Garvey. He came to Harlem from Jamaica in 1916 and founded the Universal Negro Improvement Association, which promoted self-help, racial pride and a back-to-Africa movement.

# Museo del Barrio ⑲

1230 5th Ave. **Map** 21 C5. *Tel (212) 831-7272.* Ⓜ *103rd St, 110th St.* ☐ *11am–5pm Wed–Sun (to 8pm Thu).* ● *Jan 1, Thanksgiving, Dec 25.* ♿🅿🚫⚠📷 *www.elmuseo.org*

Founded in 1969, this is North America's only museum devoted to Latin American art. It specializes in the culture of Puerto Rico. Exhibitions feature contemporary painting and sculpture, folk art, and historical artifacts. The stars of the permanent collection are about 240 wooden Santos, (carved figures of saints), and a reconstructed *bodega*, or Latino corner grocery. Exhibits change often, but some of the Santos are often on display. The Pre-Columbian collection contains rare artifacts from the Caribbean. Situated at the far end of Museum Mile, this unusual museum attempts to bridge the gap between the lofty Upper East Side and the cultural heritage of El Barrio (Spanish Harlem).

**Folk art at the Museo del Barrio: one of the Three Wise Men (left) and the Omnipotent Hand**

# FARTHER AFIELD

Though officially part of New York City, the boroughs outside Manhattan are quite different in feel and spirit. They are residential and don't have the famous skyscrapers that are associated with New York. The difference is evident even in the way residents describe a trip to Manhattan as "going into the city." Yet the outlying areas boast many attractions, including the city's biggest zoo, botanical gardens, museums, beaches, and sports arenas. For a guided walk around Brooklyn see pages 266–7.

## SIGHTS AT A GLANCE

**Historic Streets and Buildings**
Alice Austen House ㉗
George Washington Bridge ❸
Grand Army Plaza ⑱
Historic Richmond Town ㉔
Morris-Jumel Mansion ❷
Park Slope Historic District ⑲
Wave Hill ❺
Yankee Stadium ⑩

**Museums and Galleries**
Audubon Terrace ❶
Brooklyn Children's Museum ⑯
Brooklyn Museum pp250–53 ㉑

Jacques Marchais Museum of Tibetan Art ㉕
Museum of the Moving Image and Kaufman Astoria Studio ⑭
New York Hall of Science ⑬
PS1 Museum of Modern Art (MoMA), Queens ⑮
Snug Harbor Cultural Center ㉖
The Cloisters pp236–9 ❹
Van Cortlandt House Museum ❻

**Parks and Gardens**
Bronx Zoo pp244–5 ❾
Brooklyn Botanic Garden ㉒
Flushing Meadow-Corona Park ⑫

New York Botanical Garden pp242–3 ❽
Prospect Park ⑳

**Famous Theaters**
Brooklyn Academy of Music ⑰

**Cemeteries**
Woodlawn Cemetery ❼

**Beaches**
City Island ⑪
Coney Island ㉓
Jamaica Bay Wildlife Refuge Center ㉘
Jones Beach State Park ㉙

### KEY

⬛ Main sightseeing areas

0 kilometers 5

0 miles 3

### SIGHTS OUTSIDE THE CENTER

The Bronx

Upper Manhattan

Queens

Brooklyn

Staten Island

◁ **Jamaica Bay**

# Upper Manhattan

It was in Upper Manhattan that the 18th-century Dutch settlers established their farms. Now a suburban area with little of the bustle of downtown Manhattan, it is a good place to escape the inner city for some relaxed museum and landmark sightseeing. The Cloisters (see pp236–9) displays a magnificent collection of medieval art, housed within original European buildings of the period. A piece of New York history is found at the Morris-Jumel Mansion in north Harlem. From his headquarters here, George Washington mounted the defense of Manhattan in 1776.

## Audubon Terrace ❶

Broadway at 155th St. Ⓜ *157th St.*
**American Academy of Arts and Letters**; *(212) 368-5900.* ◯ *1–4pm Thu–Sun.* 🖼 **Hispanic Society of America**; *(212) 926-2234.*
◯ *10am–4:30pm Tue–Sat, 1–4pm Sun.* ● *public hols.* **Donations**.
📷 📹 www.hispanicsociety.org

This 1908 complex of Classical Revival buildings by Charles Pratt Huntington is named for the great naturalist John James Audubon, whose estate once included this land. Audubon is buried in nearby Trinity Cemetery. His gravestone, a Celtic cross, bears the symbolic images of his adventurous career: the birds he painted, his palette and brushes, and his rifles.

Facade of the American Academy of Arts and Letters

The complex was funded by the architect's cousin, civic benefactor Archer Milton Huntington. His dream was that it should be a center of culture and study. A central plaza contains statues by his wife, sculptress Anna Hyatt Huntington.

Audubon Terrace contains two theme museums that are worth seeking out. The American Academy of Arts and Letters was set up to honor American writers, artists, and composers, and 75 honorary members from overseas. On this illustrious roll are writers John Steinbeck and Mark Twain, painters Andrew Wyeth and Edward Hopper, and composer

Aaron Copland. Exhibitions feature members' work. The library (for scholars, by appointment) has old manuscripts and first editions.

The Hispanic Society of America is a public museum and library based upon a personal collection amassed by Archer M. Huntington. The main gallery, in Spanish Renaissance style, holds works by Goya, El Greco, and Velázquez. There are one-month exhibitions from March through May, and on one Sunday in late October the building is open to the public.

Bronze door, American Academy

Nearby is an interesting church. This is the Church of Our Lady of Esperanza, which stands on a knoll at 624 W 156th Street, once part of Audubon Park. It was built at the instigation of Señora de Barril, wife of the Spanish Consul-General in New York, as a church for the Spanish-speaking peoples of New York City. Built with fund provided by railroad magnate Archer Milton Huntington, the church was completed in 1912, and enlarged in the 1920s.

Statue of El Cid by Anna Hyatt Huntington at Audubon Terrace

# Morris-Jumel Mansion ❷

Corner W 160th St and Edgecombe Ave. **Tel** (212) 923-8008. M 163rd St. ◯ 10am–4pm Wed–Sun. ● public hols. 🖼 🅾 🎥 by appt. 🏠 www. morrisjumel.org

This is one of New York's few pre-Revolutionary buildings. Now a museum with nine restored period rooms, it was built in 1765 for Roger Morris. His former military colleague George Washington used it as temporary headquarters while defending Manhattan in 1776. In 1810 it was bought and updated by Stephen Jumel, a merchant of French-Caribbean descent, and his wife Eliza.

The pair furnished the house with souvenirs of their many visits to France. Her boudoir has a "dolphin" chair, reputedly bought from Napoleon. Eliza's social climbing and love affairs scandalized New York society. It was rumored that she let her husband bleed to death in 1832 so she could inherit his fortune. She later married Aaron Burr, aged 77, and divorced him three years later on the day he died.

The exterior of the Palladian-style, wood-sided Georgian house with classical portico and octagonal wing has been restored. The museum exhibits include many original Jumel pieces.

The 3,500-ft (1,065-m) span of the George Washington Bridge

# George Washington Bridge ❸

M 175th St. www.panynj.gov

French architect Le Corbusier called this "the only seat of grace in the disordered city." While not as famous a landmark as its Brooklyn equivalent, this bridge by engineer Othmar Ammann and his architect Cass Gilbert has its own character and history. Plans for a bridge linking Manhattan to New Jersey had been in the pipeline for more than 60 years before the Port of New York Authority raised the $59 million to fund the project. It was Ammann

The lighthouse under Washington Bridge

who suggested a road bridge rather than the more expensive rail link. Work began in 1927 and the bridge was opened in 1931: first across were two young roller skaters from the Bronx. Today it is a vital link for commuter traffic and is in constant use.

Cass Gilbert had plans to clad the two towers with masonry but funds did not permit it, leaving an elegant skeletal structure 600 ft (183 m) high and 3,500 ft (1,065 m) long.

Ammann had also allowed for a second deck in his plan, and this lower deck was added in 1962, increasing the bridge's capacity enormously. Now the eastbound toll collection shows a traffic level of over 53 million cars per year.

Below the eastern tower is a lighthouse that was saved from possible demolition in 1951 by public pressure. Many thousands of young New Yorkers and children all around the world have loved the bedtime story *The Little Red Lighthouse and the Great Gray Bridge,* and wrote letters to save the lighthouse. Author Hildegarde Hoyt Swift wove the tale around her two favorite New York landmarks.

The bridge is also home to the world's largest free-flying American flag, which is hung out on major federal holidays.

Morris-Jumel Mansion, built in 1765, with its original colossal portico

# The Cloisters ❹

See pp236–9.

# The Cloisters ❹

The Cloisters seen from Fort Tryon Park

This world-famous museum of medieval art resides in a building constructed from 1934 to 1938, incorporating medieval cloisters, chapels, and halls. Sculptor George Grey Barnard founded the museum in 1914; John D. Rockefeller, Jr. funded the Metropolitan Museum of Art's 1925 purchase of the collection and donated the site at Fort Tryon Park and also the land on the New Jersey side of the Hudson River, directly across from The Cloisters.

**Tomb Effigy of Jean d'Alluye**
*This tomb immortalizes the 13th-century Crusader.*

Langon Chapel

Pontaut Chapter House

Gothic Chapel

**★ Unicorn Tapestries**
*The set of beautifully preserved tapestries, woven in Brussels around 1500, depicts the quest and capture of the mythical unicorn.*

**Boppard Stained-Glass Lancets** *(1440–47)*
*Below the lancet of St Catherine, angels display the arms of the coopers' guild, of which Catherine was patron.*

**STAR EXHIBITS**

★ Annunciation Triptych by Robert Campin

★ Belles Heures de Jean, Duc de Berry

★ Unicorn Tapestries

Bonnefort Cloister

Glass Gallery

Trie Cloister

**★ Annunciation Triptych** *(about 1425)*
*The Campin Room is the location of this Robert Campin of Tournai small triptych, a magnificent example of early Flemish painting.*

## Saint-Guilhem Cloister
*Intricate floral ornamentation can be found on the capitals of this cloister.*

Romanesque Hall

Upper floor

Lower floor

Main entrance

### Virgin and Child Frescoes
*This 12th-century fresco is from the Catalonian church of San Juan de Tredós.*

### KEY TO FLOOR PLAN

☐ Exhibition space

☐ Non-exhibition space

### Cuxa Cloister
*The reconstructed 12th-century cloister features Romanesque architectural detail and motifs.*

### Enthroned Virgin and Child
*This elaborately carved ivory sculpture was made in England during the late 13th century.*

## GALLERY GUIDE
*The museum is organized roughly in chronological order. It starts with the Romanesque period (AD 1000) and moves to the Gothic (1150 to 1520). Sculptures, stained glass, paintings, and the gardens are on the lower floor. The Unicorn Tapestries are on the upper floor.*

### ★ Belles Heures
*This book of hours, commissioned by Jean, Duc de Berry, is among a rotating installation of exquisite illuminated books and folios.*

# Exploring The Cloisters

Known particularly for its Romanesque and
Gothic architectural sculpture, The Cloisters
collection also includes illuminated manuscripts,
stained glass, metalwork, enamels, ivories, and
paintings. Among its tapestries is the renowned
*Unicorn* series. The Cloisters' splendid medieval
complex is unrivaled in North America.

## ROMANESQUE ART

**A lifesized 12th-century Spanish
crucifix portraying Christ as the
King of Heaven**

Fanciful beasts and people,
acanthus blossoms and
scrollwork top the columns
around The Cloisters. Many
are in the Romanesque style
that flourished in the 11th
and 12th centuries. The
museum has numerous
masterpieces of Romanesque
art and architecture, showing
the style's powerful rounded
arches and intricate details.
Highly embellished capitals
and warm, pink marble typify
the 12th-century Cuxa Cloister
from the Pyrenees in France.
A griffin, a dragon, a centaur,
and a basilisk are among the
creatures parading over the
Narbonne Arch nearby.

In a more solemn style, the
apse from the church of
Saint-Martín in Fuentidueña,
Spain, is a massive rounded
vault constructed from 3,300
blocks of limestone. It is
decorated with a 12th-century
fresco of the Virgin and Child
and has a golden-crowned
Christ depicted as triumphant
over death.

More than 800 years ago,
Benedictine and Cistercian
monks sat on the cold stone
benches in the Pontaut Chapter
House. By the 19th century it
had become so neglected that
it was used as a stable. Its
ribbed vaulting is a foretaste of
the Gothic style to come.

**A 16th-century Flemish boxwood
rosary bead from the Treasury**

## GOTHIC ART

Where Romanesque art was
solid, the Gothic style that
followed (from 1150 to
around 1520) was open, with
pointed arches, glowing
stained-glass windows, and
three-dimensional sculpture.
Gothic depictions of the Virgin
and Child display exquisite
craftsmanship.

The Gothic Chapel's
brilliantly colored windows
show scenes and figures from
biblical stories. Lifesized tomb
sculptures include the effigy
of the Crusader knight Jean
d'Alluye. During the 1790s,

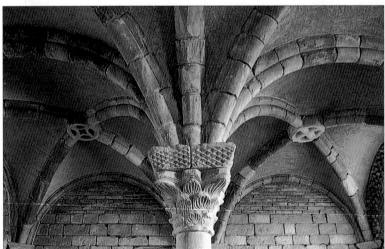

**Vaulted ceiling of the Pontaut Chapter House**

the statue's original home, La Clarté-Dieu Abbey in France, was vandalized, and the statue was used to bridge a stream.

In the Boppard Room, the lives of the saints are told in marvelous late Gothic stained glass from Germany.

Robert Campin's Flemish masterwork, the *Annunciation* altarpiece, is the focus of the Campin Room. It is an intimate room with furnishings that might have belonged to a wealthy 15th-century family.

## MEDIEVAL GARDENS

More than 300 varieties of plants grown in the Middle Ages can be found in The Cloisters' gardens. The Bonnefont Cloister has aromatic, magic, medicinal, and culinary plants. The Trie Cloister features plants shown in the *Unicorn Tapestries* and reveals the use of flowers in medieval symbolism: roses (for the Virgin Mary), pansies (the Holy Trinity), and daisies (the eye of Christ).

**Bonnefont Cloister**

## THE TAPESTRIES

The Cloisters' tapestries are full of rich imagery and symbolism, and are among the museum's most highly prized treasures. The four *Nine Heroes Tapestries* bear the coat of arms of Jean, Duc de Berry, who was a brother of the King of France and one of the greatest art patrons of the Middle Ages. These tapestries are one of only two sets that survived from the late 14th century; the other set belonged to Jean's brother, Louis, Duc d'Anjou.

Nine great heroes of the past – three pagan, three Hebrew, three Christian – are shown with members of the medieval court, from cardinals, knights, and damsels to musicians.

In an adjacent room is the magnificent *Hunt of the Unicorn*, a series of seven tapestries woven in Brussels around 1500. It depicts the symbolic hunt of the mythical unicorn and capture by a maiden.

Although they were misused in the 19th century to protect fruit trees from frost damage,

**Julius Caesar, entertained by court musicians, in a Nine Heroes tapestry**

the tapestries are remarkably well preserved. They are also astonishing in detail, with literally hundreds of minutely observed plants and animals. Their story can be read as a tale of courtly love, but the series is also an allegory of the Crucifixion and the Resurrection of Christ.

## THE TREASURY

In medieval times, precious objects were stored for safekeeping in sanctuaries. At The Cloisters, they are found in the Treasury.

The collection includes several Gothic illuminated "books of hours." These were used for the private devotions of the nobility, such as the Limbourg brothers' *Belles Heures*, made for Jean, Duc de Berry, in 1410, and the tiny, palm-sized version by Gothic master Jean Pucelle for the Queen of France, around 1325.

Other religious artifacts range from a 13th-century English ivory Virgin to the 14th-century silver gilt and enamel reliquary shrine thought to have belonged to Queen Elizabeth of Hungary, along with censers, chalices, candlesticks, and crucifixes.

Curiosities here include the "Monkey Cup," an enameled beaker probably made for the 15th-century Burgundian court, showing mischievous monkeys robbing a sleeping peddler; an intricately carved rosary bead the size of a walnut; a 13th-century boat-shaped, jeweled saltcellar; and a full set of playing cards dating to the 15th century.

**Hunting images and symbols depicted on a 15th-century deck of playing cards**

The west parlor of the Van Cortlandt House Museum

# The Bronx

Once a prosperous suburb with a famous Grand Concourse lined with apartment buildings for the wealthy, the Bronx has now become an unfortunate symbol of urban decay. Still, diverse ethnic communities, unique resources, and charming areas, such as Riverdale at the northern end, remain.

Two major attractions are the Bronx Zoo and New York Botanical Garden. There is also a new golf course at Ferry Point Park and Fulton Fish Market has relocated here. Yankee Stadium, now over 50 years old, is still a favorite for baseball fans (see p360).

## Wave Hill ❺

W 249th St. and Independence Ave, Riverdale. *Tel* (718) 549-3200. Ⓜ 231st St, then bus Bx7, 10. ◐ 9am–5:30pm Tue–Sun (to 9pm Wed Jun–Jul, to 4:30pm mid-Oct–mid-Apr). 🎟 free Tue, 9am–noon Sat, Dec–Feb. 🎫 2:15pm Sun. 🚹 **www**.wavehill.org

This 28-actre (11-ha) oasis of calm and beauty boasts fine views over to the New Jersey Palisades across the Hudson River. The former estate of financier and conservationist George W. Perkins, Wave Hill has had many distinguished tenants, including Theodore Roosevelt, Mark Twain, and

Arturo Toscanini. Perkins also owned neighboring estates, underneath which he built a subterranean recreation center complete with bowling alley, and a tunnel leading into the main building.

The house and the grounds are open to the public. The house is frequently used for concerts. They often take place in the grand Armor Hall, designed in 1928 for Bashford Dean, who was then the curator of the collection of arms and armor at the Metropolitan Museum of Art.

The gardens were originally designed by Viennese landscape gardener Albert Millard. There are also greenhouses, lawns, an herb garden, and woodlands. Exhibitions range from sculpture to horticulture.

The adjoining Riverdale Park has attractive woodland and paths along the river.

The interior of the grand Armor Hall at Wave Hill

# Van Cortlandt House Museum ❻

Van Cortlandt Park. *Tel* (718) 543-3344. Ⓜ 242nd St, Van Cortlandt Park. ◐ 10am–3pm Tue–Fri, 11am–4pm Sat, Sun (last adm: 30 mins before closing). ◑ public hols & Nov 26. 🎟 free Wed. 📷 🎫 🚹 *See The History of New York pp20–21.* **www**.vancortlandthouse.org

The facade of Van Cortlandt House

A restored 1748 Georgian Colonial country manor built of rough stone, the Bronx's oldest building was the family home of Frederick Van Cortlandt, a New Yorker who inherited great wealth and was related to many influential families of his day.

The dining room was used as one of General George Washington's headquarters; the ground behind the house was once the scene of skirmishing during the Revolutionary War.

The interior has American period furnishings as well as a superb collection of delftware and a complete 17th-century Dutch bedroom.

On the exterior, look for the carved faces in the keystones over the windows.

# Woodlawn Cemetery ❼

Webster Ave and E 233rd St.
**Tel** (718) 920-0500. M Woodlawn.
⏰ 8:30am–5pm daily.
⚫ public hols. 🅿 ♿ 📷
**www**.thewoodlawncemetery.org

For a glimpse into another kind of social history, visit Woodlawn Cemetery, burial place of many a wealthy and distinguished New Yorker. Memorials and tombstones are set in beautiful grounds. F.W. Woolworth and many members of his family are interred in a mausoleum only a little less ornate

**Entrance to the Woolworth mausoleum**

than the building that carries the family name. The pink marble vault of meat magnate Herman Armour is oddly reminiscent of a ham.

Other New York notables buried here include Mayor Fiorello LaGuardia, Roland Macy, the founder of the great department store, author Herman Melville, and jazz legend Duke Ellington.

# New York Botanical Garden ❽

See pp242–3.

# Bronx Zoo/Wildlife Conservation Park ❾

See pp244–5.

# Yankee Stadium ❿

E 161st St at River Ave, Highbridge.
**Tel** (718) 293-6000. M 161st St.
📷 noon daily (except on game afternoons); reservation advised.
See **Sport** p360. **www**.yankees.com

This is the home of the New York Yankees baseball team. Among Yankee heroes are two of the greatest players of all time: Babe Ruth and Joe

DiMaggio (who was also famous for marrying the actress Marilyn Monroe in 1954). In 1921 left-hander Babe Ruth, wearing the Yankees' distinctive pinstripes, hit the stadium's first home run – against the Boston Red Sox, his former team. The stadium was completed two years later by Jacob Ruppert, the owner of the Yankees, and became known as "the house that Ruth built".

**Joe DiMaggio in action at Yankee Stadium in 1941**

The stadium had a facelift in the mid-1970s, and now seats up to 54,000 people who come for sports, concerts, and other events. One of the largest annual gatherings has been that of the Jehovah's Witnesses and in 1950, 123,707 people attended in a single day. In 1965 Pope Paul VI celebrated mass before a crowd of more than 80,000. It was the first visit to North America by a pope – the second was made in 1979 when John Paul II also visited the stadium.

The Yankees remain one of the top teams in the American League. There are five Yankee Clubhouse stores in New York where tickets for tours and games can be purchased. Construction of a new, $1.3-billion stadium adjacent to the current one began in 2006 and is expected to be completed in 2009. The old stadium will then be demolished.

# City Island ⓫

M 6 to Pelham Bay Park, then Bx29 to City Island. **Museum** 190 Fordham St. ⏰ 1–5pm Sun.
**Tel** (718) 885-0008.
**www**.cityislandmuseum.org

Situated off the northeast shore of the Bronx and surrounded by Long Island Sound, City Island is a small nautical outpost with a very New England feel and offers a refreshing change of pace. Its scenic marinas are filled with sailboats, and its seafood restaurants would satisfy any sailor's appetite. Several Americas Cup winners have been built in its boatyards.

The **City Island Museum** is in one of the island's most historic buildings, the old Public School 17, built on an Indian burial ground at a high point on the island.

City Island is linked to the Bronx by bridge. To the north on the mainland is Orchard Beach, a crescent of white sand edged with bathing huts. The beach is popular with area residents, and it can be crowded and dirty.

**An old tugboat moored at one of City Island's piers**

# The New York Botanical Garden 8

Hibiscus

The New York Botanical Garden is 250 acres (100 ha) of dazzling beauty and hands-on enjoyment. From the nation's most glorious Victorian glasshouse to the 12-acre (5-ha) Everett Children's Adventure Garden, it is alive with things to discover. One of the oldest and largest botanical gardens in the world, it has 50 gardens and plant collections, and 50 acres (20 ha) of uncut forest. The spectacular Enid A. Haupt Conservatory has been wonderfully restored as *A World of Plants*, with misty tropical rain forests and dramatic deserts.

Entrance to Enid A. Haupt Conservatory

Seasonal Exhibition Galleries

Deserts of Africa

### Rock Garden
*Rock outcroppings, streams, a waterfall, and a flower-rimmed pond create an alpine habitat for plants from around the world* 4

### Historic Forest
*One of New York City's last surviving natural forest areas includes red oak, white ash, tulip trees, and birch* 5

Deserts of the Americas

**Everett Children's Adventure Garden** *Kids can discover the wonders of ecology and plants* 8

Entrance

6
2   3 4
1   9   5
8
Entrance     7

**LOCATOR MAP**

**Peggy Rockefeller Rose Garden**
*Over 2,700 rose bushes have been planted in the Rose Garden, laid out in 1988 according to the 1916 design* 7

### Palms of the Americas Gallery

*100 majestic palms soar into a 90-ft (27-m) glass dome. A tranquil reflecting pool is surrounded by tropical plants.*

**The Enid A. Haupt Conservatory** consists of 11 interconnecting glass galleries housing *A World of Plants*, including rain forests, deserts, aquatic plants, and seasonal exhibitions ①

### Garden Cafe

*This is a delightful spot to enjoy a meal. You can eat outside on terraces overlooking beautiful gardens ⑥*

Conservatory

### Jane Watson Irwin Perennial Garden

*Flowering perennials are arranged in dramatic patterns according to height, shade, color and blooming time ②*

Tropical Lowland Rain Forest Gallery

Courtyard Pool

### Leon Levy Visitor Center

*This modern pavilion, which opened in 2004, has a shop, a cafe, and a visitor orientation facility ⑨*

Aquatic Plants and Vines Gallery

Tropical Upland Rainforest Gallery

### Tram

*The half-hour tour of the gardens provides information about horticultural, educational, and botanical research programs. Passengers can alight at a number of stops to explore the gardens before reboarding ③*

# Bronx Zoo ❾

Opened in 1899, the Bronx Zoo is the largest urban zoo in the United States. It is home to more than 4,000 animals of 500 species, which live in realistic representations of their natural habitats. The zoo is a leader in the perpetuation of endangered species, such as the Indian rhinoceros and the snow leopard. Its 265 acres of woods, streams, and parklands include, in season, a children's zoo a butterfly garden, and a shuttle train that transports visitors around the sprawling park. Visitors are also free to walk around. For the best overview of the zoo's park areas take the SkyFari cable car (which also operates seasonally).

★ **The Congo Gorilla Forest**
*This award winning replica of a central African rain forest is home to the largest population of Western Lowland gorillas in the US, along with a host of other animals.*

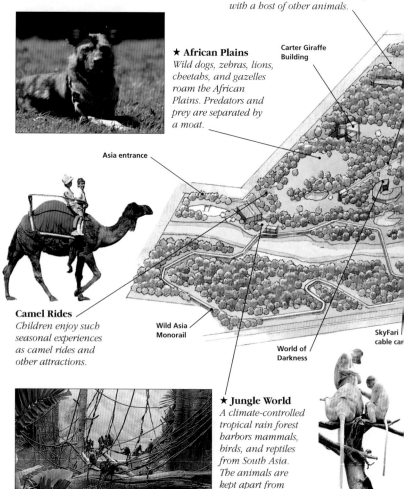

★ **African Plains**
*Wild dogs, zebras, lions, cheetahs, and gazelles roam the African Plains. Predators and prey are separated by a moat.*

Carter Giraffe Building

Asia entrance

**Camel Rides**
*Children enjoy such seasonal experiences as camel rides and other attractions.*

Wild Asia Monorail

World of Darkness

SkyFari cable car

★ **Jungle World**
*A climate-controlled tropical rain forest harbors mammals, birds, and reptiles from South Asia. The animals are kept apart from visitors by ravines, streams and cliffs.*

**Monkeys in Jungle World**

**Baboon Reserve**
*Visitors walk along a dry riverbed to see wildlife in an Ethiopian mountain habitat.*

**Children's Zoo**
*Kids can crawl through a prairie dog tunnel, climb on a spiderweb, try on a turtle shell, and pet and feed the animals.*

World of Reptiles

The Zoo Center houses elephants, rhinos and tapirs.

Butterfly Garden

Southern Boulevard entrance

owl

Madagascar

Aquatic Bird House

Sea Bird Colony

Rainey Gate entrance

Monkey House

**★ World of Birds**
*Exotic birds soar free in the lush surroundings of a rain forest. An artificial waterfall rushes down a 50-ft (15-m) fiberglass cliff in this walk-through habitat.*

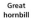

Great hornbill

Mouse-House

Bronx Parkway entrance

**Himalayan Highlands** endangered species, such as snow leopards and red pandas, are kept here.

## VISITORS' CHECKLIST

Fordham Rd/Bronx River Pkwy. *Tel* (718) 367-1010. **M** 2, 5 to Pelham Pkwy. 🚇 to Fordham Station. 🚌 Bx9, Bx12, Bx19, Bx22, Bx36, Bx39, Bx40, Bx42, BxM11 express bus, Q44. 🕐 Nov–Mar: 10am–4:30pm daily; Apr–Oct: 10am–5pm daily (5:30pm Sat–Sun). 🅿️ Wed by donation. 📷 ♿ 🎁 🍴 🚻 *Children's Zoo* 🕐 Apr–Oct. **www**.bronxzoo.com

## STAR FEATURES

★ African Plains

★ Congo Gorilla Forest

★ Jungle World

★ Tiger Mountain

★ Wild Asia

★ World of Birds

**★ Wild Asia**
*From May to October, the monorail journeys through forests and meadows, where rhinos, tigers, and Mongolian wild horses roam free.*

**★ Tiger Mountain**
*Amur tigers are on view all year. Only one inch of glass separates visitors from these magnificent wild cats.*

# Queens

A big, sprawling borough, Queens has a wide variety of attractions and residential and commercial areas, including Long Island City, where exciting new museums and restaurants are springing up all over. Development of the borough accelerated after 1909, when the construction of Queensboro Bridge made commuting easier. The city's main airports are here, and there are many different ethnic enclaves including the Greek neighborhood of Astoria and the various Asian communities in Flushing.

A 1900 Mutoscope at the Museum of the Moving Image

## Flushing Meadow–Corona Park ⑫

Ⓜ Willets Point-Shea Stadium. See **Sports** p361.

The site of New York's two World's Fairs now offers expansive waterside picnic grounds and a multitude of attractions. These include the 50,000-seat Shea Stadium, the home of the New York Mets baseball team and a popular site for rock concerts. Flushing Meadow is also home to the US Tennis Center, where the prestigious United States Open is played. The courts are open for would-be Agassis, Grafs, and Everts for the remainder of the year. In the 1920s this area was known as the Corona Dump, a nightmarish place of salt marshes and great piles of smoldering trash. In *The Great Gatsby*, author F. Scott Fitzgerald dubbed it the "valley of ashes." It reeked of rotting garbage and glowed red at night. New York's Parks' Commissioner Robert Moses was the driving force behind its transformation. A whole mountain of rubbish was removed and the river was totally re-channeled. The marsh was drained and sewage works were built, helping to restore the area. This site was to serve as the site for the 1939 World's Fair, at which a world on the brink of war saluted the elusive notion of world peace.

The Unisphere, symbol of the 1964 fair, still dominates the remains of the fairground. This giant hollow ball of green steel, built by the US Steel Corporation, is 12 stories high and weighs a massive 350 tons.

# New York Hall of Science ⑬

46th Ave and 111th St Flushing Meadow, Corona Park. **Tel** (718) 699-0005 Ⓜ 111th St. ◯ Sep–Jun: 9:30am–2pm Mon–Thu, 9:30am–5pm Fri, 10am–6pm Sat, Sun; Jul–Aug: 9:30am–5pm Mon–Fri, 10am–6pm Sat, Sun. ● Labor Day, Dec 25. 🔲◯♿🔲📷 **www**.nyscience.org

The science pavilion was built for the 1964 World's Fair, with stained glass set in concrete. It is now a hands-on museum of science and technology, with exhibits on color, light, and physics. Kids love the giant video screens, interactive video, and laser optical exhibits.

The concrete curtain wall of the New York Hall of Science

# Museum of the Moving Image and Kaufman Astoria Studio ⑭

35th Ave at 36th St, Astoria. **Museum** (718) 784-0077. Ⓜ 36th St. **Steinway Museum** ◯ 11am–5pm Wed, Thu, 11am–8pm Fri, 11am–6:30pm Sat, Sun. Screenings: 7:30pm Fri, afternoon and eves Sat–Sun. 📷 (free 4–8pm Fri). 📷 2pm Sat, Sun. ● Memorial Day, Thanksgiving, Dec 25. **Studio.** ● to public. 📷 ♿🔲📷 **www**.movingimage.us

In New York's filmmaking heyday, Rudolph Valentino, W.C. Fields, the Marx Brothers, and Gloria Swanson all made films in the Astoria Studio, which was opened in 1920 by Paramount Pictures. When the movies went west, the army took over, making training films from 1941 to 1971.

The complex stood empty until 1977 when Astoria Motion Picture and Television

The 1964 World's Fair Unisphere at Flushing Meadow-Corona Park

**Poster at the Museum of the Moving Image**

Foundation was founded to preserve it. *The Wiz*, a musical starring Michael Jackson and Diana Ross, was made here, helping to pay for restoration.

Today, the studios house the largest moviemaking facilities on the East Coast.

In 1981 one of the studio buildings was transformed into the Museum of the Moving Image, with interactive displays on production and theaters for the screening of movies and television, as well as a special lecture hall.

There is a lot of memorabilia on display, from Ben Hur's chariot to *Star Trek* costumes. The main gallery draws from the permanent collection of over 85,000 movie artifacts. A $25-million expansion of the museum is currently underway, which will double the size of the museum and include a garden for outdoor exhibitions.

## PS1 MoMA, Queens ⑮

22–25 Jackson Ave at 46th Ave, Long Island City. *Tel* (718) 784-2084. **M** E, V to 23rd St-Ely Ave; 7 to 45 Road-Courthouse Square; G to Court Sq or 21 St-Van Alst. ☐ B61, Q67. ☐ noon–6pm Thu–Mon. ● Jan 1, Dec 25. ☐ ☐ ☐ www.ps1.org

Housed in an elementary school, PS1 was founded in 1971 under a scheme to transform abandoned New York City buildings into exhibition, performance, and studio spaces for artists. The museum is affiliated to the Museum of Modern Art (*see pp172–5*) and is one of the oldest art organisations in the US devoted solely to modern art. Temporary exhibitions are hosted alongside permanent works and many pieces are interactive. In summer, music is performed in the courtyard.

# Brooklyn

**The bandstand at Prospect Park (*see p248*)**

If Brooklyn were a separate city, it would be the country's fourth largest. It has a character all of its own. Many entertainment greats – Mel Brooks, Phil Silvers, Woody Allen, and Neil Simon among them – celebrate their birthplace with great affection and humor. Brooklyn is the ultimate melting pot, with West Indians, Hasidic Jews, Russians, Italians, and Arabs living side by side. Among the diverse neighborhoods are the historic residential districts of Park Slope and Brooklyn Heights.

## Brooklyn Children's Museum ⑯

145 Brooklyn Ave. *Tel* (718) 735-4400. **M** Kingston (C, 3). ☐ 11am–6pm Sat–Sun; Sep–Jun: 1–6pm Wed–Fri; Jul–Aug: noon–6pm Tue–Thu, noon–6:30pm Fri. ● public hols. **Rooftop Theater** ☐ 6:30–8pm Fri, 10am–5pm Sat, Sun. ● public hols. ☐ ☐ ☐ ☐ www.bchildmus.org

The Brooklyn Children's Museum was the first to be designed especially for children and was founded in 1899. Since then, it has been a model, inspiration, and consultant to the development of more than 250 museums for children across the country and all over the world. Housed in a high-tech, specially designed underground building dating from 1976, it is one of the most imaginative children's museums anywhere.

The layout of the building, which has

recently doubled in size following a major renovation, is a maze of complex inter-connected passageways running off the main "people tube" – a huge drainage pipe that connects the four levels. The emphasis here is on involvement and hands-on exhibits and everywhere you look there are curiosities to be discovered, experienced, made, or played with. There is even a walk-on piano like the one in the film *Big* – children of every age find it quite irresistible.

Special exhibitions and events are designed to help children learn about the planet, resolve their fears or problems, understand other cultures, and discover the past. The squeals of laughter that are always heard are a sign of this museum's success in teaching children and the young at

**A mask at the Brooklyn Children's Museum** heart.

The facade of the Brooklyn Academy of Music

# Brooklyn Academy of Music ⑰

30 Lafayette Ave. **Tel** (718) 636 4100.
Ⓜ Atlantic Ave, Nevins St (M, N, Q, R, W, 2, 3, 4, 5). 🅿 ♿ 🏢 📷 🍴
www.bam.org See **Classic and Contemporary Music** p350.

Home to the Brooklyn Philharmonic, the Academy of Music (known as BAM) is Brooklyn's leading cultural venue and the oldest, founded in 1858. It offers outstanding performances, often tending toward the innovative and avant-garde.

The classic 1908 building was designed by Herts & Tallant, and inaugurated with a production of Gounod's opera *Faust* featuring the Neapolitan tenor Enrico Caruso. The greats who have performed here include actress Sarah Bernhardt, ballerina Anna Pavlova, musicians Pablo Casals and Sergei Rachmaninoff, poets Edna St. Vincent Millay and Carl Sandburg, and statesman Winston Churchill. Many international touring groups have made appearances here, including Britain's Royal Shakespeare Company.

The BAM Next Wave Festival has presented contemporary artists such as musicians David Byrne and Philip Glass and choreographers Pina Bausch and Mark Morris. The BAM also runs the Harvey Theater nearby, a movie theater now used for dance, drama, and music events. BAM Rose Cinemas show first-run independent films and BAMcinématek has classics, retrospectives, festivals, and sneak previews.

# Grand Army Plaza ⑱

Plaza St at Flatbush Ave. Ⓜ Grand Army Plaza (2, 3). **Arch** ☐ for occasional exhibitions.

The Soldiers' and Sailors' Arch at Grand Army Plaza

Frederick Law Olmsted and Calvert Vaux laid out this grand oval in 1870 as a gateway to Prospect Park. The Soldiers' and Sailors' Arch and its sculptures were added in 1892 as a tribute to the Union Army. The bust of John F. Kennedy here is the only official New York monument to him.

In June, the plaza is the center of the Welcome Back to Brooklyn Festival for the famous – and not-so-famous – people born in Brooklyn.

# Park Slope Historic District ⑲

Streets from Prospect Park W below Flatbush Ave, to 8th/7th/5th Aves. Ⓜ Grand Army Plaza (2, 3), 7th Ave (F).

Relief work on the Montauk Club

This wonderful enclave of beautiful Victorian town houses was developed on the edge of Prospect Park in the 1880s. It served the upper-middle-class professionals who were able to commute into Manhattan after the Brooklyn Bridge was opened in 1883. The shady streets are lined with two- to five-story houses in every architectural style popular in the late 19th century, some with the towers, turrets, and curlicues so representative of the era. Particularly fine examples are in Romanesque Revival style, with rounded entry arches.

The Montauk Club at 25 Eighth Avenue combines the style of Venice's Ca' d'Oro palazzo with the friezes and gargoyles of the Montauk Indians, for whom this popular 19th-century gathering place was named.

# Prospect Park ⑳

Ⓜ Grand Army Plaza, Prospect Park (B, Q). 🅿 & information (718) 287 3400. 📷 🍴 www.prospectpark.org

Olmsted and Vaux considered this park, opened in 1867, better than their earlier Central Park (see pp203–09). The Long Meadow, a sweep of broad lawns and grand vistas, is the longest unbroken swath of green space in New York.

Olmsted's belief was that "a feeling of relief is experienced by entering them [the parks] on escaping from the cramped, confining and controlling circumstances of the streets of the town."

The facade of the Brooklyn Public Library on Grand Army Plaza

That vision is still as true today as it was a century ago. Among the many notable features are Stanford White's colonnaded Croquet Shelter, and the pools and weeping willows of the Vale of Cashmere. The Music Grove bandstand shows Japanese influences and hosts both jazz and classical music concerts throughout the summer.

A favorite feature of the park is the Camperdown Elm, an ancient and twisted tree planted in 1872. The Friends of Prospect Park raise money to keep it and all the park trees healthy. This old elm has inspired many poems and paintings. Prospect Park has a wide variety of landscapes, from classical gardens dotted with statues to rocky glens with running brooks. A guided tour with a ranger is the best way to see the park.

Carousel horse in Prospect Park

# Brooklyn Museum ㉑

*See pp250–53.*

# Brooklyn Botanic Garden ㉒

900 Washington Ave. **Tel** (718) 623-7200. **M** Prospect Pk (B, Q), Eastern Pkwy (2, 3). **Grounds** ☐ Apr–Sep: 8am–6pm Tue–Fri (10am Sat–Sun & public hols); Oct–Mar: 8am–4:30pm (10am Sat–Sun & public hols). ☐ Jan 1, Labor Day, Thanksgiving, Dec 25. 🅿 Mar–mid-Nov: free Tue & 10am–noon Sat; mid-Nov–Feb: free for under-16s Mon–Fri. 🄾 🅱 🖬 🄷 🄿 www.bbg.org

Though it is not vast, you will find that this 50-acre (20-ha) garden holds many delights. The area was designed by the

A beluga whale at the New York Aquarium, on Coney Island

Olmsted Brothers in 1910 and features an Elizabethan-style "knot" herb garden and one of North America's largest collections of roses.

The central showpiece is a Japanese hill-and-pond garden, complete with a teahouse and Shinto shrine. In late April and early May the park promenade is aglow with delicate Japanese cherry blossoms, which have prompted an annual festival featuring typical Japanese culture, food, and music. April is also the time for tourists to appreciate Magnolia Plaza, where some 80 trees display their beautiful, creamy blossoms against a backdrop of daffodils on Boulder Hill.

The Fragrance Garden is planted in raised beds, where the heavily scented, textured and flavored plants are all labeled in Braille, giving blind visitors an opportunity to identify them as well.

The conservatory houses one of America's largest bonsai collections and some rare rain forest trees, whose extracts allow scientists to produce produce life-saving drugs.

Brooklyn Botanic Garden lily pond

# Coney Island ㉓

**M** Stillwell Ave (D, F, N, Q), W 8th St (F, Q). **New York Aquarium** Surf Ave and W 8th St, Coney Island. **Tel** (718) 265-FISH. ☐ 10am–5pm Mon–Fri, 10am–5:30pm Sat, Sun & hols (Jun–Aug: to 6pm Mon–Fri & 7pm Sat, Sun & hols; Nov–Mar: to 4:30pm daily). 🅿 last adm: 45 mins before closing. ☐ www.nyaquarium.com **Coney Island Museum** 1208 Surf Ave, nr W 12th St. **Tel** (718) 372 5159. ☐ noon–5pm Sat, Sun. 🅿 www.coneyislandusa.com

In the mid-19th century, Brooklyn poet Walt Whitman composed many of his works on Coney Island, at that time untamed Atlantic coastline. By the 1920s, Coney Island was starting to bill itself as the "World's Largest Playground." Three huge fairgrounds built by 1904 (Luna Park, Dream-land, and Steeplechase Park) provided a combination of hair-raising rides and nearby beaches. The subway arrived in 1920, and the 1921 boardwalk ensured Coney Island's popularity throughout the Depression.

A main attraction is the **New York Aquarium**, on 14 acres (6 ha) by the sea, with 350 species. **Coney Island Museum** has memorabilia, relics of old rides, and souvenirs. Coney Island is still exciting: the boardwalk yields ocean views and the Cyclone roller coaster evokes screams. The Mermaid Parade in June is a major annual event.

# Brooklyn Museum ㉑

When it opened in 1897, the
Brooklyn Museum building,
designed to be the largest cultural
edifice in the world, was the
greatest achievement of New York
architects McKim, Mead & White.

North facade, designed by McKim, Mead & White

Though only one-sixth completed, the museum
is today one of the most impressive cultural institutions
in the United States, with a permanent encyclopedic
collection of some one million objects, which are housed
in a grand structure of 560,000 sq ft (41,805 sq m).

**KEY TO FLOOR PLAN**

- Arts of Africa and the Americas
- Asian art
- Prints, drawings, and photographs
- Williamsburg Murals
- Egyptian and Classical art
- Decorative arts
- Painting and sculpture
- Special exhibitions
- Non-exhibition space

**★ Female Figurine**
*5000 years old, this rare
statuette is a highlight of
the museum's impressive
Egyptian collection.*

**Chinese Jar**
*Cobalt blue fishes and
water plants adorn this
14th-century Yuan
dynasty blue-and-white
ceramic jar.*

Iris and B. Cantor
Auditorium

**★ Beaded Crown**
*This 19th-century
crown from
Nigeria is
the ultimate
symbol of
Yoruba
kingship.*

Third floor

Mezzanine
Gallery

Second floor

South
entrance

First floor

Morris A.
and Meyer
Schapiro Wing

Main entrance

**★ An Out of Doors Study** (1889)
*Sargent's portrait of French artist Paul Helleu and his wife Alice was painted during the couple's visit to the Sargent family at Fladbury.*

Fifth floor

ce visible
orage

Luce Center for American Art

## VISITORS' CHECKLIST

200 Eastern Pkwy, Brooklyn.
**Tel** (718) 638-5000. Ⓜ 2, 3 to Eastern Parkway/Brooklyn Museum. 🚌 B41, B69, B67, B71.
◯ 10am–5pm Wed–Fri, 11am–6pm Sat & Sun, 11am–11pm first Sat in month (except Sep).
⬤ Jan 1, Thanksgiving, Dec 25.
**Donation expected**. 🅾 ♿ 🅿
📷 🔲 🎫 **Concerts, lectures**.
**www**.brooklynmuseum.org

**★ Winter Scene in Brooklyn** (1820)
*Francis Guy's depiction of downtown Brooklyn is from the American Identities Collection.*

**The Dinner Party** (1970s) *This is the centerpiece of the Elizabeth A. Sackler Center for Feminist Art.*

Fourth floor

**Moorish Smoking Room** (1865)
*This room is from a house on West 54th Street, bought by J. D. Rockefeller in 1884.*

**Alexander the Great**
*The military leader was portrayed in alabaster in the 1st century BC.*

**Ibis Coffin** (332–330 BC)
*The sacred bird of ancient Egypt merited a splendid coffin of gold leaf and silver.*

## GALLERY GUIDE

*The collection is on five floors, with African and New World art on the first; prints, drawings, and Asian art on the second; Egyptian, Classical, and European painting and sculpture on the third; decorative art on the fourth; and American art on the fifth. There is special exhibition space on the first and fourth floors.*

## STAR EXHIBITS

★ An Out of Doors Study, by John Singer Sargent

★ Beaded Crown

★ Female Figurine

★ Winter Scene in Brooklyn, by Francis Guy

# Exploring the Collection

The Brooklyn Museum houses one of the finest art collections in the United States. Its strengths include an outstanding collection of Native American art from the Southwest; American period rooms; exquisite pieces of ancient Egyptian and Islamic art; and important American and European paintings.

Seated Buddha torso in limestone, from India (late 3rd century AD)

## ARTS OF AFRICA, THE PACIFIC, AND THE AMERICAS

The Brooklyn Museum set a precedent in the United States in 1923 by exhibiting African objects as works of art rather than artifacts. Since then, the African art collection has grown steadily in both importance and size.

Exhibits include a rare intricately carved ivory gong from the Benin kingdom of 16th-century Nigeria, one of only five in existence.

The museum also has a notable collection of Native American work, including totem poles, textiles, and pottery. A 19th-century deerskin shirt, once worn by a chief of the Blackfoot tribe, depicts his brave and daring exploits in battle.

Ancient American artistic traditions are represented by Peruvian textiles, Central American gold, and Mexican sculpture. A beautifully preserved tunic from Peru, dating from AD 600, is so tightly woven that its vibrant symbolic designs appear to have been painted onto the cloth rather than woven in the traditional manner.

The Oceanic collection includes sculpture from the Solomon Islands, Papua New Guinea, and New Zealand.

## ASIAN ART

Changing exhibitions from the museum's permanent collection of Chinese, Japanese, Korean, Indian, Southeast Asian, and Islamic art are always on display. Japanese and Chinese paintings, Indian miniatures, and Islamic calligraphy complement the Asian sculpture, textiles, and ceramics. The collections of Japanese folk art, Chinese cloisonné (enamel work), and Oriental carpets are of particular note. Good examples of Buddhist art range from a variety of Chinese, Indian, and Southeast Asian Buddhas to a mandala-patterned temple banner from 14th-century Tibet, painted in rich, luminous watercolors.

Blackfoot tribe deerskin shirt, decorated with porcupine quills and glass beads (19th century)

## DECORATIVE ARTS

The decorative arts collection reflects changes in domestic life and design from the 17th century to the present.

The Moorish Smoking Room, from John D. Rockefeller's brownstone house, embodies elegant New York living in the 1880s. There is also a 1928–30 Art Deco study from a Park Avenue apartment, including a walk-in bar that was hidden behind paneling during the Prohibition era (see pp30–31).

More than 350 items from the museum's collection of silver, furniture, ceramics, and textiles are featured in the Luce Center for American Art. Although centered mostly on American art, the selection also includes pieces of Native American and Spanish colonial art.

*Normandie* chrome pitcher, by Peter Müller-Munk (1935)

The Luce galleries are arranged thematically and explore crucial moments and ideas in American visual culture over the past 300 years. Among the collection are pieces by John Singer Sargent, Frank Lloyd Wright, and Georgia O'Keeffe.

## EGYPTIAN, CLASSICAL, AND ANCIENT MIDDLE EASTERN ART

Recognized as among the world's finest, the Egyptian collection holds many masterpieces. It begins with an early female figure dating from 3500 BC, and encompasses sculptures, statues, tomb paintings, and reliefs as well as funerary paraphernalia. Of the latter, the most unusual is the coffin of an ibis, probably recovered from the vast animal cemetery of Tuna el-Gebel in Middle Egypt. The ibis was a sacred bird representing the god Thoth, and this coffin is made of solid silver and wood overlaid with gold leaf, with rock crystal for the bird's eyes. These galleries have been renovated into a state-of-the-art, high-tech installation.

Among the artifacts from the Greek and Roman civilizations are statuary, pottery, bronzes, jewelry, and mosaics.

Among the Ancient Near and Middle Eastern exhibits are an extensive collection of pottery and 12 alabaster reliefs from the Assyrian palace of King Ashurnasirpal II. These date from around 883–859 BC and depict the king fighting, overseeing his crops, and purifying the "sacred tree," a major icon in Assyrian religion.

## PAINTING AND SCULPTURE

This section contains works from the 14th century to the present, including a well-known and outstanding 19th-century French art collection with works by Degas, Rodin, Monet, Cézanne, Matisse, and Pissarro. It also boasts one of the largest holdings of Spanish

*Pierre de Wiessant* (about 1886) by Auguste Rodin, from his *Burghers of Calais* group

Colonial paintings and one of the best collections of North American paintings to be found in the United States.

The museum's 20th-century American collection includes, appropriately, *Brooklyn Bridge* by Georgia O'Keeffe.

The Sculpture Garden holds architectural ornamentation taken from demolished New York buildings, including statues rescued from the original Penn Station, and a replica of the Statue of Liberty.

## PRINTS, DRAWINGS, AND PHOTOGRAPHS

The prints section displays examples by many masters, ranging from a rare woodcut print by Dürer entitled *The Great Triumphal Chariot* and works by Piranesi to an excellent Impressionist and Post-Impressionist collection. This includes works by Toulouse-Lautrec and Mary Cassatt, the only American woman associated with the Impressionist movement. There are lithographs by James McNeill Whistler, Winslow Homer engravings, and a superb selection of

*Rotherhide*, an etching by James McNeill Whistler (1860)

drawings by Fragonard, Paul Klee, Van Gogh, Picasso, and Gorky, among others, many of them in black and white.

The photography collection consists mainly of works by major 20th-century American photographers, including a 1924 portrait of Mary Pickford by Edward Steichen and work by Margaret Bourke-White, Berenice Abbott, and Robert Mapplethorpe. All of these artworks are constantly rotated for conservation purposes.

Sandstone reliefs from Thebes in Egypt (around 760–656 BC), depicting the great god Amun-Re and his consort Mut

# Staten Island

Apart from the famous ferry ride, Staten Island and its attractions are not well known to New Yorkers in general. Residents feel so ignored, in fact, that they've talked about seceding from the city. Visitors who venture beyond the ferry terminal, however, will be pleasantly surprised to find hills, lakes, and greenery, with expanses of open space, amazing harbor views, and well-preserved early New York buildings. One of the biggest surprises here is a cache of Tibetan art that is hidden away in a replica of a Buddhist temple.

## Historic Richmond Town ❷❹

441 Clarke Ave. **Tel** (718) 351-1611. 🚌 S74 from ferry. ⏰ Sep–Jun: 1–5pm, Wed–Sun; Jul–Aug: 10am–5pm Wed–Sat, 1–5pm Sun. ⬤ Jan 1, Easter Sun, Thanksgiving, Dec 25. 🏷 ⓞ ♿ 🎁 🍴 🏠 **www**.historicrichmondtown.org

There are now 29 buildings, 14 of which are open to the public, in New York's only restored village and outdoor museum. The village was first named Coccles-town, after the local shellfish, but was soon corrupted to "Cuckoldstown," much to the annoyance of the residents. By the end of the Revolutionary War the new name of Richmondtown had been adopted. It was the county seat until Staten Island was made part of the city in 1898, and has been preserved as an example of an early New York settlement.

**Cologne at the General Store**

The Voorlezer House, built in the Dutch era before 1696, is the oldest elementary school to be found in the country. The Stephens General Store, which opened in 1837, doubled as the local post office. It has been well restored, right down to the contents of the shelves. The complex, set on 100 acres (40 ha), includes wagon sheds, a courthouse built in 1837, houses, several shops, and a tavern. There are also seasonal workshops where traditional rural crafts are demonstrated to visitors.

St. Andrew's Church, dating to 1708, and its old graveyard are just across the Mill Pond stream, and the Historical Society Museum is in the County Clerk's and Surrogate's Office. The toy room is a delight.

## Jacques Marchais Museum of Tibetan Art ❷❺

338 Lighthouse Ave. **Tel** (718) 987-3500. 🚌 S74 from ferry. ⏰ 1–5pm Wed–Sun. ⬤ public hols. 🏷 ◎ 🎁 🏠 **www**.tibetanmuseum.org

A hilltop provides a very tranquil setting for one of the largest collections of privately owned Tibetan art of the 15th to the 20th centuries outside Tibet. The main building is a replica of a mountain monastery with an

Sacred sculpture at the Jacques Marchais Center of Tibetan Art

The Voorlezer House at Richmond Town

authentic altar in three tiers, crowded with gold, silver, and bronze figures.

The second building is used as a library. The garden has some stone sculptures, including life-size Buddhas. The museum was built in 1947 by Mrs. Jacques Marchais, a dealer in Asian art. The Dalai Lama paid his first visit here in 1991.

A gazebo at the Snug Harbor Cultural Center

## Snug Harbor Cultural Center ❷❻

1000 Richmond Terrace. **Tel** (718) 448-2500. 🚌 S40 from ferry to Snug Harbor Gate. **Grounds** ⏰ dawn–dusk daily. **Art Gallery** ⏰10am–5pm Tue–Sun. 💲 donation. **Children's Museum** ⏰ noon–5pm (summer 11am–5pm) Tue–Sun. ⬤ Jan 1, Thanksgiving, Dec 25. ♿ limited. 🏷 🏠 **www**.snug-harbor.org

Founded in 1801 as a haven for aged sailors, Snug Harbor is now an arts center, with a complex of 28 buildings in various stages of restoration. There are five stately Greek Revival gems, dating from 1831 to 1880.

The oldest, the Main Hall, is the Visitors' Center. This leads through to the **Newhouse Center for Contemporary Art**, but the ships in the stained-glass windows are a reminder of its origins. Other buildings house the award-winning **Staten Island Children's Museum** and Veterans Memorial Hall, used for indoor performances. A sculpture festival and summer shows are held on the lawns. The Staten Island Botanical Garden has a noted orchid collection and a beautiful rose garden.

Snug Harbor is the legacy of a Scottish sailor, Robert Richard Randall, who became rich in the Revolutionary War and bequeathed his wealth to care for seamen. The property was bought so that the sailors could enjoy its harbor views.

Clear Comfort, Alice Austen's lifetime residence

## Alice Austen House ㉗

2 Hylan Blvd. **Tel** (718) 816-4506.
🚢 S 51 from ferry to Hylan Blvd.
⭘ noon–5pm Thu–Sun; grounds: to dusk. ● Jan, Feb, public hols. 🖼
**Donation** 📷 ♿ limited. 🎞 🚻
**www**.aliceausten.org

This small cottage built around 1690 has the delightful name of Clear Comfort. It was the home of the photographer Alice Austen, who was born in 1866 and who lived in this house for most of her life. She documented life on the island, in Manhattan, and also on trips to other parts of the country and on her travels to Europe. She lost all her money in the stock market crash of 1929, and poverty forced her into a public poorhouse at the age of 84. One year later, her photographic talent was finally recognized by *Life* magazine, which published an article about her, earning her enough money to enter a nursing home. She left 3,500 negatives dating from 1880 to 1930. Today, the Friends of Alice Austen House mounts exhibitions of her best work.

# Even Farther Afield

The village of Broad Channel at Jamaica Bay

## Jamaica Bay Wildlife Refuge Center ㉘

Cross Bay Blvd at Broad Channel. **Tel** (718) 318-4340. Ⓜ Broad Channel (A). ⭘ sunrise to sunset; visitor center: 8:30am–5pm daily. 🎞 seasonal (call ahead)
**www**.nps.gov/gate

The marshes and uplands of the Refuge cover an area almost the size of Manhattan. Over 300 species of birds live here either seasonally or all year round. On the main Atlantic migratory path, the Refuge is at its best in spring and autumn, when the skies are filled with skeins of geese and ducks. The park rangers lead hikes and nature walks for weekend visitors – be sure to wear suitable shoes and clothes, and take along a zoom-lens camera or binoculars to get the best from your visit. The only village is Broad Channel, a small collection of houses on pilings on the Cross Bay Boulevard. The Refuge and a 10-mile (16-km) stretch of beach and boardwalk at Rockaway, are accessible by subway straight from Manhattan.

## Jones Beach State Park ㉙

Beaches. ⭘ all year. 🖼 late May–Labor Day. **Tel** (516) 785-1600.
**www**.nysparks.state.ny.us/parks
🚆 Long Island Railroad: Penn Station to Jones Beach; train schedule (late May–Labor Day); (718) 217-5477.
**Jones Beach Theater**; (516) 221-1000. ♿

Jones Beach was the creation of Robert Moses, New York's Parks' Commissioner (*see p246*), who transformed this narrow spit of land into Long Island's most accessible and popular beach in 1929. There are sand dunes, surf on the Atlantic side, and sheltered water in the bay. There is also miniature golf, swimming pools, restaurants, and the **Jones Beach Theater**, which hosts concerts in the summer.

Robert Moses State Park is on the next island to the east, Fire Island, which is over 30 miles (48 km) long, yet less than 900 yds (800 m) across. Areas of the island are totally unspoiled and unpopulated, with long stretches of white sands, making it a great place for walking and bicycling in peaceful surroundings.

Fire Island's communities are small and varied. Some are favored by singles looking for the company of the opposite sex, others are sedate and family-orientated, and still others are favorites with New York's large gay community.

Sunbathers basking at Jones Beach

# SEVEN GUIDED WALKS

**W**alking in New York is an excellent way to discover the human scale of the city. The following 16 pages explore the unique character and charm of New York through seven thematic walks. These range from an exploration of Greenwich Village and SoHo's literary and artistic connections *(see pp260–61)* to a trip across the Brooklyn Bridge for spectacular views and a glimpse of 19th-century New York *(see pp266–7)*.

In addition, each of the 15 areas of Manhattan described in the *Area by Area* section of this book has a short

Sculpture outside US Custom House, Lower Manhattan

walk on its *Street-by-Street* map, taking you past many of the interesting sights in that area. Various organizations run walking tours of the city. These range from serious appraisals of architectural history to a guide to the ghosts of Broadway. Details of tour organizers are listed on page 369, or you can consult *Time Out New York* magazine. Although New York's crime rate has dropped to a record low, as in any major city take extra care of your personal belongings while walking *(see p372–3)*. Plan your route ahead and walk only during daylight hours.

**KEY**

••••• Walk routes

0 kilometers        4

0 miles        2

The Chinese Garden Court at the Metropolitan Museum of Art, Upper East Side *(see pp264-5)*

Harlem *(pp272-3)*

Upper East Side *(pp264-5)*

Greenwich Village and SoHo *(pp260-61)*

Waterfront *(pp268-9)*

Lower East Side *(pp258-9)*

East Village *(pp270-71)*

Brooklyn *(pp266-7)*

Riverfront promenade, Brooklyn *(see pp266-7)*

◁ Relaxing on Grove Street, Greenwich Village *(see pp260–61)*

# A 90-Minute Walk in the Lower East Side

This walk is through old immigrant neighborhoods that have given New York its unique flavor, and illustrates the ever-changing texture of the city as neighborhoods are rediscovered and one set of newcomers replaces another. Along the way you can experience a variety of cultures and cuisines. Sunday is the best day for local color. See more about Lower East Side on pages 92–101.

### The Lower East Side

Begin on East Houston Street, the border between the Lower East Side and the East Village, where some of the best traditional Jewish cuisine can be found at Yonah Schimmel Knish Bakery ① (137) and Russ & Daughters ② (179), run by the great-grandson of the founder and famed for smoked fish and caviar. Katz's Delicatessen ③ (205) has been a fixture for over 100 years. Continue to Norfolk Street and turn right to see the Angel Orensanz Center ④ (172), housed in New York's oldest synagogue building.

Turn right on Rivington for another synagogue survivor, the

An 1885 iron from the Lower East Side Tenement Museum ⑥

Shaarai Shomoyim First Romanian-American Congregation ⑤ (89) in a handsome 1890 brick building. The interior, while shabby, is still impressive.

The Lower East Side has been discovered by hip young New Yorkers and is now home to cutting-edge boutiques, trendy clubs, restaurants. On Rivington cool young fashion shops share the blocks with the old.

Make a left onto Orchard Street, the traditional center of the Jewish Lower East Side. Pushcarts that lined the block are gone and the sidewalk stands sell mostly cheap merchandise, but many stores offer discount designer leather and fashion. All are closed on Saturday, so Sunday is the busiest day.

A must stop for historians is the Lower East Side Tenement Museum ⑥ (108 Orchard). An original tenement has been restored to show how three immigrant families lived from 1874 to the 1930s.

A detour across Broome Street on Orchard brings you to Guss Pickles ⑦ (85–7), a new location for an old-timer, the inspiration for the 1988 film *Crossing Delancey*. Customers still line up for the crunchy pickles sold from barrels.

Come back to Broome and turn left for another unique

survivor, the Kehila Kedosha Janina Synagogue and Museum ⑧ (280 Broome), a small but fascinating congregation with a little upstairs museum.

Another left along Eldridge will take you, beyond Canal Street, to the grand Eldridge Street Synagogue ⑨ (12), the first Eastern European synagogue in New York, now open again after extensive restoration.

### KEY

··· Walk route

☀ Good viewing point

Ⓜ Subway station

### TIPS FOR WALKERS

**Starting point:** East Houston St.

**Length:** 2 miles (3.2 km).

**Getting there:** Take the subway F or V to Second Avenue; exit one East Houston at Eldridge. Other stops: F to Delancey, J, M, Z to Essex. The M15 bus stops on East Houston and on the corner of Delancey and Allen Streets, M14A and M9 run along Essex Street. Returning from Chinatown–Little Italy, Canal Street station is served by the J, M, N, Q, R, W, and 6 trains.

**Stopping-off points:** Little Italy's cafés are perfect for coffee and luscious cakes. For more substantial fare, Sweet-n-Tart at 20 Mott Street is recommended for Chinese food, or for Italian on Mulberry Street, Il Cortile (125) or Il Palazzo (151). For Jewish dairy delicacies such as blintzes, try Ratner's Dairy Restaurant at 138 Delancey Street.

0 meters       500

0 yards       500

Clothes vendors at Orchard Street market

Guss' Pickle Company ⑦

Pretzel seller on Orchard Street

Kam Man Food Products at 200 Canal Street

## Chinatown

Turn around and return to Canal Street, pausing to admire the spire of the Chrysler Building and the city skyline in view in the distance from Eldridge. Turn left and cross the Bowery, where many jewelry shops remain, remnants of the city's original Diamond District ⑩ (1). As you continue, the shops give way to stalls selling an exotic array of vegetables, and butcher shops with rows of roast ducks in the windows. At 200 Canal Street is Kam Man Food Products. One of the largest Chinese markets in the area, it is a fascinating place to explore. Turn left from Canal to Mott Street and you'll know you are right in the heart of Chinatown by all the Chinese neon signs. Even the banks and phone booths are shaped like pagodas. There are hundreds of restaurants here, from holes-in-the-wall to haute cuisine, all offering a chance to taste unusual fare. For spiritual sustenance. visit the Eastern States Buddhist Temple ⑪ in Mott Street (64b).

At Bayard Street, turn left to see all the Chinese political posters and messages on the Wall of Democracy, then turn back and walk to Mulberry Street. The curve next to Columbus Park was Mulberry Bend ⑫, once notorious for gang murders and mayhem.

An Italian deli in Little Italy ⑬

## Little Italy

Walk up Mulberry Street toward Grand Street and you are suddenly in Little Italy ⑬. Small in area though it is, and encroached on by Chinatown, this is a colorful few blocks of old-world restaurants, coffee shops, and stores selling homemade pasta, sausages, breads, and pastries. The Italian population has dwindled over the years, but a staunch group of merchants remain, determined to retain the area's Italian atmosphere. Their stronghold is Mulberry Street between Broome and Canal streets, with a few shops holding their own on Grand Street near Mulberry. If you continue to walk on Grand, however, you are quickly back into Chinatown.

The big event of the year is the Feast of San Gennaro, named for the patron saint of Naples. For 11 nights in September, Mulberry Street is jammed with locals and visitors enjoying the parades and the Italian food, with rows of sizzling sausages stalls.

# A 90-Minute Walk in Greenwich Village and SoHo

A stroll through the patchwork quilt of streets in Greenwich Village takes you to where New York's best-known writers and artists have lived, worked, and played. It ends with a tour of SoHo's galleries and museums, where today's artists show their work. For more details on sights in Greenwich Village, see pages 108–15, and for SoHo sights, see pages 102–07.

**Facade in Washington Mews ⑬**

**Author Mark Twain, who lived on 10th Street**

### West 10th Street

The junction of 8th Street and 6th Avenue ① has many book, music, and clothing stores nearby. Walk up Sixth to West Ninth Street to see (on the left at 425) Jefferson Market Courthouse ②.

Turn right at West 10th Street ③ to the Alexander Onassis Center for Hellenic Studies (58). A passageway at the front once led up to the Tile Club, a gathering place for the artists of the Tenth Street Studio, where Augustus Saint-Gaudens, John LaFarge, and Winslow Homer lived. Mark Twain lived at 24 West 10th Street, and Edward Albee at 50 West 10th.

Back across Sixth Avenue is Milligan Place ④, with 19th-century houses, and Patchin Place ⑤, where the poets e e cummings and John Masefield both lived. Farther on is the site of the Ninth Circle bar ⑥ which when it opened in 1898 was known as "Regnaneschi's." It was the subject of John Sloan's painting *Regnaneschi's Saturday Night*. Playwright Edward Albee first saw the question "Who's afraid of Virginia Woolf?" scrawled on a mirror here.

**The doorway of Chumley's ⑩**

### Greenwich Village

Turn left at Waverly Place past the Three Lives Book-store (154 West 10th St), a typical literary gathering spot, to Christopher Street and the Northern Dispensary ⑦.

Follow Grove Street along Christopher Park to Sheridan Square, the busy hub of the Village. The Circle Repertory Theater ⑧, which premiered plays by Pulitzer Prizewinner Lanford Wilson, is now closed.

Cross Seventh Avenue and bear left on to Grove Street. At the corner of Bedford Street, you can't miss "Twin Peaks" ⑨ (120 Bedford) a home for artists in the 1920s. Turn right to see Bedford: the unmarked door is Chumley's ⑩ (86), a saloon not much changed since it was a speakeasy (*see p30*). Writers Dylan Thomas, Ernest Hemingway, William Faulkner, J.D. Salinger, Jack Kerouac, and many others drank here. Covers of their books line the walls. 75½ Bedford is the narrowest house in the Village, and was once the home of feminist poet Edna St. Vincent Millay.

Walk up Carmine to Sixth Avenue and turn right at Waverly Place. At 116 Waverly ⑪, Anne Charlotte Lynch, an English teacher, held weekly gatherings in her town house for such eminent friends as Herman Melville and Edgar Allan Poe, who gave his first reading of *The Raven* here.

A detour left of half a block will bring you to MacDougal Alley ⑫, a lane of carriage houses in which Gertrude Vanderbilt Whitney had her studio. She opened the first Whitney Museum here in 1932, just behind the studio.

---

### TIPS FOR WALKERS

**Starting point:** *8th St/6th Ave.*
**Length:** *2 miles (3.2 km).*
**Getting there:** *Take subway train A, B, C, D, E, F or V to West Fourth Street-Washington Square station (Eighth Street exit). Fifth Avenue buses M2 and M3 stop at Eighth Street. From here, walk one block west to Sixth. The M5 bus loops around Washington Square back to Sixth Avenue and Eighth Street.*
**Stopping-off points:** *The Pink Tea Cup, 42 Grove Street, is good for lunch. Fanelli's Café, 94 Prince Street, has been serving customers since 1847 and was once a speakeasy.*

## Washington Square

Back on MacDougal, turn left to Washington Square North, to see the finest Greek Revival houses in the United States. Built of red brick, they have marble balustrades and entrances flanked by columns. Writer Henry James set his *Washington Square* in No. 18, his grandmother's home.

**Washington Square Park and Arch**

Pause at Fifth Avenue to look back at Washington Square Park, with its famous Washington Square Arch. Go across to Two Fifth Avenue; opposite is Washington Mews ⑬, an elegant carriage house complex. John Dos Passos, Edward Hopper, and Rockwell Kent lived in the studio at No. 14a at various times.

Go back up Washington Square North, past some elegant houses. Writer Edith Wharton lived at 7 Washington Square North. Now walk beneath the arch and across Washington Square Park. On the left as you leave the park, is the fine Judson Memorial Church and Tower ⑭ by Stanford White and the NYU Loeb Student Center. The Center was once a boarding house, known as the "house of genius," and is where Theodore Dreiser wrote *An American Tragedy*.

## SoHo

Walk south on Thompson, a typical Village street lined with clubs, cafés, and shops. Turn left at Houston, SoHo's northern limit, and right on West Broadway, lined with some of the city's most famous galleries along with a large number of chic and arty boutiques.

Turn left at Spring Street for yet more tempting shops, then right at Greene Street ⑮, which is the heart of the Cast-Iron Historic District. Many of these fine buildings now house clusters of art galleries.

Turn left at the end of Greene Street to Canal Street, the end of SoHo, to see how quickly the atmosphere of New York can change. This noisy street is full of hawkers and discount electronics stores. You can explore bargains for the next two blocks and then turn left up Broadway. Keen shoppers can turn right on Spring Street for NoLita, featuring clothes by trendy, aspiring designers.

**Cast-iron facade, Greene Street ⑮**

**KEY**

••• Walk route

☆ Good viewing point

M Subway station

0 meters 500

0 yards 500

Subway entrance in wintertime, near Bryant Park ▷

# A Two-Hour Walk in the Upper East Side

A promenade along upper Fifth Avenue and its
environs will take you past the best remaining
examples of New York's turn-of-the-century gilded age.
A detour through the old German district of Yorkville
leads to a riverside stroll to Gracie Mansion, official
residence of the city's mayor, dating from 1799. For
details on Upper East Side sights, see pages 182–203.

0 meters    500
0 yards     500

**From the Frick to the Met**
Begin at the Frick mansion
①, built for coal magnate
Henry Clay Frick in
1913–14. Allow some
extra time to see
Frick's art collection
(pp202–3). Many
such mansions were
built as New York's
first families outdid
each other with
miniature Versailles,
Loire-style châteaux
and even Venetian
palazzos. Most of
those still standing
have now become
either institutions or
museums. The apartment
building opposite the Frick is
typical of those where today's
affluent New Yorkers live.

**Church of the Holy Trinity ⑰**

East on 70th are two of
the city's top art galleries,
the Knoedler & Co (19) and
Hirschl & Adler ② (21). Walk
up Madison to the corner
of 72nd Street, to the big
Polo-Ralph Lauren store ③,
the 1898 French Renais-
sance home of Gertrude
Rhinelander
Waldo. Wander
inside to see the
elegant restored interior.

Walk back toward Fifth on
the north side of 72nd, past
two 1890s limestone beauties
that once housed the Lycée
Français de New York ④.
Continue along Fifth Avenue
to 73rd Street. Turn east to
11, Joseph Pulitzer's former
home ⑤.

A few blocks on, between
Lexington and Third, is a fine
row of town houses ⑥. Back
on Fifth
Avenue, walk
to 75th

**KEY**

••• Walk route
☸ Good viewing point
Ⓜ Subway station

**Ukrainian Institute of America ⑩**

◁ **Entrance to subway station in Bryant Park**

Street, to see No. 1, the
former residence
of Edward S.
Harkness, son
of a founder
of Standard
Oil. It is now
the Common-
wealth Fund
⑦. At 1 East
78th, the tob-
acco million-
aire James B.

Duke's 18th-century
French-style château is now
the New York University
Institute of Fine Arts ⑧.
At 79th Street and Fifth, the
former home of financier
Payne Whitney, is the
French Embassy ⑨, and 2
East 79th is the Ukrainian
Institute of America ⑩. On the
southeast corner of 82nd Street
is Duke-Semans House ⑪,
one of the few grand Fifth
Avenue residences that are still
privately owned. Save another
full day for The Metropolitan
Museum of Art ⑫ at 82nd.

Carl Schurz Park Promenade

### Yorkville

Turn east on 86th Street for the vestiges of German Yorkville – Bremen House ⑬, cross Second Avenue, then turn right to the Heidelberg Café and German deli Schaller & Weber ⑭ for a break. For cheap eats, try the famed hot dogs at Papaya King, 179 East 86th Street.

### East River and Gracie Mansion

Henderson Place ⑮ at East End Avenue is a cluster of 24 red-brick Queen Anne town houses. Carl Schurz Park opposite was named for the city's most prominent German immigrant, editor of *Harper's Weekly* and the *New York Post*. The park promenade atop the East River Drive leads to a view of Hell Gate, where the Harlem River, Long Island Sound, and New York harbor meet. From the walkway you can see the back of Gracie Mansion ⑯, the mayor's official residence. The path west along the fence leads to a better view. Walk west on 88th Street past the Church of the Holy Trinity ⑰ and at Lexington Avenue go to 92nd Street and west past two of the few wooden houses left in Manhattan ⑱.

The Cooper-Hewitt Museum ⑳

### Carnegie Hill

Back on Fifth Avenue, turn downtown past the Felix Warburg Mansion of 1908, now the Jewish Museum ⑲, and continue to 91st Street and the huge Andrew Carnegie home, now the Cooper-Hewitt Museum ⑳. Built in 1902 in the style of an English country manor, it gave the area the unofficial name of Carnegie Hill. The James Burden House ㉑ at 7 East 91st Street, built for Vanderbilt heiress Adele Sloan in 1905, has a spiral staircase under a stained-glass skylight that was known in society as "the stairway to heaven." At 1 East 91st, the financier Otto Kahn's Italian Renaissance-style residence was a show-place with a drive-through porch and interior courtyard. It is now the Convent of the Sacred Heart School.

Wooden houses on 92nd Street ⑱

# A Three-Hour Walk in Brooklyn

A trip across New York's most famous crossing leads to Brooklyn Heights, the city's first suburb. This neighborhood has a 19th-century feel, mixed with a hint of Middle Eastern cultures. The riverfront promenade has unrivaled views of Manhattan. For more details on sights in Brooklyn, see pages 247–53.

Brooklyn Bridge-
Worth Street **M**
*550yards/500m*

Fire Station on Old Fulton Street

### Fulton Ferry Landing
About 3,580 ft (1 km) long, the Brooklyn Bridge span yields thrilling views of the lower New York skyline and prize photo opportunities. Take a taxi, or if you have time, walk across to Brooklyn.

On the far side, follow the Tillary Street sign to the right, turn right at the bottom of the stairs, then take the first path through the park and walk down Cadman Plaza West ① under the Brooklyn-Queens Expressway; here Cadman becomes Old Fulton Street. You can see the bridge on the right as you head to the river at Water Street and the Fulton Ferry landing ②. During the Revolutionary War, George

Washington's troops fled to Manhattan from here. In 1814, this was the depot for the ferry connecting Brooklyn and Manhattan Island. This transformed Brooklyn Heights from a predominantly farming area to a residential district. The area is full of character and is still a very popular place to live. To the right is the River Café ③. This restaurant's fine cuisine and spectacular views of the Manhattan skyline make it one of New York's most exceptional dining spots. Double back past the former Eagle Warehouse ④ of 1893.

Eagle Warehouse ④

### Brooklyn Heights
From the landing, turn right to steep Everitt Street up Columbia Heights, on to Middagh Street, and along the streets of Brooklyn Heights. 24 Middagh ⑤ is one of the oldest, built in 1824.

Next turn right on Willow and left on Cranberry; here the town houses range from wooden clapboards to brick Federal-style to brownstones. Except for cars and a few modern buildings, you could be in the 19th century.

Many famous people have lived here. Truman Capote wrote *Breakfast at Tiffany's* and *In Cold Blood* in the basement of 70

Willow, and Arthur Miller once owned 155 Willow. Walt Whitman lived on Cranberry Street when he was editor of the *Brooklyn Eagle.* He set the type for his *Leaves of Grass* at a print shop near the corner of Cranberry and Fulton. The town houses now on the site are called Whitman Close.

Turn right along Hicks. The Hicks family, local farmers, inspired the name "hick" for a yokel. Turn left on Orange Street to the Plymouth Church ⑥, home of Henry Ward Beecher, an antislavery preacher. His sister, Harriet

Entrance to the River Café ③

Truman Capote with
feathered friend

Beecher Stowe, wrote *Uncle Tom's Cabin*. Meander along Henry and Pineapple streets. At Clark Street are marquees of once-luxurious hotels, such as the Towers. Follow Clark Street to 142 Columbia Heights, where Norman Mailer lives ⑦. Washington Roebling, architect of the Brooklyn Bridge, lived at 110.

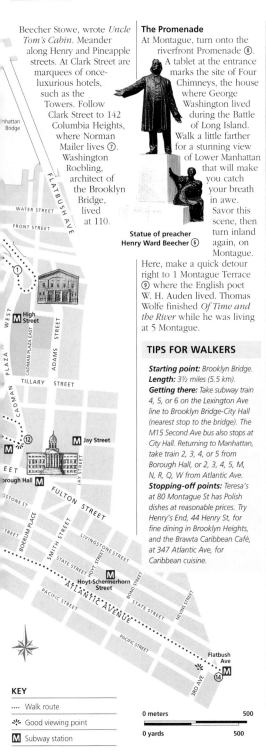

Statue of preacher
Henry Ward Beecher ⑥

## The Promenade

At Montague, turn onto the riverfront Promenade ⑧. A tablet at the entrance marks the site of Four Chimneys, the house where George Washington lived during the Battle of Long Island. Walk a little farther for a stunning view of Lower Manhattan that will make you catch your breath in awe. Savor this scene, then turn inland again, on Montague. Here, make a quick detour right to 1 Montague Terrace ⑨ where the English poet W. H. Auden lived. Thomas Wolfe finished *Of Time and the River* while he was living at 5 Montague.

## TIPS FOR WALKERS

***Starting point:*** *Brooklyn Bridge.*
***Length:*** *3½ miles (5.5 km).*
***Getting there:*** *Take subway train 4, 5, or 6 on the Lexington Ave line to Brooklyn Bridge-City Hall (nearest stop to the bridge). The M15 Second Ave bus also stops at City Hall. Returning to Manhattan, take train 2, 3, 4, or 5 from Borough Hall, or 2, 3, 4, 5, M, N, R, Q, W from Atlantic Ave.*
***Stopping-off points:*** *Teresa's at 80 Montague St has Polish dishes at reasonable prices. Try Henry's End, 44 Henry St, for fine dining in Brooklyn Heights, and the Brawta Caribbean Café, at 347 Atlantic Ave, for Caribbean cuisine.*

## KEY

···· Walk route

✹ Good viewing point

Ⓜ Subway station

0 meters 500
0 yards 500

The old Montague Street trolley, which led to the river and the ferry

## Montague and Clinton Streets

Once back on Montague Street, walk to the heart of Brooklyn Heights, with all its cafés and boutiques. The baseball team, the Brooklyn Dodgers, got their name from dodging the trolley cars that once ran down the street. Walk to the intersection of Montague and Clinton to see the stained glass of the 1834 Church of St. Ann and the Holy Trinity ⑩. Walk a block left on Clinton to Pierrepont Street for the Brooklyn Historical Society ⑪. A block farther, at Court Street, is the 1849 Borough Hall ⑫, and the subway taking you back to Manhattan.

Brooklyn's Dodgers, who got their name from dodging trolley cars

## Atlantic Avenue

Another option is to stay on Clinton Street and walk the five short blocks to Atlantic Avenue. A left turn here leads to a whole string of Middle Eastern emporia, such as Sahadi Imports ⑬ at 187 Atlantic Avenue, which stocks a huge selection of foods. The Damascus Bakery at 195 makes the most delicious filo pastries. Various other shops here sell Arabic books, tapes, publications, and CDs.

At Flatbush Avenue, look left to the Brooklyn Academy of Music ⑭ and the grand front of the Williamsburg Savings Bank. Watch for signs to the subway for your journey back to Manhattan.

# A 90-Minute Waterfront Walk

From the breezy Battery Park City Esplanade with its sweeping river views and upscale condos to the magnificent schooners moored at South Street Seaport, this waterfront amble introduces you to New York's formidable maritime legacy. The concrete jungle may lie just a few blocks inland, yet it seems worlds away, as the bleating horns and hiss of the crosstown buses are blessedly muffled. Stroll the green tip of Battery Park for a startling reminder that Manhattan is, in fact, an island. For more details on sights in Lower Manhattan, *see pp64–79.*

View of the Statue of Liberty from the waterfront promenade

The many photographs at the Museum of Jewish Heritage ⑤

### Battery Park City

Begin your walk on the Esplanade ① near Rector Place Park, just west of the Rector Street subway stop. Across the Hudson River looms the New Jersey skyline. Stroll toward the South Cove ②, where you'll catch sight, as did more than 100 million immigrants on their arrival, of Lady Liberty herself. Explore Robert F. Wagner, Jr. Park ③, named after a former New York City mayor. The leafy acres of grassy slopes, linden trees, and inviting pavilions are an important link in

Lower Manhattan's waterfront "greenbelt". Climb to the Wagner Park lookout point ④ for vistas of the Hudson River. Here, information panels chronicle New York City's seafaring history when grand schooners and coastal packets plied these waters.

### Battery Place

On Battery Place, visit the Museum of Jewish Heritage ⑤ *(see p77)* and its outdoor Garden of Stones, a calm, elegant space of dwarf oak saplings growing out of boulders. Since Manhattan is the undisputed king of tall buildings, pay homage at the sleek Skyscraper Museum ⑥, a marvel in stainless steel. Admire skyscraper history and current designs from around the world, as well as the original model, created in 1971, of the former World Trade Center.

Shiny surfaces and sharp angles at the Skyscraper Museum ⑥

Castle Clinton, an early 19th century fort built to defend the harbor ⑨

## Battery Park

On your way to nearby Battery Park, check out Pier A ⑦, which is all that remains of the 1886 grand marine firehouse. Important visitors who arrived by sea were once greeted with festive jets of water pumped into the sky by the fireboats. The clock on the pier tower used to keep time to the maritime system – eight bells and all's well. Continue along the waterfront, looking out for the American Merchant Mariners Memorial ⑧, a haunting sculpture of soldiers pulling a desperate comrade out of the waters, based on photographs of a World War II attack on an American ship. Head past Castle Clinton

**Enjoying a well-earned rest at a café, South Street Seaport ⑬**

monument ⑨, a fort built during the War of 1812. It later became an opera house, theater, and aquarium, but is now a museum. Stroll through the park where you can relax on benches in the shade of trees. Continue on to State Street, turn right on Whitehall, and then left onto South Street, passing the graceful Beaux-Arts Battery Maritime Building ⑩.

## South Street Seaport

Follow South Street, with the Brooklyn Bridge in the distance. Walk through the Vietnam Veterans Memorial Plaza ⑪ with its glass memorial etched with the poignant words from soldiers to their loved ones. Head north on Water Street, so named because it marks what was once the water's edge, and past Old Slip; all streets named "slip" are where boats used to dock between piers. Look west up the famed Wall Street ⑫ (see pp66–7) as you

cross it, for a view of the spires of Trinity Church (see p68). Turn right at Maiden Lane, then left onto the quaint and cobblestoned Front Street, which feeds into South Street Seaport ⑬ (see pp82–5), marked by the wooden masts and sails of the tall ships in the harbor. Explore New York's seafaring history at the South Street Seaport Museum, and then wander the shop-lined Fulton Street to Water Street. Take a peek into Bowne & Co Stationers at 211 ⑭, a charming old-fashioned print shop with 19th-century antique hand presses. Amble toward Pier 16 for a further glimpse of the past at the Maritime Crafts Center ⑮ where painters and carvers work at figureheads and carvings. Continue on to Pier 17 ⑯, bustling with shops and cafés. As you walk the wooden pier, look back for a memorable view of Manhattan – the masts of ancient schooners against the city's towering skyscrapers. Finish up at the inviting Paris Café in the 1873 Meyer's Hotel (see p83).

### TIPS FOR WALKERS

*Starting point: The Esplanade near Rector Place*
*Length: 2 miles (3.2 km)*
*Getting there: Take subway train 1, R, or W to Rector Street. Head west on Rector Street, cross the bridge over West Street to Rector Place, and walk to the Esplanade.*
*Stopping-off points: Gigino, on Wagner Park at 20 Battery Place, offers savory Italian fare outdoors.*

### KEY

••• Walk route

☀ Good viewing point

Ⓜ Metro station

| 0 meters | 300 |
| 0 yards | 300 |

# A 90-Minute Walk in the East Village

Originally the farm or *bouwerie* of the Stuyvesant family, this historic area now has a different appeal with its musical and artistic associations, as well as many of the city's interesting and affordable ethnic bars and restaurants. It also manages to balance a peaceful residential area with business and creativity, which is reflected in the constantly changing funky record shops, vegan cafés, craft stores, and live music clubs. For more details on sights in the East Village, *see pp116–21.*

### Astor Place
Adjacent to the Astor Place subway stop is a black steel cube called the *Alamo* ① – a meeting point for students and skateboarders. Walk towards Third Avenue through the large buildings that comprise Cooper Union ② *(see p120).* This scholarship college was founded in 1859 by Peter Cooper, an illiterate but successful businessman and proponent of free education. Across the street is the Continental ③, a live music venue that has hosted groups such as Iggy Pop and Guns N' Roses. In the East Village, 8th Street becomes St. Mark's Place ④, a former jazz, then hippie, then punk hangout. With so many sidewalk cafés and street vendors, this is one of the busiest pedestrian areas of Manhattan. St. Mark's Ale House ⑤ on the right, formerly The Five Spot, was where musicians and poets got together in the 1960s. A few steps down is Trash and Vaudeville ⑥, a clothing store that was once the Bridge Theater. The venue was repeatedly shut down due to controversial acts, then reopened. Yoko Ono held "happenings", and the US

**Locals enjoying celebrations on Ukrainian Day**

flag was burned as an anti-war protest in 1967. At 19–25 St. Mark's Place ⑦, there was a Jewish hangout, then the Italian mafia ruled, until Andy Warhol turned the space into the infamous nightclub Electric Circus in the 1960s. The Velvet Underground was among the bands who played here.

To check out their albums, stop at Kim's Video ⑧ nearby, which stocks obscure music and movies.

### Little Ukraine
Turn left onto Second Avenue, home of the largest and longest-standing Ukrainian population in the US, with restaurants, bars, and centers such as the Ukrainian National Home ⑨ on the right (140), and the good-value,

**Trash and Vaudeville store, once a venue known for controversial acts ⑥**

The style and elegance of an earlier century at Veniero's ⑫

First Avenue M

EAST 14TH STREET
EAST 13TH STREET
EAST 12TH STREET
EAST 11TH STREET
EAST 10TH STREET
EAST 9TH STREET
ST MARKS PLACE
EAST 7TH STREET
ST 6TH STREET

FIRST AVENUE
AVENUE A
AVENUE B

⑫
⑬
⑱
⑰
⑭
⑮
⑯

TOMPKINS SQUARE

Elm tree in Tomkins Square Park, a Hare Krishna memorial ⑮

**KEY**

••• Walk route

Ⓜ Metro station

0 meters 200
0 yards 200

24-hour Ukrainian eaterie Veselka ⑩ on the corner. Farther up Second Avenue, at East 10th Street, sits the St. Mark's-in-the-Bowery Church ⑪ *(see p121)*. Erected in 1795, this church was Dutch governor Peter Stuyvesant's private chapel and he is buried here. More recently, the Black Panthers and Young Lords gathered here, and Allen Ginsberg and other notable writers contributed to The Poetry Project that exists to this day. A right on 11th Street leads to Veniero's ⑫, a stylish Italian bakery that still has many of its original details, such as hand-stamped metal ceilings. Make a right and then a left onto 10th Street, past the three-story Turkish Bath House ⑬, to the northern edge of Tompkins Square Park ⑭ *(see p121)*.

## Tompkins Square Park

Built in 1834, this square has seen political activism of all kinds. It is also where a sacred elm tree in the middle of the park ⑮ commemorates the first Hare Krishna ceremony on American soil. Jazz great Charlie Parker lived across the street from the park from 1950–55 ⑯. Walk to the southwestern corner on 7th Street where 7A ⑰ serves breakfast 24 hours a day. Down the block, Turntable Lab 04 ⑱ sells DJ equipment and vinyl. If thirsty, continue west toward Second Avenue to McSorley's Old Ale House ⑲, one of the oldest bars in the city offering "dark" and "light" beer. Then get back onto Second Avenue and turn right to see where the old Fillmore East Auditorium ⑳ used to be (105). This classic rock scene featured such legends as The Doors, Jimi Hendrix, Janis Joplin, and Pink Floyd. The Who even premiered their rock opera *Tommy* here. Look left at 6th Street – "Indian Restaurant Row" ㉑ – where Bengali curry houses compete for business. Go down Second Avenue to number 80 ㉒; this was the home of Joe "The Boss" Masseria, head of the Italian mob in the 1920s. Turn right onto 4th Street where KGB bar ㉓, on the right, is a literary institution. A final left on Bowery leads to the former site of CBGB & OMFUG ㉔, or Country, Bluegrass, Blues & Other Music For Uplifting Gormandizers, birthplace of bands such as Talking Heads, which closed in 2006.

"Indian Restaurant Row" – the best street to go for a Bengali curry ㉑

# A 90-Minute Walk in Harlem

Few neighborhoods in New York are as rich in cultural history as Harlem, a haven for African-American heritage. This walk starts in Strivers' Row, one of the few areas that provided affordable housing during the 1920s and 1930s when the area flourished with creative and intellectual expression. It takes you past renowned gospel churches, jazz and blues clubs, and ends at the Apollo Theater, Harlem's famous showcase for new artists. For more details on sights in Harlem, *see pp220–31.*

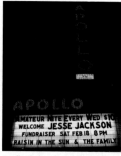

Apollo Theater, famous for televised shows and legendary acts ⑭

### Strivers' Row

The tree-lined area on 138th Street between Seventh and Eighth avenues is the St. Nicholas Historic District, commonly known as Strivers' Row ①. In the 1920s and 1930s wealthy and influential black professionals aiming for better lives moved into homes designed by such great architects as James Brown Lord and McKim, Mead & White. Signs on some of the gates still read "Private road walk your horses." A short detour left on Seventh Avenue (Adam Clayton Powell, Jr. Boulevard) and right on 139th Street leads to West 139th Street ②, where in 1932 16-year-old Billie Holiday moved into No. 108 shortly before landing her first singing job at a club in nearby "Jungle Alley."

An ornate doorway in Strivers' Row ①

internationally renowned for its magnificent Sunday gospel service. Founded in 1921 and named for the East African Americans of its first congregation, this church has hosted such notable pastors as Adam Clayton Powell, Jr. A stone's throw away on West 137th Street is the Mother Zion church ④, New York's first black church and one of America's oldest. While part of the Underground Railroad (an escape route for slaves), it acquired the nickname "Freedom Church." Continue to the Countee Cullen Regional Library where Madam C.J. Walker founded the Walker School of Hair ⑤. With her successful cosmetics line and hair-smoothing system, Walker was one of the first self-made female millionaires in the country. An active philanthropist, she donated to many African-American charities such as the National Association of

### Abyssinian Baptist Church

Turn right at Lenox Avenue and right back onto 138th Street toward the striking Abyssinian Baptist Church ③ *(see p229),* which is

Colored People (NAACP) and Tuskegee Institute. After her death in 1919, her daughter A'Leila turned the salon into an intellectual center for artists, scholars, and activists. It was named "The Dark Tower" after Harlem writer Countee Cullen's protest poem. Around the corner on Lenox Avenue is the Schomburg Center for Research into Black Culture ⑥ *(see p229),* a national research library named for the Puerto Rican-born black scholar who donated his personal collection to the library and served as its curator for six years. Down West 136th Street is Montgomery ⑦, a whimsical women's clothing store with one-of-a-kind designs. Farther down at No. 267 is "Niggerati Manor" ⑧, an artist's rooming house, so-named by Zora Neale Hurston, who lived here while collaborating with Wallace Thurman, Aaron Douglas, and Bruce Nugent on *Fire!!,* a magazine devoted

The famous Sylvia's restaurant, providing authentic soul food ⑪

to young black artists. Get back on Adam Clayton Powell, Jr. Boulevard and follow it down to "Jungle Alley" ⑨, the former highlight of Harlem nightlife, which once contained numerous bars, clubs, cabarets, and speakeasies. A detour across 131st Street will bring you to Marcus Garvey's house ⑩ (235), a major leader and fierce proponent of black unity, economic independence, and

**Art displays at the Schomberg Center for Research into Black Culture ⑥**

**The great jazz singer Billy Holiday ②**

**"Jungle Alley," where Billie Holiday first performed ⑨**

0 meters 200

0 yards 200

all performed. It is also home to the Zebra Room, a jazz spot that James Baldwin and Malcolm X frequented. In the middle of the next block is The Studio Museum in Harlem ⑬ (see pp230–31), with a variety of contemporary art exhibits, programs, lectures, and performances by artists of African descent. Its store is also worth a browse for its array of posters and books.

**Apollo Theater**

On West 125th Street is the famous Apollo Theater ⑭ (see p230), where since 1934, "stars are born and legends are made." These performers have ranged in style from Ella Fitzgerald to James Brown. Since 1987, "Amateur Night at the Apollo" has been televised nationwide and the theater has become the third-most popular tourist destination in Manhattan.

pride. Return to Adam Clayton Powell, Jr. Boulevard and make a left on 127th Street until you reach Sylvia's Restaurant ⑪ (see p230), the self-proclaimed "Queen of Soul Food." Family-owned since 1962, Sylvia's serves authentic southern favorites, such as fried chicken, catfish, and BBQ ribs. Stay on Lenox Avenue until 125th Street; here you'll find Lenox Lounge ⑫ where Billie Holiday, Miles Davis, and John Coltrane have

**KEY**

••• Walk route

Ⓜ Metro station

**TIPS FOR WALKERS**

**Starting point:** Strivers' Row.
**Length:** 1.75 miles (2.8 km)
**Getting there:** Take subway train 2 or 3 to 135th St and Lenox Ave, then walk north to 138th St and west to Seventh Ave. Or take M2, M7, or M10 bus to 135th St and walk to Seventh Ave.
**Stopping-off Points:** Sylvia's on 127th and Lenox is the famous soul food place in Harlem. Jimbo's Hamburger Joint on 125th and Lenox has great burgers and fries.

# TRAVELERS'
# NEEDS

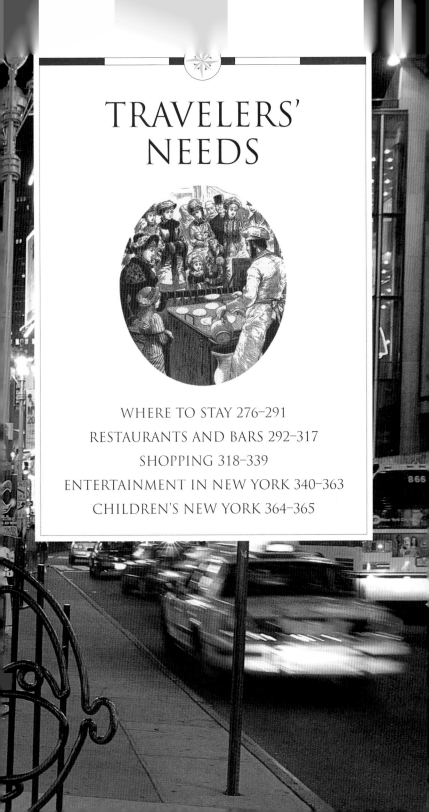

# WHERE TO STAY

With over 65,000 hotel rooms available, New York offers something for everyone. The city's top hotels are not quite as expensive as those in Paris or London, but the best news for visitors is the increase in budget hotels. While many of these are basic rather than charming, they offer good value. Other budget options are furnished apartments and studios, and bed and breakfast in private

Cole Porter's piano, in the Waldorf–Astoria bar *(see p289)*

homes, as well as youth hostels and YMCAs. From an inspection of over 200 hotels in New York, we have selected the best of their kind. *Choosing a Hotel (pp280–91)* contains detailed descriptions of the hotels, which will help you select the one best suited to your needs. Many of the hotels have a website address to enable you to book a room via the internet.

Bathroom at the Paramount, a midrange hotel in the Theater District

## WHERE TO LOOK

The East Side, roughly between 59th and 77th streets, is the traditional location for luxury hotels, but the renovation of certain landmark midtown properties, such as the St. Regis, and new hotels in famous chains from the Far East, such as the Peninsula Group, have considerably increased the competition in this price range.

Business travelers tend to favor midtown, especially the moderately priced hotels lining Lexington Avenue near Grand Central Terminal.

Those seeking relative quiet with access to midtown should look in the Murray Hill area, while theater-lovers should note the revival of the Times Square area. Hotels within walking distance of theaters offer an advantage, since performances tend to end at the same time and cabs are hard to come by.

There are a number of good, inexpensive hotels around Herald Square, which is convenient for shopping. Trendy boutique hotels have flourished in SoHo and the Meatpacking District, where there are also plenty of good bars, restaurants, and upscale shops (*see pp320–21*).

**New York & Co** (the Convention and Visitors Bureau) publishes a free, annually updated leaflet called "The New York Hotel Guide," listing current rates, toll-free numbers, and fax numbers. Staff will offer advice about hotels but do not make reservations.

## HOTEL PRICES

Some hotels offer seasonal promotional rates and other off-peak reductions. For example, business travelers vacate hotels at the end of the working week, and you can

take advantage of bargain weekend deals, even in luxury hotels, as prices drop (*see Special Rates p278*). There is a growing number of all-suite hotels available in every price category. Suites offer extra space plus cooking facilities and a refrigerator. Most suites can accommodate up to four people, which makes them popular with families.

Café Botanica at the Jumeirah Essex House *(see p286)*

## HIDDEN EXTRAS

When calculating the cost of hotels in New York, it is not enough simply to take into consideration the quoted room price. Hotel rooms have long been subject to extra taxes, but the former sliding scale, which favored rates under $100, has now given way to a blanket 13.375% hotel tax, plus $3.50 per night per room fee.

Several hotels now include continental breakfast in the room price. This is a big

Lobby phones, to reach a guest staying in the hotel.

◁ Tourists consult map on busy New York street

**Suite at the Millennium** (see p286)

saving, since standard hotel continental breakfast prices, before tax and tip, start at about $5 and soar to around $30 in some of the luxury hotels. To save money, head for the nearest deli or coffee shop and leave the hotel to business people having power breakfasts.

Hotel telephone charges are always high; it is much less expensive to use the pay phone in the lobby, particularly when you are calling overseas.

Tips are expected. Staff who take your luggage to the room are usually tipped a minimum of $1 per bag – more in a luxury hotel. The concierge need not be tipped for normal services such as arranging transportation or making dinner reservations, but should be rewarded for exceptional services.

When you order from room service, check the menu to see whether a service charge will also be included in the bill; if not, a 15–20% tip is customary. Solo travelers will find that single room rates are usually at least 80% of the double rate and are sometimes the same as for two people.

## FACILITIES

Although you'd expect hotel rooms in New York City to be noisy, most windows are double- or even triple-glazed to keep out the noise. Air-conditioning is a standard feature, so there is no need to open the windows in hot weather. Even so, some rooms are obviously quieter than others, especially if they are at the back of the hotel or overlooking a courtyard – check when reserving.

Television, radio, and at least one telephone are usually provided in every room, even in modest lodgings, and most hotel bedrooms have private bathrooms. In budget and mid-priced hotels a shower, rather than a tub, is the norm. Many of the mid-range hotels now offer fax outlets and machines in each room, a health club or exercise room, and a full concierge service. Luxury facilities include mini-bars in the room, dual phones, private phone message systems and electronic checkout.

The hotels listed here are all within a few minutes' walk of a large number of shops and restaurants. Very few hotels have their own parking, but valets may park your car in areas reserved for guests' use in nearby garages. A reduced (but still expensive) daily parking fee is normally offered. If there is no concierge at the hotel, front desk staff will be able to help with tourist information and to answer any queries.

**The Art Deco lobby of the Edison Hotel, in the Theater District**

# DIRECTORY

## TOURIST OFFICE

### NYC & Co.
*(New York Convention and Visitors Bureau)*
810 7th Ave, NY,
NY 10019. **Map** 12 E4.
*Tel (212) 484-1222.*
Publications available
at JFK Airport.
**www**.nycvisit.com

## SUITE HOTELS

### Affinia Suite Hotels
One reservation number
serves all of the following:
*Tel (212) 320-8050.*
Toll-free: *1-866-246 2203.*

**www**.affinia.com

### Affinia Dumont
150 E 34th St. **Map** 9 A2.

### Affinia Gardens
215 E 64th St. **Map** 13 B2.

### Affinia Manhattan
371 7th Ave. **Map** 8 E3.

### Affinia Plaza
155 E 50th St. **Map** 13 B4.

### Beekman Tower
3 Mitchell Pl. **Map** 13 C5.

### The Benjamin
125 E 50th St. **Map** 13 B4.

### Eastgate Tower
222 E 39th St. **Map** 9 B1.

### Shelburne–Murray Hill
303 Lexington Ave.
**Map** 9 A2.

### Surrey
20 E 76th St. **Map** 17 A5.

### The Phillips Club
155 West 66th St.
**Map** 12 D2.
*Tel (212) 835-8800.*
**www**.phillipsclub.com

## AIRPORT RESERVATIONS

### A Meegan Services
JFK International Airport
*Tel 1-800-441-1115.*

### Accommodations Plus
JFK International Airport
*Tel 1-800-733-7666.*

## DISCOUNT RESERVATION SERVICE

### Hotel con-x-ions
*Tel (212) 840-8686.*
*Fax (212) 221-8686.*
**www**.hotelconxions.com

### Quikbook
*Tel (212) 779-7666.*
**www**.quikbook.com

## HOW TO RESERVE

It is advisable to make hotel reservations at least one month in advance. While it's unlikely that the hotel will be fully booked, you may well find that the best rooms and suites have been taken, especially if a major convention is taking place. The busiest periods are at Easter, the New York Marathon week in late October or early November, Thanksgiving and Christmas.

Reserve directly with the hotel by telephone, letter or fax or over the internet. Written confirmation of your telephone booking will be required, probably with a deposit as a guarantee of your arrival; any cancellation fees may be deducted from this. You can pay by credit card, international bank draft or money order, or US traveler's check. Advise the staff if you are going to arrive at the hotel after 6pm or you will lose your reservation, unless you have prepaid with a credit card.

You can also book a hotel through your travel agent or airline. Most hotels have a toll-free telephone number for use in the United States, but these numbers do not work from Europe and the UK. If the hotel is part of an international chain, an affiliated hotel in your country should be able to reserve a room for you.

## SPECIAL RATES

Hotels are busiest during the week, when business travelers are in the city, so most of them offer budget packages to encourage more weekend business. It's often possible to move from a standard to a luxury room for the weekend at the same rate. A lower corporate rate is usually available to employees of large companies. Quite often, reservation clerks will grant corporate discounts on request without asking for a company affiliation.

Some reservation agencies offer discount rates. A good travel agent should be able to get the best current rates, but compare prices by contacting directly a discount reservation service such as Hotel con-x-ions or Quikbook *(see p277)*, which offers discounts between 20% and 50%, depending on the time of year. You reserve by credit card and receive a voucher, which you present to the hotel.

Package tours can also provide savings on the usual price. These rates may not oblige you to stay with a tour group, only to use their air and hotel arrangements. They may also include airport transfers, an additional saving. Airlines frequently have special deals, particularly during slow travel seasons. A knowledgeable travel agent should be able to tell you the current best deals, but newspapers often advertise special, limited offers that can be booked directly. At off-peak times you may net even bigger savings than with the package plans.

**Lobby of the St. Regis Hotel** *(see p287)*

## DIRECTORY

### DISABLED TRAVELERS

**Mayor's Office for People with Disabilities**
100 Gold St, 2nd floor, NY, NY 10038.
*Tel* *(212) 788-2830.*
www.nyc.gov/mopd

### BED & BREAKFAST

**At Home in NY**
*Tel* *(212) 956-3125.*
*Fax* *(212) 247-3294.*

**B & B Network in New York**
130 Barrow St, Suite 508, NY, NY, 10014.

*Tel* *(212) 645-8134* or *(800) 900-8134.*

**CountryInn The City**
*Tel* *(212) 580-4183.*
www.countryinnthecity.com

**New World B & B**
*Tel* *(212) 675-5600* or *(800) 443-3800.*

### YOUTH HOSTELS AND DORMITORIES

**Big Apple Hostel**
119 W 45th St, NY, NY 10036.
**Map** 12 E5.
*Tel* *(212) 302-2603.*
www.bigapplehostel.com

**Hosteling International, NY**
891 Amsterdam Ave at W 103rd St, NY, NY 10025.
**Map** 20 E5.
*Tel* *(212) 932-2300.*
www.hinewyork.org

**92nd St Y**
1395 Lexington Ave, NY, NY 10128.
**Map** 17 A2.
*Tel* *(212) 415-5650.*
www.92y.org

**YMCA-Vanderbilt**
224 E 47th St, NY, NY 10017.
**Map** 13 A5.
*Tel* *(212) 756-9600.*
www.ymcanyc.org

**YMCA-West Side**
5 W 63rd St, NY, NY 10023. **Map** 12 D2.
*Tel* *(212) 875-4273.*
www.ymcanyc.org

### AIRPORT HOTELS

See pp380–81 for details of the hotels to be found at *JFK* and *Newark* airports.

## DISABLED TRAVELERS

By law, new hotels must provide facilities for disabled visitors. Many older buildings have also been renovated so as to comply with this regulation.

To find out which hotels offer the best facilities, check their websites. These are provided for all the hotels listed on pp280–91. When booking, let the hotel know of any specific needs. Guide dogs are allowed in most hotels, but it is also advisable to check in advance.

The **Mayor's Office for People With Disabilities** also offers information about hotels.

## TRAVELING WITH CHILDREN

American hotels generally have a very welcoming attitude toward children. Cots or cribs as well as lists of reliable baby-sitters are normally available, and most hotel restaurants are happy to cater to young guests.

Traveling with children can be cheaper than anticipated. Many hotels do not charge for children if they stay in their parents' room, or make only a small charge for an extra bed. There is usually a limit of one or two children per room in these cases, and most hotels stipulate that the children must be under a certain age, most often 12. Parents of older children are expected to pay the full price, although the age limit is occasionally extended to 18. Ask about family rates when you make your reservation.

## BED-AND-BREAKFAST

An increasing number of bed-and-breakfast accommodations in private apartments is available in New York. These can vary from a room in an apartment with an owner-host in residence to an entire self-contained apartment with its own kitchen and bathroom, which you have to yourself while the owner is away.

Staying in a private apartment has certain advantages. It enables you to feel at home in a New York neighborhood

Entrance to the Peninsula Hotel (see p289)

and to visit local restaurants, which are usually far more reasonably priced than those in tourist areas.

Bed-and-breakfast lodgings can be found through many free booking services. Some booking agencies have a two-or-more-night minimum.

Rates for unhosted apartments vary from about $100 to $300, and for a double room start at $100 a night, depending on whether you have a private bathroom. There is a wide range of apartments, from spacious and luxurious to cramped and dowdy. Remember that, if the address is remote or inconveniently far from bus routes or subway stations, your costs will rise, as you will need frequent cabs. Ask about location and amenities when you reserve.

## YOUTH AND BUDGET ACCOMMODATIONS

New York's youth hostel and its many **YMCA** dormitories offer lodgings for those on a tight budget. For the longer-term visitor, the **92nd Street Y**, a nonsectarian hostel and lively cultural center situated in the Upper East Side, has

Sky-high swimming pool at a luxury hotel

good-value rooms, with prices starting from around $35 to $50 a night.

There are no campsites in Manhattan, and, sadly, youth hostels are not as prevalent in New York as they are in large European cities.

For the budget-minded traveler looking for the bare essentials, there is still other accommodation that can offer surprisingly good value for the price. Inexpensive rooms, often in relatively good locations for sightseeing, are available in several areas of New York, particularly in Chelsea, the Garment District and the Upper West Side, and to a lesser extent in such prime neighborhoods as the Upper Midtown. Although some of these budget-price rooms are reasonably comfortable, with private baths or showers, others may be rather small, perhaps with no air conditioning, and you may have to share a bathroom.

Finally, another way to make your budget go further is to avoid having breakfast in your hotel. Even its coffee shop is likely to be more expensive than an outside coffee shop or deli.

## USING THE LISTINGS

Hotel listings are on pages 280–291. Each hotel is listed according to its area and price category. The symbols after each hotel's address summarize the facilities it offers.

🏋 gym/fitness facilities available in hotel
🏊 swimming pool in hotel
🧒 children's facilities: cribs/cots, baby-sitting service
🛗 elevator
🅿 valet parking available
🍴 restaurant
💳 no credit cards accepted

**Price categories** for a double room inclusive of breakfast, service charges, and any additional taxes:

$ under $150
$$ $150–$250
$$$ $250–$350
$$$$ $350–$450
$$$$$ over $450

# Choosing a Hotel

These hotels have been selected across a wide price range for their good value, excellent facilities, and location. This chart lists the hotels by area of the city in the same order as the rest of the guide. Within each area, entries are listed alphabetically within each price category, from the least expensive to the most expensive.

**PRICE CATEGORIES**
For a standard double room per night, inclusive of breakfast, service charges, and any additional taxes:

$ under $150
$$ $150–$250
$$$ $250–$350
$$$$ $350–$450
$$$$$ over $450

## LOWER MANHATTAN

### Best Western Seaport Inn Downtown
$$
*33 Peck Slip, 10038* **Tel** *(212) 766-6600* **Fax** *(212) 766-6615* **Rooms** *72*     **Map** *2 D2*

You'll feel like you're stepping into a 19th-century sailor's haunt at this property with views of Brooklyn Bridge. Familes enjoy the deluxe breakfast, afternoon cookies, and lounge with coffee and tea. The 24-hour fitness center is large. Upgrade to a room with a terrace if you can. **www.seaportinn.com**

### Embassy Suites New York
$$$
*102 North End Ave, 10282* **Tel** *(212) 945-0100* **Fax** *(212) 945-3012* **Rooms** *463*     **Map** *1 A2*

This all-suite hotel is a great bet for families. Two-room accommodations feature high-speed internet and fold-out couch beds. Fantastic views of the harbor and discounted weekend rates. The hotel is located near Battery Park City and the Statue of Liberty ferry, but is quite far from the subway. **www.embassysuites.com**

### Holiday Inn Wall Street
$$$
*15 Gold St, 10038* **Tel** *(212) 232-7700* **Fax** *(212) 425-0330* **Rooms** *138*     **Map** *2 D2*

Business travelers feel right at home in rooms designed just for them with all the latest high-tech necessities. Personal computers in each room also come with fax/copier, portable phones, and all the office supplies one could need. Buffet breakfast available for those who don't have appointments elsewhere. **www.holidayinnwsd.com**

### Marriott New York City Financial Center
$$$
*85 West St, 10006* **Tel** *(212) 385-4900* **Fax** *(212) 227-8136* **Rooms** *497*     **Map** *1 B3*

This new hotel in the heart of Financial District is modern and grand, and even offers an indoor pool. All rooms have luxurious bedding and high-speed internet access. Some offer views of the Statue of Liberty and New York Harbor. Primarily a business hotel, this property sometimes offers great weekend rates. **www.nycmarriottfinancial.com**

### The Wall Street Inn
$$$
*9 South William St, 10004* **Tel** *(212) 747-1500* **Fax** *(212) 747-1900* **Rooms** *46*     **Map** *1 C3*

Rates can drop to bargain levels on weekends at this business-targeted hotel. The early-American interiors keep it from feeling stuffy, and the professional service is first class. While rooms can feel small, the beds are comfortable. Score a corner room for a whirlpool tub. Continental breakfast included. **www.thewallstreetinn.com**

### Ritz Carlton Battery Park
$$$$
*2 West St, 10004* **Tel** *(212) 344-0800* **Fax** *(212) 344-3801* **Rooms** *298*     **Map** *1 B4*

Telescopes in the elegantly modern rooms offer spectacular close-up views of the Statue of Liberty and New York Harbor. Bathrooms are huge and stocked with amenities, while special attention is paid to kids in the hotel's special children's program. Afternoon tea is served in the bar. **www.ritzcarlton.com**

## LOWER EAST SIDE

### Off SoHo Suites Hotel
$
*11 Rivington St, 10002* **Tel** *(212) 979-9808* **Fax** *(212) 979-9801* **Rooms** *38*     **Map** *5 A3*

Trendy downtown neighborhoods have enveloped this budget spot making it a good choice for those wanting to be near SoHo or the Lower East Side. Small suites share facilities, while the larger ones come with private bathrooms and full kitchens, making it a good choice for bigger groups or families. **www.offsoho.com**

### Howard Johnson Express Inn
$$$
*135 East Houston St, 10002* **Tel** *(212) 358-8844* **Fax** *(212) 473-3500* **Rooms** *46*     **Map** *5 A3*

This relatively new addition offers small yet clean budget rooms for checking out the trendy cafés and boutiques just outside. Steps away from the subway line and cheap eats, the location for young hipsters is hard to beat. Some rooms have microwaves and small fridges. The famous Katz's Deli is just a block away. **www.hojo.com**

**Key to Symbols** *see back cover flap*

# SOHO AND TRIBECA

### Cosmopolitan Hotel ⬜ $$

*95 West Broadway, 10007* **Tel** *(212) 566-1900* **Fax** *(212) 566-6909* **Rooms** *125* **Map** *1 B1*

This budget gem is located in the heart of trendy TriBeCa. While rooms are small, they are well maintained with equally tiny but clean bathrooms. The many top restaurants nearby and easy access to public transport make this a top-budget recommendation. Also great for shopping. **www.cosmohotel.com**

### Holiday Inn Downtown ⬜⬜⬜ $$

*138 Lafayette St, 10013* **Tel** *(212) 966-8898* **Fax** *(212) 941-5832* **Rooms** *227* **Map** *4 F5*

This basic property is a longtime favorite of those wishing to be close to New York's bustling downtown area. SoHo, Chinatown, the Lower East Side, and Little Italy are just steps away with boutique shops and restaurants galore. Rooms are simple but comfortable, and the in-house restaurant is good at a pinch. **www.hidowntown-nyc.com**

### Tribeca Grand Hotel ⬜⬜⬜⬜ $$$

*2 Sixth Ave, 10013* **Tel** *(212) 519-6600* **Fax** *(212) 519-6700* **Rooms** *203* **Map** *3 E5*

The atrium lobby gives this hotel a grand look. The private screening room downstairs has long made this a favorite of celebrities. Rooms are sleekly designed and the bathroom amenities first-rate. Score a corner room or studio suite for the most space, and make sure to sip a drink in the lounge to maximize star sightings. **www.tribecagrand.com**

### 60 Thompson ⬜⬜⬜⬜ $$$$

*60 Thompson St, 10012* **Tel** *(877) 431-0400* **Fax** *(212) 431-0200* **Rooms** *100* **Map** *4 D4*

This chic boutique hotel keeps getting hotter with the opening of a new restaurant and a summertime rooftop lounge/deck available only to guests and certain trendsetters. Rooms are minimalist yet comfortable with a pleasing palette tone, and have all the latest high-tech gadgets. Location is the star here. **www.60thompson.com**

### SoHo Grand Hotel ⬜⬜⬜⬜ $$$$

*310 West Broadway, 10013* **Tel** *(212) 965-3000* **Fax** *(212) 965-3200* **Rooms** *367* **Map** *4 E4*

Entertainment moguls and celebrities as well keep returning to this boutique favorite. Located in the middle of happening SoHo, the rooms are small and can seem dark despite the high windows offering views of downtown. A 24-hour room service and pet amenities keep guests happy. **www.sohogrand.com**

### The Mercer Hotel ⬜⬜⬜⬜ $$$$$

*147 Mercer St, 10012* **Tel** *(212) 966-6060* **Fax** *(212) 965-3838* **Rooms** *75* **Map** *4 E3*

This discreet boutique property comes at luxury prices, and celebrities seeking a bit more privacy have made this their choice. Rooms are designed as lofts with exposed brick and wooden floors. Bathroom tubs are large enough for two. Children are welcome – cribs featuring Frette linens are available. **www.mercerhotel.com**

# GREENWICH VILLAGE

### Abingdon Guest House $$

*13 Eighth Ave, 10014* **Tel** *(212) 243-5384* **Fax** *(212) 807-7473* **Rooms** *9* **Map** *3 C1*

This lovely guesthouse is located on one of the West Village's most beautiful brownstone- and boutique-lined streets. Each room has unique decor and is fitted with classic comforts. No on-site full-time staff means this gem is best suited to independent travelers. No breakfast, but there are coffee facilities. **www.abingdonguesthouse.com**

### Washington Square Hotel ⬜⬜⬜ $$

*103 Waverly Place, 10011* **Tel** *(212) 777-9515* **Fax** *(212) 979-8373* **Rooms** *170* **Map** *4 D2*

Just steps away from NYU, this hotel faces recently-renovated Washington Square Park. The marble lobby leads to fresh, boutique-like rooms. The central location means higher than average rates, but great bars and restaurants are just around the corner. On-site restaurant delivers good meals. **www.wshotel.com**

# EAST VILLAGE

### Union Square Inn ⬜ $

*209 East 14th St, 10003* **Tel** *(212) 614-0500* **Fax** *(212) 614-0512* **Rooms** *40* **Map** *4 F1*

All the standard comforts come at reasonable prices in this hotel. Rooms have no views and are nothing to write home about, but the beds are comfortable and bathrooms clean. European breakfast is on offer at the in-house café, which keeps limited hours. Union Square nearby is nice for peoplewatching. **www.unionsquareinn.com**

### The Bowery Hotel

🅿️🔢🚶 $$$$

*335 Bowery, 10003* **Tel** *(212) 505-9100* **Rooms** *135*

**Map** *4 F3*

From the same duo who developed the Maritime in Chelsea comes this luxury lodging. An opulent 17-story hotel, it features lobby fireplaces and wood-paneled elevators, floor-to-ceiling windows in every room, and seven rooms with private terraces, hot tubs, and outdoor showers. The bar attracts a VIP scene. **www.theboweryhotel.com**

## GRAMERCY AND THE FLATIRON DISTRICT

### Hotel 17

📶 $

*225 East 17th St, 10003* **Tel** *(212) 475-2845* **Fax** *(212) 677-8178* **Rooms** *120*

**Map** *9 B5*

Young travelers love the location of this very basic budget option. Rooms are tiny with not much flair and some share baths. Woody Allen popularized this hotel in *Manhattan Murder Mystery* and supposedly Madonna stayed here as a young singer. Some cheap eats are nearby as is good mainstream shopping. **www.hotel17ny.com**

### Hotel 31

📶 $

*129 East 31st St, 10016* **Tel** *(212) 685-3060* **Fax** *(212) 532-1232* **Rooms** *60*

**Map** *9 A3*

This sister property to Hotel 17 was recently refurnished. Each of the 60 rooms is decorated differently, although the style is typical chic floral print. Rooms have the basics such as air conditioning, televisions with cable, and some share baths. This area is a little quieter at night. **www.hotel31.com**

### Murray Hill Inn

$

*143 East 30th St, 10016* **Tel** *(212) 683-6900* **Fax** *(212) 545-0103* **Rooms** *50*

**Map** *9 A3*

The good value of this walk-up hotel atones for the small, simple, and unstylish rooms. Rooms with private bathrooms are the best, but the shared bathrooms are very clean and a good option for those with limited budgets. Murray Hill is home to young families, so can feel a little quiet at night. **www.murrayhillinn.com**

### Gershwin Hotel

📶🔢 $$

*7 East 27th St, 10016* **Tel** *(212) 545-8000* **Fax** *(212) 684-5546* **Rooms** *150*

**Map** *8 F3*

An original Andy Warhol *Campbell's Soup Can* in the lobby sets the tone of this popart-inspired hotel. More art can be found on every floor. Rooms are bright and stylishly decorated. A tourist bargain as it's just steps to the Empire State Building. Many reasonable restaurants nearby. **www.gershwinhotel.com**

### The Marcel

📶🅿️🔢 $$

*301 East 24th St, 10011* **Tel** *(212) 696-3800* **Fax** *(212) 696-0077* **Rooms** *97*

**Map** *9 B4*

Even though the rooms are on the small side, budget travelers will enjoy the contemporary feel of The Marcel. Rooms feature down duvets, CD players, and padded headboards, while built-in and comfortable fold-down beds maximize the space. The complimentary 24/7 cappuccino bar is a nice touch. Wireless Internet access is charged extra.

### Thirty Thirty

📶🔢 $$

*30 East 30th St, 10016* **Tel** *(212) 689-1900* **Fax** *(212) 689-0023* **Rooms** *253*

**Map** *9 A3*

The stylish rooms here are perfect for sophisticated travelers on a budget. While small, the rooms are quite comfortable with many twin-bedded rooms available as well as some with kitchenettes. The restaurant and lounge add to its attractions. Several trendy restaurants and shops nearby as well. **www.thirtythirty-nyc.com**

### Hotel Roger Williams

📶🔢 $$$

*131 Madison Ave, 10016* **Tel** *(212) 448-7000* **Fax** *(212) 448-7007* **Rooms** *200*

**Map** *9 A3*

A stylish option for those with a little more to spend, and the added amenities make it worth the price – free breakfast, all-day serve-yourself coffee and treats, and DVD lending. The rooms are soothing in blond woods and warm colors. Seasonal discounts can make this even more affordable. **www.rogerwilliamshotel.com**

### Hotel Giraffe

📶🔢 $$$$

*365 Park Ave South, 10016* **Tel** *(212) 685-7700* **Fax** *(212) 685-7771* **Rooms** *73*

**Map** *9 A4*

Perhaps the Flatiron District's finest full-service luxury hotel, the rooms are decorated with custom furnishings invoking the Moderne style. Suites have French doors opening onto a Juliet balcony. The restaurant downstairs offers superb cuisine and potent cocktails with a lounge scene. **www.hotelgiraffe.com**

### Inn at Irving Place

🔢 $$$$

*56 Irving Place, 10003* **Tel** *(212) 533-4600* **Fax** *(212) 533-4611* **Rooms** *12*

**Map** *9 A5*

Edith Wharton would be proud of these antique brownstones buildings, run impeccably as a luxury inn. Each room features beautiful bathrooms, as well as modern technology such as CD players. Complimentary breakfast is served in the salon, and don't miss the high tea. **www.innatirving.com**

### Gramercy Park Hotel

📶🅿️🔢 $$$$$

*2 Lexington Ave, 10010* **Tel** *(212) 920-3300* **Fax** *(212) 673-5890* **Rooms** *185*

**Map** *9 A4*

After an extensive restoration, the Gramercy Park Hotel has been unveiled as an "eclectic-Bohemian" extravagance, oozing modern art, wood paneling, velvet, and state-of-the-art gadgets. Guests can choose to relax on the private rooftop garden or in Gramercy Park itself (yes, the keys are available). **www.gramercyparkhotel.com**

**Key to Price Guide** *see p280* **Key to Symbols** *see back cover flap*

## CHELSEA AND THE GARMENT DISTRICT

### Americana Inn

*69 West 38th St, 10018* **Tel** *(212) 840-6700* **Fax** *(212) 840-1830* **Rooms** *50*

This is the place for the budget-minded traveler looking for the bare minimum essentials. Rooms have private sinks, and the baths are spotless. The central location and friendly staff make a winning combination. Just be aware that the area is always busy and can seem hectic. **www.theamericanainn.com**

### Chelsea International Hostel $

*251 West 20th St, 10011* **Tel** *(212) 647-0010* **Fax** *(212) 727-7289* **Rooms** *57*                 **Map** *8 D5*

Considered one of the city's best hostels, this complex features a series of low-rise buildings looking out on a central courtyard. Both private bunkbed rooms and shared dorm beds available, all bathrooms are shared. Facilities include two fully-equipped kitchens, laundry machines, and TVs. **www.chelseahostel.com**

### Chelsea Lodge $

*318 West 20th St, 10011* **Tel** *(212) 243-4499* **Fax** *(212) 243-7852* **Rooms** *22*                 **Map** *8 D5*

The lovingly restored townhouse in the Chelsea Historic District is the setting for this gem of a budget find. The small rooms have private sinks and showers, so guests only share toilet facilities. Perfect for independent travelers looking for a true NYC experience. **www.chelsealodge.com**

### Chelsea Star Hotel $

*300 West 30th St, 10001* **Tel** *(212) 244-7827* **Fax** *(212) 279-9018* **Rooms** *34*                 **Map** *8 D3*

After a recent renovation almost doubling the size of this hotel, its interiors are bright and upbeat if a bit garish. A life-size statue of Betty Boop greets you at the lobby. Rooms here range from dormitory style to more upscale chic with four-poster beds and DVD players. **www.starhotelny.com**

### Colonial House Inn $

*318 West 22nd St, 10011* **Tel** *(212) 243-9669* **Fax** *(212) 633-1612* **Rooms** *20*                 **Map** *8 D4*

While the owners of this lovely brownstone-turned-inn cater mostly to a gay male clientele, everyone is welcome. The well-maintained rooms have modern decor; almost half have private baths and a few feature working fireplaces. Seasonal discounts apply. **www.colonialhouseinn.com**

### Broadway Plaza Hotel $$

*1155 Broadway, 10001* **Tel** *(212) 679-7665* **Fax** *(212) 679-7694* **Rooms** *69*                 **Map** *8 F3*

The renovations in 2004 nicely updated and modernized all rooms in this budget find. New bed linens, drapes, and carpets give each room a fresh look, with extras such as high-speed internet access and two-line phones. Complimentary breakfast. The neighborhood can seem noisy at times. **www.broadwayplazahotel.com**

### Chelsea Inn $$

*46 West 17th St, 10011* **Tel** *(212) 645-8989* **Fax** *(212) 645-1903* **Rooms** *26*                 **Map** *8 F5*

Two turn-of-the-19th-century brownstones house a rambling selection of rooms and suites, many with private bathrooms. Eclectic furnishings and worn rugs add a slightly downtrodden touch, but it is clean. Complimentary breakfast vouchers are given for the café downstairs. **www.chelseainn.com**

### Chelsea Savoy Hotel $$

*204 West 23rd St, 10011* **Tel** *(212) 929-9353* **Fax** *(212) 741-6309* **Rooms** *90*                 **Map** *8 E4*

One of the more modern options in Chelsea, this hotel has a devoted following of those who appreciate the new rooms and consistent service. The rooms are pleasant though lacking in any extra touches. A good choice for those who appreciate the Chelsea restaurant, bar, and club scene. **www.chelseasavoynyc.com**

### Comfort Inn Chelsea $$

*18 West 25th St, 10010* **Tel** *(212) 645-3990* **Fax** *(212) 633-8952* **Rooms** *121*                 **Map** *8 F4*

Budget travelers enjoy the location of this modest find in hip Chelsea. The 1901 brick building offers clean rooms with TVs and refrigerators. The restaurant and coffee bar in the lobby are a draw, as is the famous Chelsea flea market around the corner on weekends. The suites, which sleep up to six, are a bargain. **www.choicehotels.com**

### Hotel Chelsea $$

*222 West 23rd St, 10011* **Tel** *(212) 243-3700* **Fax** *(212) 675-5531* **Rooms** *400*                 **Map** *8 E4*

Music history was made when punk legend Sid Vicious killed girlfriend Nancy Spungen here. Since then, famous personalities such as Sandra Bernhardt and post-Uma Ethan Hawke have stayed here. Some claim the large rooms and privacy are the draw, while others enjoy the bohemian, if somewhat dusty, furnishings. **www.hotelchelsea.com**

### Hotel Metro $$

*45 West 35th St, 10001* **Tel** *(212) 947-2500* **Fax** *(212) 279-1310* **Rooms** *179*                 **Map** *8 F2*

This Art Deco-inspired jewel is one of the best-priced mid-range hotels in midtown. Rooms are large and better decorated than most in this range. Rates include breakfast, and many enjoy the restaurant ambience and food. The real draw is the rooftop terrace with dramatic views of the Empire State Building. **www.hotelmetronyc.com**

## Wolcott
*31st St, 10001* **Tel** *(212) 268-2900* **Fax** *(212) 563-0096* **Rooms** *250*   🅿️📺   $$

**Map** 8 F3

Large rooms, low rates, and central location makes this a good choice for budget-minded travelers. While the rooms are plain, they are clean and internet access is available on the in-room TV. There are laundry facilities on the premises, and though no restaurant, cheap eats abound in the area. **www.wolcott.com**

## Inn on 23rd
*131 West 23rd St, 10011* **Tel** *(212) 463-0330* **Fax** *(212) 463-0302* **Rooms** *14*   🅿️   $$

**Map** 8 E4

This gem offers a perfect blend of bed-and-breakfast charm and full hotel service. Rooms and suites are uniquely decorated with extra touches such as pillow-top beds and plush Turkish terry towels in the bathrooms. New School Culinary Institute creates sumptuous breakfast each morning. Highly recommended. **www.innon23rd.com**

## Red Roof Inn
*6 West 32nd St, 10001* **Tel** *(212) 643-7100* **Fax** *(212) 643-7101* **Rooms** *172*   🅿️📺   $$

**Map** 8 F3

This middle-America motel chain from Accor successfully goes urban with nicely appointed rooms and professional service. In-room internet access is available. Affordable Korean restaurants line the block, which is convenient for sightseeing, shopping, and concerts at Madison Square Garden. Rates include breakfast. **www.redroof.com**

## Four Points by Sheraton
*160 West 25th St, 10001* **Tel** *(212) 627-1888* **Fax** *(212) 627-1611* **Rooms** *158*   🅿️🍴🏋️📺   $$$

**Map** 8 E4

This new budget-conscious hotel appeals to sophisticated travelers and business executives who are willing to spend a little more. Rooms are well designed with free high-speed internet access. Some have balconies with views of downtown, and good service as you'd expect from this chain. **www.starwoodhotels.com/fourpoints**

## The Maritime
*363 West 16th St, 10011* **Tel** *(212) 242-4300* **Fax** *(212) 242-1188* **Rooms** *125*   🅿️🍴📺   $$$

**Map** 8 D5

You can't help noticing the nautical theme of this hotel, since every room is centered around a porthole window with views of the Hudson River. This hip and happening place has rooms that are small but well designed, and several restaurants and bars. Has the most outdoor space in a New York hotel. **www.themaritimehotel.com**

## Radisson/Martinique on Broadway
*49 West 32nd St, 10001* **Tel** *(212) 736-3800* **Fax** *(212) 277-2702* **Rooms** *532*   🅿️🍴📺   $$$$

**Map** 8 F3

The landmarked French-Renaissance building houses this outpost of the reliable Radisson chain. Past the ornate lobby, the rooms have been restored to an elegant finish. Affordable Asian dining lines the blocks around the hotel, which is literally steps away from some of the best tourist sites on the island. **www.radisson.com**

# THEATER DISTRICT

## Big Apple Hostel
*119 West 45th St, 10036* **Tel** *(212) 302-2603* **Fax** *(212) 302-2605* **Rooms** *39*   🅿️   $

**Map** 12 E5

For prime location and clean accommodations, this hostel is perfect for young travelers. While most beds are dormitory style, a few private rooms with queen-size beds are available. Full kitchen facilities, and the backyard garden provide a respite from the harried streets of Manhattan. Book well in advance. **www.bigapplehostel.com**

## Park Savoy Hotel
*158 West 58th St, 10019* **Tel** *(212) 245-5755* **Fax** *(212) 765-0668* **Rooms** *70*   🅿️   $

**Map** 12 E3

While this very plain hotel offers the most basic of accommodation, it does so only a block away from Central Park. The rooms are clean, but they tend to be a little ragged and spartan. Expect friendly but limited service at the front desk. Grab a sandwich to go at one of the delis nearby and head to the park. **www.parksavoyhotelny.com**

## 414 Inn
*414 West 46th St, 10036* **Tel** *(212) 399-0006* **Fax** *(212) 957-8716* **Rooms** *22*   $$

**Map** 11 C5

This small and stylish hotel has an accommodating staff, who will arrange to have food delivered from nearby restaurant row. King-size rooms tend to be nicer than the double rooms, with better beds and linens. Make sure you snag a room overlooking the private courtyard for less noise. **www.414inn.com**

## Amsterdam Court Hotel
*226 West 50 St, 10019* **Tel** *(212) 459-1000* **Fax** *(212) 265-5070* **Rooms** *125*   🅿️   $$

**Map** 12 D4

This very stylish property is perfect for the sophisticated traveler with a few extra dollars to spend. Rooms are decorated in soothing whites and khakis, and offer Belgian linens with down comforters and CD players. A rooftop terrace is delightful in summer. Many great restaurants on Ninth Avenue. **www.nychotels.com**

## Belvedere Hotel
*319 West 48th St, 10036* **Tel** *(212) 245-7000* **Fax** *(212) 245-4455* **Rooms** *400*   🅿️🍴   $$

**Map** 12 D5

This quality mid-range hotel is a great choice over many hotels in this price range and location. Rooms are larger than average and relatively attractive. A very popular Brazilian steakhouse is located on the premises, a good addition to the many quality eateries just outside. A family favorite. **www.belvederehotelnyc.com**

**Key to Price Guide** *see p280* **Key to Symbols** *see back cover flap*

## Best Western President Hotel
*234 West 48th St, 10036* **Tel** *(212) 246-8800* **Fax** *(212) 974-3922* **Rooms** *334*  **Map** *12 E5*

Families prefer the junior suites with fold-out sofas for children, while the standard rooms work well for the typical traveler. This outpost of the chain hotel is well run with simple but clean rooms in a good location. Be aware that the area is always busy, so light sleepers might look elsewhere. **www.bestwestern.com**

## Broadway Inn
*264 West 46th St, 10036* **Tel** *(212) 997-9200* **Fax** *(212) 768-2807* **Rooms** *41*  **Map** *12 D5*

Fine service sets this small property apart from others in the price category. Kids stay free in the suites, and every room gets a free breakfast, making this a popular choice for families. Rooms are small, yet tastefully decorated with an Art Deco flair. Ask about free parking. **www.broadwayinn.com**

## Da Vinci Hotel
*244 West 56th St, 10019* **Tel** *(212) 489-4100* **Fax** *(212) 399-0434* **Rooms** *20*  **Map** *12 D3*

This European-style, intimate boutique property prides itself on good service. Rooms are on the small side, but well stocked and comfortable. A good choice for those who want to be close to the theater and don't mind the heavily touristed street. Meals in this area can be pricey, so watch for coffee shops and diners. **www.davincihotel.com**

## Holiday Inn New York City-Midtown-57th St
*440 West 57th St, 10019* **Tel** *(212) 581-8100* **Fax** *(212) 581-7739* **Rooms** *596*  **Map** *11 C3*

This solid choice from the famous American chain is a favorite with families thanks to the outdoor pool, and the fact that children enjoy a free breakfast. The rooms are all that you'd expect – clean, comfortable, and wired for internet access. Just blocks away from Central Park and the Theater District. **www.hi57.com**

## Hotel Edison
*228 West 47th St, 10036* **Tel** *(212) 840-5000* **Fax** *(212) 596-6850* **Rooms** *800*  **Map** *12 E5*

This enormous property offers good value for travelers who want to be in the heart of the Theater District. Rooms are well appointed, and the larger units are perfect for families. High-tech travelers will appreciate the recently added Wi-Fi access. The hotel is steps away from restaurant row. **www.edisonhotelnyc.com**

## Mayfair Hotel
*242 West 49th St, 10019* **Tel** *(212) 586-0300* **Fax** *(212) 307-5226* **Rooms** *78*  **Map** *12 D5*

While rooms are super small at this well-run property, they're also comfortable and up-to-date. Service is friendly, and the location for theatergoers is prime. The French bistro on site is a good choice for pre-theater dining, but for cheaper eats and better value, head to Ninth Avenue. **www.mayfairnewyork.com**

## Algonquin
*59 West 44th St, 10036* **Tel** *(212) 840-6800* **Fax** *(212) 944-1419* **Rooms** *174*  **Map** *12 F5*

The home of Dorothy Parker's literary "Round Table" of the 1920s has been fully refurbished and still draws literati to its doors. The comfortable rooms are small, so if possible, splurge on a literary-themed suite. The well-preserved mahogany-paneled lobby provides access to the legendary Oak Room cabaret. **www.algonquinhotel.com**

## Blakely Hotel
*136 West 55th St, 10019* **Tel** *(212) 245-1800* **Fax** *(212) 582-8332* **Rooms** *115*  **Map** *12 E4*

Formerly the Gorham, this hotel has been done up in a boutique tradition with an eye on service. From the duo who developed Chambers and Mercer, this hotel offers superb value and location in this price range. The nicely appointed rooms include details such as Egyptian linens. Keep an eye out for specials. **www.blakelynewyork.com**

## Casablanca Hotel
*147 West 43rd St, 10036* **Tel** *(212) 869-1212* **Fax** *(212) 391-7585* **Rooms** *48*  **Map** *8 E1*

This Moroccan-themed hotel is ideal for theatergoers. The rooms are small, but recently refreshed and feature fun touches such as polished rattan fixtures. Complimentary breakfast is served in the fireplace lounge. Great people-watching for the fashionistas heading in and out of *Vogue* headquarters across the street. **www.casablancahotel.com**

## Chambers
*15 West 56 Street, 10019* **Tel** *(212) 974-5656* **Fax** *(212) 974-5657* **Rooms** *77*  **Map** *12 F3*

A little downtown-style livens up this strip of midtown with a sleek design. The smallish rooms feature original modern art, Frette bathrobes, and cashmere throws. Town restaurant downstairs is one of the best in Manhattan. A perfect spot to take a break from shopping on Madison Avenue. **www.chambershotel.com**

## Doubletree Guest Suites
*1568 Broadway, 10036* **Tel** *(212) 719-1600* **Fax** *(212) 921-5212* **Rooms** *460*  **Map** *12 E5*

What this all-suite hotel lacks in charm, it more than makes up for in location and superior facilities. Some suites are designed for families, while others are perfect for business travelers. A special kids' play area makes it a favorite of families with toddlers. **www.nyc.doubletreehotels.com**

## Dream Hotel
*210 West 55th St, 10019* **Tel** *(212) 247-2000* **Fax** *(212) 974-0595* **Rooms** *228*  **Map** *12 E4*

This 1904 Beaux-Arts building was renovated, and you'll feel like you are sleepwalking the moment you walk into the lobby with its weird and over-the-top displays. The rooms are accented with blue light, and also feature pre-loaded iPods. The restaurant is well worth a stop, and check out the rooftop bar and terrace. **www.dreamny.com**

## Hilton Times Square      $$$

*234 West 42nd St, 10036* **Tel** *(212) 840-8222* **Fax** *(212) 840-5516* **Rooms** *444*     **Map** *8 E1*

You could easily miss this oasis of serenity in the midst of the Times Square madness, but don't. The design of the hotel goes way beyond chain mentality with oversize rooms and modern amenities. Rooms begin on the 23rd floor, assuring great views of the area. The upscale restaurant is a winner. **www.timessquare.hilton.com**

## Mansfield      $$$

*12 West 44th St, 10036* **Tel** *(212) 277-8700* **Fax** *(212) 764-4477* **Rooms** *124*     **Map** *12 E5*

This 1905 hotel has been made over as a boutique property with rooms featuring complimentary internet access and down comforters. The bar is a quiet spot for a drink after a hectic New York day. Tucked away on a busy street, the hotel's location is very convenient to theatergoers. **www.mansfieldhotel.com**

## Millennium Broadway      $$$

*145 West 44th St, 10036* **Tel** *(212) 768-4400* **Fax** *(212) 768-0847* **Rooms** *752*     **Map** *12 E5*

The large rooms are priced right at this Theater District favorite making it a good value in this price range. Guest rooms are outfitted in an Art Deco style, and the premier tower rooms are even larger with more amenities. The bar is a nice stop for pre-theater drinks. **www.millennium-hotels.com**

## Paramount Hotel      $$$

*235 West 46th St, 10036* **Tel** *(212) 764-5500* **Fax** *(212) 354-5237* **Rooms** *610*     **Map** *12 D5*

Originally designed by Ian Schrager, this property has been taken over by the Spanish Sol Melia chain, and the rates have subsequently dropped. The tiny rooms are shades of whites and gray, but escape the room and pose in the trendy bar. Stock up on goodies in the onsite gourmet grocery store. **www.nycparamount.com**

## Roosevelt Hotel      $$$

*45 East 45th St, 10017* **Tel** *(212) 661-9600* **Fax** *(212) 885-6161* **Rooms** *1013*     **Map** *13 A5*

Built in 1924 and meticulously renovated and restored for its 80th birthday, this "grand dame of Madison Avenue" is still a favorite of business and leisure travelers. Rooms are well appointed with comfortable beds, and the lobby will make you feel like you've stepped into history. **www.theroosevelthotel.com**

## Skyline Hotel      $$$

*725 10th Ave at 49th St, 10019* **Tel** *(212) 586-3400* **Fax** *(212) 582-4604* **Rooms** *230*     **Map** *11 C5*

Convenient for the Theater District and many of the city's best restaurants, the family-friendly Skyline has a quintessential New York lobby and facade. The recently renovated rooms are large and comfortable. The heated, indoor swimming pool is a major bonus, especially for those visiting with children. **www.skylinehotelnyc.com**

## Time      $$$

*224 West 49th St, 10019* **Tel** *(212) 320-2900* **Fax** *(212) 245-2305* **Rooms** *200*     **Map** *12 D5*

Renovated once again, this time by the celebrated designer Adam Tihany, who has used a primary color palette to create a multi-sensory experience. Many of the rooms are small, especially for the price. The lobby bar can be a scene, so stop by for a cocktail. Some can find the noise level too distracting. **www.thetimeny.com**

## Westin Times Square      $$$

*270 West 43rd St, 10036* **Tel** *(212) 201-2700* **Fax** *(212) 201-2701* **Rooms** *863*     **Map** *8 D1*

Another instant hit in Times Square is this modern, multi-colored 45-story tower hotel. Although the architecture has its critics (some say it would be more at home in South Beach), others rave about the larger rooms and the "heavenly bed" and now the "heavenly crib." Many family restaurants nearby. **www.westinny.com**

## Jumeirah Essex House      $$$$

*160 Central Park South, 10019* **Tel** *(212) 247-0300* **Fax** *(212) 315-1839* **Rooms** *515*     **Map** *12 E3*

This ornate Art Deco tower overlooking Central Park is undergoing a $70-million refurbishment that will upgrade the hotel to five-star status. The sleekly designed lobby is comfortable and understated, while the rooms are standard size. Enjoy afternoon high tea (2–6pm) in the sumptuous lobby lounge. **www.jumeirahessexhouse.com**

## Le Parker Meridien      $$$$

*118 West 57th St, 10019* **Tel** *(212) 245-5000* **Fax** *(212) 307-1776* **Rooms** *730*     **Map** *12 E3*

With outstanding service and one of the best restaurants and gyms in town, this sleek and modern hotel offers the best value in this price category. Try the cheap burger joint after going for a rooftop swim. Rooms are large and recently refurbished with high design and the latest technology. **www.parkermeridien.com**

## Michelangelo      $$$$

*152 West 51st St, 10019* **Tel** *(212) 765-0505* **Fax** *(212) 581-7618* **Rooms** *178*     **Map** *12 F4*

Italian Renaissance is the name of the game at this boutique gem that features classic rugs and weavings throughout the property. Italian espresso and pastries for breakfast start the day and Baci chocolates at bedtime finish it off. Bathrooms make good use of Italian marble. We say *la dolce vita*. **www.michaelangelohotel.com**

## Royalton      $$$$

*44 West 44th St, 10036* **Tel** *(212) 869-4400* **Fax** *(212) 869-8965* **Rooms** *205*     **Map** *12 F5*

This hotel from Ian Schrager and Philippe Starck was groundbreaking at the time, but is starting to feel a little dated. The service, however, remains consistently indifferent, while beautiful people still crowd the lobby bar and restaurant. Rooms can be tiny, albeit stylish, with funky bathrooms that don't quite work. **www.royaltonhotel.com**

**Key to Price Guide** *see p280* **Key to Symbols** *see back cover flap*

### Sofitel New York
🔲🔢🔳 $$$$

*45 West 44th St, 10036* **Tel** *(212) 354-8844* **Fax** *(212) 354-2480* **Rooms** *398*                **Map** *12 F5*

This hotel has been an instant hit in the Theater District and offers a wonderful blend of modern and classic, with helpful service. The brasserie restaurant is a nice choice with seasonal outdoor seating. Some of the top tier suites have terraces. A favorite with business travelers. **www.sofitel.com**

### W Times Square
🔲🔢🏃🔳 $$$$

*1567 Broadway, 10036* **Tel** *(212) 930-7400* **Fax** *(212) 930-7500* **Rooms** *507*                **Map** *12 E5*

This hip hotel from the Starwood Group continues to draw crowds and fans for its high-design and ultra-modern rooms – although somewhat dark, they offer fantastic views of midtown. The lounges and restaurants are always happening places. Make sure to check out Blue Fin, for some of the best sushi in town. **www.whotels.com**

### Ritz-Carlton, New York
🔲🔢🏃🔳 $$$$$

*50 Central Park South, 10019* **Tel** *(212) 308-9100* **Fax** *(212) 207-8831* **Rooms** *260*                **Map** *12 F3*

Fans rave that this is the best hotel for service in the entire Ritz-Carlton chain. Traditional in style, the large rooms are extremely comfortable and filled with the latest technology. The full-service spa and location across from Central Park make it a true winner. **www.ritzcarlton.com**

### St. Regis New York
🔲ℙ🔢🏃🔳 $$$$$

*2 East 55th St, 10022* **Tel** *(212) 753-4500* **Fax** *(212) 787-3447* **Rooms** *408*                **Map** *12 F4*

This 1904 Beaux-Arts landmark is filled with luxury and old-world glamour with chandeliers and expensive rugs. Service is very formal, but you would expect this of a grand dame that has been modernized. Internet access available. A favorite spot for weddings, it's unfortunate that the award-winning Lespinasse is now closed. **www.stregis.com**

### The London NYC
🔲🔢🏃🔳 $$$$$

*151 West 54th St, 10019* **Tel** *(866) 690-2029* **Rooms** *562*                **Map** *12 E4*

The former Rhigha Royal has undergone a facelift in the hands of new owners. The 54-story Art Deco building is within walking distance of Central Park and offers all the perks you'd expect from a hotel in this class, including an impressive concierge service and UK star chef Gordon Ramsay's first US restaurant. **www.thelondonnyc.com**

## LOWER MIDTOWN

### Hotel Grand Union
🔲🏃 $

*34 East 32nd St, 10016* **Tel** *(212) 683-5890* **Fax** *(212) 689-7397* **Rooms** *95*                **Map** *9 A3*

Extreme budget travelers of all ages find the Grand Union of good value for the level of service it offers. While rooms can be downright unattractive, they are well maintained and have all the necessary comforts. Some rooms are large enough for families. **www.hotelgrandunion.com**

### Courtyard New York
🔲🔢🏃🔳 $$

*3 East 40th St, 10016* **Tel** *(212) 447-1500* **Fax** *(212) 683-7839* **Rooms** *185*                **Map** *8 F1*

This neighborhood location can be pricey, but this hotel offers good value for its price range. It has recently been taken over by the Marriott chain and substantially renovated. Families appreciate the location since it is close to the New York Public Library and the Theater District without the noise. **www.courtyard.com**

### 70 Park
🔲🔢🏃🔳 $$$

*70 Park Ave, 10016* **Tel** *(212) 973 2400* **Fax** *(212) 973-2401* **Rooms** *205*                **Map** *9 A1*

This smart addition in the boutique category from the well-regarded Kimpton Group is stylish and well executed. Pets are welcome, and they provide extra amenities for the little critters. Business travelers appreciate the free extras such as Wi-Fi and high-speed internet. Rooms can be small, but comfortable. **www.70parkave.com**

### Affinia Dumont
🔲🏃🔳 $$$

*150 East 34th St, 10016* **Tel** *(212) 481 7600* **Fax** *(212) 889-8856* **Rooms** *248*                **Map** *9 A2*

The recently relaunched all-suite hotel is perfect for travelers who want space and comfortable design. Amenities include full kitchens with microwave ovens, and the helpful staff will even do grocery shopping for you. The on-site spa is a winner and will help travelers stay healthy. **www.affinia.com**

### Courtyard by Marriott Midtown East
🔲🔳 $$$

*866 Third Ave, 10022* **Tel** *(212) 644-1300* **Fax** *(212) 317-7940* **Rooms** *308*                **Map** *13 B4*

The spacious rooms make this a good choice for families that need to be in this neighborhood. Rooms are modern and have in-room coffee makers and free high-speed internet access. Free Wi-Fi is available in a special lounge. The neighborhood can be much quieter at night. **www.marriott.com**

### Dylan
🔲🔳 $$$

*52 East 41st St, 10017* **Tel** *(212) 338-0500* **Fax** *(212) 338-0569* **Rooms** *107*                **Map** *9 A1*

This boutique property is the former home of the Chemists Club, a 1903 Beaux-Arts building. The lobby may feel a little antiseptic, but the rooms are spacious by city standards. An excellent restaurant is on the premises, which is good, because there aren't too many good options nearby. **www.dylanhotel.com**

### Library Hotel

*299 Madison Ave, 10017* **Tel** *(212) 983-4500* **Fax** *(212) 499-9099* **Rooms** *60*     **Map** *9 A1*

This new boutique hotel has been gaining fans since it opened for its cleverly designed rooms organized around a library theme. From fairy tales to erotic literature, choose your room based upon mood, and you'll get the books to go with it. Rooftop terrace and all-day snacks make this a winning choice. **www.libraryhotel.com**

### Morgans

*237 Madison Ave, 10016* **Tel** *(212) 686-0300* **Fax** *(212) 779-8352* **Rooms** *113*     **Map** *9 A2*

The establishment that launched the boutique hotel revolution is still going strong. Surprisingly, it still draws a fashion-conscious crowd that will put up with tiny rooms and unreliable service in exchange for the lobby scene. Head down to the lobby bar and watch the action unfold. **www.morganshotel.com**

### Fitzpatrick Grand Central Hotel

*141 East 44th St, 10017* **Tel** *(212) 351-6800* **Fax** *(212) 818-1747* **Rooms** *155*     **Map** *13 A5*

An elegant hotel with charming service only steps away from Grand Central Terminal. Rooms go beyond business comforts with luscious colors, and some have canopied beds. A genuine pub on-site offers after-hours fun. Its location near many subway lines make it a good base of exploring. **www.fitzpatrickhotels.com**

### W The Court / W The Tuscany

*120–130 East 39th St, 10016* **Tel** *(212) 686-1600* **Fax** *(212) 779-8352* **Rooms** *320*     **Map** *9 A1*

This matched set of club-like properties offers boutique-style hotels with much better service. Room are equipped with the latest technology, and many offer free movie downloads. The Court has a trendier lounge scene, while the Tuscany is a little more relaxed. Both are recommended in this price range. **www.whotels.com**

### Bryant Park

*40 West 40th St, 10018* **Tel** *(212) 869-0100* **Fax** *(212) 869-4446* **Rooms** *128*     **Map** *8 F1*

Wonderful pedigree and great location makes this midtown find a winner. The stunning American Radiator Building (with all the gold leaf) is home to minimalist design luxury across from Bryant Park. The Cellar Bar is filled with fashionistas; it also has a 70-seat screening room. **www.bryantparkhotel.com**

### Kitano

*66 Park Ave, 10016* **Tel** *(212) 885-7000* **Fax** *(212) 885-7100* **Rooms** *149*     **Map** *9 A2*

Buttoned-up Japanese-style service is the name of the game at this elegant midtown hotel, which caters primarily to a business crowd. Hotel rooms are havens of serenity with complimentary Japanese green tea. The restaurant also draws a crowd. This part of Park Avenue can seem amazingly serene. **www.kitano.com**

## UPPER MIDTOWN

### Hotel 57

*130 East 57th St, 10022* **Tel** *(212) 753-8841* **Fax** *(212) 869-9605* **Rooms** *220*     **Map** *13 A3*

The hotel lives up to the label "cheap chic," effortlessly combining high design with low prices. While the rooms can be narrow and small and often share baths in the hallway, it's hard to beat the price with such a great midtown location, close to all major shopping. Great views from the 17th-floor bar. **www.hotel57.com**

### The Pod Hotel

*230 East 51st St, 10022* **Tel** *(212) 355-0300* **Fax** *(212) 755-5029* **Rooms** *320*     **Map** *13 B4*

Even after a recent refurbishing, The Pod (formerly The Pickwick) has kept its prices at rock-bottom levels, especially for the prime neighborhood. Make sure to inquire about private baths and the exact size of the room, as many can be tiny. But all are clean, and the hotel runs exceedingly well. Single rooms are a bargain. **www.thepodhotel.com**

### Doubletree Metropolitan Hotel

*569 Lexington Ave, 10022* **Tel** *(212) 752-7000* **Fax** *(212) 758-6311* **Rooms** *722*     **Map** *13 A4*

This former Loews property is now being managed by the Doubletree group, which means service remains strong with a special catering to families. Rates are reasonable, and while rooms can be small, they are well cared for. Restaurants on-site are good family dining options. **www.metropolitanhotelnyc.com**

### Kimberly Hotel

*145 East 50th St, 10022* **Tel** *(212) 755-0400* **Fax** *(212) 486-6915* **Rooms** *185*     **Map** *13 A5*

For large space and great value, this low-profile establishment is perhaps the best choice. The one- and two-bedroom apartments feel like apartments with full-size kitchens and well-appointed furniture. The location is wonderful for a little peace and quiet, yet close to good shopping. **www.kimberlyhotel.com**

### Roger Smith

*501 Lexington Ave, 10022* **Tel** *(212) 755-1400* **Fax** *(212) 758-4061* **Rooms** *130*     **Map** *13 A5*

This low-key property has a few high-design touches that separate it from the rest of the pack. Rooms are larger than normal and individually decorated. Rates include breakfast. Draws a diverse crowd, from businessmen to arty folk. The neighborhood calms down a bit when the sun goes down. **www.rogersmith.com**

**Key to Price Guide** *see p280* **Key to Symbols** *see back cover flap*

## Benjamin                                                      🛗🏃🍴      ⑤⑤⑤⑤

*125 East 50th St, 10022* **Tel** *(212) 715-2500* **Fax** *(212) 715-2525* **Rooms** *209*              **Map** *13 A4*

The modern rooms in this low-key hotel are designed for comfort. The work stations are perfect for the high-tech business traveler. Each room has a kichenette, and comes with a pillow menu to guarantee you a perfect night's sleep. Restaurant and small spa on site as well. **www.thebenjamin.com**

## Omni Berkshire Place                                          🛗🏃🍴      ⑤⑤⑤⑤

*21 East 52nd St, 10022* **Tel** *(212) 753-5800* **Fax** *(212) 754-5018* **Rooms** *396*              **Map** *12 F4*

The decor is designed for comfort at this understated hotel. Service earns high marks and the wealth of business facilities make it a great choice for the business traveler. But the hotel also caters to families, so make sure you check for discounted weekend rates. The area is a little less hectic than most. **www.omnihotels.com**

## Waldorf Astoria / Waldorf Towers                              🛗🏃🍴      ⑤⑤⑤⑤

*301 Park Ave, 10022* **Tel** *(212) 355-3000* **Fax** *(212) 872-7272* **Rooms** *1242*               **Map** *13 A5*

This New York legend is still kicking, despite complaints about indifferent service. Rates can be reasonable because the hotel is enormous, but it does have a historical feel about it. Rooms are large and have recently been refreshed. If you score a room in the exclusive Towers, expect 24-hour butler service. **www.waldorfastoria.com**

## Four Seasons New York                                         🛗Ⓟ🍽🏃🍴   ⑤⑤⑤⑤⑤

*57 East 57th St, 10022* **Tel** *(212) 758-5700* **Fax** *(212) 758-5711* **Rooms** *364*              **Map** *13 A3*

One of the crown jewels in the Four Seasons chain is this I.M. Pei-designed tower that rises 52 stories above midtown Manhattan. The lobby reeks of New York power and elegance and is worth a look. Rooms are large and extremely comfortable with fabulous views of Central Park. **www.fourseasons.com**

## New York Palace                                               🛗🍽🏃🍴     ⑤⑤⑤⑤⑤

*455 Madison Ave, 10022* **Tel** *(212) 888-7000* **Fax** *(212) 303-6000* **Rooms** *896*             **Map** *13 A4*

When the legendary restaurant Le Cirque 2000 closed its doors, this opulent property lost a bit of its lustre. But the splendid hotel, housed in a landmark 1882 house, is a wonderfully lavish establishment with old-world style and perfect service. Many think it's the most serene and calming spot in NYC. **www.newyorkpalace.com**

## Peninsula New York                                            🛗🏊🏃🍴     ⑤⑤⑤⑤⑤

*700 Fifth Ave, 10019* **Tel** *(212) 956-2888* **Fax** *(212) 903-3949* **Rooms** *239*               **Map** *12 F4*

Expect legendary Peninsula service at the small Asian chain's Big Apple outpost. Rooms are designed for ultimate comfort with the latest technology integrated seamlessly. The spa is one of the best in New York, and the rooftop bar and terrace is a prime choice for sunset drinks. Highly recommended. **www.peninsula.com**

# UPPER EAST SIDE

## Bentley Hotel                                                 🛗🍽🏃      ⑤⑤⑤

*500 East 62nd St, 10021* **Tel** *(212) 644-6000* **Fax** *(212) 207-4800* **Rooms** *197*            **Map** *13 B4*

This sleekly designed hotel is off the beaten path, but the rooms are comfortable though a bit small, so try and snag a room for more space. Bathrooms are lovely with marble tile. A great choice for leisure travelers who want to experience a true New York neighborhood. The 24-hour Cappuccino Bar is a winner. **www.bentleyhotelnewyork.com**

## Franklin                                                      🛗         ⑤⑤⑤

*164 East 87th St, 10128* **Tel** *(212) 369-1000* **Fax** *(212) 369-8000* **Rooms** *48*             **Map** *17 A3*

Rooms may be tiny at this modern hotel, but they are well appointed with romantic canopied beds, VCRs, and the like. The limited space makes it the choice for short-term travelers or light packers. Continental breakfast included. Check for seasonal rates. **www.franklinhotel.com**

## Hotel Wales                                                   🛗🍽🏃🍴     ⑤⑤⑤⑤

*1295 Madison Ave, 10028* **Tel** *(212) 876-6000* **Fax** *(212) 860-7000* **Rooms** *86*            **Map** *17 B2*

A cosy, comfortable hotel that is well located for Museum Mile. The decor and furnishing feature some nice touches, such as mahogany furniture, Belgian linen on the beds and fresh flowers in the rooms. There are some wonderful city views from the rooftop terrace. **www.waleshotel.com**

## Surrey Hotel                                                  🛗🍽🏃      ⑤⑤⑤⑤

*20 East 76th St, 10021* **Tel** *(212) 288-3700* **Fax** *(212) 628-1549* **Rooms** *130*             **Map** *17 A5*

This all-suite hotel is a lovely choice for those willing to spend extra on dramatically more space. Each suite has a fully-equipped kitchen, but the reason to stay here is the in-suite dining from the famous Café Boulud downstairs. Cheaper diners and pizzerias are all around the area. **www.affinia.com**

## Carlyle                                                       🛗🍽🏃🍴     ⑤⑤⑤⑤⑤

*35 East 76th St, 10021* **Tel** *(212) 744-1600* **Fax** *(212) 717-4682* **Rooms** *180*             **Map** *17 A5*

You'll feel like a true Upper Eastsider in a room at this legendary hotel. The elegant rooms and phenomenal service have drawn heads of state and movie stars alike. Afternoon tea attracts the who's who of New York socialites. This is true New York elegance and glamour at its best. **www.thecarlyle.com**

## Sherry-Netherland

781 Fifth Ave, 10022 **Tel** (212) 355-2800 **Fax** (212) 319-4306 **Rooms** 50

**Map** 12 F3

A little less stuffy than next-door neighbor The Pierre, this old-world style hotel defines residential living in New York City. Suites are enormous, and the service is top-of-the-class. Breakfast at the downstairs Cipriani's is included in the price, if you can handle sitting with fellow powerbrokers. **www.sherrynetherland.com**

## The Pierre

2 East 61st St, 10021 **Tel** (212) 838-8000 **Fax** (212) 940-8109 **Rooms** 203

**Map** 12 F3

Inviting service makes this very sophisticated hotel seem not so intimidating. The interiors are grand, but the rooms have a residential touch. Royalty feels right at home here with gloved elevator operators. The bar and restaurant are both recommended. **www.tajhotels.com/pierre**

# UPPER WEST SIDE

## Amsterdam Inn

340 Amsterdam Ave, 10024 **Tel** (212) 579-7500 **Fax** (212) 545-0103 **Rooms** 25

**Map** 15 C5

All rooms are well cared for in this budget establishment, but the rooms can be narrow. Some share baths, but the private ones are good value. Be sure to verify that a "double" is actually a real bed for two, rather than a single and pull-out trundle. Excellent location near Upper West Side museums. **www.amsterdaminn.com**

## Hostelling International – New York

891 Amsterdam Ave, 10025 **Tel** (212) 932-2300 **Fax** (212) 932-2574 **Rooms** 628

**Map** 20 E5

You will feel like you've gone back to college in this mammoth building that feels exactly like a dormitory. The good news is that it features all the upside of campus living – cafeteria, game room, laundry, internet access, and picnic tables. The establishment is at least 18 years old. **www.hinewyork.org**

## Hotel Newton

2528 Broadway, 10025 **Tel** (212) 678-6500 **Fax** (212) 678-6758 **Rooms** 110

**Map** 15 C2

One of the best options for the price, this well-run hotel has clean and attractive rooms with nice bathrooms. Some rooms can accommodate four travelers. Service is pleasant and professional. While there's no restaurant on premises, there are many options up and down Broadway. **www.thehotelnewton.com**

## Jazz on the Park

36 West 106th St, 10025 **Tel** (212) 932-1600 **Fax** (212) 932-1700 **Rooms** 220

**Map** 21 A5

This arty hostel is extremely popular and brings a downtown feel to the sometimes staid Upper West Side. Don't miss the coffeehouse with live music that can be a little rowdy. Dorm rooms are very basic and so are the bathrooms. Very international crowd. The area keeps getting better and better. **www.jazzonthepark.com**

## West End Studios

850 West End Ave, 10025 **Tel** (212) 749-7104 **Fax** (212) 865-5130 **Rooms** 85

**Map** 15 B1

Blocks away from Riverside Park, this is a good budget choice for those who want to experience neighborhood living. A little way from the main subway lines, the hotel offers very basic accommodation with shared baths. The family room comes with two beds and a bunkbed, but rooms can seem small. **www.westendstudios.com**

## Belleclaire Hotel

250 West 77th St, 10024 **Tel** (212) 362-7700 **Fax** (212) 362-1004 **Rooms** 180

**Map** 15 C5

The rooms in this renovated property are sparse, but well designed and stylish. Bathrooms are small, and some rooms share baths and are even less expensive. Try and get a one-bath family suite if the kids are in-tow. Very close to express subway lines, making it a great spot for exploring. **www.hotelbelleclaire.com**

## Hotel Beacon

2130 Broadway, 10023 **Tel** (212) 787-1100 **Fax** (212) 724-0839 **Rooms** 236

**Map** 15 C5

Families enjoy the extra-large rooms and laundry facilities on offer at this great-value hotel. The rooms aren't the best in town, but they have kitchenettes and often can accommodate four people. Larger groups should inquire about the two-bedroom/two-bath suites. **www.beaconhotel.com**

## Milburn

242 West 76th St, 10023 **Tel** (212) 362-1006 **Fax** (212) 721-5476 **Rooms** 114

**Map** 15 C5

This all-suite hotel is exceedingly well priced and offers all the comforts of home, including size. While not particularly smart, the rooms come with well-equipped kitchenettes and nice bathrooms. Staff is helpful and laundry facilities are also available. Good restaurants around the corner. **www.milburnhotel.com**

## Park 79

117 West 79th St, 10024 **Tel** (212) 787-4900 **Fax** (212) 496-3975 **Rooms** 106

**Map** 15 C5

This intimate hotel is on a charming street just steps away from Central Park and all the museums on the Upper West Side. The rooms are very well looked after with mahogany furniture. The private baths are some of the prettiest in this price category. A wonderful option in this price range. **www.park79.com**

**Key to Price Guide** see p280 **Key to Symbols** see back cover flap

## West Park Hotel ⌖ $$

6 Columbus Circle, 10019 **Tel** (212) 445-0200 **Fax** (212) 246-3131 **Rooms** 90      **Map** 12 D3

This hotel is working hard to style itself as a boutique property, and for the money it's a good bet for single travelers. Rooms are small and the furnishings are pleasant, if a little less plush than they should be. Bathrooms are small, but the amenities are nice. Across from the Time Warner Center, a good bet for shopping. **www.westparkhotel.com**

## Lucerne ⌖ ❚❚ ★ ⛷ $$$

201 West 79th St, 10024 **Tel** (212) 875-1000 **Fax** (212) 579-2408 **Rooms** 184      **Map** 15 C4

This lovely jewel of a mid-priced hotel is housed in an elegant 1903 building. The rooms are very well maintained and feature Americana furnishings. Rates include Continental breakfast, and don't miss the live jazz and blues in the stylish bar and grill. Other good restaurant options are just blocks away. **www.newyorkhotel.com**

## On the Ave ⌖ $$$

2178 Broadway, 10024 **Tel** (212) 362-1100 **Fax** (212) 787-9521 **Rooms** 251      **Map** 15 C5

Style is the name of the game at this mid-range budget hotel filled with modern design. Rooms have modular furniture in natural hues. A great deck offers beautiful views of the city. If possible, spring for a deluxe room, otherwise you might be too cramped. Good dining options up and down the avenue. **www.ontheave-nyc.com**

## Inn New York City $$$$

266 West 71st St, 10023 **Tel** (212) 580-1900 **Fax** (212) 580-4437 **Rooms** 4      **Map** 11 C1

Nothing but the best will do at this small, intimate, and utterly charming guesthouse. A renovated 19th-century townhouse with just four rooms, each one has its own theme – Opera, Library, Vermont, or Spa. In-suite breakfast is delightful. An over-the-top treat to be sure. **www.innnewyorkcity.com**

## Mandarin Oriental New York ⌖ ❚❚ ⛷ ★ ⛷ $$$$$

80 Columbus Circle, 10023 **Tel** (212) 805-8800 **Fax** (212) 805-8888 **Rooms** 251      **Map** 12 D3

Asian opulence comes at quite a price in this dramatic hotel. Rooms are modern-Oriental and feature terrific views of Central Park and the Hudson, if on a high floor. The spa is wonderful, but pricey. The bar and restaurants offer the same view and can be quite a scene in the evening. **www.mandarinoriental.com**

## Trump International Hotel & Tower ⌖ ❚❚ ★ ⛷ $$$$$

1 Central Park West, 10023 **Tel** (212) 299-1000 **Fax** (212) 299-1150 **Rooms** 167      **Map** 12 D3

This modern luxury hotel tower prides itself on its exclusivity, discretion, and style. Recently-refurbished rooms are decorated in soothing tones and offer the latest technology. The unobstructed views of Central Park is the real draw, as is the Jean George restaurant downstairs. **www.trumpintl.com**

# MORNINGSIDE HEIGHTS AND HARLEM

## Morningside Inn Hotel ⌖ $

235 West 107th St, 10025 **Tel** (212) 316-0055 **Fax** (212) 864-9155 **Rooms** 96      **Map** 20 E5

Sister property to the Riverside Inn, this hotel is newer and fresher, although it still retains an air of dormitory. Best for students or single travelers, try and score a double deluxe, which will assure you a private bath and air conditioning. All rooms are clean and well cared for. **www.morningsideinn-ny.com**

## Astor on the Park ⌖ $$

465 Central Park West, 10025 **Tel** (212) 866-1880 **Fax** (212) 316-9555 **Rooms** 80      **Map** 21 A5

On Central Park West at 107th street, the convenient location of this hotel more than makes up for the small, basic rooms. It is an ideal choice for visitors on a budget who plan to be out for most of the day (and night!). The bathrooms are clean, the staff friendly – and there's a complimentary breakfast. **www.nychotels.com/astor.html**

# FARTHER AFIELD: BROOKLYN

## Best Western Gregory Hotel Brooklyn ⌖ $$

8315 4th Ave, 11209 **Tel** (718) 238-3737 **Fax** (718) 680-0827 **Rooms** 70

While this hotel is a little off the beaten path, it is a good choice for those who need to be in Brooklyn. The subway is only a few blocks away. Rooms can be small, but are well maintained. Recent service problems seem to have been fixed with a change in management. Several cheap eats around the corner. **www.bestwestern.com**

## Marriott Brooklyn Bridge ⌖ P ❚❚ ⛷ ⛷ $$

333 Adams St, 11201 **Tel** (718) 246-7000 **Fax** (718) 246-0563 **Rooms** 355

The only full-service hotel in Brooklyn, this is a wonderful option for business and leisure travelers who want to explore this borough but be close to Financial District. Nine major subway lines converge outside the hotel, and the rooms are nicely decorated. Lobby is grand, and there's a large fitness center with a pool. **www.marriott.com**

# RESTAURANTS AND BARS

New Yorkers love to eat well, and in the five boroughs there are more than 25,000 restaurants catering to their wishes. City dwellers avidly read restaurant reviews in magazines such as *New York* to ensure that they are seen in the latest fashionable eatery. "In" places and cuisine change with great regularity, while some favorite places simply remain popular.

The restaurants cited in our listings have been selected as the best that New York can offer across a wide price range. While the information on pages 296–311 will help you to select a suitable restaurant, there are details of lighter refreshments on pages 312–4. *New York's Bars* on pages 315-7 highlights some of the city's best drinking spots.

**The classic Manhattan cocktail**

## RESTAURANT MENUS

Meals in most of the better restaurants consist of three courses: the appetizer (starter), an entrée (the main course) and a dessert. Virtually all New York restaurants, except fast-food places, serve you bread and butter just after you're seated, at no extra charge. In some fine restaurants you may be offered a complimentary appetizer, such as a small dollop of mousse or a tiny triangle of quiche. Appetizers at the better

**Street-corner hot dog stand**

restaurants are often the chef's most creative dishes – many diners request two appetizers and no entrée. Italian menus offer a pasta dish as a course before the main course, but in many places pasta is seen as a main course. Coffee or tea and a dessert ordinarily conclude the meal in restaurants above the coffee-shop level. Your coffee cup may be refilled until you refuse any more. Some of the better establishments now feature a cheeseboard on the menu.

To get a sense of a restaurant's cuisine, visit www. menupages.com, which features the menus of several thousand Manhattan eateries.

## PRICES

You will always find a restaurant in New York to suit your budget. At inexpensive coffee shops, diners and fast-food chains, $10 will buy you a filling meal. There are also hundreds of acceptable, even first-rate, restaurants where you can eat well at a moderate cost – around $25 per person for a filling and decent meal, not including drinks – in attractive surroundings.

For dinner at a trendy New American venue with a star chef, the bill could be upward of $70 to $100 per person, excluding drinks. Many top restaurants do, however, offer fixed-price (or, as they are known in New York, prix-fixe) meals. This is normally a much cheaper way of enjoying a good meal than choosing dishes from the à la carte menu. Lunch is also less expensive than dinner in such places and, because of the profusion of business diners, lunch is also the busiest period of the day.

## TAXES AND TIPPING

New York city sales tax of 8.625% will be added to your bill. Service is not usually included. Tipping can run from 10% at a coffee shop to 20% at the fanciest places, with 15% an average fair tip. Many people just double the sales tax for a tip.

**A typical New York deli *(see p312)***

The bill is known as the "check" in the US. The most commonly accepted credit cards are VISA, MasterCard and American Express. Traveler's checks are taken in many restaurants. Diners and coffee shops may accept cash only. In fast-food chains, you order at the counter and pay cash in advance. Some other types of establishment also take only cash.

## DINING ON A BUDGET

Despite the tales of $200 business lunches, there are ways to stretch a meal budget in New York.

Order fewer courses than you would normally. American portions are huge, and an appetizer is often big enough for a light main course. You could share one with your companion or choose two appetizers and no entrée.

"Specials of the day" may be more expensive than items on the printed menu, so be sure to check prices.

Ask your waiter if there is a prix-fixe menu. Many of the more expensive restaurants offer this at lunch and dinner – in the

**McSorley's Old Ale House *(see p317)***

early evening it may often be called the pre-theater menu. Or try a prix-fixe lunch buffet. These are popular in Indian restaurants and other places and are very reasonably priced meals.

Other options for a quick, tasty and restorative meal are the less expensive Chinese, Thai and Mexican restaurants and some Jewish delis. Italian pizzerias and French bistros, as well as the small eateries that serve fish and chips, griddle hamburgers and gourmet sandwiches and desserts also offer good value. Alternatively, go to bars featuring "happy hours." They often offer a variety of substantial hors d'oeuvres, like Spanish *tapas*, which can make a meal in themselves.

If you simply want to see inside the restaurants every visitor has heard about, just go to have a drink and soak up the atmosphere. Many restaurants post their menus or will let you see them before you are seated, good for checking prices in advance.

**Dining in style at the Oyster Bar in Grand Central Terminal** *(see p306)*

**Poolside dining at Four Seasons (see p307)**

## HOURS

Breakfast hours are usually from 7 to 10:30 or 11am. Sunday brunch, a popular meal, is served at most better restaurants between about 11am and 3pm. Lunch runs from 11:30am or noon to 2:30pm at most places, but the busiest time of the day is 1pm. Dinner is usually served from 5:30 to 6pm onward. The most popular time is around 7:30 to 8pm.

Some restaurants stop serving at 10pm during the week, or 11pm on Friday and Saturday. Certain informal restaurants are open from 11:30am to 10pm. Coffee shops are open long hours, from 7am to midnight or even 24 hours.

## DRESS CODES

Few restaurants demand that male diners dress formally, though a jacket is required at classy restaurants, and a jacket and tie at the very best. At most restaurants, for both men and women, smart "business casual" suffices.

Women tend to dress up when dining at the more expensive restaurants. If you are unsure, check what the dress code is when you make your reservation.

## RESERVATIONS

It is wise to make reservations at any restaurant above the diner/fast-food level, especially on weekends. A few of the trendiest restaurants won't even accept reservations less than two months in advance. Be sure to make reservations for lunch at a midtown restaurant. You may still have to wait at the bar, even if you have booked. Waits of an hour at the most popular spots are not unusual.

## SMOKING

Smoking is now illegal in all bars and restaurants in New York. The only exceptions are owner-operated bars that have special smoking rooms.

## CHILDREN

When eating out with children, ask if there's a child's menu with half-portions. The prices are reduced, sometimes by half. Children are accepted in most New York restaurants, but if yours are unpredictable

stick to casual spots, China-town Chinese or family-run Italian restaurants, burger bars, delis, cafés, fast food chains and diners. A few of the better restaurants have facilities for babies or toddlers; others may not be so well equipped. Dining out in the more formal New York restaurants is certainly not a family affair.

## WHEELCHAIR ACCESS

While many restaurants may be able to accommodate a wheelchair, it is always best to mention your requirements when making your reservation. Many of the smaller places cannot cater to disabled customers because of lack of space in their dining rooms.

## USING THE LISTINGS

Key to symbols in the listings on pp296–311.

🏠 outdoor eating
🧒 children welcome
👔 formal dress required
♿ disabled access
🎵 live music
💳 no credit cards accepted

**Price categories** for a three-course meal for one, including a glass of house wine and all unavoidable charges such as sales tax:

Ⓢ Under $25
ⓈⓈ $25–$40
ⓈⓈⓈ $40–$60
ⓈⓈⓈⓈ $60–$80
ⓈⓈⓈⓈⓈ Over $80

# The Flavors of New York

Few cities can match the diversity of New York's restaurants. Reflecting the city's melting pot of nationalities, foods range from the "hautest" of French and continental cuisine to the freshest sushi outside of Tokyo. Caribbean, Mexican, Thai, Vietnamese, Korean, Greek, Indian – all are well represented, and every block seems to have an Italian restaurant. The quality of the city's top restaurants is unsurpassed and their chefs are superstars, as well-known and revered as movie idols. Yet, because so many nationalities are represented in its culinary culture, only a few foods are native to the city itself.

**Dim sum**

and smoked salmon. The bagel, once synonymous with New York, has become a universal American food, but a true New York bagel is nothing like the bready imitations found in the hinterlands. It is shaped by hand, and the dough is cooked briefly in boiling water before being baked, resulting in a unique firm and chewy texture. A relative, and another New York specialty, is the bialy,

a flat, chewy flour-dusted roll with a center indentation filed with toasted onions. The finest examples of each are to be found in the kosher bakeries of the Lower East Side *(see pp92–101)*.

## THE GREENMARKET

You may well find yourself next to a well-known chef browsing at New York's greenmarkets, open-air markets where farmers from

**Fresh, local produce on display at the Greenmarket**

## DELI DINING

A large Jewish population has given rise to some of New York's best known specialties, now enjoyed by all – overstuffed corned beef and pastrami sandwiches, dill pickles, matzo ball soup, herrings, blintzes, and bagels served with cream cheese

Pastrami on rye
Blintzes
Dill pickles
Bagels with smoked salmon and cream cheese
Pickled herrings

**Selection of classic foods available at any New York deli**

## NEW YORK SPECIALTIES

While New York dining may span all nations, a few special dishes are closely associated with the city. Manhattan Clam Chowder, prepared with tomatoes rather than cream, has been popular ever since it was introduced at Coney Island beach stands in the 1880s. In the city's many steak houses, a prime selection is the "New York strip steak," a boneless sirloin cut from the short loin, the tenderest portion of beef. Italian cuisine has

**Pretzels**

often been given a New York spin. Rich and creamy New York cheesecake is made with cream cheese rather than the Italian ricotta. And, since traditional wood-burning ovens were impractical in New York, the first Italian immigrant chefs used coal ovens. Though these are rare today, purists still insist they are necessary for a true New York pizza.

**Manhattan clam chowder**
*This is a rich blend of potatoes, onions, tomatoes, oyster crackers crumbs and clams.*

Fast food cart on a Manhattan street corner, selling hots dogs and sodas

upstate New York sell fresh-picked fruits and vegetables, as well as meat, poultry and dairy products. Over 105 city restaurants patronize the greenmarkets, so you'll find ultra-fresh local produce on many menus in the city. As many as 70 vendors attend the biggest of the markets in Union Square on Monday, Wednesday, Friday, and Saturday *(see p129)*.

## STREET FOOD

Street food is a favorite choice in a fast-moving city. Sabrett hot dogs and over-size soft pretzels are classic New York choices, along with some surprisingly good food cart specialties, from falafel to soup to barbecue to Texas chile, all ready to eat on the run. In winter, vendors all over town offer hot roasted chestnuts.

## SOUL FOOD

Harlem is America's largest African-American community, and restaurants here are the place to sample specialties from the Deep South, such as fried chicken, ribs, collard

An Oriental produce store in New York's Chinatown

greens, yams, flaky biscuits or cornbread. A popular Harlem dish, fried chicken and waffles, is said to have originated to serve musicians leaving jazz clubs in the wee hours.

## ASIAN FOOD RIVALS

Chinese restaurants and dim sum parlors have long been found throughout the city, but lately they have been challenged by the arrival of many excellent Thai and Vietnamese restaurants. But all take second place to the multiplying sushi bars and new, high profile, highly praised Japanese chefs.

## DELICATESSEN CLASSICS

**Babkas** Slightly sweet, yeasted coffee cakes.

**Blintzes** Crêpes filled with sweetened soft white cheese and/or fruit and sautéd.

**Chopped liver** Chicken livers mashed with minced onion, hard-cooked eggs and *schmaltz* (chicken fat).

**Gefilte fish** Minced white fish dumplings poached in fish broth. A holiday dish.

**Knishes** Soft dough shells filled with oniony mashed potatoes.

**Latkes** Grated potato, onion and matzo-meal pancakes.

**Rugelach** Rich, cream-cheese-dough pastries filled with jam, chopped nuts and raisins.

**New York-style pizza** *Thick-or thin-crusted, a true New York pizza must be baked in a coal-fired oven*

**New York Strip Steak** *Served with creamed spinach, fries or hash-browns, this tender steak is hard to beat.*

**New York cheesecake** *This is a dense, rich, baked cake with a crust of pastry or graham crackers (digestives).*

# Choosing a Restaurant

The restaurants in this section have been selected for their good value and exceptional food. Within each area, entries are listed alphabetically within each price category, from the least to the most expensive. Details of *Light Meals and Snacks* are on pages 312–4 and for some of New York's best *Bars* see pages 315–7.

## LOWER MANHATTAN

### Les Halles
ⓈⓈ
*15 John St between Broadway and Nassau St, 10038* **Tel** *(212) 285-8585*     **Map** *1 C2*

The Financial District meets a Parisian-style brasserie at this sister restaurant of the Park Avenue Les Halles, made famous by its celebrity chef Anthony Bourdain. Expect well-executed dishes such as mussels and frites. A heaven for carnivores, with a wide selection of meats.

### Battery Gardens
ⓈⓈⓈ
*Southwest corner of Battery Park, 10004* **Tel** *(212) 809-5508*     **Map** *1 C4*

Refurbished in 2004 and formerly known as American Park at the Battery, the restaurant has fantastic views of the harbor, albeit at a price. The food is primarily seafood with a combination of Italian and Asian twists. The outside seating is unbeatable during the summer months.

### Fraunces Tavern
ⓈⓈⓈ
*54 Pearl St, corner of Broad Street, 10004* **Tel** *(212) 968-1776*     **Map** *1 C4*

This historic tavern has been in operation since 1762 and was where George Washington bid a fond farewell to his officers, on the eve of his retirement in 1783. Classic American steak and fish dishes are on offer, along with wholesome pot roasts and soups. In winter warm up in the snug lounge.

### Harry's Café
ⓈⓈⓈⓈ
*1 Hanover Sq, 10004* **Tel** *(212) 785-9200*     **Map** *1 C3*

The former Bayard's has been restyled as a clubby steakhouse offering first-rate food and wine. If you don't have an expense account and your budget is limited, you can still enjoy the atmosphere of this landmark heritage building by choosing from a short café menu. One of the few Wall Street spots open at the weekend.

## SEAPORT AND THE CIVIC CENTER

### Acqua at Peck Slip
ⓈⓈⓈ
*21–23 Peck Slip, 10038* **Tel** *(212) 349-4433*     **Map** *2 D2*

Amid the tourist traps of South Street Seaport, this Italian restaurant stands out like a beacon, serving up New American-tinged Italian dishes prepared with organic ingredients. Service can be a little slow, so just sit back and enjoy the vaulted ceilings and warm earthy tones that make this a cozy, romantic spot. The lasagna is fantastic.

### Bridge Café
ⓈⓈⓈ
*279 Water St at Dover St, 10038* **Tel** *(212) 227-3344*     **Map** *2 D2*

A charming café located just below the Brooklyn Bridge, this age-old restaurant is worth a visit while in the area. Adventurers should try the specialty – buffalo steak with gnocchi. For the tamer, there are still plenty of options – from lobster pot pie to a grilled vegetable and goats' cheese plate.

## LOWER EAST SIDE

### Grand Sichuan
Ⓢ
*125 Canal St at Bowery, 10002* **Tel** *(212) 625-9212*     **Map** *4 E5*

A never-ending menu with all kinds of Sichuan, Hunang, and "Chinese-food American style," as well as all types of hot (including spicy) and cold noodles and fried rice. It also offers a wide variety of vegetarian dishes. Spotty service and little decor may be the reason for the quite affordable prices.

**Key to Symbols** *see back cover flap*

## Katz Delicatessen
*205 East Houston St, 10002* **Tel** *(212) 254-2246*

A New York City classic, this Jewish deli continues to serve the best pastrami and corned beef towerir _
Don't expect much from service or decor – it's all in the beef and the very affordable prices. Famous for
salami to the army, way before the memorable scene from *When Harry Met Sally*.

## San Loco Mexico
*11 Stanton St, 10002* **Tel** *(212) 253-7580*

Map 5 ,

You'll be hard pressed to spend over $10 at this excellent value Mexican restaurant, which is popular with
cost-conscious locals. All the Mexican favorites are on offer and come with a choice of four potencies of homemade
sauce – mild, hot, serious, and stupid. Save room for the dessert.

## Teany Café
*90 Rivington St, 10002* **Tel** *(212) 475-9190*

($)

Map 5 A3

Rock star Moby owns this famous café offering all vegan and vegetarian sandwiches, salads, and nibblers. Great
desserts, too, such as the chocolate peanut butter bomb and the warm rhubarb pie. The "afternoon tea service" for
one or two is worth a try. Service can be patchy, and they often run out of the daily specials in just a few hours.

## Il Palazzo
*151 Mulberry St, 10013* **Tel** *(212) 343-7000*

($)($)

Map 4 F4

Among Little Italy's few good Italian restaurants, especially when it comes to service. A new glassed-in garden has
boosted its charm. Homemade pastas and risotti are always a good and inexpensive choice, try the simple but well-
done homemade spaghetti *a la chitarra*. Standard homemade desserts include cannoli and tiramisu.

## Joe's Shanghai
*9 Pell St, 10013* **Tel** *(212) 233-8888*

($)($)

Map 4 F5

When visiting this famous local restaurant, don't miss the crab and pork soup dumplings. This dish is the main
reason for long lines especially on weekends, but it's definitely worth it. The rest of the menu is hit and miss but
it's good value. Other locations may have better decor/service at the expense of food quality.

## Sammy's Roumanian
*157 Chrystie St, 10002* **Tel** *(212) 673-0330*

($)($)($)

Map 5 A4

Probably among the first "themed" restaurants in New York, the Jewish-inspired menu offers traditional fare such
as *latkes*, chopped liver, mashed potatoes with *schmaltz* (chicken fat), and a large selection of meat cuts. Enjoy the
garlic sausage with ice-cold vodka.

## The Orchard
*162 Orchard St, 10002* **Tel** *(212) 353-3570*

($)($)($)

Map 5 A3

Imaginative New American food is served up to a hip and young LES crowd. The decor is stylish, with subdued
lighting. Don't miss the steak tartare flatbread. Wines come at a good range of price points, ensuring there is
something for every budget.

## The Stanton Social
*99 Stanton St, 10002* **Tel** *(212) 995-0099*

($)($)($)

Map 5 A3

Groovy and gorgeous sums up the scene at this restaurant, where the atmosphere almost overshadows the food.
The eclectic tapas menu has many mouthwatering options – but beware: the cost adds up quickly. The cocktails
are equally inviting. It's best to go in a small group, recline on the leather banquettes and indulge. Closed Sat, Sun.

## The Tasting Room
*72 East 1st St, 10003* **Tel** *(212) 358-7831*

($)($)($)($)

Map 5 A3

An inventive "new-tapas"-style menu of mostly eclectic dishes meant to be shared in a small, yet romantic setting.
Local and exotic ingredients compose the seasonal menus – rabbit terrine, fluke carpaccio, trout and apples, or
squab with chestnuts. A great all-American wine list and a wine flight is available.

## WD-50
*50 Clinton St, 10002* **Tel** *(212) 477-2900*

($)($)($)($)

Map 5 B3

Celebrated chef Wylie Dufresne pushes avant-garde cuisine in this restaurant. A courteous and knowledgable
service will offer assortments such as fried mayonnaise and beef tongue and *foie gras* with a basil-grapefruit
crumble and *nori* (seaweed) caramel. Try the nine-course tasting menu, one of the most innovative meals around.

# SOHO AND TRIBECA

## Peanut Butter & Co.
*240 Sullivan St, 10012* **Tel** *(212) 677-3995*

($)

Map 4 D2

A sandwich shop worth the trip to see the unbelievable combinations available with peanut butter. Yes, you can even
get the famous Elvis Presley-inspired sandwich. Thankfully, you can get milk too, and plenty of other yummy desserts.
Invite friends and bring your kids and your wallet won't even notice it.

Map 5 A3
297
Map 5 A3
sandwiches,
nding

🖥🚹 $

...556 **Map 4 F5**

...itown, offering a cheap and fast choice of noodles. Try the Vietnamese rolls
...ou can even see yourself sweat in the mirrored walls in case you order any
...variety of Asian beverages.

🖥🚹 $$

**Map 4 F4**

...rick-oven baked pies come thin, charred, and oozing a delectable
...tick with pizza and don't expect dessert. A very welcome recent expansion
...ur friends to share the joy faster.

## Aquagrill
🚹🖼 $$$

*210 Spring St, 10012* **Tel** *(212) 274-0505*            **Map 4 D4**

A seafood-lovers' paradise with very fresh ingredients. An oyster bar selection to die for, a reliable kitchen, and
courteous service are all ingredients for success adding up to a busy dining room. The mussel soup with saffron
and sea scallops with a crabmeat rissotto are both highly recommended.

## L'Ecole
🔥🚹 $$$

*462 Broadway, 10012* **Tel** *(212) 219-3300*            **Map 4 E4**

A small and charming SoHo restaurant where students of the French Culinary Institute do hands-on training. The
place offers different tasting menus at reasonable prices considering the good quality of the food and courteous
service. Impress your friends and guests here!

## Le Jardin Bistrot
🚹🔥🖼 $$$

*25 Cleveland Place, 10012* **Tel** *(212) 343-9599*            **Map 4 F4**

French bistro with the usual staples such as steak tartare, pâté, *bouillabaisse*, mussels, and frites. The main draw
may not necessarily be the food but the beautiful seasonal garden for a romantic dinner. Its popularity during the
summer months may make tables hard to get.

## Lupa
🚹🔥🖼 $$$

*170 Thompson St, 10012* **Tel** *(212) 982-5089*            **Map 4 F3**

An Italian *trattoria* courtesy of celebrity chef Mario Batali offering a cheaper alternative to its flagship Babbo.
Expect a wide variety of dishes such as smoked eggplant and dried cod, excellent fresh pastas, and accomplished
entrées such as tuna belly *puttanesca* and pork *saltimbocca*. Excellent Italian wine list.

## Odeon
🚹🖼 $$$

*145 West Broadway, 10013* **Tel** *(212) 233-0507*            **Map 1 B1**

One of the first restaurants to open in TriBeCa back in the 1980s, this "faux-bistro" offers good quality French-
American fare. Don't miss the steak tartare, but the burgers are also a great experience. The decor is simple and
the place is always packed with a mixed crowd.

## Peep
🔥 $$$

*177 Prince St, 10012* **Tel** *(212) 254-7337*            **Map 4 D3**

A hip SoHo single set descends on this glamorous, hot-pink spot for tasty Thai and exotic cocktails. Be sure to stop
by the bathrooms that give the restaurant its name – don't worry, the mirrors are only one-way (looking out). Prix-
fixe lunches and dinner specials are a bargain.

## Public
🚹 $$$

*210 Elizabeth St, 10012* **Tel** *(212) 343-7011*            **Map 4 F3**

A taste of modern Down Under food with inventive creations such as Tasmanian trout and Meyer lemon ceviche,
and New Zealand snapper with bok choy and sesame ginger broth. Kiwi Peter Gordon is credited as consulting
chef. Try some of the Australian beer on offer.

## The Harrison
🚹🖼 $$$

*355 Greenwich St, 10013* **Tel** *(212) 274-9310*            **Map 4 D5**

A New England seafront house in the midst of TriBeCa offering good "re-engineered" American fare such as
biscuits and gravy with chorizo and clams and a crispy chicken with chestnut stuffing. Very popular with the
area's 30-somethings, which means long lines at times.

## Danube
🔥🚹 $$$$

*30 Hudson St, 10013* **Tel** *(212) 791-3771*            **Map 1 B1**

An eclectic menu of fine Austrian cuisine and other modern choices set in a decadently decorated setting. Chestnut
honey-glazed duck breast is but an example of the latter while port-glazed venison in huckleberry sauce and red
cabbage illustrate the former. Royal service will transport you to Vienna.

## Kittichai
🔥🚹 $$$$

*60 Thompson St, 10012* **Tel** *(212) 219-2000*            **Map 4 D4**

A high-end Thai restaurant in a beautifully designed space of the 60 Thompson hotel. A definite place to be seen.
The menu offers an expensive selection of choices including "Thai tapas" such as scallop and caviar ceviche, plus
traditional entrées such as soups, curries, and seafood dishes.

**Key to Price Guide** *see p296* **Key to Symbols** *see back cover flap*

### Montrachet
🏃 ♿ 🍸  $$$$

*239 West Broadway, 10013* **Tel** *(212) 219-2777*

**Map** 4 E5

An institution that revolutionized fine dining in TriBeCa still stands strong. This elegant high-end French restaurant offers both top-notch quality and service. A great wine list complements the classic menu featuring lobster gratin, roasted langoustines, and duck breast among other hits.

### Nobu
♿ 🍸  $$$$

*105 Hudson St, 10013* **Tel** *(212) 219-0500*

**Map** 4 D5

Chef Nobu Matsuhisa offers a menu of fantastic reach for those who can afford it and get a reservation. The menu features items such as tuna toro tartar, Peruvian-influenced ceviches and tempuras, not to mention a lengthy sushi menu. This high-profile spot attracts celebrities and mortals alike.

### Bouley
♿ 🍸  $$$$$

*120 West Broadway, 10013* **Tel** *(212) 964-2525*

**Map** 1 B1

Celebrated chef David Bouley's flagship restaurant showcases inspiring contemporary cuisine. Flawless service and knowledgable sommeliers make this place a destination for special occasions. Gems include wild salmon with tarragon corn sauce and lobster with tamarind dressing and coconut.

### Chanterelle
♿ 🍸  $$$$$

*2 Harrison St, 10013* **Tel** *(212) 966-6960*

**Map** 4 D5

A TriBeCa classic of French-haute contemporary cuisine with impeccable service and beautifully decorated settings. Ideal for a memorable occasion once you've secured the bank loan required. Butternut squash ravioli with oxtail ragout and the loin of lamb in Morrocan spices are recommended.

### Megu
🏃 ♿ 🍸  $$$$$

*62 Thomas St, 10013* **Tel** *(212) 964-7777*

**Map** 1 B1

Joining the latest trend in behemoth Japanese restaurants, Megu has an impressively decorated menu offering an outrageous option of dishes to be shared. Prime ingredients can quickly add up in the tab but some consider it the equivalent of dinner and a show. Can be noisy, especially on weekends.

## GREENWICH VILLAGE

### A Salt & Battery
🏃 ♿  $

*112 Greenwich Ave, 10011* **Tel** *(212) 691-2713*

**Map** 3 B1

The best fish-and-chips this side of the pond with rock-bottom prices. Many different combinations of fish and platters to choose from. Plenty of other sidedishes as well makes the trip worth it, especially that infamously delicious deep-fried Mars bar. Another sister restaurant has opened in the East Village at 80 Second Avenue.

### Corner Bistro
📋 🏃  $

*331 West 4th St, 10014* **Tel** *(212) 242-9502*

**Map** 3 C1

The line outside indicates this isn't your typical bistro food, but a dive that has developed a cult following for the juiciest and messiest burgers and the cheapest beer in town. Grab a spot in line that sometimes snakes by the bar and outside. Food is served on paper plates with lots of napkins.

### Cowgirl Hall of Fame
🏃 📺  $$

*519 Hudson St, 10014* **Tel** *(212) 633-1133*

**Map** 3 C2

For those homesick for down south food, this is the kitschy place. Don't expect much in service in what seems like a theme restaurant, but enjoy the cheap American regional staples such as chicken-fried steak, biscuits and gravy, green collards, and frito pie. Down them with a few margaritas.

### Florent
📋 🏃 📺  $$

*69 Gansevoort St, 10014* **Tel** *(212) 989-5779*

**Map** 3 B1

The true pioneer of the Meatpacking District scene before *Sex and the City* erased the area's seediness, this diner is famous for its (sadly gone) drag queen clientele and late night/post-clubbing dining. Still strong with great French food at even greater prices. The place really gets going around 2am.

### ino
📋 🏃  $$

*21 Bedford St, 10014* **Tel** *(212) 989-5769*

**Map** 4 D3

Cute and intimate, not to say small, panini café for a casual dinner. Despite their Atkins-related phobias, fashionistas flock to this place that can be extremely light on the wallet. It also doubles as a wine bar with an approachable Italian wine list. However, service is not the best in town.

### Moustache
📋 🏃  $$

*90 Bedford St, 10014* **Tel** *(212) 229-2220*

**Map** 3 C2

Middle-Eastern casual eatery with consistently good and cheap food, including Turkish *pitzas*, merguez sausages, and lamb. The space may be too small for the crowd and service can be slow. Try the sibling East Village spot at 265 East 19th Street that includes an indoor garden.

### Pearl Oyster Bar    🚶   $$
*18 Cornelia St, 10014* **Tel** *(212) 691-8211*    **Map** *4 D4*

Very succesful raw bar in the Village with top-of-the-line fresh ingredients and bold flavors. The lobster roll is a smash hit as are the Prince Edward Island mussels. Unlike other places that use quality ingredients, service is amicable too, but be prepared for long lines at rush hours.

### Westville    🚶🍷   $$
*210 West 10th St, 10014* **Tel** *(212) 741-7971*    **Map** *3 C2*

A no-thrills narrow eatery offering great-value meals of regional American cooking, aka comfort food staples, such as cod po'boys, burgers, mac 'n' cheese, and BLTs. Avoid rush hours since cheap prices can mean long lines. So popular it spawned an East Village sister, cleverly called Eastville.

### Blue Ribbon    🚶♿   $$$
*97 Sullivan St, 10012* **Tel** *(212) 274-0404*    **Map** *4 D3*

A SoHo staple for always reliable French fare such as beef marrow and oxtail marmalade, barbecue ribs, and escargots. Mains include paella, rack of lamb, and roast chicken done to perfection. Great for late dining with an open kitchen until 4am, including a fabulous raw bar.

### Blue Ribbon Bakery    🚶   $$$
*33 Downing Street, 10014* **Tel** *(212) 337-0404*    **Map** *4 D3*

An extensive tapas-style menu made out of cheeses and cold cuts with fantastic bread is complemented with soups, salads, and entrées such as filet mignon, duck confit, and burgers. An accessible wine list makes this an ideal place to pass time with friends and family.

### One    ♿   $$$
*1 Little West 12th St, 10014* **Tel** *(212) 255-9717*    **Map** *3 B1*

The New American menu is designed around plates for one and plates to share, with a large selection of seafood platters as a group option. Most people come here for the hopping, trendy scene rather than the food, however. There are three different lounge areas: choose one according to your mood.

### Otto    🚶♿   $$$
*1 Fifth Ave, 10003* **Tel** *(212) 995-9559*    **Map** *4 E1*

An upscale and fashionable pizzeria from chef Mario Batali. An amazing wine list and an array of sidedishes and antipasti can quickly raise your tab in this usually crowded and upbeat place. Try the famous lardo pizza, which is exactly what it sounds like – pig lard slathered on pizza crust. Don't miss the olive oil ice cream.

### Pastis    🚶🏠   $$$
*9 Ninth Ave, 10014* **Tel** *(212) 929-4844*    **Map** *3 B1*

Among the pioneers in the Meatpacking District, this gorgeous Parisian bistro offers good-quality French fare in large portions. The ambience can be loud on weekends, with plenty of celebrity sightseeing. It also serves a good weekend brunch. If you can't get a reservation, just show up and take your chances.

### The Spotted Pig    🚶   $$$
*314 West 11th St, 10014* **Tel** *(212) 620-0393*    **Map** *3 B2*

Londoners will feel at home in Brit chef April Bloomfield's Italian take on gastropub fare. This tiny spot fills up quick, so get there early during peak times and enjoy drinks at the bar. Hand-cask beer from Brooklyn Brewery is great with the first-rate shepherd's pie.

### Annisa    ♿   $$$$
*13 Barrow St, 10014* **Tel** *(212) 741-6699*    **Map** *3 C2*

Inventive chef Annisa Lo offers great value given the fresh seasonal menu on offer, the intimate setting, and attentive service. Great seafood dishes with Asian touches such as miso-marinated sable in bonito broth are mixed with gems such as Niman Ranch pig cheeks with caramel and lotus root.

### Babbo    🚶   $$$$
*110 Waverly Place, 10011* **Tel** *(212) 777-0303*    **Map** *4 D2*

Chef Mario Batali's flagship restaurant is housed in this beautiful Village duplex – paradise for high-quality pasta and offal lovers alike. Hard to get reservations and service could see some improvement given the prices. A winning wine list and trendy crowd add the magic touch to a great dining experience.

### Blue Hill    🚶♿🏠   $$$$
*75 Washington Place, 10011* **Tel** *(212) 539-1776*    **Map** *4 E4*

This new American kitchen is obsessed with the quality of its ingredients, especially with the addition of its own Stone Barns produce from upstate New York. The limited menu is a guarantee of the freshness and liveliness of the seasonal dishes. Taste the poached *foie gras* or the Berkshire pork with chestnuts.

### Da Silvano    🚶♿🏠   $$$$
*260 Sixth Ave, 10014* **Tel** *(212) 982-2343*    **Map** *4 D3*

This Tuscan restaurant is popular more for the celebrities that dine here than the food itself, which covers a wide range of pastas, some seafood antipasti, salads, and traditional entrées such as lamb chops and stewed rabbit. The coveted outdoor seating is perfect for peoplewatching in the summer months.

**Key to Price Guide** *see p296* **Key to Symbols** *see back cover flap*

### One if by Land, Two if by Sea  🛓🎵🍴  $$$$
*17 Barrow St, 10014* **Tel** *(212) 228-0822* **Map** *3 C3*

Aaron Burr's carriage house made famous in the American Revolution is now arguably one of the most romantic and historical spots in town. To some, the decor seems a tad bit kitschy. The three-course prix-fixe of casual American dining is served right next to the fireplace and candles. Piano music daily.

### Spice Market  🛓  $$$$
*403 West 13th St, 10014* **Tel** *(212) 675-2322* **Map** *3 B1*

An incredibly beautiful behemoth of a place featuring Asian-inspired "street food" by chef Jean Georges Vongerichten. With a club-like atmosphere, it is *the* place for beautiful people (including waiters) to sip fancy cocktails. The menu, however, is a hit-and-miss affair.

### Gotham Bar & Grill  🛓🍴  $$$$$
*12 East 12th Street, 10003* **Tel** *(212) 620-4020* **Map** *4 E1*

A New York classic of modern American cuisine showcasing revolutionary chef Alfred Portale's creations such as gingerbread crusted *foie gras* or roasted pheasant in a ginger and juniper marinade. Some consider the place somewhat past its prime but the bargain $25 prix-fixe lunch is worth a try.

## EAST VILLAGE

### Blue 9 Burger  📋🚶🛓  $
*92 Third Ave, 10003* **Tel** *(212) 979-0053* **Map** *4 F1*

Tasty griddle hamburgers in the East Village at very affordable prices for when you get those fast-food cravings without the need to visit a chain. Plus, they offer a mango-chili sauce with your fries. Grab it to go and head to an park nearby for a good people-watching picnic.

### Caracas Arepa Bar  🚶  $
*91 East 7th St, 10009* **Tel** *(212) 228-5062* **Map** *5 A2*

A kitschy restaurant with delicious Venezuelan fast food and slow service. *Arepas* (savoury corn cakes with a variety of fillings), sandwiches, and *tamales* are great fillers at rock-bottom prices. The premises are unbelievably small but the food keeps people coming.

### Dumpling Man  📋🚶  $
*100 St Mark's Place, 10009* **Tel** *(212) 505-2121* **Map** *5 A1*

Tiny yet trendy bar in the East Village, offering a wide variety of dumplings to meet your imagination. You get to watch what goes on behind the bar as the cooks handle the steamed or fried treasures. With rock-bottom prices, it doesn't get better than this dinner and a show.

### Minca  📋🚶  $
*536 East 5th St, 10009* **Tel** *(212) 505-8001* **Map** *5 B2*

The latest craze in dining at least in the East Village – noodle bars. Minca is a Ramen-style noodle joint that is far away from your memories of microwave noodle cups. You can choose a variety of noodles with beef, pork, vegetarian, and more. Perfect spot for cold weather after a stroll through the East Village hip boutiques.

### Counter  🚶  $$
*105 First Ave, 10003* **Tel** *(212) 982-5870* **Map** *5 A2*

Inventive vegetarian cuisine worth the trip for non-vegetarians in a sophisticated dining room. An inviting environmentally sound, organic or biodynamic, wine list is also highly recommended. Caring but nevertheless spotty service from time to time.

### Great Jones Café  🚶  $$
*54 Great Jones St, 10012* **Tel** *(212) 674-9304* **Map** *4 F2*

Get your fix of New Orleans cooking in this inexpensive, family-friendly, jukebox-equipped hole-in-the-wall. Staples include fried shrimp po'boys, andouille sausages, and jambalaya. The walls are lined with an array of hot sauces from all over the world, so feel free to dab on your entrées. Definitely down it all with a beer.

### Il Bagatto  🚶  $$
*192 East 2nd St, 10009* **Tel** *(212) 228-0977* **Map** *5 B2*

Trendy and popular Italian eatery with inexpensive and well-executed food that has New Yorkers flocking to the East Village. However, be warned of long lines and rushed service as a consequence. The reservation policy is a bit of mystery, so call ahead and see. If staying locally, order take-away.

### Lil' Frankies  📋🚶🍴  $$
*19–21 First Ave, 10003* **Tel** *(212) 420-4900* **Map** *5 A2*

Neighborhood pizzeria with an oven that claims to have lava from Vesuvius! Despite the boasting, cheap and very good pizzas draw a hip young crowd. Features a backyard garden and service is friendly if a bit on the slow side. A recent renovation has thankfully expanded into a full bar next door.

### Zum Schneider
⬛🚶♿🖼                    $$
*107 Avenue C, 10009* **Tel** *(212) 598-1098*                    **Map** *5 B2*

Oktoberfest all year round in this neighborhood favorite Bier Garten. Bring your lederhosen and enjoy the relaxed atmosphere and great sausages. Family-friendly, it usually draws big crowds on weekends when the service can be slow. As you might expect, a great selection of beer on tap from all over the world.

### Casimir
🚶🖼                    $$$
*103–105 Avenue B, 10009* **Tel** *(212) 358-9683*                    **Map** *5 B2*

Packed French bistro in the happening area of Alphabet City. Authentic fare brought by good looking, not necessarily speedy, waiters includes onion soup, steak frites, and steak tartare. Try grabbing a table at the little outside garden for extra charm, and make sure to bring your American Express (the only card accepted).

### La Palapa
🚶🖼                    $$$
*77 St Marks Place, 10003* **Tel** *(212) 777-2537*                    **Map** *5 A1*

Mexico City-style and regional Mexican cooking with authentic ingredients make this a good fiesta destination in the beautifully decorated dining room. It's easy on the wallet and serves great margaritas too. Don't miss the cod filet "Zihuatanejo style" or the duck in black mole sauce.

### Le Tableau
🚶                    $$$
*511 East 5th St, 10009* **Tel** *(212) 260-1333*                    **Map** *5 B2*

Fancy, friendly French restaurant with quality ingredients and down-to-earth prices. Cozy interiors and candlelit tables make it an enticing place to bring along a date or share with friends. Wine pairings available; there's also special wine-themed menus. The lamb is always a good choice.

### The Elephant
🚶🖼                    $$$
*58 East 1st St, 10003* **Tel** *(212) 505-7739*                    **Map** *5 A3*

A Thai-French place that is always happening with cute crowd and waiters alike. Wonderfully inventive Thai cocktails and well-executed dishes such as sticky rice with chicken and pork, and duck breast with orange confit and cinnamon prepared in a wok. The decor is a mix of funky rattan with French accents.

### The Mermaid Inn
🚶                    $$$
*96 Second Ave, 10003* **Tel** *(212) 674-5870*                    **Map** *5 A2*

Hip seafood restaurant from the duo that launched TriBeCa's The Harrison and Chelsea's The Red Cat. Attracts a young foodie crowd delighting in a prime, fresh raw bar and New England-style fare such as lobster sandwiches and chowder. A no-reservation policy usually comes with long lines attached.

### Hearth
$$$$
*403 East 12th St, 10009* **Tel** *(212) 602-1300*                    **Map** *5 A1*

A Tuscan-American restaurant with high-quality and audacious food in a romantic and chic-rustic setting. Chef Marco Canora (previously from Craft) offers interesting dishes such as *ribollita* (bean and cabbage soup), New Zealand venison, and olive oil cake. Tasting menu available.

### Jewel Bako
🍴                    $$$$
*239 East 5th St, 10003* **Tel** *(212) 979-1012*                    **Map** *4 F2*

The battle for New York's best sushi got more heated with this high-end Japanese restaurant offering fresh-from-the-sea ingredients beautifully prepared. Courteous but erractic service and the extremely tiny premises take some shine out of the expensive experience. A more casual spot just opened around the corner.

## GRAMERCY AND THE FLATIRON DISTRICT

### Ahn
🖼♿                    $
*363 3rd Ave, 10016* **Tel** *(212) 532-2848*                    **Map** *9 B4*

Stop at Ahn for delicious, authentic Vietnamese food and quick, efficient-but-friendly service. The decor is nothing to write home about, but the atmosphere is pleasant and convivial. The lunch specials are an absolute steal – try the ginger chicken baked in a clay pot.

### Chat 'n' Chew
🚶                    $$
*10 East 16th St, 10003* **Tel** *(212) 243-1616*                    **Map** *8 F5*

Kitschy comfort food destination in the Union Square area that fills the spot and is gentle on the wallet. Staples include mac 'n' cheese, a year-round Thanksgiving roast-turkey dinner, and mama's meatloaf. Don't forget the mashed potatoes, and a changing selection of cakes and pies for dessert. Good brunch spot.

### Blue Smoke
🚶                    $$$
*116 East 27th St, 10016* **Tel** *(212) 447-7733*                    **Map** *9 A3*

Danny Meyer does down south BBQ in this hip joint. Expect luscious heavy-duty pulled pork sandwiches, full racks of ribs, corn muffins, and hushpuppies (deep-fried cornmeal batter). The place features a jazz club downstairs. The large bar offers beer from around the US, and is great for large groups.

---

**Key to Price Guide** *see p296* **Key to Symbols** *see back cover flap*

## Devi

$$$

*8 East 18th St, 10003* **Tel** *(212) 691-1300*

Map 8 F5

A trendy newcomer from chefs Suvi Saran and Hemant Mathur showcasing authentic regional Indian cuisine in a gracious environment full of Indian textiles and woodcarvings. Dishes include tandoori lamb chops with pear chutney and spicy Goan shrimp, and don't miss the delectable cauliflower!

## I Trulli

$$$

*122 East 27th St, 10010* **Tel** *(212) 481-7372*

Map 9 A3

An upscale Italian restaurant specializing in Pugliese (Southern Italian) cuisine. Ideal for a romantic dinner by the fireplace in winter or in the garden during summer. A great wine list is available here and at Enoteca I Trulli, its wine bar next door. Try several wines by the glass before deciding what you want to buy.

## Pure Food and Wine

$$$

*54 Irving Place, 10003* **Tel** *(212) 477-1010*

Map 9 A5

New York's first restaurant dedicated to the raw-vegan movement – no food heated above 118°F. Expect produce with pedigree in creative dishes at this smart venue. A few examples include coconut noodles, cauliflower samosas, and an amaranth-crust pizza with hummus.

## Tamarind

$$$

*41–43 East 22nd St, 10010* **Tel** *(212) 674-7400*

Map 8 F4

A modern Indian restaurant with minimalist decorations, fantastic china, and friendly service. While pricier than your average Indian eatery, the quality of the ingredients and mix of flavors will transport you to India promptly. Ask the waiter to help you pair something from their extensive wine list.

## Craft

$$$$

*43 East 19th St, 10003* **Tel** *(212) 780-0880*

Map 9 A5

Executive chef Tom Colicchio from the acclaimed Gramercy Tavern offers a "deconstructed" menu of vibrant quality in this sleekly decorated venue. Diners have the option to "create" their entrée with a combination of ingredients and sides that can quickly push up the tab. If it seems stressful, just ask the waiter for advice.

## Fleur de Sel

$$$$

*5 East 20th Street, 10003* **Tel** *(212) 460-9100*

Map 8 F4

An intimate and charming modern French restaurant featuring the dishes of chef Cyril Renaud, formerly of Bouley. The small menu shows meticulous dedication and the attentive service completes the experience. Ideal for a romantic getaway. The service is first class, and ask the staff for help with their wine list.

## Mesa Grill

$$$$

*102 Fifth Ave, 10011* **Tel** *(212) 807-7400*

Map 8 F5

Star chef Bobby Flay's flagship restaurant showcases modern Southwestern cuisine and has pleased crowds since 1991. The creative menu includes cornmeal-crusted oysters, a "deconstructed" lamb taco, and chile- and honey-glazed salmon. The special margaritas are quite something, and the bar scene alone can get quite lively.

## Tabla

$$$$

*11 Madison Ave, 10010* **Tel** *(212) 889-0667*

Map 9 A4

A fancy Indian restaurant with a modern American twist under the direction of chef Floyd Cardoz. An elegant dining room provides the appropriate framework to a lavish, prix-fixe only, meal with dishes such as crisped shrimp with grilled pineapple and kohlrabi and lamb with chickpea spaetzle and apricots.

## Tocqueville

$$$$

*15 East 15th St, 10003* **Tel** *(212) 647-1515*

Map 8 F5

This tucked-away gem in Union Square offers French cuisine with Japanese touches, in a simple yet elegant and intimate room. Chef Marco Moreira puts out well-executed quality ingredients. Great for a special occasion that does not require a house mortgage.

## Union Square Café

$$$$

*21 East 16th Street, 10003* **Tel** *(212) 243-4020*

Map 9 A5

Among the most popular of New York City restaurants, this Danny Meyer flagship serves modern American cuisine in comfortable surroundings, drawing ingredients from the greenmarket in Union Square. The prices are anything but market level. Courteous service.

## Gramercy Tavern

$$$$$

*42 East 20th St, 10003* **Tel** *(212) 477-0777*

Map 9 A5

Acclaimed chef Tom Colicchio prepares outstanding food in a comfortable, always hopping, rustic ambience of a country inn house. An ideal place for a sophisticated dining experience without stuffy pretense. This is consistently one of the best dining experiences in the city.

## Veritas

$$$$$

*43 East 20th St, 10010* **Tel** *(212) 353-3700*

Map 9 A5

A small sleek restaurant in the Flatiron District dedicated to wine. Wine-lovers may have a coronary when reading the 2,700 plus wine list. However, the food by chef Scott Bryan rises to the occasion with jewels such as *foie gras* with a quince-Armagnac sauce and braised veal with porcini mushrooms. Prix-fixe only.

## CHELSEA AND THE GARMENT DISTRICT

### Empire Diner
210 Tenth Ave, 10011 **Tel** (212) 243-2736
$$
**Map** 7 C4

Landmark Chelsea Art Deco diner open 24 hours with standard comfort food. This is the place to have trashy American fare such as pigs in a blanket after 4am for the still-raving club-kids! A sidewalk café in the warm months is also popular for brunch, and peoplewatching the hip Chelsea crowd.

### Bottino
246 Tenth Ave, 10001 **Tel** (212) 206-6766
$$$
**Map** 7 C4

A Northern Italian restaurant in a restored 100-year-old hardware shop with minimalist decor. The place attracts a stylish crowd especially to its lovely backyard garden to enjoy traditional salads, pastas, and grilled meats. A next-door store shop and coffee bar sells items to go.

### Sueños
311 West 17th St, 10011 **Tel** (212) 243-1333
$$$
**Map** 8 D5

Traditional Mexican regional cuisine served in a colorful mid-sized space. Great tequila and margarita bar and inventive food creations, including a chile-tasting menu, provide the necessary ingredients for a pleasant, if slightly above average-priced, dining experience.

### The Red Cat
227 Tenth Ave, 10011 **Tel** (212) 242-1122
$$$
**Map** 7 C4

Modern American food in a gorgeous barnhouse setting with red- and white-painted wood that will transport you to New England. The menu features some of the best quality dishes in the neighborhood such as crispy fried oysters, wild striped bass in white wine butter, and delicious risotto fritters with blueberries.

### Buddakan
75 Ninth Ave, 10011 **Tel** (212) 989-6699
$$$$
**Map** 8 D5

Philadelphia restaurateur Stephen Starr is repeating his success with a series of New York establishments. Buddakan is the jewel in his crown, featuring jaw-dropping decor in the main hall and a series of more intimate, smaller spaces. The Asian fusion cuisine is tasty, but not the main draw to this Chelsea restaurant. Hopping bar scene.

### Matsuri
369 West 16th St, 10011 **Tel** (212) 243-6400
$$$$
**Map** 8 D5

An enormous and noisy dining space in the Maritime hotel featuring high-quality Japanese fare from chef Tadashi Ono with prime ingredients such as Kobe beef and sweet shrimp. A great sake wine list and to-die-for lemon *yuzu* crème brûlée. Plenty of star sightseeing potential so bring along your Manolos.

## THEATER DISTRICT

### Burger Joint at Le Parker Meridien
119 West 56th St, 10019 **Tel** (212) 708-7444
$
**Map** 12 E3

This kitsch joint inside the Parker Meridien hotel serves freshly cooked, mouthwatering burgers, fries, shakes, beer, and little else at rock-bottom prices. There's nothing uptight about this midtown gem hidden behind curtains in the lobby. It's the envy of all chain restaurants.

### Carve Unique Sandwiches
760 Eighth Ave, 10036 **Tel** (212) 730-4949
$
**Map** 12 D5

A new small shop where you can get all your sandwich cravings fulfilled on the cheap in the Theater District. So friendly it even has a section for the low-carb dieters with no bread, pasta, rice, or anything of the like. Lines are exasperatingly long at lunchtime, so try it in off hours.

### Pam Real Thai Food
404 West 49th St, 10019 **Tel** (212) 333-7500
$
**Map** 11 C5

If you are looking for good, inexpensive Thai food in the area, and don't care about decor, then this is the place. The usual assortment of curries, soups, pad Thai and noodle and rice dishes come in a variety of spicy degrees to order. No reservations means long waits at rush hour.

### Carnegie Deli
854 Seventh Ave, 10019 **Tel** (212) 757-2245
$$
**Map** 12 E4

You'll have to wait in long lines to glimpse one of this deli's gargantuan sandwiches and history-making cheesecakes. You'll also have to endure hostile waiters in order to experience this "quintessential" New York experience. While expensive, you probably won't eat for over a week.

**Key to Price Guide** *see p296* **Key to Symbols** *see back cover flap*

## Norma's 🏃 ⑤⑤

*118 West 57th St, 10019* **Tel** *(212) 708-7460*

**Map** *12 E3*

An unbelievable place for breakfast or brunch at the Parker Meridien hotel. Set in a slick room, the elaborate and creative menu will fulfill all of your desires. While on the pricey side, you won't eat anything else for the rest of the day, or have brunch anywhere quite like it. Weekends can see long lines, but it's very family-friendly.

## Virgil's Real Barbecue 🏃 ♿ ⑤⑤

*152 West 44th St, 10036* **Tel** *(212) 921-9494*

**Map** *12 E5*

Hopping BBQ joint in the heart of Times Square with an always bustling clientele and fast service. Ideal for pre-theater dining, provided that the heavy meal doesn't make you sleepy. Staples include over 10 different meat platters from around America, and tasty sidedishes such as biscuits, collard greens, grits, and mac 'n' cheese.

## Becco 🏃 ⑤⑤⑤

*355 West 46th St, 10036* **Tel** *(212) 397-7597*

**Map** *11 D5*

Chef Lidia Bastianich is a co-owner of this standard Italian *trattoria* on restaurant row offering a decent selection of antipasti, salads, pastas, and main courses, as well as pre-theater menus. The $25 wine list is a great deal as well; for those with more to spend, check out the more extensive regular wine list.

## Jezebel 🏃 ♿ ⑤⑤⑤

*630 Ninth Ave, 10036* **Tel** *(212) 582-1045*

**Map** *12 D5*

Sample soul-food favorites such as fried chicken, catfish, and fried okra with collard greens in this eclectic setting with porch swings, antiques, and even palm trees. Live music available from Thursday through Saturday nights. Smack dab in the middle of the Theater District, reserve early if this is the spot for pre-theater dining.

## Marseille 🏃 ♿ ⑤⑤⑤

*630 Ninth Ave, 10036* **Tel** *(212) 333-3410*

**Map** *12 D5*

Good dining in the Theater District is indeed possible at this romantic French-Mediterranean restaurant with modern twists – peanut butter tiramisu anyone? The vegetarian-friendly menu is served by a courteous staff. Check out the funky bar, Kemia, downstairs.

## Molyvos 🏃 ♿ ⑤⑤⑤

*871 Seventh Ave, 10019* **Tel** *(212) 582-7500*

**Map** *12 E4*

An upscale Greek restaurant near Carnegie Hall. The warm Mediterranean decor is the perfect setting for fresh seafood and other Greek specialties justifying the above-average prices. Try the flashy (and flaming) saganaki appetizer for your own pre-theater experience. Prix-fixe available.

## Osteria al Doge ⑤⑤⑤

*142 West 44th St, 10036* **Tel** *(212) 944-3643*

**Map** *12 E5*

Venetian cuisine in a rustic dining room with a successful power-lunch clientele and popular with early evening theater-goers. Service is expeditious and warm. The menu includes pizza, great salads, and carpaccio as well as fresh pastas at prices and quality better than other venues in the area.

## Blue Fin ♿ ⑤⑤⑤⑤

*1567 Broadway, 10036* **Tel** *(212) 918-1400*

**Map** *12 E5*

Among the coolest places in the area, this is dedicated to seafood in a big way, including a raw and sushi bar. The two-story restaurant is always hopping and some may complain about the noise level, not just from the live music. A good place to flex the expense account.

## db Bistro Moderne ♿ ⑤⑤⑤⑤

*55 West 44th St, 10036* **Tel** *(212) 391-2400*

**Map** *8 F1*

Home of the famous *foie gras* and the $29 burger filled with wine-braised short ribs and sirloin. This lively midtown restaurant offers another glimpse of Daniel Boulud's fine-dining experience with less damage to the wallet. Popular for power lunches with the publishing executive crowd who can afford it. Nice choice for upscale pre-theater dinner.

## Esca ♿ 🍴 ⑤⑤⑤⑤

*402 West 43rd St, 10036* **Tel** *(212) 564-7272*

**Map** *8 D1*

An upscale Italian seafood restaurant from the Batali-Bastianich partnership. A large variety of appetizers is followed by other dishes that reflect the great quality of its ingredients. Service can be unreliable and some think the atmosphere is a bit stale. A little formal, so not the best place for children.

## Osteria del Circo ♿ ⑤⑤⑤⑤

*120 West 55th St, 10019* **Tel** *(212) 265-3636*

**Map** *12 E4*

Northern Italian restaurant from the Maccioni family known for Le Cirque. The Adam Tihany-designed dining room is spacious and comfortable and the food is well executed amid very affable service. Save space for desserts, including the Tuscan doughnuts with cappuccino cream.

## Triomphe ♿ ⑤⑤⑤⑤

*49 West 44th St, 10036* **Tel** *(212) 453-4233*

**Map** *12 F5*

A charming oasis of quiet from the bustle of Times Square, this French restaurant in the Iroquois Hotel pairs excellent food and wine with impeccable service. Tasting menus are available, as well as quirkier events, such as gathering between 10 and 20 of your friends to enjoy dinner and a movie in the private room.

### Gordon Ramsay

♿🍴   ⑤⑤⑤⑤⑤

*151 West 54th St, 10019* **Tel** *(212) 468-8888*                                              **Map** *12 E4*

Despite UK chef Gordon Ramsay's brash reputation, his first US venture is a subdued affair. The 45-seat restaurant at the London NYC Hotel is quiet and relaxed – all the better to focus on the exquisite French cuisine. The prix-fixe lunch is a bargain for a restaurant of this class. Book well in advance, especially for the eight-seat kitchen table.

### Le Bernardin

♿🍴   ⑤⑤⑤⑤⑤

*155 West 51st St, 10019* **Tel** *(212) 554-1515*                                              **Map** *12 E4*

A dream-come-true for seafood- and fish-lovers. This superb and elegant longstanding restaurant offers an outstanding dining experience with French haute cuisine from chef Eric Ripert. Service is flawless including the sommelier advice. It's the place to propose.

### Milos Estiatorio

🍴♿   ⑤⑤⑤⑤⑤

*125 West 55th St, 10019* **Tel** *(212) 245-7400*                                              **Map** *12 E4*

Formidable Greek food with fresh out-of-the-water seafood set in a spartan, airy dining room where guests select the fish from a beautifully decorated stand. The catch of the day depends on the luck of the fishermen purveyors for this upscale restaurant. Prices are some of the most expensive in town.

## LOWER MIDTOWN

### Grand Central Oyster Bar

🍴♿   ⑤⑤⑤

*Grand Central, Lower Level, 42nd St, 10017* **Tel** *(212) 490-6650*                          **Map** *9 A1*

Cavernous space inside Grand Central where you'll be transported to the past. The very fresh seafood in simple preparations are not too pricey, and the menu features a long list of over a dozen kinds of oysters. The setting and decor is casual, so leave the fur coats at home and bring your appetite. Waiter service included.

### Riingo

🍴♿   ⑤⑤⑤

*205 East 45th St, 10017* **Tel** *(212) 867-4200*                                              **Map** *13 B5*

Very chic restaurant at the Alex hotel from chef Marcus Samuelsson and *chef de cuisine* Johan Svensson offering a marriage of Japanese and Swedish specialties in eyecatching preparations. Try their signature *nigiri-sashimi* with warm *foie gras* or Kobe beef.

### Artisanal

🍴♿   ⑤⑤⑤⑤

*2 Park Ave, 10016* **Tel** *(212) 725-8585*                                                   **Map** *9 A2*

Sparkling upscale French bistro where the main topic is cheese, including a large selection to taste either by themselves or in fondues. Non-cheese lovers need not be afraid as there are plenty of non-dairy selections available. Service can be unreliable, and reservations aren't always respected on time.

### Asia de Cuba

♿🍴   ⑤⑤⑤⑤

*237 Madison Ave, 10016* **Tel** *(212) 726-7755*                                              **Map** *9 A2*

The minimalist-chic white dining room still attracts a young hip crowd to taste Latin fusion cuisine with Asian touches. High-priced dishes include a tasting of tofu, lobster mai tai, and miso-cured black cod. Some, however, consider it's past its prime. Grab a drink and watch the crowds sharing food at large tables.

### L'Impero

♿🍳🍴   ⑤⑤⑤⑤

*45 Tudor City Place, 10017* **Tel** *(212) 599-5045*                                          **Map** *9 B1*

A cozy Italian menu from chef Scott Conant with innovative dishes, a fantastic wine list, and great service. Amazing homemade pastas, and don't forget to try the cheese course with outstanding flavor pairings. Tasting menu also available. Perfect for special occasions and another excuse to see hidden Tudor city.

### Michael Jordan's The Steakhouse NYC

🍴♿   ⑤⑤⑤⑤

*Grand Central, North Balcony, 10017* **Tel** *(212) 655-2300*                                  **Map** *9 A1*

The celebrity player steakhouse located on the beautifully renovated mezzanine of Grand Central Terminal. Expect high-quality (and high-priced) dry, aged cuts. Avoid a hot summer day because the terminal is not air conditioned. Service is casual but knowledgable and you can't beat the view of the hectic train passengers below.

## UPPER MIDTOWN

### La Bonne Soupe

🍴♿   ⑤

*48 West 55th St, 10019* **Tel** *(212) 586-7650*                                              **Map** *12 F4*

A cozy midtown haven for the thrifty, with a longstanding French bistro menu including quiches, omelettes, soups, steaks, and crêpes. Service is on the slow side. Features a small terrace for outdoor dining in the warm months. A great low-cost option in this pricey and uscale neighborhood.

**Key to Price Guide** *see p296* **Key to Symbols** *see back cover flap*

## Beacon     🚻♿     $$$
*25 West 56th St, 10019* **Tel** *(212) 332-0500*         **Map** *12 E3*

A modern American menu is offered at this striking tri-level space with dishes such as shrimp cocktail with roasted jalapeño peppers, and a lamb T-bone with black olives and lemon. Moods change with the levels – busy at the bar, intimate upstairs, and cozy near the open kitchen.

## Dawat     🚹♿     $$$
*210 East 58th St, 10022* **Tel** *(212) 355-7555*         **Map** *13 B3*

An attractive Indian restaurant with recipes from none other than famous Indian chef Madhur Jaffrey. Signature dishes include salmon rubbed with a coriander chutney and baked in a banana leaf. The clever touch is a snack car that parades to your table. If you're not an Indian food expert, ask the helpful staff for advice.

## Rue 57     🚹♿🚻     $$$
*60 West 57th St, 10019* **Tel** *(212) 307-5656*         **Map** *12 F3*

The fusion fever does not stop at Rue 57, which offers a combination of a sushi bar and French cuisine in a popular sophisticated bistro. It's good value as a breakfast option as well. Sidewalk tables available – a great peoplewatching spot in warm months, and a fine last-minute choice in midtown.

## Shun Lee Palace     🚹♿     $$$
*155 East 55th St, 10022* **Tel** *(212) 371-8844*         **Map** *13 A4*

A handsome dining room considered one of the city's premier Chinese restaurants. The menu is a Cantonese/ Szechuan blend with casserole specialties. The Grand Marnier prawns can become a serious addiction. Another location is near the Lincoln Center at 43 West 65th Street.

## Inagiku     ♿🍸     $$$$
*111 East 49th St, 10017* **Tel** *(212) 355-0440*         **Map** *13 A5*

Formal Japanese restaurant hidden away in the Waldorf-Astoria, featuring fresh sushi sent daily air express from Japan, tempura, and *kaiseki* (tasting menus). Service and decor are both charming, and a welcome respite from the tourist craze of the hotel. Perfect choice for business lunches.

## Pampano     🚹🚻     $$$$
*209 East 49th St, 10017* **Tel** *(212) 751-4545*         **Map** *13 B2*

A lovely, modern Mexican restaurant from chef Richard Sandoval and opera legend co-owner Placido Domingo. Inventive and fresh creations in a chic dining room will make you want to sing an aria or two. Don't miss the smoked swordfish appetizer or the halibut Pampano. A beautiful terrace is also available.

## Vong     ♿🍸     $$$$
*200 East 54th St, 10022* **Tel** *(212) 486-9592*         **Map** *13 B4*

Longstanding French-Thai restaurant from chef Jean Georges Vongerichten. An impossibly beautiful dining room gives way to some intriguing fusion dishes such as sautéed *foie gras* with ginger and mango or lobster with Thai herbs. Save room for the passion fruit soufflé. Treat yourself with the pre-theater prix-fixe meal.

## Aquavit     ♿🍸     $$$$$
*65 East 55th St, 10022* **Tel** *(212) 307-7311*         **Map** *13 A4*

The new minimalist space for Aquavit serves as the home of inventive Scandinavian creations from chefs Nils Noren and Marcus Samuelsson, with prime ingredients and several tasting menus available. The signature Aquavit cocktails are also a must.

## BLT Steak     🚹♿     $$$$$
*106 East 57th St, 10022* **Tel** *(212) 752-7470*         **Map** *13 A3*

Bistro Laurent Tourondel (BLT) offers fancy steaks with prime ingredients and your choice of sauces for your Angus-certified protein. A stylish room with toffee-colored booths, a zinc bar, and other eye-catching elements draws a hip, fashion-conscious crowd.

## Felidia     🍸     $$$$$
*243 East 58th St, 10022* **Tel** *(212) 758-1479*         **Map** *13 B3*

TV star chef Lidia Bastianich offers upscale Italian fare in this charming, wood-paneled townhouse with exposed bricks and flower arrangements. Conducive to romance, the seasonal menu is creative and well executed. In line with Lidia's other restaurants, an impressive wine list is also available.

## Four Seasons     ♿     $$$$$
*99 East 52nd St, 10022* **Tel** *(212) 754-9494*         **Map** *13 A4*

Restaurants come and go, but this gracious New York institution with landmark decor by Philip Johnson seems to go on forever, always among the top-rated for American-Continental food. The Grill Room is still the prime place for power lunches, and the Pool Room is a perfect setting for special-occasion dinners.

## La Grenouille     ♿🍸     $$$$$
*3 East 52nd St, 10022* **Tel** *(212) 752-1495*         **Map** *12 F4*

One of the last remaining classic French restaurants in the city with outstanding food. The dining room walls are laden with silk and velvet blanquettes, beautiful floral arrangements abound making the eating experience a memorable one. A place for special occasions.

## Lever House
       🚹  ⑤⑤⑤⑤⑤
*390 Park Ave, 10022* **Tel** *(212) 888-2700*      **Map** *13 A4*

New York City's new mecca for power lunches is a who's who in the business world. This modern dining room offers a seasonal menu with new American-influenced dishes such as lobster gazpacho and poussin with tarragon jus. Dress to impress and beware of the high noise level.

## Oceana
       🍴  ⑤⑤⑤⑤⑤
*55 East 54th St, 10022* **Tel** *(212) 759-5941*      **Map** *13 A4*

The freshest seafood ingredients this side of Le Bernardin, this posh two-level dining room seems like a private yacht, yet offers beautiful dishes with a smooth service. Chef Cornelius Gallagher provides creative dishes such as halibut with piquillo peppers and black tahini and raisins coulis. Prix-fixe only.

## The Modern
       🚹  ⑤⑤⑤⑤⑤
*9 West 53rd St, 10019* **Tel** *(212) 333-1220*      **Map** *12 F4*

In a clean, modern space at the Museum of Modern Art, overlooking the Sculpture Garden, this restaurant serves an impeccable array of New American and French cuisine, alongside an extensive wine list. Expect a high level of service. The tasting menu is popular and can be enjoyed with a wine pairing if your wallet can take the strain.

# UPPER EAST SIDE

## Brother Jimmy's BBQ
       🚶  ⑤⑤
*1485 Second Ave, 10021* **Tel** *(212) 288-0999*      **Map** *17 B5*

The original of the Brother Jimmy's chain promises a rowdy evening and some "finger-lickin"ribs and Southern favorites. All-you-can-eat specials are a popular option. This is a good destination for carnivores, though there are a few options for vegetarians. Some quieter tables can be found at the rear.

## Shanghai Pavilion
       🚶  ⑤⑤
*1378 Third Ave, 10021* **Tel** *(212) 585-3388*      **Map** *17 B5*

Newcomer offering Shanghai cuisine, as authentic as you can get outside of Chinatown. The menu has plenty of options at reasonable prices, making it a good value in this neighborhood. The service is friendly. Great dim sums, noodle dishes, and specialties such as velvet sea bass or lobster tropicana.

## Via Quadronno
       🚶  ⑤⑤
*25 East 73rd St, 10021* **Tel** *(212) 650-9880*      **Map** *12 F1*

A cute Italian-style "bar paninoteca" with a rainbow of delicious prime-ingredient sandwiches and salads worth a stop after a Museum Mile extravaganza. The small space inspired by a Milan paninoteca translates into waiting lines at peak hours. Definitely splurge on a glass of wine to go with the meal.

## Aureole
       🏢🍴  ⑤⑤⑤
*34 East 61st St, 10021* **Tel** *(212) 319-1600*      **Map** *13 A3*

Acclaimed chef Charlie Palmer continues to dazzle in this flower-filled, duplex townhouse with his elegant new American fare. Try the portobello and goats' cheese gratin or the pancetta-crusted rack of veal. The extensive wine list can take some help to get through, so ask for the sommelier.

## Maya
       🚶🚹  ⑤⑤⑤
*1191 First Ave, 10021* **Tel** *(212) 585-1818*      **Map** *13 C2*

Chef Richard Sandoval serves sophisticated and delicate main courses at this upbeat Mexican restaurant in a peach-hued setting. The drawback comes in the sound level; dine early to avoid the din. Many rave about the seafood tacos, margaritas, and guacamole.

## Café Boulud
       🚹🍴  ⑤⑤⑤⑤
*20 East 76th St, 10021* **Tel** *(212) 772-2600*      **Map** *16 F5*

Chef Daniel Boulud creates a less formal dining room with solid creations inside the Surrey hotel. An interesting array of dinner options will keep any diner intrigued – "Le Tradition" (classic French), "Le Voyager" (world cuisines), "Le Potager" (vegetarian), and "La Saison"(seasonal specialties).

## Orsay
       🚶🚹  ⑤⑤⑤⑤
*1057 Lexington Ave, 10021* **Tel** *(212) 517-6400*      **Map** *17 A5*

A spacious modern French café with an upscale feeling and so popular that it gets pretty noisy in the evenings. Still, the crowds come to try exotic creations such as the "margarita tartare" and the crispy duck leg with garlic *beignet* (a fluffy, buttery fritter). Definitely order a wine by the glass to go with the creative meal.

## Daniel
       🚹🍴  ⑤⑤⑤⑤⑤
*60 East 65th St, 10021* **Tel** *(212) 288-0033*      **Map** *13 A2*

Chef Daniel Boulud's flagship restaurant features a Venetian Renaissance-inspired dining room, one of the most luscious settings in town. His highly acclaimed creations make this a place for special occasions but be warned of the sky-high prices and occasional sub-standard service.

**Key to Price Guide** *see p296* **Key to Symbols** *see back cover flap*

## David Burke & Donatella

*133 East 61st St, 10021* **Tel** *(212) 813-2121*          **Map** *13 A3*

Creative new American dishes from chef David Burke and former Bellini hostess Donatella Arpaia. Diners cross a glamorous white gloss and stone bar to proceed to a cool dining area in bold colors and lacquered surfaces. Save room for the signature cheesecake "lollipop" dessert.

# UPPER WEST SIDE

## Wholefoods Market Café

*Time Warner Center, 10 Columbus Circle, 10019* **Tel** *(212) 823-9600*          **Map** *12 D3*

An enormous, environment-friendly supermarket with an impressive food hall stocking all sorts of cuisine from sushi to pizzas. The ideal spot to shop for your inexpensive picnic adventures in Central Park or eat in at the booths. A wine shop is available inside too. Beware of crowds at peak times.

## Gennaro

*665 Amsterdam Ave, 10025* **Tel** *(212) 665-5348*          **Map** *15 C2*

An inexpensive small café serving consistently good Italian food with large servings. With a no-reservation policy, there can be lines at busy times. All the usuals are available here, including daily pasta specials and a wine list that is pretty reasonable. When busy, service can be annoyingly slow.

## Boathouse Restaurant Central Park

*Central Park, East 72nd St & Park Drive North, 10023* **Tel** *(212) 517-2233*          **Map** *12 E1*

The setting by Central Park's lake could not be any lovelier than this boathouse. An ideal place for brunch or lunch, and a romantic dinner is available April through October. Given the prices, it's unfortunate that the inevitable touristy nature has limited its potential to serve above-average food.

## Café Fiorello

*1900 Broadway, 10023* **Tel** *(212) 595-5330*          **Map** *12 D2*

Boasting that it's "the longest running show on Broadway" this noisy Italian place features a bountiful antipasto bar. You can sample enough for a whole meal before crossing the street to the Lincoln Center. The menu also includes pizzas and standard Italian fare. Great for peoplewatching in the seasonal outside tables.

## Café Luxembourg

*200 West 70th St, 10023* **Tel** *(212) 873-7411*          **Map** *11 C1*

A classic Art Deco Parisian bistro with a zinc-topped bar, antique mirrors, and a loyal, hip clientele with the occasional celebrity sighting. Standard bistro fare with weekly specials available but don't expect flawless service. The crowd and decor make it a good choice for business dinners.

## Calle Ocho

*446 Columbus Ave, 10024* **Tel** *(212) 873-5025*          **Map** *16 D4*

It's a never-ending party in this loud and colorful Cuban restaurant filled with beautiful 20-somethings. The menu is an amalgam of Latin American dishes, all with varying degrees of success. A small kids' menu is also available. And since it's close to the American Museum of Natural History, take a break with your family and have a drink.

## Pampa

*768 Amsterdam Ave, 10025* **Tel** *(212) 865-2929*          **Map** *15 C1*

An Argentine grill that is always hip and happening with enormous meat portions and great garlic frites. Perfect for a hungry appetite and a leanish wallet. Don't miss the *humita* (corn) empanadas and the panqueques dessert with *dulce de leche*. The waitstaff is on the glamorous side, and don't miss the Peruvian beers.

## Pasha

*70 West 71st St, 10023* **Tel** *(212) 579-8751*          **Map** *12 D1*

A serene and spacious, skylit, Turkish restaurant with friendly service ideal for a good conversation amid well-executed food. The lamb dumpling appetizers are delicious as well as all of the eggplant dishes, in particular the smoky *patlican salatasi*, mashed with garlic, olive oil, and lemon.

## Rosa Mexicano

*61 Columbus Ave, 10023* **Tel** *(212) 977-7700*          **Map** *12 D2*

Popular and trendy upscale Mexican fine dining drawing a crowd of hip diners near Lincoln Center. Awesome pomegranate margaritas and guacamole made to order at your table. Try the *cochinita pibil* tacos (achiote rubbed pork steamed in banana leafs) or the Veracruz fish in tomato sauce.

## Aix

*2398 Broadway, 10024* **Tel** *(212) 874-7400*          **Map** *15 C3*

Creative modern French cuisine by chef Didier Virot in a beautiful romantic setting complemented by professional service. Aix brings a much-needed breath of fresh air to this neighborhood's dining options. Save room for dessert creations by rising star, pastry chef Jehangir Mehta.

### Café des Artistes
*1 West 67th St, 10023* **Tel** *(212) 877-3500*

🔝  $$$$

*Map 12 D2*

A romantic bistro serving French cuisine in a beautiful flower-filled dining room with the famous Howard Christy Chandler nymph murals. Dishes are no stretch of the imagination, but are nevertheless well executed if somewhat expensive. There's potential for some celebrity spotting. Brunch is also popular.

### Café Gray
*Time Warner Center, 10 Columbus Circle, 10019* **Tel** *(212) 823-6338*

♿🔝  $$$$

*Map 12 D3*

Chef Gray Kunz of L'Espinasse fame has opened his new French brasserie with Asian nuances at the Time Warner Center. The beautifully decorated room, while noisy, offers high-quality creations such as oxtail consommé with *foie gras* dumplings or the braised short ribs.

### Ouest
*2315 Broadway, 10024* **Tel** *(212) 580-8700*

🏃♿  $$$$

*Map 15 C4*

Chef Tom Valenti offers his version of new American comfort cuisine – it's an elegant restaurant that still makes you feel comfortable. The menu features nightly specials such as traditional meatloaf and other creative dishes such as poached squab with *foie gras agnoloti*. An outstanding wine list is available as well.

### Asiate
*80 Columbus Circle, 35th Floor, 10019* **Tel** *(212) 805-8881*

♿🔝  $$$$$

*Map 12 D3*

Stellar views of Central Park are available from this Asian-influenced restaurant at the Mandarin hotel. Highlights include pan-seared *foie gras* with steamed sea eel and tamarind sauce and Wagyu beef with oxtail sauce. The bar includes an interesting array of cocktails.

### Jean Georges
*1 Central Park West at Columbus Circle and West 60th St, 10023* **Tel** *(212) 299-3900*

♿🔝  $$$$$

*Map 12 D3*

Chef Jean George's flagship temple for modern French cuisine with Asian nuances. An austere yet elegant, Adam Tihany-designed room is the stage for an impressive array of delicate dishes brought in by a courteous and warm service. One of the most memorable fine dining experiences in New York.

### Masa
*Time Warner Center, 10 Columbus Circle, 10019* **Tel** *(212) 823-9800*

♿🔝  $$$$$

*Map 12 D3*

Chef Masayoshi Takayama, of the famed LA Ginza sushi-Ko, has moved to New York to break the record of most expensive meal ever. It consists of a never-ending *kaiseki*-style (tasting) menu chosen by Mr Masa using incredibly fresh ingredients. Take a seat by the sushi bar to savor the show in every detail.

### Per Se
*Time Warner Center, 10 Columbus Circle, 10019* **Tel** *(212) 823-9335*

♿🔝  $$$$$

*Map 12 D3*

Call two months in advance to score a seat in the critically-acclaimed restaurant from Thomas Keller of California's French Laundry fame. The tasting menus change daily, and many think the vegetarian option is the best. Plus, it offers spectacular views of Central Park. Service is impeccable.

### Picholine
*35 West 64th St, 10023* **Tel** *(212) 724-8585*

🔝  $$$$$

*Map 12 D2*

Terrance Brennan's elegant French-Mediterranean restaurant a few steps away from the Lincoln Center. Several prix-fixe, *a la carte*, and even tasting menus available with dishes such as John Dory with grapes, chanterelles, and truffle vinaigrette. Save room for their famous artisanal cheeses.

## MORNINGSIDE HEIGHTS AND HARLEM

### Sylvia's
*328 Lenox Ave, 10027* **Tel** *(212) 996-0660*

🏃🎵  $$

*Map 21 B1*

A New York tradition since 1962, serving good old soul food in a kitschy dining room with occasional live music. Its success brings along plenty of tourists and locals alike to enjoy the inexpensive menu of staples such as fried chicken, collard greens, and black-eyed peas. Extremely busy on Sundays after church.

## FARTHER AFIELD: BROOKLYN

### Grimaldi's
*19 Old Fulton St, 11201* **Tel** *(718) 858-4300*

🍽🏃  $

Unbelievably good coal-oven pizzas made from the milkiest mozzarella and the freshest sauce. Definitely try the pepperoni. This place is worth the trip to Brooklyn and a walk back across the bridge. Bring your family and wait in line to taste the inexpensive pies at this buzzing pizzeria.

## Song
*295 Fifth Ave, 11217* **Tel** *(718) 965-1108*

This friendly Thai spot in Park Slope draws a big crowd with its triple play – low prices, a tranquil garden, and a groovy industrial interior. The music inside can get loud, but that doesn't seem to bother the locals. Big sister restaurant Joya, in Cobble Hill, is equally popular.

## Chip Shop/ Curry Shop
*383 Fifth Ave, 11215* **Tel** *(718) 832-7701*

An outpost of British comfort food in New York City, this inexpensive shop offers fish and chips, bangers and mash, kidney pies, and curries in a kitschy dining room. Great to sit back with a group of friends and enjoy a pint of beer. Family-friendly as well. Don't forget to try the yummy fried Mars bar.

## Planet Thailand
*133 North 7th St, 11211* **Tel** *(718) 599-5758*

A trendy renovated warehouse featuring outstanding Thai specialties – try the beef and broccoli flat noodles – and a less successful sushi bar. A very hip place for large groups. Reserve ahead. Only one stop into Brooklyn on the L-train, try this spot before bar-hopping in Williamsburg.

## Patois
*255 Smith St, 11231* **Tel** *(718) 855-1535*

The French bistro that started the Smith Street restaurant revolution, offering inexpensive seasonal menus in its rustic decor environment. Dishes include veal meatballs in a caper cream sauce and a vegetarian cassoulet with smoked Gouda. Vibrant garden seating available.

## Peter Luger Steakhouse
*178 Broadway, 11211* **Tel** *(718) 387-7400*

A New York institution serving "the discerning steak connoisseur" since 1887. Try their out-of-this-world meat. Just be aware that the decor's ambience is much like a beer-hall and the waiters can be snippy. Reserve ahead and still expect to wait for a table.

## The Grocery
*288 Smith St, 11231* **Tel** *(718) 596-3335*

A charming 30-seat restaurant in Carrol Gardens, offering a delightful seasonal menu such as whole boneless trout stuffed with spaetzle and asparagus or braised duck breast with bulghur, Swiss chard, and caramelized red wine. The romantic venue also features a lovely summer garden.

## River Café
*One Water St, 11201* **Tel** *(718) 522-5200*

Unrivaled for its location featuring stunning Manhattan skyline views, this upscale Brooklyn standout offers a new American three-course, prix-fixe menu. A tasting menu is also available. An unbeatable romantic place for special occasions. Save room for their signature chocolate Brooklyn Bridge dessert.

# FARTHER AFIELD: QUEENS

## Jackson Diner
*37–47 74th St, 11372* **Tel** *(718) 672-1232*

This spacious Indian cafeteria-style restaurant pulls out all the stops for well-prepared Northern Indian (spicy) and Southern Indian (less spicy) food at very cheap prices and well worth the visit when you are at Jackson Heights. Magnificent lamb dishes and samosas and great *lassi* to wash it all down.

## Elias Corner
*24–02 31st St, 11102* **Tel** *(718) 932-1510*

Among the most famous Greek restaurants with a huge following and long lines. This no-thrills, expanded restaurant serves some of the freshest fish in town, prepared simply. A large garden also makes this a good place for group gatherings, if you don't mind the wait at rush hours, especially weekends.

## S'Agapo
*34–21 34th Ave, 11106* **Tel** *(718) 626-0303*

The name means "I love you" in Greek, and this taverna has a cheerful atmosphere where grilled fish is the specialty. Live music on weekends and a terrace for summer evenings enliven the inexpensive experience. The restaurant is close to the American Museum of the Moving Image.

## Trattoria L'incontro
*21–76 31st St at Ditmars Blvd, 11105* **Tel** *(718) 721-3532*

This Italian restaurant is spot on with flavor, large portions, and accessible prices. The decor is hardly memorable but their grilled swordfish or veal with lemon and capers are. Reserve ahead for this popular place in the Astoria, but don't be surprised if you rub shoulders with someone who looks like they're part of the Mafia.

# Light Meals and Snacks

You can get a snack almost anywhere and anytime in Manhattan. New Yorkers seem to eat endlessly – on street corners, in bars, luncheonettes, delis, before and after work, and long into the night. Casual eating in New York might include soft pretzels or char-roasted chestnuts from a corner stand; a huge sandwich from a deli; a Greek gyro sandwich (roasted lamb in pitta bread) from street vendors; a pre-theater snack at a café or coffee bar; or a post-party binge at an all-night diner or bistro. While street fare is generally cheap, the quality and culinary skills vary greatly.

## DELIS

Delicatessens are a New York institution, a great source for a hefty lunchtime sandwich. Definitely try the wonderful corned beef and pastrami sandwiches. While **Carnegie Delicatessen** in the Theater District is perhaps New York's most famous deli, **Katz's Deli** on the Lower East Side is much more authentic – and cheaper.

Most deli business is takeout and as such delis are bustling places serving huge sandwiches at relatively cheap prices. Counter staff are typically surly and impatient, and rudeness has almost become a trademark of the **Stage Deli**, which is now more of a tourist stop than the showbiz favorite it used to be.

For New York ethnic Jewish flavor, try **Barney Greengrass**, on the Upper West Side. In operation since 1929, the "Sturgeon King" serves up lox, salmon, pastrami, and, of course, sturgeon. **Zabar's** is a takeout haven for yuppies who put up with the crowds for superb smoked fish, pickles, and salads.

Aficionados say that the best pastrami sandwiches and other favorites are to be found at the **Pastrami Queen** in Manhattan.

## CAFÉS, BISTROS, AND BRASSERIES

Cafés, bistros, and the larger brasseries have become "in" places in New York in recent years. Try the upscale **Balthazar** on Spring Street for "brilliantly faux" everything except the menu, which is stellar. Even more trendy and less expensive is Balthazar's sister bistro, **Pastis**, in the Meatpacking District. The **Café Centro**, above Grand Central, is particularly busy and noisy during lunchtime, and is a favorite with business types. The Centro's Provençal/Mediterranean fare includes fish soups and some succulent desserts. **Brasserie** on East 53rd, a longtime landmark, has had an elegant remodeling. **Bistro du Nord** on Madison Avenue has a variety of French/American fare with an inventive flair. Downtown, **Odeon** is a TriBeCa favorite for its brasserie menu and late hours. **Raoul's** in SoHo is a French bistro with a relaxed ambience that keeps artists and other habitués coming back for reliable, informal food. **Elephant and Castle**, a minimally decorated café, is a Greenwich Village standby for soup-salad-omelette lunches and other light snacks. Its real forte is breakfast and brunch, served in ample portions at modest prices. The bar scene is lively too. Tiny **Chez Jacqueline** is also a favored Village spot. Its French bistro fare and proximity to several off-Broadway theaters make it popular with the young, hip, and international crowd for a moderately priced dinner or late supper.

In the Theater District, try the Cuban **Victor's Café**. Large, lively, and Latin, it is known for authentic Cuban food served in giant portions at medium prices. **Chez Josephine** is an exuberant bistro-cabaret with live jazz piano playing. The scene is the main attraction here, and the French food is excellent.

**La Boite en Bois**, small but delightfully French, serves delicious French bistro food and is conveniently close to Lincoln Center. In the same vicinity is **Vince and Eddie's**, a tiny gem known for reliable, often superb American food.

**Sarabeth's**, on the Upper West Side, defies categorizing, but might best be dubbed a café. Breakfast or weekend brunch is the best time to try waffles, French toast, pancakes, and omelettes. There are two other branches, one of which is located in the Whitney Museum of Art.

The Gramercy Park area's **Les Halles** is about as all-out French bistro as New York gets. At its late-night peak, the decibel level is high, but regulars think the *frites* and beef dishes are worth the noise and crowds.

## PIZZERIAS

Pizza is available all over New York, from street stands and fast-food places that sell it by the slice for a few dollars, to a traditional Neapolitan pizzeria.

Some pizzerias offer something more. **Arturo's Pizzeria** uses a coal oven for crisp, thin-crusted bases with the added inducement of live jazz. **Mezzogiorno** has a Tuscan menu and wonderful pizzas with unusual toppings. The crowded **Mezzaluna** also specializes in brick-oven, thin-crusted pizza, as does **John's Pizzeria**, whose fans, including Woody Allen, consider it Manhattan's best.

Brooklyn boasts a top pizzeria in Coney Island's **Totonno Pizzeria**, which is well worth the trip for real pizza aficionados, though it also has a Manhattan branch. **Trattoria Dante** in Greenwich Village is famous with students who like to sit outside in warm weather.

Generally, pizza parlors are good places to go for a cheap, simple meal, particularly with children.

Most places won't take reservations, so popular ones may have long lines.

## HAMBURGER PLACES

Apart from the hot dog stands on the street, New York has many places selling better quality burgers, even though prices for a top grade all-beef burger can go up to $10.

Burgers have even gone "upscale" with famed New York restauranteur Danny Meyer creating the **Shake Shack** in Madison Square Park. It offers good-value eats from April to November. In Midtown, the stylish Le Parker Meridien Hotel opened the **Burger Joint**, which looks like a truck-stop, and has some of the best burgers in town.

Bright and basic, the five outlets of **Jackson Hole** offer fat, juicy, meaty burgers in 28 varieties popular with kids. Adults might prefer less glare and smarter decor, but they will like the low prices. A good place to try the typical New York drink, the egg cream.

The **Beer Bar at Café Centro** in the MetLife Building, where professional types like to hang out, has an unusual beer menu and delicious burgers.

The **Corner Bistro** in Greenwich Village offers New York's best burgers, tasty and reasonably priced. The beer selection is good, too, and the 4am closing makes this a great late-night stop.

## DINERS AND LUNCHEONETTES

Diners and luncheonettes, also called sandwich or coffee shops, can be found all over town. Food is mostly bland but served in huge, cheap platefuls. They are usually open from breakfast until late evening, and you can stop in at almost any hour.

A recent trend with diners has seen 1990s replicas of the old 1930s cheap-eats places. One such retro-diner is the chic **Empire Diner** (see p138), which is a popular spot for club kids thanks to its 24-hour opening times. The

**Moondance Diner** in SoHo dates from the 1930s and also featured in the film *Spider-Man*.

**Jerry's** attracts a SoHo art and celebrity crowd who love the inventive sandwiches, salads, delicious desserts, and huge breakfasts. Also attracting a hip art crowd is **Florent**, a West Village diner with good French food served around the clock. **Big Nick's** on Broadway is the best place for a pizza, hamburger, or breakfast on the Upper WestSide. The **Coffee Shop** in Union Square serves Brazilian-American fare and is open all night.

On the Upper East Side, Eli Zabar's **E.A.T.** sells excellent but pricey Jewish favorites – such as mushroom-barley soup and challah bread, as well as some sinful desserts.

Devotees swear by **Viand**, a spic-and-span East Side luncheonette, with cheap, ample American breakfasts, good burgers, egg creams, and the best turkey sand-wiches in town. **Veselka**, not the usual New York sandwich shop, serves Polish/Ukrainian food at rock-bottom prices and has just opened a second outlet, **Little Veselka**.

## TEA ROOMS

The only place you can be absolutely sure of getting a cup of real, brewed tea is at a formal, prix-fixe afternoon tea in a lounge at one of New York's pricier hotels, from 3pm to 5pm.

For an extra-stylish tea, on Chippendale furniture, visit **Carlyle** in the Upper East Side. Another good buy in hotel prix-fixe tea is **Hotel Pierre**. Tea at the **Waldorf-Astoria** comes with Devonshire cream, while the elegant tea at **Stanhope** on Fifth Avenue is abundant enough to carry you through to a late dinner.

A variation on tea themes can be found in a new chain of teahouses called **Saint's Alp**. These delightful spots, serving frothy, flavored, colorful tea drinks poured over crushed ice, can be found at 51 Mott Street near Chinatown and in the new

Times Square area. Teatime, Japanese-style, can also be enjoyed at **The Tea Box**, in the Takashimaya department store on Fifth Avenue.

## COFFEE AND CAKES

You can get a decent cup of coffee for as little as 75 cents, with endless free refills, at most diners, luncheonettes, and coffee shops. There is a new trend for coffee bars that serve a variety of specialty coffees, such as cappuccino, espresso, and caffè latte. Ice cream parlors and patisseries also serve good coffee, along with sinfully luscious pastries.

People wait in line at **Magnolia Bakery** to sample the decadent cakes, while **Joe** boasts the world's best espresso machine. **Caffè Ferrara**, going strong since 1892, has moderately priced Italian pastries, good coffee, and outdoor seating. **Vesuvio Bakery** is an old-fashioned Italian café that sells fresh bread baked in a coal oven. **DT-UT** is known to be child-friendly.

The **Seaport Café**, in the South Street Seaport, serves fine coffee and is a good place to watch the passing scene and spectacular view.

**The Hungarian Pastry Shop** has a range of Austro-Hungarian delights and views of St. John the Divine. Located in the Hotel Edison, **Café Edison** offers reasonably priced food in an Art-Nouveau setting. **Sant' Ambroeus** is a luxurious outpost of the Milanese pasticceria selling sumptuous desserts. In addition to home delivery of pies or cakes, **Dessert Delivery** has a nifty café for tasting the pastries and coffee. Try **Serendipity 3**, famous for its Victoriana, ice cream creations, coffee, and mid-afternoon snacks. **Barnes & Noble Café** is a happy refuge for coffee and a pastry while browsing the bookstore. **Mudspot** is the new permanent set-up run by a couple who used to sell potent coffee from a bright orange van. And, like them or not, you can't ignore **Starbucks**, which has dozens of locations around town.

# DIRECTORY

## LOWER MANHATTAN

**Pastis**
9 9th Avenue.
**Map** 3 B1.

## LOWER EAST SIDE

**Caffè Ferrara**
195 Grand St. **Map** 4 F4.

**Katz's Deli**
205 E Houston St.
**Map** 5 A3.

**Saint's Alp**
51 Mott St. **Map** 4 F4.

**Seaport Café**
89 South St.
**Map** 2 E2.

## SOHO AND TRIBECA

**Jerry's**
101 Prince St. **Map** 4 D3.

**Mezzogiorno**
195 Spring St.
**Map** 4 D4.

**Moondance Diner**
80 6th Ave. **Map** 4 D4.

**Odeon**
145 W Broadway.
**Map** 1 B1.

**Raoul's**
180 Prince St. **Map** 4 D3.

**Vesuvio Bakery**
160 Prince St. **Map** 4 D3.

## GREENWICH VILLAGE

**Arturo's Pizzeria**
106 W Houston St.
**Map** 4 E3.

**Balthazar**
80 Spring St. **Map** 4 E4.

**Chez Jacqueline**
72 MacDougal St.
**Map** 4 D2.

**Corner Bistro**
331 W 4th St. **Map** 3 C1.

**Elephant and Castle**
68 Greenwich Ave.
**Map** 3 C1.

**Florent**
69 Gansevoort St.
**Map** 3 B1.

**Joe**
141 Waverly Place.
**Map** 3 C1.

**Magnolia Bakery**
401 Bleecker St.
**Map** 3 C2.

**Sant'Ambroeus**
259 W 4th St.
**Map** 3 C1.

**Trattoria Dante**
79 MacDougal St.
**Map** 4 D3.

## EAST VILLAGE

**Little Veselka**
75 E 1st St.
**Map** 4 F3.

**Mudspot**
307 E 9th St.
**Map** 4 F1.

**Veselka**
144 2nd Ave.
**Map** 4 F1.

## GRAMERCY AND THE FLATIRON

**The Coffee Shop**
29 Union Square West
**Map** 9 A5.

**Les Halles**
411 Park Ave South
**Map** 9 A3.

## CHELSEA AND THE GARMENT DISTRICT

**Empire Diner**
210 10th Ave.
**Map** 7 C4.

## THEATER DISTRICT

**Café Edison**
Edison Hotel,
228 W 47th St.
**Map** 12 D5.

**Carnegie Delicatessen**
854 7th Ave.
**Map** 12 E4.

**Chez Josephine**
414 W 42nd St.
**Map** 7 B1.

**Stage Deli**
834 7th Ave. **Map** 12 E4.

**Victor's Café**
236 W 52nd St.
**Map** 11 B4.

## EAST SIDE MIDTOWN

**Beer Bar at Café Centro**
MetLife Building,
200 Park Ave. **Map** 9 A2.

## UPPER MIDTOWN

**Barnes & Noble Café**
Citicorp Building,
160 E 54th St.
**Map** 13 A4.

**Brasserie**
100 E 53rd St.
**Map** 13 A4.

**Burger Joint**
Le Parker Meridien Hotel,
118 W 57th St.
**Map** 12 E3.

**The Tea Box**
Takashimaya,
693 5th Ave.
**Map** 12 F2.

**Waldorf-Astoria**
301 Park Ave.
**Map** 13 A5.

## UPPER EAST SIDE

**Bistro du Nord**
1312 Madison Ave.
**Map** 17 A2.

**Carlyle**
35 E 76th St. **Map** 17 A5.

**Dessert Delivery**
350 E 55th St.
**Map** 13 B4.
*Tel* 838-5411.

**DT-UT**
1626 2nd Ave.
**Map** 17 B4.

**E.A.T.**
1064 Madison Ave.
**Map** 17 A4.

**Hotel Pierre**
2 E 61st St.
**Map** 12 F3.

**Jackson Hole**
232 E 64th St.
**Map** 13 B2.
*One of five branches.*

**John's Pizzeria**
408 E 64th St.
**Map** 13 C2.
*One of three branches.*

**Mezzaluna**
1295 3rd Ave.
**Map** 17 B5.

**Pastrami Queen**
1125 Lexington Ave.
**Map** 17 A5.

**Payard Patisserie**
1032 Lexington Ave.
**Map** 13 A1.

**Serendipity 3**
225 E 60th St.
**Map** 13 B3.

**Shake Shack**
Madison Square Park.
**Map** 8 F4.

**Stanhope**
995 5th Ave. **Map** 17 A4.

**Viand**
1011 Madison Ave.
**Map** 17 A5.
*One of four branches.*

## UPPER WEST SIDE

**Barney Greengrass**
541 Amsterdam Ave.
**Map** 15 C3.

**Big Nick's**
2175 Broadway at 77th St.
**Map** 15 C5.

**La Boite en Bois**
75 W 68th St. **Map** 11 C1.

**Sarabeth's**
423 Amsterdam Ave.
**Map** 15 C4.

**Whitney Museum**
945 Madison Ave.
**Map** 17 A5.

**Vince and Eddie's**
70 W 68th St.
**Map** 11 C1.

**Zabar's**
2245 Broadway.
**Map** 15 C2.

## MORNINGSIDE HEIGHTS AND HARLEM

**The Hungarian Pastry Shop**
Amsterdam & 109th St.
**Map** 20 E4.

## BROOKLYN

**Totonno Pizzeria**
1524 Neptune Ave.
**Map** 7 C5.

# New York Bars

New York bars play a huge role in the life and culture of the city. Many New Yorkers spend the evening in a succession of bars, because each usually offers something more than just alcohol. There may be additional inducements, like excellent food, live music, dancing, or a particularly large selection of beers. Brew pubs, which serve meals and brew beer on the premises, are a recent phenomenon. Bars suiting every taste and budget are to be found in every corner.

## RULES AND CONVENTIONS

Bars generally remain open from around 11am to midnight. Some stay open to 2 or 4am, when they must close by law. Many bars have a "happy hour" between 5pm and 7pm, when they offer twofers (two drinks for the price of one) and free snacks. Bartenders can refuse to serve anyone they consider having had too much to drink. Smoking is banned and is only allowed outside or in specially ventilated rooms.

The legal minimum drinking age is 21; if the bartender suspects you are younger, you'll be "carded," or asked for identification. Children aren't usually allowed in.

It is common to "run a tab" by giving the bartender a credit card and paying your bill just before you leave. Tipping the bartender is expected – 15 percent of the bill or about $1 per drink. Shots are not pre-measured, so if you want a bigger drink, it can help to "belly up" to the bar and tip the bartender accordingly for his or her generosity. If you sit at a table, you'll be served there and be charged more. A round of drinks can be expensive. Save money by buying a quart (95 cl) or a half gallon (190 cl) pitcher of beer.

Many bars have obtained liquor licenses under an oscure cabaret law that prohibits dancing. Bars are regularly closed down for ignoring this rule, so if staff ask you to refrain from dancing to music, they are serious and should be obeyed.

## WHAT TO DRINK

Mainstream bars serve standard beers from big producers, such as Budweiser, Coors, and Miller, as well as high-profile imports including Becks, Heineken, and draft Guinness. Old pubs and chic new bars have a much wider variety of beers, imported and small domestics. These include flavorful beers, usually based on traditional European styles, made by some of New York's microbreweries. The locally brewed Brooklyn Lager is highly rated.

Other popular drinks include "designer" cocktails, rum and coke, vodka-and-tonic, gin-and-tonic, dry Martinis, and Scotch or bourbon – either "straight up" (without ice) or "on the rocks" (with ice). The "Cosmopolitan" is very New York: vodka, cranberry juice, triple sec, and lime. Most of the bars serve a range of Martinis made with vodka.

Wine is widely available at bars, and the "wine bar" concept is making a comeback with options all over the city.

## FOOD

Some bars serve food such as burgers, fries, salads, sandwiches, and spicy chicken wings throughout the day. If you are visiting the bar of a popular restaurant, you can often order bar snacks. Most bar kitchens stop serving food just before midnight.

## FASHIONABLE BARS

To get into a hip bar, you will need to look glamorous and be prepared to wait in line, unless you arrive early. Designer Robert McKinley has created a breathtaking space with high, vaulted ceilings and skylights at **PM Lounge**. The cocktails are Haitian-inspired. Within stumbling distance is **Buddha Bar NYC**, a spinoff of the Paris original. The enormous restaurant has a bar that draws a hip crowd. The only serene elements are the massive Buddha and the jellyfish-stocked aquariums. Also incorporating a giant Buddha is **Tao Bar**, located in a former theater next to the Four Seasons Hotel. The venue is spread over three floors: the top two are devoted to pan-Asian cuisine and overlook the bar below.

Despite the throng of East Village hipsters, the Australian-themed **Sunburnt Cow** has an unpretentious air. Chill out on the garden porch with an Aussie beer, a glass of wine, or a "Mootini." Formerly the Bowery Bar, the **B-Bar** still attracts a stylish crowd, though some claim its glory days are over. In the summer, the enormous outdoor space can't be beaten. **Pravda** is another favorite in nearby NoLIta. Subdued lighting creates a degree of calm in this subterranean spot decorated in Soviet chic. **The Odeon** on Broadway captures the lively SoHo-TriBeCa scene.

## BARS WITH VIEWS

The Art Deco **Beekman Tower** on the 26th floor offers unsurpassed views of the city and great piano music. Also spectacular are **Pentop Bar and Terrace** at the Peninsula Hotel, **Stone Rose Lounge** in the Time Warner Center, and **Rise** at the Ritz-Carlton in Battery Park. In warm weather, **BP Café** is a popular midtown scene. Though glitzy inside, **Tavern on the Green** has magical views of Central Park.

## HISTORIC AND LITERARY BARS

If you sample only one New York bar, it should probably be **McSorley's Old Ale House**, an Irish saloon often dubbed "McSurly's" because of its

staff. It opened in 1854, and is one of the city's oldest bars.

**The Ear Inn** dates from 1812 when the first tavern opened on this SoHo site. Now the haunt of poets and writers, its cramped interior and long wooden bar ooze authenticity.

Greenwich Village has some of the city's oldest bars, such as **Chumley's**, which retains its character as a Prohibition-era speakeasy. It's particularly snug in winter, when an open fire burns in the hearth.

Dylan Thomas's old favorite, the **White Horse Tavern**, is an unpretentious 1880s-landmark, still crowded with literary and collegiate types. It also has an outdoor café for warm weather.

**Peculier Pub** is a beer-lover's paradise, with over 360 varieties of beer from all over the world. A good, though rather touristy, place for a drink in the financial district is **Fraunces Tavern**, first built in 1719 *(see p76)*.

**Pete's Tavern** in the Gramercy Park area dates to 1864. Busy until 2am, it is known for Victoriana and the house brew called Pete's Ale. The typical Irish pub **Old Town Bar** has been serving stout since 1892, and is now favored largely by advertising types. No longer the celebrity scene it once was, **Sardi's** still appeals to *New York Times* reporters, and serves generous portions.

Hidden away in the balcony of Grand Central Terminal is **The Campbell Apartment**, the former private office of 1920s tycoon John W. Campbell. The spectacular space resembles a 13th-century Florentine palace. On the Upper East Side, the bar at **Swifty's** is a place to observe high-society trends without paying steep prices for the ordinary food.

A bustling saloon with Irish bartenders, **P. J. Clarke's** has been New York's favorite since the 1890s. **Elaine's**, also on the East Side, remains a haunt of mainly visiting literary types, though the food is so-so.

Near Carnegie Hall is the unobtrusive **P. J. Carney's**, a watering hole for musicians and artists since 1927. It serves Irish ales and a good shepherd's pie.

## YOUNG HANGOUTS

Brew pubs, where the house beer is brewed on the premises, are currently the rage with the 20- and 30-somethings, as are bars that stock a variety of micro-brews and imported beers. The **Chelsea Brewing Company** is a large, fun-filled brew pub in the Chelsea Piers sports complex. In the Gramercy neighborhood, you will find the **Heartland Brewery**, the busiest and, according to some, the best of the new brew pubs, with five beers, including the outstanding India Pale Ale, and many seasonals, such as cranberry and pumpkin ales.

The **Westside Brewing Company** uptown is a favorite youth and neighborhood hangout, popular for its house ales and fruit beers.

Serious beer drinkers will enjoy the 170 draft and bottled Belgian beers on offer at **Burp Castle**, while homesick Brits will likely head to **Manchester**. In a cozy, publike setting, you'll find Watneys or Newcastle Brown Ale on tap, just two of the 18 draft beers, and 40 bottled ones not widely available in New York.

In the East Village is bustling **d.b.a.**, which has 14 draft beers on tap, along with scores of microbrews and 50 single-malt whiskeys to choose from.

A popular beer stop uptown for the college-age crowd is the loud and noisy **Brother Jimmy's BBQ**, where you can snack on old-fashioned southern barbequed ribs.

**Park Slope Ale House** in Brooklyn is another brew pub favored by the young for its home brews and seasonal beers, as well as its decent pub grub and lively ambience.

## GAY AND LESBIAN BARS

Gay bars can be found in Greenwich Village, Chelsea, and the East Village with a few on the Upper East and West Sides. Lesbian bars are mostly in Greenwich Village and East Village. For current listings, check the free weekly gay publications *HX* (www.hx.com) and *Next*.

## HOTEL BARS

Centrally located, the **Algonquin Hotel** *(see p145)* was a famous literary haunt in the 1920s and early 1930s. Its Lobby Bar and Blue Bar are good places for a quiet pre-dinner or pre-theater drink.

The minimalist bar in the lobby lounge of the **Royalton Hotel** is a perfect spot for a drink while watching the theatrical crowds drifting in and out. Also in the Theater District, the **Whiskey Bar** has floor-to-ceiling windows and is usually frequented by fashion and theater types. In Upper Midtown there's the **Villard Bar & Lounge**, where you can recline on soft, plush red velvet seats.

The **Bull and Bear** in the Waldorf-Astoria, dating back to the Prohibition era, exudes comfort, charm, and a sense of history. There are many exotic drinks and Bull and Bear ale on tap.

The stylish **King Cole Room** at St. Regis Hotel is named after a colorful mural behind the bar, by Maxfield Parrish.

Relax to downtempo tunes at the **Grand Bar**. One of New York's trendiest nightspots, the Soho Grand's bar is a good place to people-spot. Its sister hotel, the Tribeca Grand, also draws a crowd to its **Church Lounge**.

With dark-wood panels, navy-blue color scheme, and a kitschy seafaring theme, the Maritime Hotel's **Lobby Bar** draws a young, trendy crowd. Special attractions include a roaring fire in winter and an outdoor terrace in summer.

The glass-floored **Hudson Bar** at Ian Schrager's trendy Hudson Hotel is a regular hotspot. Now that Schrager has refurbished the Gramercy Park Hotel, expect the **Rose** and **Jade** bars to be filled with fashionistas drinking in the "eclectic-Bohemian" vibe. Equally popular are **Thom Bar** at the 60 Thompson Hotel and **Bookmarks** at the Library Hotel; both attract a sophisticated scene. For those interested in joining the *Sex in the City* crowd, there's Rande Gerber's **Whiskey Blue Bar** in one of the boutique W Hotels.

# DIRECTORY

## LOWER MANHATTAN

**Fraunces Tavern**
54 Pearl St.
**Map** 1 C4.

**Rise**
2 W St. **Map** 1 B4.

## SOHO AND TRIBECA

**Church Lounge**
Tribeca Grand,
2 6th Ave.
**Map** 4 D4.

**The Ear Inn**
326 Spring St.
**Map** 3 C4.

**The Grand Bar**
Soho Grand,
310 W Broadway.
**Map** 4 E4.

**The Odeon**
145 W Broadway.
**Map** 1 B1.

**Pravda**
281 Lafayette St.
**Map** 4 F3.

**Thom Bar**
60 Thompson Hotel,
60 Thompson
**Map** 4 D4.

## GREENWICH VILLAGE

**Buddha Bar NYC**
25 Little W 12th St.
**Map** 3 B1.

**Chumley's**
86 Bedford St.
**Map** 3 C2.

**Peculier Pub**
145 Bleecker St.
**Map** 4 D3.

**PM Lounge**
50 Gansevoort St.
**Map** 3 B1.

**White Horse Tavern**
567 Hudson St.
**Map** 3 C1.

## EAST VILLAGE

**B-Bar**
40 E 4th St. **Map** 4 F2.

**Burp Castle**
41 E 7th St. **Map** 4 F2.

**d.b.a.**
41 1st Ave. **Map** 5 A1.

**McSorley's Old Ale House**
15 E 7th St. **Map** 4 F2.

**Sunburnt Cow**
137 Avenue C.
**Map** 5 C1.

## GRAMERCY

**Heartland Brewery**
35 Union Square W.
**Map** 9 A5.

**Jade Bar**
Gramercy Park Hotel,
2 Lexington Ave.
**Map** 9 A4.

**Old Town Bar**
45 E 18th St.
**Map** 8 F5.

**Pete's Tavern**
129 E 18th St.
**Map** 9 A5.

**Rose Bar**
Gramercy Park Hotel,
2 Lexington Ave.
**Map** 9 A4.

## CHELSEA AND THE GARMENT DISTRICT

**Chelsea Brewing Company**
Pier 59, 11th Ave.
**Map** 7 B5.

**Lobby Bar**
Maritime Hotel,
363 W 16th St.
**Map** 8 D5.

## THEATER DISTRICT

**BP Café**
Bryant Park.
**Map** 8 F1.

**Hudson Bar**
Hudson Hotel,
356 W 58th St.
**Map** 12 D3.

**P. J. Carney's**
906 7th Ave.
**Map** 12 E3.

**Royalton Hotel**
44 W 44th St.
**Map** 12 F5.

**Sardi's**
234 W 44th St.
**Map** 12 F5.

**Whiskey Bar**
Paramount Hotel,
235 W 46th St.
**Map** 12 E5.

## LOWER MIDTOWN

**Bookmarks**
The Library Hotel,
299 Madison Ave.
**Map** 9 A1.

**The Campbell Apartment**
Grand Central Terminal,
15 Vanderbilt Ave.
**Map** 9 A1.

## UPPER MIDTOWN

**Bar and Books**
889 1st Ave.
**Map** 13 C2.

**Beekman Tower**
3 Mitchell Place.
**Map** 13 C5.

**Bull and Bear**
Ground floor,
Waldorf-Astoria Hotel,
Lexington Ave at
E 49th St.
**Map** 13 A5.

**King Cole Room**
St. Regis Hotel,
2 E 55th St.
**Map** 12 F5.

**Manchester**
920 2nd Ave.
**Map** 13 B5.

**Pentop Bar and Terrace**
Peninsula Hotel,
700 5th Ave. **Map** 12 F5.

**P. J. Clarke's**
915 3rd Ave.
**Map** 13 B4.

**Stone Rose Lounge**
10 Columbus Circle,
4th Floor. **Map** 12 D3.

**Tao Bar**
42 E 58th St. **Map** 13 A3.

**Villard Bar & Lounge**
New York Palace Hotel,
455 Madison Ave.
**Map** 13 A4.

## UPPER EAST SIDE

**Brother Jimmy's BBQ**
1485 2nd Ave.
**Map** 17 B5.

**Elaine's**
1703 2nd Ave.
**Map** 17 B4.

**Swifty's**
1007 Lexington Ave.
**Map** 17 A5.

## UPPER WEST SIDE

**Tavern on the Green**
Central Park, W 67th St.
**Map** 12 D2.

**Westside Brewing Company**
340 Amsterdam Ave.
**Map** 15 C2.

## BROOKLYN

**Park Slope Ale House**
356 6th Ave at 5th St.

# SHOPPING

Tiffany's clock

Visitors to New York will inevitably include shopping in their action plan. The city is the consumer capital of the world: a shopper's paradise and a constant source of entertainment, with dazzling window displays and a staggering variety of goods for sale. Everything is found here, from high fashion to rare children's books, state-of-the-art electronics and a mouthwatering array of exotic food. Whether you are looking for a personal Hovercraft, read-in-the-dark eyeglass attachments, a designer bed for your pet gerbil or a Wurlitzer jukebox, this is the city of your dreams. Whether you have $50,000 or $5, New York is the place to spend it.

## BEST BUYS

New York is a bargain hunter's dream, with huge discounts on anything from household goods to designer clothes. Some of the best shops are on Orchard Street and Grand Street on the Lower East Side, where designer goods are sold at 20–50 percent below

The 1920s-style Henri Bendel store *(see p319)*

the retail price. You can find just about every imaginable item of clothing here, in addition to tableware, shoes, home furnishings, and electronics. Shops in this area are closed on Saturday – the Jewish Sabbath – but are usually open all day Sunday.

Another great area for fashion bargain hunters is the Garment District, roughly between Sixth and Eighth avenues from 30th to 40th Street. The main hub, Seventh Avenue, was renamed Fashion Avenue in the early 1970s. Several designers and manufacturers have showrooms here, some of which are open to the public. Many of their samples are put up for sales, announced on notices posted around the area. The best

time to visit them is just before one of the major gift-giving holidays. Top Button (www.topbutton.com) has comprehensive sales listings.

## SALES

One word you'll come across all over the city, anytime of the year, is "sale." So check the sale goods before you pay full price for any purchase. The best sales are during New York's sale seasons, which run from mid-June until end-July and from December 26 until February. Look up the local papers for ads. Along midtown Fifth Avenue you'll see signs announcing "Lost Our Lease" sales. Avoid them, as these signs have been up for years at many shops. Also keep your eyes peeled for "Sample Sales," where the top designers sell to the public the sample outfits they have created to show store buyers. Sample sales occur at different locations throughout the city, and are generally not advertised, so your best bet is to keep a lookout for signs announcing sample sales, particularly on Fifth Avenue and on Broadway.

The Bulgari entrance at Hotel Pierre *(see p290)*

## HOW TO PAY

Most shops accept major credit cards, although there will often be a minimum purchase price. If you want to use your traveler's checks, identification is needed. Personal checks drawn in another currency will be refused. Some stores only take cash, especially during sales.

## OPENING HOURS

Most shops are open from 10am to 6pm, Monday to Saturday. Many department stores are open through Sunday and until 9pm, at least two nights a week. Lunch hours (noon to 2:30pm), Saturday mornings, sales, and holidays are the most crowded times.

Designer dress at a New York sale

## TAXES

The New York City sales tax is 8.625 percent, although clothing and shoes under $110 are exempt. However, sales tax will be waived if the goods are shipped home.

## SHOPPING TOURS

If you dread braving the stores alone, shopping tours are a good option. Apart from the main department stores, you could visit private designer showrooms, auction houses, and fashion shows. Some operators will customize tours to suit your requirements.

## DEPARTMENT STORES AND MALLS

Most of the large department stores are in midtown Manhattan. Explore at leisure the

Window displays at Bloomingdale's *(see p181)*

ones you are interested in, since all these stores tend to be enormous, with a great range of goods. If possible, avoid weekends and vacation times when the crowds can be overwhelming. Prices are often high, but you may find some bargains during sales.

Stores such as Saks Fifth Avenue, Bloomingdale's, and Macy's provide a diverse and extraordinary range of shopping services, including actually shopping for you.

One of the biggest malls to open in Manhattan is the **Shops at Columbus Circle** in the Time Warner Center. Its stores include Williams-Sonoma, Coach, and men's clothier Hugo Boss. **Barney's New York**, favored by young professionals, specializes in excellent, though

expensive, designer clothes.

Luxurious, elegant, and understated, **Bergdorf Goodman** sells contemporary clothes by European designers at high prices. The men's store is across the street.

A visit to New York isn't complete without **Bloomingdale's** *(see p181)*, the Hollywood film star of the department stores, with many eye-catching displays and seductive goods. Its ambience is that of a luxurious wonderland, filled with young and old New Yorkers seeking out the newest in fashion. The linen and fine china departments have an undisputed reputation for quality. Check out the gourmet food section, which features a shop devoted entirely to caviar.

Extensive shopping services and amenities include a noted restaurant, Le Train Bleu, with its view of the Queensboro Bridge. There is also a SoHo branch of Bloomingdale's on Broadway. Though much smaller than the main store, it stocks a similar selection of luxury goods.

At the exclusive **Henri Bendel's**, everything from the Art Deco jewels to beautiful handmade shoes, is displayed as a priceless work of art. The store, laid out in a series of 1920s-style boutiques, sells an excellent range of innovative women's fashions.

**Lord & Taylor** is renowned for its classic and much more conservative fashions for men and women, with an emphasis on US designers. You'll need comfortable shoes and plenty of time for browsing.

**Macy's**, the self-proclaimed largest store in the world *(see p134–5)*, has ten floors selling everything imaginable from can openers to antiques.

A magnificent display offering household goods

**Saks Fifth Avenue**, known for style and elegance, has long been considered one of the city's best department stores, with service to match. It sells stunning designerwear for adults as well as children.

## ADDRESSES

**Barney's New York**
660 Madison Ave. **Map** 13 A3.
*Tel (212) 826-8900.*

**Bergdorf Goodman**
754 5th Ave. **Map** 12 F3.
*Tel (212) 753-7300.*

**Bloomingdale's**
1000 3rd Ave. **Map** 13 A3.
*Tel (212) 705-2000.*

**Bloomingdale's SoHo**
504 Broadway. **Map** 4 E4.
*Tel (212) 729-5900.*

**Convention Tours Unlimited**
*Tel (212) 545-1160.*

**Doorway to Design**
*Tel (212) 229-0299.*

**Guide Service of New York**
*Tel (212) 408-3332.*

**Henri Bendel**
712 5th Ave. **Map** 12 F4.
*Tel (212) 247-1100.*

**Lord & Taylor**
424 5th Ave. **Map** 8 F1.
*Tel (212) 391-3344.*

**Macy's**
151 W 34th St. **Map** 8 E2.
*Tel (212) 695-4400.*

**Saks Fifth Avenue**
611 5th Ave. **Map** 12 F4.
*Tel (212) 753-4000.*

**Shop Gotham**
*Tel (866) 795-4200.*

**Shops at Columbus Circle**
Time Warner Center. **Map** 12 D3.
*Tel (212) 823-6300.*

# New York's Best: Shopping

Designer shoes from
Madison Avenue

In a city where you can literally shop 24 hours a day, the best plan is to shop the way New Yorkers do, by neighborhood.
Each has its own character and specialties. Here are highlights of the best shopping districts – where they are and what you will find in each. If time is very tight, head for one of the huge department stores *(see p319)*, or if window shopping is your preference, stroll along Fifth Avenue, home to Manhattan's most glittering stores *(see opposite)*. For great bargains in a truly ethnic area, try the Lower East Side.

**Greenwich Village and the Meatpacking District**
*Quaint, eclectic, and antique choices in the Village, and gourmands will enjoy the myriad speciality food stores. Meander over to Meatpacking District for high fashion shopping (see pp112–3).*

**SoHo**
*The area bordered by Sixth Avenue, Lafayette, Houston, and Canal streets is bustling with antiques, crafts, and clothes from designer flagships. Weekend brunchtime gallery-hopping is very popular. Cross Broadway to NoLita for even trendier, cutting-edge fashion (see pp104–5).*

**East Village and Lower East Side**
*Explore around St Mark's Place for shoes, avant-garde fashions, and ethnic goods (see pp118–9). Bargains are becoming harder to find in the Lower East Side, but trendy options are increasing (see pp94–5).*

**South Street Seaport**
*This is a browser's paradise of crafts, gifts, toys, souvenirs, antiquarian and new books, and antiques with a seafaring connection (see pp82–3).*

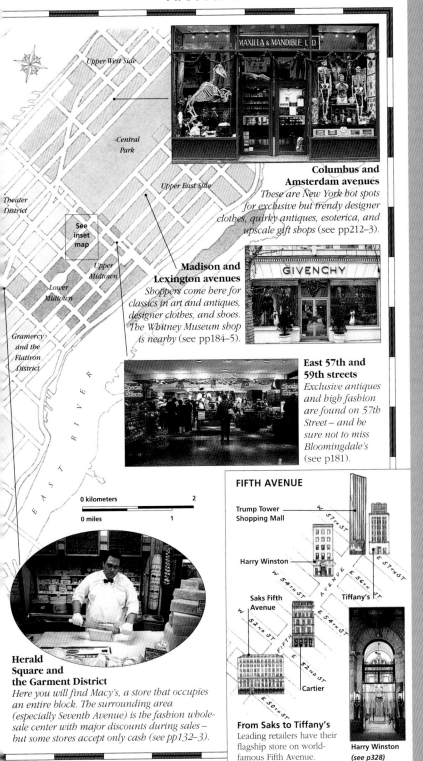

## Columbus and Amsterdam avenues
*These are New York hot spots for exclusive but trendy designer clothes, quirky antiques, esoterica, and upscale gift shops (see pp212–3).*

## Madison and Lexington avenues
*Shoppers come here for classics in art and antiques, designer clothes, and shoes. The Whitney Museum shop is nearby (see pp184–5).*

## East 57th and 59th streets
*Exclusive antiques and high fashion are found on 57th Street – and be sure not to miss Bloomingdale's (see p181).*

## Herald Square and the Garment District
*Here you will find Macy's, a store that occupies an entire block. The surrounding area (especially Seventh Avenue) is the fashion wholesale center with major discounts during sales – but some stores accept only cash (see pp132–3).*

**FIFTH AVENUE**

Trump Tower Shopping Mall

Harry Winston

Saks Fifth Avenue

Tiffany's

Cartier

### From Saks to Tiffany's
Leading retailers have their flagship store on world-famous Fifth Avenue.

**Harry Winston**
*(see p328)*

# New York Originals

New York is a city where just about any kind of shop, no matter how esoteric, will always attract customers. Dozens of tiny shops scattered around the city specialize in unusual merchandise, from butterflies and bones to traditional Tibetan treasures and Shamrock sprigs from Ireland. Coming across these in some tucked-away corner is what makes shopping in New York such an entertaining and invigorating experience.

## SPECIALTY SHOPS

For beautiful brass, onyx, and pewter chess sets, and the opportunity to play a decent game, make a move to the **Chess Shop**. For every type of pen **Arthur Brown & Bros.** stocks an enormous range, including such names as Mont Blanc and Schaeffer. For those with a bit more energy, **Blades Board & Skate** sells and rents out skates and also the trendiest skateboards plus all the safety equipment.

If you're looking for different or unusual buttons, a visit to **Tender Buttons**, which stocks millions, is a must. Whether you want enamel, wood, or Navajo silver buttons – or perhaps want your own buttons made into cuff links or earrings – here you'll find just what you want – and more. **Trash & Vaudeville** has been supplying punk and goth gear to New Yorkers for decades and is the HQ of Astor Place fashion.

**Leo Kaplan Ltd.** is the place to go if you are a keen collector of paperweights, while **Rita Ford's Music Boxes**, a 19th-century style shop, stocks a tuneful and extensive range of music boxes.

The **New York Firefighter's Friend** sells an intriguing range of items related to fire-fighting, including toy fire engines, firemen's jackets, badges, stuffed toy dalmatians and a wide selection of T-shirts, including a popular one with FDNY (Fire Department New York) on one side and "Keep back 200 feet" on the other.

Spies and conspiracy theorists will be enthralled with the extensive offering at **Quark Spy**, where you can simple choose from survival kits and camera pens up to audio intelligence rooms.

For the true romantic who wants to impress, everything sold by **Only Hearts** is heart-shaped, including pillows, soap, and jewelry. If you are artistic, or if you wish to buy a present for someone who is, visit the **Pearl Paint Co.**, which stocks everything you could need. Step straight into the space age at **Star Magic** to buy celestial maps, holograms, prisms, and scientific toys. **Forbidden Planet** is a science fiction megastore with everything from comics to models for the true fan.

Cologne made especially for George Washington and the official soap of the White House during the Eisenhower era are just some of the many fascinating items for sale at **Caswell-Massey Ltd.**, the oldest pharmacy in the city.

Guitar gurus will want to visit **Rudy's**, **Manny's**, or Sam Ash's guitar shop. Not only is there a chance you'll bump into Eric Clapton or Lou Reed – both have their guitars made in this area – but you'll find the widest and best choice of instruments in the city.

Bibliophiles will find a range of gifts in both the **New York Public Library Shop** (see p146) (such as bookends of the lions guarding the main entrance) and the **Morgan Library Shop** (see pp164–5), including bookmarks and writing paper.

University logos and college colors dominate the many knickknacks and accessories at **The Yale Club** gift shop and **The Princeton Club**.

**Weisburg Religious Articles** carries one of the largest selections of Jewish religious items in the city.

**The Cathedral Shop** at the Cathedral of St. John the Divine on Amsterdam Avenue is a large store selling books, artworks, herbs, jewelry, and religious items made locally.

## MEMORABILIA

At Lincoln Center, the **Metropolitan Opera Shop** has records, cards, librettos, small binoculars, and many other opera-related items. The **Performing Arts Shop** downstairs is a real treasure trove of theater, opera, ballet, and music memorabilia. For theater fans, everything from scripts and vocal scores to CDs can be found at **One Shubert Alley**. For thousands of rare and classic film stills and posters visit **Jerry Ohlinger's Movie Material Store** on 242 W 14th Street.

The **Carnegie Hall Shop** carries musically themed cards, T-shirts, games, posters, tote bags, and much more. For something truly original and very American, be sure to visit **Lost City Arts** and **Urban Archaeology** in SoHo. Between these two shops, you'll unearth all sorts of relics from America's past, from Barbie Doll lunch boxes to furniture from traditional ice-cream parlors.

## TOYS, GAMES, AND GADGETS

For children's gifts, don't miss the legendary **F.A.O. Schwarz**. This is a massive store crammed from floor to ceiling with luxury toy cars, enormous stuffed animals and every kind of electronic toy imaginable. There are shoulder-to-shoulder crowds at Christmas, when you might have to line up to get in.

The **Children's General Store** is one of the city's newest and cleverest – children's toy stores.

**Penny Whistle Toys** sells a huge selection of quality toys, games, and all kinds of dolls. **Red Caboose** is for fans of model railways. On three floors, the **Toys 'R' Us** flagship glass building on Broadway is the largest toy store in the world, with a 60-ft (20-m) ferris wheel.

**Dinosaur Hill** on Second Avenue offers handmade puppets and toys, mobiles, and beautifully made children's clothes. It's expensive but worth it. Since 1848, **Hammacher Schlemmer** have been encouraging shoppers to buy gadgets for home, office, and recreation that they didn't know they wanted. **The Sharper Image** has a similar philosophy – be careful or you may find yourself shipping home a massage chair.

## MUSEUM SHOPS

Some of New York's best souvenirs can be found in the city's many museum shops. In addition to the usual range of books, posters, and cards, there are reproductions of the exhibits on display, including jewelry and sculpture. The **Museum of Arts & Design** (see p149) has an excellent selection of American crafts as well as original works for sale. In addition to realistic model dinosaurs, rubber animals, minerals, and rocks, the **American Museum of Natural History** (see pp216–17) has a variety of recycled products

and earth-awareness gifts, which include posters, bags, and T-shirts with environmental messages, and a large selection of Native American handicrafts. There is also a kids' shop with reasonably priced items such as shell sets, magnets, and toys.

The **Asia Society Bookstore and Gift Shop** (see p187) has a striking selection of Oriental prints, posters, art books, toys, and jewelry. Items related to interior design are offered at the **Cooper-Hewitt** (see p186). One of New York's largest collections of Jewish ceremonial objects, including menorahs and Kiddush cups, books, and jewelry, is found in the small shop at the **Jewish Museum** (see p186).

For reproduction prints of famous paintings and other exquisite gifts a visit to the **Metropolitan Museum of Art** (see pp190–97) gift shop is a must. There is also an enormous book department and a children's gift shop. The traditional **American Folk Art Museum** (see p171) prides itself on its American country crafts, including wooden toys, quilts, and weathervanes, which are

mostly original. Works by craftspeople who currently have pieces on display in the museum are also sold.

The **Museum of the City of New York** (see p199), specializes in pictures of old New York. The **Museum of Modern Art/MOMA Design Store** (see pp172–75) has a highly praised selection of innovative home furnishings, toys and kitchenware inspired by international designers such as Frank Lloyd Wright and Le Corbusier. The store will remain open during the reconstruction.

For a selection of nautical items, including charts, maps, model ships, and scrimshaw, go to the **South Street Seaport Museum Shops** (see pp82–85). The **Whitney Museum's Shop** (see pp200–201) stocks American-made items, including jewelry, wooden toys, books, and posters complementing current exhibitions. The **Museum of Jewish Heritage** (see p77) has a gift shop with an unusual array of gifts, souvenirs, and educational material about Jewish life. Open to ticketed visitors only.

## THE BEST OF THE IMPORTS

New York is a massive melting pot of different nationalities, cultures, and ethnic groups, all of which have made their mark on its diverse culture in one way or another. Many ethnic shops specialize in food or goods of a particular group. Some of the most interesting and unusual shops include **Alaska on Madison**, which has a huge collection of Eskimo art, and the **Chinese Porcelain Company,** for exquisite Chinese decorative arts and furniture. **Pearl River Mart** has been a staple for Asian goods for thirty years, and **Himalayan Crafts and Tours** stocks everything from paintings to Tibetan rugs. **Sweet Life**, on the Lower East Side, is a tiny but charming

old-fashioned candy shop with delicacies from around the world. **Things Japanese** has beautifully made crafts and unusual books. **Surma** is a Ukrainian general store that sells hand painted eggs and linens. **Common Ground** sells Native American arts, and **Astro Gems** has a large collection of jewelry and mineral specimens from Africa and Asia. Nearby, Chinatown is packed with stalls and shops selling everything from eclectic souvenirs to leather goods, all at wonderfully low prices.

### ADDRESSES

**Alaska on Madison**
937 Madison Ave. **Map** 17 A1.
*Tel* (212) 879-1782.

**Astro Gems**
185 Madison Ave. **Map** 9 A2.
*Tel* (212) 889-9000.

**Chinese Porcelain Company**
475 Park Ave. **Map** 13 A3.
*Tel* (212) 838-7744.

**Common Ground**
55 W 16th St. **Map** 8 F5.
*Tel* (212) 989-4178.

**Himalayan Crafts and Tours**
2007 Broadway. **Map** 11 C1.
*Tel* (212) 787-8500.

**Pearl River Mart**
477 Broadway. **Map** 4 E4.
*Tel* (212) 431-4770.

**Sweet Life**
63 Hester St. **Map** 5 B4.
*Tel* (212) 598-0092.

**Surma**
11 E 7th St. **Map** 4 F2.
*Tel* (212) 477-0729.

**Things Japanese**
127 E 60th St. **Map** 13 A3.
*Tel* (212) 371-4661.

# DIRECTORY

## SPECIALTY SHOPS

**Arthur Brown & Bros.**
2 W 46th St. **Map** 12 F5.
*Tel (212) 575-5555.*

**Blades Board & Skate**
120 W 72nd St.
**Map** 12 D1.
*Tel (888) 552-5233.*
*One of several branches.*

**Caswell-Massey Ltd.**
518 Lexington Ave.
**Map** 13 A5.
*Tel (212) 755-2254.*

**The Cathedral Shop**
Cathedral of St. John the
Divine, 1047 Amsterdam
Ave. **Map** 20 E4.
*Tel (212) 222-7200.*

**Leo Kaplan Ltd.**
114 E 57th St.
**Map** B A3.
*Tel (212) 355-7122.*

**Morgan Library Shop**
Madison Ave at 36th St.
**Map** 9 A2.
*Tel (212) 685-0610.*

**New York Firefighter's Friend**
263 Lafayette St.
**Map** 4 F3.
*Tel (212) 226-3142.*

**New York Public Library Shop**
5th Ave at 42nd St.
**Map** 8 F1.
*Tel (212) 930-0869.*

**Only Hearts**
386 Columbus Ave.
**Map** 15 D5.
*Tel (212) 724-5608.*

**Pearl Paint Co**
308 Canal St. **Map** 4 E5.
*Tel (212) 431-7932.*

**The Princeton Club**
15 W 43rd St. **Map** 8 F1.
*Tel (212) 596-1200.*

**Quark Spy**
240 E 29th St. **Map** 9 B3.
*Tel (212) 683-9100.*

**Rita Ford's Music Boxes**
19 E 65th St. **Map** 12 F2.
*Tel (212) 535-6717.*

**Rudy's**
169 W 48th St.
**Map** 12 E5.
*Tel (212) 391-1699.*

**Star Magic**
745 Broadway. **Map** 4 E2.
*Tel (212) 228-7770.*

**Tender Buttons**
143 E 62nd St.
**Map** 13 A2.
*Tel (212) 758-7004.*

**The Chess Shop**
230 Thompson St.
**Map** 4 D3.
*Tel (212) 475-9580.*

**Trash & Vaudeville**
4 St. Mark's Pl.
**Map** 5 A4.
*Tel (212) 982-3590.*

**Weisburg Religious Articles**
45 Essex St. **Map** 5 B4.
*Tel (212) 674-1770.*

**The Yale Club**
50 Vanderbilt Ave.
**Map** 13 A5.
*Tel (212) 661-2070.*

## MEMORABILIA

**One Shubert Alley**
1 Shubert Alley.
**Map** 12 E5.
*Tel (212) 944-4133.*

**The Carnegie Hall Shop**
881 7th Ave. **Map** 12 E3.
*Tel (212) 903-9610.*

**Forbidden Planet**
840 Broadway.
**Map** 4 E1.
*Tel (212) 473-1576.*

**Jerry Ohlinger's Movie Material Store**
253 W 35th St.
**Map** 8 D2.
*Tel (212) 989-0869.*

**Lost City Arts**
18 Cooper Square.
**Map** 4 F2.
*Tel (212) 375-0500.*

**Metropolitan Opera Shop**
Metropolitan Opera
House, Lincoln Center, 136
W 65th St. **Map** 11 C2.
*Tel (212) 580-4090.*

**Performing Arts Shop**
Metropolitan Opera
House, Lincoln Center, 136
W 65th St. **Map** 11 C2.
*Tel (917) 441-1195.*

**Urban Archaeology**
143 Franklin St.
**Map** 4 D5.
*Tel (212) 431-4646.*

## TOYS, GAMES, AND GADGETS

**The Children's General Store**
Grand Central Station.
**Map** 9 A1.
*Tel (212) 682-0004.*

**Dinosaur Hill**
306 E 9th St, 2nd Ave.
**Map** 4 F1.
*Tel (212) 473-5850.*

**F.A.O. Schwarz**
767 5th Ave. **Map** 12 F3.
*Tel (212) 644-9400.*

**Hammacher Schlemmer**
147 E 57th St.
**Map** 13 A3.
*Tel (212) 421-9000.*
*One of two branches.*

**Penny Whistle Toys**
448 Columbus Ave.
**Map** 16 D4.
*Tel (212) 873-9090*
*One of several branches.*

**Red Caboose**
23 W 45th St.
**Map** 12 F5.
*Tel (212) 575-0155.*

**The Sharper Image**
98 Greene St. **Map** 4 E4.
*Tel (917) 237-0221.*
*One of several branches.*

**Toys 'R' Us**
1514 Broadway,
Times Square. **Map** 8 E2.
*Tel (646) 366-8800.*

## MUSEUM SHOPS

**Museum of Arts & Design**
40 W 53rd St. **Map** 12
F4. *Tel (212) 956-3535.*

**American Folk Art Museum**
45 W 53rd St. **Map** 12 F4.
*Tel (212) 265-1040.*

**American Museum of Natural History**
W 79th St at Central Park
W. **Map** 16 D5.
*Tel (212) 769-5100.*

**Asia Society Bookstore and Gift Shop**
725 Park Ave.
**Map** 13 A1.
*Tel (212) 288-6400.*

**Cooper-Hewitt**
2 E 91st St. **Map** 16 F2.
*Tel (212) 849-8400.*

**Jewish Museum**
1109 5th Ave.
**Map** 16 F2.
*Tel (212) 423-3200.*

**Metropolitan Museum of Art**
5th Ave at 82nd St.
**Map** 16 F4.
*Tel (212) 535-7710.*

**Museum of the City of New York**
5th Ave at 103rd St.
**Map** 21 C5.
*Tel (212) 534-1672.*

**Museum of Jewish Heritage**
18 1st Place, Battery Park
City. **Map** 1 B4.
*Tel (646) 437-4200.*

**Museum of Modern Art/MOMA Design Store**
44 W 53rd St.
**Map** 12 F4.
*Tel (212) 767-1050.*

**South St. Seaport Museum Shops**
12 Fulton St.
**Map** 2 D2.
*Tel (212) 748-8600.*

**The Whitney Museum's Store Next Door**
943 Madison Ave.
**Map** 13 A1.
*Tel (212) 570-3676.*

# Fashion

Whether you're looking for a secondhand pair of 501s or the kind of ballgown Ivana Trump would be proud to wear, you're sure to find it in New York. The city is the fashion capital of America and an important center of clothing manufacture and design. New York's clothing stores, like its restaurants, reflect the city's dramatically different styles and cultures. To save time it's probably best to visit one area at a time and wander from store to store. Alternatively, visit one of the major department stores for an excellent selection of fashion for everyone.

## AMERICAN DESIGNERS

Many American designers sell their creations in boutiques within the large department stores, or have exclusive shops of their own. One of the most famous is Geoffrey Beene, known for sophisticated looks that are casual and comfortable.

Bill Blass is the king of American fashion whose clothes feature loads of different colors, wild patterns, innovative shapes, and a lot of wit. Liz Claiborne's designs are always elegantly simple, casual, and reasonably priced, including everything you could possibly need from tennis whites to casual professional wear for women.

Marc Jacobs, known for his sportswear, has his own label and store in Greenwich Village. James Galanos is an exclusive designer for the rich and famous, making one-of-a-kind *couture* clothes, and Betsey Johnson is popular with women able to wear figure-hugging fashions in fabulous fabrics.

In the last decade, Donna Karan has become a name that appears everywhere. Her simple, stylish, and great-looking designs work for everything from work-out clothes to black tie wear. Calvin Klein now has his name on place settings and sunglasses in addition to underwear, jeans, and a whole range of clothes. He is renowned for comfortable, sensuous, and well-fitting – as well as very hip – looks. Ralph Lauren is very well known for his aristocratic and expensive clothes, a

"look" favored by the exclusive and posh Ivy League, horsey set. For those with a taste for more experimental designs, Joan Vass specializes in moderately priced but exciting, colorful, and innovative knitwear.

## DISCOUNT DESIGNER CLOTHES

If you're on the lookout for discount designer clothes, **Designer Resale**, **Encore**, and **Michael's** sell a wide range. Oscar de la Renta, Ungaro, and Armani are just some of the leading labels available. Clothes are either new or worn but near-perfect.

One of New York City's best kept secrets is the **Century 21 Department Store** in Lower Manhattan. The designer discount emporium has reopened in its original location and sells European and American designer fashions discounted up to an amazing 75 percent off regular retail prices. **Filene's Basement**, one of Manhattan's longest-running discount department stores, offers designer clothes, shoes, and accessories at bargain prices.

## MEN'S CLOTHES

In the center of midtown, you'll find two of the city's most highly regarded menswear stores: **Brooks Brothers** and **Paul Stuart**. Brooks Brothers is something of a New York institution, famous for its traditional, conservative clothing such as smart button-down shirts and Chinos. There's an ultra-conservative woman's line too. Paul Stuart

prides itself on its very British look and offers a stylish array of superbly tailored fashions. Go to the high-quality department store **Bergdorf Goodman Men** to find beautifully made Turnbull & Asser shirts and marvelous suits by Gianfranco Ferré or Hugo Boss.

**Barney's New York** has one of the most comprehensive men's departments in America, with a truly massive range of clothes and accessories. **Rothman's** offers international styles at great bargain prices.

**The Custom Shop Shirtmakers** specializes in custommade suits and shirts in beautiful materials. Go to **Burberry Limited** if you are looking for classic British trenchcoats and traditional outdoor wear.

**J. Press** sells classic, conservative yet elegant clothes while **John Varvatos** is famous for luxurious, sporty designs with superb detail. Uptown designer menswear boutiques include the renowned **Beau Brummel** with a selection of very stylish European clothes and **Thomas Pink** whose bright colors and fine fabrics make this store a celebrity favorite. Many of these men's stores also carry striking women's fashions. Watch for the new Hickey-Freeman store on Fifth Avenue for a wide range of men's traditional clothing.

## CHILDREN'S CLOTHES

In addition to an excellent selection within the large department stores, there are several shops around the city that sell children's clothing exclusively. A good example is **Bonpoint**, which has a world of French-style charm.

**GapKids** and **BabyGap** shops, often in the **Gap** shops, have comfortable, long-lasting cotton overalls, sweat pants, denim jackets, sweatshirts, and leggings. The wonderfully named **Peanut Butter & Jane** sells trendy but particularly comfortable togs. **Space Kiddets** has everything from booties to Western wear.

## WOMEN'S CLOTHES

Women's fashion is subject to design trends, and New York stores keep pace with them all. Most of the city's most fashionable shops are found in the midtown area around Madison and Fifth Avenues. These include some of the major department stores (see p319), which stock a range of American designers, including Donna Karan, Ralph Lauren and Bill Blass.

Leading international names such as **Chanel, Fendi**, and **Valentino** also have shops here, as does one of the outstanding American designers, **Geoffrey Beene**. There is also a handful of popular ready-to-wear stores, including **Ann Taylor**, which is much favored by young, busy professionals looking for stylish, comfortable clothing.

Right at the heart of this area stands the pink-marbled Trump Tower, which houses a selection of exclusive shops. Madison Avenue is packed with designers for the smart set, who have everything you could ever need, including **Givenchy** who sells showstopping formal gowns at phenomenal prices, Valentino who has classic Italian clothes and **Emanuel Ungaro** who is relatively unintimidating and has something to suit most tastes and physiques from beautifully tailored jackets to more matronly full-figured and boldly patterned print dresses. **Missoni** is famous for richly textured sweaters in sumptuous wools and colorful patterns. **Yves St Laurent Rive Gauche** has evening gowns, one-of-a-kind jackets, silks and extravagant blouses, and beautifully cut pants suits.

Sophisticated Italian looks are also available from Italian style kings **Giorgio Armani** and **Gianni Versace. Dolce & Gabbana** sells only unique, one-of-a-kind Italian clothing. **Gucci**, one of the oldest Italian shops in America, is only for the wealthy and status-conscious.

The Upper West Side has many shops competing for attention with contemporary fashions, including **Betsey Johnson's** shop, with her whimsical, relatively inexpensive designs. **Calvin Klein** now has a store on the East Side, specializing in ultra-hip, casual fashions. **French Connection** is known for its affordable separates, both casual and for the office. **Scoop** is *the* place to get a little black dress.

The villages – the East Village in particular – are the best places to go for secondhand clothing and 1950s rock 'n' roll gear, with ever-changing interesting shops run by new and young designers and art school graduates. For a range of affordable, well-cut clothes from classic to casual, try **APC**.

**Cheap Jack's** carries a huge selection of secondhand Levi's as well as hundreds of denim and leather jackets. **Loehmann's** offers discounted fashion clothes, and it's the place to shop if you want top-of-the-line fashions at unbelievable discounts. **Big Drop** has a great selection of perfectly fitting little black dresses. **Screaming Mimi's** is where you could unearth that pair of velvet bellbottoms or go-go boots you've always dreamed of having. A more mainstream shop is **The Gap**, a chain store selling lots of moderately-priced, casual and comfortable clothes for men, women and children.

Recently SoHo has come to rival Madison Avenue for designer boutiques specializing in expensive but interesting clothes – the fashions here are far more avant-garde. You'll find **Yohji Yamamoto**, among other exclusive stores. **Comme des Garçons** sells minimalist Japanese chic.

**Cynthia Rowley** is a prominent New York designer who sells flirty fashions for women and **What Comes Around Goes Around** is the place to go for vintage jeans.

## SIZE CHART

For Australian sizes follow the British and American conversions.

**Children's clothing**

| | | | | | | | | |
|---|---|---|---|---|---|---|---|---|
| American | 2–3 | 4–5 | 6–6x | 7–8 | 10 | 12 | 14 | 16 (size) |
| British | 2–3 | 4–5 | 6–7 | 8–9 | 10–11 | 12 | 14 | 14+ (years) |
| Continental | 2–3 | 4–5 | 6–7 | 8–9 | 10–11 | 12 | 14 | 14+ (years) |

**Children's shoes**

| | | | | | | | | | |
|---|---|---|---|---|---|---|---|---|---|
| American | 7½ | 8½ | 9½ | 10½ | 11½ | 12½ | 13½ | 1½ | 2½ |
| British | 7 | 8 | 9 | 10 | 11 | 12 | 13 | 1 | 2 |
| Continental | 24 | 25½ | 27 | 28 | 29 | 30 | 32 | 33 | 34 |

**Women's dresses, coats and skirts**

| | | | | | | | | |
|---|---|---|---|---|---|---|---|---|
| American | 4 | 6 | 8 | 10 | 12 | 14 | 16 | 18 |
| British | 6 | 8 | 10 | 12 | 14 | 16 | 18 | 20 |
| Continental | 38 | 40 | 42 | 44 | 46 | 48 | 50 | 52 |

**Women's blouses and sweaters**

| | | | | | | | |
|---|---|---|---|---|---|---|---|
| American | 6 | 8 | 10 | 12 | 14 | 16 | 18 |
| British | 30 | 32 | 34 | 36 | 38 | 40 | 42 |
| Continental | 40 | 42 | 44 | 46 | 48 | 50 | 52 |

**Women's shoes**

| | | | | | | | |
|---|---|---|---|---|---|---|---|
| American | 5 | 6 | 7 | 8 | 9 | 10 | 11 |
| British | 3 | 4 | 5 | 6 | 7 | 8 | 9 |
| Continental | 36 | 37 | 38 | 39 | 40 | 41 | 44 |

**Men's suits**

| | | | | | | | | |
|---|---|---|---|---|---|---|---|---|
| American | 34 | 36 | 38 | 40 | 42 | 44 | 46 | 48 |
| British | 34 | 36 | 38 | 40 | 42 | 44 | 46 | 48 |
| Continental | 44 | 46 | 48 | 50 | 52 | 54 | 56 | 58 |

**Men's shirts**

| | | | | | | | | |
|---|---|---|---|---|---|---|---|---|
| American | 14 | 15 | 15½ | 16 | 16½ | 17 | 17½ | 18 |
| British | 14 | 15 | 15½ | 16 | 16½ | 17 | 17½ | 18 |
| Continental | 36 | 38 | 39 | 41 | 42 | 43 | 44 | 45 |

**Men's shoes**

| | | | | | | | | |
|---|---|---|---|---|---|---|---|---|
| American | 7 | 7½ | 8 | 8½ | 9½ | 10½ | 11 | 11½ |
| British | 6 | 7 | 7½ | 8 | 9 | 10 | 11 | 12 |
| Continental | 39 | 40 | 41 | 42 | 43 | 44 | 45 | 46 |

# DIRECTORY

## DISCOUNT DESIGNER CLOTHES

**Century 21 Department Store**
22 Cortland St.
**Map** 1 C2.
*Tel (212) 227-9092.*

**Designer Resale**
324 E 81st St.
**Map** 17 B4.
*Tel (212) 734-3639.*

**Encore**
1132 Madison Ave.
**Map** 17 A4.
*Tel (212) 879-2850.*

**Filene's Basement**
4 Union Square South.
**Map** 9 A5.
*Tel (212) 358-0169.*
*One of several branches.*

**Michael's**
1041 Madison Ave.
**Map** 17 A5.
*Tel (212) 737-7273.*

## MEN'S CLOTHES

**Barney's New York**
660 Madison Ave.
**Map** 13 A3.
*Tel (212) 826-8900.*

**Beau Brummel**
421 W Broadway.
**Map** 4 E3.
*Tel (212) 219-2666.*
*One of several branches.*

**Bergdorf Goodman Men**
754 5th Ave.
**Map** 12 F3.
*Tel (212) 753-7300.*

**Brooks Brothers**
346 Madison Ave.
**Map** 9 A1.
*Tel (212) 682-8800.*

**Burberry Limited**
9 E 57th St.
**Map** 12 F3.
*Tel (212) 757-3700.*

**The Custom Shop Shirtmakers**
618 5th Ave.
**Map** 12 F4.
*Tel (212) 245-2499.*
*One of several branches.*

**J. Press**
7 E 44th St. **Map** 12 F5.
*Tel (212) 687-7642.*

**John Varvatos**
149 Mercer St.
**Map** 4 E3.
*Tel (212) 965-0700.*

**Paul Stuart**
350 Madison Ave.
**Map** 13 A5.
*Tel (212) 682-0320.*

**Polo/Ralph Lauren**
Madison Ave at 72nd St.
**Map** 13 A1.
*Tel (212) 606-2100.*

**Rothman's**
200 Park Ave South.
**Map** 9 A5.
*Tel (212) 777-7400.*

**ThomasPink**
520 Madison Ave.
**Map** 13 A4.
*Tel (212) 838-1928.*

## CHILDREN'S CLOTHES

**Bonpoint**
1269 Madison Ave.
**Map** 17 A3.
*Tel (212) 722-7720.*

**GapKids**
60 W 34th St.
**Map** 8 F2.
*Tel (212) 760-1268.*
*One of several branches.*

**Peanut Butter & Jane**
617 Hudson St.
**Map** 3 B1.
*Tel (212) 620-7952.*

**Space Kiddets**
46 E 21st St.
**Map** 8 F4.
*Tel (212) 420-9878.*

## WOMEN'S CLOTHES

**Ann Taylor**
645 Madison Ave.
**Map** 13 A3.
*Tel (212) 832-2010.*
*One of several branches.*

**APC**
131 Mercer St.
**Map** 4 E3.
*Tel (212) 966-9685.*

**Betsey Johnson**
248 Columbus Ave.
**Map** 16 D4.
*Tel (212) 362-3364.*
*One of several branches.*

**Big Drop**
174 Spring St.
**Map** 3 C4.
*Tel (212) 966-4299.*

**Calvin Klein**
654 Madison Ave.
**Map** 13 A3.
*Tel (212) 292-9000.*

**Chanel**
15 E 57th St.
**Map** 12 F3.
*Tel (212) 355-5050.*

**Cheap Jack's**
841 Broadway.
**Map** 4 E1.
*Tel (212) 777-9564.*

**Comme des Garçons**
520 W 22nd St.
**Map** 8 F3.
*Tel (212) 604-9200.*

**Cynthia Rowley**
376 Bleecker St.
**Map** 3 C2.
*Tel (212) 242-3803.*

**Dolce & Gabbana**
434 W Broadway.
**Map** 4 E3.
*Tel (212) 965-8000.*

**Emanuel Ungaro**
792 Madison Ave.
**Map** 13 A2.
*Tel (212) 249-4090.*

**Fendi**
677 5th Ave.
**Map** 12 F3.
*Tel (212) 759-4646.*

**French Connection**
700 Broadway.
**Map** 4 E2.
*Tel (212) 473-4486.*
*One of several branches.*

**The Gap**
250 W 57th St.
**Map** 12 D3.
*Tel (212) 315-2250.*
*One of many branches.*

**Geoffrey Beene**
783 5th Ave.
**Map** 12 F3.
*Tel (212) 935-0470.*

**Gianni Versace**
647 5th Ave.
**Map** 12 F4.
*Tel (212) 317-0224.*

**Giorgio Armani**
760 Madison Ave.
**Map** 13 A2.
*Tel (212) 988-9191.*

**Givenchy**
710 Madison Ave.
**Map** 13 A1.
*Tel (212) 688-4005.*

**Gucci**
685 5th Ave.
**Map** 12 F4.
*Tel (212) 826-2600.*

**Loehmann's**
101 7th Ave.
**Map** 8 E1.
*Tel (212) 352-0856.*

**Missoni**
1009 Madison Ave.
**Map** 13 A1.
*Tel (212) 517-9339.*

**Saks Fifth Avenue**
611 5th Ave.
**Map** 12 F4.
*Tel (212) 753-4000.*

**Scoop**
532 Broadway
(near Spring St).
**Map** 4 E4.
*Tel (212) 925-2886.*
*One of two branches.*

**Screaming Mimi's**
382 Lafayette St.
**Map** 4 F2.
*Tel (212) 677-6464.*

**Valentino**
747 Madison Ave.
**Map** 13 A2.
*Tel (212) 772-6969.*

**What Comes Around Goes Around**
351 W Broadway.
**Map** 4 E4.
*Tel (212) 343-9303.*

**Yohji Yamamoto**
103 Grand St.
**Map** 4 E4.
*Tel (212) 966-9066.*

**Yves St Laurent Rive Gauche**
855 Madison Ave.
**Map** 13 A1.
*Tel (212) 517-7400.*

# Accessories

In addition to the following shops, all of the major
Manhattan department stores have extensive accessory
departments stocking a range of hats, gloves, bags,
jewelry, watches, scarves, shoes, and umbrellas.

## JEWELRY

Midtown Fifth Avenue is
where to find the most
dazzling jewelers. By day,
windows glisten with gems
from around the world; by
night they are empty – the
jewels safely locked away.
The most sensational shops
are all within a couple of
blocks of one another and
include the museum-like
**Harry Winston**, which showcases its coveted jewels from
around the world. **Buccellati**
is well respected for its
innovative Italian creations
and excellent workmanship.
**Bulgari** has an impressive
collection that ranges in price
from a mere couple of hundred
to over a million dollars.

Housed in a Renaissance-
style palazzo, **Cartier** is a jewel
in itself and sells its beautiful
baubles at unthinkable prices.
**Tiffany & Co**. has ten floors of
glittering crystal, diamonds,
and other jewels just waiting
to be packed up for you and
taken away in the store's
signature sky blue boxes.

Diamond Row, a one-block
area on 47th Street (between
Fifth and Sixth Avenues), is
lined with shops displaying
hundreds of thousands of
dollars worth of diamonds,
gold, pearls, and other exotic
jewels from around the world.
Try not to miss the **Jewelry
Exchange**, a complex where
60 different crafts-people sell
their ware direct to the
public. Boisterous bargaining
is very much alive here, so be
prepared to play the game.

## HATS

New York's oldest hat shop
is **Worth & Worth**, which
also has the largest collection
of hats in the city. You can
get everything you could
possibly want here, ranging
from original Australian bush
hats to silk toppers, to slouch
hats and boaters. **Suzanne**

**Millinery** is the hat-maker to
the stars, as she has proved
very popular with celebrities
such as Whoopi Goldberg
and Ivana Trump. **Lids** sells
baseball caps in dozens of
varieties, with logos ranging
from sports teams to the
evergreen "I HEART NY".

## UMBRELLAS

The minute it starts to rain in
New York, hundreds of street
vendors selling umbrellas seem
to sprout like mushrooms.
Their umbrellas, which sell at
just a few dollars, are without
doubt the cheapest in the
city, but unlikely to last much
longer than the downpour
itself. For good-quality umbrellas, you'll find a fine selection
of Briggs of London at **Worth
& Worth**. There is a wide
range of different sizes, trendy
patterns, and traditional tartans
and stripes at **Barney's New
York**, and there's always **Macy's**
*(see p319)* for the usual sizes
and styles. World-famous
**Gucci** has umbrellas to match
its ties. Subway-themed ones
can be found at the **NY Transit
Museum Store**, and doorman-
sized ones in solid black or in
the university's traditional
colors of black and orange
at **The Princeton Club**.

## HANDBAGS AND
BRIEFCASES

Twice a year, during the
January and August sales,
a serpentine line of buyers
wraps around the corner
of 48th Street and Madison
Avenue waiting to get into
**Crouch & Fitzgerald**, an old
New York institution, selling
handbags, briefcases, and
luggage. All the well-known
brands are sold here, including
Judith Leiber, Ghurka, Dooney
& Bourke, and Louis Vuitton,
as well as the firm's own line.
Elsewhere in the city are such
exclusive shops as **Bottega
Veneta**, and **Prada**, where

handbags are displayed like
precious art, with prices to
match. Younger and trendier
places include **Furla**, well-
respected for its Italian
designs, and the stylish **Il
Bisonte**. Current must-have
designer Rafé Totengco's soft
suede pastel pouches are
found at **TG-170** and **Big Drop**.
**The Coach Store** is known for
its simple, classic leather
handbags. Designer **Kate
Spade's** stylish yet practical
rectangular handbags, in a
plethora of prints and colors,
have become modern classics,
and add a chic touch to any
woman's wardrobe.

For discount designer
handbags go to the legendary
**Fine & Klein**, and for bargain
briefcases from slim enve-
lopes to thick lawyer's bags,
a visit to the **Altman Luggage
Company** is a must.

## SHOES AND
BOOTS

Manhattan shoe stores are
famous for their extensive
selections of shoes and boots,
and if you shop around you
are sure to find what you
want at a reasonable price.

Most of the large depart-
ment stores in New York also
have shoe departments where
you can find designer-label
shoes in addition to other
brands. **Bloomingdale's** *(see
p181)* has a huge women's
footwear department, and
**Brooks Brothers** has one of
the best selections of traditional men's shoes in the city.

For both men's and women's
shoes, the most exclusive
shops are around the midtown
area. **Nadine & David** has
beautiful shoes made from
suede and leather, in various
elegant styles. **Ferragamo**
sells classic styles crafted in
Florence. Go to **Botticelli** for
whimsical shoe fashions.
For stylish shoes at decent
prices, head for **Sigerson
Morrison** in Little Italy.

For cowboy boots, head
for **Billy Martin's**. There's
an enormous selection of
handmade boots, from basic,
no-frills "ropers," which real
American cowboys wear, to

crocodile leather boots that sell for thousands of dollars. Billy Martin's stocks western garb and accessories, so you can dress in western gear from head to toe. For beautiful custom-made boots, try **Buffalo Chips Bootery**.

For the best in children's shoes, **East Side Kids** stocks the trendiest fashions for kids, while **Shoofly** has imported shoes in all styles. **Harry's** carries a wonderful selection of sensible shoes.

The **Jimmy Choo** boutique offers a plethora of sexy, stylish heels. Popular among Manhattan's chic set are the beautiful women's shoes,

particularly the flattering heels, at **Manolo Blahnik**. **Christian Louboutin** rounds out the stiletto heavyweights. Spain's most popular brand, **Camper**, has an airy SoHo store featuring their signature comfy, funky, and colorful shoes for women and men.

For discounted shoes, the greatest concentration of shops is around West 34th Street and West Eight Street between Fifth and Sixth Avenues, and Orchard Street on the Lower East Side. The **DSW** discount shoe store sells row upon row of brand-name shoes and boots at a fraction of the regular price.

## LINGERIE

Expensive imports from Europe, which are sexy yet elegant, can be found at **La Petite Coquette**.

More affordable is **Victoria's Secret** on 57th Street, which offers two floors of beautifully made lingerie in satin, silk, and many other fine fabrics. **Henri Bendel's** lingerie department offers a sumptuous array of lingerie, from naughty to nice. The Italian **La Perla** features seductive lingerie and undergarments in sensual fabrics from tulle and chiffon to satin.

# DIRECTORY

## JEWELRY

**Buccellati**
46 E 57th Ave.
**Map** 12 F3.
*Tel (212) 308-2900.*

**Bulgari**
730 5th Ave. **Map** 12 F3.
*Tel (212) 315-9000.*

**Cartier**
653 5th Ave. **Map** 12 F4.
*Tel (212) 753-0111.*

**Harry Winston**
718 5th Ave. **Map** 12 F3.
*Tel (212) 245-2000.*

**Jewelry Exchange**
15 W 47th St. **Map** 12 F5.

**Tiffany & Co**
5th Ave at 57th St.
**Map** 12 F3.
*Tel (212) 755-8000.*

## HATS

**Lids**
243 W 42nd St. **Map** 8
E1. *Tel (212) 575-8555.*
*One of several branches.*

**Suzanne Millinery**
27 E 61 St. **Map** 13 A3.
*Tel (212) 593-3232.*

**Worth & Worth**
101 W 55th St, Suite 3N.
**Map** 12 E4.
*Tel (212) 265-2887.*

## UMBRELLAS

**Barney's New York**
*See p319.*

**Gucci**
*See p327.*

**NY Transit Museum Store**
Grand Central Terminal.
**Map** 9 A1.
*Tel (212) 878-0106.*

**The Princeton Club**
*See p324.*

## HANDBAGS AND BRIEFCASES

**Altman Luggage Company**
135 Orchard St. **Map** 5 A3.
*Tel (212) 254-7275.*

**Big Drop**
*See p327.*

**Il Bisonte**
120 Sullivan St. **Map** 4
D4. *Tel (212) 966-8773.*

**Bottega Veneta**
635 Madison Ave. **Map** 13
A3. *Tel (212) 371-5511.*

**The Coach Store**
595 Madison Ave. **Map** 13
A3. *Tel (212) 754-0041.*

**Crouch & Fitzgerald**
400 Madison Ave.
**Map** 13 A5.
*Tel (212) 755-5888.*

**Fine & Klein**
119 Orchard St. **Map** 5
A3. *Tel (212) 674-6720.*

**Furla**
727 Madison Ave.
**Map** 13 A3.
*Tel (212) 755-8986.*
*One of two branches.*

**Kate Spade**
454 Broome St. **Map** 4 E4.
*Tel (212) 274-1991.*

**Prada**
49 E 57th St. **Map** 12 F3.
*Tel (212) 308-2332.*

**TG-170**
170 Ludlow St. **Map** 5 A3.
*Tel (212) 995-8660.*

## SHOES AND BOOTS

**Billy Martin's**
220 E 60th St. **Map** 13
B3. *Tel (212) 861-3100.*

**Botticelli**
620 5th Ave. **Map** 12 F4.
*Tel (212) 582-6313.*

**Bloomingdale's**
*See p319.*

**Brooks Brothers**
*See p327.*

**Buffalo Chips Bootery**
355 W Broadway.
**Map** 4 E4.
*Tel (212) 625-8400.*

**Camper**
125 Prince St. **Map** 4 E3.
*Tel (212) 358-1842.*

**Christian Louboutin**
941 Madison Ave.
**Map** 17 A5.
*Tel (212) 396-1884.*

**DSW**
40 E 14th St, 3rd Floor.
**Map** 9 A5.
*Tel (212) 674-2146.*

**East Side Kids**
1298 Madison Ave. **Map**
17 A2. *Tel (212) 360-5000.*

**Ferragamo**
655 5th Ave. **Map** 12 F3.
*Tel (212) 759-3822.*

**Harry's**
2299 Broadway. **Map** 15
C2. *Tel (212) 874-2035.*

**Jimmy Choo**
645 5th Ave. **Map** 12 F4.
*Tel (212) 593-0800.*

**Manolo Blahnik**
31 W 54th St. **Map** 12 F4.
*Tel (212) 582-3007.*

**Nadine & David**
1029 3rd Ave. **Map** 13
B3. *Tel (212) 753-1822.*

**Shoofly**
42 Hudson St. **Map** 1 B1.
*Tel (212) 406-3270.*

**Sigerson Morrison**
28 Prince St. **Map** 4 F3.
*Tel (212) 219-3893.*

## LINGERIE

**Henri Bendel**
*See p319.*

**La Perla**
93 Greene St. **Map** 4 E3.
*Tel (212) 219-0999.*

**La Petite Coquette**
51 University Place. **Map** 4
E1. *Tel (212) 473-2478.*

**Victoria's Secret**
34 E 57th St. **Map** 12 F3.
*Tel (212) 758-5592.*
*One of several branches.*

# Beauty, Manicures and Pedicures, and Hair Salons

You can shop 'til you drop in New York City – and when you do, rest assured that rejuvenation (and a heavenly foot massage) is just around the corner. There are plenty of well-stocked beauty stores, manicure and pedicure specialists, and sleek hair salons. Many of the manicurists and salons cater to New Yorkers and their hectic schedules, so they often accept same-day appointments that can easily fitted in between rounds of sightseeing and shopping. After a pamper session or two (or three…), you'll be ready to hit the shops again, this time with the prettiest toes and silkiest hair around.

## BEAUTY STORES

The French-owned **Sephora** is a cosmetics megastore that offers its shoppers row upon row of beauty products, from skin cleansers to cosmetics and fragrances, and, thankfully, a no-pressure sales staff. For all-natural essences and products, try **Erbe** ("herbs" in Italian), a soothing sanctuary with a plethora of hypo-allergenic products, all made with fresh herbs and free from mineral oils, animal products, waxes, synthetic fragrances, or dyes. The royal jelly nutrient moisturizer and Pennywort exfoliating cream are popular choices.

The high-ceilinged **MAC Cosmetics** store is always busy. Their face powders, particularly the Studio Fix line, are unsurpassed. Best of all, you can be glamorous and giving at the same time when you buy the Viva Glam lipstick – proceeds go to the MAC Aids fund. The promise of creamy Swedish skin (at a reasonable price) lures shoppers to **FACE Stockholm**, where they stock natural, botanical skin products plus lipstick and nail polish in a rainbow of colors. Since 1851, **Kiehl's** has been creating cleansers, toners, balms, and masques "in purposefully utilitarian" packaging as the natural ingredients speak for themselves.

The nature-friendly **Fresh** sells fragrant body creams and fruity perfume. **Sabon** sells a luxurious range of bath and beauty products that are 100 percent natural

and irresistibly scented. Soaps can be bought by the pound here, and they are gift-wrapped for free.

For good quality makeup that stands the test of time, visit SoHo's stylish **Make Up for Ever**, which stocks everything from liquid face foundations and creamy lipsticks, to sparkling body powders. Head to earthy **Origins** and select from their plethora of plant-based lotions, an antioxidant moisturizer made with white tea, and body creams sensitive enough for a baby's skin. Also worth visiting is **Shu Uemura**, which showcases an array of top-notch cosmetics.

Most of New York's large department stores, including **Bloomingdale's**, **Lord & Taylor**, **Saks Fifth Avenue**, **Barney's New York**, and **Macy's** offer well-stocked makeup counters.

## MANICURES AND PEDICURES

Young Korean entrepreneur Ji Baek's **Rescue Beauty Lounge** started out as a cozy SoHo salon, but it proved so popular that she had to open a second outpost. As well as manicures and pedicures, you can have waxing and browse hard-to-find makeup lines. **Eve's** may look somewhat bland and institutional, but appearances can be deceiving. Their long-lasting manicures and pedicures are top-notch. **Dashing Diva Nail Spa & Boutique** not only offers excellent manicures and pedicures at a bargain price (starting at $10). The

whole experience is made all the more alluring, however, as they offer treats with their treatments. On Thursdays and Fridays, they serve Cosmopolitans and turn up the music, and on Sundays through to Wednesdays, you can sip Mimosas while beauticians tend to your hands and feet.

Experience the ultimate in hand and nail care at **Sweet Lily Natural Nail Spa & Boutique**. The range includes an intoxicating blend of warm milk and almond oil for your hands, and a moisturizing honey walnut mask with a honey walnut manicure ($36). The hot lavender cream manicure includes a wonderful conditioning treatment for cuticles that contains tea tree and citrus oil. The boutique is not just for adults, as there is also a manicure for little girls: the Little Miss Mani includes a choice of nail art.

## HAIR SALONS

If you're in the mood for a new hair do, or just want to refresh your current cut, try one of New York City's cutting-edge hair salons.

The stylists at the downtown **Arrojo Studio** will update your style, so that you walk out of the salon looking as hip as they do. Follow the celebrities, and get your hair cut, styled, and/or colored by stylist Frederic Fekkai or one of his associates at the chic **Frederic Fekkai Beaute de Provence**. This top salon is very much a cut above the rest. Korean stylist Younghee Kim, formerly of Vidal Sassoon, offers hip cuts and colors starting at $110 at her eponymous hair salon, **Younghee Salon** in TriBeCa. The stylists at the **Rumor Salon** are well-known to be czars with scissors, creating simple yet fashionable and flattering cuts amid a spare salon awash in warm lighting. Set in a classy, sun-flooded loft, the **Aveda Institute** offers superb cuts, colors, and scalp massages. Pick up one of their plant-based beauty and bath products. The institute also offers the opportunity to receive a discount haircut by one of the trainee hairdressers. A great choice for men is **La Boite a Coupe**, whose clientele includes many advertising and media personalities. Moroccan-French stylist Laurent De Louya has been cutting hair here since 1972. The upscale, Asian-accented **Le Salon Chinois**,

never fails to create a sleek cut that will turn heads. They also offer excellent scalp treatments, hair aroma-therapy, and effective straightening treatments. Head to the lovely **TwoDo Salon**, where you can get an expert cut and color amid a rustic, colorful decor of fresh flowers and brick walls hung with paintings by local artists. Styling stalwart **Vidal Sassoon** is still going strong. Visit the elegant downtown salon where accomplished stylists and colorists – all of whom have gone through the com-

pany's rigorous training – turn out impeccable, eye-catching cuts and colors. **Toni & Guy**, a premiere hair salon from the UK, is renowned for its consistently good cuts. The NYC salon is the US training headquarters, where creative stylists offer the boldest cuts around. Toni & Guy colorists have also been lauded for their tinting and highlighting skill. For more great cuts and colors, try the hip favorites **Antonio Prieto** and **Bumble & Bumble**, the refined **John Masters Organics**, and the elite **Oscar Blandi**.

# DIRECTORY

## BEAUTY STORES

**Erbe**
196 Prince St.
**Map** 4 D3.
*Tel (212) 966-1445.*

**FACE Stockholm**
10 Columbus Circle.
**Map** 12 D3.
*Tel (212) 823-9415.*

110 Prince St, SoHo.
**Map** 4 E3.
*Tel (212) 966-9110.*

**Fresh**
57 Spring St at
Lafayette St. **Map** 4 F4.
*Tel (212) 925-0099.*

**John Masters Organics**
77 Sullivan St near
Broome St. **Map** 4 D4.
*Tel (212) 343-9590.*

**Kiehl's**
109 3rd Ave. **Map** 9 B5.
*Tel (212) 677-3171.*

**MAC Cosmetics**
113 Spring St. **Map** 4 E4.
*Tel (212) 334-4641.*

**Make Up for Ever**
409 W Broadway at
Spring St. **Map** 4 E4.
*Tel (212) 941-9337.*

**Origins**
175 5th Ave at 23rd St.
**Map** 8 F4.
*Tel (212) 677-9100.*

**Sabon**
93 Spring St. **Map** 4 E4.
*Tel (212) 925-0742.*
*One of three branches.*

**Sephora**
555 Broadway.
**Map** 4 E3.
*Tel (212) 625-1309.*
*One of several branches.*

**Shu Uemura**
121 Greene St, near
Prince St. **Map** 4 E3.
*Tel (212) 979-5500.*

## MANICURE AND PEDICURES

**Barney's New York**
660 Madison Ave.
**Map** 13 A3.
*Tel (212) 826-8900.*

**Bloomingdale's**
1000 3rd Ave.
**Map** 13 B3.
*Tel (212) 705-2000.*

**Bloomingdale's SoHo**
504 Broadway.
**Map** 4 E4.
*Tel (212) 729-5900.*

**Dashing Diva Nail Spa & Boutique**
41 E 8th St. **Map** 4 E2.
*Tel (212) 673-9000.*

**Eve**
400 Bleecker St.
**Map** 3 C2.
*Tel (212) 807-8054.*

**Lord & Taylor**
424 5th Ave. **Map** 8 F1.
*Tel (212) 391-3344.*

**Macy's**
151 W 34th St.
**Map** 8 E2.
*Tel (212) 695-4400.*

**Rescue Beauty Lounge**
8 Centre Market Pl.
**Map** 4 F4.
*Tel (212) 431-0449.*
34 Gansevoort St.
**Map** 3 B1.
*Tel (212) 206-6409.*

**Saks Fifth Avenue**
611 5th Ave. **Map** 12 F4.
*Tel (212) 753-4000.*

**Sweet Lily Natural Nail Spa & Boutique**
222 W Broadway,
between N Moore &
Franklin sts. **Map** 4 E5.
*Tel (212) 925-5441.*

## HAIR SALONS

**Antonio Prieto**
25 19th St, between 5th
& 6th aves. **Map** 8 F5.
*Tel (212) 255-3741.*

**Arrojo Studio**
180 Varick St.
**Map** 4 D3.
*Tel (212) 242-7786.*

**Aveda Institute**
233 Spring St. **Map** 4 D4.
*Tel (212) 807-1492.*

**La Boite a Coupe**
18 W 55th St.
**Map** 12 F4.
*Tel (212) 246-2097.*

**Bumble & Bumble**
415 13th St near 9th Ave.
**Map** 3 B1.
*Tel (212) 521-6500.*

**Frederic Fekkai Beaute de Provence**
15 E 57th St.
**Map** 12 F3.
*Tel (212) 753-9500.*

**Oscar Blandi**
746 Madison Ave.
**Map** 13 A2.
*Tel (212) 988-9404.*

**Le Salon Chinois**
44 W 55th St, 4th Floor.
Between 5th & 6th aves.
**Map** 12 F4.
*Tel (212) 956-1200.*

**Rumor Salon**
15 E 12th St, 2nd Floor.
**Map** 4 E1.
*Tel (212) 414-0195.*

**Toni & Guy**
673 Madison Ave,
Suite 2 at 61st St.
**Map** 13 A3.
*Tel (212) 702-9771.*

**TwoDo Salon**
210 W 82nd St,
between Broadway &
Amsterdam. **Map** 15 C4 .
*Tel (212) 787-1277.*

**Vidal Sassoon**
90 5th Ave, Suite 90.
Between 14th & 15th sts.
**Map** 8 F5.
*Tel (212) 229-2200.*

**Younghee Salon**
64 N Moore St.
**Map** 4 D5.
*Tel (212) 334-3770.*

# Books and Music

As the publishing capital of America, it's not surprising that New York has the country's best selection of bookstores. These range from vast general interest stores to hundreds of esoteric bookstores specializing in everything from sci-fi to suspense, selling new books and old. Music lovers will also find sounds for all tastes at reasonable prices, plus thousands of rare recordings.

## GENERAL INTEREST BOOKSTORES

One of the most well-known of New York's bookstores – for best prices as well as selection of titles – is **Barnes & Noble** on Fifth Avenue, reputedly the world's largest bookstore and packed high with over three million books on every imaginable subject. There are branches all over the City, plus the sales annex across the street, with amazing bargains.

Several blocks away is the main branch of New York's famous **Strand Book Store**, with an astonishing two million copies of new and secondhand books. There is also a large rare book room for first editions.

**Westsider Bookshop** is as comprehensive as its music counterpart, as it stocks an enormous collection of used books and country/bluegrass LPs. **12th Street Books** has a good selection of new and used books, and art books. **Borders Books & Music** offers a choice of CDs and books of all genres.

**Rizzoli** has an enormous selection of photography, foreign language, music, and art books plus children's books and videos. **Gotham Book Mart**, a New York institution, is a tiny shop with hundreds of out-of-print books and limited editions. The beloved **Coliseum**, New York's largest independent bookstore, has just reopened. **Shakespeare & Co.** offers a sensational selection of titles and is open late every night.

## SPECIALTY BOOKSTORES

For the best selection of art books in the city, visit **Hacker -Strand Art Books**. **Urban Center Books** has titles on urban planning and other conservation issues. The city's largest selection of theatrical books and publications is found at **Drama Book Shop**. Jewish books and music abound at **J. Levine Judaica**. Rare books, books out-of-print, and old books about New York are the *raison d'être* of **JN Bartfield Books**. The **Biography Bookshop** is the only midtown store specializing in diaries, letters, biographies, and auto-biographies. Theater buffs should try **Applause Theater & Cinema Books**.

Books on murder and suspense are the focus of **Mysterious Bookshop**. Try **Forbidden Planet** for old and new science-fiction books and comics. **Midtown Comics** has two spacious locations and offers a good range of comics at affordable prices, mostly from the late 1980s to the present. Vintage collectors might prefer **Jim Hanley's Universe**, across from the Empire State Building. The store is open until 11pm Mondays to Saturdays and until 9pm on Sundays. Collectible merchandise here ranges from reasonable to "ask Santa" in price.

**Bank Street Book Store** has one of the best selections of current children's books. Visit **Books of Wonder** for a variety of hardcover and rare children's books.

**The Complete Traveler** stocks a wide selection of brand-new and antique travel books and guides for your trip. The staff is very knowledgeable and more than helpful.

For an excellent range of maps visit the **Hagstrom Map & Travel Store**. Cookbooks are on the menu at **Kitchen Arts & Letters**, with many out-of-print books and first editions. Radicals should head for **Revolution Books** or **St. Mark's Bookstore**, which also has an excellent selection of literary and art titles. The **Oscar Wilde Memorial Bookshop** has a wide selection of gay and lesbian texts.

## RECORDS, TAPES, AND COMPACT DISCS

The best Manhattan record-store chain is **Virgin**, which has several megastore branches. **J&R Music World** is a complete home-enter-tainment store with one of the best CD selections in the city.

For out-of-print records, go to **Westsider Records**, a treasure trove for collectors, with an excellent choice of classical, jazz, and opera recordings. **House of Oldies** has a massive stock of deleted and rare records to suit all tastes. **Bleecker Bob's Golden Oldies** record shop has everything from imports, rock, and punk to rare jazz. Try **Midnight Records** for imports, reissues, American garage rock, and psychedelia.

DJs and vinyl lovers still have options for deep house, disco, and electronica. Check out **Rebel Rebel**, **Dance Tracks**, and **Satellite** in Manhattan, or the lively **Halcyon** in Brooklyn. True music enthu-siasts should head to **Other Music**, which stocks obscure gems, from hot electronica to 70's free jazz. **Disc-O-Rama** has some of the cheapest CD prices around.

## SHEET MUSIC

Just behind Carnegie Hall is one of the best stores for classical sheet music, **Joseph Patelson Music House Ltd.** The **Frank Music Company** has a huge collection of classical music scores. **Charles Colin Publications** specializes in jazz. For chart music and pop tunes try **Colony Record and Music Center** in the Brill Building on Broadway.

# DIRECTORY

## GENERAL INTEREST BOOKSTORES

**Barnes & Noble**
105 5th Ave. **Map** 8 F5.
*Tel (212) 807-0099.*
*One of several branches.*

**Borders Books & Music**
461 Park Ave.
**Map** 17 A3.
*Tel (212) 980-6785.*
*One of several branches.*

**Coliseum Books**
11 W 42nd St.
**Map** 8 F1.
*Tel (212) 803-5892.*

**Gotham Book Mart**
16 E 46th St.
**Map** 12 F5.
*Tel (212) 719-4448.*

**Rizzoli**
31 W 57th St.
**Map** 12 F3.
*Tel (212) 759-2424.*

**Shakespeare & Co.**
716 Broadway.
**Map** 4 E2.
*Tel (212) 529-1330.*
*One of several branches.*

**Strand Book Store**
828 Broadway.
**Map** 4 E1.
*Tel (212) 473-1452.*

**12th Street Books**
11 East 12th St.
**Map** 4 F1.
*Tel (212) 645-4340.*

**Westsider Bookshop**
2246 Broadway.
**Map** 15 C4.
*Tel (212) 362-0706.*

## SPECIALTY BOOKSTORES

**Applause Theater & Cinema Books**
19 W 21st St.
**Map** 8 F4.
*Tel (212) 575-9265.*

**Bank Street Book Store**
610 W 112th St.
**Map** 21 A4.
*Tel (212) 678-1654.*

**Biography Bookshop**
400 Bleecker St.
**Map** 3 C2.
*Tel (212) 807-8655.*

**Books of Wonder**
16 W 18th St.
**Map** 8 E5.
*Tel (212) 989-3270.*

**The Complete Traveler**
199 Madison Ave.
**Map** 9 A2.
*Tel (212) 685-9007.*

**Drama Book Store**
250 W 40th St.
**Map** 8 E1.
*Tel (212) 944-0595.*

**Forbidden Planet**
840 Broadway.
**Map** 4 E1.
*Tel (212) 473-1576.*

**Hacker-Strand Art Books**
45 W 57th St.
**Map** 12 F3.
*Tel (212) 688-7600.*

**Hagstrom Map & Travel Store**
57 W 43rd St.
**Map** 8 F1.
*Tel (212) 398-1222.*
*One of two branches.*

**Jim Hanley's Universe**
4 W 33rd St.
**Map** 8 F2.
*Tel (212) 268-7088.*

**J. Levine Judaica**
5 W 30th St.
**Map** 8 F3.
*Tel (212) 695-6888.*

**JN Bartfield Books**
30 W 57th St.
**Map** 12 F3.
*Tel (212) 245-8890.*

**Kitchen Arts & Letters**
1435 Lexington Ave.
**Map** 17 A2.
*Tel (212) 876-5550.*

**Midtown Comics**
200 W 40th St.
**Map** 8 E1.
459 Lexington Ave.
**Map** 13 A5.
*Tel (212) 302-8192.*

**Mysterious Bookshop**
58 Warren St. **Map** 1 B1.
*Tel (212) 582-1011.*

**Oscar Wilde Memorial Bookshop**
15 Christopher St.
**Map** 3 C2.
*Tel (212) 255-8097.*

**Revolution Books**
9 W 19th St.
**Map** 7 C5.
*Tel (212) 691-3345.*

**St. Mark's Bookshop**
31 3rd Ave.
**Map** 5 A2.
*Tel (212) 260-7853.*

**Urban Center Books**
457 Madison Ave.
**Map** 13 A4.
*Tel (212) 935-3592.*

## RECORDS, TAPES, AND COMPACT DISCS

**Bleecker Bob's Golden Oldies**
118 W 3rd St.
**Map** 4 D2.
*Tel (212) 475-9677.*

**Dance Tracks**
91 E 3rd St.
**Map** 5 A2.
*Tel (212) 260-8729.*

**Disc-O-Rama**
186 W 4th St.
**Map** 4 D2.
*Tel (212) 206-8417.*

**Halcyon The Shop**
57 Pearl St at Water St,
Dumbo, Brooklyn.
**Map** 2 F2.
*Tel (718) 260-WAXY.*

**House of Oldies**
35 Carmine St.
**Map** 4 D3.
*Tel (212) 243-0500.*

**J&R Music World**
23 Park Row.
**Map** 1 C2.
*Tel (800) 806-1115.*

**Midnight Records**
263 W 23rd St.
**Map** 8 D4.
*Tel (212) 675-2768.*

**Other Music**
15 E 4th St.
**Map** 4 F2.
*Tel (212) 477-8150.*

**Rebel Rebel Records**
319 Bleecker St.
**Map** 4 D3.
*Tel (212) 989-0770.*

**Satellite Records**
259 The Bowery.
**Map** 4 F3.
*Tel (212) 995-1744.*

**Virgin Megastore**
45th & Broadway.
**Map** 12 E5.
*Tel (212) 921-1020.*
*One of several branches.*

**West Sider Records**
233 W 72nd St.
**Map** 11 D1.
*Tel (212) 874-1588.*

## SHEET MUSIC

**Charles Colin Publications**
315 W 53rd St.
**Map** 12 D4.
*Tel (212) 581-1480.*

**Colony Record and Music Center**
1619 Broadway.
**Map** 12 E4.
*Tel (212) 265-2050.*

**Frank Music Company**
244 W 54th St.
**Map** 12 D4.
*Tel (212) 582-1999.*

**Joseph Patelson Music House Ltd.**
160 W 56th St.
**Map** 12 E4.
*Tel (212) 757-5587.*

# Art and Antiques

Any art-loving visitor to New York could easily spend several days gallery-hopping around the several hundred galleries found throughout New York. Antique lovers can find an exciting variety of goods, including Americana and many bargains, at the many flea markets; or they can browse through European and American fine antiques in one of the more exclusive antiques centers. To find out what's happening, pick up the free monthly *Art Now Gallery Guide*, available at most galleries, or check the local papers.

## ART GALLERIES

One of the city's best-known galleries is **Leo Castelli**, an important showcase for Pop Art during the early 1960s and now spotlighting new artists. **Mary Boone Gallery** features Neo-Expressionist artists such as Julian Schnabel. **Pace Wildenstein Gallery** exhibits current stars, especially well-known painter-photographers. **Postmasters** is a treasure trove of conceptual pieces. **Marian Goodman Gallery** features the European avant-garde.

In Chelsea, the **Mathew Marks Gallery** and **Marianne Boesky Gallery** are usually worth a visit. **Paula Cooper** often hosts controversial shows in her beautiful loft space. The **Gagosian Gallery** exhibits paintings by modern masters, with great works by Lichtenstein and Johns. It also has an outlet in the Upper East Side where you can find **Knoedler & Company**, and the **Hirschl & Adler Galleries** with a good selection of European and American fine art. **Max Protech** is very architecture-friendly, while **Esso** displays Pop Art. **Barbara Gladstone** is another heavy hitter in the art scene, and **Exit Art** is famed for its multimedia exhibitions.

## AMERICAN FOLK ART

If you're in the market for American folk art, **Susan Parrish Antiques** has a wide selection of hooked rugs and other Americana, but is open only by appointment. Similar goods are at **Laura Fisher Quilts** in Manhattan Art & Antiques Center, who sells everything from decoys to hooked rugs.

## ANTIQUES CENTERS AND SECONDHAND ANTIQUES

In addition to hundreds of small shops selling everything from tiger teeth to multimillion-dollar paintings, Manhattan is home to **The Manhattan Art & Antiques Center**, which has dozens of dealers under one roof. The **Chelsea Antiques Building** is home to more than 100 galleries of antiques over twelve floors. Collectibles include Hollywood memorabilia and rare personal items of stars such as Garbo and Bogart.

## AMERICAN FURNITURE

For furniture from the 17th-, 18th-, and 19th-centuries, try **Bernard & S. Dean Levy**, or **Leigh Keno American Furniture**. **Judith & James Milne** sell early American country furniture and a splendid collection of quilts. Go to **Woodard & Greenstein American Antiques & Quilts** for a truly wonderful selection of Shaker furniture.

Collectors of Art Deco or Art Nouveau furniture should pay a visit to **Alan Moss**, which is full of furniture and decorative items. **Macklowe Gallery** has a massive collection of fine Art Nouveau furniture. **Lillian Nassau** has Tiffany lamps and many Art Nouveau and Art Deco pieces. New York has a handful of retro shops, though numbers are growing all the time. Two of the best are **Depression Modern** and **Mood Indigo**

on Prince Street, which have treasures from the 1930s and 1940s.

## INTERNATIONAL ANTIQUES

If you're looking for English antiques, try **Florian Papp** and **Kentshire Galleries**. For European pieces, you'll have plenty of choices; try **Betty Jane Bart Antiques**, **Kurt Glückselig Antiques**, **Linda Horn Antiques**, and **Les Pierres**. La Belle Epoque stocks antique posters. Oriental dealers include **Doris Leslie Blau**, **E. & J. Frankel**, and **Flying Cranes Antiques**.

## FLEA MARKETS

New York has a number of year-round weekend markets. Most flea markets officially open at 9 or 10am, but the haggling starts as early as 6am. If you arrive early, you could unearth some valuable piece of cultural Americana like a Barbie lunch box or a Soupy Sales record.

Visit the **Annex Antiques Fair and Flea Market** for everything from secondhand clothing to antique furniture. The weekend **Canal Street Flea Market** has bric-a-brac; the **Columbus Avenue Flea Market** has new and second-hand clothing and furniture. For information on all street fairs and flea markets, check Friday's *The New York Times*.

## AUCTION HOUSES

Manhattan's two most celebrated auction houses are **Christie's** and **Sotheby's**, selling collectibles ranging from coins, jewels, and vintage wines to fine and decorative arts. **Doyle New York** and **Phillips de Pury & Co.** are both well-respected names for fine art, jewelry, and antiques. Items for sale are previewed several days before the auctions, so check the Friday and Sunday *Times*. The venerable **Swann Galleries** auctions prints, books, maps, posters, autographs, and photographs.

# DIRECTORY

## ART GALLERIES

**Barbara Gladstone**
515 W 24th St.
**Map** 7 C4.
*Tel (212) 206-9300.*

**Esso Gallery**
531 W 26th St, 2nd Floor.
**Map** 7 C4.
*Tel (212) 560-9728.*

**Exit Art**
475 10th Ave.
**Map** 7 C2.
*Tel (212) 966-7745.*

**Gagosian Gallery**
555 W 24th St.
**Map** 7 C4.
*Tel (212) 741-1111.*
*One of two galleries.*

**Hirschl & Adler Galleries**
21 E 70th St.
**Map** 12 F1.
*Tel (212) 535-8810.*

**Knoedler & Company**
19 E 70th St.
**Map** 13 A1.
*Tel (212) 794-0550.*

**Leo Castelli**
18 E 77th St.
**Map** 17 A5.
*Tel (212) 249-4470.*

**Marian Goodman Gallery**
24 W 57th St.
**Map** 12 F3.
*Tel (212) 977-7160.*

**Marianne Boesky Gallery**
535 W 22nd St.
**Map** 7 C4.
*Tel (212) 680-9889.*

**Mary Boone Gallery**
745 5th Ave.
**Map** 12 F3.
*Tel (212) 752-2929.*
*One of two galleries.*

**Mathew Marks Gallery**
523 W 24th St.
**Map** 7 C4.
*Tel (212) 243-0200.*

**Max Protech**
511 W 22nd St.
**Map** 7 C4.
*Tel (212) 633-6999.*

**Pace Wildenstein Gallery**
534 W 25th St.
**Map** 7 C4.
*Tel (212) 929-7000.*
*One of two galleries.*

**Paula Cooper**
534 W 21st St.
**Map** 7 C4.
*Tel (212) 255-1105.*

**Postmasters**
459 W 19th St.
**Map** 7 C5.
*Tel (212) 727-3323.*

## AMERICAN FOLK ART

**Laura Fisher Quilts**
Manhattan Art
& Antiques Center,
1050 2nd Ave.
**Map** 13 B4.
*Tel (212) 838-2596.*

**Susan Parrish Antiques**
*Tel (212) 807-1561.*
*By appointment only.*

## ANTIQUE CENTERS AND SECOND-HAND ANTIQUES

**Chelsea Antiques Building**
110 W 25th St.
**Map** 8 F4.
*Tel (212) 929-0909.*

**The Manhattan Arts & Antiques Center**
1050 2nd Ave.
**Map** 13 A3.
*Tel (212) 355-4400.*

## AMERICAN FURNITURE

**Alan Moss**
436 Lafayette St.
**Map** 4 F2.
*Tel (212) 473-1310.*

**Bernard & S. Dean Levy**
24 E 84th St.
**Map** 16 F4.
*Tel (212) 628-7088.*

**Depression Modern**
150 Sullivan St.
**Map** 4 D3.
*Tel (212) 982-5699.*

**Judith & James Milne**
506 E 74th St.
**Map** 17 C5.
*Tel (212) 472-0107.*
*One of two branches.*

**Leigh Keno American Furniture**
127 E 69th St.
**Map** 17 A5.
*Tel (212) 734-2381.*

**Lillian Nassau**
220 E 57th St.
**Map** 13 B3.
*Tel (212) 759-6062.*

**Macklowe Gallery**
667 Madison Ave.
**Map** 13 A3.
*Tel (212) 644-6400.*

**Mood Indigo**
181 Prince St. **Map** 4 E3.
*Tel (212) 254-1176.*

**Woodard & Greenstein American Antiques**
506 E 74th St.
**Map** 17 A5.
*Tel (212) 988-2906.*

## INTERNATIONAL ANTIQUES

**La Belle Epoque**
280 Columbus Ave.
**Map** 12 D1.
*Tel (212) 362-1770.*

**Betty Jane Bart Antiques**
1225 Madison Ave.
**Map** 17 A3.
*Tel (212) 410-2702.*

**Doris Leslie Blau**
724 5th Ave. **Map** 12 F3.
*Tel (212) 586-5511.*
*By appointment only.*

**E. & J. Frankel**
1040 Madison Ave.
**Map** 17 A5.
*Tel (212) 879-5733.*

**Florian Papp**
962 Madison Ave.
**Map** 17 A5.
*Tel (212) 288-6770.*

**Flying Cranes Antiques**
1050 2nd Ave.
**Map** 13 B4.
*Tel (212) 223-4600.*

**Kentshire Galleries**
37 E 12th St. **Map** 4 E1.
*Tel (212) 673-6644.*

**Kurt Gluckselig Antiques**
200 E 58th St. **Map** 13 B3.
*Tel (212) 758-1805.*

**Linda Horn Antiques**
1015 Madison Ave.
**Map** 17 A5.
*Tel (212) 772-1122.*

**Les Pierres**
369 Bleecker St.
**Map** 3 C2.
*Tel (212) 243-7740.*

## FLEA MARKETS

**Annex Antiques Fair and Flea Market**
26th St at 6th Ave,
112 W 25th St (Annex).
**Map** 8 E4.
*Tel (212) 243-5343.*
*Open Sat and Sun.*

**Canal Street Flea Market**
335 Canal St. **Map** 4 E5.
*Open every weekend
Mar–Dec.*

**Columbus Avenue Flea Market**
Columbus Ave, between
76th and 77th St.
**Map** 16 D5.
*Tel (631) 873-4790.*
*Open Sun.*

## AUCTION HOUSES

**Christie's**
20 Rockefeller Plaza.
**Map** 12 F5.
*Tel (212) 636-2000.*

**Doyle New York**
175 E 87th St.
**Map** 17 A3.
*Tel (212) 427-2730.*

**Phillips de Pury & Co.**
450 W 15th St.
**Map** 7 C5.
*Tel (212) 940-1200.*

**Sotheby's**
1334 York Ave. **Map** 13
C1. *Tel (212) 606-7000.*

**Swann Galleries**
104 E 25th St. **Map** 9 A4.
*Tel (212) 254-4710.*

# Gourmet Groceries, Specialty Food, and Wine Shops

New York's striking cultural and ethnic diversity is celebrated in its food – the city's food shops provide a truly international feast. There is also a dazzling array of coffee stores and wine shops available almost everywhere you turn.

## GOURMET GROCERIES

Scattered around town are several famous food emporiums that are tourist attractions in themselves. Remember, too, to visit the department stores, which often rival the specialty food stores.

At **Dean & DeLuca** on Broadway, a chic delicatessen, food is elevated to an art form – don't miss the huge selection of take-out food. **Russ & Daughters** on Houston Street, one of the oldest gourmet shops, is known as an "appetizing" store, full of ethnic food and famous for smoked fish, cream cheese, chocolates, and bagels. The **Gourmet Garage** on Broome Street sells all kinds of delicious fresh food, in particular organic produce. **Zabar's** on Broadway is perhaps the finest food store in the world, with huge crowds jostling for the excellent smoked salmon, bagels, caviar, nuts and candies, cheese, and coffee.

**William Poll** on Lexington Avenue offers picnic hampers as well as a great variety of prepared dishes. For pâté de foie gras, Scottish smoked salmon, beluga, and caviar, go to **Caviarteria**.

**Whole Foods**, famed for their superb selection of natural, organic, wholesome foods, draws devoted shoppers from throughout the city. The new Whole Foods that opened in Columbus Circle is now the largest supermarket in Manhattan, with row upon gleaming row of quality food "in its purest state" with no artificial additives, sweeteners, or preservatives. **Fairway Market** on Broadway, established over 55 years ago, offers premium groceries from fresh produce to smoked fish and baked goods.

## SPECIALTY FOOD

Fabulous bread and cake shops abound but one of the best is **Poseidon Greek Bakery**, renowned for its filo pastry. **H & H Bagels** bakes 60,000 of the best bagels every day. **Vesuvio** has Italian bread and some unusual pepper biscuits. Try the delicious Chinese pastries at **Fung Wong**, or the pretzel croissants and great tarts at **City Bakery**. Instantly recognizable by the line of happy customers at the door, **Magnolia Bakery** is famed for its beautifully decorated and superb-tasting cupcakes.

Great confectionery shops include **Li-Lac** for handmade chocolates and **Mondel Chocolates** for chocolate animals. **Economy Candy** has a huge range of dried fruit but for a real treat go to **Teuscher Chocolates**, which has fresh champagne truffles flown in direct from Switzerland.

**Myers of Keswick** imports English food. For something more exotic, **Kam Man Market** is an Oriental grocery selling Chinese, Thai, and other oriental products. The **Italian Food Center** has great olive oils, dried pastas, and sausages. Go to **Jefferson Market** for meat and fish, and **Citarella** for its fine seafood. **Angelica's Herbs and Spices** has a selection of 2,000 varieties of herbs and spices.

For a wide choice of cheese, as well as olives and *charcuterie*, visit **Murray's Cheese Shop**. The intoxicating wafts that greet you at the front door are sure to lure you in. Named New York's Best Cheese Shop by many of the city's newspapers, it is heaven for cheese-lovers, with over 250 types of cheese from around the world, from bloomy rinds like Camembert to moist Ricotta. Feel free to sample; the friendly staff happily offers tastings from the mind-boggling selection. Make a picnic out of it, and pick up some of their fresh breads and olives to accompany your pungent purchases.

If you are looking for true old Eastern European pickle recipes then **The Pickle Guys** is the right place. In addition to pickles, they also store pickled tomatoes, mushrooms, olives, hot peppers, sweet kraut, sauerkraut, herring, and sun-dried tomatoes.

## COFFEE STORES

New York also has many fine coffee stores. Among the best are **Oren's Daily Roast**, **The Sensuous Bean**, and **Porto Rico Importing Company**, each with a mouth-watering selection. For fruit and vegetables at reasonable prices, visit a farmers' green market, but get there early. Among the most popular are **Upper West Side**, **St. Mark's in-the-Bowery**, and **Union Square**. The cozy **McNulty's Tea & Coffee Company**, one of the nation's oldest coffee stores, sells excellent coffees and teas. For information about the city's markets, phone: (212) 788-7476.

## WINE SHOPS

**Acker, Merrall & Condit** have been selling wines since 1820 and have an excellent selection. Go to **Garnet Liquors** for fine wines and champagnes at bargain prices. **SoHo Wines and Spirits** has an extensive selection of single-malt Scotch whisky. **Sherry-Lehmann** is New York's leading wine merchant. **Astor Wines & Spirits**, New York's largest wine store, features a massive selection of premium and discount wines and spirits. Every month they highlight their Top 10 choices under $10, where you can pick up superb bottles at nice prices. **Union Square Wines and Spirits** offers terrific a variety of wines, and features tastings every week.

# DIRECTORY

## GOURMET GROCERIES

**Caviarteria**
502 Park Ave.
**Map** 13 A3.
*Tel (212) 759-7410.*

**Dean & DeLuca**
560 Broadway.
**Map** 4 E3.
*Tel (212) 226-6800.*
*One of several branches.*

**Fairway Market**
2127 Broadway.
**Map** 15 C5.
*Tel (212) 595-1888.*

**Gourmet Garage**
453 Broome St.
**Map** 4 E4.
*Tel (212) 941-5850.*
*One of several branches.*

**Russ & Daughters**
179 E Houston St.
**Map** 5 A3.
*Tel (212) 475-4880.*

**Whole Foods**
10 Columbus Circle.
**Map** 12 D3.
*Tel (212) 823-9600.*
*One of several branches.*

**William Poll**
1051 Lexington Ave.
**Map** 17 A5.
*Tel (212) 288-0501.*

**Zabar's**
2245 Broadway.
**Map** 15 C4.
*Tel (212) 787-2000.*

## SPECIALTY FOOD

**Angelica's Herbs and Spices**
147 1st Ave.
**Map** 5 A1.
*Tel (212) 677-1549.*

**Citarella**
2135 Broadway.
**Map** 15 C5.
*Tel (212) 874-0383.*

**City Bakery**
3 W 18th St.
**Map** 8 F5.
*Tel (212) 366-1414.*

**Economy Candy**
108 Rivington St.
**Map** 5 A3.
*Tel (212) 254-1531.*

**Fung Wong**
41 Mott St.
**Map** 4 F3.
*Tel (212) 267-4037.*

**H & H Bagels**
2239 Broadway.
**Map** 15 C4.
*Tel (212) 595-8003.*
*One of two branches.*

**Italian Food Center**
186 Grand St.
**Map** 15 C4.
*Tel (212) 925-2954.*

**Jefferson Market**
450 Ave of the Americas.
**Map** 12 E5.
*Tel (212) 533-3377.*

**Kam Man Market**
200 Canal St.
**Map** 4 F5.
*Tel (212) 571-0330.*

**Li-Lac**
120 Christopher St.
**Map** 3 C2.
*Tel (212) 242-7374.*

**Magnolia Bakery**
401 Bleecker St.
**Map** 3 C2.
*Tel (212) 462-2572.*

**Mondel Chocolates**
2913 Broadway.
**Map** 20 E3.
*Tel (212) 864-2111.*

**Murray's Cheese Shop**
257 Bleecker St.
**Map** 4 D2.
*Tel (212) 243-3289.*
*One of two branches.*

**Myers of Keswick**
634 Hudson St.
**Map** 3 C2.
*Tel (212) 691-4194.*

**The Pickle Guys**
49 Essex St.
**Map** 5 B4.
*Tel (212) 656-9739.*

**Poseidon Greek Bakery**
629 9th Ave.
**Map** 12 D5.
*Tel (212) 757-6173.*

**Teuscher Chocolates**
25 E 61st St.
**Map** 12 F3.
*Tel (212) 751-8482.*

620 5th Ave.
**Map** 12 F4.
*Tel (212) 246-4416.*

**Vesuvio Bakery**
160 Prince St.
**Map** 4 E3.
*Tel (212) 925-8248.*

## COFFEE STORES

**McNulty's Tea & Coffee Company**
109 Christopher St.
**Map** 3 C2.
*Tel (212) 242-5351.*

**Oren's Daily Roast**
1144 Lexington Ave.
**Map** 17 A4.
*Tel (212) 472-6830.*
*One of several branches.*

**Porto Rico Importing Company**
201 Bleecker St.
**Map** 3 C2.
*Tel (212) 477-5421.*
*One of several branches.*

**St. Mark's in-the-Bowery Greenmarket**
E 10th St at 2nd Ave.
**Map** 4 F1.
*Open Tue.*

**The Sensuous Bean**
66 W 70th St.
**Map** 12 D1.
*Tel 1-800-238-6845.*

**Union Square Greenmarket**
E 17th St & Broadway.
**Map** 8 F5.
*Open Mon, Wed, Fri, and Sat.*

**Upper West Side Greenmarket**
Columbus Ave at 77th St.
**Map** 16 D5.
*Open Sun.*

## WINE SHOPS

**Acker, Merrall & Condit**
160 W 72nd St.
**Map** 11 C1.
*Tel (212) 787-1700.*

**Astor Wines & Spirits**
399 Lafayette St.
**Map** 4 F2.
*Tel (212) 674-7500.*

**Garnet Liquors**
929 Lexington Ave.
**Map** 13 A1.
*Tel (212) 772-3211.*

**SoHo Wines and Spirits**
461 W Broadway.
**Map** 4 E4.
*Tel (212) 777-4332.*

**Sherry-Lehmann**
679 Madison Ave.
**Map** 13 A3.
*Tel (212) 838-7500.*

**Union Square Wines and Spirits**
33 Union Square West.
**Map** 9 A5.
*Tel (212) 675-8100.*

# Electronics and Housewares

From flat-screen TVs and top-of-the-line sound systems to swanky designer home furnishings, New York City abounds with electronics and housewares stores. Perhaps the most competitive retailers in New York are the ones that sell electronics, so it pays to shop around. Be particularly careful with electronics stores on the heavily touristed streets and those around the major tourist sights, such as Fifth Avenue near the Empire State Building. Many of these stores sell mediocre, sometimes faulty equipment at inflated prices, and it's a hassle or near impossible to get a refund once you've returned home. If you're buying electronic goods to take to Europe, make sure they have compatible voltages and formats (many in the US are made to different standards).

## SOUND SYSTEMS AND EQUIPMENT

For the latest in cutting-edge stereo equipment, head to **Sound by Singer**. **J&R Music World** sells competitively priced equipment and has the best jazz CD collection in the city. The Danish **Bang & Olufsen** showcases a range of sleek, minimalist sound systems that can dress up even the humblest flat. **Harvey Electronics** sells top-notch stereos and electronics with the bonus of a friendly, informative staff. Browse the quality systems at **Lyric Hi-Fi**, a longtime favorite that's been around since 1959. The perennially jam-packed **Sony Style** delivers on its wide assortment of top-shelf sound systems and plenty of impulse-buy gizmos. True to its name, the chain store **Best Buy** does offer some of the best buys on an enormous range of stereo systems and home-entertainment products. For high-end stereo equipment and components, check out **Innovative Audio Video Showrooms**. Also stop to look around at the wide range of both used and new stereos at the friendly **Stereo Exchange**.

## PHOTOGRAPHY

**B & H Photo** is where amateur and professional photographers can find everything they need. Check the newspapers for **Willoughby's**, they have good sales on photographic equipment and supplies. The appropriately named **Olden Camera** on Broadway eschews anything digital offering instead quality, old-school cameras and gear. Head to Chelsea's **Foto Care** for a wide range of cameras and accoutrements. **Alkit Pro Camera** offers a large assortment of cameras, components, and lighting equipment plus rentals and film developing and processing. Make for **Adorama** in the Flatiron District, and browse the spectacular displays of digital cameras and accessories, point-and-shoots, and disposables, and also affordable prices on film developing and processing. Don't miss the quality, high-end cameras and equipment at the elegant **The Photo Village**.

## COMPUTERS

The immense, airy **Apple Store SoHo** on Prince Street is undoubtedly the Macintosh mecca of Manhattan. Macphiles flock here to peruse and test-drive the latest models, plug in to iPods, and attend seminars geared to both novices and experts. **CompUSA** offers an enormous range of computers, from laptops to desktops. If you brought your computer from home and find that you need a repair, head to **Amnet PC Solutions**, where a tech whiz will – keep your fingers crossed – be able to fix whatever ails your computer. If you'd rather not haul your computer across town in a cab, they also do house calls starting at $95 an hour. The specialty at **Tekserve** is Mac repairs, where you can get a free estimate and also browse for upgrades.

## KITCHENWARE

Most of the department stores offer a wide range of household goods. For a specialized shop, try **Broadway Panhandlers** on Broome Street, a cook's heaven with outstanding baking and pastry-making equipment. **Bridge Kitchenware** is a household name among most restauranteurs. **Williams-Sonoma** has a wide range of kitchenware, utensils, and cookbooks. The East Village, particularly on and around Bowery Street, has long been the nucleus for restaurant supply stores, where you can find top-quality kitchenware at bargain prices. **Leader Restaurant Equipment & Supplies** sells all the kitchenware you can think of, from heavy cutlery to sushi platters and chopsticks.

## HOUSEWARES AND FURNISHINGS

**Baccarat**, **Lalique**, and **Villeroy & Boch** are where you'll find the finest crystal, china, and silverware. **Orrefors Kosta Boda** and **Tiffany & Co**. are among other fashionable shops. Go to **Avventura** for crystal and china and, for the best of inexpensive, utilitarian china, visit **Fishs Eddy**. Try **Ceramica**, which stocks lovely handmade Italian pottery, and **La Terrine** and **Stuben Glass** for hand-painted ceramics. Browse the hip SoHo showcase of designer **Jonathan Adler**, whose eye-catching pottery of natural shades and primitive and organic shapes will stand out from everything else in your living room. His collection includes a "family" of playful decanters in the shapes of man, woman, and child, plump vases of smiling suns and fish plates, and a menagerie of pottery animals, including bookends shaped like the front and back of a charging bull. **ABC Carpet & Home** on Broadway has an enviable reputation for home furnishings. For low prices on housewares, shop on **Grand Street** on the Lower East Side.

For elegant furniture, from soft leather sofas to luxurious beds, and sleek tableware, try Giorgio Armani's posh **Armani Casa. Dune** on Franklin Street in TriBeCa offers chic furniture by

contemporary designers, including wool sofas and convertible lounges. Browse the classy furnishings, by designers such as Philippe Starck and Paola Navone, at **M at Mercer** in SoHo. If you lean towards retro, then make a beeline for **Restoration Hardware** on Broadway, where you can choose from updated Art Deco furnishings, lighting fixtures, and patinated bronze accessories.

## LINENS

Linens (...)
departr(...)
sheets (...)
visit **Porthau...**
The Italian **Frette**, on Mad... Avenue, sells thick towels and robes and wonderfully soft cotton sheets and bedding. **Bed, Bath & Beyond** offers a varied selection of bed linens, kitchen, and bath accessories.

# DIRECTORY

### SOUND SYSTEMS AND EQUIPMENT

**Bang & Olufsen**
952 Madison Ave.
**Map** 17 A5.
*Tel (212) 879-6161.*

**Best Buy**
60 W 23rd St. **Map** 8 E4.
*Tel (212) 366-1373.*

**Harvey Electronics**
2 W 45th St. **Map** 12 F5.
*Tel (212) 575-5000.*

**Innovative Audio Video Showrooms**
150 58th St. **Map** 13 A4.
*Tel (212) 634-4444.*

**J & R Music World**
31 Park Row. **Map** 1 C2.
*Tel (212) 238-9100.*

**Lyric Hi-Fi**
1221 Lexington Ave.
**Map** 17 A4.
*Tel (212) 439-1900.*

**Sony Style**
550 Madison Ave.
**Map** 13 A4.
*Tel (212) 833-5336.*

**Sound by Singer**
18 16th St. **Map** 8 F5.
*Tel (212) 924-8600.*

**Stereo Exchange**
627 Broadway.
**Map** 4 E3.
*Tel (212) 505-1111.*

### PHOTOGRAPHY

**Adorama**
42 18th St. **Map** 8 F5.
*Tel (212) 741-0052.*

**Alkit Pro Camera**
222 Park Ave S.
**Map** 9 A5.
*Tel (212) 674-1515.*

**B & H Photography**
420 9th Ave. **Map** 8 D2.
*Tel (212) 444-6615.*

**Foto Care**
136 W 21st St. **Map** 8 E4.
*Tel (212) 741-2990.*

**Olden Camera**
1263 Broadway, 4th floor.
**Map** 8 F3.
*Tel (212) 725-1234.*

**The Photo Village**
1133 Broadway, Suite 824.
**Map** 8 F4.
*Tel (212) 989-1252.*

**Willoughby's**
298 5th Ave.
**Map** 8 F3.
*Tel (800) 378-1898.*

### COMPUTERS

**Amnet PC Solutions**
229 E 53rd St.
**Map** 13 B4.
*Tel (212) 593-2425.*

**Apple Store SoHo**
103 Prince St. **Map** 4 E3.
*Tel (212) 226-3126.*

**CompUSA**
420 5th Ave. **Map** 8 F1.
*Tel (212) 764-6224.*

**Tekserve**
119 W 23rd St. **Map** 8 E4.
*Tel (212) 929-3645.*

### KITCHENWARE

**Bridge Kitchenware**
214 E 52nd St.
**Map** 13 B4.
*Tel (212) 688-4220.*

**Broadway Panhandlers**
477 Broome St. **Map** 4 E4.
*Tel (212) 966-3434.*

**Leader Restaurant Equipment & Supplies**
191 Bowery. **Map** 4 F4.
*Tel (212) 677-1982.*

**Williams-Sonoma**
10 Columbus Circle.
**Map** 12 D3.
*Tel (212) 823-9750.*
*One of several branches.*

### HOUSEWARES & FURNISHINGS

**ABC Carpet & Home**
888 Broadway. **Map** 8 F5.
*Tel (212) 473-3000.*

**Armani Casa**
97 Greene St. **Map** 4 E3.
*Tel (212) 334-1271.*

**Avventura**
463 Amsterdam Ave.
**Map** 15 C4.
*Tel (212) 769-2510.*

**Baccarat**
625 Madison Ave.
**Map** 13 A3.
*Tel (212) 862-4100.*

**Ceramica**
59 Thompson St.
**Map** 4 D4.
*Tel (212) 941-1307.*

**Dune**
88 Franklin St. **Map** 4 E5.
*Tel (212) 925-6171.*

**Fishs Eddy**
889 Broadway.
**Map** 8 F5.
*Tel (212) 420-9020.*

**Grand Street**
Lower East Side.
**Map** 4 E5.

**Jonathan Adler**
47 Greene St. **Map** 4 E4.
*Tel (212) 941-8950.*

**Lalique**
712 Madison Ave.
**Map** 13 A3.
*Tel (212) 355-6550.*

**M at Mercer**
49 Mercer St. **Map** 4 E4.
*Tel (212) 966-2830.*

**Orrefors Kosta Boda**
200 Lexington Ave.
**Map** 9 A2.
*Tel (212) 684-5455.*

**Restoration Hardware**
935 Broadway. **Map** 8 F4.
*Tel (212) 260-9479.*

**Stuben Glass**
667 Madison Ave.
**Map** 13 A3.
*Tel (212) 752-1441.*

**La Terrine**
1024 Lexington Ave.
**Map** 13 A1.
*Tel (212) 988-3366.*

**Tiffany & Co.**
See p329.

**Villeroy & Boch**
41 Madison Ave.
**Map** 9 A4.
*Tel (212) 213-8149.*

### LINENS

**Bed, Bath & Beyond**
620 Ave of the Americas.
**Map** 8 F5.
*Tel (212) 255-3550.*

**Frette**
799 Madison Ave.
**Map** 13 A1.
*Tel (212) 988-5221.*

**Porthault**
18 E 69th St. **Map** 12 F1.
*Tel (212) 688-1660.*

**Pratesi**
829 Madison Ave. **Map** 13
A2. *Tel (212) 288-2315.*

# ...TERTAINMENT IN NEW YORK

New York City is a non-stop entertainment extravaganza, every day, all year round. Whatever your taste, you can be sure the city will satisfy it on both a grand and an intimate scale. The challenge is to take advantage of as many of the entertainments as possible. If it's theater, you can enjoy a mainstream success on Broadway or take a chance on an experimental production in a loft. If it's music, there's the magnificence of opera at the Met or a jazz group blowing in a club in the Village. You can catch a spectacle of avant-garde dance in a café or try your own avant-garde dancing in one of the city's warehouse-sized clubs. Movie theaters abound. But perhaps best of all is wandering and watching the vast show that is New York.

**Performance by the New York City Ballet**

## PRACTICAL INFORMATION

Find out what events there are to choose from in the arts and leisure listings of the *New York Times* and the *Village Voice* newspapers and in *Time Out New York* and

**TKTS discount ticket booth**

*The New Yorker* magazines. These briefly describe the current entertainment and tell you which credit cards are accepted at the venue. At your hotel ask for *Where*, a free weekly magazine containing maps and information on the many attractions.

Hotel staff may be able to answer some of your questions and should also carry a wide selection of brochures and leaflets. In addition, they may be willing to reserve tickets for you. Some hotel TVs have a New York visitor information channel.

The **NYC & Company** is the city's official source for everything to do and see in the city. Touch-screen kiosks provide information and sell general admission tickets to the city's top attractions. Multilingual counselors, discount coupons, free maps, brochures, tour information and ATMs

are available. **NYC On Stage** is a phone hotline for theater, dance, and music events; **Broadway Inner Circle** gives brief descriptions of current shows, schedules, and prices; **Moviefone** gives recorded information on all the films; and **ClubFone** has up-to-date information on nightlife.

## BOOKING TICKETS

Popular shows may be sold out for weeks ahead, so book early. Box offices are open daily, except Sundays, from 10am until one hour after the performance begins. Call in person, or phone the box office or a ticket agency and order your seats by credit card. The biggest agencies are **Telecharge**, **Ticketmaster**, and **Ticket Central**; they will charge a small fee of a few dollars. An independent ticket

agent may also be able to find seats for you – try **Prestige Entertainment**; others are listed in the Yellow Pages. Fees vary according to demand. **Broadway Ticket Center** in the Times Square Information Center sells full-price tickets.

## DISCOUNT TICKETS

Established in 1973 to the advantage of theaters and theatergoers alike, the non-profit **TKTS** company sells unsold tickets on the day of the performance for all Broadway shows. Discounts range from 25 to 50 percent, but the price will include a small handling fee and must be paid for in cash or by traveler's check.

The **TKTS** booth at Duffy Square sells matinée tickets from 10am to 2pm every Wednesday and Saturday and from 11am to 3pm on Sundays; evening tickets are sold from 3pm to 8pm, and Sunday tickets from 11am until closing. The booths at Front and John Streets sell evening tickets from 10am to 6pm Monday through Friday, and from 11am to 7pm on Saturdays. All matinée tickets and Sunday performances are sold the day before. The booth in Times Square is in the heart of town, making it easily accessible. Evening tickets are sold Monday to Saturday from 3pm to 8pm, and Sunday from 3pm to closing (times vary); matinée tickets are sold Wednesday and Saturday

**A band playing at a cozy New York jazz club**

The Booth Theater on Broadway (see p345)

## USEFUL CONTACTS

**Broadway Bucks**
226 W 47th St. **Map** 12 E5.
*Tel 1-800-223-7565, ext. 214.*
www.bestofbroadway.com

**Broadway Inner Circle**
*Tel (212) 563-2929.*
www.broadwayinnercircle.com

**ClubFone**
*Tel (212) 777-2582.*
www.clubfone.com

**Delacorte Theater**
Entrance via 81st St at Central
Park W. **Map** 16 E4.
*Tel (212) 539-8750.*
www.publictheater.org
*Summer time only.*

**Hit Show Club**
8th Fl, 630 9th Ave. **Map** 12 D5.
*Tel (212) 581-4211.*
www.hitshowclub.com

**Movie Tickets Online**
www.movietickets.com
www.fandango.com
www.moviefone.com

**Network Tickets** *See p349.*

**New York Convention Center & Visitors Bureau (NYC & Co.)**
810 7th Ave. **Map** 12 E4.
*Tel (212) 484-1222.*
www.nycvisit.com

**NYC On Stage**
1501 Broadway. **Map** 12 D2.
*Tel (212) 768-1818.*

**Prestige Entertainment**
*Tel 1-800-243-8849.*

**Tap (Theatre Access Project)**
*Tel (212) 221-1103 (Voice).*
www.tdf.org

**Telecharge**
*Tel (212) 239-6200, 1-800-432-7250.* www.telecharge.com

**Ticket Central**
*Tel (212) 279-4200.*
www.ticketcentral.org

**Ticketmaster**
*Tel (212) 307-4100, 1-800-755-4000.* www.ticketmaster.com

**TKTS**
*Tel (212) 221-0013.*
Duffy Square. **Map** 12 E5.
Front & John Sts. **Map** 2 D2.
Times Square.
47th St & Broadway. **Map** 12 E5.
*Tel (212) 221-0885, ext. 446.*

from 10am to 2pm, and Sunday from 11am to 3pm.

You can purchase day-of-performance tickets from **Ticketmaster** at discounts of 10 to 25 percent (with a small commission charge) by telephone. The **Hit Show Club** sells vouchers that can be exchanged at box offices for discounted tickets. Some shows offer standing-room tickets on the day at a bargain price. It's often the only way to catch a sold-out show on short notice, but you might not get the best view. You can also get discount tickets for shows at **Broadway Bucks**.

### "SCALPERS" AND TOUTS

If you buy from a "scalper" (a ticket tout), you risk getting tickets for the wrong day, counterfeit tickets, and paying outrageous prices. The police often monitor sports and theater venues for scalpers and their customers.

### FREE TICKETS

Free tickets to TV shows, concerts, and special events are sometimes offered at **NYC & Co.** (New York Convention & Visitors Bureau), which is open from 8:30am to 6pm Monday to Friday and 9am to 5pm on weekends. Free or deeply discounted tickets to film or theater premieres are often advertised in the *New York Times, Daily News*, or *Time Out New York*. The "Cheap Thrills" section in the *Village Voice* lists poetry readings, recitals, and experimental films. The Shakespeare Festival at the **Delacorte Theater** in Central Park offers free tickets – one per person – on a first-come, first-served basis (be prepared to queue).

Royale Theater in the heart of Broadway (see p345)

### DISABLED ACCESS

Broadway theaters reserve a few spaces and cut-price tickets for the disabled. Call **Ticketmaster** or **Telecharge** well in advance for information and to reserve your tickets. For Off-Broadway theaters, call their box offices. Some theaters offer special equipment for the hearing-impaired patrons. **Tap** can arrange sign language for Broadway theaters.

# New York's Best: Entertainment

**Greenwich Village jazz club**

New York is one of the great entertainment capitals of the world. Top names in every branch of the arts are drawn here to perform and often to live and work. Major sports events are also constant, and as for nightlife, New York lives up to its reputation as "the city that never sleeps." From the huge choice offered, there are some venues and events that stand out as classics of their kind; this selection has been chosen from the listings on pages 344 to 363 as among those not to be missed. Even if you experience only one of them, you will have been part of something as essentially New York as the Empire State Building.

**Avalon**
*Formerly the Limelight, this converted church has remained a firm favorite with New York's night owls (see p354).*

**Madison Square Garden**
*Top sporting action is found at "the Garden," including home games for basketball's New York Knicks and ice hockey's Rangers, plus the Golden Gloves boxing tournament (see p360).*

**Film Forum**
*At New York's most stylish arts movie theater you can see the latest foreign and American independent releases or catch up with a classic in a wide range of retrospectives (see p349).*

**Village Vanguard**
*The jazz clubs of Greenwich Village have played host to all the great names in jazz. Fans can catch the stars of today and tomorrow at the world-famous Village Vanguard and the Blue Note (see p352).*

*Upper West Side*

*Central Park*

*Upper East Side*

*Upper Midtown*

*ercy the iron rict*

E A S T   R I V E R

**Philharmonic Rehearsals**
*The Thursday-morning rehearsals at Avery Fisher Hall are often open to the public at a fraction of the normal ticket price (see p350).*

**Metropolitan Opera House**
*Reserve well ahead and prepare to pay high prices to see the giants of the opera world (see p350).*

**Shakespeare in Central Park**
*If you are a summer visitor, set aside a time to get one of the rare free tickets for the Delacorte Theater's open-air Shakespeare featuring top Hollywood and Broadway names (see p344).*

**The Nutcracker**
*The Christmas event for children of every age is performed each year at Lincoln Center by the New York City Ballet (see p346).*

| 0 kilometers | | 2 |
|---|---|---|
| 0 miles | | 1 |

**Public Theater**
*Founded in 1954, the Public has a mandate to create theater for all New Yorkers. Its year-round Shakespeare Festival is part of a commitment to classical works, but new plays are also developed here (see p120).*

**Carnegie Hall**
*Conveniently situated in the Theater District, Carnegie Hall is famous the world over as a show-case for the best in the musical arts. A backstage tour gives a fascinat-ing insight into "the house that music built" (see p350).*

# Theater and Dance

New York is famous for its extravagant musicals and its ferocious critics. It is one of the world's greatest theater and dance centers, featuring every kind of production imaginable. Whether your preference is for the glitz and glamour of a Broadway blockbuster or something truly experimental, you'll find it here.

## BROADWAY

Broadway has long been synonymous with New York's Theater District, but the majority of Broadway theaters are actually scattered between 41st and 53rd streets and from Sixth to Ninth Avenues, with a few around the much-improved Times Square. Most were built between 1910 and 1930, during the heyday of vaudeville and the famous Ziegfeld Follies. The **Lyceum** (see p144) is the oldest theater still in operation (1903), the **American Airlines Theater**, permanent home of the Roundabout Theater Co., is the newest, and the historic **Biltmore Theater** opened in 2003 after a 14-year closure.

Many Broadway theaters went through a slump in the 1980s but are now enjoying a revival, using big names to draw in the crowds. This is where you will find the "power productions" – the big, highly publicized dramas, musicals and revivals starring Hollywood luminaries in (it is hoped) sure-fire earners. Hits have included imports such as *Les Misérables*; New York originals such as *Cats* and *The Producers*; the popular children's favorite *The Lion King*; and great revivals like *42nd Street*. There have also been glitzy adaptations from popular movies, such as *Hairspray*; shows celebrating 60s and 70s pop favorites, such as ABBA in *Mamma Mia!* and Monty Python's *Spamalot*.

## OFF-BROADWAY AND OFF-OFF-BROADWAY

There are about 20 Off-Broadway stages and 300 Off-Off-Broadway stages whose works will sometimes transfer to Broadway. Off-Broadway theaters have from 100 to 499 seats, and Off-Off-Broadway showplaces have fewer than 100. Both range from the well-appointed to the improvised, sited in lofts, churches, and even garages. Off-Broadway became very popular during the 1950s as a reaction to the commercialism of Broadway. It was also an ideal place for cautious producers to try out works considered too avant-garde for Broadway at lower operating costs. During the past two decades, Off-Off-Broadway theaters have staged more experimental pieces by these same producers.

Off-Broadway theaters are found all over Manhattan – from the **Douglas Fairbanks Theater**, where the irreverent *Forbidden Broadway* plays, to Central Park's open-air **Delacorte Theater**. Some are even in the Broadway district, such as the **Manhattan Theater Club**. Farther afield are the **Brooklyn Academy of Music (BAM)** (see p248), and the **92nd Street Y**. In these venues you will find lively, unusual, and experimental showcases for new talent as well as lots of uninhibited productions.

The Off-Broadway theaters mounted the first productions in New York of the works of playwrights Sean O'Casey, Tennessee Williams, Eugene O'Neill, Jean Genet, Eugene Ionesco, and David Mamet. Samuel Beckett's *Happy Days* premiered at the **Cherry Lane Theatre** in 1961, a venue that still promotes cutting-edge writing. Off-Broadway theaters host new and very often irreverent treatments of the classics.

Sometimes a more intimate, smaller Off-Broadway stage suits a production better than a larger more established theater would, as proved by such long-running successes as *The Fantasticks* along with the *Threepenny Opera*, which has been shown at the **Lucille Lortel Theater** since 1955.

## PERFORMANCE THEATERS

This extremely avant-garde art form can be found in several Off- and Off-Off-Broadway locations. Accurate descriptions and categorizations are almost impossible, but expect the bizarre and outlandish. The most likely venues to find this are **La MaMa**, **P.S. 122**, **HERE**, **Actor's Playhouse**, **92nd Street Y**, **Symphony Space**, and the **Joseph Papp Public Theater** (see p120). The latter is perhaps the most influential theater in New York. It was founded in the 1950s by the late director Joseph Papp, who introduced neighborhood tours to bring theater to people who had never seen it before.

The Public Theater created hits such as *A Chorus Line*; and *Hair*; it is most famous for its free summer performances of Shakespeare at the Delacorte Theater in Central Park (see p208). It usually has several productions running, and at 6pm on the day of performance, "Quiktix" tickets (limited to two per person) are sold in the Public Theater lobby.

## THEATER SCHOOLS

New York is the best place in the country to see actors learning their trade. Foremost among the acting schools is **The Actors' Studio**. The late Lee Strasberg, the advocate of method acting – in which the actor aims for complete identification with the character being played – was its guru. His students included Dustin Hoffman, Al Pacino, and Marilyn Monroe. "In progress" productions feature trainees and are open to the public and free. Sandy Meisner trained many actors, including the late Lee Remick, at the **Neighborhood Playhouse School of the Theater**. Its plays are not open to the public. The **New Dramatists** began in 1949 to develop new playwrights, helping the careers of the likes of William Inge. Play readings are open to the public and free.

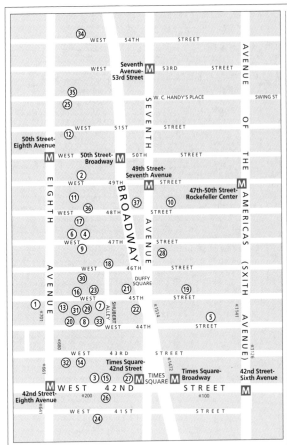

For other theaters
see p347.

## BROADWAY THEATERS

**① Al Hirschfield**
302 W. 45th St.
*Tel (212) 239-6200.*

**② Ambassador**
219 W. 49th St.
*Tel (212) 239-6200.*

**③ American Airlines Theater**
227 W. 42nd St.
*Tel (212) 719-1300.*

**④ Barrymore**
243 W. 47th St.
*Tel (212) 239-6200.*

**⑤ Belasco**
111 W. 44th St.
*Tel (212) 239-6200.*

**⑥ Biltmore**
261 W. 47th St.
*Tel (212) 239 6200.*

**⑦ Booth**
222 W. 45th St.
*Tel (212) 239-6200.*

**⑧ Broadhurst**
235 W. 44th St.
*Tel (212) 239-6200.*

**⑨ Brooks Atkinson**
256 W. 47th St.
*Tel (212) 307-4100.*

**⑩ Cort**
138 W. 48th St.
*Tel (212) 239-6200.*

**⑪ Eugene O'Neill**
230 W. 49th St.
*Tel (212) 239-6200.*

**⑫ Gershwin**
222 W. 51st St.
*Tel (212) 307-4100.*

**⑬ John Golden**
252 W. 45th St.
*Tel (212) 239-6200.*

**⑭ Helen Hayes**
240 W. 44th St.
*Tel (212) 239-6200.*

**⑮ Hilton**
213 W. 42nd St.
*Tel (212) 307 4100.*

**⑯ Imperial**
249 W. 45th St.
*Tel (212) 239-6200.*

**⑰ Longacre**
220 W. 48th St.
*Tel (212) 239-6200.*

**⑱ Lunt – Fontanne**
205 W. 46th St.
*Tel (212) 307-4747.*

**⑲ Lyceum**
149 W. 45th St.
*Tel (212) 239-6200.*

**⑳ Majestic**
247 W. 44th St.
*Tel (212) 239-6200.*

**㉑ Marquis**
211 W. 45th St.
*Tel (212) 307-4100.*

**㉒ Minskoff**
200 W. 45th St.
*Tel (212) 307-4100.*

**㉓ Music Box**
239 W. 45th St.
*Tel (212) 239-6200.*

**㉔ Nederlander**
208 W. 41st St.
*Tel (212) 307-4100.*

**㉕ Neil Simon**
250 W. 52nd St.
*Tel (212) 307-4100.*

**㉖ New Amsterdam**
214 W. 42nd St.
*Tel (212) 307 4100.*

**㉗ New Victory**
209 W. 42nd St.
*Tel (212) 239-6200.*

**㉘ Palace**
1564 Broadway.
*Tel (212) 307-4100.*

**㉙ Plymouth**
236 W. 45th St.
*Tel (212) 239-6200.*

**㉚ Richard Rodgers**
226 W. 46th St.
*Tel (212) 307-4100.*

**㉛ Royale**
242 W. 45th St.
*Tel (212) 239-6200.*

**㉜ St. James**
246 W. 44th St.
*Tel (212) 239-6200.*

**㉝ Shubert**
225 W. 44th St.
*Tel (212) 239-6200.*

**㉞ Studio 54**
254 W. 54th St.
*Tel (212) 719 3100.*

**㉟ Virginia**
245 W. 52nd St.
*Tel (212) 239-6200.*

**㊱ Walter Kerr**
219 W. 48th St.
*Tel (212) 239-6200.*

**㊲ Winter Garden**
1634 Broadway.
*Tel (212) 239-6200.*

## BALLET

At the heart of the dance world is Lincoln Center (see p214), where the New York City Ballet performs pieces in the **New York State Theater**. This company was created by the legendary brilliant choreographer George Balanchine (see p49) and is probably still the best in the world. The current director, Peter Martins, was one of Balanchine's best dancers and continues the strict policy of ensemble dancing rather than "star turns." The season runs from November to February and late April to early June. The ballet school at the **Juilliard Dance Theater** also presents a spring workshop every year, and this is a good chance to see budding stars.

The American Ballet Theater appears at the **Metropolitan Opera House**, which also hosts many visiting foreign companies, such as the Kirov, Bolshoi, and Royal ballets. Its repertoire includes 19th-century classics, such as *Swan Lake*, and works by modern choreographers such as Twyla Tharp and Paul Taylor.

## CONTEMPORARY DANCE

New York is the center of many of the most important movements in modern dance. The **Dance Theater of Harlem** is world famous for its modern, traditional, and ethnic productions. Other havens of experimental dance include the **92nd Street Y** and the **Merce Cunningham Studio** in Greenwich Village. The unusual **Dance Theater Workshop** has a packed program as well as an art gallery. **The Kitchen**, **La MaMa**, **Symphony Space**, and **P.S. 122** are all multimedia venues with the latest in contemporary dance, performance art and avant-garde music. Choreographer Mark Morris's company performs at the brand new **Mark Morris Dance Center** in Brooklyn; **City Center** (see p148) is a favorite spot for dance fans. It used to house the New York City Ballet and the

American Ballet Theater before Lincoln Center was built. As well as featuring the Joffrey Ballet, City Center has held performances by all the great contemporary artists, including Alvin Ailey's blend of modern, jazz, and blues and the companies of modern dance masters Merce Cunningham and Paul Taylor. Avoid the mezzanine as the view is restricted.

The city's single most active venue for dance is probably the **Joyce Theater**, where such well-established companies as the Feld Ballet, along with bold newcomers and visiting troupes, perform.

Each spring the Festival of Black Dance at the **Brooklyn Academy of Music (BAM)** (see p248) features everything from ethnic dance to hip-hop. During autumn the "Next Wave" festival of music and dance is held, celebrating international and American avant-garde dance and music. During winter, the American Ballet Festival is held here.

During June, **New York University** (see p115) holds a Summer Residency Festival with lecture-demonstrations, rehearsals, and performances, and **Dancing in the Streets** organizes summertime dance performances all over the city.

Throughout the month of August, **Lincoln Center Out of Doors** has a program of free dance events on the plaza, with such experimental groups as the American Tap Dance Orchestra.

The new **Duke Theater** presents many contemporary dance companies and participates in events such as the New York Tap Festival.

At different times of the year, **Radio City Music Hall** holds several spectacular shows, with different companies from all over the world. At Christmas and Easter, it features the famously precise Rockettes dance troupe.

Choreographers and dance companies frequently present works-in-progress and recitals to the public. Among the most interesting venues for these is **Alvin Ailey's Repertory Ensemble**, famous for promoting black cultural expression,

which is opening the country's largest dance facility in 2004. The **Hunter College Dance Company** performs new works by its student choreographers, and the **Isadora Duncan Dance Foundation** recreates Duncan's original dances. To see contemporary choreographers the best place to go is **Juilliard Dance Theater**.

## PRICES

Theater is extremely expensive to produce, and ticket prices tend to reflect this. Even Off- and Off-Off-Broadway tickets are not cheap anymore. At one time, all tickets to previews of new plays sold at a much-reduced price, but not so today. Preview tickets are easier to get hold of, though, and it's fun to see a show before the reviews are in so you're able to make up your own mind.

For a Broadway theater ticket you can expect to pay $80 or more; for musicals, up to $100; Off-Broadway, $25 to $40. For dance, $20 to $50 is the usual range, with up to $115 for the American Ballet Theater.

## TIMES OF PERFORMANCE

The general rules for theater-hours are: closed on Mondays (except for most musicals), with matinees on Wednesdays, Saturdays, and sometimes Sundays. Matinees usually begin at 2pm, with evening performances at 8pm. Be sure to check the correct dates and times of the performance beforehand.

## BACKSTAGE TOURS AND LECTURES

For those interested in the mechanics and anecdotes of the theater, your best bet is to go on one of the theater tours. The **92nd Street Y** organizes insider's views of the theater, with famous directors, actors, and choreographers taking part. Writers are invited along to read or discuss their current works. **Radio City Music Hall** also holds tours.

# DIRECTORY

## OFF-BROADWAY

**92nd Street Y**
1395 Lexington Ave.
**Map** 17 A2.
*Tel (212) 415-5500.*

**Actors' Playhouse**
100 Seventh Ave S.
**Map** 3 C1.
*Tel (212) 463-0060.*

**Brooklyn Academy of Music**
30 Lafayette Ave.,
Brooklyn.
*Tel (718) 636-4100.*

**Cherry Lane Theatre**
38 Commerce St.
**Map** 3 C2.
*Tel (212) 239-6200.*

**HERE Art Center**
145 6th Ave.
**Map** 4 D4.
*Tel (212) 647-0202.*

**Circle in the Square**
1633 Broadway.
**Map** 12 E4.
*Tel (212) 307-0388.*

**Delacorte Theater**
Central Park. (81st St.)
**Map** 16 E4.
*Tel (212) 539-8750.*
*Summer time only.*

**Douglas Fairbanks Theater**
432 W 42nd St.
**Map** 7 C1.
*Tel (212) 239-6200.*

**Lambs Theater**
130 W 44th St.
**Map** 12 E5.
*Tel (212) 575-0300.*

**Lucille Lortel Theater**
121 Christopher St.
**Map** 3 C2.
*Tel (212) 924-2817.*

**Manhattan Theater Club**
311 W 43rd St.
**Map** 8 D1.
*Tel (212) 399-3000.*

**New York Theater Workshop**
79 E 4th St.
**Map** 4 F2.
*Tel (212) 460-5475.*

**Public Theater**
425 Lafayette St.
**Map** 4 F2.
*Tel (212) 539-8500.*

**Symphony Space**
2537 Broadway.
**Map** 15 C2.
*Tel (212) 864-5400.*

**Vivian Beaumont**
Lincoln Center.
**Map** 11 C2.
*Tel (212) 362-7600.*

## OFF-OFF-BROADWAY

**Bouwerie Lane Theater**
330 Bowery.
**Map** 4 F2.
*Tel (212) 677-0060.*

**The Kitchen**
512 W 19th St.
**Map** 7 C5.
*Tel (212) 255-5793.*

**Performing Garage**
33 Wooster St.
**Map** 4 E4.
*Tel (212) 966-3651.*

**York Theater at St. Peter's Church**
Citigroup Center,
619 Lexington Ave.
**Map** 13 A4.
*Tel (212) 935-5820.*

## PERFORMANCE THEATER

**La MaMa**
74a E 4th St.
**Map** 4 F2.
*Tel (212) 475-7710.*

**P.S. 122**
150 First Ave.
**Map** 5 A1.
*Tel (212) 477-5288.*

**Public Theater**
*See Off-Broadway.*

## THEATER SCHOOLS

**The Actors' Studio**
432 W 44th St.
**Map** 11 B5.
*Tel (212) 757-0870.*

**New Dramatists**
424 W 44th.
**Map** 11 C5.
*Tel (212) 757-6960.*

## DANCE

**92nd Street Y**
*See Off-Broadway.*

**Alvin Ailey American Dance Center**
211 W 61st St.
**Map** 11 C3.
*Tel (212) 767-0590.*

**Brooklyn Academy of Music**
*See Off-Broadway.*

**City Center**
130 W 56th St.
**Map** 12 E4.
*Tel (212) 581-1212.*

**Dance Theater of Harlem**
466 W 152nd St.
*Tel (212) 690-2800.*

**Dance Theater Workshop**
219 W 19th St. **Map** 8 E5.
*Tel (212) 924-0077.*

**Dancing in the Streets**
55 6th Ave. (offices)
*Tel (212) 625-3505.*

**Hunter College Dance Company**
695 Park Ave.
**Map** 13 A1.
*Tel (212) 772-4490.*

**Isadora Duncan Dance Foundation**
141 W 26th St.
**Map** 20 D2.
*Tel (212) 691-5040.*

**Joyce Theater**
175 Eighth Ave at 19th St.
**Map** 8 D5.
*Tel (212) 242-0800.*

**Juilliard Dance Theater**
60 Lincoln Center Plaza,
W 65th St.
**Map** 11 C2.
*Tel (212) 769-7406.*

## PERFORMANCE VENUES

**Duke Theater**
229 W 42nd St.
**Map** 8 E1.
*Tel (646) 223-3000.*

**The Kitchen**
*See Off-Off Broadway.*

**La MaMa**
*See Performance Theater.*

**Lincoln Center Out of Doors**
Lincoln Center, Broadway
at 64th St. **Map** 11 C2.
*Tel (212) 362-6000.*

**Manhattan Center**
311 W 34th St. **Map** 8 D2.
*Tel (212) 279-7740.*

**Mark Morris**
3 Lafayette Ave. (Brooklyn)
*Tel (718) 624-8400.*

**Merce Cunningham Studio**
55 Bethune St. **Map** 3 B2.
*Tel (212) 255-8290.*

**Metropolitan Opera House**
Lincoln Center, Broadway
at 65th St. **Map** 11 C2.
*Tel (212) 362-6000.*

**New York State Theater**
Lincoln Center, Broadway
at 65th St. **Map** 11 C2.
*Tel (212) 870-5570.*

**New York University**
Tisch School of the Arts
(TSOA), 111 2nd Ave.
**Map** 4 F1.
*Tel (212) 998-1920.*

**P.S. 122**
*See Performance Theater.*

**Radio City Music Hall**
50th St at Ave of the
Americas. **Map** 12 F4.
*Tel (212) 307-7171.*

**Symphony Space**
*See Off-Broadway.*

## BACKSTAGE TOURS

**92nd Street Y**
*See Off-Broadway.*

**Radio City Music Hall**
*Tel (212) 307-7171.*

**Events Guide**
www.broadway.org
www.livebroadway.com
www.playbill.com
www.newyork.citysearch.com

# Movies

New York is a film buff's paradise. Apart from new US releases, which show months in advance of other countries, many classic and foreign films are screened here.

The city has always been the testing ground for new developments in films, and it continues to be a hotbed of new and innovative talent. Many of the movies' most famous directors – Spike Lee, Martin Scorsese, and Woody Allen – were born and raised in New York, and the city's influence can be seen in many of their films. They, and others, can often be seen filming on the streets of the city; many of New York's landmarks have become famous after appearing in films. Most of the TV networks based in New York offer free tickets to the taping of their shows. Watching a show, such as *The David Letterman Show*, is popular with visitors.

## FIRST-RUN MOVIES

New York reviews and box office returns are so vital to a film's success that most major American films have their premieres in Manhattan's theaters. First-run films are shown mainly at the City Cinema chains, Loews, United Artists and Cineplex Odeon, which are scattered around the city. Some theaters have recorded information giving the names and duration of the different films showing, with starting times and ticket prices.

Programs start at 10am or 11am and are repeated every two to three hours until midnight. You should expect to line up for most evening and weekend performances of the more popular films. Making reservations using a credit card is possible at some theaters for an additional charge of about $1 per ticket. Matinees (usually before 4pm) are easier to get into. Senior citizens pay a reduced price for tickets: the required age may be over 60, 62, or 65 depending on the policy of the theater.

## NEW YORK FILM FESTIVAL

A high point of the year for film buffs is the New York Film Festival, now in its third decade. Organized by the **Film Society of Lincoln Center**, the festival starts in late September and continues for two weeks at the many Lincoln Center theaters. Outstanding new films from the US and abroad are entered in a competition for the huge prestige of winning an award. Many of the films shown during the festival are later released and can usually be seen only in art houses.

The **TriBeCa Film Festival**, created in part by director and actor Robert De Niro, was launched in 2002 to celebrate New York City as a filmmaking capital and to contribute to the long-term recovery of Lower Manhattan. The festival showcases a wide range of films, including classics, documentaries, and premieres, and usually takes place in late April and early May. Every spring, **Docfest** (the New York International Documentary Festival) presents five days of film and video documentaries from around the world, followed by panel discussions with the filmmaker.

## FILM RATINGS

Films in the United States are graded as follows:
**G** General audiences; all ages admitted.
**PG** Parental guidance suggested; some material unsuitable for children.
**PG-13** Parents strongly cautioned; some material inappropriate for children under age 13.
**R** Restricted. Children under 17 need to be accompanied by a parent or an adult guardian.
**NC-17** No children under 17 admitted.

## ON LOCATION

Many New York locations have played starring roles in films. Here are a few:

**The Brill Building** (1141 Broadway) contained Burt Lancaster's penthouse in *Sweet Smell of Success*.
**The Brooklyn Bridge** was a great backdrop in Spike Lee's *Mo' Better Blues*.
**Brooklyn Heights** and the **Metropolitan Opera** appeared in *Moonstruck*.
**Central Park** has shown up in countless films, including *Love Story* and *Marathon Man*.
**55 Central Park West** will be remembered as Sigourney Weaver's home in *Ghostbusters*.
**Chinatown** played a major role in *Year of the Dragon*.
**The Dakota** was where Mia Farrow lived in the classic *Rosemary's Baby*.
**The Empire State Building** is still standing after *King Kong*'s last battle. The observation deck is where Cary Grant waited in vain in *An Affair to Remember;* here Meg Ryan finally met Tom Hanks in *Sleepless in Seattle*.
**Grand Central Station** is famous for Robert Walker's meeting with Judy Garland in *Under the Clock* and the magical ballroom sequence in *The Fisher King*.
**Harlem** hosted the jazz musicians and dancers in *The Cotton Club*.
**Katz's Deli** was the setting for the café scene between Billy Crystal and Meg Ryan in *When Harry Met Sally...*.
**Little Italy** appeared in *The Godfather I* and *II*.
**Madison Square Garden** was the setting for the dramatic climax of *The Manchurian Candidate*.
**Tiffany & Co**. was Audrey Hepburn's favorite shop in *Breakfast at Tiffany's*.
**The United Nations Building** featured in *North by Northwest*.
**Washington Square Park** was where Robert Redford and Jane Fonda walked *Barefoot in the Park*.

## FOREIGN FILMS AND ART HOUSES

For the latest foreign and independent films, go to the **Angelika Film Center**, which also has an upscale coffee bar. Other good places are the **Rose Cinemas** at the BAM, the **Film Forum**, and **Lincoln Plaza Cinema**. The Plaza has a busy program of art and foreign films. For Asian, Indian, and Chinese films, you should visit the **Asia Society**. The **French Institute** screens many French films with English subtitles on Tuesdays. The **Quad Cinema** shows a wide selection of foreign films, often quite rare. **Cinema Village** runs special film events, such as the Festival of Animation.

The **Walter Reade Theater** houses the Film Society of the Lincoln Center, offering retro-spectives of international movies as well as celebrations of contemporary works, such as the popular annual Spanish Cinema Now festival.

## CLASSIC FILMS AND MUSEUMS

Retrospectives of films by particular directors or featuring specific actors are shown at

the **Public Theater** and the **Whitney Museum of American Art** *(see pp200–01)*. The **Museum of the Moving Image** *(see p246)* screens old films and also has many exhibits of memorabilia from the film industry. The **Museum of Television and Radio** *(see p171)* has regular screenings of classic films; you can also see or hear specific television or radio programs. Students interested in classic, new and experimental movies will appreciate the collection of the **Anthology Film Archives**.

The sky shows at the **Rose Center for Earth and Space** at the **American Museum of Natural History** are well worth a whole day's visit.

On summer evenings in Bryant Park, you can watch free classic movies, and on Saturday mornings, the **Film Society of Lincoln Center**, where special children's shows are held.

## TELEVISION SHOWS

A number of TV programs originate in New York. The popular *David Letterman* and *Saturday Night Live* shows are almost impossible to get tickets for, but tickets for many other shows can be

obtained online, by calling the networks such as **NBC**, **ABC**, and **CBS**, or sometimes on standby.

Another good source of free tickets is the Times Square Information Bureau *(see p368)*. On weekday mornings on Fifth Avenue around **Rockefeller Plaza**, free tickets for a number of TV programs are sometimes distributed by the program's production staff. There's absolutely no way that you can plan for this. It's simply a matter of good luck and being in the right place at the right time.

For those who want to get a glimpse behind the scenes of TV, NBC organizes tours around the studios, from 8:30am to 5:30pm Monday to Saturday and 9:30 to 4:30pm on Sunday.

## CHOOSING WHAT TO SEE

If you feel bewildered by the huge range of films offered in New York, check the listings in *New York* magazine, the *New York Times*, the *Village Voice* and *The New Yorker*. The following Internet guides give show times and locations:
**www**.moviefone.com
**www**.movietickets.com

# DIRECTORY

**ABC**
*Tel (212) 580-5176.*
**www**.abc.com.

**American Museum of Natural History**
Central Park W at 79th St.
**Map** 16 D5.
*Tel (212) 769-5650.*

**Angelika Film Center**
18 W Houston St.
**Map** 4 E3.
*Tel (212) 995-2000.*

**Anthology Film Archives**
32 2nd Ave at 2nd St.
**Map** 5 C2.
*Tel (212) 505-5181.*

**Asia Society**
725 Park Ave. **Map** 13 A1.
*Tel (212) 517-2742.*

**CBS**
*Tel (212) 247-6497.*

**Cinema Village**
22 E 12th St. **Map** 4 F1.
*Tel (212) 924-3363.*

**Docfest**
*Tel (212) 668-1100.*
**www**.docfest.org

**Film Forum**
209 W Houston St.
**Map** 3 C3.
*Tel (212) 727-8110.*

**French Institute**
55 E 59th St. **Map** 12 F3.
*Tel (212) 355-6160.*

**Lincoln Plaza Cinema**
1886 Broadway.
**Map** 12 D2.
*Tel (212) 757-2280.*

**Museum of Modern Art**
11 W 53rd St. **Map** 12 F4.
*Tel (212) 708-9480.*

**Museum of the Moving Image**
35th Ave & 36th St.
Astoria, Queens.
*Tel (718) 784-0077.*

**Museum of Television & Radio**
25 W 52nd St. **Map** 12 F4.
*Tel (212) 621-6600.*

**NBC**
Standby: 30 Rockefeller
Plaza at 49th St
(before 9pm).
*Tel (212) 664-3056.*
**www**.nbc.com

**Public Theater**
425 Lafayette St.
**Map** 4 F4.
*Tel (212) 539-8500.*

**Quad Cinema**
34 W 13th St.
**Map** 4 D1.
*Tel (212) 255-8800.*

**Rockefeller Plaza**
47th–50th St, 5th Ave.
**Map** 12 F5.

**Rose Cinemas**
Brooklyn Academy of
Music (BAM), 30 Lafayette
Ave, Brooklyn.
*Tel (718) 636-4100.*

**TriBeCa Film Festival**
*Tel (212) 941-2400.*
**www**.tribecafilmfestival.
org

**Walter Reade Theater**
70 Lincoln Center Plaza.
**Map** 12 D2.
*Tel (212) 875-5600.*

**Whitney Museum of American Art**
945 Madison Ave.
**Map** 13 A1.
*Tel 1-800-944-WHITNEY.*

# Classical and Contemporary Music

New Yorkers have a voracious appetite for music. Live concerts by the world's most celebrated musical performers may be enjoyed at famous halls throughout the year, and younger, newer artists, and exotic imports always find receptive audiences.

## TICKETS

Find out what you can choose from in New York by checking out the listings in the *New York Times* and the *Village Voice* and in *Time Out New York* and *The New Yorker* magazines.

## CLASSICAL MUSIC

The Orchestra in residence at **Avery Fisher Hall** in Lincoln Center *(see p215)* is the New York Philharmonic. It is also the annual site for the popular "Mostly Mozart" series and Young People's Concerts. **Alice Tully Hall**, in Lincoln Center, is an acoustic gem and home to the Chamber Music Society.

One of the world's premier concert halls is the revamped **Carnegie Hall** *(see p148)*. Upstairs in the Weill Recital Hall there are quality performances for reasonable prices.

The **Brooklyn Academy of Music (BAM)** *(see p248)* is the home of the Brooklyn Philharmonic. The **New Jersey Performance Arts Center** in Newark is the newest star in the music venue crown. Classical music, dance, opera, jazz, and world music all find an audience here.

The **Merkin Concert Hall** is host to some top chamber ensembles and soloists. For really excellent acoustics, go to the **Town Hall**. The **92nd Street Y's** Kaufmann Concert Hall also offers a lively menu of music and dance. There's also the **Frick Collection** and

### CLASSICAL RADIO

New York has three FM radio stations that broadcast classical music: WQXR at 96.3, the National Public Radio station WNYC at 93.9 and WKCR 89.9.

**Symphony Space**, both of which offer a varied program ranging from gospel to Gershwin, classical to ethnic. The beautiful Grace Rainey Rogers Auditorium in the **Metropolitan Museum of Art** is for chamber music and soloists, while the **Florence Gould Hall**, at the Alliance Française, presents a varied program of chamber music and orchestral pieces.

The **Juilliard School of Music** and the **Mannes College of Music** are both considered excellent. Their students and faculties give free recitals, and there are shows by leading orchestras, chamber music groups, and opera companies. The **Manhattan School of Music** offers an excellent program of over 400 events per year, from classical to jazz.

At 9:45am on the Thursdays of the New York Philharmonic concerts, the evening show is rehearsed at **Avery Fisher Hall** in Lincoln Center. Audiences are often admitted to listen, and rehearsal tickets are available at low prices. The **Kosciuszko Foundation** hosts the annual Chopin Competition. **Corpus Christi Church** has an active concert schedule, presenting such groups as the Tallis Scholars.

## OPERA

Dominating the city's operatic scene is **Lincoln Center** *(see p212)*, home to the New York City Opera, and the **Metropolitan Opera House**, which has its own opera company. The Met is the jewel in the crown, offering top international performers. More accessible and dynamic is the New York City Opera. Its performances range from *Madame Butterfly* to *South Pacific*, with subtitles above the stage to help the audience understand the plot. Lower-priced quality performances

are staged by the up-and-coming singers at the **Village Light Opera Group**, the **Amato Opera Theater**, the **Kaye Playhouse** at Hunter College, and the students at the **Juilliard Opera Center** in Lincoln Center.

## CONTEMPORARY MUSIC

New York is one of the most important places in the world for contemporary music. Exotic, ethnic, and experimental music is played in many first-rate venues. The **Brooklyn Academy of Music (BAM)** is the standard-bearer of the avant-garde. Each autumn the Academy holds a festival of music and dance called "Next Wave," which has helped launch many musical careers.

An annual festival of serious modern music called "Bang on a Can" is performed at the **Ethical Culture Society Hall** and features works by Steve Reich, Pierre Boulez, and John Cage. Experimentalists, such as Davie Weinstein with his "audio-visual acid test" music – a mix of CD players, amplified instruments, keyboards, and sound effects – perform at the **Dance Theater Workshop**.

Other venues include the **Asia Society** *(see p187)*, with its jewel of a theater for many visiting Asian performers, and **St. Peter's Church**.

## BACKSTAGE TOURS

Behind-the-scenes tours are offered by **Lincoln Center** and **Carnegie Hall**.

## RELIGIOUS MUSIC

Few experiences are more moving than an Easter concert in the vast **Cathedral of St. John the Divine** *(see pp226–7)*. Seasonal music is also offered at many of the city's museums and in almost every other available space – from Grand Central Terminal's main concourse *(see pp156–7)* to bank and hotel lobbies. For jazz vespers in a stunning modern building, visit **St. Peter's Church** *(see p177)*.

Most of these concerts are free, but you are encouraged to contribute.

## ALFRESCO

Free outdoor summer concerts occur in **Bryant Park**, **Washington Square**, and **Lincoln Center's Damrosch Park**. The annual concerts on Central Park's Great Lawn and in Brooklyn's Prospect Park are performed by the New York Philharmonic and the Metropolitan Opera. In good weather, strolling musicians perform at South Street Seaport, on the steps of the **Metropolitan Museum** of Art *(see pp190–97)*, and in the area around Washington Square.

## MUSIC FOR FREE

Throughout the year free musical performances are given at **The Cloisters** *(see pp236–9)* and the **Whitney Museum's** Philip Morris Building *(see p152)*. Sunday-afternoon recitals are held at Rumsey Playfield and the Naumburg Bandshell in Central Park *(see p208)*, as well as the Summerstage. Call **The Dairy** for more information. You will also find music in the **Federal Hall** *(see p68)*, while at **Lincoln Center**, don't miss the exciting free performances held in the **Juilliard School of Music**. Other very popular venues include the **Greenwich House Music School** (free student recitals) and the **Winter Garden** at the World Financial Center *(see p69)*. Numerous free concerts and talks take place in the city's churches, including **St. Paul's Chapel** and **Trinity Church Wall Street** *(see p68)*.

## INTERNET EVENTS GUIDE

www.nymag.com
www.nytoday.com
www.newyork.citysearch.com

# DIRECTORY

**92nd Street Y**
1395 Lexington Ave.
Map 17 A2.
*Tel (212) 415-5500.*

**Amato Opera Theater**
319 Bowery at 2nd St.
Map 4 F2.
*Tel (212) 228-8200.*

**Asia Society**
725 Park Ave.
Map 13 A1.
*Tel (212) 517-2742.*

**Brooklyn Academy of Music**
30 Lafayette Ave, Brooklyn.
*Tel (718) 636-4100.*

**Bryant Park**
Map 8 F1.
*Tel (212) 768-4242.*

**Carnegie Hall**
881 7th Ave. Map 12 E3.
*Tel (212) 247-7800.*

**Cathedral of St. John the Divine**
1047 Amsterdam Ave & 112th St. Map 20 E4.
*Tel (212) 316-7540.*

**The Cloisters**
Fort Tryon Park.
*Tel (212) 923-3700.*

**Corpus Christi Church**
529 W 121st St.
Map 20 E2.
*Tel (212) 666-9350.*

**The Dairy**
Central Park at 65th St.
Map 12 F2.
*Tel (212) 794-6564.*

**Dance Theater Workshop**
See Dance p347.

**Ethical Culture Society Hall**
2 W 64th St.
Map 12 D2.
*Tel (212) 874-5210.*

**Federal Hall**
26 Wall St.
Map 1 C3.
*Tel (212) 825-6888.*

**Florence Gould Hall (at the Alliance Française)**
55 E 59th St.
Map 13 A3.
*Tel (212) 355-6160.*

**Frick Collection**
1 E 70th St. Map 12 F1.
*Tel (212) 288-0700.*

**Greenwich House Music School**
46 Barrow St. Map 3 C2.
*Tel (212) 242-4770.*

**Kaye Playhouse (Hunter College)**
695 Park Ave. Map 13 A1.
*Tel (212) 772-4448.*

**Kosciuszko Foundation**
15 E 65th St. Map 12 F2
*Tel (212) 734-2130.*

**Lincoln Center**
155 W 65th St.
Map 11 C2.
*Tel (212) 546-2656.*
Tours of various venues at Lincoln Center can be arranged by calling:
*Tel (212) 875-5350.*

**Alice Tully Hall**
*Tel (212) 875-5050.*

**Avery Fisher Hall**
*Tel (212) 875-5030.*

**Damrosch Park**
*Tel (212) 875-5000.*

**Juilliard Opera Center**
*Tel (212) 769-7406.*

**Juilliard School of Music**
*Tel (212) 799-5000.*

**Metropolitan Opera House**
*Tel (212) 362-6000.*

**Manhattan School of Music**
120 Claremont Ave.
Map 20 E2.
*Tel (212) 749-2802.*

**Mannes College of Music**
150 W 85th St.
Map 15 D3.
*Tel (212) 580-0210.*

**Merkin Hall**
129 W 67th St.
Map 11 D2.
*Tel (212) 501-3330.*

**Metropolitan Museum of Art**
1000 5th Ave at 82nd St.
Map 16 F4.
*Tel (212) 535-7710.*

**New Jersey Performance Arts Center**
1 Center St, Newark, NJ.
*Tel 1-888-466-5722.*

**St. Paul's Chapel**
Broadway at Fulton St.
Map 1 C2.
*Tel (212) 233-4164.*

**St. Peter's Church**
619 Lexington Ave.
Map 13 A4.
*Tel (212) 935-2200.*

**Symphony Space**
2537 Broadway.
Map 15 C2.
*Tel (212) 864-5400.*

**Town Hall**
123 W 43rd St.
Map 8 E1.
*Tel (212) 997-1003.*

**Trinity Church**
Broadway at Wall St.
Map 1 C3.
*Tel (212) 602-0800.*

**Village Light Opera Group**
Perform at: Haft Auditorium, Fashion Institute of Technology, 227 W 27th St.
Map 8 E3.
*Tel (212) 352-3101.*

**Washington Square**
Map 4 D2.

**Whitney Museum**
Philip Morris Building, 120 Park Ave at 42nd St.
Map 9 A1.
*Tel 1-800-944-8639.*

**Winter Garden**
World Financial Center, West St.
Map 1 A2.
*Tel (212) 945-2600.*

# Rock, Jazz, and World Music

There's every imaginable form of music in New York, from international stadium rock to the sounds of the 1960s, from Dixieland jazz or country blues, soul, and world music to talented street musicians. The city's music scene changes at a dizzying pace, with many new arrivals (and departures) almost daily, so there's no way to predict what you may find when you arrive. Musical standards also vary.

## PRICES AND PLACES

At clubs, expect to pay a cover charge and possibly a one- or two-drink minimum (at $7 or more) requirement. The prices for concerts range from $50 to $150 for the major venues. Many of the smaller concert venues are arranged for seating in certain areas and dancing in others – often with different prices for each.

The top international bands are usually to be found in the huge arenas at the **Meadowlands** or **Madison Square Garden** (see p135). Here the likes of Elton John, Bruce Springsteen, and the Stones perform. Tickets for these events sell out very fast, so buy as many as you need as soon as you hear of a concert, unless you don't mind paying a lot for them through an agent or a scalper (see p341). During the summer, big outdoor concerts are held at Jones Beach (see p255) and **Central Park SummerStage**.

Medium-sized venues for mainstream bands include the Art Deco palace of **Radio City Music Hall**, the **Manhattan Center** (formerly the Hammerstein Ballroom), and the **Beacon Theater**. One of the newest on the scene, and booking an impressive line up of acts, is the **Nokia Theater** in Times Square. This state-of-the-art venue is known for its top-notch acoustics. The most popular live-music venues are in the Upper West Side area.

Many leading rock venues are basically bars with music. They will often book different bands every night, so check the listings in the *New York Times*, *Village Voice*, or *Time Out New York* or phone the place to find out what's happening and at what time during that particular week.

## ROCK MUSIC

Rock comes in many forms: gothic, industrial, techno, psychedelic, post-punk funk, indie, and alternative music are among the latest crazes. If you prefer to see more of a band than a giant video screen, the following venues have a much more intimate, friendly atmosphere.

The **Knitting Factory** has live jazz and new music while the **Mercury Lounge** is one of the most happening music spots, featuring hot new bands being groomed for MTV. **Irving Plaza** is where relatively unknown and sometimes known rock groups play, as do the occasional famous country and blues musicians.

The opening of the **Bowery Ballroom** in 1998 helped revive the Lower East Side, boasting superior acoustics and sightlines and usually booking well-known touring acts and local bands.

A converted bodega, **Arlene's Grocery** has been attracting a loyal crowd since 1995, thanks to acts ranging from rock to country and comedy. **Joe's Pub** draws those who appreciate the eclectic roster of rock, jazz, hip-hop, and lounge music. A more upscale venue **Crash Mansion** showcases up-and-coming talents of any musical persuasion, from rock and punk to Brazilian and jazz, as well as featuring established performers such as Norah Jones.

## JAZZ

The original Cotton Club and Connie's Inn, which were once crucibles of jazz, are long gone, as are the former speakeasies of West 52nd Street. But living legends such as Maynard Ferguson still play, while others carry on the old traditions of Dave Brubeck, Les Paul, Duke Ellington, Count Basie, and other big bands. In Harlem, the stylish yet informal **Lenox Lounge** features contemporary jazz on the weekends.

In Greenwich Village, jazz temples from the 1930s survive and continue to foster great music. Foremost among them is the **Village Vanguard**, where some of the most highly revered jazz memories linger and newer ones are being fashioned by such groups as the McCoy Tyner and Branford Marsalis trios. **Blue Note** hosts big bands at high prices but has a great atmosphere. **Smalls** is under new management and offers cutting-edge jazz, with four sets a night from two different bands (Mon–Sat). The **Knitting Factory** features contemporary and avant-garde jazz.

**Smoke** is an intimate nightspot offering a divergent roster of musicians, and **Birdland** features ex-Mingus alumni and musicians such as Bud Shank.

**Café Carlyle**, an East Side spot once famed for late jazz pianist and singer Bobby Short, now features clarinetist-filmmaker Woody Allen playing with Eddy Davis and his New Orleans Jazz Band. **Jazz Standard**, with an ample underground performance space, showcases top-notch jazz performers most nights of the week.

A sophisticated club and restaurant, **Iridium** features progressive jazz. If you're in New York in June, don't miss the annual **JVC Jazz Festival**, where such famous jazz and blues icons as Oscar Peterson, and B.B. King play at various clubs all around Manhattan.

**Jazz at Lincoln Center** events are scheduled throughout the year, including concerts by the renowned Lincoln Center Jazz Orchestra under the direction of Wynton Marsalis. The music ranges from Duke Ellington's New York sounds to Johnny Dodds' traditional

New Orleans-style jazz. Jazz at Lincoln Center now has its own home since it moved into the world's first performing arts center specifically for jazz. It is housed in the new Time Warner Center. A multi-room facility perched above Central Park, with bandstands posed against sparing walls of glass and a dance floor beneath the moon and stars. Finally, Friday night at the **Rose Center** (at **AMNH**) offers live jazz concerts.

## FOLK AND COUNTRY MUSIC

Folk, rock music, and R&B (rhythm and blues) can be found at the famed but much-faded **Bitter End**, which once showcased James Taylor and Joni Mitchell but now special-izes in promising new talent as does **Kenny's Castaways**. Also worth checking out is the **Sidewalk Café**.

## BLUES, SOUL, AND WORLD MUSIC

For blues, soul, and world music, options include the **Apollo Theater** in Harlem (see p230). For nearly 60 years the near-legendary Wednesday Amateur Nights have been responsible for discovering and launching stars, including James Brown and Dionne Warwick.

The **Cotton Club** is no longer located in its original spot, but the modern venue offers good blues, jazz, and a Sunday real Gospel brunch on Harlem's main street.

The **B.B. King's Blues Club** lineup often features legendary jazz and gospel performers. Food is also served, but can be pricy. Don't miss "Mambo Mondays" with Nestor Torres at **SOB's** (Sounds of Brazil), a world music club specializing in Afro-Latin rhythms.

**Terra Blues**'s bar doubles as an interesting music venue. The blues artists that appear here can range from authentic Chicago acoustic players to more modern blues acts. In the East Village, **The Stone** showcases an eclectic range of artsy acts. Part community center and café, part jazz and experimental music space, the **5C Café** is a throwback to old New York and has a laidback vibe.

# DIRECTORY

## MUSIC VENUES

**Beacon Theater**
2124 Broadway.
Map 15 C5.
Tel (815) 477-5076
(ticketline).

**Central Park SummerStage**
Rumsey Playfield.
Map 12 F1.
Tel (212) 360-2777.

**Continental Arena Meadowlands**
50 Route 120 E
Rutherford, NJ.
Tel (201) 935-3900.

**Madison Square Garden**
7th Ave & 33rd St.
Map 8 E2.
Tel (212) 465-6741.

**Manhattan Center**
311 W 34th St. Map 8
D2. Tel (212) 279-7740.

**Nokia Theater**
1515 Broadway. Map 12
E5. Tel (212) 930-1959.

**Radio City Music Hall**
See p347.

## ROCK MUSIC

**Arlene's Grocery**
95 Stanton St. Map 5 A3.
Tel (212) 995-1652.

**Bowery Ballroom**
6 Delancey St. Map 4F3.
Tel (212) 533-2111.

**Crash Mansion**
199 Bowery. Map 4 F3.
Tel (212) 982-7767.

**Joe's Pub**
Public Theater, 425
Lafayette St. Map 4 F2.
Tel (212) 539-8770.

**Knitting Factory**
74 Leonard St. Map 4 E5.
Tel (212) 219-3132.

**Mercury Lounge**
217 E Houston St.
Map 5 A3.
Tel (212) 260-4700.

**Irving Plaza**
17 Irving Pl. Map 9 A5.
Tel (212) 777-6800.

## JAZZ

**Birdland**
315 W 44th St. Map 12
D5. Tel (212) 581-3080.

**Blue Note**
131 W 3rd St. Map 4 D2.
Tel (212) 475-8592.

**Café Carlyle**
95 E 76th St. Map 17 A5.
Tel (212) 744-1600.

**Iridium**
1650 Broadway.
Map 12 D2.
Tel (212) 582-2121.

**Jazz at Lincoln Center**
Tel (212) 258-9800.

**Jazz Standard**
116 E 27th St. Map 9 A3
Tel (212) 576-2232.

**JVC Jazz Festival**
Tel (212) 501-1390.

**Lenox Lounge**
288 Malcolm X Boulevard.
Map 21 B2.
Tel (212) 427-0253.

**Rose Center**
79th St at CPW. Map 16
D5. Tel (212) 769-5100.

**Smalls**
183 W 10th St. Map 3
C2. Tel (212) 252-5091.

**Smoke**
2751 Broadway. Map 20
E5. Tel (212) 864-6662.

**Village Vanguard**
178 7th Ave S.
Map 3 C1.
Tel (212) 255-4037.

## FOLK AND COUNTRY

**Bitter End**
147 Bleecker St. Map 4
E3. Tel (212) 673-7030.

**Kenny's Castaways**
157 Bleecker St.
Map 4 E3.
Tel (212) 979-9762.

**Sidewalk Café**
94 Ave A. Map 5 B2.
Tel (212) 473-7373.

## BLUES, SOUL, AND WORLD MUSIC

**Apollo Theater**
253 W 125 St.
Map 19 A1.
Tel (212) 531-5305.

**B.B. King's Blues Club**
237 W 42nd St.
Map 8 E1.
Tel (212) 997-4144.

**Cotton Club**
656 W 125th St. Map 22
F2. Tel (212) 663-7980.

**5C Café**
68 Avenue C. Map 5 C2.
Tel (212) 477-5993.

**SOB's**
204 Varick St. Map 4 D3.
Tel (212) 243-4940.

**Terra Blues**
149 Bleecker St.
Map 4 E3.
Tel (212) 777-7776.

**The Stone**
Avenue C at 2nd St.
Map 5 C2.
www.thestonenyc.com

# Clubs, Dance Halls, and Gay and Lesbian Venues

New York's nightlife and club scene is legendary, and deservedly so. Whatever your preference – be it for a noisy disco, stand-up comedy, or the soothing melodies of a Harry Connick, Jr., sound-alike in a piano bar – you'll be really amazed at the choice. There was a rash of big discos in the 1980s, but relatively few of these have survived the recent trend toward the comfort and style of supper clubs.

## WHEN AND WHERE

The best and hippest time for clubbing is during the week – it's also a lot cheaper. Take a fair amount of money and some ID to prove that you're old enough to drink (which is over 21) – but beware, all the drinks are very expensive.

The trendiest clubs roll on until 4am or later. Fashions and club nights change all the time, so go to Tower Records on Broadway for all the latest leaflets, check club details in the listings magazines (see p340) and read the Village Voice. The most interesting places nowadays are often popularized by word of mouth. Your best bet is to go somewhere like the **Avalon** (the old Limelight) and hope someone will tell you where to go on to – often invitations to other clubs are given out there as well.

## DANCING

New Yorkers thrive on music and dancing. The dance floors available all around the city range from the ever-popular **SOB's** – for jungle, reggae, soul, jazz, and salsa – to a few huge basketball-court-sized places, such as **Roseland**. This has ballroom dancing every Thursday and Sunday and is New York's classic Broadway ballroom, revealing a tantalizing glimpse of older Broadway culture. It also has a good megasize, 700 - seater, restaurant with a fully stocked bar.

If you want to sample something different, try **Barbetta**, where Boris and Yvgeny play a combination of gypsy music and Viennese waltzes. The **Copacabana**, which when it originally opened starred the likes of Dean Martin and Frank Sinatra, is now a disco alternating with live bands. It also stages wild parties on the last Thursday of every month, with go-go boys, drag queens, and disco divas.

The **Avalon**, which is a mixed venue with ground-floor dancing and spectator seats up in the balconies, was renovated in 1998, and the new, improved club is well worth a visit.

The trendy **Studio Mezmor** (formerly Crobar), with its stylish bar and enormous dance floor, draws massive crowds who groove to contemporary hits. The legendary club **Pacha**, which started out in Ibiza, has opened a swanky four-floor venue in the heart of Times Square and is consistently booking top international DJs to make the most of the colossal sound system. **Marquee** is another A-list spot in Chelsea, with a glass-enclosed VIP mezzanine that draws Hollywood starlets. Bring some models if you want to get in. Those who prefer a more underground house scene should head to **Apt** for top DJ tunes. **Home** is exclusive, dim, and sexy in Chelsea, while **Cielo** welcomes the beautiful Meatpacking District set to groove to the music spun by the legendary François K. Swanky. **The Plumm** fills with trendy clubbers, celebs, and those who have come to spot them. Join the crowd cutting moves on the dance floor to hip-hop, funk, rock, and classics. The door policy can be strict, so dress up in your hippest duds. Spacious **Mannahatta** fills with a hip yet informal crowd who enjoy a tipple at the inviting bar before heading downstairs to dance to everything from hip-hop to pop classics, depending on the night of the week.

## NIGHTCLUBS

Nightclubs are the places to see a show. NY shows are less flashy than in the 1940s and 1950s but they still boast a wide variety of acts. Expect to pay a cover charge; many of the clubs also require that you have at least two drinks.

The **Rainbow Grill** on the 65th floor of the RCA Building has a fine piano bar. The chic **Supper Club** surrounds you with gold lamé draperies and features big band music downstairs. Cabaret singers perform upstairs in their intimate Blue Room. **Joe's Pub** at the Public Theater has very decent food and serves the likes of John Hammond and Mo Tucker. Central Park has an indoors/outdoors club, **Tavern on the Green**, which offers jazz in its Chestnut Room, and **Feinstein's at the Regency** is the epitome of classic cabaret.

## GAY AND LESBIAN VENUES

The past two decades have seen the arrival of clubs and restaurants specifically geared to gay and lesbian clientele. Although the entertainment is varied, transvestite revues predominate. Though all the clubs are open to heterosexuals and often to the opposite sex, too, some can make "interlopers" feel extremely uncomfortable. The current popular gay cabarets include the **Duplex**, which has a mix of stand-up comics, comedy sketches and singers.

The very fashionable nightclubs and bars for men include the trendy uptown **Town House**, a piano bar with restaurant, and **Don't Tell Mama**, a long-established gay bar that presents good musical revues and spoofs. **Henrietta Hudson** caters solely to women, as does **Grolier**. **Marie's Crisis** piano bar is a mixed venue. The *Village Voice*, *HX*, and *Next* have good listings of what's happening in the gay communities, and the *Gay Yellow Pages* covers the gay scene. If you need more information, phone the **Gay and Lesbian Switchboard**.

The Chelsea neighborhood, particularly around Eighth Avenue, is the bustling heart of gay life. The Hell's Kitchen area, around the mid 40s between Eighth and 10th avenues, also thrums with gay nightlife. The inviting and stylish **G Lounge** serves a potent selection of cocktails and flavored coffees, and is the perfect spot for a drink before hitting the clubs.

Lively **Barracuda** features drag shows and draws a diverse crowd of regulars and newcomers, all out for a good time. **Rawhide** stays hopping throughout the evening, with a popular happy hour every night until 10pm. **Stonewall Inn**, the famed site of the Stonewall riots and birth of the modern gay movement, has just undergone a multimillion-dollar refurbishment. The comfy neighborhood lounge **Posh** pulls in a friendly crowd for the popular happy hour 4–8pm.

Casual, friendly **Rubyfruit Bar and Grill** on Hudson Street fills with women who are out for cocktails and conversation. The imaginatively decorated **Cubby Hole** is a cozy lesbian bar where regulars often sing along to the jukebox.

# DIRECTORY

## DANCING

**Apt**
419 W 13th St.
**Map** 3 C1.
*Tel (212) 414-4245.*

**Avalon**
660 6th Ave.
**Map** 8 E5.
*Tel (212) 807-7780.*

**Barbetta**
321 W 46th St.
**Map** 12 D5.
*Tel (212) 246-9171.*

**Cielo**
18 Little W 12th St.
**Map** 3 B1.
*Tel (212) 645-5700.*

**Copacabana**
560 W 34th St.
**Map** 8 E2.
*Tel (212) 239-2672.*

**Home**
532 W 27th St.
**Map** 8 D4.
*Tel (212) 273-3700.*

**Knitting Factory**
74 Leonard St.
**Map** 4 E5.
*Tel (212) 219-3132.*

**Mannahatta**
316 Bowery St.
**Map** 4 E3.
*Tel (212) 253-8644.*

**Marquee**
289 10th Ave.
**Map** 7 C4.
*Tel (646) 473-0202.*

**Pacha**
618 W 46th St.
**Map** 12 E5.
*Tel (212) 209-7500.*

**Roseland**
239 W 52nd St.
**Map** 12 E4.
*Tel (212) 247-0200.*

**SOB's**
204 Varick St.
**Map** 4 D3.
*Tel (212) 243-4940.*

**Studio Mezmor**
530 W 28th St.
**Map** 7 C3.
*Tel (212) 629-9000.*

**The Plumm**
246 W 14th St.
**Map** 3 C1.
*Tel (212) 675-1567.*

## NIGHTCLUBS

**Feinstein's at the Regency**
540 Park Ave.
**Map** 13 A3.
*Tel (212) 339-4095.*

**Joe's Pub**
425 Lafayette St
(Public Theater).
**Map** 4 F2.
*Tel (212) 539-8777.*

**Rainbow Grill**
30 Rockefeller Plaza.
**Map** 12 F4.
*Tel (212) 632-5000.*

**Tavern on the Green**
Central Park,
West side at 67th St.
**Map** 12 D2.
*Tel (212) 873-3200.*

**The Supper Club**
240 W 47th St.
**Map** 12 D5.
*Tel (212) 921-1940.*

## GAY AND LESBIAN VENUES

**Barracuda**
275 W 22nd St.
**Map** 8 D4.
*Tel (212) 645-8613.*

**Don't Tell Mama**
343 W 46th St.
**Map** 12 D5.
*Tel (212) 757-0788.*

**Duplex**
61 Christopher St.
**Map** 3 C2.
*Tel (212) 255-5438.*

**G Lounge**
223 W 19th St.
**Map** 8 E5.
*Tel (212) 929-1085.*

**Gay and Lesbian Switchboard**
*Tel (212) 989-0999.*

**Henrietta Hudson**
438 Hudson St.
**Map** 3 C3.
*Tel (212) 924-3347.*

**Marie's Crisis Café**
59 Grove St.
**Map** 3 C2.
*Tel (212) 243-9323.*

**Posh**
405 W 51st St.
**Map** 11 C4.
*Tel (212) 957-2222.*

**Rawhide**
212 8th Ave.
**Map** 8 D4.
*Tel (212) 242-9332.*

**Rubyfruit Bar and Grill**
531 Hudson St.
**Map** 3 C2.
*Tel (212) 929-3343.*

**Stonewall Inn**
53 Christopher St.
**Map** 3 C2.
*Tel (212) 488-2705.*

**The Cubby Hole**
281 W 12th St.
**Map** 3 C1.
*Tel (212) 243-9041.*

**Town House**
236 E 58th St.
**Map** 13 B4.
*Tel (212) 754-4649.*

# Comedy, Cabaret, and Literary Events

From Jack Benny and Rodney Dangerfield to Woody Allen and Jerry Seinfeld, New York has spawned almost as many comics as it has jokes about itself, including the requisite quips: on crime – "In New York crime is getting worse. When I was there the other day, the Statue of Liberty had both hands up"; and on driving – "Always look both ways when running a red light." Comedy is a cut-throat business here. This is good news for punters, because it means that no matter what comedy club you walk into, you'll be howling after just a few sets. NYC is also a consummate romancer, judging by its plethora of cabarets and lounges. An unforgettable New York experience is to be serenaded by a lounge singer in a dusky piano bar. New York also boasts a booming literary scene, with superb weekly readings and lectures.

## COMEDY SHOWCASES

Many of New York's best current comedy clubs or showcases have evolved from earlier "improvisational" comedy. Part of the allure of New York comedy clubs is that you never know who might get behind the mic to deliver their spiel. Anyone from Dennis Miller to Roseanne Barr to Robin Williams could show up. A word of caution: if you don't want to be singled out and made fun of, sit away from the stage. Many of the larger comedy clubs offer meals, and at the more popular clubs, it's always a good idea to make reservations to ensure admission.

Leading the comedy club pack is the **Broadway Comedy Club** in the Theater District, which has formed from a merger of Chicago City Limits and NY Improv. As the city's largest club, it draws big names nightly. **Caroline's** also has big-name comics perform in elegant surroundings. The famous catchphrase of the bug-eyed New York comedian Roger Dangerfield was "I get no respect," but judging from the lasting fame of his **Dangerfield's Comedy Club**, which draws top acts from around the country, he seems to have gotten respect after all. The **Upright Citizens Brigade Theatre** has sassy, Chicago-style improv on Sundays (7:30pm, 9:30pm).

Many of the UCB's weekly late shows are free. The **Gotham Comedy Club** in the Flatiron District, presents a wide range of comics in a sophisticated setting. **Comic Strip Live**, on the East Side, has hosted a slew of top comics, including Eddie Murphy, and continues to introduce many new comics to the scene. The basement-level **Comedy Cellar** in Greenwich Village presents a nightly lineup of new and established comics. Also good are **Stand-Up New York**, **NY Comedy Club**, **Rose's Turn**, **The Underground**, and **The Laugh Factory**.

## CABARETS AND PIANO BARS

Cabarets have become a New York institution. Such cozy, just-for-listening places are often called "rooms" and are located in hotels. Most operate from Tuesday to Saturday (usually with a cover charge or a drink minimum), and most take credit cards.

The Algonquin's **Oak Room** has song stylists. For a classic piano lounge with a panoramic Manhattan view, visit the **Top of the Tower** at the Beekman Tower Hotel. The "long-distance hummer" award goes to the late Bobby Short, who played his piano for over 25 years at the Café Carlyle in the **Carlyle Hotel**. Now Woody Allen plays there on Mondays with Eddy Davis's New Orleans Jazz Band.

Also in the Carlyle is **Bemelman's Bar**, with its whimsical murals; it attracts a relaxed crowd who enjoy first-class crooners. A jacket is required if you visit the **5757 Bar** at the Four Seasons Hotel, but the opulence is worth it.

There's a piano player at the Hilton Hotel's **Lobby Lounge**, and **Cafe Pierre's** singer-pianist Kathleen Landis holds court at the Pierre Hotel. There's also piano music at the **Ambassador Lounge** in the Regal UN Plaza Hotel. The spirited cabaret **Don't Tell Mama** showcases emerging and established performers who belt out their songs with equal gusto. **Ars Nova** in Hell's Kitchen is an informal, anything-goes cabaret where you may see show tunes and experimental comedy, and has attracted the likes of Liza Minnelli and Tony Kushner. For Manhattan's choicest cabaret, kick back and enjoy the show at lively **Duplex**, the longest-running cabaret venue in New York City. Relax to the tinkling of keys at the downstairs piano bar, or head upstairs for superlative classic cabaret shows, one-act plays, and top-notch comedy. A mixed crowd, including the talented staff, croons along at **Brandy's Piano Bar**. For a memorable evening of song and music, head to **Feinstein's at the Regency Hotel**, where top-of-the-line performers entertain Tuesday through Saturday. Enjoy sultry cabaret, theater, and musical ensembles at the plush showroom in **Dillon's Restaurant and Lounge**, nestled in the heart of the Theater District.

## LITERARY EVENTS AND POETRY SLAMS

As the birthplace of some of the greatest American writers, from Herman Melville to Henry James, and the adopted home of countless others, New York has long been a writer's city. The literary tradition is celebrated often and throughout the year, with readings and talks that take place at bookstores, libraries, cafés, and community centers across the city. Readings are usually free, but expect long lines for the better known names. The **92nd Street Y** hosts readings by some of the greatest writers to pass through New York, including many Nobel- and Pulitzer-prize winning authors. Most NYC bookstores present a weekly or monthly reading series, including **Barnes & Noble** (the Astor Place and Union Square branches usually attract the highest profile authors) and **Borders Books and Music**. The **Mid-Manhattan Library** also presents readings. Enjoy spirited readings by playwrights at the **Drama Book Shop**. Check out *The New Yorker* magazine, available in bookstores and at many newsstands, for current listings of readings and talks.

Poetry slams (sometimes called Spoken Word), are just what the name implies, an evening of freeform poems, raps, and storytelling, usually raucous and entertaining, often unpredictable, and never boring. The **Nuyorican Poets Café** in Alphabet City, often heralded as the progenitor of spoken word in New York, serves up a nightly mix of poetry slams, readings, and performances. The **Bowery Poetry Club**, established as a performance space for spoken word in all its incarnations, presents an eclectic range of performances, from poetry jams to various performance arts. The **Poetry Project** at St. Mark's Church has hosted readings and events since 1966.

## DIRECTORY

### COMEDY SHOWCASES

**Broadway Comedy Club**
318 W 53rd St.
Map 12 E4.
*Tel (212) 757-2323.*

**Caroline's**
1626 Broadway.
Map 12 E5.
*Tel (212) 757-4100.*

**Comedy Cellar**
117 MacDougal St.
Map 4 D2.
*Tel (212) 254-3480.*

**Comic Strip Live**
1568 2nd Ave.
Map 17 B4.
*Tel (212) 861-9386.*

**Dangerfield's**
1118 1st Ave.
Map 13 C3.
*Tel (212) 593-1650.*

**Gotham Comedy Club**
34 W 22nd St.
Map 8 F4.
*Tel (212) 367-9000.*

**NY Comedy Club**
236 W 78th St.
Map 15 C5.
*Tel (212) 595-0850.*

**Rose's Turn**
55 Grove St. Map 3 C2.
*Tel (212) 366-5438.*

**Stand-up New York**
236 W 78th St.
Map 15 C5.
*Tel (212) 595-0850.*

**The Laugh Factory**
303 W 42 St. Map 8 D1.
*Tel (212) 586-7829.*

**The Underground**
955 W End Ave.
Map 20 E5.
*Tel (212) 531-4759.*

**Upright Citizens Brigade Theatre**
307 W 26th St.
Map 8 D4.
*Tel (212) 366-9176.*

### CABARETS AND PIANO BARS

**5757 Bar**
Four Seasons Hotel,
57 E 57th St.
Map 12 F3.
*Tel (212) 758-5700.*

**Ambassador Lounge**
Regal UN Plaza Hotel,
1 UN Plaza at 44th St.
Map 13 C5.
*Tel (212) 758-1234.*

**Ars Nova**
511 W 54th St.
Map 12 E4.
*Tel (212) 489-9800.*

**Brandy's Piano Bar**
235 E 84th St.
Map 17 B4.
*Tel (212) 650-1944.*

**Café Pierre**
Pierre Hotel, 2 E 61st St.
Map 12 F3.
*Tel (212) 940-8195.*

**Carlyle Hotel**
35 E 76th St.
Map 17 A5.
*Tel (212) 744-1600.*

**Dillon's Restaurant and Lounge**
245 W 54th St.
Map 12 D4.
*Tel (212) 307-9797.*

**Don't Tell Mama**
343 W 46th St.
Map 12 D5.
*Tel (212) 757-0788.*

**Duplex**
61 Christopher St.
Map 3 C2.
*Tel (212) 255-5438.*

**Feinstein's at the Regency Hotel**
540 Park Ave.
Map 13 A3.
*Tel (212) 759-4100.*

**Lobby Lounge**
Hilton Hotel,
53 Ave of the Americas.
Map 12 E4.
*Tel (212) 586-7000.*

**Oak Room**
Algonquin Hotel,
59 W 44th St.
Map 12 F5.
*Tel (212) 840-6800.*

**Top of the Tower**
Beekman Tower Hotel,
3 Mitchell Pl.
Map 13 C5.
*Tel (212) 355-7300.*

### LITERARY EVENTS AND POETRY SLAMS

**92nd Street Y**
1395 Lexington Ave.
Map 17 A2.
*Tel (212) 415-5729.*

**Barnes & Noble**
4 Astor Place.
Map 4 F2.
*Tel (212) 420-1322.*
33 E 17th St.
Map 9 A5.
*Tel (212) 253-0810.*

**Borders Books and Music**
461 Park Ave.
Map 17 A3.
*Tel (212) 980-6785.*

**Bowery Poetry Club**
308 Bowery.
Map 4 F3.
*Tel (212) 614-0505.*

**Drama Book Shop**
250 W 40th St.
Map 8 E1.
*Tel (212) 944-0595.*

**Mid-Manhattan Library**
455 Fifth Ave at 40th St.
Map 8 F1.
*Tel (212) 340-0833.*

**Nuyorican Poets Café**
236 E 3rd St.
Map 5 B2.
*Tel (212) 505-8183.*

**Poetry Project**
St. Mark's Church,
131 E 10th St.
Map 4 F1.
*Tel (212) 674-0910.*

# Late-Night New York

New York is indeed a city that never sleeps. If you wake up in the middle of the night – with a craving for fresh bread, a need to be entertained, or an urge to watch the sun rise over the Manhattan skyline – there are always plenty of options to choose from.

## BARS

The best and friendliest bars are often the Irish ones. **O'Flanagan's** or **Scruffy Duffy's** are both loud, have late-night dancing, and cater to regulars. Go for a late-night dry martini at the **Temple Bar**. The best piano bars are in the hotels: try the Café Carlyle in the **Carlyle Hotel**, Feinstein's at the **Regency**, or the Oak Room in the **Algonquin Hotel**.

For hot American jazz until 4am, go to **Joe's Pub** or the **Blue Note**. **Cornelia Street Café** is a lively nook for prose, poetry, and theater readings. Poetry, theater, and Latin music can be found at the **Nuyorican Poets Café**. If you're in the Village, stop in at **Rose's Turn** for open mike, piano bar, and late-night ambience.

## MIDNIGHT MOVIES

Special midnight showings and a youthful crowd can be found the Angelika Film Center and the Film Forum (*see p349*). New multi-plexes often show movies at midnight on weekends.

## SHOPS

Shakespeare & Company Booksellers on Broadway and the St. Mark's Bookshop are open until late. The **Apple Store** on Fifth Ave is open 24 hours and well worth a visit at any time of the day. In the evening, DJs bring the store to life, while during the day, more than 300 Mac specialists are available for training and consultations. Check out **TLA Video** on Eighth Street if you've forgotten to rent a DVD – it's open every day until 11pm. Among the many Village clothing stores that stay open late is **Trash and Vaudeville** (open till 8pm Mon–Sat);

**Macy's** at Herald Square is open daily until 9:30pm. For health essentials, numerous **Duane Reade** and **Rite Aid** pharmacies are

## TAKE-OUT FOOD AND GROCERIES

A few take-out food stores are open 24 hours a day, including numerous **Gristedes** emporiums and the **West Side Supermarket**. Many Korean greengrocers also stay open all night. The **Food Emporium** is a supermarket chain usually open until midnight. Liquor stores are usually open until 10pm and many deliver.

For the best in bagels, go to **H & H Bagels**, **Bagels On The Square**, and **Jumbo Bagels and Bialys**. There are many pizzerias and Chinese restaurants that stay open late, and most deliver.

## DINING

The trendy set often frequent **Balthazar**, **Florent**, and **Les Halles** for good French dishes. Twentysomethings will seek out the **Coffee Shop** for late-night beer and Brazilian food. You'll find delicious and legendary sandwiches at the **Carnegie Deli**. **Caffè Reggio** in Greenwich Village has been a favorite for late-night coffee and desserts since 1927. Other good options include **Blue Ribbon** and **Odeon. The Dead Poet** is a real Upper West Side neighborhood hangout, with a jukebox, a lively bar, and late-night bar food. Downtown, the party crowds flock to **Bereket Turkish Kebab House** for excellent kebabs, or to the **Empire Diner** in Chelsea. Both are open 24 hours a day.

## SPORTS

There is late-night play at **Slate Billiards** until 4am or until 5am at the **Billiard**

**Club** on weekends. Have latenight beers and burgers with the New York University crowd at **Bowlmor Lanes** bowling alley. Monday night's glow-in-the-dark bowling is very popular. **24–7 Fitness Club** offers a no-frill gym around the clock.

## SERVICES

**Midnight Express Cleaners** picks up garments in Manhattan until midnight and has them ready the next day. Note that this service does not pick up or deliver to major hotels. On Thursdays hair-dresser **George Michael of Madison Avenue/Madora Inc** is open until 9pm and will also make house calls. Primarily for women, the no-nonsense Korean spa **Juvenex** provides massages and saunas at any time of the day or night. If you are locked out, try **Mr Locks Inc**. For stamps, head to the General Post Office, open 24 hours.

## TOURS AND VIEWS

One of New York's most enjoyable walks is along the Hudson River at the World Financial Center's **Battery Park City**, open (and safe) at all hours. Piers 16 and 17 at South Street Seaport attract strollers and revelers all night long and the **Harbour Lights** restaurant on Pier 17 is often open until 2am for a middle of the night pick-me-up. Enjoy the city lights by taking a **Circle Line** two-hour tour of the nighttime harbor.

Try the Riverview Terrace at Sutton Place: the benches offer a peaceful place to watch the sun rise over the East River, Roosevelt Island, and Queens. Two of the most sensational views with the Manhattan backdrop are (looking west) from the **River Café** and (looking east) from **Arthur's Landing** restaurant.

Take a trip on the **Staten Island Ferry** (*see p76*) to see the Statue of Liberty and the Manhattan skyline in the dawn light, or a take a taxi across Brooklyn Bridge (*see* *pp86–9)* to watch the sun rise over New York Harbor. Go to the **Beekman Tower Hotel**'s Top of the Tower for some panoramas of the city's East Side up to 1am. The ultimate view is from the **Empire State Building**: its observation decks *(see pp136–7)* stay open until 2am. **Top of the Rock**'s observation decks *(see p144)* are open until midnight. **Rise**, the 14th-floor bar of the Ritz-Carlton Hotel in Battery Park has great views of the harbor and Statue of Liberty.

**Château Stables** has rides in horse-drawn carriages and **Liberty Helicopters** run flights over the city at sunset. If you want something a little bit different, try **Marvelous Manhattan Tours**' escorted evening barhopping walks. And if you still can't sleep, stroll along the Upper West Side and grab a couple of hot dogs at the famous **Gray's Papaya**.

# DIRECTORY

## BARS

**Algonquin Hotel**
See p357.

**Blue Note**
See p353.

**Carlyle Hotel**
See p357.

**Cornelia Street Café**
29 Cornelia St.
**Map** 4 D2.
**Tel** (212) 989-9318.

**Joe's Pub**
See p353.

**Nuyorican Poets Café**
236 E 3rd St. **Map** 5 A2.
**Tel** (212) 505-8183.

**O'Flanagan's**
1215 1st Ave. **Map** 13 C2.
**Tel** (212) 439-0660.

**Rose's Turn**
See p357.

**Scruffy Duffy's**
743 8th Ave. **Map** 12 D5.
**Tel** (212) 245-9126.

**Temple Bar**
332 Lafayette St.
**Map** 4 F4.
**Tel** (212) 925-4242.

## SHOPS

**Apple Store**
767 5th Ave.
**Map** 12 F3.
**Tel** (212) 336-1440.

**Duane Reade Drugstores**
224 W 57th (Broadway).
**Map** 12 D3.
**Tel** (212) 541-9708.

1279 3rd Ave at E 74th St.
**Map** 17 B5.
**Tel** (212) 744-2668.

**Macy's**
See p134.

**RiteAid Pharmacy**
See p373.

**TLA Video**
52 W 8th St. **Map** 4 D2.
**Tel** (212) 228-8282.

**Trash and Vaudeville**
See p324.

## TAKE-OUT FOOD AND GROCERIES

**Bagels On The Square**
7 Carmine St. **Map** 4 D3.
**Tel** (212) 691-3041.

**Gristedes Food Emporium**
See the Yellow Pages for locations.

**H & H Bagels**
Broadway at 80th St.
**Map** 15 C4.
**Tel** (212) 595-8003.

**H & H Midtown Bagels East**
1551 2nd Ave.
**Map** 17 B4.
**Tel** (212) 734-7441.

**Jumbo Bagels and Bialys**
1070 2nd Ave.
**Map** 13 B3.
**Tel** (212) 355-6185.

**West Side Market**
2171 Broadway. **Map** 15 C5. **Tel** (212) 595-2536.

## DINING

**Balthazar**
80 Spring St. **Map** 4 E4.
**Tel** (212) 965-1414.

**Bereket Turkish Kebab House**
187 E Houston St. **Map** 5 A3. **Tel** (212) 475-7700.

**Blue Ribbon**
See p300.

**Caffè Reggio**
119 MacDougal St. **Map** 4 D2. **Tel** (212) 475-9557.

**Carnegie Deli**
See p314.

**Coffee Shop**
See p314.

**The Dead Poet**
450 Amsterdam Ave.
**Map** 15 C4.
**Tel** (212) 595-5670.

**Empire Diner**
See p138.

**Florent**
See p314.

**Gray's Papaya**
Broadway at 72nd St.
**Map** 11 C1.
**Tel** (212) 260-3532.

**Les Halles**
See p314.

**Odeon**
See p298.

## SPORTS

**24–7 Fitness Club**
47 W 14th St. **Map** 4 D1.
**Tel** (212) 206-1504.

**Billiard Club**
220 W 19th St. **Map** 8 E5. **Tel** (212) 206-POOL.

**Bowlmor Lanes**
110 University Pl. **Map** 4 E1. **Tel** (212) 255-8188.

**Slate Billiards**
See p361.

## SERVICES

**General Post Office**
See p135.

**George Michael of Madison Avenue/ Madora Inc**
422 Madison Ave. **Map** 13 A5. **Tel** (212) 752-1177.

**Juvenex Spa**
25 W 32nd St, 5th Floor.
**Map** 8 F3.
**Tel** (646) 733-1330.

**Midnight Express Cleaners**
**Tel** (718) 392-9200.

**Mr Locks Inc**
**Tel** (866) 675-6257.

## TOURS AND VIEWS

**Arthur's Landing**
Port Imperial Marina,
Pershing Circle,
Weehawken, NJ.
**Tel** (201) 867-0777.

**Battery Park City**
West St. **Map** 1 A3.

**Beekman Tower Hotel**
1st Ave 49th St. **Map** 13 C5. **Tel** (212) 355-7300.

**Château Stables**
608 W 48th St.
**Map** 15 B3.
**Tel** (212) 246-0520.

**Circle Line**
W 42nd St. **Map** 15 B3.
**Tel** (212) 563-3200.

**Marvelous Manhattan Tours**
**Tel** (718) 846-9308.

**Empire State Building**
See pp136–7.

**Harbour Lights**
89 South St Seaport.
Pier 17. **Map** 2 D2.
**Tel** (212) 227-2800.

**Liberty Helicopters**
**Tel** (212) 487-4777.

**Rise**
Ritz-Carlton, Battery Park.
**Map** 1 B4.
**Tel** (212) 344-0800.

**River Café**
See p311.

**Staten Island Ferry**
See p76.

**Top of the Rock**
See p144.

# Sports

Many New Yorkers are ardent sports fans, and you'll find a range of sports events, both to watch and participate in, going on throughout the year. The city boasts two professional baseball teams, two hockey teams, a basketball team, and two football teams. Madison Square Garden plays host to an extraordinary variety of spectator sports, including basketball, hockey, boxing, and track and field events. Tennis fans can take in the US Open and Virginia Slims tournaments, and those who follow track and field events swarm to the Millrose Games, where top runners and other athletes compete.

## TICKETS

The easiest way to get hold of your tickets is through **Ticketron** or **Ticketmaster**. For the big games, you may need a ticket agent. You can also buy tickets at the stadium box office itself, though these tickets often sell out quickly, so you'll have to call or stop by far in advance. Keep your eyes peeled for ticket offers in the free entertainment weeklies that are distributed throughout town.

## FOOTBALL

The city's two professional football teams are the New York Giants and the New York Jets. They both play their home games across the river at the **Giants Stadium** in New Jersey, though there are plans in the works for the construction of a new Giants Stadium on the West Side of Manhattan. Tickets for the Giants, a popular team with an impressive number of NFL and Super Bowl championships under their belt, are near impossible to obtain, but they may be available for the Jets.

## BASEBALL

To capture the essence of this American institution, baseball fans should try to see the famed New York Yankees in action at the **Yankee Stadium** in the Bronx. The team's legendary accomplishments are manifold, and include winning the most World Series titles and boasting such celebrated players as Joe DiMaggio and Jackie Robinson. The New York Mets, the other major baseball team, plays at **Shea Stadium** in Queens. Catching a game of "America's favorite pastime" on a crisp summer day at the hallowed Yankee Stadium is memorable, from the crack of the bat and the baseball soaring into the clear blue sky to the seemingly effortless slides into base and the roar of the crowd. If you can, try and catch a game when the Yankees are playing the Boston Red Sox. The baseball season runs from April to October.

## BASKETBALL

The New York Knicks play their home games at **Madison Square Garden**; note that tickets are pricey and difficult to attain, so you'll need to reserve far in advance through Ticketron or Ticketmaster. The ever-popular Harlem Globetrotters also play their games at The Garden.

## BOXING

Professional boxing matches are more often seen on Paramount's wide TV screen than in the flesh at Madison Square Garden. Also at the Garden are the Daily News Golden Gloves in mid-April, the largest and oldest amateur boxing tournament in the United States, with boxers from New York's five boroughs competing. Past Golden Glove winners, many of whom have gone on to become Olympic gold medalists and world champions, have included Sugar Ray Robinson and Floyd Patterson.

## HORSE RACES

A day at the races may not be quite the lavish affair it once was, but the high-stakes races still draw the society crowd – hats, summer dresses and all – along with lively crowds who have come to cheer, jeer, and bet on their lucky horse. Harness racing, in which horses pull sulkies (small carts), takes place year-round at the **Yonkers Raceway**. Flat races are held daily, except Tuesday, October to May, at the **Aqueduct Race Track** in Queens, and May to October at the **Belmont Park Race Track** in Long Island.

## ICE HOCKEY

Fists and ice fly when the New York Rangers meet their competition at Madison Square Garden. The New York Islanders are also fierce hockey contenders, with exciting matches at the **Nassau Coliseum** in Long Island. The hockey season runs from October to April.

## ICE-SKATING

There are three good places to go ice skating out of doors. One is the **Rockefeller Plaza Rink**, which looks beautiful at Christmas. The others are in Central Park: **Wollman Memorial Rink** and **Lasker Ice Rink**. For indoor sites, try the Sky Rink at **Chelsea Piers**.

## MARATHON

To be one of the 30,000 who enter the New York Marathon, you have to sign up six months in advance. The race is held on the first Sunday in November. Phone (212) 423-2249 for information.

## TENNIS

The top tennis tournament in New York is the US Open, played each August at the **National Tennis Center**. Also good is the women's Virginia Slims Championships in November at **Madison Square Garden** (see p135). If you want to play tennis rather than watch it, look in the telephone directory under "Tennis Courts: Public and Private." For private courts, you can expect to pay about $50–70 an hour. The **Manhattan Plaza Racquet Club** offers both courts and lessons by the hour. For public courts, you will need a $50 permit, available from the **NY City Parks & Recreation Department**. You will also need an identity card and a reservation coupon.

## TRACK AND FIELD

The Millrose Games, which draws top athletes from around the world, are normally held in early February at **Madison Square Garden**. The 100-meter sprint, pole vault, and high jump competitions are particularly exciting. The Amateur Athletic

Union (AAU) championships, where many renowned student athletes compete, are held in late February at the Garden. Chelsea Piers also has a complete track and field complex.

## SPORTS BARS

New York City is crammed with sports bars, often unmissable for their big screens, sports banners, and cheering (or booing), beer-guzzling patrons. For a slice of American sports life, step into a sports bar when a big game is on, and you'll soon be whooping it up with the rest of them. Try **Time Out** or **Mickey Mantle's**, both of which have giant scoreboards and multiple video screens. **ESPN Zone**, in Times Square, offers a plethora of screens so that you can follow the action

no matter where you are, even in the bathroom. **Bar None** and the friendly, Irish **Pioneer Bar** are also favorites, and for soccer, try the amiable **Nevada Smith's** in the East Village, with an infectious vibe thanks to the friendly, Guinness-fueled crowds.

## OTHER ACTIVITIES

In Central Park, options include renting rowboats from **Loeb Boathouse** or playing chess – pick up the pieces from The Dairy *(see p208)*. Rent rollerblades at **Blades Board & Skate** and have a free lesson on stopping at Central Park before making a circuit. Bowling is available at **Chelsea Piers** and a few other lanes throughout the city. **Slate Billiards** and many bars offer pool and darts.

# DIRECTORY

**Aqueduct Race Track**
Ozone Park, Queens.
*Tel (718) 641-4700.*

**Bar None**
98 3rd Ave.
Map 4 F1.
*Tel (212) 777-6663.*

**Belmont Park Race Track**
Hempstead Turnpike,
Long Island.
*Tel (718) 641-4700.*

**Blades Board & Skate**
120 W 72nd St.
Map 12 D1.
*Tel (212) 787-3911.*

**Chelsea Piers Sports & Entertainment Complex**
Piers 59–62 at 23rd St & 11th Ave (Hudson River).
Map 7 B4–5.
*Tel (212) 336-6000.*
www.chelseapiers.com

**ESPN Zone**
1472 Broadway at W 42nd St.
Map 8 E1.
*Tel (212) 921-3776.*

**Giants Stadium**
Meadowlands,
E Rutherford, NJ.
*Tel (201) 935-8111.*
www.giants.com

*Tel (516) 560-8200.*
www.newyorkjets.com

**Lasker Ice Rink**
Central Park Drive East at 108th St.
Map 21 B4.
*Tel (212) 534-7639.*

**Loeb Boathouse**
Central Park.
Map 16 F5.
*Tel (212) 517-2233.*

**Madison Square Garden**
7th Ave at 33rd St.
Map 8 E2.
*Tel (212) 465-6741.*
www.thegarden.com

**Manhattan Plaza Racquet Club**
450 W 43rd St.
Map 7 C1.
*Tel (212) 594-0554.*

**Mickey Mantle's**
42 Central Park South.
Map 12 E3.
*Tel (212) 688-7777.*

**Nassau Coliseum**
1255 Hempstead Turnpike.
*Tel (516) 794-9303.*
www.nassaucoliseum.com

**National Tennis Center**
Flushing Meadow Park, Queens.
*Tel (718) 595-2420.*
www.usta.com

**Nevada Smith's**
74 3rd Ave.
Map 4 F1.
*Tel (212) 982-2591.*

**NY City Parks & Recreation Department**
Arsenal Building,
64th St & 5th Ave.
Map 12 F2.
*Tel (212) 408-0100.*

**Pioneer Bar**
218 Bowery.
Map 4 F3.
*Tel (212) 334-0484.*

**Plaza Rink**
1 Rockefeller Plaza,
5th Ave.
Map 12 F5.
*Tel (212) 332-7654.*

**Shea Stadium**
126th St at Roosevelt Ave,
Flushing, Queens.
*Tel (718) 507-8499.*

**Slate Billiards**
54 W 21st St.
Map 8 E4.
*Tel (212) 989-0096.*

**Ticketmaster**
*Tel (212) 307-4100.*
www.ticketmaster.com

**Ticketron**
*Tel (212) 239-6200,
1-800-432-7250.*
www.telecharge.com

**Time Out**
349 Amsterdam Ave.
Map 15 C5.
*Tel (212) 362-5400.*

**Wollman Memorial Rink**
Central Park,
5th Ave at 59th St.
Map 12 F2.
*Tel (212) 439-6900.*

**Yankee Stadium**
River Ave at 161st St,
The Bronx.
*Tel (718) 293-4300.*

**Yonkers Raceway**
Yonkers,
Westchester County.
*Tel (914) 968-4200.*

# Fitness and Wellbeing

New York City may be (in)famous for its concrete, crowds, and cacophony, but the urban jungle is a boon for sports and fitness aficionados. A host of possibilities beckon, from pedaling on the sun-washed riverfront and jogging under the shadow of Manhattan's signature skyline at the Central Park Reservoir to scaling a soaring climbing wall at one of the city's many upscale gyms, indulging in a massage at gorgeous spa strewn with rose petals and finding your inner Om in the lotus position at a yoga class.

## CYCLING

There's nothing like being stuck in midtown traffic to make you long for pedaling the open road. While Manhattan may be one of the most crowded islands on the planet, it offers a surprising 120 km (75 miles) of bike trails. At the last count, Manhattan boasted more than 110,000 everyday cyclists. One of the most pleasant places to cycle is in Central Park during the weekend, when it's closed to cars. Bikes may be rented from **Central Park Bike Rentals** on Columbus Circle. If you would like to feel the river breeze in your hair, pedal the well-maintained bike path along the West Side Highway that runs parallel to the Hudson River, or hit the bike trails in Riverside Park. On summer weekends, the paths can get exasperatingly congested, but if you go early or late in the day, or in the winter months, you can often coast solo.

The friendly folks at **Bicycle Habitat** on Lafayette Street rent bikes and dole out tips on getting around New York by bike.

## FITNESS CENTERS, GYMS, AND HEALTH CLUBS

In New York, a weekly workout has become almost de rigueur for even the most extreme workaholics. Gyms and health clubs have sprouted across the city to accommodate the demand, and serious sweating goes on at all hours, day and night. The options are endless: Get your aggression out with a punch bag, increase your heart rate on the stairmaster, or pump iron. Most major hotels have fitness centers. Many commercial gyms and health clubs are open only to members, but an increasing number of gyms now offer day passes. Check out the **Chelsea Piers Sports & Entertainment Complex** on Piers 59–62 near Hudson River; there's something for everyone at this enormous facility. It's one-stop shopping at the multilevel **May Center for Health, Fitness, and Sport at the 92nd Street Y**, with exercise studios, weight-training, racquetball courts, a boxing room, and an indoor track. Day passes cost $30. With its well-maintained gym along with an array of personal diet and exercise programs, the **Casa Spa & Fitness at the Regency Hotel** on Park Avenue lives up to its promise to be "your health and fitness oasis when you're away from home".

You can enjoy a wide range of activities at **YMCA** (one in West Side and the other on 47th Street) fitness centers. The state-of-the-art training equipment, a number of gymnasiums, swimming pools, aerobics studios, running/walking tracks, and various courts for different games, add to your enthusiasm of working out. The center also has special programs for elderly people designed to suit their physical stature for a healthy life.

## GOLF

Practice your swing at **Randalls Island Golf Center** on Randalls Island, **Chelsea Golf Club**, or play mini-golf at the **Wollman Memorial Rink** in Central Park. The city owns several courses in the boroughs, such as **Pelham Bay Park** in the Bronx and **Silver Lake** on Staten Island.

## JOGGING

Some parks are safe for joggers, others are not, so be guided by your concierge. None is safe after dark, at dusk or before dawn. The most popular and beautiful route is around the reservoir in Central Park. The **NY Road Runners** on 89th Street have weekly running clinics and races, as does **Chelsea Piers Sports & Entertainment Complex**.

## PILATES

All you have to lose are your love handles. Work your abs and torso for lean, toned muscles at a Pilates class. The philosophy behind Pilates is based on the premise that the body's core is the "powerhouse" for the peripheral parts of the body. Challenge your muscles at a **Grasshopper Pilates**, Franklin Street, class ($20), taught by a professionally trained dancer in a TriBeCa loft. **Power Pilates** also hold strengthening classes ($15) throughout the city.

## YOGA

It's easier to get in touch your spiritual center when you can do it in a place like the airy **Exhale Mind Body Spa** on Madison Avenue, with its high ceilings and hard-wood floors. "Journey into the Core", "Ride the Vinyasa Wave", and "Dance into Trance" at a variety of yoga sessions, the ideal antidote to the city's madness. And, lest you should think yoga isn't enough of a work-out, then you haven't tried the core fusion power pack abs session. **YogaMoves** on Sixth Avenue also offers a wide range of yoga classes, from beginner to advanced.

## SPAS

Pamper yourself at one of New York City's choice spas and you'll emerge fresh as a daisy – and ready to take on the urban jungle once again. Most spas offer packages where you can enjoy several treatments at a lower price. If you're travelling with your significant other, bond over a couples' massage. The intoxicating wafts of Native American incense that greet you at the front door of the fragrant, low-lit **Clay** are just a hint of the luxurious massage that awaits within.

At the comfy, casual **Oasis Day Spa** at Union Square, select from six aromatherapy massages ($100) in aromas of uplift, refresh, balance, passion, calm, or relief. Men's specials include a Dead Sea salt scrub, an algae facial, or a muscle meltdown massage ($100 for an hour). For a slice of heaven, Bali style, disappear into the **Acqua Beauty Bar** on 14th Street and enjoy a botanical

purifying facial ($115), orchid pedicure ($45), or Indonesian ritual of beauty ($170), where your skin is scrubbed with ground rice and kneaded with fragrant oils. Enter **Bliss** on 57th Street and you'll soon discover that there's nothing a carrot and sesame body buff ($195) or fully loaded facial ($195) can't cure. Top it off with a decadent double chocolate pedicure, accompanied by a cup of creamy cocoa. Pure bliss.

Celebrities including Antonio Banderas and Kate Moss swear by **Mario Badescu** on 52nd Street whose facials and body scrubs, including the fresh fruit body scrub, with plump raspberries and strawberries, are as legendary as the beauty products, which are perfect to bring home as gifts.

## SWIMMING

Many Manhattan hotels have pools with free access during your stay. You can also swim and surf at the Surfside 3

Maritime Center at **Chelsea Piers**. For a day trip, go to Jones Beach State Park *(see p255)* along Long Island's shoreline.

## INDOOR SPORTS

**Chelsea Piers** has it all: roller rinks, bowling, indoor soccer, basketball, rock-climbing walls, fitness centers, golf, a field house for gymnastics, sports medicine, spa centers, and of course, swimming pools. This huge complex, which is spread over four old West Side piers, is open to everyone.

Apart from providing fitness centers, gymnasium facilities, and indoor sports activities **YMCA** also offers exercise, balance, and flexibility classes; organizes day trips; special events; and sports and volunteer opportunities. If you are planning an adventurous day out for your children with fitness on the agenda or for burning extra calories then the club is worth a visit.

# DIRECTORY

**Acqua Beauty Bar**
7 E 14th St. **Map** 8 F5.
*Tel (212) 620-4329.*

**Bicycle Habitat**
244 Lafayette St.
**Map** 4 F3.
*Tel (212) 431-3315.*

**Bliss**
19 E 57th St.
**Map** 12 F3.
*Tel (212) 219-8970.*
*(Also has a SoHo location).*

**Casa Spa & Fitness at the Regency Hotel**
540 Park Ave.
**Map** 13 A3.
*Tel (212) 223-9280.*

**Central Park Bike Rental**
2 Columbus Circle.
**Map** 12 D3.
*Tel (212) 541-8759.*

**Chelsea Piers Sports & Entertainment Complex**
Piers 59–62 at 23rd St & 11th Ave (Hudson River).
**Map** 7 B4–5.
*Tel (212) 336-6000.*
www.chelseapiers.com

**Clay**
25 W 14th St.
**Map** 4 D1.
*Tel (212) 206-9200.*

**Exhale Mind Body Spa**
980 Madison Ave.
**Map** 17 A5.
*Tel (212) 561-6400.*

**Grasshopper Pilates**
116 Franklin St.
**Map** 4 E5.
*Tel (212) 431-5225.*

**NY Road Runners**
9 E 89th St.
**Map** 17 A3.
*Tel (212) 860-4455.*

**Mario Badescu**
320 E 52nd St.
**Map** 13 B4.
*Tel (212) 758-1065.*

**May Center for Health, Fitness, and Sport at the 92nd Street Y**
1395 Lexington Ave.
**Map** 17 A2.
*Tel (212) 415-5729.*

**Oasis Day Spa**
108 E 16th St.
**Map** 9 A5.
*Tel (212) 254-7722.*
*One of several branches.*

**Pelham Bay Park**
The Bronx,
870 Shore Rd.
*Tel (718) 885-1461.*

**Power Pilates**
49 W 23rd St,
10th floor.
**Map** 8 F4.
*Tel (212) 627-5852.*

**Randalls Island Golf Center**
Randalls Island.
**Map** 22 F2.
*Tel (212) 427-5689.*

**YMCA West Side**
1395 Lexington Ave.
**Map** 17 A2.
*Tel (212) 415-5500.*

**Silver Lake**
915 Victory Blvd.
Staten Island.
*Tel (718) 447-5686.*

**Wollman Memorial Rink**
Central Park, 5th Ave at 59th St. **Map** 12 F2.
*Tel (212) 439-6900.*

**YMCA 47th St**
224 E 47th St.
**Map** 13 B5.
*Tel (212) 756-9600.*

**YogaMoves**
1026 6th Ave.
**Map** 8 E1.
*Tel (212) 278-8330.*

# CHILDREN'S NEW YORK

Young visitors soon catch the contagious excitement in the air in New York. Attractions for all ages abound, and plenty are designed especially for children. More than a dozen theater companies, two zoos, and three imaginative museums are for just the young, backed up with special events at many museums and parks. The chance to visit a TV studio is a treat, and New York's own Big Apple Circus is a perennial delight. With more to do than can ever be squeezed into a single visit, you'll never hear the cry "I'm bored!" Best of all, there's no need to spend a fortune to have fun.

**A young visitor making New York his very own playground**

## PRACTICAL ADVICE

New York is family-friendly. Many of its hotels allow children in parents' rooms free, and will supply cots or cribs if needed. Most museums charge half price or less for children, while others are free. Children under 112 cm (44 in) also ride free on subways and buses when accompanied by an adult. Travel between 9am and 4pm to avoid rush hours.

Supplies such as diapers and medicines are readily available, and the Rite Aid Pharmacy (see p373) is open 24 hours a day. Finding changing tables in public toilets is less easy, but no one objects if a counter is used. Best bets are the facilities in libraries, hotels, and department stores. Most hotels will arrange babysitters; try **Baby Sitters' Guild** or **Pinch Sitters**.

To find out more about the range of current activities for children, get a copy of the free quarterly calendar of events, available from the New York Convention and Visitors Bureau (see p368). Weekly listings can be found in *New York* magazine or *Time Out New York*.

## NEW YORK ADVENTURES

The city can seem like a giant amusement park for youngsters. Elevators whisk you sky-high for bird's-eye views from atop the world's highest buildings. You can set sail on the classic **Circle Line** tour around Manhattan; the sailboat **Pioneer** (see p84), or charter your own paddle-wheeler from the marina at E. 23rd St; or the free round-trip on the Staten Island Ferry (see p76). The Roosevelt Island Tram (see p181) is a Swiss cable car offering an airborne ride over the East River. Central Park (see pp204–9) is a source of rides of every kind – from the old-fashioned charm of the carousel to real horseback and ponycart rides. Children who prefer a faster pace can join the skateboarders and in-line skaters who cruise around the traffic-free park every weekend.

**Cooling off in a playground in Central Park**

## MUSEUMS

While many of New York's museums appeal to all ages, some are designed just for the young. High on the list are the Children's Museum of Art (see p107), where kids can paint and sculpt, and the Children's Museum of Manhattan (see p219), a multimedia world in which children produce their own videos and newscasts. Farther afield are the **Staten Island Children's Museum**, where a huge climb-through anthill is one of the favorite items, and the Brooklyn Children's Museum (see p247). The *Intrepid* Sea-Air-Space Museum (see p149) is a real aircraft carrier. Finally, don't miss the dinosaur display at the American Museum of Natural History (see pp216–7).

## OUTDOOR FUN

In summer, all of New York comes out to play. Central Park is a child's wonderland, from skating rinks to

**Skating with Santa at Rockefeller Center**

boating lakes, bicycle paths to miniature golf. The park offers free entertainment – such as guided walks by park rangers on Saturdays, toy sailboat races and summer storytelling. The Central Park Wildlife Center and the Tisch Children's Zoo are favorites.

Children of all ages will be fascinated by the Bronx Zoo/ Wildlife Conservation Park which is home to over 500 species (see pp244–5).

Coney Island (see p249) is just a subway ride away. Winter brings the chance to skate at Rockefeller Center (see p144) or in Central Park on a rink fringed with views of skyscrapers.

## INDOOR FUN

New York children's theater is of a quality and variety matching that for adults. Some favorite companies are the **Paper Bag Players** and **Theaterworks USA**, whose shows sell out fast; get schedules and reserve seats early.

The **Swedish Marionette Theater** in Central Park has shows at 10:30am and noon Tuesdays through Fridays, and Saturdays until 1pm.

The New York City Ballet's annual Christmas production of *The Nutcracker* at Lincoln Center (see p212) opens at the same time that the **Big Apple Circus** sets up its tent nearby. Ringling Brothers and Barnum & Bailey Circus is in action at Madison Square Garden (see p135) each spring.

Opportunities for youngsters to work off energy in winter are many, from indoor skating rinks to mini-golf and bowling alleys at **Chelsea Piers**. Kids can create video games, movies, and music for free at **Sony Wonder Technology Lab**.

Centerpiece clock at toy store F.A.O. Schwarz

## SHOPPING

There will be no complaints about shopping trips if they include the huge **F.A.O. Schwarz** or **Toys 'R' Us** for a vast range of wonderful toys and other items. For more information on other toystores see New York Originals on pages 322–4. Youngsters are welcomed for storytelling sessions at **Books of Wonder**.

## EATING OUT

Hamburger-and-pasta joint **Ottomanelli's Café** is very popular with children, and even adults find it hard to finish their huge burgers. The lively **Hard Rock Café** is another hit, and most children enjoy the foods sold around Chinatown and Little Italy. Drop into the **Chinatown Ice Cream Factory** for some strange and wonderful flavors. For a quick hot snack, try pizza-by-the-slice or pretzels and hot dogs from street vendors. There are also scores of fast food places, including White Castle, Burger King, or McDonalds.

# DIRECTORY

## PRACTICAL ADVICE

**Baby Sitters' Guild**
*Tel* (212) 682-0227.

**Pinch Sitters**
*Tel* (212) 260-6005.

## ADVENTURES

**Circle Line**
Pier 83, W 42nd St. **Map** 7 A1.
*Tel* (212) 563-3200.

## MUSEUMS

**Staten Island Children's Museum**
1000 Richmond Terr, Staten Is.
*Tel* (718) 273-2060.

## INDOOR FUN

**Big Apple Circus**
*Tel* (212) 268-2500.

**Chelsea Piers**
*Tel* (212) 336-6800.
www.chelseapiers.com

**Paper Bag Players**
*Tel* (212) 663-0390.

**Sony Wonder Technology Lab**
550 Madison Ave. **Map** 13 A3.
*Tel* (212) 833-8100.

**Swedish Cottage Marionette Theater**
*Tel* (212) 988-9093.

**Theaterworks USA**
787 7th Ave. **Map** 12 E4.
*Tel* (212) 627-7373.

## SHOPPING

**Books of Wonder**
16 W 18th St. **Map** 8 C5.
*Tel* (212) 989-3270.

**F.A.O. Schwarz**
767 5th Ave. **Map** 12 F3.
*Tel* (212) 644-9400.

**Toys 'R' Us**
See p324.

## EATING OUT

**Chinatown Ice Cream Factory**
65 Bayard St. **Map** 4 F5.
*Tel* (212) 608-4170.

**Hard Rock Café**
1501 Broadway. **Map** 8 E1.
*Tel* (212) 343-3355.

**Ottomanelli's Café**
1626 York Ave. **Map** 17 C3.
*Tel* (212) 772-7722.

Storytelling session at South Street Seaport

# SURVIVAL GUIDE

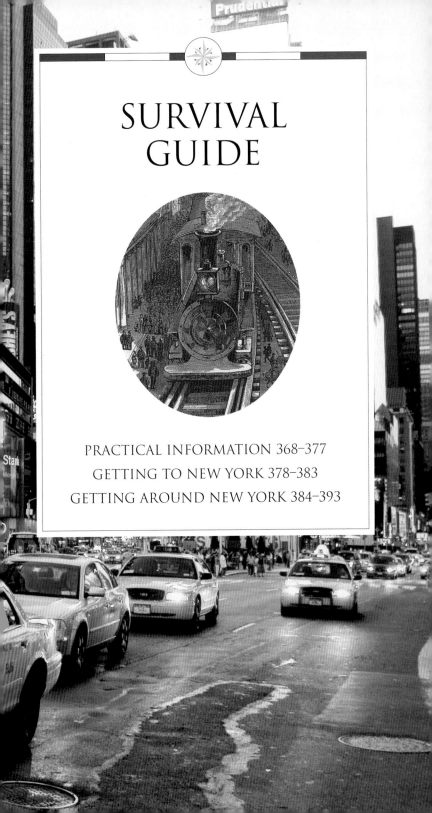

# PRACTICAL INFORMATION

Visitors to New York are treated very much the same as anyone else. While you may not be given special treatment, as long as you follow a few guidelines on personal security (see pp372–3) you'll be able to explore the city as freely as any native New Yorker. Buses and subway trains (pp388–9) are reliable and cheap; there

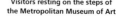

Visitors resting on the steps of the Metropolitan Museum of Art

are plenty of cash machines (pp374–5), and money can be easily exchanged at banks, hotels, and foreign money brokers. The wide range of prices offered by the many hotels (pp280–91), restaurants, (pp296–311) and entertainment venues (pp340–65) in the city means that your New York trip can be both fun and affordable.

## SIGHTSEEING TIPS

New York's rush hours extend from 8am to 10am, 11:30am to 1:30pm, and 4:30 to 6:30pm, Monday to Friday. During these times, every form of public transportation will be crowded, and the streets will be much harder to navigate on foot.

It's worth trying to visit a cluster of sights in the same area – see the *Street-by-Street* plans of each area – instead of exhausting yourself rushing from one distant attraction to another. Buses are a comfortable and reliable way to get around, and you'll see the city as you travel.

It's best to avoid passing through certain areas of the city, especially at particular times (see pp372–3). Public toilets in bus stations should be avoided. They attract drug users and the homeless. It is best to find a large hotel, department store, coffee shop, or bookstore if you need a restroom.

If you need help with street directions or feel a need to get off the street, ask a policeman or find a hotel doorman. There is one on duty at the entrance to most hotels 24 hours a day.

## OPENING HOURS

Business hours are generally from 9am to 5pm with no lunchtime closing. Only some banks close earlier, at 4pm, although some do have longer

Hotel doorman

hours (8am–6pm) and open on Saturday mornings. Many museums close on Mondays and major holidays. Some open on Tuesday or Thursday evenings during certain seasons (phone for details).

## MUSEUMS

In New York, *museum* is used as a blanket term to include institutions that offer diverse holdings. The city's flagship museums are described on pages 36 to 39. Museums either charge admission, starting at around $2, or ask for a "donation," which can be $6 to $12. There are discounts for senior citizens, students, and children. The leading museums schedule free guided tours and lectures. Museum Mile (see pp184–5), on and near Fifth Avenue, groups some major museums close together.

## ETIQUETTE

It is illegal to smoke in *any* public place or building in New York. Some restaurants now provide separate rooms for smokers, but it is best to phone ahead for details.

Tipping is an integral part of New York life: for taxi drivers leave 10 to 15%; waiters 15 to 20%, cocktail waiters 15%, hotel room service 10% (when not added to the bill); coat check $1; hotel maids $1 or $2 per day after the first day; hotel bellhops about $1 per bag; hair stylists 15 to 20%, and barbers 10 to 20%.

## INTERNET CAFES

Internet cafés offer safe access to the world wide web. Some, such as the **easyInternetcafé**, are huge. Others, including **Cyber Café**, give more emphasis to the snacks and coffee available. Expect to pay about $6 for 30 minutes. **Web2Zone** offers cheap rates at quiet times.

**Cyber Café**
250 W 49th St. **Map** 11 B5.
*Tel* (212) 333-4109.

**easyInternetcafé**
234 W 42nd St. **Map** B1.

**Web2Zone**
54 Cooper Square. **Map** 4 F2.
*Tel* (212) 614-7300.

## TOURIST INFORMATION

Advice on any aspect of life in New York is available from the New York Convention and Visitors Bureau, known as **NYC & Co.** (see pp340–41). Their 24-hour touch-tone phone service offers help outside office hours. Information kiosks can also be found at the **Times Square Information Bureau**.

**Useful information**
NYC & Co, 810 7th Ave. **Map** 12 E4.
*Tel* (212) 484-1222.
**www**.nycvisit.com
Times Square Information Center
1560 Broadway. **Map** 12 E5.
◻ 8am–8pm daily.
**www**.timessquarenyc.org
New York City information
**www**.nyc.gov
On-line guide to everything in NYC:
**www**.jimsdeli.com
New York State information
**www**.state.ny.us

◁ **Taxis queue below Stars and Stripes**

## ENTERTAINMENT LISTINGS

A number of inexpensive or even free publications listing current exhibitions and leisure activities are available at newsstands, hotels or galleries throughout New York.

Among the more popular ones are *New York* magazine, *The New Yorker's* "Goings On About Town," roster and *Time Out New York*, which list offerings at the city's many museums, clubs, theaters, galleries, restaurants, cinemas, colleges, and libraries, plus impending auctions. The *Village Voice*, a free magazine, focuses on events in SoHo, TriBeCa, and Greenwich Village, plus other major

cultural activity in the city. *The New York Times* Friday and Sunday editions list current visual and performing arts events in their respective "Weekend" and "Arts and Leisure" sections. *Art News* is a monthly magazine that lists major art events and auctions and reviews exhibits.

There are also various free magazines. The weekly *Where* is distributed through hotel concierges and lists major museums, their opening hours, locations, and any exhibitions. *Art Now/New York Gallery Guide* is released in art galleries each month. It lists current exhibitions and has useful maps showing where they are located.

*New York magazine has weekly comprehensive entertainment listings for all of New York*

## GUIDED TOURS

Whichever way you want to see New York – with the help of a pre-recorded walk or by an exciting trip in a helicopter, boat, or horse-drawn carriage – organized sightseeing trips, planned by someone else, can save a lot of time, effort, and often money.

### Boat Tours
Circle Line Sightseeing Yachts, Pier 83, W 42nd St.
**Map** 7 A1.
*Tel (212) 563-3200.*
*A three-hour trip circum-navigating Manhattan.*

Circle Line Statue of Liberty Ferry
South Ferry, Battery Park.
**Map** 1 C4.
*Tel (212) 269-5755.*

Spirit of New York
W 23rd and 8th Ave.
**Map** 8 D4.
*Tel (866) 211-3805.*
*Cruises with lunch/dinner.*

World Yacht, Inc
Pier 81 W 41st St.
**Map** 7 A1.
*Tel (212) 630-8100.*
*Cruises with lunch/dinner and entertainment.*

### Carriage Tours
59th St at Fifth Ave and along Central Park S.
*Horse-drawn carriages gather outside the Plaza Hotel (**Map** 12 F3). Route takes in Central Park.*

### Bus Tours
Gray Line of New York
42nd St and 8th Ave.
**Map** 8 D1.
*Tel (212) 397-2620.*

Short Line Tours/American Sightseeing NY
166 W 46th St.
**Map** 12 F5.
*Tel (800) 631-8405.*

### Bicycle Tours
Bite of the Apple Tours, 2 Columbus Circle, 59th St & Broadway. **Map** 12 D3.
*Tel (212) 541-8759.*
*A two-hour spin around Central Park. $35 with bike rental. 10am, 1pm, and 4pm.*

### Helicopter Tours
Liberty
W 30th St and 12th Ave South Ferry.
**Map** 7 B3.
*Tel (212) 967-6464.*

### Walking Tours
Adventures on a Shoestring
300 W 53rd St

**Map** 12 E4
*Tel (212) 265-2663.*
*Theme and neighborhood tours.*

Big Apple Greeters
1 Centre St, Suite 2035.
**Map** 4 F4.
*Tel (212) 669-8159.*
*Free tours by New York natives.*

Big Onion Walking Tours
Columbia University.
**Map** 20 E3.
*Tel (212) 439-1090.*
*Historical and ethnic.*

Harlem Spirituals, Inc.
690 8th Ave. **Map** 8 D1.
*Tel (212) 391-0900.*
*Harlem's history and culture. Apr–Oct only.*

Heritage Trails
Four free do-it-yourself historical trails begin at Federal Hall; brochures at Federal Hall. **Map** 1 C3.

Museum of the City of New York
103rd St and Fifth Ave.
**Map** 21 C5.
*Tel (212) 534-1672.*
*Architecture and history.*

NBC Studio Tour
30 Rockefeller Plaza.
**Map** 12 F5.
*Tel (212) 664-7174.*

92nd Street Y
1395 Lexington Ave.
**Map** 17 A2.
*Tel (212) 415-5500.*
*Culture and history.*

PhotoTrek Tours
*Tel (212) 410-2514.*
*Tours aimed at creating a CD with 75–100 pictures of yourself in New York.*

Walkin' Broadway.
1619 Broadway.
**Map** 12 E5.
*Tel (212) 997-5004.*
*Broadway audio guide.*

**Carriage ride in Central Park**

## DISABLED TRAVELERS

Disabled people may find New York a challenging city. Only 21 of Manhattan's subway stations are wheelchair-accessible and, while all buses are equipped for wheelchair access, some major boarding areas are not.

Many hotels, restaurants, and tourist attractions are equipped for disabled visitors, but it is wise to check. Also ask about accessibilty to rest rooms.

Some museums offer tours for deaf, blind, or disabled people, and all Broadway theaters have devices for the hearing-impaired. An excellent resource is *Access Guide to New York City*, available from the **Mayor's Office for People with Disabilities**.

**Useful information** Mayor's Office for People with Disabilities. *Tel (212) 788-2830.* **www**.nyc.gov/mopd Hospital Audiences Inc. *Tel (212) 575-7660.* **www**.hospaud.org

A New York city bus "kneeling" to help the elderly board

## CUSTOMS AND IMMIGRATION

Citizens of Britain, New Zealand, Australia, and 26 other countries do not need visas if they are staying in the US for 90 days or less. Canadians need only proof of citizenship and a photo ID. Students do need proper visas. All travelers need round-trip or onward passage tickets and must show proof that they have $500 or more. Check with a US embassy or travel agent if in doubt.

Customs allowances per person when you enter the US are 200 cigarettes, 100 cigars or 4.4 pounds (2 kilograms) of tobacco; no more than 2 pints (1 liter) of alcohol; gifts worth no more than $100; no meat or meat products (even in cans), and no seeds, growing plants, or fresh fruit.

Upon arrival at one of New York's airports, follow signs stating "other than American passports" to immigration counters, where your passport will then be inspected and stamped. Once you have reclaimed your baggage from the appropriate area (again, follow the signs), you will be approached by a Customs officer. He or she will examine the Customs declaration you should have received and filled in on your flight and direct you either toward the exit or to a Customs inspector, who will then search your luggage. According to US Customs officials, around 5% of all travelers will have to have their luggage searched. There are no red or green Customs channels – you're cleared and free to go once the Customs officer has seen your fully completed declaration.

## STUDENT TRAVELERS

Many museums and theaters allow students a discount on admission. To receive this, however, you will need to carry proof of your student status at all times.

An International Student ID Card can be purchased quite cheaply, provided you have the right credentials, from the **Council Travel**, which has two branches in New York. At the same time, ask for a copy of the *ISIC Student Handbook*. This invaluable booklet identifies places and services throughout the US that offer a range of discounts to card-holders. Included are selected accommodations, various museums, theaters, tours, attractions, nightclubs, and restaurants.

Although it is normally extremely difficult to obtain permission to work in the US, students are an exception to this rule, being eligible to work as part of exchange programs, or as interns. The Student Travel Association in the UK, Australia, or New Zealand will provide you with details of working holidays in New York. In London, contact the **Council on International Educational Exchange**.

## STUDENT INFORMATION

**Bunac Summer Camps USA**
P.O. Box 430, Southbery, CT 06488.
*Tel (203) 264-0901. Summer only.*

**Council on International Educational Exchange**
633 3rd Ave. **Map** 9 B1.
*Tel (212) 822-2700.*
52 Poland St, London W1V 4JQ.
*Tel +44 (207) 478-2000.*

**STA Travel**
10 Downing St. **Map** 4 D3.
205E 42nd St. **Map** 9 B1.
*Tel (212) 627-3111; (800) 781-4040.*
**www**.statravel.com
Two of four branches.

## CONVERSION CHART

Bear in mind that 1 US pint (0.5 liter) is a smaller measure than 1 UK pint (0.6 liter).

**Imperial system:**
1 inch = 2.5 centimeters
1 foot = 30 centimeters
1 mile = 1.6 kilometers
1 ounce = 28 grams
1 pound = 454 grams
1 US pint = 0.47 liter
1 US gallon = 3.8 liters

**Metric system:**
1 millimeter = 0.04 inch
1 centimeter = 0.4 inch
1 meter = 3 feet 3 inches
1 kilometer = 0.6 mile
1 gram = 0.04 ounce

International Student ID Card

**New York daily newspapers**

**A newspaper vending machine**

## NEWSPAPERS, TELEVISION AND RADIO

You can buy foreign newspapers, usually the previous day's issue, at **Universal News**, airports, hotels, and newsstands near international business areas like the World Financial Center or Wall Street.

TV program schedules can be found in the weekly *TV Guide* magazine and the television section of the Sunday edition of *The New York Times*.

The choice of TV stations available in New York is vast. CBS operates on channel 2, NBC on channel 4, ABC on channel 7 and WNYW (Fox) on channel 5. PBS offers cultural and educational fare, including some vintage BBC programs, on channel 13. Cable TV offers everything from the Arts and Entertainment Network (channel 16) to public access programs.

AM radio stations include WCBS News (880AM) and WFAN Sports (660AM). Some FM stations are WWFS contemporary (102.7FM), WBGO jazz (88.3FM) and WQXR classical (96.3FM).
**Information** Universal News, 234 W 42nd St. **Map** 8 D1. **Tel** (212) 221-1809. One of several branches.

## ELECTRICAL APPLIANCES

All American electric current flows at a standardized 110 to 120 volts AC (alternating

current). You will need to bring an adapter plug and a voltage convertor that fits standard US electrical outlets. US plugs have two flat prongs.

Most modern New York hotels provide wall-mounted electric hair dryers in bathrooms. In addition, some hotels have wall plugs capable of powering both 110- and 220-volt electric shavers, but little else – not even radios. It can, in fact, be dangerous to connect anything more powerful. If you bring along sophisticated electrical appliances with you, be certain to take a battery pack as well. You will also need an adapter to recharge your spare batteries.

Few New York hotel rooms provide irons or coffee-makers. However, room service should be able to provide you with an iron upon request.

**Standard plug**

### EMBASSIES AND CONSULATES

**Australia**
150 E 42nd St. **Map** 9 A1.
**Tel** (212) 351-6500.
www.australianyc.org

**Britain**
845 Third Ave. **Map** 13 B4.
**Tel** (212) 745-0200.
www.britainusa.com/ny

**Canada**
1251 Sixth Ave at 50th St. **Map** 12 E4. **Tel** (212) 596-1628.
www.canada-ny.org

**Ireland**
345 Park Ave. **Map** 13 A4.
**Tel** (212) 319-2555.
www.irelandemb.org

**New Zealand**
37 Observatory Circle, NW, Washington, DC 20008.
**Tel** (202) 328-4800.
www.nzemb.org

### RELIGIOUS SERVICES

There are some 4,000 places of worship in New York, catering to almost any faith. Most hotels have lists of local organizations and service times. Among the leading churches and temples are:

**Baptist**
Riverside Church
122nd St at Riverside Dr.
**Map** 20 D2.
**Tel** (212) 870-6700.

**Catholic**
St. Patrick's Cathedral
Fifth Ave at 50th St.
**Map** 12 F4.
**Tel** (212) 753-2261.

**Episcopal**
St. Bartholomew's
109 E 50th St. **Map** 13 A4.
**Tel** (212) 378-0200.

**Jewish**
Reform
Temple Emanu-El
Fifth Ave at 65th St.
**Map** 12 F2.
**Tel** (212) 744-1400.

Orthodox
Fifth Avenue Synagogue
5 E 62nd St. **Map** 12 F2.
**Tel** (212) 838-2122.

**Lutheran**
St. Peter's
619 Lexington Ave. **Map** 17 A4. **Tel** (212) 935-2200.

**Methodist**
Christ Church United Methodist
520 Park Ave. **Map** 13 A3.
**Tel** (212) 838-3036.

**Riverside Church**

# Personal Security and Health

**Police badge**

In 1998, New York was rated the safest among large US cities with a population of more than one million. This ranks New York 166th among cities with population of over one hundred thousand. The city's police force concentrates on foot and bicycle patrols in tourist areas, and security has been beefed up in midtown, in the transportation system and at airports. While there are places where any traveler would be foolish to tread after dark – and sometimes in daylight – if you keep your wits about you and stick to the following guidelines, you should enjoy a trouble-free visit.

**New York City police patrol using a range of transportation**

## LAW ENFORCEMENT

The New York police department has around-the-clock foot, horse, bike, and car patrols. These are concentrated in specific areas at critical times – for instance, the theater district during show times. There are police who ride the subways and buses, and the recent dramatic drop in crime statistics reflects this.

You may also see youths wearing red berets. As their T-shirts proclaim, they are Guardian Angels. Always unarmed, these safety patrols "police" the subways and midtown streets. Although tolerated by the police and often a welcome sight, they have no official powers.

## GUIDELINES ON SAFETY

Under the leadership of former mayor Rudolph Giuliani, New York became a relatively safe place to roam. Common sense still rules, however, so be alert and walk as if you know where you're going. Avoid eye contact and confrontations with down-and-outs. If someone asks you for money, be careful and do not be drawn into conversation.

Avoid deserted streets. At night, if you can't afford a taxi, try to travel with a group and keep away from the Lower East Side, Chinatown, midtown west of Broadway (except Lincoln Center and Times Square), and any place off the beaten path. The Financial District (except for the World Financial Center) is deserted after business hours, and some TriBeCa and SoHo streets can be risky after dark.

Parks are often used for drug dealing. They are safest when there is a crowd for a rally, concert or other event, although you should still take precautions to avoid being pick-pocketed. If you want to go for a jog, ask your hotel concierge for a map of safe routes and follow his or her advice. When walking in the park or street, keep your wallet in an inconspicuous place and have enough change handy for phone calls and bus fares. It's best not to have to dig into your purse or wallet while standing in line. Never stop to count your money on the street, and be aware of strangers watching at bank machines. Defeat purse snatchers by carrying your bag with the clasp facing toward you and the shoulder strap across your body.

Leave valuable jewelry at home or stored at your hotel; do not allow anyone except hotel and airport personnel to carry your luggage or parcels; and stow your valuables and camera in a locked suitcase or closet safe when you leave your hotel room.

**Mounted police officers patrolling the streets to keep the city safe**

## LOST AND FOUND

The chances are poor of recovering anything lost in New York City. There is no city-wide lost and found. The lost-and-found rooms at Grand Central and Penn Station, however, are well-run with helpful staff. Most taxi and transport firms also have lost and found departments.

In the event of loss or theft, report all missing items to the police and make sure you get a copy of the police report for

**As a general rule, be alert when you walk down the street**

**Cap and badge worn by city police**

your insurance claim. Keep a record of your valuables' serial numbers and receipts as proof of possession.

## USEFUL INFORMATION

### Lost and Found Offices
Bus and subway services
**Tel** (212) 712-4500.

Taxis **Tel** 311.
*From outside New York:*
*(212) NEW-YORK.*

### Stolen or Lost Credit Cards
American Express
**Tel** (800) 528-4800 (free).

Diners Club
**Tel** (800) 234-6377 (free).

JCB
**Tel** (800) 366-4522 (free).

MasterCard
**Tel** (800) 627-8372 (free).

VISA
**Tel** (800) 336-8472 (free).

## TRAVEL INSURANCE

Travel insurance is highly recommended, mainly because of the high cost of medical care. There are many types of coverage, with prices dependent on the length of your trip and the number of people covered on the policy.
Among the most important features are: accidental death, dismemberment, emergency medical and dental care, trip cancellation, and baggage and travel document loss. There are many policies that include all these items. Your travel agent or insurance company should recommend a suitable policy.

## MEDICAL TREATMENT

Be prepared to undergo an expensive experience: some of the city's practitioners and facilities are among the best

around, and medical fees in the US are unregulated. Be sure to protect yourself well with insurance. A few physicians and dentists may accept credit cards, but they are much more likely to want payment in cash or traveler's checks. Hospitals accept most credit cards *(see p374).*

**A 24-hour pharmacy, one of several in the city**

## EMERGENCIES

In the event of your being involved in a medical emergency, proceed at once to a **Hospital Emergency Room.** Should you need an ambulance, telephone 911 and one will be sent. If your medical insurance is properly in order, you won't have to worry about costs.
Unless you are impoverished, it is better to avoid the city-owned hospitals listed in the telephone book Blue Pages. Instead, choose one of the many private hospitals listed in the Yellow Pages. Dial 411 and ask the operator to give you the number of the nearest public or private hospital. Other options include asking your hotel to call a doctor or dentist to visit you in your room, or finding one yourself through the **NY Hotel Urgent Medical Services** or **NYU Dental Care**. The Beth Israel Medical Center has an excellent walk-in clinic, **DOCS**. For more general advice and information call **Travelers' Aid**, a national organization geared to helping travelers.

## CRISIS INFORMATION

### All Emergencies
**Tel** 911 (or 0). This alerts police, fire, and medical services.

### Crime Victims Hot Line
**Tel** (212) 577-7777.

### DOCS
55 E 34th St.
**Map** 8 F2.
**Tel** (212) 252-6000.
One of three branches.

### Hospital Emergency Rooms
St. Vincent's, 11th St and Seventh Ave. **Map** 3 C1.
**Tel** (212) 604-7998.

St. Luke's Roosevelt, 58th St and Ninth Ave.
**Map** 12 D3.
**Tel** (212) 523-6800.

### National Organization for Women (NOW)
**Tel** (212) 627-9895.

### NY Hotel Urgent Medical Services
**Tel** (212) 737-1212.

### NYU Dental Care
345 E 24th St/1st Ave.
**Map** 9 B4.
**Tel** (212) 998-9800
(9am–6:30pm Mon–Thu, 9am–4pm Fri), (212) 998-9828 (weekends and after 9pm).

### Pharmacy (24-hour)
Rite Aid, 50th St/8th Ave.
**Map** 12 D4.
**Tel** (212) 247-8384.

### Poison Control Center
**Tel** (212) 764-7667.

### Sex Crimes Report Line
**Tel** (212) 267-7273.

### The Samaritans
**Tel** (212) 673-3000.

### Travelers' Aid
JFK Airport, Terminal 410.
**Tel** (718) 656-4870.

**New York ambulance**

# Banking and Currency

New York is the nation's banking center. It has a wealth of local, regional and major national banks, plus some retail branches of the leading foreign banks. Fleet Bank and Barclays are well represented in New York; the banks of Australia, Canada, Ireland, Scotland, Tokyo, and Turkey all have offices or branches.

American Express charge cards

## BANKING

New York banks are generally open weekdays from 9am to 3pm. There are, however, a number of banks that open earlier or close later in the evening to suit commuters' needs. Tellers are behind a counter. At most banks, all the tellers will cash traveler's checks and exchange your foreign currency.

Automated teller machine (ATM)

## AUTOMATED TELLER MACHINES

A convenient development in banking has been the introduction of the automated teller machine (ATM). These are found in nearly all bank lobbies and enable you to obtain American currency 24 hours a day by electronically tapping into your own bank account. ATMs usually issue American banknotes in $20 denominations.

Before you leave for New York, check with your bank about which New York City banks and ATM systems will accept your bank card and what fees and commissions will be charged on each transaction. Most ATMs are part of either the Cirrus or

the Plus network. They accept various US bank cards, MasterCard and VISA cards and certain others. Among the many advantages of ATMs is the swift, secure exchange of your money at the whole-sale rate used between the banks when they make their million-dollar deals.

On a more cautionary note, always be aware of your surroundings when using an unlocked ATM. It is best to use them only in daylight hours or when the streets are crowded.

## CREDIT CARDS

Mastercard, American Express, VISA, JCB and Diners Club cards are widely accepted throughout the United States, regardless of which company or bank issues them. These cards can also be used to obtain cash advances from various ATMs. They may be upgraded to confer higher spending limits.

In the United States you can use a credit card to pay for nearly everything imaginable, from groceries to restaurant and hotel bills, and for movie and theater tickets booked by telephone. Major expenses such as tours, travel packages and expensive rentals are all best paid for by credit card. Using a card also means that you can avoid carrying huge sums of money around with you.

## CASHING CHECKS

Traveler's checks issued in dollars by American Express and Thomas Cook are widely accepted without a fee by most department stores, shops, hotels and restaurants in New York. Traveler's checks in other currencies, including sterling, are not

universally accepted. However, they can usually be exchanged by your hotel cashier, but may require a visit to a bank. Exchange rates for foreign currency are printed daily in the *New York Times* and *Wall Street Journal*, and may be posted in bank windows. American Express checks are exchanged without a fee at American Express offices. Major hotels have cashiers that will exchange traveler's checks.

Foreign exchange brokers are few. Among the most solidly established are **Travelex Currency Services Inc**. and **American Express**. Those listed on the opposite page have late hours. Others are listed in the city's telephone Yellow Pages under *Foreign Money Brokers*. When you use the services of a foreign exchange broker, expect to pay a fee, which will vary widely from one place to the next. There will also be a commission.

**Chase Manhattan Bank** offers exchange in more than 400 locations and there are scores of hole-in-the-wall check-cashing shops in Manhattan. **Commerce Bank** also has branches throughout Manhattan that are open weekends and until 8pm weekdays. Both banks are listed in the Yellow Pages classified section.

## MONEY WIRES

In emergencies, you can arrange to have money wired to you through Moneygram or Western Union.

**Moneygram**
*Tel (800) 926-9400.*

**Western Union**
*Tel (800) 225-5227.*

## Coins

*American coins come in 50-, 25-, 10-, 5- and 1-cent pieces. The new gold-tone $1 coins are now in circulation as are the State quarters, which feature an historical scene on one side. Each value of coin has a popular name: 25-cent pieces are called quarters, 10-cent pieces are called dimes, 5-cent pieces called nickels and 1-cent pieces called pennies.*

25-cent coin
(a quarter)

10-cent coin
(a dime)

5-cent coin
(a nickel)

1-cent coin
(a penny)

A one-dollar coin
or 'buck'

### Bank Notes (Bills)

*Units of currency in the United States are dollars and cents. There are 100 cents to a dollar. Notes come in $1, $5, $10, $20, $50 and $100s. The new $10, $20, and $50 bills are now in circulation; security features include subtle colour hues and improved colour-shifting ink in the lower right hand corner of the face of each note.*

## FINANCIAL SERVICES

### American Express
822 Lexington Ave. **Map** 13 A2.
**Tel** *(212) 758-6510.* 9am–6pm Mon–Fri, 10am–4pm Sat.
Marriot Marquis Hotel,
1535 Broadway. **Map** 12 E5.
**Tel** *(212) 575-6580.*
7am–8pm daily.
Helpline **Tel** *(800) 333-AMEX.*

### Choice Forex
Grand Central Terminal.
**Map** 9 A1. **Tel** *(212) 661-7600.*
7am–9pm Mon–Fri,
10am–6pm Sat–Sun.

### Cirrus/MasterCard
**Tel** *(800) 424-7787 (ATM locator).*

### VISA Plus
**Tel** *(800) 843-7587.*

### Travelex
1590 Broadway. **Map** 12 E5.
**Tel** *(212) 265-6063.*
1271 Broadway. **Map** 8 F3.
**Tel** *(212) 679-4365.*
9am–7pm Mon–Sat,
9am–5pm Sun.
Also at: 510 Madison Ave and
29 Broadway. 9am–5pm daily.
**Tel** *(800) CURRENCY.*

1-dollar bill ($1)

5-dollar bill ($5)

10-dollar bill ($50)

20-dollar bill ($20)

50-dollar bill ($50)

100-dollar bill ($100)

# Using New York's Phones

**Sign for public payphones**

Public pay phones can be found at many street corners, in hotel and office lobbies, restaurants, bars, theaters, and department stores. Few use credit cards, but you can now buy prepaid phone cards. Most phones are coin-operated and take 5-, 10-, and 25-cent coins. In 2003 Neptune 800 internet pay phones were introduced to the streets of New York. These have a color monitor, keyboard, and webcam, and offer customers internet access at 25 cents per minute.

## NEW YORK TIME

New York is on Eastern Standard Time. When making international calls, calculate the time in the country you are calling. For the UK add 5 hours; for Australia add 15 hours; and for New Zealand add 17 hours.

## PUBLIC TELEPHONES

The standard pay phone has a hand receiver and 12-button keypad and is pillar- or wall-mounted. In some locations the pay phone may belong to an independent company. The independents are often more expensive and less reliable. Regulations require each public pay phone to post information about charges, toll-free numbers, and how to make calls using other carriers. Look

**Independently operated pay phone**

for the Verizon logo on the box to be sure the phone will reach all numbers at standard rates. To complain about service, call the **Public Service Commission**.
**Useful information**
Public Service Commission
**Tel** *(800) 342-3355 (toll-free number).*

**To check e-mail**
Times Square Information Center, 1560 Broadway, **Map** 12 E5; many New York Public Libraries also have internet desks, but there is usually a time limit for use. See also p368.

## PAY PHONE CHARGES

Within all boroughs of New York City, the standard charge, around 25 cents, buys three minutes' talking time. If your call lasts longer, the operator will request an additional payment.

Many newsstands now sell prepaid phone cards for long-distance calls; they can be bought in $5, $10, and $25 amounts. The cards offer substantial savings compared to standard rates. However, the calls are connected over the internet and so the sound quality may not be as good as calls using a standard carrier.

## USING A COIN-OPERATED PHONE

**1** Lift the receiver.

**3** Dial or press the number.

**Coins**
*Make sure you have the correct coins available before you dial.*

**5 cents**

**10 cents**

**25 cents**

**2** Insert the necessary coin or coins. The coin drops as soon as you insert it.

**4** If you do not want to complete your call or it does not get through, retrieve the coin(s) by pressing the coin return.

**5** If the call is answered and you talk longer than the allotted three minutes, the operator will interrupt and ask you to deposit more coins. Pay phones do not give change.

**A typical public pay phone stand**

International long-distance rates for calls dialed direct vary from country to country. For calls to the UK, the discount rate starts at 1pm, then drops to an economy rate from 6pm until 7am the next day.

## USEFUL NUMBERS

**Directory Inquiries**
*Tel 411 or 10-10-9000.*

**US Post Office**
*Tel (800) ASK-USPS.*

**Operator Assistance**
*Tel 0.*

**Speaking Clock**
*Tel (212) 976-1616.*

**International Directory Inquiries**
*Tel 00.*

### REACHING THE RIGHT NUMBER

• Five area codes are used in New York: 212, 917, 646 for Manhattan; the other boroughs use 718 and 347. Calls to 800, 888, and 877 numbers are free.
• To call a number outside your own area, first dial 1. For example, to dial Queens from Manhattan dial 1 (718) (number). To call inside your area, dial the area code first.
• To call long distance from a pay phone: dial 0 followed by the area code and then the number. The operator will answer and tell you how much money you need to deposit.
• To make an international direct call: dial 011 followed by the country code (New Zealand: 64; Australia: 61; UK: 44), then the city or area code (minus the first 0) and the local number.
• To make an international call via the operator: dial 01 followed by the country code, the city code (minus the first 0) and then the local number.
• International Directory Inquiries are on 00. International operator assistance is on 01.
• **In an emergency, phone 911**.

# Sending A Letter

US postal service logo

Apart from post offices, letters can be mailed at your hotel concierge desk (which usually also sells stamps); in letter slots in office building lobbies; in air, rail, and bus terminals; and in the occasional street mailbox. These are always painted blue, or red, white, and blue. Mail in most

mailboxes is not picked up on weekends. Post offices are shown on the *Street Finder* maps *(see pp394–5).*

## POSTAL SERVICES

The city's main **General Post Office** is open 24 hours a day. Stamps can be bought here or from branch offices (a handy one is in the Empire State Building) or from coin-operated machines in pharmacies, department stores, and bus and train stations. All letters go first class.

US stamp

The post office offers three special mail delivery services: **Express Mail** service for next-day delivery, **Priority Mail** service for two-day delivery, and **International Express Mail** for overseas. Priority Mail will also pick up letters on weekdays for an extra charge. Private express mail can be arranged through hotel

concierges or with one of the delivery services listed in the telephone book.

**Useful information**
General Post Office, 421 8th Ave. **Map** 8 D2. *Tel (800) ASK-USPS. **Tel** (800) 222-1811* Priority and Express Mail. ***Tel** (800) 463-3339* FedEx. ***Tel** (800) 225-5345* DHL. ***Tel** (800) 782-7892* UPS.

**Internet guides**
www.bigyellow.com
www.usps.com

## HELD MAIL

Mail will be held for you for up to 30 days at the General Post Office's General Delivery window. Mail can be sent to any local post office by giving the zip code or name. Address mail with: Name, General Delivery, US Post Office, New York, NY 10001.

**Express Mail**     **Priority Mail**

**Mailboxes**
*Mailboxes can be few and far between on New York streets, and it may be easier to find a post office (see Street Finder pp394–5). Instructions on how to use the mailbox are written on the box. If you use Express or Priority services, weigh your letters at a post office to figure out the postage needed.*

**Standard mailbox**

# GETTING TO NEW YORK

Many international airlines have direct flights to New York. The city is also very well served by charter and domestic services. Price wars between airlines have reduced fares, and domestic flights now prove a viable alternative to buses and trains; group tour package prices are often unbeatable.

**Grand Central Terminal**

The *QM2* is one of several cruise ships that dock in the city. Long-distance trains serving New York are clean and comfortable, and interstate and long-distance buses usually have air-conditioning, video screens, and on-board toilets. For information on arriving in New York see the map on pages 382–3.

## AIR TRAVEL

New York can be reached by air direct from most major cities. The flight from London takes about eight hours. However, there are no direct flights from Australia or New Zealand. Instead, the airlines fly to the West coast or Asia, which takes around 10–14 hours, land, refuel, and then continue on to New York.

Among the main carriers to New York are **Air Canada, Delta, Continental, British Airways, American Airlines, Virgin Atlantic,** and **United Airlines.** All international flights arrive at Newark or JFK airports *(see pp380–81).*

APEX (Advance Purchase Excursion) tickets for the scheduled airlines are usually the cheapest return fares apart from package tours. But they must be bought in advance and are valid for a stay of 7 to 30 days. Some airlines offer cheaper fares if you limit your stay to specified periods. Senior citizens may also receive discounts on some flights.

## AIRLINE NUMBERS

Air Canada **Tel** *(888) 247-2262.*
**www**.aircanada.ca

American Airlines **Tel** *(800) 433-7300.*
**www**.aa.com

British Airways **Tel** *(800) AIRWAYS.*
**www**.british-airways.com

Continental **Tel** *(800) 231-0856.*
**www**.flycontinental.com

Delta **Tel** *(800) 241-4141.*
**www**.delta.com

Qantas **Tel** *(800) 227-4500.*
**www**.qantas.com

United Airlines **Tel** *(800) 241-6522.*
**www**.united.com

Virgin Atlantic **Tel** *(800) 862-8621.*
**www**.virgin-atlantic.com

## OCEAN TRAVEL

New York is a regular port of call for many cruise liners, in addition to the *QM2,* which docks there, via Southampton, 25 times a year. You can also take the *QM2* from

**Long-distance Greyhound bus**

New York to Australia and New Zealand. Ships dock at the Hudson River piers in midtown Manhattan.

## LONG-DISTANCE BUSES

All long-distance buses such as **Greyhound Lines** arrive in the city at the **Port Authority Bus Terminal.** Buses from here also connect with the three airports. With over 6,000 buses arriving and leaving daily, and carrying some 172,000 passengers, the atmosphere is chaotic. Many hotels are also accessible directly from the terminal.
**Useful information** Greyhound Bus Lines **Tel** *(800) 231-2222. (24 hrs).*
**www**.greyhound.com Port Authority Bus Terminal. W 40th St and Eighth Ave. **Map** 8 D1. **Tel** *(212) 564-8484 (24 hrs).* **www**.panynj.gov

## TRAIN TRAVEL

Amtrak trains from Canada, upstate New York, southern, northeastern and western states all stop at Penn Station *(see p392).* Metro-North lines from upstate New York and Connecticut arrive at Grand Central Terminal *(see p392).*

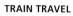

**Ocean liner anchored in Manhattan**

# New York Airports

The three main airports (Newark, JFK, and LaGuardia) are all well connected to central Manhattan. Look for uniformed "skycaps" – scarlet-capped porters wearing distinctive badges, who will help you with your luggage. Never trust anyone else to help carry your bags – you may never see them again. Taxi dispatchers will help you into a licensed taxi at the taxi area.

## GETTING INTO MANHATTAN

The ground Transportation center at each airport will give you information on the ways you can continue your trip. The most useful services, operating from LaGuardia and JFK, are the **New York Airport Service** and **Super Shuttle**. The former stops at Grand Central, Port Authority, or Penn Station; the latter will drop you anywhere in Manhattan. New Jersey Transit buses and **Olympia Airport Express** also go to and from each airport into the city. The fare on the Olympia buses is one of the best bargains.

Shared vehicle rides are offered at JFK and La Guardia by **Classic Limousine** and **Connecticut Limo**. You can sometimes share a taxi into Manhattan. For the price of a subway ride, the "A" line connects with a shuttle bus and takes passengers to and from JFK. The M60 city bus

Taxi dispatcher

also goes to and from LaGuardia. Most car rental firms have courtesy telephones at the baggage-claim areas. Telephone numbers and web addresses for advance reservations are listed on page 386. For up-to-date transport information, call (800) AIR-RIDE.

## COMPANIES

**New York Airport Service**
*Tel (718) 875-8200.*

**Classic Limousine**
*Tel (800) 666-4949.*
www.classictrans.com

**Super Shuttle**
*Tel (212) BLUE-VAN;
(800) BLUE-VAN.*
www.supershuttle.com

**Olympia Airport Express**
*Tel (212) 964-6233.*
www.olympiabus.com

**Connecticut Limo**
*Tel (800) 472-5466.*
www.ctlimo.com

## LAGUARDIA (LGA)

Principally serving business travelers, LaGuardia lies 8 miles (13 km) east of Manhattan on the north side of Long Island in Queens.

Upon arrival, you can rent luggage trolleys from the baggage-claim area next to the luggage carousels. Skycaps are on hand to assist you. Baggage can also be left in the Tele-Trip business center on the departure level. Foreign exchange desks are located around the Central Terminal.

Uniformed taxi dispatchers at the airport are on duty at peak hours. Only use yellow taxis licensed by the city. The cost of tolls, plus a small surcharge after 8pm and all day Sunday, will be added to the fare shown on the meter (about $20–$30 to midtown).

### Useful information
Airport Information Service **Tel** (718) 533-3400. www.laguardia airport.com www.panynj.gov

**Transatlantic jet**

### Plan of LaGuardia Airport
*A free bus service runs between each of the terminals and parking areas every 10–15 minutes from 5am to 2am. Buses and taxis into the city and its suburbs depart from the front of every terminal building.*

Central Terminal building (B)
Marine Air Terminal
Terminal A
Delta Shuttle Terminal
USAirways Terminal (C)
USAirways Shuttle (C)
Delta Terminal (D)

Grand Central Parkway to New York

**KEY**

P Parking

🚌 Bus service between terminals

To Eastern Long Island

## JFK AIRPORT

New York's main airport, JFK, is 15 miles (24 km) southeast of Manhattan, in the borough of Queens. American Airlines, British Airways, Continental, Delta, and United have their own arrivals buildings. Other international airlines use terminals 1, 5 and 6.

Luggage trolleys are free on arrival in the meeting area for international flights. Foreign exchange offices are located in all terminals and hotels can be booked at the

**Airport information signs at JFK**

**Main Hall at the International Arrivals Building, JFK**

Meegan Services desk in the arrivals section at Terminal 3.

Transportation to Manhattan can be arranged 24 hours a day at the Ground Transportation desk on the ground level near the baggage-claim. Courtesy phones are provided by car rental companies. Most have a shuttle service to their rental offices. Taxis wait outside terminals. A trip to Manhattan takes up to an hour; there is a flat fee of $45 plus tolls. The New York Airport Service buses go to Grand Central,

Penn Station and the Port Authority and cost $15; the Super Shuttle costs $17–$19.

A light-rail system, AirTrain JFK, connects to the A train at Howard Beach and the E, J, and Z trains and Long Island Railroad (for Penn station) at Jamaica. The AirTrain costs $5, the subway $2. The 10-minute helicopter ride to East 34th Street costs $850.

### USEFUL ADDRESSES

**Airport Information Service**
(718) 244-4444.

**Best Western JFK Airport**
144–25 153rd Ave, Queens.
*Tel* (718) 977-2100.

**Holiday Inn JFK**
144–02 135th Ave, Queens.
*Tel* (718) 659-0200.

Helicopter Flight Services
*Tel* (212) 355-0801. **www**.heliny.com
Liberty Helicopters *Tel* (888) 692-4354. **www**.libertyhelicopters.com

American Airlines (international) (8)

American Airlines (internal) (9)

Garage

Air Canada, British Airways, Qantas, United Airlines (7)

Jet Blue (6)

Van Wyck Expressway to New York

Terminal 5

Terminal 1

Garage

Garage

Continental (2)

Virgin Atlantic (4)

Delta (3)

**KEY**

🚌 Bus stops for all buses

🅿 Parking

■ ■ AirTrain JFK

**Plan of JFK Airport**
*The free AirTrain stops at the terminals, parking lots and car rental agencies, departing every 2–4 minutes from 6am to 11pm, and every 8 minutes from 11pm to 6am. For a faster, but more expensive, transfer, take a taxi. Cabs leave from clearly marked stands just outside the air terminal arrival areas.*

# NEWARK AIRPORT

**KEY**

| | |
|---|---|
| P | Parking |
| 🚌 | Bus stop |
| -- | Newark AirTrain |

**Plan of Newark Airport**
*The free AirTrain service connects the airport's terminals and parking lots. Trains run every 3 minutes from 5am to midnight, and every 15–24 minutes from midnight to 5am. The journey time between terminals is 7–11 minutes. Taxis wait outside the terminal arrival areas.*

**Bus terminal at Newark Airport**

Terminal B (international arrivals)

Terminal C

Terminal A

Terminal C-3

Hotel Courtesy pickup

Marriott Hotel

Roads to Manhattan

Rental cars

---

Newark, New York's second-largest international airport, is about 16 miles (26 km) southwest of Manhattan, in New Jersey.

Most international flights arrive at Terminal B. Baggage trolleys are free for passengers arriving on international flights. There is no baggage room. Foreign exchange desks are available in each terminal.

The Ground Transportation services desk, open 24 hours a day, is next to the baggage-claim area. Courtesy phones are provided by limousine and car rental firms. Many of these have a free shuttle service to their rental offices.

Taxi stands are located outside most arrival areas, and uniformed taxi dispatchers will also help you hail a cab. Never accept a ride into town from anyone who approaches you in the terminal: they may not have insurance and could charge an outrageous fare.

The taxi ride into Manhattan takes about 40–60 minutes and will cost you up to $50.

Buses to Manhattan can take 40 minutes to over an hour, but cost about $12. Electronic boards around the terminal list departure times. AirTrain Newark (www.airtrainnewark. com) connects you to NJ Transit and Amtrak trains; it then continues to New York Penn Station. The 25-minute journey costs $11.55, as does the NJ Transit, while Amtrak is $32. The Super Shuttle costs $15–$19.

Hotels can be booked on arrival through the courtesy phones that are linked directly to various Manhattan hotels. At Newark, these are located in all the terminals.

## USEFUL ADDRESSES

**Port Authority at Newark Airport**
*Tel* (888) 397-4636.
www.newarkairport.com

**Holiday Inn International**
1000 Spring St, Elizabeth, N J.
*Tel* (800) 465-4329.

**Marriott Hotel**
Newark Airport grounds.
*Tel* (800) 228-9290.

**Arrival and departure monitors at Newark Airport**

# Arriving in New York

This map shows the links between New York's three airports and the center of Manhattan. It also illustrates rail connections linking New York to the rest of the United States and Canada. Travel information, including travel times for subway, bus, rail, and helicopter services, is listed in each information box. The passenger ship terminal, New York's key point of arrival for the flood of post-war immigrants, is located a short distance from the center of Manhattan. Port Authority Bus Terminal, on the West Side, provides services across the city.

Ships at the passenger terminal

## 🚢 PASSENGER SHIP TERMINAL
*Piers 88–92 for QM2 and other cruise ship arrivals and departures.*

## KEY

| | |
|---|---|
| ✈ | Airport *see pp379–81* |
| 🚢 | Seaport *see p378* |
| 🚉 | Rail link *see p378* |
| 🚌 | Bus station/link *see p378* |
| 🚁 | Helicopter links *see p380* |
| ▬ | New York Airport Service and Super Shuttle *see p379* |
| ▬ | Helicopters *see p380* |
| ▬ | Long Island Rail Road *see pp392–3* |
| ▬ | New Jersey Transit buses *see p379* |
| ▬ | Olympia Airport Express *see p379* |
| ▬ | Shuttle bus *see p380* |
| ▬ | Subway A *see p390* |

## 🚌 PORT AUTHORITY BUS TERMINAL
*All long-distance buses arrive and depart here; links to all city airports.*

## 🚉 PENN STATION
*Long-distance trains serve the US and **Canada**; commuter trains to **Long Island** and **New Jersey**; AirTrain Newark to **Newark Airport**.*
🚉 *Amtrak, Long Island Rail Road and New Jersey Transit services.*
Ⓜ *A, C, E, 1, 2, 3.*

Passenger Ship Terminal

Port Authority Bus Terminal

West 30th St Heliport

Penn Station

*Chelsea and the Garment District*

*Super Shuttle buses take passengers to any point between Battery Park and 227th St.*

*Greenwich Village*

*SoHo and TriBeCa*

*East Village*

*Seaport and the Civic Center*

*Lower East Side*

*Lower Manhattan*

Pier 11

## ✈ NEWARK
🚌 **Olympia Airport Express**
*4am–11pm, every 20–30 mins to **Penn Station, Grand Central** and **Port Authority**.*
🚌 **New Jersey Transit** *Every 15–20 mins to **Port Authority**.*
🚉 **AirTrain to Penn Station**
*5am–midnight, every 3 mins; midnight–5am, every 15–24 mins*
🚁**Helicopters** *to 34th St heliport.*

*The Port Authority of New York and New Jersey, operator of JFK, Newark, and La Guardia airports, has invested $2.7 billion in AirTrain, a new rail link that connects JFK and Newark to the city subway system.*

**Amtrak railroad train**

*Morningside
Heights
and Harlem*

*Upper West
Side*

*Central Park*

**Grand Central Terminal**

🚉 **GRAND CENTRAL**
Daily commuter train service to
upstate **New York** and **Connecticut**.
🚇 Metro-North.
Ⓜ 4, 5, 6, 7, S.

*Upper
East Side*

✈ **LA GUARDIA**
🚌 *New York Airport Service*
7.20am–11pm, every 20–30 mins
to **Grand Central, Port
Authority** and **Penn Station**.
🚌 *Super Shuttle* service to your
choice of destination,
7am–11:30pm.
🚌 *M60* to 125th St, 5am–1am.
🚉 Shuttle to **Jamaica, Queens**,
station of the **Long Island Rail
Road** every half hour; then trains
every 5–10 mins to **Penn Station**
(25 mins).
🚁 *Chartered helicopter* to
midtown.

*Upper
Midtown*

*Lower
Midtown*

st 34th
St. Pier

port

**Jamaica**
🚉 *Long Island Rail Road.
Airtrain JFK.
E, J, Z subway*

**Chartered helicopter service to
and from all three airports**

✈ **JFK**
🚌 *New York Airport Service*
6:15am–11:10pm: every 15–30
mins to **Grand Central, Port
Authority Bus Terminal** and
**Penn Station**.
🚌 *Super Shuttle* service to your
choice of destination, 24hrs.
🚌 *Bus Q10 to Kew Gardens*
every 15 mins, with transfers to A,
J, Z, E and F trains to Manhattan.
🚉 *AirTrain JFK to Howard
Beach* and **Jamaica** – 24 hours,
frequent departures.
🚁 *Chartered helicopters* fly
frequently from all airports to the
**East 34th Street Heliport**, the
**West 30th Street Heliport**, and the
**Downtown Manhattan Heliport**.

**Howard Beach**
🚉 *AirTrain JFK.
Subway A*

ilometers                 2

miles              1

# GETTING AROUND NEW YORK

With over six thousand miles of streets, walking around New York could prove difficult. But the city is a network of districts and many of the major sites can be visited area by area. Taxis are the best option for door-to-door transit, but they can be held up in traffic jams, especially during rush hours. The city's bus service is reliable and cheap but often slow. Subways are quick, reliable, and cheap, and make stops throughout central Manhattan. There are weekly and day passes that are valid for all public transportation. These are the best value when visiting the sights of the city.

Stretch limousine, the preferred
vehicle for New York's glitterati

## NEGOTIATING THE AVENUES AND STREETS

Manhattan's avenues run approximately north to south; its streets (except in the older areas) run east to west. Fifth Avenue is used to divide East and West Street addresses; Five West 40th Street is, for example, a few doors west of Fifth Avenue on 40th Street, and Five East 40th is a few doors to the east.

Most streets in midtown are one-way. In general, traffic is eastbound on even-numbered streets and westbound on odd-numbered streets. Avenues also tend to be one-way, alternating northbound or southbound. First, Third (above 23rd Street), Madison, Eighth, Avenue of the Americas (6th Ave), and Tenth avenues are all northbound, while Second, Lexington, Fifth, Seventh, and Ninth avenues, and Broadway below 59th Street are southbound. There is two-way traffic on York, Park, Eleventh, and Twelfth avenues and on Broadway above 60th Street.

Although most city blocks north of Houston Street are rectangular, they are not very uniform: east–west blocks are three or even four times longer than north–south blocks.

Certain streets have more than one name, for instance, Avenue of the Americas is also Sixth Avenue. Note too that Park Avenue South is not the same as Park Avenue. Many intersections and plazas have titles commemorating people or events. The maps in this guide use the names most often used by New Yorkers.

Rush-hour gridlock in Manhattan

## FINDING AN ADDRESS

A useful formula has been devised to help pinpoint any **Avenue Address**. By dropping the last digit of the address, dividing the remainder by 2, then adding or subtracting the **Key Number** given here, you will discover the nearest cross street. For example: To find No. 826 Lexington Avenue, first you have to drop the 6; divide 82 by 2, which is 41; then add **22** (the key number). Therefore, the nearest cross street is 63rd Street.

**MADISON AVENUE**

A road sign for Madison Avenue positioned at an intersection with a street

| Avenue Address | Key Number | Avenue Address | Key Number |
|---|---|---|---|
| 1st Ave | +3 | 9th Ave | +13 |
| 2nd Ave | +3 | 10th Ave | +14 |
| 3rd Ave | +10 | Amsterdam Ave | +60 |
| 4th Ave | +8 | Audubon Ave | +165 |
| 5th Ave, up to 200 | +13 | Broadway above | |
| 5th Ave, up to 400 | +16 | 23rd St | -30 |
| 5th Ave, up to 600 | +18 | Central Park W, divide | |
| 5th Ave, up to 775 | +20 | full number by 10 | +60 |
| 5th Ave 775–1286, | | Columbus Ave | +60 |
| do not divide by 2 | -18 | Convent Ave | +127 |
| 5th Ave, up to 1500 | +45 | Lenox Ave | +110 |
| 5th Ave, up to 2000 | +24 | Lexington Ave | +22 |
| (6th) Ave of the | | Madison Ave | +26 |
| Americas | -12 | Park Ave | +35 |
| 7th Ave below | | Park Ave South | +08 |
| 110th St | +12 | Riverside Drive, divide | |
| 7th Ave above | | full number by 10 | +72 |
| 110th St | +20 | St Nicholas Ave | +110 |
| 8th Ave | +10 | West End Ave | +60 |

## PLANNING YOUR JOURNEY

The streets and sidewalks are busiest during the rush hours – 8 to 10 am, 11:30 am to 1:30 pm and 4:30 to 6:30 pm, Monday to Friday. Throughout these periods it is better to face the crowds on foot than attempt any journey by bus, taxi, or subway. At other times of day and during certain holiday periods (see p53), the traffic is often much lighter and you should reach your destination quickly.

There are, of course, a few exceptions. Fifth Avenue should always be avoided on parade days (St. Patrick's Day and Thanksgiving Day are the worst). Celebrity visits or one of the regular demonstrations at City Hall (see p90) can cause major disruption to the traffic. The area around Seventh Avenue, south of 42nd Street, is likely to be busy during the day with the truck and handcart traffic of New York's garment industry.

## WALKING

Most intersections between avenues and streets have lampposts with name-markers and electric traffic signals. The traffic lights show red (stop) and green (go) for vehicles and "Walk–Don't Walk" for pedestrians. However, most New Yorkers rely on their own judgment rather than on the numerous "Walk" signs.

Remember that vehicles keep to the right. There are no

**Pedestrian crossing**

**Do not cross the street**

**You may cross the street**

**Staten Island Ferry leaving Battery Park**

**Circle Line tour boat**

cautionary "Look Left" signs to alert you to the direction of oncoming traffic. There are, however, numerous one-way streets, so it's best to look both ways before you cross. Beware, too, of cars, trucks and taxis turning the corner behind you as you start to cross the street.

There are pedestrian crossings at some intersections. These are officially designated pedestrian crossing points (at Rockefeller Center for instance) and are closely monitored by the police. The city has a few underground walkways for pedestrians in Central Park.

## WATER TAXI

The New York water taxi arrived in 2002 and runs from East 90th Street Pier to Pier 84. Visit www.nywatertaxi. com for more information.

## FERRIES

There are two ferries of interest to visitors (see also p369): the Circle Line runs a ferry to the Statue of Liberty and Ellis Island several times each day from Battery Park at the southern tip of Manhattan – **www**.circleline.com. The 24-hour Staten Island ferry from Battery Park travels the channel and offers splendid views of lower Manhattan, the Statue of Liberty, Ellis Island, the bridges, and Governors Island. The round trip is the best bargain in New York; it's free.

## CYCLING

Cycling in the city is safest on the park pathways (Central Park and along the East and Hudson rivers) in daylight hours. You can rent bikes at Columbus Circle or the Loeb Boathouse in Central Park.
**Useful information**
Central Park Bike Rental, 2 Columbus Circle. **Map** 12 D3. **Tel** (212) 541-8759. **www**.centralparkbiketour.com

**Cyclist in Central Park**

# Driving in New York

Heavy traffic and expensive rental cars make driving in New York a frustrating experience. You must wear a seat belt. The speed limit is 30 mph (48 km/h) – which is difficult to exceed because of Manhattan's pot-holes and traffic. Most streets are one-way, and there are traffic lights at every corner. Driving is on the right.

**Busy traffic heading down Sixth Avenue**

## RENTING A CAR

To rent a car you must be at least 25 years old, or pay a surcharge. You will need a valid driver's license (for foreign visitors an International Driver's License is useful), a passport, and a credit card.

Unless you are adequately covered by your own insurance policy, you should also take out damage and liability protection, as personal injury lawsuits are very expensive. Also remember to refill with gas before you return the car or you'll pay double the normal price for fuel. It is cheaper to rent a car in the city than at the airports.

**Traffic signs**
*Black-and-white markings on many street crossings mean that pedestrians have right of way. At intersections, they indicate that traffic should keep out when the light is red. Unlike the rest of New York State, you can never turn right on a red light unless there is a sign indicating otherwise.*

**Traffic flows in a single direction**

## PARKING

Parking in Manhattan is difficult and costly. Parking areas and parking garages post their rates at the entrance. Some hotels include parking charges in their room rates.

In some areas there are meters at the curb for short-term (20 – 60 minutes) parking. Don't be tempted to park at out-of-order meters – you may receive a parking ticket. Yellow street and curb markings mean no parking.

"Alternate-side" parking applies on most of the city's side streets. Cars may usually be left all day and night but must be moved to the other side of the street before 8am the next day. For specific information call the **Transportation Department**.

## PENALTIES

If you receive a parking ticket, you have seven days to pay the required fine or to appeal against it. If you have any queries about your ticket call the **Parking Violations Bureau** between 8:30am and 7pm on any weekday.

New York's tow-away crews are extremely active, and one-third of cars towed suffer damage. If you cannot find your car at its parking place, first of all call the traffic department's tow-away office. The pound is open 24 hours a day, Monday to Saturday. You can redeem your car for a hefty fine of $150, plus $10 per day storage fee. Traveler's checks, certified checks, money orders, and cash are all accepted. There is an ATM machine (*see p374*) on the premises. If you have rented the car, the contract must be produced, and only the authorized driver may redeem the car. If the car is not at the pound, report it to the police.

**Useful information**
Police emergencies only **Tel** *911*; Parking Violations Bureau **Tel** *(718) 802-3636*; Traffic Dept, Tow Pound, Pier 76, W 38th St and 12th Ave. **Map** 7 1B; uptown at the 207th St. Pound **Tel** *311*; Transportation Dept **Tel** *311*.

## BRIDGE TOLLS

Most major access routes in and out of New York City levy tolls. These vary in price from $1.50 for some of the smaller bridges, to $6.00 for the George Washington Bridge between New York and New Jersey. The bridges of the Triborough Bridge Authority charge $3.50 each way. All tolls must be paid in cash. Avoid E-Z Pass lanes, marked with purple signs, which are only for holders of pre-paid passes.

## CAR RENTAL AGENCIES

If you need to rent a car while in New York, agencies are listed in the telephone directory under *Automobile Renting*. The major rental companies include:

**Avis Tel** *(800) 331-1212.*
**www**.avis.com

**Budget Tel** *(800) 527-0700.*
**www**.drivebudget.com

**Dollar Tel** *(800) 800-4000.*
**www**.dollar.com

**Hertz Tel** *(800) 654-3131.*
**www**.hertz.com

**National Tel** *(800) CAR RENT.*
**www**.nationalcar.com

**Entry prohibited**

**50 mph (80 km/h) speed limit**

**Give way to all vehicles**

**Stop at intersection**

# New York's Taxis

**New York taxi cab**

All licensed taxi cabs are yellow. If their roof numbers are lit up, they are available and can be flagged down. Occupied cabs have their top lights switched off. Taxis that are not on duty have their "Off-Duty" sign lit. Only licensed cabs are authorized to pick up people who hail them from the street; accepting a ride from anyone else can be dangerous and expensive.

## TAKING A CAB

There are more than 12,000 Yellow Cabs in New York. Each one has a meter, and many can issue printed receipts. A taxi can carry up to four passengers with a single fare covering everyone on board.

Taxi stands are scarce; hotels, Penn Station and Grand Central Terminal are by far the best places to seek cabs.

**A printed receipt available from most taxi cabs**

Licensed taxis undergo periodic inspections and are insured against accidents and losses. Non-licensed or "gypsy" cabs are unlikely to have these safeguards, and are not recommended.

Once the cab driver accepts a passenger the meter starts ticking at $2.50. The fare increases 40 cents after each additional 292 yards (267 meters) or every 120 seconds of waiting time. There is an additional 50-cent charge between 8pm and 6am, and a $1 charge between 4pm and 8pm on weekdays.

A few drivers now accept credit cards but most will want to be paid in cash. Tip the driver about 15%.

Cab driving is a traditional occupation of newly arrived immigrants and, as such, communication can be a problem. Although owners of licensed cabs

must pass exams in English comprehension and the layout of the city, they will not necessarily understand either. Make sure your driver understands exactly where you want to go before you start your ride. By law, a driver must take you anywhere in the city unless the off-duty sign is lit and the roof light is off. The driver should not ask you your destination until after you've sat down, and must follow your requests not to smoke, to open or close a window, and to pick up or drop off passengers as you direct. If he or she doesn't comply you can report them to the **Taxi & Limousine Commission**.

Each yellow cab displays the driver's photograph and registered number next to the meter. Drivers can be sullen, or try to overcharge or not cooperate with some of your requests. Make a note of the driver's number or the license or receipt number (if you have requested one), and report it to the Commission.

**Yellow taxi cabs dominating one of the city's avenues**

## TAXI NUMBERS

**Taxi & Limousine Commission**
*Tel 311.*

**Lost and Found**
*Tel 311.*

If you would prefer to use a taxi that has been radio-dispatched, rather than hailing one on the street, call:

**Allstate Car & Limousine**
*Tel (800) 453-4099 (toll free).*

**Chris Limousines**
*Tel (718) 356-3232.*

**Limo Resinet**
*Tel (212) 777-7171.*

**A meter** will display your fare as it mounts up. Additional costs are then shown separately.

**The roof-light** illuminates the cab's number as well as the driver's "Off-Duty" sign.

# Traveling by Bus

The city's more than 4,000 blue-and-white buses cover more than 200 routes in the five boroughs. Many run 24 hours a day, every day. The buses are modern, clean, and air-conditioned. Traveling by bus is a good way to take in many of New York's sights. Buses are also considered safe and tend not to get crowded. Smoking is forbidden on all public buses, and animals except service animals (guide dogs) are not allowed.

**The fare box** is just inside the entrance doors, next to the driver.

## FARE

You can pay the fare on a bus using a MetroCard *(see p390)* or exact change (these must be in coins only). Bus drivers cannot make change, and fare boxes do not accept dollar bills, half dollars or pennies. You can buy the MetroCard at any subway station booth.

If you are need to take more than one bus to reach your destination, you are eligible for a free transfer. If you pay your bus fare with a Metro-Card, a free bus-to-subway, subway-to-local bus, or local bus-to-bus transfer is electronically placed on the card. If you pay with exact change, be sure to ask the driver for a transfer ticket when you pay.

There are discount fares for senior citizens and the disabled. All buses can "kneel," which helps elderly people to board *(see p370)*, and they are also accessible to wheelchairs via a lift at the rear or front.

### Recognizing Your Bus

*Each bus stop serves more than one route, so look for the route number posted on the lighted strip above the windshield on the front of the bus. Ask the driver if he or she will be stopping at your destination or close to it.*

**Exit the bus** through the double doors toward the rear.

## RIDING THE BUS

Buses will stop only at the designated bus stops. They follow north–south routes on the major avenues, stopping every two or three blocks. Crosstown buses, running east–west, stop at every block *(see p384)*. Many routes run a 24-hour daily service, which becomes a lot less frequent during the evening and at night; other bus services operate only during the peak hours of 7am to 10pm.

Bus stops are marked by red, white, and blue signs and yellow paint along the curb. Most also have bus shelters. A route map and schedule is posted at each stop. When you have identified your bus, enter at the front door and put your MetroCard in the fare box. Request a transfer if you will be changing to another bus. The majority of New York's bus drivers are very friendly and will call out your stop if you ask them to.

**Bus stops** often have three-sided, glass-walled shelters.

**This bus map** shows the route and main stopping-off points for route M15.

To request a stop when traveling on the bus, press the yellow or black vertical call strip between the windows. A "Stop Requested" sign near the driver will then light up. If the bus is crowded, it is worth starting to move toward the exit door when you are a few blocks from your stop.

Leave through the double door located toward the rear of the bus. The driver will activate the door release as soon as the bus has stopped, but you then have to push the yellow stripe on the door, not the door itself. This automatically opens the door and keeps it open.

**Route numbers** appear on the front and side of the bus.

**Enter the bus** through the doors at the front.

## LONG-DISTANCE & COMMUTER BUSES

Buses to the rest of the US and Canada leave from the **Port Authority Bus Terminal**. Another terminal, at the Manhattan end of the George Washington Bridge, is for local buses to northern New Jersey and New York's Rockland County.

Bus tickets at Port Authority are on sale in the main concourse. The long-distance bus companies, Greyhound, Peter Pan, and Adirondack and the commuter Short Line and NJ Transit have their own ticket counters. There are no reservations taken on any of these bus lines.

There are bathrooms open from 6am to 10pm, but caution is advised. The homeless congregate in Port Authority.

A Greyhound bus arriving in New York en route to Port Authority

## BUS INFORMATION

### Route Maps
*Available from MTA/NYCT, Customer Services Center, 3 Stone Street, Lower Manhattan.*

### MTA Travel Information
*Tel (718) 330-1234 (24 hrs).* www.mta.info

### Port Authority Bus Terminal
West 40th St and Eighth Ave. **Map** 8 D1. *Tel (212) 564-8484.* www.panynj.gov

### George Washington Bridge Terminal
*178th St and Broadway. Tel (800) 221-9903.* www.panynj.gov

### Lost Property
*Tel (212) 712-4500.*

## SIGHTSEEING BY BUS

For a pleasant and cheap alternative to a tour bus, hop on a city bus and see New York with the New Yorkers. Bus routes M1 and M6 down Fifth and Seventh Avenues to the Battery, returning north via the Wall Street area, Madison Avenue, and Sixth Avenue. Route M5 gives fine views of the Hudson River as buses travel north on Riverside Drive to the George Washington Bridge at 178th Street. Route M104 travels from the United Nations at First Avenue across 42nd Street, through Times Square, then follows Broadway north by Lincoln Center to Columbia University at 125th Street.

KEY
— Route M1
— Route M5
— Route M104

# Using the Subway

**New York City Subway**

New York subway logo

The subway is the quickest and most reliable way to travel in the city. The vast system extends over 233 route miles (375 km) and has 468 stations. Most routes operate 24 hours a day throughout the year. Night services are less frequent, and fewer trains run on weekends. In the past few years the subway system has been completely upgraded, and the trains are now air-conditioned, well lit, safer and more comfortable.

## NEW YORK SUBWAY

Many subway entrances are marked by illuminated spheres: green where the station booth is manned around the clock, red means that there is restricted entry. Others are marked by a sign bearing the name of the station and the numbers or letters of the routes passing through it.

Altought the subway system runs 24 hours a day, not all routes operate at all times. The basic service is between 6am and midnight.

Bear in mind that there are two types of trains. Local trains stop at all stations, and express trains are faster and stop at fewer stations. Both types of stops are distinguished on every subway map.

In general, the safest, but most crowded, times to travel on the subway, are weekdays between 7am and 7pm. Use common sense, stand in the "Off-Hour Waiting Area" on the platforms, and always be sure of where you are going

when you use the subway. It is safe to travel to outer boroughs, although it is not a good idea for anyone to travel alone after 10pm. Use the central cars and avoid all eye contact with any unsavory characters. If it is very hot, try to avoid the more crowded carriages.

In an emergency, contact either the station agent in the station booth or a member of the train crew, who are located either in the first car or in the middle of the train.

## SUBWAY FARE

The fare is $2 no matter how far you travel. The MetroCard has replaced tokens as means of fare. A one-day FunPass for $7 for unlimited travel all day is one option for visitors. Other options are a $10 MetroCard (allowing five rides, plus one free ride), a $20 MetroCard (good for 10 rides, plus two free rides), or a $24 7-Day Unlimited Ride MetroCard. MetroCard, which can also be used on buses *(see p388)*, is sold at 3,500 locations around the city as well as at subway stations where you can pay with cash or credit card.

**Subway information**
MTA/NYCT **Tel** *(718) 330-1234.*
Metrocard Customer Service
**Tel** *(212) 638-7622.* **www**.mta.info

---

## READING THE SUBWAY MAP

Each route is identified on the subway map *(see inside back cover)* by color, by the names of the stations at each end of the line, and by a letter or number. Local and express stops and interchange points are identified. The letters and numbers below the station names indicate which routes serve that particular station. A letter or number in heavy type indicates that trains on that route stop there between 6am and midnight; letters in lighter type mean that the route is served by a part-time service only; a boxed letter or number shows the last stop on the line. Express trains are indicated on subway maps with a white (rather than solid) circle. The maps posted in all the subway stations have a comprehensive guide that explains the trains and timetable of each route.

**A** — Line letter

— Local stop

— Express stop

— Express and local stop

Free local transfers

Free express transfers

**42 Street– Times Square**
N·R [S]
1·2·3 [7] 6

Light type
Part-time service

Boxed type
Last stop on this line (full or part-time)

Express and local stops

Free transfers from line to line

**Bold type** Full-time service

---

**23 Street Station**
Uptown & The Bronx
6

This station's green sphere shows that it is staffed continuously

## MAKING A TRIP BY SUBWAY

Subways run north–south up and down the city on Lexington Avenue, 6th Avenue, 7th Avenue/Broadway, and 8th Avenue. The N, R, E, F, V, and W trains to Queens run east to west.

**1** There is a map of the subway system on the back inside cover of this book. Large-scale maps are also positioned in prominent areas in every station. Maps are also available at www.mta.info

**Subway map**

**Booth with agent**

**2** Buy a MetroCard from a station subway booth or MetroCard vending machine. The machines accept most credit cards and bills up to $50, but no pennies. Vending machines can also be used to refill MetroCards.

**3** Use MetroCard to pass through the turnstile onto the platform.

**Entry turnstile**

**4** Follow the directions for the train you want. For safety, stay in sight of the booth as you wait for your train; at night, stay in one of the yellow off-hours waiting areas.

**Off-hours waiting area**

**5** Each train displays its route number or letter in the appropriate color and the names of the terminal stations.

**Route indicator**

**6** On every platform, you will find a line map, while on each train there is a system map next to the door on each side of the car. Newer trains have electronic maps that light up overhead. Stops are announced on the public address system, and you will see station names at each platform. The doors are operated by the conductor.

**7** After leaving the train, look for signs giving directions to the exit. If you need to change trains, just follow the signs to the connecting platforms.

# Traveling by Train

New York has two main train stations. Grand Central Terminal is served by commuter trains from NYC's northern suburbs and Connecticut, while Pennsylvania (Penn) Station is the terminal for service for the eastern suburbs, along with long distance services throughout the US and Canada. Most commuter trains have no buffet cars on board, so it's best to buy any food and drink you want before boarding the train. Seat reservations are available only on the long-distance intercity services.

**An Amtrak train**

## GRAND CENTRAL TERMINAL

Grand Central Terminal *(see pp156–7)* on Park Avenue between 41st and 42nd streets is the main terminal for **Metro-North Railroad** trains (Hudson, New Haven and Harlem lines), which run north and east of New York and serve southwest Connecticut and Westchester, Dutchess, and Putnam counties. From Grand Central you might travel by train to such destinations as the Bronx Zoo *(see pp244–5)*, the New York Botanical Garden and President Franklin D. Roosevelt's Hyde Park estate.

The 4 and 5 trains on the green (Lexington) line and number 7 on the purple (Flushing) line serve Grand Central subway station, below the main terminal. A shuttle service links Grand Central to Times Square. Many bus lines stop at Grand Central.

**MTA**

**Long Island Rail Road**

Long Island Rail Road logo

## PENN STATION

Penn Station, between Seventh and Eighth avenues and from 31st to 33rd streets, is a modern terminal that was rebuilt in 1963 underneath the Madison Square Garden complex *(see p135)*. Commuter trains, New Jersey Transit trains, and **Amtrak** trains from Canada and other parts of the US terminate at this station. There are no luggage trolleys, but redcap porters will help.

You will find taxis at street level. Buses run downtown on Seventh Avenue and uptown on Eighth Avenue. The blue (8th Avenue) subway lines, A, C, and E run on the Eighth Avenue side of the station; the red (Broadway) lines, 1, 2, and 3 run on the Seventh Avenue side of the station. The ticket counters and waiting rooms are one level below; the trains leave from an even lower level.

From Penn Station, you could head out to New Jersey and Long Island or venture farther on Amtrak trains to Canada, Philadelphia or Washington. Also in Penn Station are ticket offices and departure points of the **Long Island Rail Road (LIRR)**, mainly a commuter line, but with trains to such Long Island resorts, as the Hamptons, Montauk Point, and Fire Island.

## PATH TRAINS

Path trains operate round the clock between New Jersey stations (Harrison, Hoboken, Jersey City, and Newark) and Penn Station in Manhattan. They also stop at Christopher Street, the World Trade Center, 9th, 14th, 23rd, and 33rd Streets and Avenue of the Americas (6th Avenue).

**LIRR train at Penn Station**

## AMTRAK

Amtrak is the US national railroad passenger service linking New York with other US cities and Canada. Some Amtrak trains have cars with reclining seats; others have dining facilities and lounge cars. Sleeper cars are available on all long-distance routes. The new express trains operate on certain Amtrak routes, such as the **Acela** between Boston and Washington via New York.

Tickets can be bought at Penn Station, as well as from Amtrak Travel Centers. Buy your ticket before getting on the train as there is a penalty for buying tickets on board. Senior citizens receive a 15% discount; the conductor will ask for proof of age. There are no student discounts. Seat reservations made by phone with a credit card need to be made at least 10 days in advance of travel if you want the tickets mailed to you.

Amtrak also offers a Great American Vacations package and various promotional fares during the year. Ask for information when you book.

**Grand Central Terminal**

**Information board at Penn Station**

## TICKETS AND TRAVEL

Ticketing areas at all train stations are well lit and generally crowded at all times of the day. Ticket offices will accept most credit cards, as well as cash. There are a variety of ticket types, most based on a one-way fare; a return fare is twice the single fare. If you are planning a number of trips, Metro-North and LIRR offer weekly and off-peak passes that will save you money.

Train times, destination and gate numbers are continually updated on numerous large information boards. Watch for signs indicating the major interim stops and transfer points, listed next to the gate for departing trains. Wait for the opening of the gate posted for your train. Metro-North and LIRR cars are all one class, and have no reserved seating. Amtrak trains offer both services. The conductor will ask to see your ticket after the train has left the station.

Penn Station and Grand Central Terminal have good facilities, including bathrooms, banks, shops, bars, and restaurants.

## TRAIN INFORMATION

### Amtrak Travel Centers
*Tel (800) USA-RAIL or (800) 872-7245.* www.amtrak.com

### Acela
*Tel (800) 523-8720.*
www.amtrak.com

### Long Island Rail Road (LIRR)
*Tel (718) 217-LIRR (Information).*
*Tel (212) 643 5228 (Lost property).*
www.mta.info

### Metro-North
*Tel (212) 532-4900 (Information).*
*Tel (212) 340-2555 (Lost property).*
www.mta.info

### Path Trains
*Tel (800) 234-7284.*
www.panynj.com

## DAY TRIPS BY TRAIN

There are some beautiful places outside New York city, which, if your time allows, are well worth a visit. Below is a list of some recommended sights within 125 miles (200 km) of New York city center. For further details, call the New York Convention and Visitors Bureau *(see p368).*

**Phillipsburg Manor, Tarrytown**

### Stony Brook
Peaceful north shore village. Entrance to the Three Villages historic district.
🚉 *58 miles (93 km) east. Long Island Rail Road from Penn Station. 2 hrs.*

### The Hamptons
Chic bars and boutiques in a weathered, historic setting. The Beverly Hills of Long Island.
🚉 *100 miles (161 km) east. Long Island Rail Road from Penn Station. 2 hrs, 50 min.*

### Montauk Point
State park on the easternmost tip of Long Island; windswept ocean views.
🚉 *120 miles (193 km). LIRR from Penn Station. 3 hrs.*

### Westbury House, Old Westbury
John Phipps's 1906 re-creation of a Charles II mansion with exquisite English formal gardens.
🚉 *24 miles (39 km) east. Long Island Rail Road from Penn Station. 40 min.*

### Tarrytown
Washington Irving's home "Sunnyside" and Jay Gould's mansion.
🚉 *25 miles (40 km) north. Metro-North from Grand Central, then taxi. 40–50 min.*

### Hyde Park
Springwood estate of Franklin D. Roosevelt and the Vanderbilt mansion.
🚉 *74 miles (119 km) north. Metro-North from Grand Central to Poughkeepsie, then bus. 2 hrs.*

### New Haven, Connecticut
Home of Yale University.
🚉 *74 miles (119 km). Metro-North from Grand Central Terminal. 1 hr, 46 min.*

### Hartford, Connecticut
Mark Twain's riverboat-style house, Atheneum Museum and Old State House.
🚉 *112 miles (180 km) north. Amtrak from Penn Station. 2 hrs, 45 min.*

### Winterthur, Delaware
Henry du Pont's collection of Early American art, museum and gardens.
🚉 *116 miles (187 km) south. Amtrak from Penn Station to Wilmington, then bus to Winterthur. 2 hrs.*

**Yale University in New Haven, Connecticut**

# STREET FINDER

The map references given with all sights, hotels, restaurants, bars, shops, and entertainment venues described in this book refer to the maps in this section ( *see* How the Map References Work *opposite*). These maps cover the whole of Manhattan. A complete index of street names and all the places of interest marked on the maps can be found on the following pages.

The key map *(below)* shows the areas covered by the *Street Finder*, within the various districts. The maps include all of Manhattan's sight-seeing areas (which are color-coded), with all the districts important for hotels, restaurants, bars, shops, theaters, and entertainment.

**Browsing at South Street Seaport**

0 kilometers 2

0 miles 1

Inset on Map 1

## KEY TO STREET FINDER

Major sight

Other sight

Station building

M Subway station

Heliport

Ferry terminal

Bus terminal

P Parking

i Tourist information office

Hospital with emergency room

Police station

Church

Synagogue

Post office

Railroad line

Pedestrian street

## SCALE OF MAP PAGES

0 meters       200

0 yards        200

1:11,500

Inset on Map 19

## HOW THE MAP REFERENCES WORK

**The first figure** tells you which Street Finder map to turn to.

## Theodore Roosevelt Birthplace ➐

28 E 20th St. **Map 9 A5.** *Tel* 260-1616. **M** *14th St–Union Sq.* ◯ *9am–5pm Wed–Sun (last adm: 4:30pm).* ⬤ *public hols.* 🏛 📷 ☑ *Lectures, concerts, films & video* 🌐 www.nps.gov/thrb

**A letter and number** give the grid reference. Letters go across the map's top and bottom, numbers on its sides.

**The map** continues on map 5 of the *Street Finder.*

# Street Finder Index

Each place name is followed by its borough (unless in Manhattan) and then by its Street Finder reference

Each place name is followed by its borough (unless in Manhattan) and then by its Street Finder reference

Each place name is followed by its borough (unless in Manhattan) and then by its Street Finder reference

**11**

A      **15**      B      C

WEST 72ND STREET
VERDI SQUARE
72nd Street
«300 «200 «10

The Dorilto

WEST 71ST SHERMAN SQUARE STREE

**1**

WEST 70TH STREET

WEST
END

FREEDOM PLACE

HENRY HUDSON PARKWAY

# WEST SIDE

BROADWAY

AMSTERDAM

CONRAIL
PIERS
(ABANDONED)

WEST 66TH STREET

Ala
Tue
Ho
The
Juilliard
School

WEST 65TH STREET

Lincoln
Center

WEST 64TH STREET

Metropolitan
Opera House

**2**

Hudson

AVENUE

AVENUE

DAMROSCH
PARK
Guggenheim
Bandshell

MILLER HIGHWAY

WEST 61ST STREET

Fordbam
University

River

WEST 60TH STREET

PIER 99

WEST 59TH STREET

Roosevelt
Hospital
Center

ELEVENTH

TENTH

**3**

PIER 98

WEST 58TH STREET

PIER 97

WEST 57TH STREET
«600 «823 «500 «400

PIER 96

WEST 56TH STREET

PIER 95

WEST 55TH STREET

AVENUE

AVENUE

PIER 94

WEST 54TH STREET

DE WITT
CLINTON
PARK

WEST 53RD STREET

P

**4**

PIER 92

WEST 52ND STREET

TWELFTH

WEST 51ST STREET

N.Y.C. Passenger Ship Terminal
(Port Authority)

ELEVENTH

TENTH

PIER 90

WEST 50TH STREET

WEST 49TH STREET

PIER 88

WEST 48TH STREET

AVENUE

**5**

WEST 47TH STREET

PIER 86

WEST 46TH STREET

AVENUE

AVENUE

Intrepid Sea-Air-Space Museum

WEST 45TH STREET

PIER 84

A      **7**      B WEST 44TH STREET      C

«560 «589 «614

Harlem

River

1

EAST   127TH   STREET

EAST   126TH   STREET

T H I R D

S E C O N D

n Street

(MARTIN LUTHER KING, JR BOULEVARD)

«2298

«2281

200»

Wills Avenue Bridge

Triborough  Bridge

RANDALL'S

LOUIS
GUVILLIER
PARK

FRANKLIN D ROOSEVELT DRIVE

PALADINO

ISLAND

A V E N U E

A V E N U E

RONALD E MCNAIR
PLACE

S E C O N D

PARK

2

AVENUE

SYLVAN PL

T H I R D

F I R S T

EAST   120TH   STREET

PLEASANT

FRANKLIN D ROOSEVELT DRIVE (EAST RIVER DRIVE)

EAST   119TH   STREET

EAST   118TH   STREET

A V E N U E

A V E N U E

A V E N U E

EAST   117TH   STREET

AVENUE

«2254

3

h Street

«2120

(LUIS   MUÑOZ   MARIN   BOULEVARD)

«2103

0»

200»

300»

«2238

400»

EAST   115TH   STREET

EAST 114TH STREET

EAST 113TH STREET

JEFFERSON

EAST   112TH   STREET

PARK

EAST   111TH   STREET

«2135

FRANKLIN D ROOSEVELT DRIVE (EAST RIVER DRIVE)

Harlem

4

«2002

EAST  110TH   STREET

h Street

«1981

EAST   109TH   STREET

EAST 108TH STREET

S E C O N D

Benjamin
Franklin
Plaza

F I R S T

T H I R D

RECREATION
PIER

River

EAST 107TH STREET

EAST   106TH   STREET

A V E N U E

A V E N U E

A V E N U E

EAST   105TH   STREET

5

EAST   104TH   STREET

«2001

103rd Street

EAST 103RD STREET

Foot Bridge

# General Index

# Acknowledgments

Dorling Kindersley would like to thank the many people whose help and assistance contributed to the preparation of this book.

**Main Contributor**
Eleanor Berman has lived in New York for almost 40 years. Her travel articles are widely published and she is the author of *Away for the Weekend: New York*, a favorite since 1982. Her other books include *Away for the Weekend* guides for the Mid-Atlantic, New England and Northern California, *Travelling on Your Own* and *Reflections of Washington, DC*.

**Museum Contributors**
Michelle Menendez, Lucy O'Brien, Heidi Rosenau, Elyse Topalian, Sally Williams.

Dorling Kindersley wishes to thank editors and researchers at Websters International Publishers: Sandy Carr, Matthew Barrell, Sara Harper, Miriam Lloyd, Ava-Lee Tanner, Celia Woolfrey.

**Additional Photography**
Rachel Feierman, Andrew Holigan, Edward Hueber, Eliot Kaufman, Karen Kent, Dave King, Norman McGrath, Howard Millard, Ian O'Leary, Susannah Sayler, Paul Solomon, Chuck Spang, Chris Stevens.

**Additional Illustrations**
Steve Gyapay, Arshad Khan, Kevin Jones, Dinwiddie MacLaren, Janos Marffy, Chris D. Orr, Nick Shewring, John Woodcock.

**Cartography**
Maps Uma Bhattacharya, Andrew Heritage, Suresh Kumar, James Mills-Hicks, Chez Picthall, John Plumer (Dorling Kindersley Cartography), Kunal Singh. Advanced Illustration (Cheshire), Contour Publishing (Derby), Europmap Ltd (Berkshire). Street Finder maps: ERA-Maptec Ltd (Dublin) adapted with permission from original survey and mapping by Shobunsha (Japan).

**Cartographic Research**
Roger Bullen, Tony Chambers, Ruth Duxbury, Ailsa Heritage, Jayne Parsons, Laura Porter, Donna Rispoli, Joan Russell, Jill Tinsley, Andrew Thompson.

**Design and Editorial**
*Managing Editor* Douglas Amrine
*Managing Art Editors* Stephen Knowlden, Geoff Manders
*Senior Editor* Georgina Matthews
*Series Design Consultant* Peter Luff
*Editorial Director* David Lamb
*Art Director* Anne-Marie Bulat
*Production Controller* Hilary Stephens
*Picture Research* Susan Mennell, Sarah Moule
*Dtp Designer* Andy Wilkinson
Keith Addison, Eleanor Berman, Vandana Bhagra, Jon Paul Buchmeyer, Ron Boudreau, Linda Cabasin, Rebecca Carman, Michelle Clark, Sherry Collins, Carey Combe, Diana Craig, Maggie Crowley, Guy Dimond, Fay Franklin, Tom Fraser, Anna Freiberger, Jo Gardner, Alex Gray, Michelle Haimoff, Marcus Hardy, Sasha Heseltine, Rose Hudson, Pippa Hurst, Kim Inglis, Jaqueline Jackson, Mathew Kurien, Maite Lantaron, Shahid Mahmood, Susan Millership, Jane Middleton, Helen Partington, Pollyanna Poulter, Leigh Priest, Pamposh Raina, Nicki Rawson, Marisa Renzullo, Amir Reuveni, Ellen Root, Liz Rowe, Sands Publishing Solutions, Anaïs Scott, Shailesh Sharma, AnneLise Sorensen, Anna Streiffert, Clare Sullivan, Andrew Szudek, Alka Thakur, Shawn Thomas, Ros Walford, Lucilla Watson.

**Special Assistance**
Beyer Blinder Belle, John Beatty at the Cotton Club, Peter Casey at the New York Public Library, Nicky Clifford, Linda Corcoran at the Bronx Zoo, Audrey Manley at the Morgan Library, Jane Fischer, Deborah Gaines at the New York Convention and Visitors Bureau, Dawn Geigerich at the Queens Museum of Art, Peggy Harrington at St. John the Divine, Pamela Herrick at the Van Cortlandt House, Marguerite Lavin at the Museum of the City of New York, Robert Makla at the Friends of Central Park, Gary Miller at the New York Stock Exchange, Laura Mogil at the American Museum of Natural History, Fred Olsson at the Shubert Organization, Dominique Palermo at the Police Academy Museum, Royal Canadian Pancake House, Lydia Ruth and Laura I. Fries at the Empire State Building, David Schwartz at the American Museum of the Moving Image, Joy Sienkiewicz at the South Street Seaport Museum, Barbara Orlando at the Metropolitan Transit Authority, the staff at the Lower East Side Tenement Museum, Msgr. Anthony Dalla Valla at St. Patrick's Cathedral.

**Research Assistance**
Christa Griffin, Bogdan Kaczorowski, Steve McClure, Sabra Moore, Jeff Mulligan, Marc Svensson, Vicky Weiner, Steven Weinstein.

**Photographic Reference**
Duncan Petersen Publishers Ltd.

**Photography Permissions**
Dorling Kindersley would like to thank the following for their kind permission to photograph at their establishments: American Craft Museum, American Museum of Natural History, Aunt Len's Doll and Toy Museum, Balducci's, Home Savings of America, Brooklyn Children's Museum, The Cloisters, Columbia University, Eldridge Street Project, Federal Hall, Rockefeller Group, Trump Tower.

**Picture credits**
t = top; tc = top center; tr = top right; cla = center left above; ca = center above; cra = center right above; cl = center left; c = center; cr = center right; clb = center left below; cb = center below; crb = center right below; bl = bottom left; bc = bottom center; br = bottom right.

Works of art have been reproduced with the permission of the following copyright holders: © ADAGP, Paris and DACS, London 2006: 67ca (April 1971–July 1972, by Jean Dubuffet), 107cl, 162tr (donated by the Norwegian Government, 1952), 172bl, 188cl, 189cra, 189crb; © ARS, NY and DACS, London 2006:185cr, 201crb; Jose de Creeft ©DACS, London/VAGA, New York 2006: 53cl, 207cl; © DACS, London 2006: 161cr, 163tc; *Charging Bull* © Arturo Di Modica 1998 73tl; © Sucession Picasso/DACS, London 2006: 36tr, 115tc, 173cb, 174cr, 188bl, 189bl, 190cla; © Estate of Stuart Davis/DACS, London/VAGA, New York 2006: 201cr; DK IMAGES: Judith

Miller/Wallis & Wallis, Sussex 58br; © Kingdom of Spain, Gaia - Salvador Dali Foundation, DACS, London 2006: 174cl; © Marisol Escobar/DACS, London/VAGA, New York 2006: 55bc; © Jasper Johns/DACS, London/VAGA, New York 2006: 201ca; ©The Estate of Roy Lichtenstein/DACS, London 2006: 175tl, 200clb; © Estate of David Smith/ DACS, London/VAGA, New York 2006: 201bl; © 1993 The Georgia O'Keeffe Foundation/ARS, New York and DACS, London 2006: 200c; © 1993 Frank Stella/ARS, New Yorkamd DACS, London: 192tr; By permission of E Jan Nadelman: 201br; Printed by permission of the Norman Rockwell Family Trust © 1961 the Norman Rockwell Family Trust: 163br; © Licensed by The Andy Warhol Foundation for the Visual Arts, Inc/ARS, New York and DACS, London 2006: 200cla; © The Whitney Museum of American Art: 37br, 200bl.

The Publishers are grateful to the following museums, companies and picture libraries for permission to reproduce their photographs:

Agence France Presse: Doug Kanter 33tr; Alamy Images: Ambient Images Inc./Joseph A. Rosen 171c; E J Baumeister Jr. 387tl; Comstock Images 295c; Wendy Connett 96cr; Kevin Foy 73tl; Jeff Greenberg 268cla; Bob Jones 111b; PCL 295tl; Yadid Levy 366–7; Pictures Colour Library 108; Alex Segre 294cla; tbkmedia.de 340bc; Algonquin Hotel, N.Y: 280bl; American Airlines: 379tl; American Museum-Hayden Planetarium, NY: D. Finnin 218t; American Museum of the Moving Image: Carson Collection © Bruce Polin 247t; American Museum of Natural History, NY: 39bl, 216ca; D. Finnin 216bl; Angel Orensanz Center: Laszlo Regas 101cl; Aquarius, UK: 171tr; Ashmolean Museum, Oxford: 17tc; The Asia Society, NY: 187cl; Avery Fisher Hall: © N McGrath 1976 351tr.

© The George Balanchine Trust: *Apollo*, choreography by George Balanchine, photo by P Kolnik 5tc; *Stravinsky Violin Concerto*, choreography by George Balanchine, photo by P Kolnik 340tc; George Balanchine's *The Nutcracker*, SM, photo by P Kolnik 343cb; The Bettmann Archive, NY: 18bcl, 19cra, 19cr, 19bl, 20cl, 22cbr, 22bl, 22–23, 25br, 27cra, 28cla, 28cra, 28crb, 32cla, 33tl, 43tl, 45cbl, 49c, 54-55b, 71tl, 74cla, 79crb, 79br, 111bl, 177cla, 185br, 209t, 212cl, 225cr, 231t, 241tr, 267tr; Bettmann Newsphotos/Reuters: 33tr; Bettmann/ UPI: 29cra, 29bc, 30cbr, 31br, 32cra, 32bl, 32br, 46cl, 48cl, 49bl, 72c, 72ca, 78cl, 153c, 163c, 266br, 267cr; Bloomingdale's: 29cbr; © Roy Export Company Establishment 173tr; The British Library, London: 16; Brooklyn Historical Society: (detail) 89tl; The Brooklyn Museum: 38bl, 39c, 250c, 250cra, 250bl, 251t, 251cra, 251c, 251bl, 251b, 252t, 252br, 253cr, 253bl; Lewis Wick Hine, *Climbing Into The Promised Land*, 1908 – 36clb; J Kerr 250c, 252bl; P Warchol: 251cr; The Cantor Collection 253cl; Adam Husted 250t; Brown Brothers: 67br, 71bl, 82cra, 90t, 106br.

Camera Press: 30cbr, 30bl, 33cb, 127cr; R Open 48tr; T Spencer 32cb; The Carlyle Hotel, NY: 281tr; Carnegie Hall: © H. Grossman 343br; J Allan Cash: 33bl, 378cr; Cathedral of St. John The Divine: Greg Wyatt 1985, 227tl; CBS Entertainment/Desilu too: "Vacation from Marriage" 171br; Chelsea Piers: Fred George 33bl;

Children's Museum of the Arts: 107cl; Colorific!: A Clifton 389cl; Colorific/ Black Star: 79cra; T Cowell 223cr; R Fraser 74t; H Matsumoto 384cr, 387tr; D Moore 31bl; T Spiegel 15cr, 364tr; Corbis: Bettmann 137cl, 273ca, 383c; Jacques M. Chenet 272tl; Randy Duchaine 99cl; Kevin Fleming 271tl; Bob Krist 10cra; Todd Gipstein 75t; Gail Mooney 207b, 269tr, 271br; Bill Ross 12t; Michael Setboun 268tr; Steven E. Sutton 51b; Michael Yamashita 273cb; Mike Zens 262–3. Culver Pictures, Inc: (inset) 9, 19crb, 20cbl, 21bl, 23tl, 23br, 26tl, 26cl, 29cb, 29bl, 48br, 49tr, 74bl, 75cra, 75cb, 76tl, 78crb, 83c, 121bl, 124tc, 127bl, 137cr, 147c, 149cl, 229t, 229bc, 229cr, 261crb. Daily Eagle: (detail) 89cl; Daily News: 370tl, 370tr. Essex House, NY: 276cr; Esto: P Aaron 342bl; Mary Evans Picture Library: 24br, 87br, 106bl; Chris Fairclough Colour Library: 385bcl; The Forbes Magazine Collection, NY: 114tl; Four Seasons Hotel: Peter Vitale 281cr; Fraunces Tavern Museum, NY: From the exhibit "Come All You Gallant Heroes" The World of the Revolutionary Soldier December 4, 1991 to August 14, 1992: 22cla; Copyright The Frick Collection, NY: 37bl (*St Francis In The Desert* by Giovanni Bellini), 202ca, 202cl, 202clb, 202b, 202tr, 203ca, 203cr, 203bc, 203br.

Garrard The Crown Jewellers: 145c; The Solomon R Guggenheim Museum, NY: photo by D Heald 188tl, 188bl, 188bc, 188br, 189tr, 189cra, 189crb, 189bl; Robert Harding Picture Library: 378tc; Harpers New Monthly Magazine: 87tl; Harpers Weekly: 367c; Milton Hebald: *Prospero and Miranda* 205t, *Romeo and Juliet* 343cr; The Hotel Millenium, NY: 277tl. The Image Bank: front endpaper bl, 89br; P McConville 393c; M Melford 393br; P Miller 383tr; A Satterwhite 75br. The Jewish Museum, NY: 184tr, 186c. Copyright © 1993 K-III Magazine Corporation: All rights reserved. Reprinted with the permission of *New York* Magazine 368tr; The Kobal Collection: 213tc; Lebrecht Music: Toby Wales 149t; Frank Leslie's Illustrated Newspaper: 86br, 87tr, 275c; Library of congress: 20bc, 23cla, 27bl, 27br; Life Magazine © Time Warner Inc/Katz/A Feininger: 8–9; Georg John Lober: *Hans Christian Andersen*, 1956, 206br; The Lowell Hotel, NY: 281cl; Mary Ann Lynch: 318bc, 372cl.

Madison Square Garden: 134r, 342cr; Magnum Photos: © H Cartier-Bresson 175c; Erwitt 35cr; G Peres 14br, 92; Jacques Marchais Center of Tibetan Art: 254bc; Masterfile UK: Gail Mooney 33br; Metro-North Commuter Railroad: F English 156tr, 156cla; The Metropolitan Museum of Art, NY: 35bl (*Young Woman With A Waterjug* by Johannes Vermeer), 37crb (*Figure of a Hippopotamus*, faience, Egypt, 12th Dynasty), 182tc, 190cla, 190clb, 190bc, 190br, 191tl, 191tr, 191cr, 191bl, (photo Al Mozell) 191br, 192tr, 192c, 192bl, 192br, 193tl, 193tr, 193c, 193bl, 194tl, 194tr, 194b, (detail) 195tl, 195tr, 195b, 196t, 196cl, 196cr, 196b, 197tl, 197cr, 197bl, 236tr, 236cl, 236cr, 236b, 237ca, 237cr, 237bl, 237br, 238tl, 238tr, 239tr, 239c, 239b; Metropolitan Transit Authority: 388bca, 390tl, 391cla/ca, 392c; Collection of The Morgan Library, NY: 36cr (*Blanche of Castille and King Louis IX of France, author dictating to a scribe*, moralized Bible, c1230), 164br, *Song of Los* David A. Loggie (gift of Mrs Landon K Thorne) 164la, *Biblia Latina* David A. Loggie 164lb, 165tl, 165c, 165bl, 165br; Morris-Jumel Mansion, Inc NY: 19tl; A Rosario 23crb; The Museum of the City of New York: 17b,

18cra, 18–19, 19tr, 20ca, 21crb (photo J Parnell), 22tl, 22cbl, 24tl (attributed to Samuel Lovett Waldo), 24cla, 24clb, 25cr, 25crb, 25bc, 26cb, 27tl, 27crb, 27cb, 28bl, 29tr, 30tl, 30cr, 31tc, 31c, 32tr, 37tr (silver porringer), 87cr (Talfour); The Museum of Modern Art, NY: 172c, 172bl, 173tc, 173cra, 173crb, 173cb, 173bl, 174cl, 174cr, 175tl, 175b; *The Bather*, c. 1885, Paul Cézanne 174bc; Cisitalia "202" GT car 167tc; ©2004 Photo Elizabeth Felicella, architectural rendering Kohn Pedersen Fox Associates, digital composite Robert Bowen 172tl; ©2005 Timothy Hursley 168cl, 172tr; *The Goat* by Pablo Picasso, 1950, 36t; *The Starry Night* by Vincent Van Gogh, 1889, 35ca.
National Baseball Library, Cooperstown, NY: 4tr, 25bl, 30cl; National Museum of The American Indian/Smithsonian Institution: 18c; National Park Service: Ellis Island Immigration Museum 78ca, 78br; Statue of Liberty National Monument 75bl; The New Museum of Contemporary Art, NY: 167cl; New York Botanic Garden: Tori Butt 242b, 243t/cl/b; Jason Green 242cr; Muriel Weinerman 243b; New York City Fire Department: 359br; New York City Transit Authority: 390bc; Phil Bartley 391tc, 391ca, 391cl; New York Police Department: Photo Dept 372cl; The New Yorker Magazine Inc: Cover drawing by Rea Irvin, © 1925, 1953, All rights reserved, 30bcl; The New York Palace, NY: 27tr; New York Post: 370tl; New York Public Library: Special Collection Office, Schomburg Center for Research in Black Culture 30ca, 31cla; Stokes Collection 23tr; New York State Department of Motor vehicles: 386b; New York Stock Exchange: 71ra; The New York Times: 370tl; NPA: © CNES 1993 12b; The Peninsula, NY: 279bc; Performing Arts Library: Clive Barda: 212bl; The Pickle Guys: Alan Kaufman 100bl; Popperfoto: 31cra, 31cr, 262cla; Plaza Hotel, NY: 280tr.

Collection of The Queens Museum of Art: purchased with funds from the George and Mollie Wolfe World's Fair Fund 31cbr; Official souvenir, purchase 32cbr; Rensselaer Polytechnic Institute: 86–87, 87bl; Rex Features Ltd: 392tl; Sipa-Press 52tr, 52br; Courtesy of the Rockefeller Center © The Rockefeller Group, Inc: 31cbl. Luis Sanguino: *The Immigrants*, 1973, 258b; The St. Regis, NY: 278c; Scientific American: 18 May 1878 edition 86tr; 9 November 1878 edition 88bl; Skyscraper Museum: Robert Polidori 55tl; 72br; 268bl; The Society of Illustrators: 198tl; South Street Seaport Museum: R.B. Merkel 83bl, 84bl; Spectrum Colour Library: 392bl; Frank Spooner Pictures: Gamma 160cl; Gamma/B Gysenbergh 383tl; Liaison/Gamma/ Anderson front endpaper clb, 160tl, 161cla; Liaison/Levy/Halebian: 44tr, 47c;

Theater Development Fund: David LeShay 340cl; Turner Entertainment Company: 137br, 185br. United Nations, NY: 161cra, 162tr, 162bc, 163tc, 163cla, 163br; United Nations Photo: 160tr; © 2007 USPS. All Rights Reserved: 377c, 377t; Used with permission; UN Plaza Hyatt Hotel, NY: 281bl.

© Jack Vartoogian, NY: 61bc, 158t. Judith Weller: *The Garment Worker* 130t; Lucia Wilson Consultancy: Ivar Mjell 2–3, 15br, 166; Collection of The Whitney Museum of American art, NY: 200cla, 200c, 200clb, 201t, 201ca, 201cr, 201crb (purchase with funds from a public fundraising campaign in May 1982. One half of the funds were contributed by the Robert Wood Johnson Jr. Charitable Trust. Additional major donations were given by The Lauder Foundation; the Robert Lehman Foundation, Inc.; the Howard and Jean Lipman Foundation, Inc; an anonymous donor; The TM Evans Foundation, Inc.; MacAndrews & Forbes Group Incorporated; the DeWitt Wallace Fund, Inc; Martin & Agnes Gruss; Anne Phillips; Mr and Mrs Laurance S. Rockefeller; the Simon Foundation, Inc.; Marylou Whitney; Bankers Trust Company; Mr and Mrs Kenneth N Dayton; Joel and Anne Ehrenkranz; Irvin and Kenneth Feld; Flora Whitney Miller. More than 500 individuals from 26 states and abroad also contributed to the campaign), 201bl, 201br (purchased with funds from the Mr and Mrs Arthur G Altschul Purchase Fund, the Joan and Lester Avnet Purchase Fund, the Edgar William and Bernice Chrysler Garbisch Purchase Fund, the Mrs Robert C Graham Purchase Fund in honour of John I H Baur, the Mrs Percy Uris Purchase Fund and the Henry Schnakenberg Purchase Fund in honor of Juliana Force); Wheeler Pictures: 78t; Wildlife Conservation Society, Bronx Zoo: Dennis DeMello 244bl; Julie Maher 244tr, 244cl, 245br, 245bl; Robert Wright: 43t, 140b, 142tr, 142cr, 142bl; 143tl/br, 156br, 157tl/r, 293tr, 372cl, 373c. Yu Yu Yang: *Untitled*, 1973, 57br.

All other images © Dorling Kindersley. See www.dkimages.com for further information.

Front Endpapers
Alamy Images: Pictures Colour Library ftl; Magnum Photos: G. Per bl; Lucia Wilson Consultancy: Ivar Mjell tr
Jacket
Front - DK Images: Michael Moran bl; Getty Images: Image Bank/Michel Setboun main image. Back - ©The Solomon R. Guggenheim Foundation, New York: cla; Image State: Mark Segal clb; Robert Wright: tl, bl. Spine - DK Images: Max Alexander b; Getty Images: Image Bank/Michel Setboun t.

## SPECIAL EDITIONS OF DK TRAVEL GUIDES

# The Manhattan Subway

## How to Use this Map

MTA New York City Transit subway service operates 24 hours a day. On this map, **bold** identification letters or numbers below station names indicate a full-time service. A light letter or number shows a part-time service at the station. For more information, and to check the latest opening times, call (718) 330-1234 or visit **www.mta.info**.

Throughout this guide, the subway station closest to each sight is listed. For more details on traveling on the New York subway, see pages 390–1.

## Wheelchair Accessible Stations

For further information on accessible service, call (718) 596-8585 (6am–9pm daily). For information regarding the accessibility status of elevators and escalators, call (800) 734-6772 (24 hours).

### Routes Station

MANHATTAN

| Routes | Station |
|---|---|
| A C E L | 14 St/8 Av |
| L N Q R W | 14 St/Union Sq |
| B D F N Q R V W | 34 St/Herald Sq |
| 1 2 3 | 34 St/Penn Station |
| A C E | 34 St/Penn Station |
| A C E | 42 St/8 Av (Port Authority Bus Terminal) |
| N R W | 49 St *northbound only* |
| C E | 50 St/8 Av *southbound only* |
| 6 | 51 St |
| 1 | 66 St/Lincoln Center |
| 6 | 72 St |
| A B C D | 125 St |
| 4 5 6 | 125 St |
| A | 175 St |
| 4 5 6 | Brooklyn Bridge/City Hall |
| 6 | Canal St |
| R | Cortlandt St *southbound only* |
| 4 5 6 7 | Grand Central/42 St |
| A | Inwood/207 St |

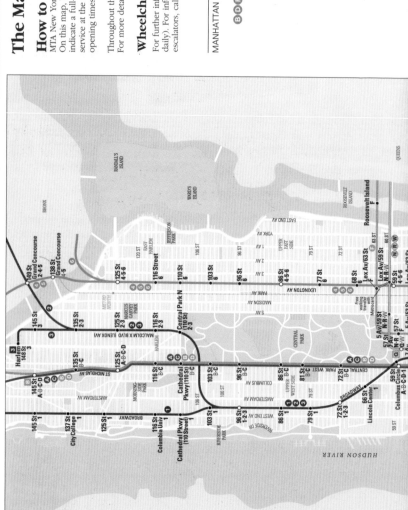